ZION
ON THE MISSISSIPPI

Martin Stephan. The white Meissen china cup is banded in gold, and the image is hand painted in color. The cup is of the exact size as this reproduction.

PLATE I

ZION
on the
MISSISSIPPI

THE SETTLEMENT OF THE SAXON LUTHERANS
IN MISSOURI 1839—1841

by

Walter O. Forster
ASSOCIATE PROFESSOR OF HISTORY AND GOVERNMENT
PURDUE UNIVERSITY

CONCORDIA PUBLISHING HOUSE · SAINT LOUIS

Paperback Edition

Original cloth edition copyright 1953

Manufactured in the USA

14 15 16 17 18 19 20 30 29 28 27 26 25 24

To Lydia

SINE QUA NON

PREFACE

It is more than a hundred years since the first book appeared on the Stephanite Emigration from Saxony to the United States. Since that time much has been written on the movement. But, as no comprehensive and thorough study of the sources was made, the growing volume of literature in the field offered little that was new and much that was partisan. Unfortunately, these Saxons and their descendants are not alone in seeing the vigorous chronicle of their critical years dissipated by that familiar trinity of corrosive forces which unfailingly attacks the immigrant saga: disintegration in family chests, distortion in anniversary publications, and dilution in personal histories.

A noted student of immigration to the United States, Carl Wittke, in speaking of the tremendous task of research remaining to be done in that field, has remarked: "Much of the work now completed has been done by descendants of some particular group, and therefore many of the accounts are unreliable and exaggerated." [1] This is bad. But the treatment of religious movements among the emigrants is worse. As early as 1913, Henry Pratt Fairchild, writing at the very climax — and, as it was to prove, near the end — of an epoch in the history of immigration to the United States, pointed out: "The effects of immigration upon the religious life of the immigrant and of the United States constitute a great field of research which has been surprisingly neglected." [2] The "Saxons" deserve a better fate. They are an excellent example not only of the effect of religion upon immigration, but of that which Fairchild is doubly right in pointing out as neglected, namely, the effect of immigration upon the religious life of the immigrant, and then their influence upon the religious life of the United States.

Accordingly, the following pages constitute a critical examination of the abundant source material available. The resulting vol-

---

[1] Wittke, *We Who Built America*, xvii.

[2] Fairchild, *Immigration*, 293.

ume presents considerable additional information on the Saxon Immigration and revises some of the ideas prevalent on the events and men connected with it. An attempt is made to bring the religious phase of the movement, which has always been recognized, into proper focus with the social, political, and economic factors involved, which have received scant attention. This approach also makes possible some contributions to the history of German immigration to the United States and to the social history of St. Louis and the West a century ago. Research has centered about the manuscripts in the Concordia Historical Institute in St. Louis. This collection alone contains enough of the records and correspondence of the Stephanite *Gesellschaft* to create for the student an *embarras de richesse*. In addition, however, extensive use was made of contemporary newspapers and periodicals, manuscript court records in Saxony and the United States, and manuscripts in church archives and private collections. The study was originally prepared as a doctoral dissertation at Washington University in St. Louis. It has since been expanded and revised.

Among numerous acknowledgments which I wish to make, the first is due Professor Ralph P. Bieber. Not only was the original thesis written under his direction, but his patient advice and scholarly guidance have been freely given over a period of years since that time. I am also greatly indebted to Ida Parker Bieber (Mrs. Ralph P. Bieber) for a critical reading of the manuscript. For invaluable assistance in every phase of the study I am deeply grateful to my wife, Lydia Treichel Forster. My father, the late Rev. Frederick Forster, formerly Assistant House Editor of Concordia Publishing House, rendered substantial help in making translations and offered many useful suggestions. I am obligated to the following institutions and individuals for various forms of aid and many courtesies extended to me in the course of my search for material: Concordia Historical Institute and its present curator, the Rev. August R. Suelflow; Pritzlaff Memorial Library, Concordia Seminary; the Saxon *Hauptstaatsarchiv,* Dresden; the Saxon *Landeskirchenamt,* Dresden; Missouri Historical Society, St. Louis; State Historical Society of Missouri, Columbia; St. Louis Public Library; St. Louis Mercantile Library Association; Washington University Library; Trinity Lutheran Church, Altenburg, Mo.; Concordia Lutheran Church, Frohna, Mo.; Trinity Lutheran Church, St. Louis; the late Prof. William G. Polack, Concordia Seminary, and the former president of that institution, Louis E. Fuerbringer; Chaplain Herbert C. W. Albrecht, U. S. N., Great Lakes, Ill.; the Rev. E. J. Buerger, Ellicottville, N. Y.; Mr. Ralph Killian, Clerk of the Perry County, Mo., Circuit Court; Miss Alice Stover, West Lafayette, Ind.; the Rev. Mr. and Mrs. A. O. Gebauer, Granite City, Ill.; and Mr. and Mrs. F. G. Hensel, Chicago, Ill. The illustrations were made possible through the collaboration of Concordia Historical Institute and the Art Department of Concordia Publishing House; specifically, contributions by Miss Esther Carlson of the Publishing House staff may properly be described as indispensable. The index is largely the product of Prof. William Schaller's patient labors.

The following holders of copyrights have generously granted permission to quote from the publications named: Ginn and Company, from George M. Stephenson's *A History of American Immigration,* 1926; Cambridge University Press, from Sir Adolphus Ward's *Germany, 1815—1890,* 1916; Brown University Press, from Vernon L. Parrington Jr.'s *American Dreams,* 1947; Carl Wittke, Dean of the Graduate School, Western Reserve University, from *We Who Built America,* 1939; the Macmillan Company, from Henry P. Fairchild's *Immigration,* 1913; Manchester University Press, from C. H. Herford, ed., *Germany in the Nineteenth Century,* 1915; the University of Georgia Press, from Carl Mauelshagen's *American Lutheranism Surrenders to Forces of Conservatism,* 1936; Harvard University Press, from Marcus Hansen's *The Atlantic Migration, 1607—1860,* 1940; The University of Chicago Press, from H. H. Maurer's series of articles on "The Sociology of Religion," in the *American Journal of Sociology,* Volumes XXX, XXXI, and XXXIII; the *American Historical Review,* from Carl Wittke's article on "The German Forty-Eighters in America," Volume LIII of the *Review;* the State Historical Society of Missouri, from articles by M. A. Owens and P. E. Kretzmann in Volumes XV and XXXIII of the *Missouri Historical Review.*

Fairchild conjectured that subjects such as that with which this volume is concerned have not received the attention they merit, perhaps "because of the difficulty of securing reliable data and establishing definite conclusions, perhaps because" they have "not seemed of sufficient importance to warrant exhaustive study." [3] The question of whether the present study has surmounted the difficul-

---

[3] *Ibid.*

ties of "securing reliable data" to the point of warranting "definite conclusions" is, of course, left to the judgment of that final arbiter, the reader. Conversely, the question of whether the aspects of migration here considered are "of sufficient importance to warrant exhaustive study" had to be answered in the writer's mind before he set himself the task. The work would neither have been begun nor completed had he lacked an abiding conviction of the transcendent importance of the things of the spirit in the life of man. His only hope is that the product will have sufficient merit to reflect the great and lasting significance of these Lutheran pioneers who came to the West to build a "Zion" in the New World.

Purdue University
December, 1952

WALTER O. FORSTER

TABLE OF CONTENTS

	Preface	VII
I.	European Background	1
II.	Rise of Stephanism in Saxony, 1810—1837	27
III.	Transformation of Stephanism into Separatism	60
IV.	Development of the Emigration Idea in Stephanite Separatism	83
V.	Planning an American Zion, 1837—1838	113
VI.	Organization of the *Auswanderungs-Gesellschaft*	137
VII.	Parting and Departing	171
VIII.	The Voyage from Bremerhaven to St. Louis, 1838—1839	202
IX.	The Saxons and Their New Home	226
X.	The Forerunners of the Forty-Eighters in the West	245
XI.	Establishing the Episcopacy	278
XII.	First Contact with Religious Conditions in the West	305
XIII.	Problems of Communal Living in St. Louis	325
XIV.	Founding the Perry County Colony	352
XV.	Discrediting Stephan's Leadership	390
XVI.	Stephan's Expulsion from the *Gesellschaft*	411
XVII.	Retrenchment and Reappraisal	443
XVIII.	Disorganization and Reorganization, 1839—1841	473
XIX.	Zion Re-Defined	507
	Appendices	535
	Bibliography	584

LIST OF ILLUSTRATIONS

PLATE

I Martin Stephan Miniature on a China Cup
Courtesy of Concordia Historical Institute, St. Louis, Missouri

Between pages 32 and 33

II St. John's Church, Dresden, Saxony, 1840

III Religious Questions and the Phenomenon of Emigration Discussed in the Saxon Press

IV Notice of Escape, Description, and Appeal for Apprehension of Franz Julius Biltz

V Scene from "Call of the Cross," Superintendent Expostulating with Pastor and Parishioners
Courtesy of The Lutheran Church — Missouri Synod

Between pages 96 and 97

VI Benjamin Kurtz's Report in the *New York Observer*

VII Artist's Drawing of G. H. Hillmer's Painting of the *Olbers*
Courtesy of Concordia Historical Institute, St. Louis, Missouri

VIII Ship's List of the *Olbers*
Courtesy of Immigration Bureau, New Orleans, Louisiana

IX Gotthold Heinrich Löber Miniature, by Gustav Pfau
Courtesy of Concordia Historical Institute, St. Louis, Missouri

Between pages 150 and 151

X Map, Origins of Saxon Immigration

Between pages 240 and 241

XI Map of St. Louis, Missouri
Courtesy of Missouri Historical Society, St. Louis, Missouri

XII View of St. Louis, Missouri, About 1840
Courtesy of Missouri Historical Society, St. Louis, Missouri

XIII View of Front Street, St. Louis, Missouri, in 1840
Courtesy of Missouri Historical Society, St. Louis, Missouri

XIV The Saxons Landing at St. Louis, Missouri, by G. H. Hillmer and F. Nuderscher
Courtesy of Concordia Historical Institute, St. Louis, Missouri

Between pages 320 and 321

XV Signatures on the "Confirmation of Stephan's Investiture"
Courtesy of Concordia Historical Institute, St. Louis, Missouri

XVI Stephan's Signatures
Courtesy of Concordia Historical Institute, St. Louis, Missouri

XVII Portion of Louise Günther's Confession
Courtesy of Concordia Historical Institute, St. Louis, Missouri

XVIII Sickbed Scene from "Call of the Cross"
Courtesy of The Lutheran Church — Missouri Synod

Between pages 384 and 385

XIX Carl Ferdinand Wilhelm Walther, by Gustav Pfau
Courtesy of Concordia Historical Institute, St. Louis, Missouri

XX Chest Used by Martin Stephan, and Book of Accounts Kept by the *Auswanderungs-Gesellschaft*
Courtesy of Concordia Historical Institute, St. Louis, Missouri

XXI Page from the Book of Accounts
Courtesy of Concordia Historical Institute, St. Louis, Missouri

XXII Christ Episcopal Church, St. Louis, Missouri
Courtesy of Missouri Historical Society, St. Louis, Missouri

Between pages 450 and 451

XXIII Map of the Saxon Colonies in Perry County, Missouri, 1838, Owners of Lots in Altenburg, Owners of Lots and Lands in Seelitz and Dresden
Courtesy of Walter A. Eggers, Farrar, Missouri

Between pages 512 and 513

XXIV Early Reports in Dresden of the Crisis in the *Gesellschaft's* Affairs

XXV Daring Advertising for Saxon Newspapers in 1839

XXVI Sustained Repercussions in the Homeland

XXVII The Altenburg Debate, Scene from "Call of the Cross'
Courtesy of The Lutheran Church — Missouri Synod

ZION
ON THE MISSISSIPPI

CHAPTER ONE

EUROPEAN BACKGROUND

ORGANIZED MIGRATION from the German states to the Americas was rare in 1838. In Saxony such movements were virtually unknown. Therefore, when the first detachment of a large group of colonists left Dresden in October of that year, a news-conscious artist commemorated the event in a painting. The crowds at the Leipzig fair established his canvas as one of the exposition's chief attractions. But at the city's university the painter's subject was regarded as an obscurantist aberration. Clerical circles viewed the incident which the picture portrayed as a matter either for ridicule or regret.

These varied reactions were only a few of the many responses to the Stephanite emigration of 1838—1839.

In Dresden the story created headlines — not only in the sense that the events leading up to the departure appeared in them, but also because its sequel made the Dresden typesetters reach for a larger font than they had ever used before. So, for the public it was a sensation. For King Fredrick Augustus II it was a political problem. Bremen encountered it in the form of an open conspiracy to evade the anti-emigration laws or policies of several German states. Yet among the Bremen police the pathos of the drama evoked sufficient feeling to make their leniency verge on co-operation.

Readers of the *New York Observer* had the movement represented to them a sort of Protestant hejira, although "the Prophet" was somewhat more numerously and solicitously attended than his prototype. In New Orleans the colonists were just another of the many groups whose outfitting and transportation were an important piece of that bustling city's business. To the generally sympathetic St. Louis public the bumptious German press pictured the entire project as a mass hoax, whose victims were doomed to failure.

To themselves, these "victims" appeared to be the family of the faithful, fleeing from "Sodom and Gomorrah." The careful chronicler of Americana will take note of them as one of the most publicized emigrant groups in a century known for its migrations.

And an historian, who sees them in the perspective of national development, is likely to agree with Marcus Hansen that they "warrant attention because, as forerunners of the hosts to follow, they were the fathers of an exodus destined to people the broad prairies."

Usually this migration of the Saxon Lutherans to Missouri in 1839 has been regarded as exclusively religious in origin and effect. While this view is an oversimplification of a complex subject, it is nevertheless true that the religious cast of the movement serves as the most suitable point of departure in considering its history, for the group represented a conservative minority in the Saxon State Church. In 1837 one of their leaders, a Dresden clergyman named Martin Stephan, was suspended from office because of his official and private actions. He thereupon organized an emigration association which was readily joined by many conservatives who were stimulated by a fear of damnation if they remained and a hope of economic and social betterment if they went. During November, 1838, six hundred and sixty-five persons left Bremen for St. Louis in five chartered ships, one of which was lost at sea. Traveling via New Orleans, they arrived in Missouri, where their number was augmented by more than two hundred additional colonists. They soon established a hierarchy with Stephan as bishop and placed him in control of certain phases of their civil affairs. About forty-five hundred acres of land were purchased in Perry County, Missouri, as the site for a semiautonomous, theocratic community.

But before the end of the Saxons' first year in Missouri, Stephan was deposed on charges of immorality and maladministration. A contest for authority ensued between the remaining clerical and lay leaders. This controversy developed into a theological dispute, which threatened with dissolution both the St. Louis and Perry County branches of the colony and intensified the hardships of the poverty-stricken settlers. In 1841, however, C. F. W. Walther, a clergyman, effected a settlement of the differences by formulating a platform satisfactory to the majority. During the reconstruction period which followed, the St. Louis group and four of the original seven communities in Perry County survived; local antagonism expressed by the *Anzeiger des Westens* was overcome; a college, founded in 1839, was maintained; churches and schools were built; and Saxon pastors were stationed at points as distant as Wisconsin and New York. In 1847, under the leadership of Walther, and with the Saxons as a nucleus, the Missouri Synod was established by organizing independent Lutheran congregations and clergymen on a national scale.

It was a circumstance of the first consequence for the development of the Saxon movement and the influence the group was to exert, that its arrival, orientation, and organization had taken place by 1847. For in that year the United States stood on the threshold of several generations of unparalleled immigration, in which the Germans played a significant part.

A few German immigrants had reached American shores as early as the seventeenth century, and more followed them in the eighteenth; but in the nineteenth century a marked increase in their numbers occurred. The extent of the later immigration can be determined with comparative accuracy, because on March 2, 1819, Congress passed an act requiring that, at the port of entry, ships' officers make a manifest of the passengers on their vessels. The first returns under this law, which date from September 30, 1820, mark the beginning of reliable information on immigration.[1] During the next eight decades (to 1902), the period of the greatest influx, no less than 20,408,677 immigrants came to our shores, or about twice as many as the entire population of the United States in 1820;[2] of this total, 5,098,005, or 24.98 per cent, were Germans.[3]

---

1 Fairchild, *op. cit.*, 62.

2 P. Hall, *Immigration and Its Effects upon the United States*, 342. The appearance of Prescott Hall's name with the initial gives occasion for a brief comment on the policy followed in this regard. Because of the family character of the Saxon emigration and the fact that the writings of a number of its more prominent members and their descendants have appeared in print, this study contains an unusual number of similar names, not only in the narrative, but also in references to both manuscript and printed material. In order to avoid unnecessary repetition of initials or Christian names, they have not been used each time a surname occurs which is borne by another person appearing in these pages. On the contrary, they have been eliminated wherever possible. Clarity was the only criterion. Accordingly, if the context, or a reference to the bibliography, or a glance at the lists of emigrants will suffice to establish the identity of such a person, the initial has not been given. Wherever there is likelihood of reasonable doubt, the initial or Christian name is inserted. In addition the following rules have been observed: The names of women appearing in the lists of emigrants are always preceded by their initials or Christian names, except in cases where the context or some other designation eliminates the possibility of confusion. However, when a duplication of surnames occurs in the case of two or more persons whose names appear in the list of emigrants, then the use of the surname, without initials or Christian name, indicates the male head of the family. In those cases where there are several families of the same name or several adult males in the same family the initials or Christian name are also given each time such a name occurs, unless the context renders this unnecessary. The single exception to the latter is Martin Stephan, Sr., who had not only a son

The coincidence of this vast migration with the climax of our westward expansion and with the period of the greatest development of the United States in almost every field is a fact that has often been noted. However, the exact relationship between these occurrences and the degree of their interaction upon each other is not always clearly indicated. Furthermore, historians have partly neglected an important portion of the larger period of immigration, namely, the portion from 1820 to 1848, into which the present study falls. The German immigrants of these years were the advance guard of their people in a new empire — the West — and to them, rather than to their more numerous compatriots of later decades, must go much of the credit for the creative influence of the pioneer. This new element made its influence felt especially in the region west of the Appalachian Mountains.

The Germans who came to the United States after 1820 tended to migrate to the West.[4] In the specific case of Missouri, Faust asserts that in 1821 no Germans of European birth lived in the State.[5] In 1824 Duden came to Missouri from Germany. Three years later, according to one writer, "there were less than a dozen German families in St. Louis." [6] And a usually reliable observer, Georg Engelmann, claimed that as late as 1832 there were only "twenty or thirty" Germans in St. Louis.[7] But from 1839 to 1847 German immigrants poured into St. Louis by the thousands, many of them coming by way of New Orleans.[8] Of the 68,069 immigrants who came to the United States in 1839, 21,028 were Germans.[9] Of the entire total, in turn, 10,306 arrived in New Orleans, and of these 2,691 came from Germany.[10] Approximately one third of the latter

---

of the same name, but also an unrelated namesake with the same initial, all three of whom appear in the lists. The names of the younger Martin and of Michael Stephan occur so seldom that when they do, these two are identified clearly. In all other cases, where the simple name Stephan is used without initial, Martin Stephan, Sr., is meant.

[3] *Ibid.*, 39.

[4] Fairchild, *op. cit.*, 71, 84.

[5] Faust, *The German Element in the United States*, I, 440.

[6] Crawford, *The Immigrant in St. Louis*, 9.

[7] Schneider, *The German Church on the American Frontier*, 98, footnote 1.

[8] *Daily Evening Gazette*, April 23, 1839, Jan. 9, 1843; *Anzeiger des Westens*, Jan. 10, 1843; *St. Louis New Era*, June 28, 1841, Jan. 9, 1843, April 20, 1844; *Daily Missouri Republican*, Jan. 7, 1847.

[9] Ferenczi-Willcox, *International Migrations*, I, 377.

[10] *Senate Docs.* 26 Cong., 1 Sess., No. 594, pp. 22—25.

belonged to a compact, well-organized association of colonists from Saxony, whose leader was Martin Stephan.

In order to understand the German immigrant, some attention must be paid to economic and political, religious and intellectual movements in both Germany and the United States. These alone can reveal his motives for leaving his native land, his character, and the aspirations which he brought with him; these alone make possible an evaluation of his attitudes, influences, and achievements in the New World. These factors, with the exception of the religious, have frequently been neglected in the history of the Stephanites. Yet, "how shall we understand the . . . clash of cultures and creeds . . . without a knowledge of the Old World environment?"[11] Obviously no attempt at completeness can be made here in describing this environment, especially in the Old World, which demands immediate consideration. The aim must be to present only essentials and to keep them in rough proportion to their relative importance as underlying factors in the emigration.

The history of nineteenth-century Germany has often been divided into three periods, the first of which usually includes all or most of the first fifty years. This period was noted in the political field for the Napoleonic era and the Congress of Vienna, and in the religious field for the Union and the *Erweckung*.[12] It was a period of readjustment in several respects; and while this statement is true in some sense of every era, a brief explanation may help to show why it was true in a particular sense at the time of the Saxon emigration.

The decade following 1830 found Germany in the throes of a twofold political struggle. The one phase was a battle between liberalism and conservatism, the other a clash between particularism and nationalism. The focal point was the German Confederation, which served as a living reminder that Germany was not yet unified. The nationalist movement had failed at the Congress of Vienna; thirty-nine autonomous political units remained; and the nearest approach to the ideal of a greater Germany was the Confederation. However, this Confederation did little more than provide a back-

---

11 Stephenson, *A History of American Immigration 1820—1924*, p. 3. See also *ibid.*, 4, 7.

12 The origin of the term is discussed in Hennig, *Die sächsische Erweckungsbewegung im Anfange des 19. Jahrhunderts*, 9—10.

ground for the ensuing contest between Prussia and Austria, and serve as an instrument for the aggressive "reaction." Under the leadership of Metternich the forces of conservatism were largely successful in crushing the liberal movements prior to 1848. The revolutions of 1830 were generally only a prelude to the period of the severest reaction.

During this time there is noticeable a thorough reconstruction of the German intellectual attitude and the German educational system. This trend was colored by a nationalistic fervor of an idealistic, romantic type, which was "inspired by a patriotic enthusiasm and by a passionate belief in the political value of intellectual achievement."[13] In the regeneration of Germany, education and general cultural influences were considered important agencies for developing the spiritual power and morale of the youth. An already strong intellectual tradition emphasized the principles of freedom of thought and teaching. Since there was also a general conviction of the necessity for universal education, both the *Gymnasium* and the elementary school were reorganized and imbued with the ideals of personal and intellectual freedom. The demand for political liberalization was only a natural concomitant of these developments. Educational reorganization was by no means completed by 1830, but it was already creating serious difficulties for the conservatives.

The most pressing problem for Saxony, however, was her political future. After her dismemberment at Vienna in 1815 she was left with less than half of her former territory and with little more than four sevenths of her population. A corresponding decrease in strength and prestige relegated her definitely to the ranks of second-rate German states. In 1815 Prussia, in partial fulfillment of her secret agreement with Russia, had obtained the northern half of the Saxon kingdom, including Wittenberg, whose university was then merged with that of Halle. In Dresden and Leipzig, as well as in a considerable fringe of territory around them, the monarchy was restored under mediocre Fredrick Augustus I (III), whose long reign extended from 1763 to 1827. There remained, then, Albertine Saxony, the original electorate, but since 1806 a kingdom, and Ernestine Saxony, the Thuringian ducal estates, headed by relatives of the royal line. Of the various Saxonies the kingdom and the

---

[13] Herford (ed.), *Germany in the Nineteenth Century*, 106.

duchy of Saxe-Altenburg are most important for the Stephanite movement, which centered in Dresden. Fredrick Augustus died on May 5, 1827, and was succeeded by his younger brother, Anton (1755—1836). Both of these rulers attempted to ignore the real situation as far as possible and to maintain the former traditions at court and in the administration of their territory. Suggested constitutional and administrative changes, which were adopted later, were then anathema. Political reform made little progress, and liberalization of the government none.

In June, 1830, mild disturbances broke out in Leipzig and some a little more serious in Dresden. Led by students at the universities, they subsided quickly and constituted no serious threat to the monarchy. But when they began to recur in September of the same year, King Anton considered it advisable to make limited concessions, the first of which was to accept his nephew, Prince Fredrick Augustus, as co-regent, on September 13, 1830. On the same day Anton's minister and trusted adviser, Count Detlev von Einsiedel, was forced to resign.[14] The count was succeeded by von Lindenau, a progressive and capable minister. On September 4, 1831, a new constitution was promulgated, establishing a limited monarchy with a bicameral legislative assembly. Although the new order did not satisfy the liberals, some progress had been made. Upon Anton's death in 1836, Prince Fredrick Augustus, an enlightened ruler, ascended the throne. "There ensued in Saxony a decade of measured political progress, which gradually transformed the kingdom into a constitutional state." [15]

Just prior to the Saxon emigration to the United States the industrialization of Germany was still in its incipient stages. Far behind her future industrial and commercial rivals, Germany was still an agrarian territory with a predominantly agricultural economy. Such industry as was carried on was in a rather primitive state. "In general, Germany was a rural country and its industries were home industries. . . . It was a poor country with very low wages and small incomes." [16] A glance at Saxony and its textile

---

[14] Von Treitschke, *Deutsche Geschichte im Neunzehnten Jahrhundert*, IV, 143—146.

[15] Ward, *Germany, 1815—1890*, I, 277. See also von Treitschke, *op. cit.*, IV, 149—151.

[16] Herford (ed.), *op. cit.*, 88—89.

industry, important for both the country at large and the emigrants of 1838, will serve to illustrate these points.

Although Saxony was one of the more advanced states in the very backward Germany of the 1830's, she still retained the guild system even after 1840. As late as 1846 it was considered a mark of progress that there were "nearly as many cotton looms in the factory as in the home," but even of those in the factories "by far the greater number were hand looms." [17] Only a fraction of the land was owned by the nobility, and small individual holdings were the rule. So the workers, besides being employed in weaving, were frequently doing some farming as well. In the case of the linen weavers, the proportion engaged in agriculture was as high as 80 per cent. However, Saxony's somewhat more rapid industrialization did not mean that she had attained any independence economically. In 1834, in accord with an agreement with Prussia during the previous year, Saxony joined the *Zollverein.* This move was a measure of economic self-defense, necessitated by the fact that the Middle German Customs Union, which Saxony had helped to found on December 8, 1828, was breaking up. Saxony had to prevent her economic isolation; so she capitulated to her more powerful neighbor. In fact, Saxony's industrialization at this time meant rather that she experienced the effects of the industrial revolution much sooner than the rest of Germany. Britain's superior mechanization of manufacture and her domination of the world market, combined with the unequal competition of cheap American cotton, reduced Saxony's linen weavers to a pitiable state.[18]

Industrial troubles in Saxony were aggravated by a decade of agrarian crises which had their beginning in the earlier twenties. After a particularly hard winter from 1829 to 1830 the sufferings of the people had become so acute that they attracted the attention of the government. During the ensuing investigation of the country's economic status a pastor from the stricken areas testified as follows about the condition of the people: "All houses and other establishments are mortgaged. Much property is being auctioned

---

[17] *Ibid.,* 87.

[18] Henderson, *The Zollverein,* 67, 85; Clapham, *The Economic Development of France and Germany 1815—1914,* pp. 84, 95, 100; Herford (ed.), *op. cit.,* 87—89; Rosenthal, *Die Auswanderung aus Sachsen im 19. Jahrhundert (1815—1871)*, pp. 24, 35. Cf. Gebauer, *Die Volkswirtschaft im Königreiche Sachsen,* 191 ff.

off and sold. They are not able to pay taxes and parish dues. . . . Poverty prevails not only among the unskilled and day laborers, but also among the crafts and the peasantry."[19] The sufferings of the people were termed "almost indescribable." The poorer classes were subsisting largely on potatoes, when these were available; often they were not to be had. Begging was rare, stealing more frequent. The only ready relief from this misery was provided by a potato whiskey, which was described as the "most wretched."[20]

It is not surprising that, when confronted by such economic circumstances, many people looked about them for an escape from their native land, or that others, who wished to emigrate for different reasons, found little in the economic situation to hold them. During the thirties a strong urge arose in Saxony for removal from the fatherland to less developed countries. This movement fixed its greatest hopes upon America. Its vanguard and example, regardless of motives, were the Stephanite emigrants of 1838. For while there had been plans for mass emigration from Saxony prior to this date, none of them was sufficiently well organized to become a reality.[21]

Religious factors exerted a more direct influence upon the Stephanite movement and played an even greater part in the emigration of 1838 than the political and economic conditions just considered. In attempting to understand the religious controversies in Germany at that time, it is helpful to review briefly the history of conflicting German religious movements during the post-Reformation era. A contest had begun already in the latter part of the sixteenth century and early part of the seventeenth with a clash between strict doctrinalism and syncretism. The latter was a movement which advocated the union of all Christian denominations on such common ground as could be found. Lutheranism spent its energies in the violence of the quarrel with syncretism, drifted into formalism, and became an easy prey to other forces — at first to Pietism and later to Rationalism. Meanwhile syncretism had been successful to the extent that among certain elements it had created

[19] Rosenthal, *op. cit.*, 24. This translation is by the present writer, as are all others in this work unless otherwise indicated.

[20] *Ibid.*, 25. In supplementing the newspaper account which the author cites, she adds: "Such and similar portrayals of need are found in the most diverse newspapers." *Ibid.*

[21] *Ibid.*, 24–25, 29, 33, 51, 67; Hennig, "Die Auswanderung Martin Stephans," *Zeitschrift für Kirchengeschichte*, LVIII, 164–165.

a frame of mind that offered little resistance to the further dilution of traditional dogmas.

During the second half of the seventeenth century and the first part of the eighteenth conditions in the Protestant Church of Germany produced in Pietism a reaction that emphasized Christian life at the expense of Christian doctrine. The leaders of the Pietist attack upon formalism and indifferentism were Philipp Jakob Spener (1635—1705) and August Hermann Francke (1663—1727). Pietism's primary effects were a renewed emphasis upon the study of the Bible, a revival of dynamic preaching, a high degree of emotionalism in religion, a renewal of lay activity in the Church, the abandonment of the doctrinal forms of the old Lutheran theology, the stressing of a moral life and practical philanthropy, and a separatistic tendency within the Church. Yet, just as Pietism had recoiled from the preceding tendency in the Church, it itself called forth a counteraction that was greatly intensified because it coincided with the developments in the Age of Enlightenment.

The overshadowing intellectual influence of the late seventeenth century and entire eighteenth century was the *Aufklärung.* The remarkable achievements attained in the domain of natural science by the application of the inductive method of reasoning led to the assumption that the universe was governed by immutable natural laws which reason could discover, and that constant advancement in the discovery of these laws could not fail to produce the progressive betterment of mankind from era to era. The optimistic feeling was rather general that the light of reason was dawning and was about to dispel all the evils of the world. On the basis of the *Aufklärung* a new approach to all problems was developed, which led in the field of politics first to enlightened despotism and ultimately to the French Revolution, and in the field of economics to the theories of Adam Smith. Theology was not spared the impact of these new forces. The attempt to apply the new line of reasoning to religion was called Rationalism.

In the early stage of its development the aim of Rationalism was to make theological truth self-evident, to prove it. The implication clearly was that if it could not be proved, it was not worthy of acceptance. To the Rationalists of the early eighteenth century this attitude toward theological problems appeared a firm defense against skepticism. To their orthodox critics it was skepticism itself; and they predicted that the principle that religion was to stand or fall by its reasonableness would lead to a fundamental denial of revealed theology. Events proved that they had been correct, for Rationalism subsequently advanced along more independent lines.[22] The theory of the reign of immutable natural law entailed the exclusion of the idea of miracles, which to the Rationalist were violations of such natural laws. At the same time divine activity was relegated to the very beginning of things, that is, to the establishment of these same laws, whose operation now governed the universe independently of a God. Such profound changes in theological thought not only were hostile to tradition, but precluded in theory and practice the acceptance of the principle of authority in religion. Philosophy of the Rationalistic type and science as then understood became the basis of a new *Vernunftreligion.* The concept of revealed theology was openly rejected, and the Bible was assailed with the tools of higher criticism.[23]

Rationalist philosophy at one time penetrated every stratum of German society, but its easiest conquest was at the universities among the educated leaders of the Church itself.[24] Mass popularization was more difficult and had to be conducted largely from the rostrum of the pulpit. Theological students, thoroughly saturated with the new religio-philosophical ideas, entered the service of the state churches and sought to pass on the torch to their parishioners.[25] The lengths to which this attempt was carried and the degree in which it was successful naturally varied greatly, and Rationalism consequently assumed a corresponding variety of forms. For instance, a milder Rationalistic wing, the Supernaturalists, insisted

---

22 Seeberg, *Die Kirche Deutschlands im neunzehnten Jahrhundert,* 5—6, 15.

23 *Ibid.;* Schaff, *Germany, its Universities, Theology and Religion,* 70.

24 Stöckhardt, *Die kirchlichen Zustände Deutschlands . . . im 19. Jahrhundert,* 3. The name of Stöckhardt presents for the first time one of the difficulties in spelling that is occasioned in a study of this kind by the German *Umlaut* in the case of the vowels "a," "o," and "u." Not only do later generations of a family (such as the Büngers, Bürgers, and others) often Anglicize the spelling of their names by inserting an "e" as a substitute for the *Umlaut,* but such variant spellings even occur in the name of the same person at the same period of time when, as was sometimes done, Latin letters are used. Therefore a variant spelling resulting from an *Umlaut* or the absence of it may never be taken as indicating a different person or even a different family. The initials will have to determine who is meant. Throughout this study the *Umlaut* is used unless the original to which reference is made had dropped it.

25 Von Treitschke, *op. cit.,* V, 353.

upon the existence of revelation. Yet even they still subjected all alleged revelation to a rationalizing process that produced much the same effect as that achieved by the outright Rationalists themselves. "Therefore Rationalistic and Supernaturalistic sermons are often so similar, that it is impossible to distinguish to which tendency the preacher belonged."[26] The problems of religious life were neglected, and sermons were devoted to a discussion of current events, scientific discourses, and homespun advice on a variety of subjects, such as stall feeding, vaccinia, coffee drinking, drunkenness, careless bathing, the culture of silkworms, intelligent agriculture, the profitableness of potato raising, the necessity of tree planting, and the importance of genuine sanitation.[27]

Rationalist preaching became more and more prevalent and often went to extremes. Miracles were summarily dismissed as fables or explained with rather strained textual and historical interpretations.[28] Eventually it became possible to state from the pulpit, as one preacher did in 1800: "I declare every so-called revealed religion to be a lie";[29] or for another to assert: "A matter which I cannot conceive and picture to myself does not exist for me."[30] Under the influence of the Rationalists, "Protestantism" (which they understood only as opposition to the dogmatism of the Roman Catholics and as man's right of free inquiry and loyalty to his convictions) was given a new meaning that was openly opposed to the chief tenets upon which the original protest had been based. Doctrines such as the vicarious atonement and justification by faith were dismissed as untenable in an enlightened age. The practice of continuing to appropriate the name and form of the old Protestant Church was defended by claiming that "Whoever finds these doctrines contrary to reason and to Scripture and consequently rejects them, proves his Protestantism through that very act."[31] In other words, Rationalism regarded itself as identical with Protestanism.

---

[26] Uhlhorn, *Geschichte der deutsch-lutherischen Kirche*, II, 84—85. See also Hagenbach, *History of the Church in the Eighteenth and Nineteenth Centuries*, II, 106.

[27] Uhlhorn, *op. cit.*, II, 55; C. F. W. Walther, *The Proper Distinction Between Law and Gospel* (hereafter cited as *Law and Gospel*), 259.

[28] Herford (ed.), *op. cit.*, 147; Schnabel, *Deutsche Geschichte im neunzehnten Jahrhundert*, IV, 369—370.

[29] Stöckhardt, *op. cit.*, 4.

[30] Seeberg, *op. cit.*, 16.

[31] Stöckhardt, *op. cit.*, 3.

Accordingly, the Rationalists, still operating officially within the scope of historic church organizations, effected a fundamental modification of Christianity into a moral system. Gradually hymnals, catechisms, and other religious books were made to conform to the new ideas.

The outstanding effect produced upon the Church by these forces, and the one most significant for Stephanism and the Stephanite emigration, was that they precipitated a bitter struggle between two major groups or factions within the Church. The one desired a variety of revisions in religious attitudes and creeds, the other a maintenance of traditional views and doctrines and, insofar as there had already been a departure from them, a return to the historic faiths. Hence, for the orthodox elements, of which the Stephanites were a part, the philosophical and scientific problems raised by the *Aufklärung* were overshadowed by the fundamental theological question: Was the rationalizing approach to spiritual matters found in most trends of thought then current, regardless of their philosophical viewpoint or religious tendency, to be adopted by the Church, or was the principle of faith to be retained as the basis of spiritual life? If the latter were accepted, to what extent and in what form?

While there were many people who secretly resented the change that had been wrought in the Church, effective opposition to its conquest by Rationalism was lacking until the early nineteenth century. Those who disapproved lacked a dynamic leadership and were forced to take recourse to private devotional reading and the Sacraments. Confessionalism, which might have served as a nucleus of opposition, was thrust so far into the background that even in the nineteenth century it was still a matter of pride to Heinrich Zschokke that from 1808 to 1842 no one could determine whether his devotional publication, known as *Stunden der Andacht,* was the product of a Roman Catholic or a Protestant.[32] Throughout the period of the *Aufklärung* the revisionist element in the Church enjoyed the advantage of both a numerical superiority and a dynamic vitality. In fact, of the two major schools of thought in religion, only that which desired a revision of historic Christianity was articulate at the beginning of the nineteenth century.

---

[32] Schnabel, *op. cit.,* IV, 371.

But Rationalism in its eighteenth-century form was to fall by its own weight, or, in the words of Seeberg: "A surfeited and ripe Rationalism sat on the throne at the beginning of the [nineteenth] century." [33] The signs of this development became apparent almost immediately after the movement had reached the climax of its influence in the latter part of the preceding century, and are noticeable simultaneously from the top to the bottom of the intellectual scale. At the same time that Rationalism began to stagnate, a variety of opinions, diverging to a greater or lesser degree from its prevalent premises, began to gain ground. Rationalism was found wanting by both the philosopher and the common man, on theoretical and practical grounds alike.[34] Some of the leaders in thought began to see that in the rationalization of the world the fact had been overlooked that man was anything but a completely rational being. "It was discovered that there were other spheres of human life besides that of reason." [35] As H. H. Maurer has more dramatically described it: "With the opening of the nineteenth century the retreat of religion before 'rationalism' had come to a standstill. Religion faced about, prepared to meet its pursuer." [36]

However, the strongest force opposing Rationalism did not have its origin in the ranks of the philosophers and the professors, the poets and the preachers, who were dominating the thought life of Germany at that time, but in the ranks of the simple laymen. This force was a surge of deeper religious feeling whose various movements may be grouped under the collective term *Erweckung*.[37] The common man could not delve deeply into the mysteries of metaphysical speculation. He did not care to, nor did he try. Consciously or unconsciously many people preferred the faith which they could feel, to the "reason" which they could not understand. Yet the *Erweckung* cannot be regarded merely as the revolt of the uneducated against a new idea. On the contrary, Rationalism even as a philosophic movement had run its course. Furthermore, the prac-

---

33 Seeberg, *op. cit.*, 15.

34 *Ibid.*, 8, 15.

35 Schnabel, *op. cit.*, IV, 294.

36 Maurer, "Studies in the Sociology of Religion, IV, The Problems of Group-Consensus; Founding the Missouri Synod," *American Journal of Sociology,* XXX, 665.

37 Schnabel, *op. cit.*, IV, 289; Hennig, *op. cit.*, 9—10.

tical effect of the Age of Enlightenment upon the spiritual life of Germany had been highly unsatisfactory. Even liberalistic leaders agreed that the Church had suffered damage in fiber and prestige.[38]

Impetus was given to the *Erweckung* by the War of Liberation. Under the impact of the times men felt the need of religion and returned to Bible reading and prayer. Preaching became more earnest; pastoral work was resumed. Moreover, the excesses of the French Revolution, which was in part the outcome of the *Aufklärung,* had cast discredit upon the entire intellectual movement of which religious Rationalism was only a single phase. When these tendencies were given further momentum by a wave of Romanticism, there was a strong disposition to return to tradition and traditional institutions in religion as well as in other fields, and the combined effect became a threat to the Rationalists against which they inveighed in their publications. While the break with Rationalism was rapid among some classes, its influence nevertheless survived well into the nineteenth century among the *bourgeoisie* and some of the clergy, just as the faith of the orthodoxists had previously not been completely smothered by their opponents.[39]

However, what was occurring in Germany was not merely the restoration of the old forms of Protestant denominationalism. The senses had been dulled to that type of theology by the experiences of the preceding century. Instead, the *Erweckung* usually styled itself more inclusively as merely Christian, or evangelical, or Protestant, or, at the very most, evangelical-Lutheran. By the same token the distinctions between orthodox Protestantism and Pietism had shrunk perceptibly, and events pointed to a possible amalgamation of the two.[40] The main purpose of both these religious groups was to call forth a real religious "awakening" and to oppose a domineering Rationalism whose "liberalism" all too frequently did not include the tolerance of divergent opinions.[41] Furthermore, the spirit of nationalism, which the struggle against Napoleon had evoked and which was most evident in Prussia, proved to be a new enemy to Lutheran conservatism. For nationalism engendered a

---

38 Seeberg, *op. cit.,* 3, 17; Schnabel, *op. cit.,* IV, 293, 295.

39 Seeberg, *op. cit.,* 9, 17.

40 Schnabel, *op. cit.,* IV, 287—289, 380; Hennig, "Die Auswanderung Martin Stephans," *Zeitschrift für Kirchengeschichte,* LVIII, 143.

41 Seeberg, *op. cit.,* 55.

spirit of devotion to the State and demanded a religious unity within it that necessitated a church with doctrinal standards comprehensive enough to include Protestants of all views, Reformed as well as Lutherans.

Thus there was thrust into the tempest of conflicting forces and ideologies of the early nineteenth century a new idea, or rather, the partial revival of an old one — the union of the Protestant churches. A beginning was made in Prussia during 1817. The ruling house of Hohenzollern had been Calvinist for about two hundred years, while the majority of its subjects were still of the Lutheran faith. Now the indifference toward traditional theological disputes, which Rationalism had begotten and which the *Erweckung* had done little to change, made a fusion possible. Accordingly, the elaborate celebration of the Reformation on the tercentenary of the posting of Luther's Ninety-Five Theses was seized upon as an opportune moment for launching "the Union." The merger of the churches in Prussia was based upon the usual assumptions of unionistic movements among Protestants: that the features which the Reformed and Lutherans had in common were the essential ones; that their differences were on relatively minor points; and that such differences should be sacrificed, or at least permitted to exist side by side.

The methods of effecting the Union were chiefly the joint celebration of the Sacrament and the introduction of a new, neutral liturgy. These measures were reinforced during the next few decades by the consolidation of some Lutheran and Reformed congregations; by the suppression of any strong confessional position and of opinions unfavorable to the Union; by the suspension of orthodox clergymen, such as Pastor Guericke of Halle, who was removed from office in 1835,[42] or Pastor J. G. Scheibel, who had to flee from Silesia to Saxony in 1832;[43] by the appointment of those favoring the State's policies; and by dragonnades. Notwithstanding very moderate petitions by the non-conforming Prussian congregations, the organization of a "free" or independent church was not permitted until 1841. Before that time those who did not comply faced

---

[42] Testimony of Guericke, Halle, March 13, 1835, G. H. Löber, Diary, Feb. 24, 1835, MSS., Concordia Historical Institute (hereafter abbreviated C. H. I.).

[43] Fischer, *Das falsche Märtyrerthum oder die Wahrheit in der Sache der Stephanianer*, 38.

the possibility of fines or imprisonment unless they took refuge in flight.[44] Pastor Grabau led one group to the United States, Pastor Fritsche another to Australia. The total number who fled in 1837 has been estimated by a contemporary at two thousand.[45]

Despite the severity of the methods used to achieve the Union, it is incorrect to picture it as willful tyranny on the part of the government. The policy of working for union was quite in keeping with the views of the majority of the people, and the aim, although frequently not the method, of the government at first enjoyed the active support of a wing of the Church led by Schleiermacher.[46]

The struggle in Prussia was only one phase of the religious conflict throughout Germany. The Prussian example influenced to a greater or lesser extent many smaller German states, in almost all of which similar unions of the Protestant church bodies were effected. And as in Prussia, so elsewhere in Germany the most conservative element opposed the tendency from the beginning. For in the eyes of strict Lutherans the unionistic tendency was an apostasy from full orthodoxy. Consequently, with the extreme right-wing Protestants, the conservative reaction against Rationalism in the late eighteenth century and early nineteenth became, after 1817, not only a dissent from Rationalism as such, but also a counteraction against what they held were its effects, including the Union in Germany and the latitudinarianism represented in the churches of the United States.

In the same year that the Prussian Union was consummated, conservative Lutheranism received a stimulus from a new set of ninety-five theses written by Klaus Harms, archdeacon at Kiel, as a parallel to Luther's theses three hundred years before. They were a powerful Jeremiad on conditions in the Church and pointed out the wide divergence of the current rationalizing, critical, and

---

44 Scheibel, *Archiv für historische Entwickelung und neueste Geschichte der lutherischen Kirche,* 239—243; Testimony in the case of Christian Schneider *et al.*, Zanthau (Breslau), May 11, 1837—Oct. 20, 1838, MSS., C. H. I.; Minutes of the *Berathungscomite* of the Stephanite Emigration Association, April 14, 1838, Bound MSS., No. 12. Fasc. III. Protokolle über die Vorbereitungen zur sächs. Auswanderung (hereafter cited as Protokolle über die . . . Auswanderung, Bound MSS., III), C. H. I.; J. F. Bünger, Diarium per iter Dresd. in Americam 1838 et 1839 (hereafter cited as Diarium), Oct. 25, 1838, MS., Fürbringer Papers, St. Louis; Schnabel, *op. cit.*, IV, 347, 354.

45 Scheibel, *op. cit.*, 245.

46 Schnabel, *op. cit.*, IV, 326—327.

unionistic trends from historic Protestantism. Harms's dramatic warning had a mildly explosive effect. Within a short time approximately two hundred pamphlets for and against these theses appeared in Germany. The reaction of the Rationalists was prompt and violent. "The thrust had gone home, and it hurt." [47] To the conservative element Harms had a correspondingly strong appeal. For instance, G. H. Löber, one of the pastors of the Saxon emigration, thought highly of Harms and was in touch with him.[48]

Meanwhile numerous isolated orthodox pastors and communities throughout Germany had survived the era of Rationalism. They were known by a variety of names: Old-Lutherans, Orthodoxists, New Orthodoxists, or by more personal designations, such as Stephanites. They had long been an inarticulate and ineffective though zealous minority. But they had been strengthened in many cases by the Pietist element; now they were encouraged by the *Erweckung,* and their indignation was incited by the Union. During the decades immediately following the latter event, the anti-Rationalists were led by men like J. G. Scheibel, Guericke, Rudelbach, Krafft, Hengstenberg, and Tholuck, who made their protest heard. Many pastors and lay leaders joined the movement, adhering tenaciously to their beliefs. Some of the more conservative Lutherans even went so far as to cross state boundaries (*e. g.,* from Prussia into Saxe-Altenburg) to have their children baptized or to take Communion from an orthodox pastor.[49]

The response to the *Erweckung* and to more conservative and more distinctly Lutheran movements was slight among the middle class, which had been impregnated with the spirit of Rationalism for a century. But the effect upon the upper and lower classes was profound, and especially among the humbler folk the preachers of the *Erweckung* created a sensation. "People of every station in life and of every confession streamed together where such a preacher stood in the pulpit each Sunday. 'The people crowded around the doors

---

[47] Seeberg, *op. cit.,* 66.

[48] Dau (ed.), *Ebenezer, Reviews of the Work of the Missouri Synod during Three Quarters of a Century,* 6. Occasionally Löber had his doubts even about Harms. G. H. Löber, Diary, April 5, 1831, MS., C. H. I.

[49] Putzer to G. H. Löber, Dec. 16, 1836, Lossagung vom Stephanismus, G. H. Löber, Diary, Jan. 23—25, March 19, and entries for July, 1836, MSS., C. H. I.; Lochner, "Ottomar Fürbringer," *Der Lutheraner,* XLIX, 163.

and climbed up to the windows on ladders,' so reads a contemporary account." [50]

In Saxony the same influences were felt as in the rest of Germany, but with different force and effect. These variations can be summed up by saying that extremes were the exception and changes were slower. Rationalism was present, but it was often tempered by one of the countless nuances of Supernaturalism. On the other hand, it maintained itself longer. Similarly, the Saxon Pietists did not go to the lengths attained elsewhere. The same observation can be made concerning confessionalism. Orthodoxy itself was qualified.[51] Except for the personal following of Martin Stephan, no one in the Kingdom during 1838 was prepared to adopt so pronounced a position as his. Even such thoroughgoing Lutherans as Rudelbach continued their activity in the State Church, while the Stephanites were shaking the dust of an unappreciative Dresden from their feet.

Nevertheless, in the history of Stephanism one fact must be emphasized as of vital importance, namely, that, despite the changes beginning to take place as a result of the *Erweckung,* there still existed an unmistakably Rationalistic tendency in the Protestant Church of that day, and particularly in the Saxon Lutheran Church and among some of its leaders. The generalization of Lamprecht that "the atmosphere which pervaded the Protestant churches during the first decades of the nineteenth century was that of the old, individualistic Rationalism," [52] and his similar remarks of a more specific nature about the year 1830,[53] became more pointed in the words of L. Fischer, an opponent of Stephanism, who wrote in 1839: "The evangelical-Protestant Church has become in its scope the refuge of freethinkers." [54] Fischer fortified his claim with quotations

---

[50] Schnabel, *op. cit.,* IV, 399. See also Löber-Eichenberg (ed.), "VI. Von Altenburg (Sachsen-Altenburg) nach Altenburg in Nordamerika (Mo.). Ein Briefwechsel aus den Jahren 1838 bis 1844 als Beitrag zur Geschichte der Stephan'schen Auswanderung," *Mitteilungen des Vereins für Geschichts- und Altertumskunde zu Kahla und Roda* (hereafter cited as "Ein Briefwechsel," *Mitteilungen . . . Kahla*), VII, 126; C. F. W. Walther, *Kurzer Lebenslauf des weiland ehrwürdigen Pastor Joh. Friedr. Bünger* (hereafter cited as *Bünger*), 39. This biography first appeared serially as "Pastor Johann Friedrich Bünger," *Der Lutheraner,* XXXVIII, 41—42, 49—51, 57—59, 66—68, 73—74, 82—84, 89—90, 105—106, 113—114. References in succeeding pages always cite the more easily accessible book form.

[51] Hennig, *op. cit.,* 12, 14—15, 208; Fischer, *op. cit.,* 37.

[52] Lamprecht, *Deutsche Geschichte,* X, 453.

[53] *Ibid.,* 488—489.

[54] Fischer, *op. cit.,* 104.

of extreme Rationalistic statements by leading churchmen in Saxony.[55] Franz Delitzsch, a scholar in his own right and a Stephanite who broke away from the movement at the time of the emigration, stated in 1842 that the bulk of Rationalistic publications was appearing in Saxony.[56]

In Saxe-Altenburg, the duchy from which many of the emigrants of 1838 came, the Church officially admitted that Rationalism had a strong representation, but claimed that it was on the wane.[57] A later opinion on Saxe-Altenburg was that "In Germany and also in our smaller fatherland [Saxe-Altenburg] Rationalism then [at the time of the emigration] reigned. The preachers who presented the pure Gospel were few, and one traveled many miles to them." [58] The opposition to Rationalism and other liberalistic tendencies in the Saxon Church, noticeable ever since 1800, was the determining factor in the development of Stephanism.

The State Church of Saxony was Lutheran, and until 1818 this was the only recognized Protestant group in the country. Citizenship implied membership in the State Church, except for the members of the one major independent establishment, the Roman Catholic Church, and of a few small bodies, such as the Reformed, which in 1838 had only two congregations, one in Dresden and another in Leipzig.[59] Normally the head of the State would have been head of the Church as well, but in Saxony the ruler had not been a member of the State Church since 1697, when Fredrick Augustus I

---

55 *Ibid.*, 109—110.

56 Delitzsch, *Wer sind die Mystiker?* 77.

57 *Bedenken der theologischen Facultäten der Landesuniversität Jena und der Universitäten zu Berlin, Göttingen, und Heidelberg über das Rescript des Herzoglichen Consistoriums zu Altenburg vom 13. Nov. 1838* (hereafter cited as *Bedenken der theologischen Facultäten*), 14.

58 Löber-Eichenberg (ed.), "Ein Briefwechsel," *Mitteilungen . . . Kahla*, VII, 126. See also G. F. Löber to G. H. Löber May 29, 1839, *ibid.*, 148—151; Stephan to B. Kurtz, March, 1833, Bound MSS., No. 9. Fasc. I. Verhandlg. u. Correspondenz d. Auswanderung betr. (hereafter cited as Bound MSS., I), C. H. I.; Fischer, *op. cit.*, 27, 35—38, 97—111; Delitzsch, *Lutherthum und Lügenthum*, 73; Schnabel, *op. cit.*, IV, 320; "Theology in Germany," *Biblical Repertory and Princeton Review for the Year 1853*, XXV, 446. Representative of the attempt to deny the prevalence of Rationalism in Saxony is Hennig, "Die Auswanderung Martin Stephans," *Zeitschrift für Kirchengeschichte*, LVIII, 144. But see *ibid.*, 145—147, 150. Löber's complaints about Rationalism in the Church were, of course, frequent, *e.g.*, G. H. Löber, Diary, Feb. 9, Aug. 15, 1831, MS., C. H. I.

59 Haan-Ramming, *Kirchlich-statistisches Handbuch für das Königreich Sachsen*, 331—332.

adopted Catholicism in order to qualify for the Polish crown. However, the majority of the people remained Protestant and were extremely distrustful of the Catholic Church, especially its clergy. Consequently the ruler and his co-religionists, who never amounted to more than a small percentage of the population, were very carefully watched and easily fell under suspicion.[60]

Since the apostasy of the electoral-royal line from Lutheranism, the crown's prerogative of governing the Church was exercised by an ecclesiastical council. This body and a consistory, which was entrusted with the administrative affairs of the Church, had their headquarters in the capital. These agencies of government were also in charge of the educational system, eleemosynary institutions, and literary censorship. The Church, accordingly, was a department of State and was administered as such, especially after the reorganization of the government in 1831, when (December 1) the Ministry of Worship and Public Instruction was established.[61] The new constitution of that year contained the following provisions: Ecclesiastical officials were to be responsible to the Ministry of Worship and Public Instruction; the head of the Ministry of Worship and two members of the cabinet were to be of the "evangelical" faith;[62] complaints concerning the misuse of ecclesiastical authority could be carried to the highest secular court of appeal; and Church and education were subject to the State in civil affairs.[63]

As has been indicated in the foregoing, there were elements in Saxony working for a modification of the Confessions of the State Church. There were those who felt that the Symbols should conform more closely to their individual ideas of Rationalistic liberalism, and there were others who felt that the creedal basis should more nearly approach the amalgamation of Lutheran and Reformed doctrine found in the churches of the Union. However, a frank revision of the Lutheran Confessions of the State Church could be accomplished only by formal action of the government. Such action

---

[60] Von Treitschke, *op. cit.*, IV, 153.

[61] Schilling, *Handbuch des geistlichen Geschaeftstyls und der geistlichen Geschaeftsverwaltung*, 9—25; Ziehnert, *Praktisches Evangelisches Kirchenrecht*, I, 20—32; Mayer, *Das Staatsrecht des Königreichs Sachsen*, 226.

[62] The term used is "evangelisch," but this is a reference to its nature and is not to be confused with the name of a denomination. The symbols of the Saxon Church were Lutheran.

[63] *Verfassungsurkunde des Königreichs Sachsen vom 4. September 1831*, Pars. 41, 57—59, pp. 21, 24.

proved too difficult for them to achieve. At the same time, none of the existing recognized organizations represented the viewpoint of either revisionist group. The establishment of new independent organizations was forbidden. Only by working from within the State Church could the aims of these factions be realized. In the face of this dilemma, men who shared the views of either of these groups remained in the State Church, where, without formal organization, but by sheer force of numbers and by expressing their personal convictions, they exerted a potent influence.

These circumstances had the effect of assuring that, in spite of administrative changes, the institutions and confessions of the State Church remained the same as they had been during the Reformation Era. Outwardly the Church appeared intact. However, the forms of religious expression were being infused with a meaning so different from that which they had formerly been understood to have, that their traditional sense appeared anachronistic through its incongruity with the background of the new interpretation supplied by the Rationalists and Unionists. The remarks of Schnabel on the infiltration of Rationalism into the German churches in general during an earlier period described what was occurring also in Saxony at this time: "In the ecclesiastical constitutions the institutions as well as the creeds . . . were usually left unchanged. But the silent adjustment of the liturgy to the new era was either permitted or required, so that the caprice of the parsons was given free rein." [64] The claim of the Stephanites was that "the Union had been accomplished in Saxony not in theory, but in fact," and one of their opponents, L. Fischer, admitted this to be at least partially true.[65]

Strict Lutheran groups in Saxony, such as the Stephanites, were opposed to both Unionism and Rationalism. But their bitterest quarrel was with the latter, that is, with all liberalistic tendencies within the Church, which in the nomenclature of the controversy were grouped under the designation of *Neologie*. Before and after Stephan came to Dresden, the Rationalists were waging a vigorous campaign against an orthodoxy that was branded literalist, medieval, unenlightened, mystical, hypocritical, and a variety of other things.[66]

---

[64] Schnabel, *op. cit.,* IV, 289—290.

[65] Fischer, *op. cit.,* 38, 99—102.

[66] *Ibid.,* 111, 129—132; Pleissner, *Die Kirchlichen Fanatiker im Muldenthale,* 3. Stephan came to Dresden as pastor in 1810.

The conservatives insisted that Rationalism had insinuated itself into the Church through an insincere aquiescence in the orthodox doctrine it was now attempting to abrogate. If this attempt to overthrow traditional creeds had been made from outside the organization, it would undoubtedly have aroused serious opposition. But in Saxony all State-Church clergymen were pledged to the Lutheran Confessions by oath; and in fact, throughout the formulas used in issuing a call, in ordination, and in installation, the pastors were bound to these same Symbols.[67] Thus the anticonfessional movement centered among the very men who were obligated to defend the tenets of the Church, and the bitterness created among their conservative opponents was even greater.[68] While it must be admitted that the Stephanites, for instance, gave to the Confessions the strictest and most literal interpretation, it is also true that many of the opposing clergymen openly derided the Symbols to which they were pledged, or at least no longer accepted them in the full force of their historic implications. Furthermore, the very men who were expected to defend the institutions and creeds of the Church — its highest officials — frequently condoned or even encouraged such laxness.[69]

Indeed, some men advocated an outright change and wished to abolish the pastors' pledge to the Symbols. Others wished to

---

67 The oath of the clergymen is quoted in Fischer, *op. cit.*, 144, and in Pöschel, *Glaubensbekenntniss der Gemeinde zu St. Johannis in Dresden*, 73—74. The latter writer also gives the formula for installation. *Ibid.*, 74. Examples of both a call issued to a Saxon pastor and of the formula used at his ordination are found in E. M. Bürger, Selbstbiographie von Ernst Moritz Bürger luther. Pastor emer. (hereafter cited as Selbstbiographie), 75—80, MS., E. J. Buerger Papers, Ellicottville, N. Y.

68 A pronounced attitude of this kind is represented in Einige Bemerkungen über die bekannten Vorgänge mit dem Pastor der böhmischen Gemeinde zu St. Joh., Martin Stephan, Bound MSS., No. 11. Fasc. V. Untersuchung P. St. betr. (hereafter cited as Bemerkungen über . . . Stephan, Bound MSS., V), C. H. I.

69 Von Falkenstein (the consistory) to E. M. Bürger, July 31, 1835, in E. M. Bürger, Selbstbiographie, 108—111, MS., E. J. Buerger Papers, Ellicottville, N. Y. See also *ibid.*, 80—85, 104—108; Bemerkungen über . . . Stephan, Bound MSS., V, C. H. I.; *Leipziger allgemeine Zeitung*, July 24, 1838; C. F. W. Walther to O. H. Walther, August, 1833, quoted in M. Günther, *Dr. C. F. W. Walther*, 15. The latter biography first appeared as a series of articles under the title: "Ehrendenkmal des seligen Dr. Carl Ferdinand Wilhelm Walther," *Der Lutheraner*, XLIV—XLV, *seriatim.* See also Fischer, *op. cit.*, 35—37, 44—46, 64—65, 99—102, 104—110; Delitzsch, *Lutherthum und Lügenthum*, 73; Delitzsch, *Wer sind die Mystiker?* 77; von Polenz, *Die öffentliche Meinung und der Pastor Stephan*, 53, 73; *Bedenken der theologischen Facultäten*, 1; C. F. W. Walther, *Bünger*, 32—33.

revise the Confessions to make them conform to the prevalent conception of Protestantism and thus to eliminate the necessity of forcing a liberalistic interpretation upon them. At the same time the consistorial form of polity was to be replaced by a synodical or presbyterial system, which, it was hoped, would be more responsive to the wishes of the non-conservative majority and thus facilitate the introduction of further changes in the Church.[70] Stephan and others were horrified at these suggestions. Yet such a revision could have had a salutary effect if it had clarified the situation.

It was just the insidiousness of the change that had taken place that caused much of the trouble. Had there been an open break between Rationalism and orthodox Lutheranism in Saxony, the solution to the problem would have been simpler. Either one would have been forced to give way, or they would have been obliged to evolve a *modus vivendi* side by side. At the very least, the lines for the struggle would have been clearly drawn, which they were not under existing circumstances. As it was, incompatibles were to be forced into the same organization, and as a result no one was occupying a consistent or logically tenable position. Thus while L. Fischer, in writing against the emigration, accused the Stephanites of being separatistic, he also admitted that conditions tolerated in the Saxon Church fairly drove them into such a position.[71]

The Protestant Church of Saxony was professedly Lutheran, nominally conservative. Yet because of the conflicting elements it contained, no one was clear in his own mind that it was either of these. The liberalistic element was attempting to remake the Church along lines sympathetic to its philosophy, which it identified

---

[70] Stephan to G. H. W. Walther, Jan. 18, 1831, MS., C. H. I.; Stephan to B. Kurtz, March, 1833, Bound MSS., I, C. H. I.; C. F. W. Walther to O. H. Walther, August, 1833, quoted in M. Günther, *op. cit.*, 15; C. F. W. Walther in Köstering, *Auswanderung der sächsischen Lutheraner im Jahre 1838* (hereafter cited as *Auswanderung*), 11; Keyl, *Offene Bekenntnisse des vormaligen Pfarrers Keyl in Niederfrohna über seine Gemeinschaft mit Stephan und die darin begangenen Versündigungen*, 13. Keyl's confession appeared first in the Rudelbach-Guericke journal, *Zeitschrift für die gesammte lutherische Theologie und Kirche*, III, No. 1, pp. 94—114. There is also a manuscript copy in the Concordia Historical Institute, which may be the original draft by Keyl, or (more likely) a contemporary copy. To simplify references the pamphlet form in which it later appeared was used here and in subsequent citations. See also Fischer, *op. cit.*, 184.

[71] Fischer, *op. cit.*, 67. See also von Polenz, *op. cit.*, 73; C. F. W. Walther, *Bünger*, 35; Schnabel, *op. cit.*, IV, 320.

with true Protestantism. Its aim was to make old forms fit a new faith, an attempt exemplified in von Ammon's *Fortbildung des Christenthums zur Weltreligion.*[72] The defenders of the traditional Confessions were either attempting to revive the Church or to recreate it, depending upon their individual opinions on the degree of its decadence. Their aim was to force a new faith back into the old forms.[73] The other elements affected by the *Erweckung* occupied an intermediate position. Since none of these groups was permitted to leave the formal organization of the State Church, the result was an internecine struggle within it, "owing partly to the want of full liberty outside of the establishments, and the excess of liberty within. . . ." [74] The struggle was a bitter one, although the Stephanites and other orthodox groups were, by their own admission, a distinct minority.[75]

The liberalists were aided in their efforts to bring about a change in the Church by the fact that many of the higher officials were adherents of this school of thought. As has been noted, these men either were actively engaged in the undertaking themselves or at least approved of activity directed toward that end. At the same time the University of Leipzig was saturated with the philosophy of the *Aufklärung,* even in its theological faculty. C. F. W. Walther asserted that during his student days there were only three members of this department whom he would not have called "coarse Rationalists." [76] While his judgment in a matter of this kind is not likely to be mild, it is authoritative assurance that they were not orthodoxists. Leipzig produced pastors and teachers who presented the viewpoint of the faculty to the people in the congrega-

---

[72] Fischer, *op. cit.,* 35—37, 97—102, 109—110; Delitzsch, *Lutherthum und Lügenthum,* 73.

[73] Fischer, *op. cit.,* 54—56.

[74] Schaff, *op. cit.,* 135. See also Fischer, *op. cit.,* 104—113.

[75] Stephan to B. Kurtz, March, 1833, Bound MSS., I, C. H. I.; G. H. Löber, Diary, July 28, Aug. 15, 1831, Aug. 29, 1836, MS., C. H. I.

[76] C. F. W. Walther, *Bünger,* 10. See also Schaff, *op. cit.,* 79—80; Bürger, *Sendschreiben an die evangelisch-lutherische Kirche zunächst in Wisconsin, Missouri, Preussen und Sachsen,* 9; C. F. W. Walther in Köstering, *Auswanderung,* 3; Hennig, "Die Auswanderung Martin Stephans," *Zeitschrift für Kirchengeschichte,* LVIII, 145. There was similar trouble in Saxe-Altenburg. G. H. Löber, Diary, Aug. 2, 1831, MS., C. H. I. A description of conditions, men, and curricula at Leipzig and at an outstanding *Gymnasium* are given in E. M. Bürger, Selbstbiographie, 34—37, 40—45, MS., E. J. Buerger Papers, Ellicottville, N. Y.

tions and to the children in the schools. The careers of students who were not disposed to do so were effectively checked.

> In order to qualify for appointment as a preacher in Saxony at that time, one had to pass a twofold examination after the completion of his university studies. The first was called "*examen pro licentia concionandi*," that is, the test for obtaining permission to preach anywhere in the State Church on request, an examination which since 1833 had to be passed before a commission of professors in Leipzig. The second examination, to which one could not be admitted until two years later, was called the "*examen pro candidatura*," that is, the examination before the state consistory in order to qualify for appointment. . . . At that time it was almost an impossibility for an orthodox candidate, who confessed and practiced his faith, to get a place in Saxony under royal patronage through the unbelieving state consistory.[77]

What had not yet been accomplished in the case of the Confessions had been effected in the liturgy. In 1812 a revision was made of the formulae for the rites of the Church and a new *Agenda* published.[78] The revisions were of such a nature that they frequently either rendered the forms meaningless by their empty phrasing or frankly changed them and the doctrines they involved.[79] The charge was also made that the extreme liberalists were permitted by indulgent authorities to change even these revised formulae, but that the conservatives were made to adhere to them strictly.[80] However, there was usually a choice of forms, and one or more of the rituals had been left intact, as in the case of Baptism.[81] The intention was that the new forms should not offend anyone, primarily the revisers. They did, nevertheless, antagonize the remaining conservative groups, of which there were many in Saxony.[82] Among the dissatisfied elements, the Stephanites were the most unyielding; their history is the principal subject of this study.

---

77 C. F. W. Walther, *Bünger,* 20, 16. See also Lossagung vom Stephanismus, MS., C. H. I.

78 *Kirchenbuch für den evangelischen Gottesdienst der Königlich Sächsischen Lande auf allerhöchsten Befehl herausgegeben,* 2 vols. (hereafter cited as *Kirchenbuch*).

79 Rudelbach, *Die Sacramentworte . . . Nebst zwei theologischen Gutachten über die Sächsische Kirchen-Agende von 1812,* pp. 95—101; Fischer, *op. cit.,* 114—121; C. F. W. Walther in Köstering, *Auswanderung,* 3, 11.

80 C. F. W. Walther, *Bünger,* 33.

81 *Kirchenbuch,* II, 167—201.

82 Hennig, *op. cit.,* 172—206.

CHAPTER TWO

RISE OF STEPHANISM IN SAXONY 1810—1837

MARTIN STEPHAN was born in Stramberg, Moravia, on August 13, 1777. The death of his poverty-stricken father and mother left him an orphan at an early age. His parents, originally of the Roman Catholic faith, had been converted to Protestantism before the birth of their son. He was given a strict Biblical training at home, but his elementary schooling seems to have been meager indeed. The lad was taught a trade, as his father had been, and came to Breslau in 1797 or 1799 as a journeyman linen weaver. In Breslau, Stephan established contact with the local Pietists and, beginning in 1802 or 1803, was enabled, through their kindness, to continue his education at St. Elizabeth's *Gymnasium*.[1] A clergyman of this conservative group, the elder Pastor Scheibel (Johann Ephraim), deacon at St. Elizabeth's Church and professor at the University of Breslau, took a special interest in Stephan and gave him free access to the church library. There the young man read avidly, laying the groundwork for a relatively conservative theological outlook and obtaining a creditable command of church history.[2] Later Stephan was to repay his benefactor by treating his son with bitter enmity.[3]

Although Stephan was gifted in many ways, a study of the classics seems to have had little attraction for him. He failed to master the requisite Greek and Latin at the *Gymnasium*, but he was permitted to continue his studies and, with the financial assistance of Count von Hohenthal, entered the University of Halle in 1804. Two years later he entered the University of Leipzig, where he remained until 1809. The same distaste for the prescribed curriculum manifested itself at the universities as it had at the *Gym-*

---

1 Lütkemüller, *Die Lehren und Umtriebe der Stephanisten*, 46—47; Fischer, *op. cit.*, 6—8; Hasse, *Abriss der meissnischen-albertinisch-sächsischen Kirchengeschichte*, 386—387; C. F. W. Walther, *Bünger*, 22; Stephan, *Der christliche Glaube*, Introductory Prayer; Hennig, "Die Auswanderung Martin Stephans," *Zeitschrift für Kirchengeschichte*, LVIII, 144.

2 Vehse, *Die Stephan'sche Auswanderung nach Amerika*, 1.

3 Stephan to G. H. Löber, Feb. 20, 1836, MS., C. H. I.; von Polenz, *op. cit.*, 10, 54—57.

nasium, and much of his time was spent in reading Pietist publications of all kinds, which were more to his liking than scholarship and "carnal erudition." Since such reading was of little help in mastering his studies, he discontinued his work at Leipzig in 1809 without taking the examination. In the same year he accepted a pastorate at Haber, Bohemia, where he was active for approximately one year.[4]

Meanwhile, in Dresden, the pulpit at St. John's had become vacant, and in 1810 Stephan accepted a call to this so-called "Bohemian" congregation.[5] This occurrence marks a turning point in Stephan's career. The history of this congregation is of some significance for the Stephanite emigration, since the exercise of its traditional rights in Stephan's peculiar fashion led to many of his subsequent difficulties. The facts can be stated only briefly here.

During the Thirty Years' War numerous Protestant fugitives from Bohemia found a haven in Saxony. However, when the war was ended in 1648, many of them did not return to their native land. Two years later, on May 15, 1650, they were formally recognized by the government, and the structure of St. John's Church in Dresden was assigned to them. Although they became a part of the State Church, their irregular religious gatherings, common in Bohemia, but prohibited in Saxony, were specifically allowed them, as well as the free choice of their elders and pastor and the exercise of their system of church discipline. They had brought along a sum of 12,000 gulden, formerly the property of a church in Prague from which many of them had come. This money was placed in trust with the government, to be administered as a fund for paying a part of the pastor's salary and for poor relief. In 1837 the church had a handsome endowment of 50,000 thaler. By that time almost all its members were natives of Saxony and understood German; in fact, only a minority could speak the language of their forefathers. The character of the congregation had changed, but its charter rights

---

[4] Von Polenz, *op. cit.,* 9; Fischer, *op. cit.,* 16—17; Lütkemüller, *op. cit.,* 47; Hennig, "Die Auswanderung Martin Stephans," *Zeitschrift für Kirchengeschichte,* LVIII, 144—145. A date for the events of 1809 is suggested by the fact that Stephan was ordained on April 3 of that year. Stephan to Flügel, Oct. 12, 1841, MS., C. H. I.

[5] Lütkemüller, *op. cit.,* 22. The inscription on a picture of Stephan in the Concordia Historical Institute states that he was pastor of St. John's since April 13, 1810. In recent years the church has been called *Erlöserkirche.* Stephan's address was *Pirnaische Strasse, No. 6.* Hennig, *op. cit.,* 26—27.

remained the same.[6] It was exercising one of its special privileges rather freely when, in 1810, it chose Stephan as its pastor, for he was not qualified for another position in the Saxon State Church. The situation was plainly a delicate one. Some jealous Saxons did not hesitate to point out that the "Bohemians" were no longer exiles, yet were enjoying a great degree of independence as a result of courtesies extended to them almost two centuries before, when they had not been, as they were in 1810, assimilated with the Saxon population.[7]

Stephan's tenure of office as pastor of St. John's Church in Dresden continued uninterruptedly for almost twenty-eight years, during all but one of which he was in active service. The story of his work during that time, which in a general sense is the story of Stephanism, can be divided into two major periods of nearly equal length. The first period, from 1810 to 1823, comprises the more constructive, peaceful years of Stephan's career, the beginnings of concerted opposition to his teachings and practices, and the efforts on his part to meet this criticism. The second period extends from 1823 to 1837, when the plan for emigration was launched. These years are characterized by a great increase in the number of his followers, the development of a remarkable ascendancy over his adherents, the degeneration of his activity into a personal movement, and the elevation of his idiosyncrasies into a system. Quite naturally these changes invited attacks upon his person and character, which, in turn, produced vehement controversy between his supporters and his opponents. When the plans for emigration matured, a new phase of development was encountered.

At first the activity of the new Bohemian pastor, who owed his position to the recommendation of Court Preacher Döring, attracted little attention and practically no opposition. It is true that Stephan was regarded as ultraconservative; yet he was generally accepted, and even attained some prominence, in the religious life of the city and of the kingdom.[8] In 1820 his edition of the *Petersburger Cate-*

---

6 Fischer, *op. cit.*, 7—14; von Polenz, *op. cit.*, 46—49; Stephan, *Herzlicher Zuruf . . . zwei Predigten*, 9—12. G. H. Löber claimed the fund was 70,000 thaler. G. H. Löber, Diary, 1836, p. 28, MS., C. H. I.

7 Complaint to the consistory against Stephan by a number of Dresden clergymen, June 23, 1820, MS., Stephanakten, Landeskirchenamt, Dresden, I, 1—3; von Polenz, *op. cit.*, 23—24, 46—47.

8 Lütkemüller, *op. cit.*, 48; Fischer, *op. cit.*, 17.

chismus appeared, and two years later, in collaboration with the Pietist Leonhardi, Stephan edited the *Christliche Katechismusübungen.*[9] His prestige was further enhanced by his connection with the Saxon Bible Society from the time of its organization in Dresden on August 10, 1814.[10] The society brought together an extremely heterogeneous group of men who were not agreed on its basic function and purpose. A glance at the roster of charter members justifies the exclamation: "A Stephan next to a von Ammon!" [11] But as time passed, the anti-Rationalist elements assumed a progressively greater control of the affairs and policies of the organization, and men like von Ammon were retained merely as figureheads to assure the *imprimatur* of the State Church. Stephan was a member of the board of the society for many years and preached the anniversary sermons as late as 1825 and 1829.[12]

Another of Stephan's public enterprises was his work in the Dresden Mission Society. In this activity he was once more associated with men who had no real compunctions about unionism — men like Leonhardi, treasurer of the organization — who wished to pledge their workers only to Christian fundamentals, such as the Ecumenical Creeds. Again the conservative element prevailed. Just as in the Bible Society, the Lutheran Confessions were retained, although it was then not customary for German mission societies to bind their emissaries to specific symbols.[13]

During these early years there was still an active group of Pietists in Dresden who held views similar to Stephan's and with whom he consorted. However, when personal differences and some divergence of opinion developed between Stephan and the group, he turned upon it. The maneuver was successful, and once more Stephan triumphed. The prestige of this society waned as Stephan's star rose, and with such remarkable co-ordination that during the

---

[9] Hennig, "Die Auswanderung Martin Stephans," *Zeitschrift für Kirchengeschichte,* LVIII, 147.

[10] Hennig, *op. cit.,* 98—102.

[11] *Ibid.,* 100. See also Hennig, "Die Auswanderung Martin Stephans," *Zeitschrift für Kirchengeschichte,* LVIII, 159—160. Von Ammon was regarded by the Stephanites as the evil genius of Saxon Protestantism. Bemerkungen über . . . Stephan, Bound MSS., V, C. H. I.

[12] Hennig, *op. cit.,* 100, 102; C. F. W. Walther, *Bünger,* 10.

[13] Hennig, *op. cit.,* 117—123; Hennig, "Die Auswanderung Martin Stephans," *Zeitschrift für Kirchengeschichte,* LVIII, 160; Stübel to Vehse *et al.,* Sept. 12, 1839, Bound MSS., VI, C. H. I.; Schneider, *op. cit.,* 8—10, 13.

last years of the Napoleonic Wars many members of the Pietist organization joined the growing number of Stephan's admirers, preferring to attend his services and prayer meetings rather than their own. Through a simple transfer of personnel the organized society of Pietists dissolved for a time into a group, as yet unorganized, who followed the Bohemian preacher.[14] Thus, at the very beginning of Stephan's influence a factor is noticeable which was to become highly significant for the emigration — the man was the loadstone: a personal leadership had been established.

These early years also reveal several other distinctive characteristics of the later Stephanite system. Foremost was the turn which Stephan gave to that wing of the *Erweckung* of which he was a part, by serving notice that he was taking a stand for the Lutheran Confessions and that all who wished to follow him must do likewise.[15] The Pietists reluctantly did so,[16] while at first most of the other anti-Rationalistic elements did not. Eventually, however, he was to win his battle with them also, although he lost in his struggle with the State Church.[17] Both Pietism and the *Erweckung* were properly undenominational, evangelical movements, and "the transition to confessionalism in the middle of the thirties meant the end of the *Erweckungsbewegung*." [18] A natural corollary of this part of Stephan's viewpoint was his negative attitude toward the unionistic movement, the distinct nature of which in Saxony has been described above.

Brief mention must also be made of another feature of the later Stephanite system, which is in evidence from the very beginning, although it did not come to full fruition for several decades. This feature was the custom of holding religious gatherings in addition

---

14 Lütkemüller, *op. cit.*, 13, 48—49; Fischer, *op. cit.*, 16, 179—181; Hennig, *op. cit.*, 26—28; Hennig, "Die Auswanderung Martin Stephans," *Zeitschrift für Kirchengeschichte*, LVIII, 148; von Polenz, *op. cit.*, 21—23, 67—72; J. S. Günther to the St. Louis congregation, n. d. [*ca.* 1842], MS., C. H. I.

15 Fischer, *op. cit.*, 181—197; C. F. W. Walther, *Bünger*, 22. The distinction between Stephanism and the general trend of the *Erweckung* is emphasized in the following document: Document zur Inlage des Grundsteins der Dreieinigkeitskirche in St. Louis, Mo., den 22. Juny 1842 (hereafter cited as Document . . . des Grundsteins . . . St. Louis . . . 22. Juny 1842), MS., C. H. I. An interesting psychological analysis of the possible motives for this action by Stephan is found in von Polenz, *op. cit.*, 11—13.

16 Hennig, *op. cit.*, 28.

17 Delitzsch to G. H. Löber, March 13, 1834, Bound MSS., Invoices, C. H. I.

18 Hennig, *op. cit.*, 10.

to the regular church services. In Saxony fear of political conspiracy had prompted the enactment of laws regulating such gatherings and prohibiting some of them, especially certain types of separatistic meetings, called conventicles, which had originated with the Pietist element and were held in cordial contempt by the public.[19] Feeling secure because of his congregation's charter rights, Stephan lost no time in availing himself of his opportunity for disregarding these laws. However, serious trouble was certain to develop when the questions were raised: Are these meetings conventicles? Are they within the law? That day was not distant.[20]

Meanwhile, Stephan's influence was steadily growing. Attendance at his services and devotional meetings increased remarkably through the addition of people from all parts of Dresden and its vicinity.[21] Yet this success in itself was a factor in making trouble for him. The members of his original congregation were by no means unanimous in their approval of his activity, and the elders protested against it as early as 1814 and 1816.[22] Aside from the fact that some of the members did not share their pastor's conservative views, they were displeased at being deluged by a wave of newcomers. Of course, these very newcomers strengthened the element favorable to Stephan and prevented effective protest by the others.

Later, members of his congregation and some of his personal followers charged that he grossly neglected his pastoral duties, especially among those who were actually members of his congregation.[23] They asserted that Stephan was no longer pastor of St. John's, but of a motley company of personal adherents who normally would have had no connection with the "Bohemian" congregation, but who

---

[19] Complaint to the consistory against Stephan by a number of Dresden clergymen, June 23, 1820, MS., Stephanakten, Landeskirchenamt, Dresden, I, 1—3; von Polenz, *op. cit.*, 41—46.

[20] Siebenhaar, "IV. Nachrichten über zwei der neuesten Religionsschwärmer im Königreiche Sachsen," *Zeitschrift für die historische Theologie*, XII, Zweites Heft, 157—158; von Polenz, *op. cit.*, 41—47; C. F. W. Walther, *Bünger*, 24.

[21] Fischer, *op. cit.*, 58; *New York Observer*, March 16, 1839, quoting B. Kurtz from *The Lutheran Observer* (most of this article is reprinted in Polack, "An Interesting Contemporary Clipping on the Saxon Centennial," *Concordia Historical Institute Quarterly*, XII, 21—24); C. F. W. Walther in Köstering, *Auswanderung*, 5.

[22] Hennig, "Die Auswanderung Martin Stephans," *Zeitschrift für Kirchengeschichte*, LVIII, 149.

[23] Stübel to Vehse *et al.*, Sept. 12, 1839, Bound MSS., VI, C.H.I.; Lütkemüller, *op. cit.*, 24—26; Fischer, *op. cit.*, 53—54, 104, 111.

St. John's Church, Dresden, Saxony, 1840

PLATE II

Mittwochs **No. 89.** 7. November 1838.

Chemnitzer Anzeiger.

(Herausgeber und Verleger: A. L. Kretschmar.)

Mit Königl. Sächs. allergnädigster Concession.

Auswanderungen nach Amerika um des Glaubens willen.

(Fortsetzung und Beschluß aus Nr. 87.)

Sehr nahe Verwandte finden sie aber in den Mystikern, wenn sie gleich in ihrem Glaubensbekenntnisse mehr Grund und Anhalt haben, als diese in dem ihrigen. Beide halten es mit der Gefühlsreligion, und in beiden ist das zur wahren Religiosität erforderliche Gleichgewicht der Seelenkräfte gänzlich aufgehoben, indem sie die Vernunft verschmähen, der nicht ganz zu entbehrende Verstand aber bei ihnen nur deutelt, klügelt und künstelt, die Einbildungskraft dagegen übermächtig geworden ist. Beide sind unduldsam gegen Andersdenkende und treiben den Eifer für ihren Glauben leicht bis zur Verfolgungssucht, wodurch sie zu Fanatikern werden. Das eigentliche Gebiet und Element des Mystikers ist aber das Geheimnißvolle in der Religion, und er erweitert dieses Gebiet nach allen Seiten hin, indem er dem natürlichen Sinne der Aussprüche heiliger Schriften immer noch einen geheimen unterlegt und sich dabei auf sein besonderes Wahrheitsgefühl, als auf ein inneres untrügliches Licht beruft, auch Anderen zumuthet, daß sie ihm blindlings glauben und nachempfinden sollen. Er mißbraucht die Offenbarung zu allen nur denkbaren Schwärmereien, die um so abenteuerlicher und gefährlicher werden, je roher überhaupt und je sittlich ungebildeter insbesondere der Schwärmer ist. Die mystischen Secten aller Völker alter und neuer Zeit, bis auf die Königsberger und andere Mucker unsrer Tage, liefern den traurigen Beweis, daß es, wenn einmal die Vernunft aufgegeben ist, keinen Aberglauben, keinen Unsinn, kein Verbrechen giebt, die nicht auf dem Boden der Schwärmerei gedeihen könnten. Darum sollen sich auch die neuerdings wieder hier und da gehegten, weit verbreiteten, so thätigen und einflußreichen Jesuiten im Geheimen hinter die christlichen Schwärmer verstecken, um dieselben, ohne daß sie es zum Theil wissen, zu Werkzeugen ihrer finstern Macht zu benutzen.

Daß der Mysticismus jeder Art leicht zum Katholicismus hinüberführt, ist eine durch Thatsachen, namentlich durch den Uebertritt so mancher gelehrten Schwärmer eben so ausgemachte Wahrheit, als daß auch die sinnloseste Schwärmerei, wird sie nur mit recht zuversichtlicher Miene gepredigt, ihre Anhänger um so gewisser findet, je mehr sie der feinen oder der groben Sinnlichkeit schmeichelt. Doch wir treten nun, nach diesen flüchtigen Umblicken in den Irrgängen auf dem Gebiete der Religion, unsern frommen Auswanderern wieder näher. Wir wollen sie keineswegs zu den Schwärmern der ärgsten Art zählen, nicht einmal dem Verdachte glauben, daß sie mit den gefährlichsten Secten in Verbindung stehen, und uns gegen die hohe Meinung, die sie von ihrer Rechtgläubigkeit hegen, in keinen Streit einlassen. Es finden sich übrigens unter ihnen manche Abstufungen in Beziehung auf ihren Eifer und ihr ganzes Verhalten, nach Maßgabe ihrer geistigen Bildung und ihrer Charaktereigenthümlichkeit. Ob der Eine und der Andere von ihnen mehr zu den altgläubigen Stocklutheranern, wie sie in Schlesien hervortreten, oder zu den Pietisten, oder zu den Mystikern gehöre, das mögen diejenigen entscheiden, die die Einzelnen von ihnen näher kennen. Doch die Classen dieser Sonderlinge grenzen nahe an einander, greifen in einander ein und vermischen sich leicht unzertrennlich.

Welches können nun aber die Beweggründe seyn, die unsere neuen Auswanderer aus dem Vaterlande vertreiben? Verfolgung um ihres Glaubens willen? Nimmermehr! Von oben her läßt man in Sachsen, Gott sey Dank, Jeden, der die bürgerliche und kirchliche Ordnung nicht stört und nicht geradezu der öffentlichen Sittlichkeit gefährlich wird, seines Glaubens leben. Man hat die pietistischen Conventikel geduldet und sie nur von fern beobachtet. Die Prediger dieser Partei durften die heilige Schrift auf ihre Weise auslegen, wie sie wollten, durften gegen die Andersdenkenden von den Canzeln und sonst zu Felde ziehen, selbst ihre Amtsbrüder als Ungläubige und Verführer der christlichen Gemeinde verdächtigen und verdammen, so viel sie Lust

Religious questions and the phenomenon of emigration prominently discussed in the Saxon press

PLATE III

abzusprechen, so ist es doch keineswegs ihre gottesfürchtige Gesinnung, weßhalb man sie fromme oder Heilige nennt; es geschieht um der Aeußerung ihrer religiösen Gefühle willen, von denen sie so durch und durch erfüllt zu seyn scheinen, daß sie dieselben überall kund thun und ihr ganzes Wesen dadurch ein eigenthümliches Gepräge erhält.

Sünde und Erlösung, im Sinne der alten Kirchensymbole gedacht, sind aber die Gegenstände, mit denen ihr Gefühl vornehmlich zu thun hat. Sie seufzen vor aller Welt tief und laut über die eigenen und über fremde Sünden, wozu sie auch alle Freude an der Welt, selbst die unschuldigste, alles Lachen und die Theilnahme an geselliger Fröhlichkeit zählen. Sie gehen in demüthiger Stellung, mit gesenktem Haupte, wie in tiefen Gram versunken, einher, und wenn sich ihr Blick erhebt, so kehrt sich das Auge auf eigenthümliche Weise nach oben, als wären sie in seliger Entzückung und liebelten mit überirdischen Wesen. Sie tragen ihre Wiedergeburt, den Durchbruch der göttlichen Gnade an ihren Herzen zur Schau, beklagen und verdammen Alle, die nicht wie sie empfinden, als sträfliche Weltkinder, von denen sie sich mit einem nicht zu verkennenden Stolze möglichst entfernt halten. Mit dem Heilande stehen sie in so enger Verbindung, daß er ihnen sogar persönlich erscheint und in allen Anliegen des äußern und innern Lebens Hülfe leistet. Sie empfinden für ihn eine Zärtlichkeit, wie die Braut für ihren Geliebten, schmachten nach den Liebesblicken des Seelenbräutigams, betten sich in seine Wunden, laben und heilen sich an seinem Blute und treiben mit dem Gotteslamme das süßeste Spiel. Die kräftigste Anregung ihrer frommen Gefühle und die reichste Nahrung dafür finden sie in ihren Conventikeln, in den Zusammenkünften mit ihren frommen Brüdern und Schwestern, wo sie in Gemeinschaft seufzen, singen und beten, einander nach ihrer Weise die Schrift erklären, wozu sich Jeder von ihnen berufen fühlt, sobald er eine innere Erweckung gewahr wird, sich überdieß an den Tractätchen oder kleinen Schriften erbauen, die von den Erleuchtetsten unter ihnen ausgegangen sind. Diese Werkchen des Glaubens, die neben manchem Guten die seltsamsten Wundergeschichten aus der Gemüthswelt, allerlei Teufelsbesitzungen und die unglaublichsten Wirkungen gläubiger Gebete erzählen, streuen sie auf allen Wegen aus, um die Weltkinder zu sich zu bekehren und ihren Anhang zu vergrößern. So phantasiren sie sich in einen unnatürlichen Zustand hinein, in welchem die Frömmigkeit zur Frömmelei wird; so ziehen sie Gegenstände tiefer Verehrung in das Gebiet der sinnlichen Liebe hinab, wo sie von Gefahren bedroht werden, die sie nicht ahnen. Ihre Tändeleien widern das gesunde Gefühl anderer Christenherzen an, und es darf die Pietisten nicht befremden, wenn ihr pharisäischer Anstrich den Verdacht der Heucheley erweckt, mag man auch damit manchem unter ihnen Unrecht thun.

(Der Schluß folgt in Nr. 89.)

Bekanntmachungen.

*** Donnerstags den 1. Novbr. Abends 6 Uhr Versammlung des Schulvorstandes.

1. Wir machen hiermit bekannt, daß der 17. November d. J. der letzte Termin ist, bis zu welchem wir die noch rückständigen Einzahlungen auf Theater-Actien annehmen werden. — Es sind demnach vom 18. Novbr. an alle Interimsquittungen ungültig und die Inhaber von solchen nicht fortgesteuerten Actien ihrer Rechte verlustig, ohne auf Rückgabe der bereits gezahlen Beträge Anspruch machen zu können.

Chemnitz, den 24. October 1838.

Das Directorium der Theater-Actien-Gesellschaft.

Adolph Wex, Stellvertreter.

2. Nach einer so eben erstatteten Anzeige sind in der verflossenen Nacht vom 27. zum 28. October die nachstehend signalisirten Individuen und zwar der sub I. genannte Bilz aus der Behausung seines Altersvormunds, die sub II. genannte Martin aber aus der Behausung ihres Vaters allhier, heimlich und ohne alle Legitimation entwichen, ohne daß ihr Aufenthalt, oder wohin selbige sonst ihren Weg genommen, bis jetzt hat ermittelt werden können.

Da nun dringender Verdacht vorhanden, daß diese beiden Individuen, insonders aber der Knabe Bilz, von auswanderungslustigen Personen aus hiesiger Gegend verleitet worden, ihnen auf dem Wege nach Nordamerika nachzufolgen, ja vielleicht von solchen Auswanderern gar mitgenommen worden sind: so bringen wir diesen Vorfall hiermit zur öffentlichen Kenntniß, und ersuchen alle Criminal- und Polizeibehörden des In- und Auslandes, besonders die Gensdarmerie, dringend, gedachten beiden Individuen streng zu invigiliren, sie im Betretungsfalle zu verhaften und mittelst Schubtransportes anher abzuliefern.

Sollte hierbei gegen die oder die nächsten Begleiter Bilz's und der Martin der oben beregte Verdacht als begründet sich ergeben: so bitten wir auch, selbige, Behufs der wider sie einzuleitenden Untersuchung, mittelst Zwangspasses in ihren bisherigen Wohnort zurück zu weisen und uns hiervon schleunige Mittheilung zu thun.

Mittelfrohne, am 28. Oct. 1838.

Die Gräflich Schönburgschen Gerichte.

Eduard Otto Börner, Ger. Dir.

Signalement.

I. Franz Julius Bilz ist 12½ Jahr alt, hat die Statur seines Alters, gesunde Gesichtsfarbe, blaue Augen, proportionirte Nase, blonde Haare, einen breiten Mund, und ist bekleidet mit einem blauen Tuchoberrock, ein Paar grauen Tuchbeinkleidern, neuen langen zweinäthigen Stiefeln, einer blauen Tuchmütze mit Schirm und einer weißen Weste mit bunten Blümchen versehen.

Notice of escape, description, and appeal for apprehension of Franz Julius Biltz, thirteen years old, who fled from his guardian to accompany the emigrants. (See page 153, note 83)

PLATE IV

Rationalistic superintendent of Saxon State Church expostulating with pious pastor. The scene is from Call of the Cross, *full-length film produced in 1938 to commemorate the centennial of the Saxon immigration*

PLATE V

were attracted by its pastor. Furthermore, few of Stephan's colleagues were willing to permit their parishioners to depart in peace to St. John's. These ministers alleged that Stephan drew followers from far and near by means of flagrant encroachments upon the parishes and pastoral functions of his fellow clergymen, a practice for which the consistory reproved him even before 1820.[24]

It was not long before Stephan was serving groups which were in effect two congregations. The one was the "Bohemian" congregation, to which he had been called; the other was the "German congregation," built up on Stephan's own initiative from his own admirers with complete disregard of parish lines.[25] The claim was made that from 1809 to 1820 the membership of St. John's increased sixfold and that by 1819 it exceeded a thousand, although there were not more than thirty families properly in the membership of the "Bohemian" congregation.[26] An interesting observation in this connection was made by von Polenz, who stated that the *Beichtgeld* from this large congregation was one of the chief sources of revenue for Stephan.[27]

In his small, modest church Stephan held services several times each Sunday in both German and "Bohemian" (Czech).[28] There was nothing sensational about his delivery; he could be called an orator only in the sense that any speaker who genuinely impresses his audience must possess something of the forensic art. Stephan spoke with a "Bohemian" accent in a dignified, almost restrained,

---

24 Complaint to the consistory against Stephan by a number of Dresden clergymen, June 23, 1820, MS., Stephanakten, Landeskirchenamt, Dresden, I, 1—3; Fischer, *op. cit.*, 12. Charges of interference in other parishes were also made against other pastors in the emigration. *Bedenken der theologischen Facultäten*, 67. See also Hanewinckel Notes, 20—21, MS., C. H. I.

25 The difference between these groups is given the greatest emphasis in Hennig, "Die Auswanderung Martin Stephans," *Zeitschrift für Kirchengeschichte*, LVIII, 149, 162.

26 Complaint to the consistory against Stephan by a number of Dresden clergymen, June 23, 1820, MS., Stephanakten, Landeskirchenamt, Dresden, I, 1—3.

27 Von Polenz, *op. cit.*, 24—25.

28 Complaint to the consistory against Stephan by a number of Dresden clergymen, June 23, 1820; MS., Stephanakten, Landeskirchenamt, Dresden, I, 1—3; Fischer, *op. cit.*, 11; Hochstetter, *Die Geschichte der Evangelisch-lutherischen Missouri-Synode in Nord-Amerika*, 9. These references show some disagreement as to the time and arrangement for these services, but that they were held in two languages is clear. The presumption is that the foreign language was Czech, although that term was not used in any sources available to the writer, all of which referred to the language as "Böhmisch."

manner and achieved his purpose by a dispassionate, shrewd appeal to conscience and by the power of his message rather than by a highly emotional or polished address.[29] Many people sought his personal pastoral advice and service, and in this field Stephan did considerable good over a wide area and for a long period of time. His integrity and sincerity during the early years of his ministry have not been questioned, and for a time many approved of his activity.[30] Rudelbach, for instance, sanctioned association with Stephan because of the good he did, although Rudelbach disapproved of the man personally.[31] However, Stephan's definite stand for an unbending conservatism was unwelcome to the Rationalists and to other liberalistic elements, who saw in him a rallying point for the confessionalism they decried; so they moved forward to the attack.[32] With this development the second period of Stephan's activity begins.

The resentment against Stephan arose during the latter part of the first decade of his residence in Dresden and thenceforth became steadily more voluble. The objects of criticism were chiefly his insistence upon the Lutheran Confessions, his religious gatherings, his pastoral methods, and his person.[33] For some years Stephan paid no attention to the attacks upon him. Finally, on August 25, 1821, an article appeared in *Der Correspondent von und für*

---

[29] Fischer, *op. cit.*, 58; Lütkemüller, *op. cit.*, 10; von Polenz, *op. cit.*, 19, 29—32.

[30] Nachrichten an unsere Nachkommen, denen einst vielleicht diese Blätter zu Gesichte kommen (hereafter cited as Nachrichten an unsere Nachkommen), March 11, 1844, MS., C. H. I. This document, probably from the pen of G. H. Löber, is translated in Frank, "Records for Our Posterity," *Concordia Historical Institute Quarterly*, VII, 66—77. The copies in the Concordia Historical Institute are not contemporary. But a contemporary or very early copy is contained in Bound MSS., I, Documents Pertaining to the Early History of Trinity Congregation, Altenburg, Mo. (hereafter cited as Bound MSS., I), Trinity Church Records, Altenburg, Mo. See also Kurzer Lebenslauf des selig vollendeten Hrn. Julius Otto Nitzschke, abgelesen in der Kirche Dom. Rogate 1862 (hereafter cited as Lebenslauf des . . . Nitzschke), MS., C. H. I.; von Polenz, *op. cit.*, 13—15; Fischer, *op. cit.*, 17, 54—56; C. F. W. Walther in Köstering, *Auswanderung*, 5—6; *New York Observer*, March 16, 1839.

[31] C. F. W. Walther, *Bünger*, 29.

[32] Fischer, *op. cit.*, 104—111; Bemerkungen über . . . Stephan, Bound MSS., V, C. H. I.

[33] Complaint to the consistory against Stephan by a number of Dresden clergymen. June 23, 1820, MS., Stephanakten, Landeskirchenamt, Dresden, I, 1—3; *Chemnitzer Anzeiger*, Oct. 30, 1838; E. M. Bürger, Selbstbiographie, 34—37, MS., E. J. Buerger Papers, Ellicottville, N. Y.; Siebenhaar, "IV. Nachrichten über zwei der neuesten Religionsschwärmer im Königreiche Sachsen," *Zeitschrift für die historische Theologie*, XII, Zweites Heft, 157—158.

Deutschland,[34] which made him break his silence. Just how far the campaign against him had been carried before he was goaded into making a reply, can be seen from this article. It accused him of being a separatist, a mystic, and the cause, through his extreme teachings, of several cases of criminal insanity. The latter charge was made at intervals throughout the years Stephan spent in Dresden, and was leveled also against at least one of the clergymen associated with him, Pastor Keyl.[35]

Nothing daunted, Stephan in his reply, which appeared in the *Nationalzeitung der Deutschen* on November 21, 1821, categorically denied the charges against him. As for the cases of criminal insanity, the Dresden pastor emphasized that the people referred to were not members of his church, although they might have come to listen to him. Yet even had they been his members, Stephan pointed out, this fact alone could not have been considered proof that either his doctrine or his method had caused their derangement. In regard to his faith and practice, Stephan defended himself in the following terms:

> I am not a member of any sect, old or new; I hate all sectarianism. . . . I am an evangelical Lutheran preacher and preach the Word of God as it is written in the Bible. . . . I possess and preach the apostolic religion, which Luther preached in its purity with such courage. . . . I have no peculiar religious tenets, nor do I preach in a strange, mystic sense, but in the spirit of our pious forefathers — my religion is neither above the Bible nor beneath it, but in the Bible.[36]

Obviously nothing conclusive had resulted from the exchange, and for two years the *status quo ante* continued. Then, in December, 1823, when Stephan published a pamphlet containing two sermons and a foreword, he took up the cudgels a second time. This occasion was the last time that he expressed himself in public print in his own defense until that day, fifteen years later, when he left Germany and issued his *Farewell.* In the foreword to these sermons

---

[34] Pöschel, *op. cit.,* 3, 63; Fischer, *op. cit.,* 18. In this article, as well as in others appearing at this time, the followers of Stephan were first referred to as *Stephanianer* and *Stephanisten.* Fischer, *op. cit.,* 57.

[35] Pöschel, *op. cit.,* 43—45, 51—56; Siebenhaar, "IV. Nachrichten über zwei der neuesten Religionsschwärmer im Königreiche Sachsen," *Zeitschrift für die historische Theologie,* XII, Zweites Heft, 157, 160, 166—167, 178; C. F. W. Walther to O. H. Walther, August, 1833, in M. Günther, *op. cit.,* 15; von Polenz, *op. cit.,* 23—24.

[36] This article is quoted in full in Pöschel, *op. cit.,* 63—66.

Stephan addressed himself directly to the Dresden public and again repudiated the tales of insanity among his followers and the slanders against his person. Once more he stated his doctrinal position and challenged a refutation of it. Until this refutation was forthcoming, he claimed, he stood vindicated of the charges of both mysticism and separatism, for it was just as preposterous to claim that meetings fostered sectarianism because they were held at his home as it would have been to maintain that two congregations having services in different churches did so. The place was of no importance, but the teaching was; and the latter could easily be tested, for the doors to his meetings were always open. An appeal to the fairness of the public and to the charter rights of St. John's concluded this reply.[37] Thereafter Stephan lapsed into official silence. But his opponents and his supporters did not, and their quarrels are a part of what has been designated above as the second phase of Stephanism.

So far, attention has been directed exclusively toward Stephan and the principal events in his career. It now becomes necessary to examine the extension of his movement, the character of the group which followed him, and its personal relationship to him. For Stephanism was nothing if not personal; it was a personal faith, a personal leadership, a personal allegiance.

The growth of Stephan's following in Dresden has been noted. As early as 1820, however, his activity was extending beyond the city.[38] One of the most important sources of recruits outside the capital was the University of Leipzig, where Stephanism became effective through its connection with an independent group of Pietistic laymen and students. For a time these students were interested in a *collegium philobiblicum* conducted by conservative Professor Lindner in imitation of August Hermann Francke's meetings. But leadership of this informal association soon passed into the hands of a candidate of theology, named Kühn,[39] who was largely responsible for determining its character. Stephan's control of this group did not begin until after 1832, with the death of Kühn, who during his

---

[37] Stephan, *Herzlicher Zuruf . . . zwei Predigten,* 3—14; Pöschel, *op. cit.,* 3. A partial reprint of this foreword is contained in Pöschel, *op. cit.,* 66—73.

[38] Complaint to the consistory against Stephan by a number of Dresden clergymen, June 23, 1820, MS., Stephanakten, Landeskirchenamt, Dresden, I, 1—3.

[39] C. F. W. Walther, *Bünger,* 11.

lifetime had refused to bow before the claims of authority advanced by Stephan and Stephan's followers.[40] But the Leipizg group took shape in the early twenties; hence it must be considered at this point.

Kühn was a graduate of the theological school at Leipzig and, like many other theological candidates in Germany at that time, was forced to wait many years for an appointment. A candidate forty years of age was no rarity.[41] Kühn had arrived at his personal religious convictions through harrowing spiritual experiences that colored his entire life. His days at the university had been embittered by the scorn of his fellow students and teachers, who considered him a religious fanatic. After his graduation, while teaching in Leipzig, he provided the guidance for the small group of students and laymen mentioned above. These people were not unusual products of the *Erweckung;* they were deeply and seriously concerned about their salvation but uncertain how to attain it. The group, especially the students, held regular theological discussions and prayer meetings.[42] Just what period the activity of Kühn covered is not clear; but it is certain that his work was under way by 1824 and that it continued until 1831, when he was placed at the parish of Lunzenau by the Counts von Schönburg. There he died on August 24, 1832, after about one year of service.[43]

Kühn's "awakening,"[44] or veering from the Rationalism of the previous century, took an unfortunate turn. He was undoubtedly sincere; but sincerity is found also in the fanatic, and evidently there was an element of fanaticism in Kühn's character. Even the men who felt they were greatly indebted to him were later willing to admit that his system was morbid.[45] Kühn's very earnestness led

---

40 Candidate Kühn to O. Fürbringer, Feb. 29, 1832, MS., C. H. I.; Fischer, *op. cit.*, 61.

41 C. F. W. Walther, *Bünger*, 15—16, 25.

42 *Ibid.*, 11—12; Candidate Kühn to O. Fürbringer, May 24, Aug. 8, 1831, MSS., C. H. I.

43 Candidate Kühn to —, Oct. 20, 1831, MS., C. H. I. The tale that Kühn was poisoned because of opposition to his orthodoxy is told in Bürger, *op cit.*, 10. The story is rejected in C. F. W. Walther, *Bünger*, 16—17; Fischer, *op cit.*, 26—27. One source gives the date of his death as August 23, 1832. Brohm to O. Fürbringer, Aug. 28, 1832, MS., C. H. I.

44 The Leipzig group used the term in speaking of themselves. C. F. W. Walther, *Bünger*, 13. See also G. H. Löber, Diary, Jan. 1, 1836, MS., C. H. I.

45 *Ibid.*, 12, 17—18; E. M. Bürger, Selbstbiographie, 46—47, MS., E. J. Buerger Papers, Ellicottville, N. Y.; C. F. W. Walther, *Law and Gospel*, 141—142.

him to presume that anyone who did not arrive at his religious convictions through a period of trial similar in intensity to his own was unconverted and unawakened. The spirit not utterly crushed in a protracted battle with an overstimulated conscience was irrevocably damned. Peace of mind was to be attained only after the bitterest of struggles.[46] "They [*i. e.*, the followers of Kühn] erred, inasmuch as they made a Savior of repentance, fear, and alarm.[47]

Accordingly, Kühn did his best to produce what he considered the necessary degree of distress in his associates and to mold them into what has been described as "a group of legalistic Pietists." [48] The designation is apt, for Kühn's religious system was Pietism of the old school, and that not in its most appealing aspects. Favorites of the group were such authors as H. Müller, Rambach, Arndt, Bogatzky, A. H. Francke, Spener, Steinmetz, and Fresenius—staunch Pietists all, and severe enough.[49] However, the neophytes, in order not to retard their awakening, omitted the more attractive passages of even these writers as being too seductively mild. The demands of Kühn's formula drove some of the impressionable youths who came under his influence almost to distraction. The climax was reached in the actions of men like Bünger and the younger Walther, both of whom seriously impaired their health with self-imposed spiritual exercises. The two men just mentioned went so far as to deprive themselves of the necessary nourishment and relaxation, for these things they considered sinful distractions. Ascetic zeal contributed to physical breakdown.[50] Yet their religious aber-

---

[46] Candidate Kühn to O. Fürbringer, June 27, Aug. 8, 1831, MSS., C.H.I.; Candidate Kühn to C. F. W. Walther, April 5, 1831, Bound MSS., Invoices, C.H.I.; C. F. W. Walther, *Bünger,* 11—13; C. F. W. Walther, *Law and Gospel,* 253. Löber had similar attitudes toward his own and others' spiritual condition. G. H. Löber, Diary, Introduction to the year 1834, Close of 1834, July 5, 1831, 1836, pp. 53—54, MS., C.H.I.

[47] E. M. Bürger, Selbstbiographie, 47—48, MS., E. J. Buerger Papers, Ellicottville, N. Y.

[48] Dallmann-Dau-Engelder, *Walther and the Church,* 1.

[49] E. M. Bürger, Selbstbiographie, 53, MS., E. J. Buerger Papers, Ellicottville, N. Y.; C. F. W. Walther in Köstering, *Auswanderung,* 8; Erstes Protokollbuch der Dreieinigkeitsgemeinde vom Dec. 1839 bis Dec. 1853 (hereafter cited as Erstes Protokollbuch), Jan. 11, 25, March 1, 1841, MS., Trinity Church Records, St. Louis. The works cited above, supplemented by several others, served Löber also. G. H. Löber, Diary, May 30, 1831, 1834, p. 9, Nov. 24, 1834, March 13, 1835, MS., C.H.I.

[50] C. F. W. Walther, *Bünger,* 12—13, 17—20; Candidate Kühn to O. Fürbringer, June 27, Aug. 8, 1831, MSS., C.H.I.

rations were all intensely real to these men. When Brohm's sister joined an amateur dramatic group in Waldenburg, C. F. W. Walther felt in conscience bound to notify Brohm of the event with great sorrow.[51]

As for doctrinal position, the group, in the true spirit of the *Erweckung,* had none for a long time. Then, in the course of their private discussions, the question came up: What are we? Lutheran, Reformed, or something quite different? The majority reached the questionable conclusion that they were Lutherans. Those who disagreed were eliminated.[52] Thus for nearly a decade before Stephan took charge of the group, Kühn's influence was an important factor in molding the characters of the men who were to lead the emigration, and thus indirectly in preparing for the emigration itself. The names of these men are familiar ones in the history of the movement.

Ernst Gerhard Wilhelm Keyl (May 22, 1804—August 4, 1872)[53] was the second son of a well-to-do tax official at Leipzig. His mother died when Keyl was four years old; his father followed her in 1820. The elder Keyl, although himself only self-taught, provided his sons with a good general education as well as some training in the fine arts, and Ernst Gerhard became a finished musician of professional caliber. Until 1815 Keyl was taught by private tutors; then his father sent him to the *Nicolai Gymnasium* in Leipzig. In 1822, after his father's death, he entered the university of his native city to prepare for the ministry,[54] and there came under the influence of Kühn.

---

[51] C. F. W. Walther to Brohm, Jan. 15, 1834, MS., C. H. I.

[52] C. F. W. Walther, *Bünger,* 11—12.

[53] Köstering, *Leben und Wirken des Ehrw. Ernst Gerhard Wilh. Keyl* (hereafter cited as *Keyl*), 7—21. Keyl himself related the essential facts concerning his early life in a brief autobiographical sketch, written in his own hand and signed by him. The manuscript is undated, but it was penned between 1829 and 1838, probably during the first of these years or very shortly thereafter. Keyl, Autobiographical Sketch, MS., C. H. I. This document was evidently unknown to Keyl's biographer, Köstering, and corrects or supplements the latter's account in several instances. See also C. F. W. Walther, "Lebensabriss des . . . Keyl," *Der Lutheraner,* XXVIII, 189—190.

[54] Keyl, Autobiographical Sketch, MS., C. H. I. Köstering gave the impression that Keyl's father urged him to take up the study of theology after Ernst Gerhard's graduation from the *Gymnasium* and at the time of his entering the university in 1822. However, this date was two years after the elder Keyl's death. The discrepancy can be explained by Köstering's admission: "What his [E. G. W. Keyl's] age was at this time, we are not quite sure." Köstering, *Keyl,* 12.

While the latter aroused the young man's conscience and called forth the spiritual uncertainty which the Kühn system usually induced, Keyl attained the peace and conviction he sought only through the help of a simple Leipzig cobbler named Götsching. Keyl completed his studies in 1827 and spent the next two years in touring Germany with Count von der Recke, in occasional preaching, and in private tutoring in Leipzig. Then, in 1829, Keyl's period of waiting was suddenly cut short through his appointment by Count von Einsiedel to a rather large parish, one of the Count's advowsons. Within five weeks after Keyl had preached his trial sermon, he was established as pastor at Nieder-Frohna, Saxony, with neighboring Mittel-Frohna as a second charge. The two parishes together totaled 1,340 souls.[55]

In Leipzig, during 1828, Keyl had his first contact with Stephan. Greatly impressed by the older man as a theologian and preacher, Keyl soon came to confide in him. Stephan showed only his better side to Keyl at that time, according to the latter; and, although in no way subservient to him, Keyl frequently followed the Dresden pastor's advice. This relationship continued until 1831.[56] In that year, however, a serious clash occurred between the two when they disagreed violently over the question of what degree of obedience was due the government. The original cause of the quarrel, which finally drew in Wege, Welzel, Pöschel, Kühn, and Böhme, was soon submerged in the broader and more far-reaching issue of whether Stephan could demand submission to himself and his opinions. From that point the affair developed into a contest to determine whether the authority of the Dresdeners, primarily of Stephan, was to be asserted over the Leipzigers, or whether this group was to remain independent. So long as Kühn was living, there was little prospect that the Leipzigers would capitulate. But after his death, in the following year, Stephanism won the day. Although Keyl held out for a time, he, too, was finally persuaded to swallow his "pride." He made his "pilgrimage to Canossa" in 1834, apologized to Stephan, and resumed a relationship with him that was to become constantly more intimate and to make Keyl more and more dependent upon the pastor of St. John's. And all these developments could take place

---

[55] Köstering, *Keyl,* 19—20.

[56] Keyl, *op. cit.,* 4—5.

without effecting any clarification of the original point of dispute! [57] In view of the fact that Keyl was by nature not a submissive person, this incident is a noteworthy example of the force of Stephan's personality and the manner in which he employed it.

Ernst Moritz Bürger (1806—1890), the next student to enter the Leipzig circle,[58] was a descendant of a long line of Lutheran pastors. His father was clergyman at Arnsfeld, Saxony, when Ernst Moritz was born. Ernst Moritz was the younger of two sons in a family of six children. When he was two years old, his father was transferred to Seelitz, Saxony. At the age of thirteen Ernst Moritz went to Holy Cross *Gymnasium* in Dresden and six years later, in 1825, entered the University of Leipzig. During the four years he spent there he was exposed to the extreme viewpoints of Rationalism and conservatism. Although his father was strongly influenced by the former, Bürger himself was predisposed, by previous experiences, toward the latter. Kühn, Keyl, Pastor Wolf (a conservative clergyman of some note at St. Peter's Church in Leipzig), and cobbler Götsching all assisted in bringing about his "awakening." [59] Bürger, however, had less liking than fear for their teachings. In 1829, after Bürger's graduation from the university and his entry into the ministry as his father's assistant, he met Stephan. The Bohemian pastor gave him competent advice and a measure of mental rest, but exacted a high price; before long Bürger was also under Stephan's sway. Meanwhile, the young preacher had

---

[57] The only really lucid account of what Candidate Kühn called "this hellish quarreling" is given by Kühn himself. See Candidate Kühn to O. Fürbringer, Feb. 29, 1832, MS., C. H. I. The essential facts are also stated less clearly by Keyl. Keyl, *op. cit.*, 4—5. In view of this incident and others discussed below, it is surprising that Th. Buenger should have made the generalization: "But they [the candidates of the emigration] did not follow him [Stephan] blindly, nor did they accept his views rashly," and then cite this very case of Keyl in an attempt to substantiate the statement. Dau (ed.), *op. cit.*, 7. Note also the more recent attempt of Hennig to absolve Stephan of any desire to domineer and that writer's transformation of Stephan's inferiority complex (which probably was the root of some of his excesses in the opposite direction) into "innate modesty." Hennig, "Die Auswanderung Martin Stephans," *Zeitschrift für Kirchengeschichte*, LVIII, 150. Neither Stephan nor his followers can be cleared of responsibility for the relationship which developed.

[58] The most complete information on Bürger's life, especially for the years prior to the emigration, is found in E. M. Bürger, Selbstbiographie, 1—122, MS., E. J. Buerger Papers, Ellicottville, N. Y. See also Bürger, *op. cit.*, 9—12; *Der Lutheraner*, XLVI, 66.

[59] E. M. Bürger, Selbstbiographie, 45—48, MS., E. J. Buerger Papers, Ellicottville, N. Y.; C. F. W. Walther, *Bünger*, 16.

found a kindred spirit in Keyl, stationed only a few miles from Seelitz.[60] Religious differences between Bürger and his father occasioned violent altercations between them and resulted in the younger man's refusal to take Communion from his father. Ernst Moritz felt miserable in his position and therefore in 1832 gladly accepted the appointment offered him by the Counts von Schönburg as Kühn's successor at Lunzenau, a Schönburg advowson. Within a year Bürger's father died, and he himself was married to Kühn's former fiancée.[61]

Theodor Julius Brohm (September 12, 1808—September 24, 1881) was a native of Oberwinkel (near Waldenburg), Saxony. He attended the *Gymnasium* at Altenburg from 1821 to 1827, during which time his father died (1825). The young student decided to follow theology and arrived in Leipzig at Easter, 1827, about the time that Keyl was leaving. There Brohm became acquainted with Kühn and his group of religious zealots and had the usual unpleasant experiences with the rigors of Kühn's spiritual exercises. Brohm remained at the university from 1827 to 1832 and in the latter year passed his examination *pro candidatura* in Dresden. While a student at the university, he met Stephan, and after graduation refused to accept a position in the Saxon State Church, acting on the older man's advice. Instead, Brohm spent several years in Leipzig, studying, but by 1834 was back in Dresden, where he assisted Candidate Welzel as a teacher in the latter's private school in that city, preached occasionally for Stephan, and finally became secretary to the pastor of St. John's, following the dismissal of Pöschel from that office.[62]

Ottomar Fürbringer (June 30, 1810—July 12, 1892) was not a native of the kingdom of Saxony. He was born at Gera, Thuringia, but attended the University of Leipzig from 1828 to 1831. While

---

60 E. M. Bürger, Selbstbiographie, 53—57, MS., E. J. Buerger Papers, Ellicottville, N. Y.

61 *Ibid.*, 69—71, 86; Pleissner, *op. cit.*, 60.

62 J. F. Bünger, "Ehrengedächtniss des . . . Brohm," *Der Lutheraner*, XXXVII, 188—190; Fuerbringer-Engelder-Kretzmann (eds.), *The Concordia Cyclopedia*, 96; L. Fuerbringer, *80 Eventful Years*, 213. Bünger's statement in the article just cited, that Stephan did not want Brohm to take a call because of the imminence of the emigration (in four to six years), is contradictory both to the claims of other Stephanites that their leader had not then made a definite resolve to leave Germany, and to Stephan's own advice to C. F. W. Walther as late as 1836 to take a call.

studying theology there, he was brought into Kühn's circle. Fürbringer won Kühn's esteem and enjoyed the friendship of others in the group, notably Brohm, Bünger, and the Walthers. "From [April 24,] 1831 to 1838 he was instructor at an institute for boys at Eichenberg, conducted by Pastor G. H. Löber." [63] This "institute" at times boasted of an enrollment of five. By correspondence Fürbringer learned to know Welzel in Dresden, and the latter brought him into touch with Stephan, whom Fürbringer did not meet until 1832.

Fürbringer greatly admired Stephan and sought his advice when, in 1836, the candidate was being considered for the position of director of the seminary of the Dresden Mission Society. Stephan's advice was of such a nature that negotiations between Fürbringer and von Einsiedel, who was corresponding with him on the matter, broke down.[64] Fürbringer accordingly remained at Eichenberg until the time of the emigration. He became a Stephanite before Löber did, was in some respects more strictly conservative in his views than Löber was, and at all times displayed a real enthusiasm in proselyting for the Dresden pastor. Despite this zealotry and the strain which it placed on Fürbringer's environment, Löber liked him, respected his sincerity, and made it a point to become acquainted with the Fürbringer family. The two men were on cordial terms with each other for years, notwithstanding the difficulties which Fürbringer's violent manner occasionally created.[65]

Johann Friedrich Bünger (January 2, 1810—January 23, 1882) was born at Rosswein, Saxony. The families of both his parents boasted of a long line of clerics of considerable prominence.[66] After a desultory early training, Bünger was conditionally accepted as a

---

[63] Fuerbringer-Engelder-Kretzmann (eds.), *op. cit.*, 276; G. H. Löber, Diary, April 24, 1831, MS., C.H.I.; L. Fuerbringer, *80 Eventful Years*, 7—9. L. Fürbringer described his father's position more accurately when he said: "He . . . became a private teacher in the home of Pastor Gotthold Heinrich Loeber. . . ." It appears that girls were also accepted in this "institute." *Ibid.*, 8.

[64] Candidate Kühn to C. F. W. Walther, April 5, 1831, Bound MSS., Invoices, C.H.I.; Candidate Kühn to O. Fürbringer, May 24, June 27, Aug. 8, 1831, Feb. 29, 1832, MSS., C.H.I.; Lochner, "Ottomar Fürbringer," *Der Lutheraner*, XLIX, 155—156, 163—164, 171—172; Dau (ed.), *op. cit.*, 6; M. Günther, *op. cit.*, 17.

[65] G. H. Löber, Diary, May 1, 2, Sept. 20, Oct. 7, Nov. 7, 28, 1831, Nov. 12, 1835, MS., C.H.I.

[66] C. F. W. Walther, *Bünger*, 3—8. This work by Walther is the main source of information on J. F. Bünger.

student at the ducal academy at Meissen in 1823. He completed his course of studies at this school in six years and then passed his examination for matriculation at the university.[67] Bünger entered the theological school of the University of Leipzig at Easter, 1829, but he did not make the acquaintance of Kühn and his group until after a quiet year of study. Although delayed, his "awakening" was none the less rude, and he gave himself up completely to the extreme views and rigorous practices of the Pietistic system. By the time Bünger entered the group, its founders had left or were leaving the university. Brohm, however, still remained in Leipzig and lived in the same boardinghouse as Bünger. After 1832, when Brohm had left the university, Bünger became closely associated with C. F. W. Walther.[68]

Of the entire university group, Bünger and C. F. W. Walther were the two who experienced the most violent reaction to the goading of consciences already abnormally disturbed. Neither of the two exerted a wholesome influence on the other, for both were in a brooding fit of despondency. They finally drove matters so far that they had to suspend their studies and return to their homes because their health was seriously affected. Bünger appeared to be suffering from an incurable lung ailment; so after a brief visit to his home, from Easter until August, 1833, he went to Bad Radeberg, a health resort near Dresden.[69] There he recuperated so rapidly that he was soon allowed to rejoin his friend Brohm, then in Dresden, and to prepare for his first examination, which he passed in March, 1834. He declined to take his second examination until 1837, both because of his health and because of his scruples about entering the ministry in the State Church.[70] Meanwhile, he returned to his home and tutored some of his younger brothers and sisters. In 1836, when his father died, and during the following years, while the family was separated, he took teaching positions, first at Pirna, later at Dresden.

---

67 *Ibid.*, 8—9. These notes on his early educational training were made by J. F. Bünger himself.

68 *Ibid.*, 17—18; J. F. Bünger, "Ehrengedächtniss des . . . Brohm," *Der Lutheraner*, XXXVII, 189.

69 C. F. W. Walther, *Bünger*, 18—20. The date there given, 1883, is obviously a misprint.

70 *Ibid.*, 20. This incident is probably the one referred to in Hasse, *op. cit.*, 411.

During his two sojourns in Dresden and in the intervening years Bünger came under the influence of Stephan, in whom the young man thought he saw the sole pillar of Lutheranism in Saxony. Despite the fact that rumors concerning Stephan's personal life were already widely circulated and some of the abuses of the Stephan system were very apparent, Bünger became intimately associated with him.[71]

Otto Hermann Walther (September 23, 1809—January 21, 1841) and Carl Ferdinand Wilhelm Walther were sons of Gottlob Heinrich Wilhelm Walther (who died on January 13, 1841) and of Wilhelmine Zschenderlein Walther.[72] Like Bünger's, theirs was a name well known in German clerical circles, and G. H. W. Walther was pastor of Langenchursdorf, Saxony, during all of the several decades here under discussion. Besides Otto Hermann and his brother Carl Ferdinand, two of the Walther daughters are of some importance for the emigration. Amalia was married to Pastor Keyl of near-by Nieder-Frohna in 1836, and the eldest sister was married to H. F. W. Schubert, rector of the *Gymnasium* at Schneeberg, Saxony.[73]

The attention directed toward the "younger Walther," or Carl Ferdinand, has left many facts in the life of Otto Hermann rather obscure, but it is known that the elder brother came to the University of Leipzig in 1827 and was one of the earlier group of students gathered about Kühn.[74] When Carl Ferdinand came to Leipzig in 1829, his elder brother introduced him to the circle. Otto Hermann was appointed his father's assistant at Langenchursdorf by the patron of that parish, Count von Schönburg, Otto Viktor I,[75] and continued in that capacity from November 11, 1834, until 1838.

---

[71] C. F. W. Walther, *Bünger*, 22, 28—31.

[72] Information on the Walther family and the careers in Germany of the two brothers who took part in the emigration is contained in M. Günther, *op. cit.*, 1—33; Dau (ed.), *op. cit.*, 21—22.

[73] M. Günther, *op. cit.*, 2, 4. Keyl's marriage made him the brother-in-law of Hermann and Ferdinand Walther, not their father-in-law, as Hennig states. Hennig, "Die Auswanderung Martin Stephans," *Zeitschrift für Kirchengeschichte*, LVIII, 157.

[74] Polack, *The Story of C. F. W. Walther* (hereafter cited as *Walther*), 8—9.

[75] This man is discussed at length in Hennig, *op. cit.*, 163—165. However, Hennig's statement is open to question when he says that the "Prince von Schönburg-Waldenburg" called no Stephanites to his advowsons. *Ibid.*, 163.

Just when he began his association with Stephan is not definitely known, but his sentimental nature helped to make him one of the most devoted and submissive followers of the Dresden pastor. Despite this fact he was highly regarded in other circles as well, for he was one of the most gifted of the emigrants and possessed a capacity for energetic action.[76]

Carl Ferdinand Wilhelm Walther (October 25, 1811—May 7, 1887), the next youngest brother of Otto Hermann, was born at Langenchursdorf.[77] Until he was eight years old, he received his training from his father at home and from local elementary schools. Then he was sent to the city school at Hohenstein, where he remained until 1821. In July of that year he was advanced to the *Gymnasium* at Schneeberg, which he attended until September 23, 1829.[78] Earlier that year, on February 8, Walther, who was a capable musician and loved music devotedly, made the oft-quoted entry in his diary that he felt himself "born for music." But his father's opposition to the idea, and the impetus given his religious interests at that time, dissuaded him from adopting music as a career.[79]

In October, 1829, Walther began his studies at the University of Leipzig and was promptly introduced into the Pietist circles of the university and the city.[80] Consumption and the effects of the severity of Kühn's religious discipline forced him to suspend his studies during the winter of 1831—1832; so he returned home and devoted himself to the perusal of Luther's writings.[81] Delitzsch described Walther's condition at the time he was forced to leave the

---

[76] Köstering, *Auswanderung,* 57—58; Hanser, *Geschichte der Ersten ev.-lutherischen Dreieinigkeitsgemeinde in St. Louis, Mo.,* 101; Hennig, "Die Auswanderung Martin Stephans," *Zeitschrift für Kirchengeschichte,* LVIII, 157.

[77] Accounts of C. F. W. Walther's early life are given in a fragment (twelve pages) of an undated account (*ca.* 1835) by C. F. W. Walther himself, which describes his life in the early 1830's (hereafter cited as C. F. W. Walther, A Fragment of an Account of His Early Life), Bound MSS., Invoices, C. H. I.; "An Autobiographical Sketch of Dr. Walther," *Theological Monthly,* II, 137—140; M. Günther, *op. cit.,* 1—33; Dau (ed.), *op. cit.,* 21—26; Polack, *Walther,* 1—30.

[78] Report on leaving Schneeberg *Gymnasium,* Sept. 23, 1829, Bound MSS., Invoices, C. H. I.; M. Günther, *op. cit.,* 4.

[79] C. F. W. Walther, Tagebuch gehalten von F. Walther, Primaner zu Schneeberg (hereafter cited as Tagebuch), Feb. 8, Oct. 15, 1829, MS., C. H. I.; M. Günther, *op. cit.,* 6.

[80] M. Günther, *op. cit.,* 7—8. Note the change in the tone of his diary as early as November, 1829. C. F. W. Walther, Tagebuch, Nov. 5, Dec. 9, 1829, March 5, 1830, MS., C. H. I.

[81] M. Günther, *op. cit.,* 12.

university in these words: "During that period of struggle he was wasted like a skeleton, coughed blood, suffered from insomnia, and experienced the terrors of hell. He was more dead than alive." [82] Partially recuperated, Walther returned to the university in 1832 and finished his course of study during the following year, but he did not then expect to be able to stand the physical strain of caring for a parish.[83]

Walther's connection with Stephan dates from the early thirties, when the former wrote to Dresden on the advice of Brohm and of several pastors. The reply gave him, at least temporarily, the peace and assurance he had been seeking.[84] Walther felt himself deeply indebted to Stephan and sought his advice on later occasions, although Walther's friend Professor Rudelbach had warned him against becoming too dependent upon this counselor.[85] Returning to his home once more after completion of his university work, Walther resumed his private preparation for the first examination, which he passed at Leipzig in September, 1833.[86]

Another period of enforced idleness at home created considerable friction between him and his father and caused both to yearn for a change.[87] An incident in connection with this change, when it finally came, is illuminating, as it shows the intimate association between the members of Stephan's following and the influence of Keyl, although the latter at that time was not in the good graces of the Dresdeners. Early in 1834, Brohm wrote to Walther about a position as private tutor for the Löber family in Kahla. However, the letter was of such a nature that Walther did not care to show it to his father. But he was not reluctant to show it to Keyl, for on

---

82 Delitzsch to relatives of C. F. W. Walther, "Pfingstmontag, 1887," quoted in *Lehre und Wehre*, XXXIII, 289—290.

83 Brohm to O. Fürbringer, "Oster-Heiligenabend 1832," quoted in M. Günther, *op. cit.*, 12.

84 C. F. W. Walther, A Fragment of an Account of His Early Life, Bound MSS., Invoices, C. H. I. This letter from Stephan, the first Walther ever received from him, was the one which Walther opened only after a prayer. C. F. W. Walther, *Bünger*, 29; Dau (ed.), *op. cit.*, 7. Consequently Th. Buenger's assertion that Walther demonstrated his deliberateness in accepting Stephan's views generally is an unwarranted conclusion. Dau (ed.), *op. cit.*, 7. Certainly Walther did not follow Stephan "rashly" at this time. *before* he came under his influence. The answer to the question of what Walther's relationship to Stephan was, if it is to be raised, depends upon what happened *after* this time.

85 C. F. W. Walther, *Bünger*, 29.

86 M. Günther, *op. cit.*, 13.

87 C. F .W. Walther to Brohm, Jan. 15, March 15, 1834, MSS., C. H. I.

the very day he received the letter he went to Nieder-Frohna and sought Keyl's advice. On the same day Walther wrote to Brohm from Nieder-Frohna and indicated his readiness to accept the position, but asked that the offer be repeated in a letter which might be better suited to parental inspection.[88]

Actually, of course, Brohm was only partially responsible for placing Walther. G. H. Löber was asked by his brother to secure a teacher and, upon receiving Stephan's advice, recommended Walther. With the influence of these several people behind him, it is not surprising that by Easter, 1834, Walther was employed as tutor in the home of Friedemann Löber in Kahla, instructing Friedemann's children and those of his younger brother, Judge August Löber.[89] Walther thus had considerable contact with his friend Fürbringer and with the clergyman Löber, second of the three Löber brothers, who stood high in the estimation of Walther and influenced his doctrinal views.[90]

Walther remained at Kahla in the Löbers' employ until November, 1836. On the previous April 26 he had taken his examination before the consistory in Dresden. By the end of that year he had been called to fill the vacancy created by the death of a certain Pastor Niedner in a small parish at Bräunsdorf, Saxony, near to his former home and to Keyl, now his brother-in-law through Keyl's marriage to Amalia Walther. Ferdinand Walther's father had acted as vacancy pastor.[91] Despite previous scruples about entering the ministry, C. F. W. Walther accepted the call to Bräunsdorf, a von Einsiedel advowson, after consulting with Stephan.[92] Walther was called by Count von Einsiedel on December 11, 1836, and was or-

---

88 C. F. W. Walther to Brohm, March 15, 1834, MS., C.H.I. The elder Walther never shared the extreme conservatism of his sons. G. H. Löber, Diary, 1836, p. 25, MS., C.H.I.; Dau (ed.), *op. cit.*, 25.

89 G. H. Löber, Diary, 1834, p. 11, MS., C.H.I.; M. Günther, *op. cit.*, 16—17.

90 G. H. Löber, Diary, 1834, p. 11, MS., C.H.I.; Dau (ed.), *op. cit.*, 6. Hennig claims that Friedemann Löber strongly colored the theological outlook of Walther, but does not indicate how this was accomplished. Hennig, "Die Auswanderung Martin Stephans," *Zeitschrift für Kirchengeschichte*, LVIII, 155—156.

91 G. H. Löber, Diary, 1836, pp. 22, 25, 28, MS., C. H. I.; M. Günther, *op. cit.*, 17—19. Bräunsdorf was not in Saxe-Altenburg, as stated in Dau (ed.), *op. cit.*, 25.

92 C. F. W. Walther to Stephan, n. d. [December, 1836], MS., C.H.I. Walther had not been entirely happy at Kahla, complaining about Fürbringer and Mrs. G. H. Löber. G. H. Löber, Diary, 1836, p. 50, MS., C.H.I.

dained and installed on January 15, 1837.[93] In a letter to his patron Walther expressed the opinion that the sermon of his superintendent, Siebenhaar, on the occasion of the installation was an "un-Christian address." [94] The young pastor's estimate of his own congregation was no more flattering. The same letter assured the Count: "Now, first of all, as far as the . . . condition of the congregation is concerned, I soon came to the conclusion that real spiritual life is not to be found in a single one of its members." [95] Walther's determination to correct this condition was soon to cause some friction.

Several other names must be added to the roster of the Leipzig group. Friedrich August Fröhlich deserves mention, because contemporary writers testify to his fanaticism and to the harshness of his judgment in supporting Stephan's every dictum and in prosecuting the less zealous before the tribunal of Stephan's displeasure, whenever dissent raised its unwelcome head among the Stephanites.[96] One of these contemporary writers was Ludwig Paul Wieland Lütkemüller. During the early thirties he was intimately associated with Stephan and his followers, but before the end of the decade he had come under the influence of Dr. Scheibel, who allegedly instigated Lütkemüller's polemical writing against his former friends, *Die Lehren und Umtriebe der Stephanisten.*[97] Then there was Candidate Friedrich Wilhelm Pöschel, Stephan's secretary, who was active in taking the stenographic notes that made possible the publication of Stephan's sermons (beginning with 1824), and who was supposed to have been the author of the *Glaubensbekenntniss*

---

93 The documents relative to C. F. W. Walther's call are contained in Bound MSS., Invoices, C. H. I. See also Bound MSS., Auszug aus den Acten der evangel. Superintendur Chemnitz betreffend Wahl, Ordination & Amts-Einführung des sel. Professor Dr. *C. F. W. Walther* ins Pfarramt zu *Bräunsdorf in Sachsen* sowie den Zwist zwischen den Nagel'schen Eheleuten 1836 bis 1838 (hereafter cited as Acten der . . . Superintendur Chemnitz), C. H. I.; M. Günther, *op. cit.,* 19—20. Neither the date for Walther's call nor for his ordination was "the second Sunday in Advent, 1837," as stated in Dau (ed.), *op. cit.,* 25.

94 C. F. W. Walther to von Einsiedel, n. d. [January, 1837], quoted in M. Günther, *op. cit.,* 22.

95 *Ibid.*

96 Fischer, *op. cit.,* 61; F. A. E. F. [Friedrich August Ernst Fröhlich] to L. Fischer, n. d., quoted in *ibid.,* 153—159; Fröhlich to Marbach, June 17, 1838, Bound MSS., VI, C. H. I.; Fröhlich to Marbach, Oct. 23—24, 1838, MS., C. H. I.

97 Fischer, *op. cit.,* 90.

der Gemeinde zu St. Johannis of 1833.[98] In 1835, two years after he had acted as Stephan's apologete, he was "excommunicated" by Stephan.[99] One of the candidates who actually took part in the emigration was Georg Albert Schieferdecker (1815—1891), a native of Leipzig and a student at the university there from 1833 to 1836. Between 1836 and 1838 he taught in Breitenbrunn and Chemnitz and served as tutor for the von Schönburg-Waldenburg family. Schieferdecker is noteworthy mainly for his later activity in the Missouri Synod, in which he became a controversial figure, and as the author of a story of the Perry County settlement, where he served as pastor.[100]

Carl Ludwig Geyer (March 16, 1812—March 6, 1892) was a cousin of the Walthers who joined their circle at Leipzig when he attended the university (1833—1836). After graduation he became Ferdinand Walther's successor in the Löber household.[101] Johann Jakob Gönner (1807—1864), also a candidate from Leipzig, later became the first rector of the college in Perry County. Karl Wilhelm Welzel, another one of the Leipzig group, was a member of the committee which organized the emigration, and lost his life on the *Amalia,* of which he was in charge. Some of the other candidates besides the above were Moritz Wege and Gottlieb Klügel. The latter had also been preaching and teaching in Saxe-Altenburg and the Saxon Province of Prussia for a number of years. He had served the Löbers and was on intimate terms with G. H. Löber, Gruber, Fürbringer, Keyl, C. F. W. Walther, and others. Although inclined to be legalistic and make trouble, he was generally well thought of among the Stephanites.[102] Still others belonged to the

---

[98] Not of the year 1822, as stated in von Polenz, *op. cit.,* 26. Pöschel's clerical work led to a bitter but pointless controversy between Lütkemüller and Stephan's attorney, W. E. Krause, because the former claimed that Stephan had not "written" the sermons himself. Lütkemüller, *op. cit.,* 6—9. For Pöschel, see also Hennig, "Die Auswanderung Martin Stephans," *Zeitschrift für Kirchengeschichte,* LVIII, 152; *Der Lutheraner,* XIII, 125; Hasse, *op. cit.,* 386.

[99] Hasse, *op. cit.,* 389; Lochner, "Ottomar Fürbringer," *Der Lutheraner,* XLIX, 171.

[100] *Geschichte der ersten deutschen lutherischen Ansiedlung in Altenburg, Perry Co., Mo.* For Schieferdecker, see Köstering, "Ehrengedächtniss des . . . Schieferdecker," *Der Lutheraner,* XLVIII, 144—145, 151—152, 167—168, 175—176, 182—183, 193—194; *Der Lutheraner,* XLVII, 199.

[101] G. H. Löber, Diary, 1836, p. 53, MS., C. H. I. C. F. W. Walther [?], "Carl Ludwig Geyer," *Der Lutheraner,* XLIX, 34—36, 43—44; Stellhorn, "Carl Ludwig Geyer," *Concordia Historical Institute Quarterly,* XII, 3—12.

[102] G. H. Löber, Diary, Feb. 15, April 3, May 2, Aug. 8, Oct. 10, 1831, 1836, p. 50, MS., C. H. I.

group for a time, but left or were expelled before the emigration took place.[103]

Franz Delitzsch (1813—1890), the eminent philologian and Old Testament critic, is worthy of special mention because of his intimate connection with the Stephanite movement. Before the emigration he was still a young man whose sincerity and earnest search for truth made him highly receptive to the counsel of Stephan and to the simple faith of Stephan's followers.[104] But even then his scholarly and literary bent was asserting itself. In 1838 he published *Wissenschaft, Kunst, Judenthum,* and in 1839 *Lutherthum und Lügenthum.* One of the most glowing tributes paid Stephan came from the pen of Franz Delitzsch in the introduction to the former of these two works, where he said: "Martin Stephan is a beautiful, a significant name; the spirit of Martin Luther, the believing enthusiasm of the first blood-witnesses of the Church grace him who bears it." [105] Even Fischer, who was opposed to the emigration and to Stephanism, bears witness to the ability and integrity of Delitzsch.[106] Eventually Delitzsch did not accompany the emigrants to America, but remained deeply attached to some of the clergymen of the emigration and continued to correspond with them after they had arrived in the United States.[107]

In the history of the emigration the importance of the Leipzig group can hardly be overrated.[108] There is no evidence that the

---

[103] Von Polenz, *op. cit.*, 26—27.

[104] Delitzsch to G. H. Löber, March 13, 1833 [or 1834], Bound MSS., Invoices, C. H. I.; G. H. Löber, Diary, 1836, pp. 40, 53, MS., C. H. I.; Fischer, *op. cit.*, 14; Stoeckhardt, "Franz Delitzsch," *Lehre und Wehre,* XXXVI, 202; *Der Lutheraner,* XLVI, 66.

[105] Delitzsch, *Wissenschaft, Kunst, Judenthum,* 2; Delitzsch to L. Fischer, n. d., quoted in Fischer, *op. cit.*, 147—153.

[106] Fischer, *op. cit.*, 144—146.

[107] Delitzsch to F. W. Barthel, Dec. 8, 1839, MS., C. H. I.; O. Fürbringer to Delitzsch [?], Sept. 7, 1839, quoted in L. Fürbringer, "Aus vergangenen Tagen und vergilbten Blättern," *Der Lutheraner,* LXXXVI, 118; Delitzsch to C. F. W. Walther, March 30, 1845, quoted in "Aus einem Briefe Herrn Dr. Delitzsch'ens an den Herausgeber," *ibid.*, I, 90—91; Delitzsch to relatives of C. F. W. Walther, "Pfingstmontag 1887," quoted in *Lehre und Wehre,* XXXIII, 289—290. See also Delitzsch's extravagant address to his former associates in the dedication of his book *Vom Hause Gottes oder der Kirche,* quoted in Fritschel, *Geschichte der lutherischen Kirche in Amerika* (hereafter cited as *Geschichte*), 177—178.

[108] The failure to recognize the significance of this phase of developments (to which he devotes only a few lines) is one of the fundamental mistakes in Hennig's portrayal of the movement. Hennig, "Die Auswanderung Martin Stephans," *Zeitschrift für Kirchengeschichte,* LVIII, 159.

idea of emigration originated with these men, but without them the emigration would have been extremely unlikely — especially under a Stephanite system, where the clergy were a factor of the first magnitude. Stephan established contact with all of these men while they were comparatively young and attached them firmly to himself. Later some of them became pastors and multiplied the number of Stephan's adherents.[109] How striking a factor their youthfulness was, is demonstrated by the fact that of all the pastors and candidates who left Germany with Stephan only one was over thirty-five years of age at the time of the emigration, and half of them were thirty or less. All of them had come under his influence several years before, many of them during their early student days when they were just past twenty.[110] On the other hand, of the older dissenting theologians with whom Stephan had contact, such as Guericke, Rudelbach, Scheibel, and others, not one followed him when he left Germany. They had been exposed to his influence when they were more mature and more experienced. Although there is no conclusive evidence to prove that their refusal to follow him was a result of their age, it is worth pointing out that it was uniformly these men who maintained their independence of Stephan, no matter how conservative their views. A similar fact in the case of Kühn has already been noted. Stephan impressed most noticeably the young and unstable.[111]

Furthermore, the Leipzig background gave these men a sense of unity and compactness which later proved invaluable for Stephan and his emigration project as well as for the men themselves when they had to rebuild their lives in America. There were primarily two reasons for this feeling. On the one hand the joint religious exercises, discussions, and whatever else belonged to the Kühn formula for "awakening," supplemented by subsequent contacts between these men, served to unite them with the closest bonds. They felt themselves crusaders all, and were ready to do spiritual battle for each other. Co-operation of any kind is likely to call forth a degree of *camaraderie,* and in their case the result was a feeling of veritable brotherhood, which they never quite lost, even in later

---

109 Keyl, *op. cit.,* 7, 11; Fischer, *op. cit.,* 23; von Polenz, *op. cit.,* 27.

110 See List I, Appendix A.

111 C. F. W. Walther in Köstering, *Auswanderung,* 6.

life.[112] On the other hand, the negative side of the picture, the entire movement was carried out in an atmosphere of high consecration and martyrdom. The fellow students and teachers of Kühn's adherents were largely responsible for the attitude of his group, scorning Kühn and his followers as mystics, Pietists, obscurantists, and bigots.[113] These epithets were not entirely undeserved. But since most criticism of the group emanated from those whose opposing views were equally extreme, it is no wonder that such criticism failed to make a favorable impression. Under the influence of this attack Kühn and the others drew ever closer together. When the candidates realized that they would be confronted with similar opposition in the liberalistically dominated State Church, some of them revolted openly (*e. g.*, Brohm and Bünger) and refused to accept appointments from the ecclesiastical authorities. Here was a field for Stephanism.

The two other pastors who emigrated under Stephan's influence did not live in the kingdom of Saxony, but in the duchy of Saxe-Altenburg. One of them, Theodor Carl Friedrich Gruber, a friend of Keyl and Löber since his university days [114] and pastor at Reust since 1825, did not accompany Stephan in 1838. However, Gruber followed the emigrants to America the next year, although Stephan was no longer in charge of the movement, and thus, belatedly, became a part of the Stephanite emigration.

The second of these men was Gotthold Heinrich Löber (January 5, 1797—August 19, 1849), pastor at Eichenberg, near Kahla. Löber came from a highly respected and well-to-do family. Orphaned at an early age by the death of his father, a superintendent in the State Church of Saxe-Altenburg, the boy was provided with a thorough secular and theological training by his mother. He attended the *Gymnasium* at Altenburg from 1810 to 1815 and the Uni-

---

112 C. F. W. Walther to Brohm, Jan. 15, 1836, MS., C. H. I.; Candidate Kühn to C. F. W. Walther, April 5, 1831, Bound MSS., Invoices, C. H. I.; C. F. W. Walther to Sihler, Jan. 2, 1845, in L. Fürbringer (ed.), *Briefe von C. F. W. Walther*, I, 6; C. F. W. Walther to Emilie Bünger Walther, Oct. 11, 1851, *ibid.*, 72—76; J. F. Bünger, "Ehrengedächtniss des . . . Brohm," *Der Lutheraner*, XXXVII, 189. The entire presentation in C. F. W. Walther's biography of J. F. Bünger illustrates this point, but note especially C. F. W. Walther, *Bünger*, 15—19.

113 Candidate Kühn to O. Fürbringer, Aug. 8, 1831, MS., C. H. I.; C. F. W. Walther, *Bünger*, 11.

114 Gruber, "Ehrengedächtniss des . . . Gotthold Heinrich Löber," *Der Lutheraner*, VI, 145; Dau (ed.), *op. cit.*, 6.

versity of Jena from 1816 to 1819, but was little touched by the spirit that pervaded the latter institution. Löber's first position was that of private tutor from 1819 to 1824. In the latter year, after passing the examination before the consistory, he received a call to Eichenberg and Bibra from his elder brother, Friedemann, who was patron of these parishes.[115] During his fourteen years at Eichenberg he worked with marked success, both among his own people and among those of other parishes who sought him out because of his reputation as an orthodox Lutheran preacher of the old school.[116] For a number of years Löber's and Gruber's religious leanings were distinctly Pietistic, and both were in close touch with the Moravians.[117] But later the influence of Stephan counteracted their inclinations toward Pietism. In 1830 Löber published a memorial on the anniversary of the Augsburg Confession, and in 1834 an edition of selected writings of Luther. Neither sold in any appreciable quantities, a fact which led Löber to exclaim: "O tempora!" [118]

During the middle thirties, Löber was brought under the influence of Stephan. An exact point of time is difficult to fix, but by 1834 references to "Past. Stephan" began to appear in Löber's diary. Fürbringer, it seems, was the apostle of Stephanism to Saxe-Altenburg during these years, assisted at various times by Klügel and C. F. W. Walther. An effort on Löber's part to meet Stephan personally in Leipzig, during January, 1834, failed when Stephan became ill; instead, Löber came to know the Barthel family there.

---

115 Many of the facts of G. H. Löber's career are readily available in Gruber, "Ehrengedächtniss des . . . Gotthold Heinrich Löber," *Der Lutheraner,* VI, 145—146, 152—155. See also Nitzschke to C. F. W. Walther, Aug. 20, 1849, Bound MSS., Invoices, C.H.I.; Köstering, *Auswanderung,* 140—144, 149; Löber-Eichenberg (ed.), "Ein Briefwechsel," *Mitteilungen . . . Kahla,* VII, 127, 191. The date of Löber's death is given as both August 13 and August 19 in Hochstetter, *op. cit.,* 57, 171. Other sources agree that the latter date is the correct one.

116 Among his personal following from points outside his parish, were the Schmidts of Kahla, Putzers and Hermanns of Naumburg, the Ottos of Jena-Löbnitz, and T. Mylius of Möhrsdorf. G. H. Löber, Diary, 1836, pp. 19, 43, 47—48, MS., C.H.I.

117 G. H. Löber, Diary, May 30, July 5, 25, Aug. 7, Nov. 28, 1831, Nov. 24, 1834, March 13, 1835, MS., C.H.I.

118 G. H. Löber, Diary, 1834, p. 11, MS., C. H. I.; Gruber, "Ehrengedächtniss des . . . Gotthold Heinrich Löber," *Der Lutheraner,* VI, 145—146; Lochner, "Ottomar Fürbringer," *ibid.,* XLIX, 172; Dau (ed.), *op. cit.,* 6; Hennig, "Die Auswanderung Martin Stephans," *Zeitschrift für Kirchengeschichte,* LVIII, 158.

Later that year Löber displayed some interest in securing Stephan's approval of his editorial work, and correspondence was maintained between Eichenberg and Dresden.[119]

Then Löber began to doubt whether Stephan could be trusted, and little is said about Stephan in Löber's diary for more than a year and a half. But late in 1835 there is a revealing entry which permits a reconstruction of what had happened. The entry is the draft of a letter from Löber to Stephan, dated November 12, 1835. This letter makes it clear that the kind of treason of which Löber was guilty could not be tolerated in Stephan's version of the City of God. Fürbringer apparently had denounced Löber to the faithful in Dresden and Leipzig, and the Altenburg pastor was severely taken to task. Confronted by exclusion from the only circles which he thought had *the* truth, chided by his friend Fürbringer, reproved by the celebrated Stephan himself, and in the habit of accusing himself of every manner of laxness and insincerity, Löber did not have the stamina to keep the issue long in doubt. As Keyl had done before him, Löber surrendered, apologized to Stephan, and was again received into the fold.[120] And all this before Löber had even met Stephan!

The relationship between Löber and Gruber, meanwhile, had been growing steadily more intimate. The two families maintained frequent contact, and the men acted as confessor and counselor, each to the other.[121] Gruber seems to have had some difficulty in adjusting himself to his environment. His marital relationship was somewhat strained at this time. He was in trouble with church officials. He was at odds with his father. Klügel and he were not too friendly. He was frequently not at peace with himself.[122] Finally he committed the unpardonable sin of not accepting Stephan's leadership. In fact, with Löber's example before him, he nevertheless permitted himself to become suspicious of Stephan. This attitude was enough to alienate from Gruber his few remaining friends. Furthermore, it was a challenge to the new orthodoxy —

---

119 G. H. Löber, Diary, Introduction to the year 1834, Jan. 8, 14, 1834, and 1834, p. 11, MS., C. H. I.

120 *Ibid.*, Draft of a letter to Stephan, Nov. 12, 1835.

121 *Ibid.*, Feb. 3, April 9, June 22, 29, July 1, Sept. 19—20, 1831, Jan. 14, 1834, March 1, 1835, April 13, 1836.

122 *Ibid.*, March 3, 1831, March 1, 1835, April 13, 1836, and 1836, pp. 21, 50.

the orthodoxy of Stephanism. The situation was dealt with in a way that was assuming a pattern of pressure among the Stephanites. In October, 1836, Löber and Fürbringer went to Leipzig for one of their meetings with the group at that place. Although Stephan was not there, it was decided to force the issue with Gruber, and he was summoned to Leipzig by letter. He came. If Löber had not been able to hold out, there was no prospect that Gruber would. In fact, Löber, who had gone through a similar experience only a short time before, was instrumental in having Gruber humble himself before Stephan in a written request for forgiveness. He received a strictly qualified reply from the Dresden pastor, but it was enough to enable him to be one of the inner circle again.[123]

Members of the clergy usually furnished the leadership for the Stephanite movement in Germany, whereas the part laymen were permitted to play was generally of secondary importance until their services and abilities were needed to facilitate the emigration. However, one of the laymen, J. F. Winter, a teacher at Planena in the Saxon Province of Prussia, made a contribution of importance. He had been an open opponent of the Prussian Union since 1834. When he was suspended from office, he became instrumental in organizing, under Pastor Guericke, an independent congregation of separatists which sought an escape from the government measures against the conservatives. Later, when the Saxons decided to emigrate, Winter induced a considerable number of Prussians to join the Stephanite venture and led one group of emigrants to Bremen.[124]

The highest-ranking layman among Stephan's followers was Count Detlev von Einsiedel, prominent in the Saxon *Erweckung,* as well as a political figure of some importance. Strongly contrasting forces of progressivism and conservatism clashed in his personality, although the latter plainly dominated. Von Einsiedel was of a prominent Herrnhuter family, was decidedly anti-Rationalistic, associated with the Pietists, and used his political power freely (as long as he enjoyed it) in the interests of the Saxon *Erweckung.*[125]

---

[123] *Ibid.,* 1836, pp. 50, 52.

[124] Delitzsch to G. H. Löber, March 13, 1833 [or 1834], Bound MSS., Invoices, C. H. I.; Bekenntniss, MS., C. H. I.; Köstering, "Johann Friedrich Winter," *Der Lutheraner,* XXX, 33—38; Kuehnert, "Teacher Johann Friedrich Ferdinand Winter," *Lutheran School Journal,* LXXIV, 247—254.

[125] Hennig, *op. cit.,* 150—162; Pleissner, *op. cit.,* 45—51, 59—61; *Lehre und Wehre,* VII, 157.

> Therefore the Count sought, wherever possible, both as patron and minister of state, to give preference in the matter of appointment [of clergymen] to representatives of the *Erweckung* Pietism. That men like Pötzschke, Kranichfeld, Meurer, Keyl, Bürger, etc., were drawn into Saxony, at times to the detriment of 'natives,' created much bitterness in the country, but that he was guilty of overreaching himself cannot be proved.[126]

Von Einsiedel watched the struggles of a rising confessionalism with a benign neutrality, for they interested him little; and emigration, of course, was far from his mind. But he thought very highly of Martin Stephan and his work.[127] It was von Einsiedel who brought Stephan and Pastor Benjamin Kurtz of the General Synod together in 1827.[128] Two of the pastors connected with the movement were his appointees, one of whom, C. F. W. Walther, acted as Stephan's apologist to the count when Stephan got into serious difficulties in 1837 and 1838 and Walther's patron became somewhat suspicious.[129]

Baron von Uckermann was a product of the Saxon *Erweckung,* who took up the literary cudgels against the Rationalism of Professor Krug and von Ammon in *Sendschreiben an den Hrn. Prof. W. Tr. Krug zu Leipzig.* This publication precipitated a more extended exchange, in which von Ammon replied with *Geistesverwirrung des Baron von Uckermann,* and the baron again retaliated with *Kritik der Geistesverwirrung.*[130] Von Uckermann had frequent contact with Stephan and his followers, and at one time even made substantial financial contributions to their cause. However, he objected to the legalism of the Stephanite system and eventually severed relations with Stephan prior to the emigration.

Friedrich Wilhelm Barthel (April 2, 1791—July 4, 1859), tax official at Leipzig, and his wife were among the lay members of the *Erweckung* movement in that city. Their home became a haven for some members of the Leipzig group, especially C. F. W. Walther and Bünger. The former characterized them as "the only family in

---

126 Hennig, *op. cit.,* 156. The names of Keyl and E. M. Bürger are, of course, misplaced. Both were natives of Saxony.

127 *Ibid.*

128 *New York Observer,* March 16, 1839.

129 Meurer [?] to C. F. W. Walther, Jan. 27, 1838, C. F. W. Walther to von Einsiedel, Feb. 3, 1838, MSS., C. H. I.

130 Fischer, *op. cit.,* 1, 43—47; Bemerkungen über . . . Stephan, Bound MSS., V, C. H. I.

Leipzig which understood us."[131] Barthel became treasurer of the emigrant group and left Germany with his family in 1838. Two other Leipzigers, the merchants F. A. Böhlau (from 1830 on a member of the Leipzig group)[132] and A. H. Döderlein, later became of some importance in the emigration.

In Dresden there were also several prominent men who became attached to Stephan in a personal way. A number of them, notably Doctors Stübel, Vehse, and Marbach, were well-educated and highly trained men. Carl Eduard Vehse (1802—1870) was, since 1833, curator of the Saxon State Archives and later became the author of a well-known, gossipy work on the ruling houses of Saxony.[133] Franz Adolph Marbach, Vehse's brother-in-law, was a lawyer by profession and at one time in the Saxon civil service. He was capable, energetic, with a kinetic personality, and given to grandiose plans of various kinds, of which the emigration was one.[134] Vehse and Marbach left Germany with Stephan, but Stübel did not.

There was also a constellation of lesser lights. Heinrich Ferdinand Fischer was a Dresden merchant prominently associated with the movement. Gustav Pfau (1808—1884), a painter at the

---

[131] C. F. W. Walther, *Bünger,* 19. See also: G. H. Löber, Diary, Jan. 14, 1834, MS., C. H. I.; C. F. W. Walther, "Todesnachricht," *Der Lutheraner,* XV, 207; L. Fuerbringer, *Persons and Events,* 97—98. Löber, in the pasage of his diary just cited, reports that at one of these meetings which he attended as a guest while on a trip to Leipzig, twelve to sixteen persons were present, including such well-known names of the movement as Fröhlich, Schütz, Delitzsch, Gönner, Schieferdecker, and "Belau" (Böhlau).

[132] C. F. W. Walther [?], "Ehrengedächtniss," *Der Lutheraner,* XIX, 71; G. H. Löber, Diary, Jan. 14, 1834, MS., C. H. I.

[133] *Geschichte der Höfe des Hauses Sachsen,* 7 vols., Hamburg, 1854. See also *Lehre und Wehre,* XVI, 256; L. Fuerbringer, *Persons and Events,* 84—85.

[134] Stübel to Vehse *et al.,* Sept. 12, 1839, Marbach to — ["Hochgeehrter Herr Geheimrat"], May 8, 1840, Bound MSS., VI, C. H. I.; *Chemnitzer Anzeiger,* Oct. 30, 1838; Marbach, An meine unter Pastor Stephan mitausgewanderten deutschen Landsleute, March 3, 1841 (hereafter cited as Marbach, An meine . . . Landsleute), MS., C. H. I. It seems that at one time Marbach was mayor of Zwickau. Von Lindenau (the Ministry of the Interior) to "Mayor Marbach at Zwickau," 1832, Bound MSS., VI, C. H. I. In an address given at Marbach's funeral (he died June 6, 1860), Pastor Ahlfeld referred to him as "the man who had been mayor in one of the most important cities of our country." L. Fuerbringer, *Persons and Events,* 93. A fuller report of the address from which Fuerbringer translated this and a few other passages is contained in Ahlfeld, "Grabrede . . . dem . . . Franz Adolph Marbach . . . gehalten," *Der Lutheraner,* XVII, 9. Marbach is also said to have been mayor of Dresden. Stellhorn, "The Saxon Centennial and the Schools," *Lutheran School Journal,* LXXIV, 296.

Royal Art Gallery in Dresden, was a close friend of Stephan.[135] Julius Otto Nitzschke (November 12, 1805—May 15, 1862) was factor at the royal china warehouse in Dresden. He was one of Stephan's converts from Rationalism and was completely under his sway.[136] Gustav Jäckel, a cashier, and J. G. Gube, a wealthy farmer, complete the roster of the inner circle. The last five named became members of the emigrant group.

All the men who have been individually mentioned possessed considerable ability. Collectively they afforded a versatile panel from which to draw keymen for the movement. Only two who left Germany were over forty years of age at the time, namely, Gube and Barthel.[137] Most of them had been associated with Stephan for years, and every one of them was devoted to the Bohemian pastor. Stephan attracted people from all walks of life, but he achieved his greatest success with professional men, students, merchants, and officials in the government service. These men became his lieutenants and the leaders of the emigration. Without them it would scarcely have been possible to carry out the project, at least on the scale on which it was executed. Their individual contributions will be discussed later.

---

135 For a brief sketch of his life, see Wyneken, "Herr Gustav Pfau," *Der Lutheraner,* XL, 37; L. Fuerbringer, *Persons and Events,* 94—96.

136 Lebenslauf des . . . Nitzschke, MS., C. H. I.

137 See List I, Appendix A.

CHAPTER THREE

TRANSFORMATION OF STEPHANISM INTO SEPARATISM

The physical growth of Stephanism is equaled or exceeded in importance by a parallel development of its conceptual and functional aspects during the decade and a half before the actual emigration. A glance at the nature of this development is necessary for an understanding of the character of the movement, a character which was inseparable from that of its leader. This strong personal influence makes it impossible, in an examination of the growth of the movement or of its ideas, to proceed entirely from a set of principles or doctrines. They would provide a false basis of judgment even in the case of a religious group so intent on doctrine as the Stephanites. However, the question is further complicated by the fact that Stephan's character was, in some respects, even less consistent than that of the average person. In fact, it was less the principles of Stephan than their application — and in some cases even their violation — which constituted the distinguishing characteristics of the system, which were found objectionable by many people, and which lent color to the emigration.[1]

Thus, while there are two readily distinguishable determining features in the history of the Stephanite movement, the ideas and the man — that is, the religious principles involved and the personality of the leader, Stephan — it is a mistake to try to separate these two factors. Stephanism would not have been Stephanism, nor would there have been an emigration, in the absence of either of these influences or without a blending of the two. Such a misleading separation occurs when the movement is portrayed either as the result solely of a clash between religious oppression and religious zeal, or solely of an irreligious mass hoax perpetrated by a conscienceless old rogue.

While it is difficult to find even one person among Stephan's

[1] Marbach, An meine . . . Landsleute, MS., C. H. I.; Fischer, *op. cit.*, 21, 54—56, 178.

critics who does not have something to say in the man's favor, commendatory statements are confined largely to his earlier activity, that is, before 1823 or 1830.[2] A change came over Stephan during the twenties, in both his public and his private life, that grew constantly more pronounced. This change, whatever its nature, was not produced by any formal modification of his theology. Stephan's doctrine and preaching remained consistent with his original profession. The very rigidity of his adherence to the Confessions was one of the chief objects of attack by his critics and of admiration from his supporters.[3] Nevertheless, a change did gradually occur, the reality or significance of which is in no way minimized by the difficulty of defining exactly what it was. That change took place in the personal relationship of Stephan to his followers and his opponents.

Whether or not Stephan sought it, his power was increasing in an unwholesome manner, and he was well on his way toward earning Maurer's epithet, "ordained spellbinder."[4] More and more people looked to him for spiritual leadership. When persons in trouble came to him for aid and found it, they went away not only, perhaps not even primarily, as converts to orthodoxy, but as personal champions of Stephan, and they, in turn, directed others to him.[5] The pastors, and the candidates who later became pastors, were naturally in the best position for proselyting, but teachers and laymen often did effective work also.[6] Stephan usually had an

---

[2] Document . . . des Grundsteins . . . St. Louis . . . 22. Juny 1842, Lossagung vom Stephanismus, Bekenntniss, Nachrichten an unsere Nachkommen, MSS., C. H. I.; Fischer, *op. cit.*, 17, 54—56; C. F. W. Walther in Köstering, *Auswanderung*, 5—6; von Polenz, *op. cit.*, 23—24, 46—47.

[3] Nachrichten an unsere Nachkommen, Marbach, An meine . . . Landsleute, MSS., C. H. I.; Stephan, *Herzlicher Zuruf . . . zwei Predigten*, 6; Pöschel, *op. cit.*, 9—15, 41—42; Fischer, *op. cit.*, 20—23, 54—56; 80—83; Lütkemüller, *op. cit.*, 10, 12; C. F. W. Walther in Köstering, *Auswanderung*, 5. Later Stephan was frequently attacked as un-Lutheran, non-confessional, Pietistic, and Chiliastic. *Ibid.*, 8, 31, 35; Vehse, *op. cit.*, 24.

[4] Maurer, "Studies in the Sociology of Religion, IV, The Problem of Group Consensus; Founding the Missouri Synod," *American Journal of Sociology*, XXX, 674.

[5] Nachrichten an unsere Nachkommen, Document . . . des Grundsteins . . . St. Louis . . . 22. Juny 1842, MSS., C. H. I.; Keyl, *op. cit.*, 7, 11; von Polenz, *op. cit.*, 27, 81.

[6] Note the case of Michael Walz, who brought a group of Württemberg and Baden people into touch with Stephan. Walz to Stephan, Dec. 9, 1837, Jan. 3, 1838, Walz to Marbach, Aug. 23 [28?], Dec. 10, 1837, Jan. 3, April 6, 1838, MSS., C. H. I. The replies of both Marbach and Stephan are contained in Bound MSS., VI, C. H. I. See also Bekenntniss, MS., C. H. I.

answer to the problems of those who came to him, for besides being an excellent practical psychologist who could deal expertly with people in all stations of life, he was a capable pastor and met the individual's problems adroitly. Even persons who had never seen him wrote to him for advice, while others journeyed to Dresden to lay their troubles before him in an interview, to hear his sermons, and to attend his meetings. The members of his own congregation often could not get into the pews of their own church. Stephanism was no longer local in scope, but was spreading beyond the borders of Saxony to other German states.[7] Stephan was an able man, and his far-flung activities did immeasurable good for many years; yet his character, and with it the movement, suffered from the conditions which resulted.[8]

From the status of being a branch of a movement — the *Erweckung* — Stephanism developed into a movement itself, sufficiently self-conscious and purposeful not to hesitate even at levying financial contributions.[9] Stephanism had been a viewpoint; it became a system. This system was a hierarchical-mystical one, with a peculiar concept of relationships in a Christian community, based upon a leadership so purely personal that it led to various abuses in practice. Its most important and fundamental characteristic — the one which gave rise to most of the others — was an inordinate veneration of the office of the ministry and of Stephan's person and views, or as Fischer incisively termed it, "a subtle apotheosis" and "the new papacy." [10]

It may quite plausibly be argued that the first impulse in the wrong direction came not from Stephan himself, but from the more enthusiastic of his adherents, some of whom elevated his personality over his teaching and practice.[11] People as deeply and emotionally

---

[7] *Ibid.* Saxe-Altenburg, Saxe-Weimar, Württemberg, Baden, and Prussia (Silesia) are mentioned in Fischer, *op. cit.*, 32, 38, 63. See also the list of subscribers to Stephan's sermon book, *Der christliche Glaube.*

[8] Stübel to Vehse *et al.*, Sept. 12, 1839, Bound MSS., VI, C. H. I.; Fischer, *op. cit.*, 17, 37, 54—56; von Polenz, *op. cit.*, 13—15; Lütkemüller, *op. cit.*, 10.

[9] Delitzsch to G. H. Löber, March 13, 1833 [or 1834], Bound MSS., Invoices, C. H. I.; Bürger, *op. cit.*, 11; Pleissner, *op. cit.*, 40—42.

[10] Fischer, *op. cit.*, 130—132.

[11] All of the documents relative to Stephan's elevation to the episcopacy, which will be discussed below, reveal this attitude. Furthermore the entire set of Codes illustrates this point. Appendix B. See also Document . . . des Grundsteins . . . St. Louis . . . 22. Juny 1842, Lossagung vom Stephanismus, Bekenntniss, Marbach, An meine . . . Landsleute, Stephan to G. H. Löber,

religious as, for instance, C. F. W. Walther, who felt himself transported "from hell to heaven" through Stephan's instrumentality, naturally had an extremely high regard for him and were submissive to him without any effort on his part to produce such an effect.[12]

Yet the primary responsibility remains with Stephan. His mistake, of course, if he really did not desire such a relationship as developed, and if he was "innately modest,"[13] lay in his failure to make known his aversion for the adulation heaped upon him and effectively to discourage it. In fact, such speculation is hypothetical in the extreme. It requires unusual credulity to think that Stephan attained the position he did against his wishes. On the contrary only people who were subservient to Stephan succeeded in getting along with him. At least all the people who were allowed to advance in the Stephanite hierarchy and to play important roles stood in an intimate relationship of this kind to him. Later, during the emigration, there were many in the group who were unacquainted with Stephan. But such people seldom attained any prominence; in any event they usually came from the congregations of men implicitly devoted to him. Their relation to their pastors resembled their pastors' relation to Stephan; hence the general effect was much the same.

In the eyes of his followers Stephan became the champion of orthodoxy, the defender of the faith. They firmly asserted that the means of grace were dependent upon his person and that, if he were silenced, the Lutheran Church would cease to exist in Saxony. Stephan's doctrine was unerringly true, his solution of a question inevitably correct. Any criticism of or opposition to the Dresden pastor was condemned in the harshest terms. Stephan became an

---

Feb. 20, 1836, Candidate Kühn to O. Fürbringer, Feb. 29, 1832, MSS., C. H. I.; Fröhlich to Marbach, June 17, 1838, Stübel to Vehse *et al.*, Sept. 12, 1839, Bound MSS., VI, C. H. I.; Fröhlich to L. Fischer, May 30, 1838, quoted in Fischer, *op. cit.*, 153—159; Delitzsch to L. Fischer, n. d., *ibid.*, 144—146, 190—197; Keyl, *op. cit.*, 9—11; C. F. W. Walther in Köstering, *Auswanderung*, 6—10; *ibid.*, 37—38; Pleissner, *op. cit.*, 3; Lütkemüller, *op. cit.*, 13.

[12] C. F. W. Walther, *Bünger*, 29; Gönner to Stephan, Oct. 10, 1838, Bound MSS., I, C. H. I.; C. F. W. Walther to Brohm, Jan. 15, 1834, Aug. 17, 1837, Meurer [?] to C. F. W. Walther, Jan. 27, 1838, C. F. W. Walther to von Einsiedel, Feb. 3, 1838, MSS., C. H. I. These letters do not bear out claims made concerning C. F. W. Walther's alleged independence of Stephan, *e. g.*, in Hochstetter, *op. cit.*, 20—21; Köstering, *Auswanderung*, 38—39.

[13] Hennig, "Die Auswanderung Martin Stephans," *Zeitschrift für Kirchengeschichte*, LVIII, 150.

oracle, and all who disagreed with him, or with whom he disagreed, were wrong. Since Stephan eventually disagreed with almost everyone, the simple conclusion was that all other views represented in the Church were false; only Stephanism was right. In fact the claim was finally made not only that Stephanism was the only right Church ("die wahre Kirche im Extracte," as Marbach phrased it), but that it alone was a Church. The Stephanites were *the Church!* [14]

The Advisory Committee (which organized the emigration) recorded in its minutes, without protest, the statement of one of its members: "The health and life of the Pastor [Stephan] are at stake, and with them the chief means of grace for us." Similarly Candidate Fröhlich wrote to L. Fischer: "Everything depends upon your coming to Pastor Stephan. If you do not seek him out, the light of grace will be withheld from you." [15] When von Uckermann expressed his doubts about the personal integrity of Stephan, Marbach issued the dire warning:

> You have judged the servant of Christ [Stephan] 1 Corinth. 4:5. — May the grace of the Holy Ghost lead you to him again before the Last Judgment, where Christ will judge him and you, each according to his works — may you soon be converted from a blasphemer, who outrages the office of Jesus Christ, to a penitent sinner.[16]

---

[14] Protokolle über die . . . Auswanderung, Dec. 6, 13, 1837, Feb. 15, 16, April 14, May 11, 18, 1838, Bound MSS., III, C. H. I.; Gönner to Stephan, Oct. 10, 1838, Stephan to —, Oct 6, 1838, Marbach to O. H. Walther, Oct. 16, 1838, Bound MSS., I, C. H. I.; Bemerkungen über . . . Stephan, Bound MSS., V, C. H. I.; Stübel to Vehse *et al.*, Sept. 12, 1839, Fröhlich to Marbach, June 17, 1838, Marbach to Walz, Jan. 12, 1838, Bound MSS., VI, C. H. I.; Delitzsch to G. H. Löber, March 13, 1833 [or 1834], Bound MSS., Invoices, C. H. I.; Candidate Kühn to —, Sept. 30, 1830, Candidate Kühn to O. Fürbringer, Jan. 20, Feb. 29, 1832, C. F. W. Walther to O. H. Walther, May 4, 1840, Marbach, An meine Landsleute, Document . . . des Grundsteins . . . St. Louis . . . 22. Juny 1842, Lossagung vom Stephanismus, Bekenntniss, G. H. Löber, Diary, April 27, May 3, 1836, and 1836, pp. 12, 40, and undated entry (June—Dec.), 1840, MSS., C. H. I.; J. F. Bünger, Diarium, Oct. 22, 1838, MS., L. Fürbringer Papers, St. Louis. See also Fischer, *op. cit.*, iii-iv, 29—30, 35—43, 133—135; Pöschel, *op. cit.*, 60—62; von Polenz, *op. cit.*, 15—17, 27; Lütkemüller, *op. cit.*, 8—9, 13—16, 48—52; Pleissner, *op. cit.*, 65—66, 84—85; Bürger, *op. cit.*, 11; Keyl, *op. cit.*, 5—6; C. F. W. Walther in Köstering, *Auswanderung*, 5—10; Schieferdecker, *op. cit.*, 7.

[15] Protokolle über die . . . Auswanderung, Feb. 16, 1838, Bound MSS., III, C. H. I.; Fröhlich to L. Fischer, May 30, 1838, quoted in Fischer, *op. cit.*, 153—159. The documents relative to Stephan's elevation to the episcopacy, which will be discussed below, contain similar ideas. See also the Codes, Appendix B.

[16] Marbach to von Uckermann, Dec. 27, 1837, Bound MSS., VI., C. H. I. See also von Uckermann to Marbach, Jan. 9, 1838, Marbach to von Uckermann, May 28, 1837, *ibid.*

Such an attitude on the part of Stephan himself is not as noticeable before the second decade of his ministry as afterwards, when he came into contact with the younger men who were to emigrate under his leadership. At first Stephan passively allowed such veneration without doing anything to check it. Then he accepted it as his due. Finally he demanded unqualified agreement with his views, not on the basis of conviction, but simply because of his insistence. How this system worked has been indicated in the case of Keyl; it was applied also to others — for instance, to Löber.[17]

Stephan's contact with the Prussian Lutherans provides additional illustrations. When the younger Scheibel was exiled from Prussia in 1832, he took refuge in Dresden. His contact with Stephan while in that city was direct but not congenial. In 1834 Scheibel ordained Guericke in a house in Leipzig, although the latter was still under the jurisdiction of the Prussian government, since his residence remained at Halle. By 1836 Scheibel and his followers had broken with Stephan because of what they termed his "papacy." This action on Scheibel's part led to a rift between him and his fellow Prussian Guericke, who then came to Eichenberg and consulted with his good friend Löber and wrote to Stephan, applying for advice about the best way to sever his connections with the Silesians (Scheibel). Stephan, of course, readily obliged, as he and his followers were seizing every opportunity to discredit and criticize Scheibel. But Guericke did not become permanently allied to Stephan either, for in 1838 he remained behind, while Winter, as remarked above, led those of Guericke's and his own followers who wished to emigrate, into Stephan's camp.[18]

But while some of the men in the group clashed with Stephan in the earlier years of their contact with him, most of them capitulated in the end, and after about 1832 resistance to him was almost negligible. Stephan's domination was not only accepted, but even welcomed by many of his docile converts.[19] A power over the lives

---

[17] Stephan to G. H. Löber, Feb. 20, 1836, Marbach, An meine . . . Landsleute, Document . . . des Grundsteins . . . St. Louis . . . 22. Juny 1842, Lossagung vom Stephanismus, Bekenntniss, MSS., C. H. I."

[18] G. H. Löber, Diary, Feb. 24, 1835, Jan. 1, 23—25, April 26, 1836, and 1836, pp. 12, 42A, Stephan to G. H. Löber, Feb. 20, 1836, MSS., C. H. I.; Fischer, *op. cit.*, 63; Kluge, *Geschichte der christlichen Kirche von der Reformation bis auf unsre Tage*, 438—448.

[19] Marbach, An meine . . . Landsleute, Gönner to Stephan, Oct. 10, 1838, MSS., C. H. I. C. F. W. Walther's description of the oppressiveness of the situation seems to be a retroactive judgment. C. F. W. Walther in Köstering,

of his followers was thus placed into his hands which few men could have used with discretion; and Stephan was not one of the few.

Adulation was something Stephan could not resist. The observation has been made with some justice that the personal deference shown him was the beginning of his decline.[20] The submissiveness of his followers caused Stephan to have an opinion of himself that entailed the absence of any sense of responsibility to public opinion and to the demands of propriety.[21] This attitude of Stephan probably accounts for his failure to make an open defense of his person, practices, and principles after 1823. The public was quick to sense the state of affairs, and a hostile feeling soon developed among the people that prepared the way for the charges later made against him, including those of irresponsibility, imperiousness, a desire for unlimited power, and immoral conduct. Criticism rose in a steady crescendo, with the result that as early as 1825 it was considered a disgrace in some circles to go to hear Stephan.[22]

Stephan's lack of a sense of accountability during the second period of his ministry is illustrated in the changed nature of the meetings held by him. As previously stated, he had conducted gatherings from the very beginning of his pastorate at Dresden. He, as well as others, asserted that the regular spiritual fare on these occasions was prayer, the singing of hymns, and a catechetical review of Stephan's sermons. Besides, he sent out candidates into the homes of his followers to conduct "Concordia hours," so called because the Formula of Concord was the chief subject of discussion.[23] Then he developed the custom of holding a kind of "question-

---

Auswanderung, 9. In 1836, Walther himself went out of his way to consult Stephan when Walther could have acted independently. C. F. W. Walther to Stephan, n. d. [December, 1837], MS., C. H. I. See also Meurer [?] to C. F. W. Walther, Jan. 27, 1838, C. F. W. Walther to von Einsiedel, Feb. 3, 1838, MSS., C. H. I.; von Polenz, *op. cit.*, 31.

20 Bekenntniss, MS., C. H. I.

21 Lossagung vom Stephanismus, MS., C. H. I.; Stübel to Vehse *et al.*, Sept. 12, 1839, Bound MSS., VI, C. H. I.; Lütkemüller, *op. cit.*, 8.

22 E. M. Bürger, Selbstbiographie, 34—37, MS., E. J. Buerger Papers, Ellicottville, N. Y. Complaint to the consistory against Stephan by a number of Dresden clergymen, June 23, 1820, MS., Stephanakten, Landeskirchenamt, Dresden, I, 1—3.

23 An die Kirchen-Inspection zu Dresden Appellation des Pastor Martin Stephan zu Dresden gegen das unter dem 17. März 1836 an ihn erlassene Verbot, March 28, 1836 (hereafter cited as Appellation des . . . Stephan, March 28, 1836), Bound MSS., V, C. H. I.; C. F. W. Walther, *Bünger*, 24, 30; von Polenz, *op. cit.*, 32.

and-answer hour," in which he dispensed spiritual advice on topics suggested by those attending.[24] Time and again such gatherings called forth the accusation that they were conventicles and evidence of the formation of a new sect.[25] Hennig asserts that such meetings had been forbidden to Stephan as early as 1820.[26] The controversy about these meetings was one of long standing, but never led to any definite conclusion, although on the charge of holding conventicles Stephan was legally absolved by the Ministry of Worship as late as 1837.[27]

During the second decade of Stephan's ministry, however, a storm of protests was called forth by the addition of a new element to some of the gatherings held at his instigation; they were given a personal, social touch. A meeting place was rented as a clubroom for the entertainment of his followers. There, it is related, chess and billiards were played, and beer was dispensed. This arrangement was not a congregational project, but a private club of the faithful, with admission restricted to those who were accepted by vote of the club members and who signed the set of rules which had been drawn up by Stephan. The exclusiveness of the gatherings was immediately unpopular; and pastimes on the program, although of a relatively harmless nature, became the object of attack and suspicion when Stephan himself adopted the custom of appearing on the scene at a very late hour and when some club members allegedly failed to return home all night.[28]

Stephan had taken cognizance of slanders against his person as early as 1823.[29] However, serious trouble did not develop until

---

[24] Von Polenz, *op. cit.*, 47.

[25] Bemerkungen über . . . Stephan, Bound MSS., V, C. H. I.; Fischer, *op. cit.*, 41; Pleissner, *op. cit.*, 20.

[26] Hennig, "Die Auswanderung Martin Stephans," *Zeitschrift für Kirchengeschichte,* LVIII, 162.

[27] Mittheilungen über die Verhandelungen des Landtags, Dresden, den 9ten November 1837 (hereafter cited as Mittheilungen . . . Verhandelungen des Landtags, Nov. 9, 1837), Bound MSS., VI, C. H. I. The date in the title of this manuscript is misleading. November 9 is the day on which the transactions appeared in print. The declaration itself was made in the *Landtag* on October 20, 1837. *Ibid.* See also Fischer, *op. cit.*, 19, 80—83.

[28] Graphic descriptions are given in Fischer, *op. cit.*, 49—51; von Polenz, *op. cit.*, 49—50. The claim that public reaction was artificially stimulated by Stephan's opponents is made in Bemerkungen über . . . Stephan, Bound MSS., V; C. H. I. The characterization of this enterprise as a "workingmen's club" can be found in Hansen, *The Atlantic Migration,* 136.

[29] Stephan, *Herzlicher Zuruf . . . zwei Predigten,* 4.

after 1830, when still further embellishments of his social-pastoral habits were followed by rumors concerning his private life.[30] Louise Günther, who spoke with some authority in this matter, also placed the beginning of irregularities in Stephan's personal life in 1831 or 1832.[31]

For some time Stephan had been accustomed to taking extended walks as the only form of exercise in which he indulged. Frequently he felt the need for this relaxation at night. Gradually it became customary for one or more of his intimates, men or women, to join him on these strolls, either to or from some meeting place, or merely for the purpose of halting and resting somewhere in the open around a campfire. Since lighting such fires was a violation of forestry regulations, they drew both the ire and the official protests of the foresters and were, in themselves, sufficient to focus unfavorable publicity on the practices of the group. Stephan found nothing unusual about gatherings that lasted until "2 o'clock or occasionally later." Subsequently these nocturnal meetings assumed another form when his followers rented a lodge for him in a vineyard in the Hoflösnitz, a short distance outside the city.[32] The fact that Stephan accepted such favors from his followers is not surprising in view of the fact that at times he received outright gifts of cash for his own personal use and that there was an established system of collections to which his followers were strongly urged to contribute and for which no accounting was ever given.[33] At times Stephan's associates of both sexes went to the lodge directly by carriage, while he himself walked through the woods to the rendezvous in the company of a single female companion, his servant. These meetings at the lodge often lasted until late at night, and not infrequently the return to Dresden was delayed until the following morning. Nothing was ever proved to have transpired at these

---

30 Von Karlowitz (the Ministry of Worship and Public Instruction) to the *Kreisdirektion* at Dresden, Oct. 24, 1837, MS., Stephanakten, Landeskirchenamt, Dresden, I, 172; Fischer, *op. cit.*, 28, 32; Bemerkungen über . . . Stephan, Bound MSS., V, C. H. I.

31 Bekenntnis der Louise Guenther, MS., C. H. I.

32 Appellation des . . . Stephan, March 28, 1836, Bemerkungen über . . . Stephan, Bound MSS., V, C. H. I.; Lossagung vom Stephanismus, MS., C. H. I.; *Leipziger allgemeine Zeitung*, Nov. 22, 1837; Fischer, *op. cit.*, 49; Lütkemüller, *op. cit.*, 23—24, 52—53; von Polenz, *op. cit.*, 46—50.

33 Schwabe to Stephan, Feb. 25, 1838, Stephan to Schwabe, March 29, 1838, Bound MSS., VI, C. H. I.; Draft on Keyl's account, Oct. 30, 1838, MS., C. H. I.; Keyl, *op. cit.*, 11.

gatherings that was reprehensible, not to say criminal.[34] But it is worth noting that W. Sihler, who later was associated with the Saxons in the founding of the Missouri Synod and who was in Dresden during these years, found these meetings so questionable that he did not attend them.[35] The custom itself, which Stephan's most recent apologist, Hennig, can bring himself to call "harmless," was rather irregular and certain to cause unfavorable comment, especially since, during the latter years, the excesses of the Königsberg separatists had become notorious, and the fear had become widespread that their activities were being duplicated in Dresden.[36]

Conjectures as to what might be transpiring at these allegedly religious gatherings of Stephanites were given added impetus by the pastor's well-known marital difficulties. Stephan was living in an unsuccessful marriage with a woman of a respected Dresden family, whom some have pictured as a more refined person than the pastor himself, others as a veritable Xanthippe.[37] His family, which numbered eight or ten children, seems to have enjoyed a minimum of the father's attention.[38] Stephan claimed he received about a like amount from his wife.[39] His confidants were told that he was entirely innocent of any blame for his domestic unhappiness and that it was merely another of the crosses he was called upon to bear as a champion of Christ.[40] His critics, however, interpreted the

---

34 Appellation des . . . Stephan, March 28, 1836, Bemerkungen über . . . Stephan, Bound MSS., V, C. H. I.; Document . . . des Grundsteins . . . St. Louis . . . 22. Juny 1842, Lossagung vom Stephanismus, Bekenntniss, MSS., C. H. I.; Fischer, *op. cit.*, 49.

35 Sihler, *Lebenslauf von W. Sihler*, I, 94—95.

36 Fischer, *op. cit.*, 37; Hennig, "Die Auswanderung Martin Stephans," *Zeitschrift für Kirchengeschichte*, LVIII, 162—163. The moral delinquencies of Leonhardi, whose activity had closely paralleled that of Stephan and who had associated with the Bohemian pastor, gave rise to the fear that Stephan was traveling the same road. *Ibid.*; Hennig, *op. cit.*, 145; E. M. Bürger, Selbstbiographie, 36—37, MS., E. J. Buerger Papers, Ellicottville, N. Y.

37 Bemerkungen über . . . Stephan, Bound MSS., V, C. H. I.; Lossagung vom Stephanismus, MS., C. H. I.; von Polenz, *op. cit.*, 28; Fischer, *op. cit.*, 39—40; Lütkemüller, *op. cit.*, 53—54; Vehse, *op. cit.*, 4; C. F. W. Walther in Köstering, *Auswanderung*, 7.

38 Protokolle über die . . . Auswanderung, Feb. 15, 19, 1838, Bound MSS., III, C. H. I.; Bemerkungen über . . . Stephan, Bound MSS., V, C. H. I.; von Polenz, *op. cit.*, 28—29.

39 Bemerkungen über . . . Stephan, Bound MSS., V, C. H. I.

40 *Ibid.*; Marbach to Walz, Jan. 12, 1838, Bound MSS., VI, C. H. I.; Bekenntniss der Louise Guenther, Document . . . des Grundsteins . . . St. Louis . . . 22. Juny 1842, G. H. Löber to Nitzschke, Feb. 27, 1845, MSS., C. H. I.

matter differently and claimed that one of the reasons for his desire to leave Germany was to rid himself of his wife and family.[41]

All other objections to the offensiveness of his habits, his adherents dismissed with the assertion that persecution of his orthodoxy prompted a malicious interpretation of his every act.[42] If even Hennig can accept such an interpretation,[43] then to a following as devoted as Stephan's such a defense must have seemed highly plausible. When Keyl was told of the charges against Stephan, he stated that he could not believe them, but that if they were true, he was certain Stephan had repented.[44] The attacks of Stephan's antagonists made little impression on his blind supporters. If one of them did dare to question the wisdom of continuing the nocturnal meetings, as some did, he was promptly disciplined.[45] Opposition merely served to unify the faction which defended him and to enhance his position as a seer and martyr.[46] Stephan's tenacity and "Spartan stubbornness" in insisting upon the continuation of these meetings led impartial observers and even a few of his own followers to the conclusion that he was not willing to sacrifice a personal whim for the sake of public peace and his office.[47] When, after

---

41 This idea was commonly held; it was even published in the newspapers. Fischer, *op. cit.*, 39—40; Lütkemüller, *op. cit.*, 27, 53—54.

42 Bemerkungen über . . . Stephan, Appeal of Stephan to Fredrick Augustus II, Oct. 20, 1838, Bound MSS., V, C. H. I.; Document . . . des Grundsteins . . . St. Louis . . . 22. Juny 1842, Lossagung vom Stephanismus, Bekenntniss, Nachrichten an unsere Nachkommen, Marbach, An meine . . . Landsleute, MSS., C. H. I.; C. F. W. Walther in Köstering, *Auswanderung*, 7—8.

43 Hennig, "Die Auswanderung Martin Stephans," *Zeitschrift für Kirchengeschichte*, LVIII, 162—163.

44 Keyl, *op. cit.*, 5.

45 Candidate Kühn to O. Fürbringer, Jan. 20, 1832, Lossagung vom Stephanismus, Bekenntniss, MSS., C. H. I.; Marbach to von Uckermann, May 28, Dec. 27, 1837, von Uckermann to Marbach, Jan. 9, 1838, Bound MSS., VI, C. H. I.; Fischer, *op. cit.*, 49, 52, 61; C. F. W. Walther in Köstering, *Auswanderung*, 7; Lochner, "Ottomar Fürbringer," *Der Lutheraner*, XLIX, 171. The cases of Löber and Gruber are described elsewhere.

46 This is the trend of thought throughout the documents relative to Stephan's elevation to the episcopacy. See also Bemerkungen über . . . Stephan, Bound MSS., V, C. H. I.; Marbach to von Uckermann, May 28, Dec. 27, 1837, Feb. 7, 1838, von Uckermann to Marbach, Jan. 9, 1838, Marbach to Walz, Jan. 12, 1838, Bound MSS., VI, C. H. I.; E. M. Bürger, Selbstbiographie, 117—119, MS., E. J. Buerger Papers, Ellicottville, N. Y.; Meurer [?] to C. F. W. Walther, Jan. 27, 1838, C. F. W. Walther to von Einsiedel, Feb. 3, 1838, G. H. Löber, Diary, 1836, p. 20, MSS., C. H. I.; Keyl, *op. cit.*, 5; C. F. W. Walther in Köstering, *Auswanderung*, 7—8; Hengstenberg, "Der Pastor Stephan," *Evangelische Kirchen-Zeitung*, XXVI, 249—250.

47 Stübel to Vehse *et al.*, Sept. 12, 1839, Bound MSS., VI, C. H. I.; Fischer, *op. cit.*, 48, 52, 55—56.

years of this conduct, Stephan refused to do the little that was asked of him and to confine himself to the clearly religious meetings, which were never denied him, then the government stepped in and investigated.[48]

It is extremely difficult to understand how all of the men associated with Stephan in leading the emigration could have been completely deceived, as they later claimed they were. Brohm was Stephan's private secretary, but is supposed to have been entirely devoid of even a suspicion of immorality on Stephan's part. Yet G. H. Löber, Gönner, and Winter, all of whom were less intimately associated with Stephan than Brohm was, later admitted that the deception, even in their own case, was "incomprehensible," and some of the confessions which were drawn up in the Missouri colonies reached the same conclusion. Indeed, several of them, such as Pastors Gruber and Löber, could not have forgotten that they had been severely disciplined for having "suspicions" of Stephan.[49] To J. L. Gruber, who later became personally acquainted with many of the emigrants, it was "a riddle" how they could have been duped, and in the case of C. F. W. Walther he found it "still more inexplicable." [50] Again, it must be pointed out that Sihler did not permit himself to be taken in, and von Uckermann also had strong suspicions of Stephan's immorality.[51] In fact, when C. F. W. Walther in 1838 presented to one of his friends [Meurer?] documents which Walther considered proof of Stephan's innocence, the friend found that, although he himself was predisposed in Stephan's favor, at least two of these documents, intended as a defense of the "slandered" Dresden pastor, created an unfavorable rather than a favorable impression of Stephan's case and did more to arouse suspicions than to allay them.[52]

The charges current against Stephan certainly merited a thor-

---

48 Fischer, *op. cit.,* 27, 33, 53.

49 Nachrichten an unsere Nachkommen, Bekenntniss, G. H. Löber, Diary, Nov. 12, 1835, 1836, p. 12, entry in late 1840, MSS., C. H. I.; J. F. Bünger, "Ehrengedächtniss des . . . Brohm," *Der Lutheraner,* XXXVII, 189. See also G. Günther, *Schicksale und Abenteuer der aus Sachsen ausgewanderten Stephanianer,* 1—2.

50 Gruber, *Erinnerungen an Professor C. F. W. Walther und seine Zeit,* 33.

51 Sihler, *op. cit.,* I, 94—95; Marbach to von Uckermann, May 28, Dec. 27, 1837, von Uckermann to Marbach, Jan. 9, 1838, Bound MSS., VI, C. H. I.

52 Meuer [?] to C. F. W. Walther, Jan. 27, 1838, C. F. W. Walther to von Einsiedel, Feb. 3, 1838, MSS., C. H. I.

ough examination from his associates, as some of them subsequently admitted.[53] But this examination was never made, despite the fact that the evidence advanced was as valid as that on which Stephan was denounced and deposed in America. Keyl was told of the charges, but as has been related above, investigation was far from his mind; Bünger knew about them but ignored them.[54] While the preparations for the emigration were at their height, a Caroline Dittrich wrote from Troppau to Marbach at "Lügau" [Liegau], appealing to be taken along to America. She warned Marbach that her request would not receive favorable consideration from Stephan, for he was ill-disposed toward her since she had repulsed improper advances on his part and would not respond to the encouragement of his maid, Louise Günther, to accede to his demands. Caroline Dittrich added: "If nothing else can be done and it is required of me, I am also ready to undergo a judicial examination, can also cite a witness who had [similar ex . . .] . . . periences after me." [55] It is not known that legal action was ever taken on this accusation, which certainly warranted investigation, whether it proved Stephan guilty or innocent. Less than a year later, in cross-examining Louise Günther, Marbach did not hesitate to use Caroline Dittrich's testimony.[56]

The difficulties which the movement encountered were by no means limited to Dresden. Opposition was noticeable wherever Stephanites, particularly Stephanite pastors, were active. Broadly speaking, the same charges were raised everywhere: Literalism in interpretation of Scripture and the Confessions, legalism, undue submissiveness to, and veneration of, Stephan, sectarianism, obscurantism, and mysticism, the last of which was always linked with the question of conventicles.[57]

---

[53] *Anzeiger des Westens*, Dec. 31, 1842; Lossagung vom Stephanismus, MS., C. H. I.; *Leipziger allgemeine Zeitung*, Nov. 22, 1837.

[54] C. F. W. Walther, *Bünger*, 31.

[55] Caroline Dittrich to Marbach, Aug. 28, 1838, MS., C. H. I. Whether this girl is the one who brought formal charges against Stephan in October, 1838, is not clear. Fischer, *op. cit.*, 54. See also Sihler, *op. cit.*, I, 95.

[56] Bekenntnis der Louise Guenther, MS., C. H. I.

[57] *Chemnitzer Anzeiger*, Oct. 30, Nov. 7, 1838; C. F. W. Walther to O. H. Walther, August, 1833, quoted in M. Günther, *op. cit.*, 15; Pleissner, *op. cit.*, 3, 6—7, 20; Fischer, *op. cit.*, 56—71, 161—196. The same accusations were made in Saxe-Altenburg. The consistory of Saxe-Altenburg to Duke Joseph, Sept. 4, 1838, quoted in *Bedenken der theologischen Facultäten*, 35—46.

Thus, for example, soon after Keyl took office, he became an object of suspicion and opposition for the Rationalistically inclined pastors and laymen in his and neighboring parishes, and a period of strife began in his own congregations.[58] Leading the opposition against Keyl was Wenzel (teacher at the parish school in Nieder-Frohna), whose violent and irresponsible attacks did not stop short of writing lampoons of his pastor and acting as secret informer to Keyl's superintendent, Friedrich Otto Siebenhaar, at Penig, with whom Wenzel was on intimate terms.[59] This superintendent was another factor of importance for the development of the emigration. In the course of time he came to have under him several of the pastors who later left with Stephan; and his open favoritism for Wenzel and all who opposed the Stephanites, as well as his hostility not only toward Stephanite peculiarities, but toward confessionalism as well, did much to develop the impression among Keyl, Walther, and others that their position in Saxony was deliberately being made difficult.[60]

Keyl became a rallying point for Stephanism in the valley of the Mulde, where a rather compact organization was built up through his active proselyting among both pastors and laymen.[61] If the Muldenthal movement ever was "independent of Dresden," [62] it was not so after Keyl's capitulation to Stephan in 1834. The young pastor's revivalistic sermons, which aroused the emotions of his hearers until "it seemed the whole packed church was swimming

---

58 Summons to Keyl to appear before the superintendent at Chemnitz, Nov. 22, 1832, MS., C. H. I; Siebenhaar to the *Kreisdirektion,* July 10, 1836, July 14, 1837, The *Kreisdirektion* to Siebenhaar, July 28, 1836, Bound MSS., Auszug der Acta Ephoralia den des Mysticismus und Separatismus öffentlich beschuldigten Herrn Pfarrer Keyl betreffend. No. 18. Niederfrohna No. Lit. K. Vol. II Eingegangen bei der Superintendur Penig 1836. Sect. VI. Lit. No. 16 (hereafter cited as Acta Ephoralia . . . Keyl betreffend), C. H. I.; Keyl, *op. cit.,* 10.

59 Fischer, *op. cit.,* 66; Köstering, *Keyl,* 20—21; Proceedings, Aug. 20, 1836, Siebenhaar to Wenzel, Nov. 12, 1836, Siebenhaar to Keyl, Nov. 12, 1836, Bound MSS., Acta Ephoralia . . . Keyl betreffend, C. H. I.

60 Bemerkungen über . . . Stephan, Bound MSS., V, C. H. I.; M. Günther, *op. cit.,* 24—28; Siebenhaar to the *Kreisdirektion,* July 10, Oct. 12, 1836, July 14, 25, 1837, Feb. 19, 1838, Bound MSS., Acta Ephoralia . . . Keyl betreffend, C. H. I. In 1839 Siebenhaar revealed his attitude even more clearly in his *Discourses Relating to the Stephanist Movement,* as they are cited in the article on "Stephan" in M'Clintock-Strong, *Cyclopaedia,* IX, 1008.

61 Pleissner, *op. cit.,* 39; Fischer, *op. cit.,* 26—27.

62 Hennig, "Die Auswanderung Martin Stephans," *Zeitschrift für Kirchengeschichte,* LVIII, 157.

in tears,"[63] attracted widespread attention even in the Pietistic Muldenthal and drew pilgrimages of the "awakened" students, such as C. F. W. Walther and others of the subsequent emigration, from as far away as Leipzig, where they were carrying on the Kühn-Keyl tradition at the university.[64] Keyl's open friendship with Stephan cost him dearly. In the early thirties Stephan made a tour of the outposts of conservatism in Saxony and Silesia, and the homage Keyl paid Stephan and his satellites while they were visiting him created violent objections among his members that helped to disrupt his congregation.[65]

The young pastor also had a prolonged and bitter controversy with Teacher Wenzel and Superintendent Siebenhaar over what sermons were to be read by the teacher in services held by the congregation during Keyl's infrequent absences. The teacher, supported by Siebenhaar, refused to read Stephan's sermons, as demanded by Keyl, who had von Einsiedel on his side. The tactlessness of Siebenhaar in attempting to tell a pastor what to read or have read in his own church was matched by Keyl's in insisting that of all the books approved by the Saxon State Church only those by Stephan and Luther were usable.[66] His choice, incidentally, was made in that order.[67] The consistory, confronted with a delicate decision, compromised between its anti-Stephanite superintendent and its pro-Stephanite pastor by authorizing the use of Luther.[68] The bickerings about sermons, of which this incident is only one example, continued until March 3, 1838. Such episodes lent weight to the charge of sectarianism.

After 1830 Keyl was the most prominent of the small group of young Stephanite pastors in the vicinity of Nieder-Frohna, which

---

[63] C. F. W. Walther, "Lebensabriss des . . . Keyl," *Der Lutheraner*, XXVIII, 189. See also Hennig, "Die Auswanderung Martin Stephans," *Zeitschrift für Kirchengeschichte*, LVIII, 153—154.

[64] Siebenhaar to the *Kreisdirektion*, July 14, 1837, Bound MSS., Acta Ephoralia . . . Keyl betreffend, C. H. I.; Pleissner, *op. cit.*, 39; Köstering, *Keyl*, 22—25.

[65] Fischer, *op. cit.*, 31—32; Pleissner, *op. cit.*, 10, 37—38.

[66] Wenzel to Siebenhaar, Nov. 12, 1836, Siebenhaar to Wenzel, Nov. 12, 1836, Siebenhaar to Keyl, Nov. 12, 1836, Jan. 14, 1837, Keyl to Siebenhaar, Jan. 14, 1837, Feb. 8, 1837 [1838?], Siebenhaar to the *Kreisdirektion*, July 25, 1837, the *Kreisdirektion* to Siebenhaar, July 6, Nov. 29, 1837, the *Kreisdirektion* to Keyl, Nov. 29, 1838, Bound MSS., Acta Ephoralia . . . Keyl betreffend, C. H. I.

[67] Keyl to Siebenhaar, Feb. 8, 1837 [1838?], *ibid.*

[68] *Kreisdirektion* to Siebenhaar, March 3, 1838, *ibid.*

included C. F. W. Walther, Bürger, O. H. Walther, and, for a time, Kühn. Their personal contact with, and in some cases allegiance to, Stephan, and the practices to which this led them, occasioned some of the most acrimonious attacks upon them. Whether or not the Stephanites were a sect is a profitless argument, worthy of mention only because it occupied a prominent place in the polemical exchanges of that day.[69] The matter can be reduced to a question of definition. If a sect is a group which severs connections with an established church and adopts new creeds and doctrines, then Stephan and his followers were not a sect. If, on the other hand, a sect is a group which distinguishes itself, either inside or outside an established church, by its disagreement with the doctrinal views of the majority within that body, by its insistence upon the introduction of customs and practices different from those of the main body, and by the clannishness of its members in their associations with each other and in their adherence to some leader, then, by their own admission, the Stephanites were a sect.[70]

The accusation of separatism received additional stimulus from other incidents in the Muldenthal. On May 17, 1831, the Muldenthal Pastoral Conference was organized under the leadership of Rudelbach for the purpose of making the Saxon Church a confessional Church. Keyl and G. H. W. Walther were two of its charter members. When Keyl and several of the other Stephanites, like C. F. W. Walther, who belonged to it, failed to convert it into a legalistic body with a Stephanite cast, Keyl, at least, withdrew "for reasons of conscience." [71] To claim a feeling of moral necessity for severing connections with one of the most conservative groups within the State Church, at the same time that official membership

---

[69] Pöschel, *op. cit.*, 42—44; Pleissner, *op. cit.*, 20, 43; Fischer, *op. cit.*, 19, 25, 41, 56—92.

[70] "We had become a sect," Bürger, *op. cit.*, 11. "The congregation under Stephan was a crowd that had been misled into separatism from the Lutheran Church in Saxony . . .," C. F. W. Walther, in an unsigned and undated statement, probably written in preparation for the Altenburg Debate, MS., C. H. I. See also Marbach, An meine . . . Landsleute, Lossagung vom Stephanismus, C. F. W. Walther to O. H. Walther, May 4, 1840, MSS., C. H. I.; Pöschel, *op. cit.*, 42—44.

[71] Köstering, *Keyl*, 52. See also Hennig, "Die Auswanderung Martin Stephans," *Zeitschrift für Kirchengeschichte*, LVIII, 161; Hennig, *op. cit.*, 206—207; Fischer, *op. cit.*, 32. The date of organization has also been given as June 15, 1831. Engelder, "Die Muldentaler Konferenz," *Concordia Theological Monthly*, III, 227—229.

in the State Church was maintained, invited the conclusion that the real objection to the Muldenthal Conference was that it refused to be dominated, and made charges of willfulness, stubbornness, and separatism seem plausible.

The case did not rest on conjecture. Where the so-called conventicles were concerned, the opponents of the Stephanites seemed to have an even clearer issue. Stephan in his church, with its charter of 1650, might plead legal right and precedent, but the other pastors had no such charter to which to take recourse. Yet the Muldenthal group also followed Stephan when it instituted meetings similar to those conducted at St. John's in Dresden. Both C. F. W. Walther and Keyl were accused before Siebenhaar of holding such gatherings.[72] Neither made an effort to deny that he had done so, although they insisted, of course, on the harmlessness of the meetings. Löber, too, conducted devotional meetings of various kinds over a period of years.

The charges of personal immorality made against Stephan were never leveled against Löber and seldom against the pastors in the Muldenthal. And when such complaints occurred, it seems they were based upon gross exaggerations and perhaps distortions of actions which, in themselves, did not justify specific accusations. But the people in the Muldenthal resented the fact that mixed gatherings were held until late at night and that female parishioners were received at hours rather unusual for dispensing spiritual advice.[73] There is no reason to believe that this practice was anything but an indiscretion, and, except for the request of the authorities that Keyl refute the rumors it had occasioned, no official notice was taken of it until the actual time of departure. This fact

---

[72] Proceedings, April 9—13, 1838, Keyl to Siebenhaar, April 24, 1838, The *Kreisdirektion* to the *Kirchen-Inspektion* at Nieder-Frohna, July 6, 1838, Bound MSS., Acta Ephoralia . . . Keyl betreffend, C. H. I.; Proceedings, 13—14, Bound MSS., Acten der . . . Superintendur Chemnitz, C. H. I.; Proceedings, July 30, 1838, Siebenhaar to the *Kreisdirektion*, Aug. 1, 1838, Bound MSS., II B. 83. Abschrift der Acten betrffd. die Beschwerde des Gärtners J. Gottlieb Pester in Bräunsdorf gegen den Herrn P. Walther, später Dr. *Professor C. F. W. Walther, St. Louis, Mo.* Bräunsdorf Superintendur Penig 1838. Sect. VI. Lit. B. no. 83 (hereafter cited as Acten . . . Pester . . . *C. F. W. Walther*), C. H. I.

[73] Proceedings, April 13, 1838, Bound MSS., Acta Ephoralia . . . Keyl betreffend, C. H. I.; G. H. Löber, Diary, Jan. 3, July 4, Aug. 1, 1831, 1834, p. 10, Jan. 6, 1836, MS., C. H. I.; Keyl, *op. cit.*, 8, 11. An example of the scurrilousness with which these events were described is found in Pleissner, *op. cit.*, 24, 57. For a contemporary evaluation of Pleissner's remarks, see Fischer, *op. cit.*, 67—68.

further strengthens the conclusion that, despite some exceptions, the authorities were not so ready to restrict religious liberty or the exercise of essential religious functions as they were to prevent improper conduct and unnecessary strife.[74]

Keyl and C. F. W. Walther were also charged with condemning as godless and unchristian all who opposed their doctrines and practices, and with interfering in the private affairs of their parishioners, partly through the use of auricular confession. Each of them later conceded that both accusations were true, although at the time they denied at least the second charge.[75] One case, in which C. F. W. Walther finally filed suit for divorce on behalf of a married woman in his congregation, the mother of seven children, was climaxed by personal violence on the part of the husband against a candidate [Schieferdecker?], whose home sheltered the woman while she was awaiting the outcome of the legal action. The fact that Walther claimed the woman's husband had struck her violently as she was leaving the pastor's home late one night after an edificatory meeting only partly explains his and the candidate's role in the affair.[76] G. H. Löber sheltered a girl, a minor, in his home against the wishes of her mother, because he objected to the elder woman's religious beliefs.[77] These and similar cases show that, whatever the extenuating circumstances may have been, the pastors used their positions in a fashion which was almost certain to arouse resent-

---

[74] Keyl to Siebenhaar, April 24, 1838, Bound MSS., Acta Ephoralia . . . Keyl betreffend, C. H. I.; Marbach, An meine . . . Landsleute, Bekenntniss, C. F. W. Walther to Brohm, Jan. 15, 1834, MSS., C. H. I.; E. M. Bürger, Selbstbiographie, 95—99, MS., E. J. Buerger Papers, Ellicottville, N. Y.; Stübel to Vehse *et al.*, Sept. 12, 1839, Bound MSS., VI, C. H. I.; *Chemnitzer Anzeiger*, Nov. 7, 1838; von Polenz, *op. cit.*, 43—44; Pleissner, *op. cit.*, 44, 50; Fischer, *op. cit.*, 27, 33, 92—95, 114, 126—128. In the opinion of Guericke, "It is a fact that the . . . afore-mentioned preachers enjoyed to the very last moment full freedom of the Lutheran Word and Sacrament in their fatherland, and were by no means driven from it," quoted in *ibid.*, 33. Keyl later admitted outright that it would have been better to dispense with these meetings as plainly unessential, since they created avoidable antagonism. Keyl, *op. cit.*, 10—11.

[75] Lossagung vom Stephanismus, Bekenntniss, C. F. W. Walther to Brohm, Aug. 17, 1837, C. F. W. Walther to O. H. Walther, May 4, 1840, MSS., C. H. I.; Proceedings, 13—17a, Bound MSS., Acten . . . Pester . . . *C. F. W. Walther*, C. H. I.; Proceedings, April 3—9, 1838, Keyl to Siebenhaar, April 24, 1838, Bound MSS., Acta Ephoralia . . . Keyl betreffend, C. H. I.; Fischer, *op. cit.*, 64—65; Pleissner, *op. cit.*, 22, 29, 38, 57.

[76] Proceedings, 13—17a, Bound MSS., Acten . . . Pester . . . *C. F. W. Walther*, C. H. I.; Pleissner, *op. cit.*, 24; Köstering, "Ehrengedächtniss des Schieferdecker," *Der Lutheraner*, XLVIII, 145.

[77] G. H. Löber, Diary, May 24, June 15—18, 1831, MS., C. H. I. See also *ibid.*, Jan. 1—15, 1836.

ment.[78] However, such patriarchal interference in the personal life of their parishioners was not original with them. Stephan himself frequently intervened in the strictly family or private affairs of his followers and was consulted by them on every manner of subject, including even business matters.[79]

Repeated references to G. H. Löber have shown that in many respects the separatistic community which built up around him in Saxe-Altenburg was strikingly similar to those in Dresden, Leipzig, and the Muldenthal. Löber, too, was active at first in mission and Bible societies, trying to do constructive work, as Stephan had in the early years.[80] But the atmosphere of gloom and doom eventually became as heavy in Eichenberg as in Dresden. By 1836 Löber prophetically designated the year as "apocalyptic" even before it was well under way, and the mission society was seldom, if ever, mentioned.[81] A sense of martyrdom, persecution, and exaggerated importance permeated Löber's thoughts, which seemed to become more and more like those of the Leipzig group. As early as 1831 he was prompted to compare his position at an impending meeting of the local clergy to that of Luther at Worms.[82] Remarks such as this became symptomatic of Löber's atrophying sense of proportion. Every occasion became for him a testimonial to his Confessions, whether they were pertinent or not. In view of the fact that people of Löber's persuasion were a hopeless minority, tact, at the very least, seemed to be called for. Instead, Löber and Gruber were challenging and stubborn. When a revision of the *Agenda* of Saxe-Altenburg was considered by the authorities in 1836, reasonable principles and a moderate approach were applied, and all the pastors were to have an opportunity to express themselves on the project as such and on specific questions. It surely did not help Löber's cause that, on the advice of Stephan and in co-operation

---

78 Proceedings, April 3—9, 1838, Keyl to Siebenhaar, April 24, 1838, Bound MSS., Acta Ephoralia . . . Keyl betreffend, C. H. I.; Lossagung vom Stephanismus, Bekenntniss, MSS., C. H. I.

79 Lossagung vom Stephanismus, Bekenntniss, C. F. W. Walther to Brohm, Aug. 17, 1837, MSS., C. H. I.; Fischer, *op. cit.*, 32—42; Keyl, *op. cit.*, 7; G. H. Löber, Diary, Jan. 23—25, 1836, MS., C. H. I. One of the more interesting instances of applied Christianity is Stephan's opinion that a Christian might ride on trains in an emergency. *Ibid.*, April 26, 1836. See also his remarks at the teachers' conference in Dresden, 1836. *Ibid.*, 1836, pp. 11—15.

80 G. H. Löber, Diary, Feb. 28, May 24, 1831, MS., C. H. I.

81 *Ibid.*, 1836, p. 2.

82 *Ibid.*, July 28, Aug. 15, 1831.

with Gruber, he informed the authorities in writing: Any change of any nature in the hundred-year-old *Agenda* would be unacceptable to the conservatives. In the privacy of his diary he added that if the officials went ahead with their plan of revision (*not* if they revised the *Agenda* in a way particularly offensive to him), this action would be the sign that it was time to emigrate.[83]

Löber frequently performed official acts, such as Baptisms, for people who came across the border from Prussia. He seemed to get a certain satisfaction out of the conspiratorial atmosphere which prevailed on such occasions. In fact, these incidents occurred so frequently that the Prussian government finally interpreted its laws in such a way as to permit people to go to pastors beyond the Prussian border or to have such pastors come into the country to oblige the conservatives.[84] Even then some of the more rabid were not satisfied. Yet, despite the provocations he gave, Löber was displeased because the Kahla paper was not friendly to his viewpoint.[85] General Superintendent Hesekiel was such a sincere and moderate man that the liberals regarded him as a "mystic," and he was such a gentleman that even Löber seemed instinctively to like him. But these reactions by no means indicated that Löber was going to be satisfied. In fact, if there was any danger that one of the "awakened" pastors or candidates in Saxe-Altenburg might be satisfied with something in the Church, as Löber threatened to be in 1836, one of the others would be sure to find something wrong with it, as Gruber did on that occasion.[86]

The schools were another source of controversy and complaint on the part of the leaders and members of the emigration. Stephan complained bitterly that the *Landtag* was charged with the task of liberalizing religious education in the schools, a purpose usually effected by the introduction of Rationalistic textbooks and teachers.[87] Walther, at Bräunsdorf, went farther than mere complaint;

---

83 *Ibid.*, 1836, p. 51.

84 *Ibid.*, March 19, 1836, 1836, pp. 1, 19, and 1838, pp. 42 B—43.

85 *Ibid.*, 1836, p. 1.

86 *Ibid.*, 1836, pp. 4—5, 48.

87 Nachrichten an unsere Nachkommen, Lossagung vom Stephanismus, Excerpts from G. H. Löber's Diary, May 13, 1838, Bekenntniss, MSS., C. H. I.; Stephan to B. Kurtz, March, 1833, Bound MSS., I, C. H. I.; Öhrling to Stephan, Oct. 12, 1838, Quellmalz to Stephan, Aug. 3, 1838, Schmitte to Stephan, Sept. 25, 1838, Bound MSS., No. 17. Fasc. II. Applicationen, an der sächsischen Auswanderung teilzunehmenden (hereafter cited as Bound MSS., II), C. H. I.; *Bedenken der theologischen Fakultäten*, 56.

he simply refused to permit the use of books selected by the parish teacher and approved by the school board. The matter went before the authorities, and, of course, Siebenhaar supported the teacher. Walther eventually won his point when a donation by von Einsiedel of the conservative books Walther desired convinced the school board and the congregation that it was sound economy to use them. Walther, however, had to pay the costs of the case.[88]

Keyl's struggle in Nieder-Frohna was much more bitter. In 1834 the right to supervise the school in his own parish was taken from him.[89] Two years later, on the petition of his teacher at Mittel-Frohna and the school board at Nieder-Frohna, but against the advice of Siebenhaar, this prerogative was partially restored to him.[90] Keyl did little to justify this action, for although he had agreed to the arrangement in writing at the time it was instituted, he subsequently refused to have anything to do with the school unless he was placed in complete charge. His conduct was plainly irresponsible, and Siebenhaar made the most of it in his reports to the consistory, which censured Keyl for his conduct.[91] In Saxe-Altenburg, Löber never made a great issue of his dissatisfaction with his teachers, but he, too, was convinced that their religious views were not satisfactory.[92]

Bürger's preaching attracted people from other towns, brought about the "awakening" of some of his parishioners, the enmity of others, and the opposition of eighty-year-old Teacher Gäberlein, who had been stationed at the parish school in Lunzenau for fifty years. Gäberlein took to writing pasquils against Bürger and complaints to the consistory, which accomplished his purpose of embroiling Bürger with the ecclesiastical authorities. Bürger remained at Lunzenau, however, until the emigration, in 1838, and by that time Gäberlein had died. When Bürger left, he took with

---

[88] C. F. W. Walther to Brohm, Aug. 17, 1837, MS., C. H. I.; M. Günther, *op. cit.*, 25—27; C. F. W. Walther, *Bünger*, 34—35. The congregation restored the costs to Walther on the day he left. *Ibid.*, 35.

[89] C. F. W. Walther to Brohm, Jan. 15, 1834, MS., C. H. I.

[90] The *Kreisdirektion* to Siebenhaar, June 16, July 28, 1836, Siebenhaar to the *Kreisdirektion,* July 10, 1836, Bound MSS., Acta Ephoralia . . . Keyl betreffend, C. H. I.

[91] Proceedings and correspondence, Aug. 12, Dec. 24, 1836, July 12, 14, Nov. 29, Dec. 8, 1837, Jan. 29, Feb. 8, March 3, July 30, Aug. 8, 1838, *ibid.*

[92] G. H. Löber, Diary, Introductory remarks to the year 1835, MS., C. H. I.

him one of the largest personal followings among the emigrant pastors.[93]

A further cause for trouble was the liturgy in the *Agenda* of 1812. The attempt, referred to above, to embrace widely divergent views in the same church organization was plainly evident in these books, especially in the second volume, which contained the ritual for Baptism, the Sacrament, marriage, and other rites. The objection of the conservatives against ambiguous phrasing — which they felt perverted the spirit and intention of the rites — was often well founded. For instance, there were five forms for the administration of Baptism,[94] only one of which, the oldest, was acceptable to the Stephanites,[95] although Stephan admitted that the rite was valid even when a Roman Catholic or a Unionist performed it.[96] Some other conservatives, like Dr. Rudelbach, objected to them all.[97] The question as to which form was to be used created difficulty every time a pastor and a layman differed in their religious views, especially in cases where the parents of the child were of conservative bent and had the task of persuading a pastor to use a formula distasteful to him.[98] Often ultraconscientious laymen would travel considerable distances or cross state boundaries to a Stephanite pastor who had the reputation of using only the most conservative formulas.[99] The pastors of these people naturally objected to the fact that their members left their own parishes[100] When obstacles became too numerous, conservative laymen resorted to the subterfuge

93 E. M. Bürger, Selbstbiographie, 85—114, MS., E. J. Buerger Papers, Ellicottville, N. Y.; F. E. Schneider to Vehse, Sept. 3, 1838, MS., C. H. I.; Fischer, *op. cit.*, 60, 66.

94 *Kirchenbuch*, 1812, II, 167—201.

95 C. F. W. Walther, *Bünger*, 36. The phrase Walther employed was "tolerable to a certain extent."

96 Stephan to G. H. Löber, Feb. 20, 1836, MS., C. H. I. Marbach did not share this viewpoint with Stephan, considering the rite valid only when Stephan performed it. Marbach to Walz, Jan. 12, 1838, Bound MSS., VI, C. H. I.

97 Rudelbach, *op. cit.*, 95—97.

98 C. F. W. Walther, *Bünger*, 36—38. There really was no ground for claiming invalidity, no matter who performed the rite, for the Trinitarian formula, which should have satisfied even the most conservative, was contained in each form. *Kirchenbuch*, II, 167—201; C. F. W. Walther, *Bünger*, 36.

99 Fischer, *op. cit.*, 63—64; Putzer (of Naumburg, Prussia) to G. H. Löber, Dec. 16, 1836, MS., C. H. I.

100 Complaint to the consistory against Stephan by a number of Dresden clergymen, June 23, 1820, MS., Stephanakten, Landeskirchenamt, Dresden, I, 1—3.

of "emergency Baptism," not always quite honestly, which gave the parents or someone else the opportunity of performing the ceremony as they chose.[101] Since the ritual was not to be changed by the pastor,[102] many differences arose over the question of the forms, such as that for Absolution.[103] Annoying as these difficulties were, it still remains to be demonstrated that they led any of the younger men in Saxony, on their own initiative, to conceive of emigration as a solution for their problems.

In the last two chapters Stephanism has been treated as a force in Saxon religious life and as an independent, compact organization. However, the permanent importance of the movement, the characteristic distinguishing it from most of the similar contemporary phenomena, was the emigration. The emigration, in turn, was the result of opposition experienced by Stephan. This opposition has been described above in a general way, but it now becomes necessary also to discuss in detail the events in Stephan's career during the period just prior to the emigration.

---

101 Stephan recommended such a procedure. Stephan to G. H. Löber, Feb. 20, 1836, MS., C. H I.

102 *Kirchenbuch*, II, iii.

103 Complaint to the consistory against Stephan by a number of Dresden clergymen, June 23, 1820, MS., Stephanakten, Landeskirchenamt, Dresden, I, 1—3; Siebenhaar to the *Kreisdirektion*, Oct. 12, 1836, Bound MSS., Acta Ephoralia . . . Keyl betreffend, C. H. I.; E. M. Bürger, Selbstbiographie, 99—101, MS., E. J. Buerger Papers, Ellicottville, N. Y.; Siebenhaar to C. F. W. Walther, July 31, 1837, Bound MSS., Invoices, C. H. I.; Fischer, *op. cit.*, 64—65. 103, 115—121, 124—125.

CHAPTER FOUR

DEVELOPMENT OF THE EMIGRATION IDEA IN STEPHANITE SEPARATISM

When the decision to emigrate matured in Stephan's mind is not known. A specific date could be fixed almost only by his own statement, and this statement he was careful not to make, for it would have appeared too incongruous with his insistence that developments in Saxony in the last years were forcing the emigration upon him. It seems clear, however, that he had toyed with the idea of leaving Germany for a long time before he announced his intention publicly.[1]

The earliest indication of a desire on Stephan's part to emigrate dates back to the year 1811. One of his quondam intimates, Vehse, asserted that Stephan claimed to have contemplated leaving Germany since the year after he came to Dresden.[2] Stephan is then supposed to have considered Australia as a possible goal; indeed, it is said he remained of the same opinion for years. Eventually, however, he decided against "handing himself over to the British on discretion." [3] Stephan's part in the activities of the State Church for the next fifteen years and his co-operation with the leaders of the liberalist movement argue against laying too much stress upon these early thoughts of leaving. His sermon for the Reformation Festival of 1823 showed that the idea was running through his mind, yet he spoke with confidence of "the present time, when no persecution of the evangelical faith is yet taking place." [4] But tangible evidence does appear in 1825, a few years after the opposition against him began to crystallize. In a sermon of that year this expression of Stephan's attitude is found:

---

1 Protokolle über die . . . Auswanderung, Feb. 16, 1838, Bound MSS., III, C. H. I.; von Polenz, *op. cit.*, 73.

2 Vehse, *op. cit.*, 3; Stübel to Vehse *et al.*, Sept. 12, 1839, Bound MSS., VI, C. H. I.; C. F. W. Walther in Köstering, *Auswanderung*, 10.

3 Vehse, *op. cit.*, 3.

4 Stephan, *Herzlicher Zuruf . . . zwei Predigten*, 32.

> So must all Christians act if the temporal power wishes to rob them of their faith. They make modest, humble representations, they plead for justice and protection; if one does not hear them, if one does not grant their plea, they are still far from rebelling; but they leave a land that no longer tolerates them and seek one in which they find the freedom of religion for which they long.[5]

Thenceforth a clearer development of the emigration idea is traceable. By 1827 Stephan was applying these generalities to himself. When Pastor Benjamin Kurtz of Hagerstown, Maryland, was in Dresden in February, 1827, he was taken to services at St. John's and introduced to its pastor by Count von Einsiedel. Kurtz later gave the following account of the interview:

> [Stephan] complained of the difficulties attending the faithful discharge of ministerial duty in Dresden, of the awful progress that neology and infidelity and looseness of morals had made among the clergy in Germany, of the restrictions imposed by the police upon him and his flock in carrying on their religious exercises, the opposition and even persecution suffered in consequence of his adherence to the antiquated orthodoxy of the Bible, and especially of the fact that ministers of the Gospel were compelled in a sense to be officers of government and to prostrate themselves and the church to political subservience, etc. And then the good man sighed for a land of perfect religious freedom, for a peaceful and retired home for himself and his congregation, where they might worship God according to the conviction of their own judgment without being subjected to arbitrary restraints, vexatious requirements, etc., on the part of the government. He finally remarked that he at times had serious thoughts of emigrating to the United States and his congregation were anxious to accompany him, with no other view than to enjoy liberty — liberty of conscience, of opinion and expression, of religious worship, in a word, liberty in that broad and rational sense in which it is enjoyed *im Abendlande* (the Western World).[6]

Although Kurtz was a prominent leader of the rather liberal General Synod in the United States, he was alarmed at the condition of

---

[5] Stephan, *Der christliche Glaube,* II, 576, quoted in Fischer, *op. cit.,* 24—25.

[6] B. Kurtz in the *Lutheran Observer,* quoted in the *New York Observer,* March 16, 1839. See also Bente, *American Lutheranism,* II, 26. The year was not 1826, 1829, or 1830, as stated by a number of writers.

the Church in Germany and expressed a profound admiration for Stephan and sympathy with his complaints.[7]

The years 1830 and 1831 were critical ones for Stephan and his adherents. The political upheavals of those years of revolution, the revision of the constitution, the overthrow of the conservative political element friendly to the more orthodox wing of the Church, the change toward a more popular and hence more liberal *Landtag* (which had the power to legislate concerning ecclesiastical affairs), the reorganization of government departments, and the subsequent establishment of the Ministry of Worship and Public Instruction — all these things roused the apprehensions of Stephan.[8] The resignation of von Einsiedel from the cabinet was a real blow to the Stephanite movement, for he had always extended a measure of protection to the conservative element. Even after he was out of office, he continued to use his remaining power and influence in behalf of Stephan and his associates. It was during the thirties, when von Einsiedel's effectiveness had been greatly curtailed, that Stephan and his followers experienced their first clash with the civil authorities and were subjected to official investigation. How different the course of events might have been if von Einsiedel had remained in favor, is, of course, a matter of conjecture. But it is plain that his withdrawal from the cabinet could affect the Stephanites only unfavorably. Furthermore, the death of King Anton and the accession of Fredrick Augustus to full power came only two years before the emigration, just at the time when the affairs of the group had reached their first crisis.

It was in 1830 that Stephan first mentioned his plan of emigration to Keyl and others.[9] If the position of the pastor at St. John's had been made uncomfortable before, it was now going to be diffi-

---

[7] *New York Observer*, March 16, 1839; Stephan to B. Kurtz, March, 1833, Bound MSS., I, C. H. I.

[8] Stephan to G. H. W. Walther, Jan. 18, 1831, MS., C. H. I.; Stephan to B. Kurtz, March, 1833, Bound MSS., I, C. H. I.; Stephan, *Wir sind Pilgrime in dieser Welt, eine Predigt, gehalten am Sonntage Jubilate 1831*, pp. 3, 4, 8, 20. Changes in the government always alarmed the religious conservatives, especially as such changes at this time generally tended in the direction of some form of constitutional government. Löber, Fürbringer, and C. F. W. Walther decided in 1835 that this tendency in Europe was deplorable. G. H. Löber, Diary, March 1, 1835, MS., C. H. I. See also *ibid.*, April 24, May 12, 1831.

[9] Keyl, *op. cit.*, 11; C. F. W. Walther in Köstering, *Auswanderung*, 10—11.

cult to maintain at any cost. At least this was the development which Stephan and his associates feared. Stephan's elaborate celebration of the tercentenary of the Augsburg Confession had been overshadowed by the almost simultaneous riots leading to the changes in government, which he deplored.[10] Stephan himself attempted unsuccessfully to unite the conservative clergymen and induce them to make a joint written protest to the consistory and the *Landtag*.[11] Some difficulties did in fact come to a head during the thirties, while the emigration prevented others from becoming clear-cut issues. But unquestionably Stephan felt the situation to be more oppressive during his last ten years in Germany than it had previously been.[12] And any such feeling could only have been strengthened by a new series of attacks upon him in the early thirties. The fact that the anti-Stephan campaign reached one of its high points in 1833[13] probably accounts for Stephan's renewed interest in emigration and for his efforts to draw a wider circle of his acquaintances into such a movement approximately at this time.[14] It was also in 1833 that Stephan re-established contact with Pastor Benjamin Kurtz, in order to reopen the question of emigration to the United States.

In a letter written during March, 1833, Stephan appealed to Kurtz for advice.[15] Stephan represented the condition of the Church

---

[10] Th. Graebner, "The Three-Hundredth Anniversary of the Augsburg Confession in Saxony, 1830," *Concordia Historical Institute Quarterly*, III, 41—43.

[11] Stephan to G. H. W. Walther, Jan. 18, 1831, MS., C. H. I.; Leonhardi is supposed to have been associated with Stephan in this or a similar effort. Hennig, "Die Auswanderung Martin Stephans," *Zeitschrift für Kirchengeschichte*, LVIII, 150.

[12] Stephan to B. Kurtz, March, 1833, Bound MSS., I, C. H. I.

[13] Pöschel, *op. cit.*, 1—2. Pleissner's first essay against the Stephanites appeared in Röhr's *Kritische Predigerbibliothek*, 1833, H. 5, which also contained an anti-Stephanite article by von Ammon. Pleissner, *op. cit.*, v, 19. According to Fischer, several newspapers, prominent among them the *Peniger Wochenblatt*, were making it their "business to deliver invectives against them [the Stephanites]." Fischer, *op. cit.*, 27—28, 32.

[14] C. F. W. Walther, *Bünger*, 32.

[15] Stephan to B. Kurtz, March, 1833, Bound MSS., I, C. H. I. Neither any available documents nor internal evidence (Stephan referred to the Ministry of Worship, organized in December, 1831) bear out the claim that Stephan approached Kurtz as early as 1830, as stated in Vehse, *op. cit.*, 3, and repeated by C. F. W. Walther in Köstering, *Auswanderung*, 10; C. F. W. Walther, *Bünger*, 32; Th. Gräbner, *Lutherische Pioniere, I. Unsere Pilgerväter*, 5; Mezger (ed.), *Denkstein zum fünfundsiebzigjährigen Jubiläum der Missourisynode*, 5.

in Germany as even worse than it had been "several years ago." However, he did not indicate on what he based the statement, except for a complaint about the Ministry of Worship, whose personnel consisted, according to Stephan, of a number of young and irreligious jurists and of one clergyman who was a "blasphemer." [16] The Prussian Union he viewed with alarm. Saxony was the only German state, Stephan asserted, which had not succumbed to the trend toward the Union and where the rights of the Lutheran Church were still respected. But even there the faithful were looking into a "grave and very sorrowful future," for there were reasons to fear that Saxony, too, would momentarily fall into line with the formal policy of union.[17] Stephan lamented the fact that the authorities did not adopt repressive measures, especially censorship of the press, against the liberalistic element, although he had admitted even before this time that this element was in the majority.[18] He believed that the time had come for every Lutheran to ask himself:

> Will it not soon come to this that we must leave Babylon and Egypt and emigrate? . . . Whither shall we turn? In the German states we can find no refuge. Everywhere there is great hatred and deprecation of the pure Lutheran doctrine. In Russia a great despotism crushes everything down. So my eyes and those of many others were directed to North America, where there dwells not only political freedom, but love for the pure Lutheran religion as well.[19]

Stephan sought Kurtz's advice as to the best location for settlement with "a not inconsiderable number" of followers: "In Mary-

---

[16] A similar judgment on the Ministry of Worship is contained in Bemerkungen über . . . Stephan, Bound MSS., V, C. H. I.

[17] Even opponents of Stephanism were ready to admit that several signs pointed in that direction. Fischer, *op. cit.*, 38.

[18] Stephan to G. H. W. Walther, Jan. 18, 1831, MS., C. H. I.; Stephan to B. Kurtz, March, 1833, Bound MSS., I, C. H. I. That actual freedom of religion and separation of Church and State were things Stephan did not understand, loudly as he clamored for them, is illustrated in the Codes, Appendix B, especially in the Code for the Civil Community, par. 13.

[19] Stephan to B. Kurtz, March, 1833, Bound MSS., I, C. H. I. A desire for the religious freedom of America was frequently expressed by the emigrants. E. M. Bürger, Pathenbrief des Stephanus Keyl, July 4, 1838 (quoted in full in Rösener, *Unser erster Emigrantenmissionar, Pastor Stephanus Keyl*, 11—12), Stephan to G. H. Löber, Feb. 20, 1836, MSS., C. H. I.; Marbach to Walz, Jan. 12, 1838, Stephan to Schwabe, March 29, 1838, Bound MSS., VI, C. H. I.; *New York Observer*, March 16, 1839; Brief Outline of the Emigration Code, par. 2, Appendix B; Vehse, *op. cit.*, 3—4.

land, or in Florida, or in Georgia, or in Virginia, or on the Mississippi, or where else?" He asked Kurtz to take into consideration the economic problems of a large and professionally diversified group, including pastors, candidates, teachers, all kinds of craftsmen, secretaries, artists, "and probably even farmers." Finally, he requested that Kurtz take special care that no word of his intentions appear in the public press, for they might become known in Europe before the time was ripe; then he and his followers might be subjected to much "derision and tribulation." Stephan assured Kurtz that he had a "high purpose" in keeping his plans secret.[20]

This letter did not reach Baltimore until August 12, 1833. By that time Kurtz's health was failing, although earlier that same year he had assumed the editorship of the *Lutheran Observer*. But his uncle, John Daniel Kurtz, replied to the appeal from Dresden, Benjamin adding only a short personal note.[21] D. Kurtz assured Stephan that if freedom was what the Stephanites were looking for, the United States was the place to find it — a place "where people of all conceivable religious views live in peace, without hating or persecuting each other because of their beliefs." As to the location for a colony, he explained that Maryland and Pennsylvania were undesirable because of the relatively high price of land, which sold at $10 to $60 per acre. It was inadvisable to settle in Ohio for the same reason, although it was true that many German-Americans were living there. Virginia's plantation system would create formidable difficulties both in securing land and in obtaining employment for a large number of skilled European craftsmen. Georgia and Florida were ruled out because of their climate.

The advice of Benjamin Kurtz and his uncle, as well as that of several other competent people whom they had consulted, was that a colony of the kind proposed should be established on the banks of the Missouri River. Some Germans had already settled there, and more were coming all the time. The air was clear, the region healthful, the climate pleasant, and land was to be had for one and a half Spanish dollars per acre. For a more detailed description of this favored region the Dresdeners were referred to the famous

---

[20] Stephan to B. Kurtz, March, 1833, Bound MSS., I, C. H. I.

[21] J. D. Kurtz and B. Kurtz to Stephan, Aug. 20—24, 1833, Bound MSS., I, C. H. I.

work of Duden, published only four years before.[22] They were urged to send agents ahead to inquire about a location and possibly even contract for the land. The route advocated by the Kurtzes was the one eventually adopted, namely, directly from a German port to New Orleans, then by steamboat up the Mississippi to St. Louis. A final bit of advice, which the Stephanites did not heed, was that the candidates would do well to acquire a working knowledge of the English language if they wished to make themselves really useful in the United States.[23]

Despite the information supplied by Benjamin Kurtz and his uncle and the opposition experienced in Saxony, nothing more was heard about emigration for several years. Meanwhile, Stephan continued to adhere to his policy of ignoring the controversies he and his actions had aroused. He thereby added another complaint to those already lodged against him, namely, that he had made of himself a controversial figure, yet refused to maintain his position when it was challenged. The excuse was that he had answered all criticism and that any further attacks upon him were merely malicious repetition of the old stories, simple persecution.[24] The martyr complex was developing. Even Stephan's adherents felt the impropriety of his procedure, and, although publicly they claimed to respect his silence, they decided in 1833 on the paradoxical action of defending him nevertheless.[25] In that year the *Glaubensbe-*

---

22 *Bericht über eine Reise nach den westlichen Staaten Nordamerika's.* Much of this work has been translated in W. Bek, "Gottfried Duden's 'Report,' 1824—1827," *Missouri Historical Review,* XII, XIII, *seriatim.* This instance is one of the few references to Duden or his book in the records of the Saxon emigrants. Nevertheless, it has frequently been asserted that the Saxons followed the course they did as a result of Duden's influence. Vehse, *op. cit.,* 3; C. F. W. Walther in Köstering, *Auswanderung,* 10; Faust, *op. cit.,* I, 448; Schneider, *op. cit.,* 103; Hennig, "Die Auswanderung Martin Stephans," *Zeitschrift für Kirchengeschichte,* LVIII, 164. Even though some of these assertions come from contemporaries of the emigration, the emphasis on Duden is not borne out by the facts. While some attention was paid to him, especially in 1836 (G. H. Löber, Diary, May 3, 1836, MS., C. H. I.), other sites than Missouri, which he advocated, were seriously considered after that time. As will become apparent later, it is likely that a relatively obscure St. Louis merchant named Kimm had as much to do with the decision to settle in Missouri as anyone.

23 J. D. Kurtz and B. Kurtz to Stephan, Aug. 20—24, 1833, Bound MSS., I, C. H. I.

24 Pöschel, *op. cit.,* 1—3; Fischer, *op. cit.,* 29—31; Bemerkungen über . . . Stephan, Bound MSS., V, C. H. I.; Document . . . des Grundsteins . . . St. Louis . . . 22. Juny 1842, Bekenntniss, MSS., C. H. I.

25 Pöschel, *op. cit.,* 3, 6—8.

kenntniss der Gemeinde zu St. Johannis appeared. It was probably written by Pöschel, one of the candidates closely attached to Stephan.[26] The charges this work was intended to answer were much the same as those previously preferred. Pöschel had taken his cue from Stephan. The defense of doctrine and practice was the standard one, an appeal to the Scriptures and the Confessions, and on this basis was unassailable, even by admission of the Minister of Worship.[27] However, this attempt at a formal defense was evidence both of the renewed violence of the attack upon Stephan since the beginning of 1833 and of the difficulty created by his refusal to meet it. The greatest significance of the *Glaubensbekenntniss* is that it appeared.

Stephan's "high purpose" in maintaining secrecy regarding his plans for emigration seems to have held good for three years, although there is no evidence to show that opposition to orthodoxy was less bitter from 1833 to 1835 than it was in 1833, 1836, or 1838. This double question accordingly presents itself: Why was action deferred, and why was it then taken when it was taken? The most plausible answer can be found in the fact that after 1833 a lull in the attacks upon Stephan set in, but that opposition to him rose markedly in 1836, when he was arrested by the civil authorities for the first time.[28] On the night of February 1 Stephan was present in the Falkenhof at a gathering in the home of Mr. Nitzschke, who has been referred to above. The police raided the house, broke up the meeting on the ground that it was a disturbance of the peace, and arrested Stephan.[29] Although it was not immediately apparent, this incident marked a turning point in the history of Stephanism; thenceforth, the logical development of events was to lead almost inevitably to the emigration.

The action which followed a few weeks later was more annoying to Stephan than even the events on the night of February 1. The police closely examined many of Stephan's followers, especially

---

26 Lütkemüller, *op. cit.*, 23.

27 Mittheilungen . . . Verhandelungen des Landtags, Nov. 9, 1837, Bound MSS., VI, C. H. I.; Pöschel, *op. cit.*, 9—15, 41—42.

28 Fischer seems to have been under the impression that this event occurred in 1835. Fischer, *op. cit.*, 37. The dates here given are those in the documents on the case.

29 Appellation des . . . Stephan, March 28, 1836, Bemerkungen über . . . Stephan, Bound MSS., V, C. H. I.; G. H. Löber, Diary, 1836, pp. 20, 28, MS., C. H. I.

the candidates, and reported the incident to the ecclesiastical authorities. On the basis of this report, made out by Sergeant Pöschek [?], and of previous complaints on December 16 and 17, 1835, the *Kirchen-Inspection* on March 17, 1836, issued an injunction against Stephan's activity. The injunction prohibited "the preacher at the Bohemian congregation, Martin Stephan, . . . from any further participation in nocturnal meetings of this nature, within the city or outside it, which give offense already because of the unseemly time chosen." To assure that Stephan would not act contrary to the order, the police were charged with its execution. The injunction was issued on March 17, the local authorities received their instructions on March 22, and on the following day they notified Stephan of the action taken.[30]

Within five days the *Kirchen-Inspection* at Dresden received a lengthy document, prepared by Marbach, entitled the "Appeal of Pastor Martin Stephan from the order issued against him March 17, 1836." [31] The appeal forms the most comprehensive written defense of himself made by Stephan to the authorities. Divided into six points of "complaint," it began with an assertion on oath that all and sundry charges against him were false and that he was being deeply wronged. In the first point of "complaint" he attacked the procedure adopted in his case, which, he claimed, seriously infringed upon his civil rights. He charged, in this connection, that the action restricting his movements had been taken before giving him a hearing and without notifying him of the charges against him.[32]

In the remainder of his appeal Stephan departed from his insistence upon his legal rights and launched into a prolonged explanation of his personal life and movements. He declared that he did not "arrange for" meetings, since these had existed at St. John's for

---

30 The *Kirchen-Inspektion* (Dr. Carl C. Seltenreich, Superintendent) to Stephan, March 17, 1836, the *Kreisdirektion* (von Wintersheim) to the Superintendent of the Second Judicial District (von Biesko) and the Dresden City Council, March 22, 1836, Appellation des . . . Stephan, March 28, 1836, Bound MSS., V, C. H. I. As noted above, Hennig claims that Stephan was forbidden (probably only by his ecclesiastical superiors) to hold such meetings as early as 1820. If this assertion is correct, it can only emphasize the statements previously made in this study regarding the inadvisability of Stephan's action. Hennig, "Die Auswanderung Martin Stephans," *Zeitschrift für Kirchengeschichte*, LVIII, 162.

31 Appellation des . . . Stephan, March 28, 1836, Bemerkungen über . . . Stephan, Bound MSS., V, C. H. I.; G. H. Löber, Diary, 1836, pp. 20, 28, MS., C. H. I.

32 Appellation des . . . Stephan, March 28, 1836, Bound MSS., V, C. H. I.

two hundred years prior to his time.[33] Such terminology led to some inconsistencies. If, as was implied in his appeal to tradition and directly stated elsewhere,[34] he was characterizing his meetings as religious gatherings, he would have had difficulty in demonstrating that they had always been so. In fact Stephan himself contradicted this claim in another portion of the appeal when he said: "Frequently, however, I am also invited for purely social reasons . . . and I may not entirely . . . withdraw from these invitations . . ."[35] Again Stephan may have gone too far when he said: "I have never arranged for any nocturnal gatherings, in fact no gatherings of any kind. . . . Likewise I have never taken part in any nocturnal gatherings."[36] That the "Concordia hours" were his work or that he actually was at Nitzschke's must have been hard to deny.

He also attempted to justify his actions on the basis of his physical condition. Then his argument ran like this:

> Above all things this circumstance is to be taken into consideration, that from my early youth I have had a disposition for staying up late. In fact, ever since I was a little child, I have been unable to sleep until several hours after midnight, a peculiarity which I have been unable to overcome despite all my efforts to do so, which have almost made me ill. This affects the entire schedule of my day; therefore I have time for taking a walk only late in the evening — to which must be added a further circumstance, namely, that the night air is especially beneficial to me — which prompts me to accept invitations only for late in the evening, and whoever wishes to invite me must accommodate himself to me. But no one urges him to do so except his own free will.
>
> This division of my time I cannot alter unless I want simply to destroy my nature . . . and furthermore, this peculiarity of nature is not unique, but occurs not infrequently in individual persons as well as among whole peoples, at least whole classes of people.[37]

This defense was followed by an elaboration upon it, in which Stephan confused social and pastoral calls and then sought to justify

---

33 *Ibid.*

34 Marbach to von Uckermann, May 28, 1837, Bound MSS., VI, C. H. I.

35 Appellation des . . . Stephan, March 28, 1836, Bound MSS., V, C. H. I.

36 *Ibid.*

37 *Ibid.;* Bemerkungen über . . . Stephan, Bound MSS., V, C. H. I. Stübel stated outright that Stephan's complaints about his physical condition were unfounded. Stübel to Vehse *et al.,* Sept. 12, 1839, Bound MSS., VI, C. H. I.

his conduct by claiming a professional immunity to criticism in either case. Furthermore, he asserted that his conduct had been uniformly decorous and unobjectionable. The excursions to the vineyard lodge in the Hoflösnitz, he declared, were indispensable to his health, and any restriction upon his freedom of movement would make a sick man of him in a fortnight.[38] Even these representations did not make the authorities relent. It is not known that any official answer was ever made, but in any event no favorable action seems to have resulted.

Meanwhile, the unfavorable reaction of the populace had been almost immediate. The insidious effect of the injunction's ambiguous phrasing and of its disgracing provision for police supervision of Stephan's activities was heightened by the publication of stories which Stephan denounced as flagrant falsehoods. For example, in the *Penig-Bornaisches Volksblatt* Stephan was pictured as blessing a bowl of punch during the course of the now famous evening at Nitzschke's.[39] Marbach and Vehse attempted to insert a public defense of Stephan into the *Dresdener Anzeiger* a few days after Stephan's arrest. The pastor gave his written approval to this touching knight-errantry on the part of two of his most faithful followers, who virtually staked their own reputations upon their ability to defend his. But the *Dresdener Anzeiger* refused to accept the statement for publication on the ground that it was against the ordinances of the board of censorship for the public press to print discussions on the character of local clergymen.[40] Apparently, however, the brothers-in-law were successful in making public their sentiments in some journal, for by the middle of February they were in receipt of an anonymous letter reviling them for their defense of Stephan.[41] They even took the matter up with von Lindenau personally.[42]

Stephan's appeal indicates the general attitude and procedure

---

38 Appellation des . . . Stephan, March 28, 1836, Bound MSS., V, C. H. I.

39 *Ibid.; Penig-Bornaisches Volksblatt,* No. 12, 1836 (the date is not given on the copy in Concordia Historical Institute), Bound MSS., V, C. H. I.

40 Marbach and Vehse to the *Dresdener Anzeiger,* Feb. 5, 1836, Bound MSS., VI, C. H. I. Stephan's statement, dated Feb. 6, 1836, and the *Anzeiger's* rejection, dated March 1, 1836, are on the same manuscript.

41 "Ein wahrer Protestant" to Marbach [?], Feb. 15, 1836 [?], Bound MSS., VI, C. H. I.

42 G. H. Löber, Diary, 1836, p. 20, MS., C. H. I.

on the part of both Stephan and his opponents.[43] Furthermore, it is a basic document for the bitterly controverted point which cannot be entirely ignored: Was Stephan subjected to undue pressure by the civil authorities? The incident is one of the highlights in the activity of the Dresden police against him during a period of three years, 1836 to 1838, when Stephan and the authorities were in almost constant conflict. He had complained previously of opposition on the part of the civil authorities, but it was largely on the basis of incidents in the latter years that Stephan and his supporters pictured him a martyr. Stephan, they claimed, was not only pilloried in the press, slandered by the public, and harassed by the liberalist element among the clergy, but, because of his orthodox position, was being "persecuted" by the police in violation of his legal rights and being subjected to "political pressure," so that his final action, the emigration, was forced upon him.[44] It was even claimed that von Lindenau himself had decided to eliminate this "sect,"[45] and Stephan summed up this attitude when he wrote: "A stealthy persecution by powerful enemies over a period of years forced me to emigrate to North America."[46]

Perhaps the key to the dispute between Stephan and the authorities is that Stephan did have legal right on his side for many years. He was never convicted of a single criminal charge, how-

---

[43] An outstanding example of this line of argument is contained in the extended defense of Stephan, Bemerkungen über . . . Stephan, Bound MSS., V, C.H.I.

[44] Stephan to B. Kurtz, March, 1833, Jäckel to G. H. Löber, Sept. 4, 1838, Bound MSS., I, C.H.I.; Protokolle über die . . . Auswanderung, Dec. 13, 1837, Feb. 15, 16, 19, March 24, April 14, May 11, 18, 1838, Bound MSS., III, C.H.I.; Appellation des . . . Stephan, March 28, 1836, Bemerkungen über . . . Stephan, Appeal of Stephan to Fredrick Augustus II, Oct. 20, 1838, Bound MSS., V, C.H.I.; Marbach to von Uckermann, May 28, Dec. 27, 1837, Jan. 9, Feb. 7, 1838, Marbach to Walz, Jan. 12, 1838, Stephan to Walz, n.d. [Jan. 20, 1838?], Stephan to Schwabe, March 29, 1838, Stephan to —, Oct. 6, 1838, Bound MSS., VI, C.H.I.; Stephan to G. H. W. Walther, Jan. 18, 1831, C. F. W. Walther to von Einsiedel, Feb. 3, 1838, Marbach, An meine . . . Landsleute, Document . . . des Grundsteins . . . St. Louis . . . 22. Juny 1842, Bekenntniss, Lossagung vom Stephanismus, Ein Lebewohl der aus Sachsen nach Nord-Amerika ziehenden altlutherischen Gemeinde, Nov. 18, 1838 (hereafter cited as Lebewohl; it has been reprinted a number of times, *e.g.*, Fischer, *op. cit.*, 210—211), MSS., C.H.I.; O. H. Walther. *Exulanten-Lieder auf dem Meere,* 3—16 (note the full title); Brief Outline of the Emigration Code, par. 2, Appendix B. The Stephanite viewpoint is adopted by Hennig, "Die Auswanderung Martin Stephans," *Zeitschrift für Kirchengeschichte,* LVIII, 148, 163.

[45] G. H. Löber. Diary, 1836, p. 20. MS., C.H.I.

[46] Stephan to Flügel, Oct. 12, 1841, MS., C.H.I.

ever small, although it cannot be overlooked that some of the most serious and strongest cases against him were interrupted by his departure. The burden of proof rested with Stephan's opponents, and this proof they never produced. Until his very last months in Germany his followers were able to point out that Stephan had emerged from all investigations without a single conviction, despite the fact that it seems reasonably clear that some of the meetings he held were extra-legal. Almost at the very time of his suspension from office, the Minister of Worship in an oft-quoted declaration admitted before the *Landtag* that not a single charge against the Bohemian pastor had been proved.[47]

But many people did not observe legal punctilio, and a defense such as Stephan's served, if anything, to prejudice his case before the public. The feeling developed that instead of avoiding whatever would offend, as might be expected of a man in his position, he was hiding behind technicalities while courting censure. Many people thought his conduct was so unbecoming a public figure, his petty insistence upon offensive personal habits so out of keeping with the character of a clergyman, that they had little sympathy for his defense; and it failed to carry conviction even among those who accepted his statements at face value.[48] In general, Stephan's opponents asserted, the attitude of both the civil and ecclesiastical authorities, regardless of what their personal sentiments may have been, was constrained in the face of constant and deliberate provocation, and their policy was usually considerate.[49]

As far as the incident of 1836 is concerned, both sides seem to have overshot the mark. While the authorities may, as charged, have infringed upon some of Stephan's civil rights, their action in no way absolved Stephan. Interference with his allegedly religious meetings did not begin until they had become notorious, were, even by his own admission, no longer purely religious, and hence were

---

[47] Mittheilungen . . . Verhandelungen des Landtags, Nov. 9, 1837, Bound MSS., VI, C. H. I.; Jäckel to G. H. Löber, Sept. 4, 1838, Bound MSS., I, C. H. I.; Bemerkungen über . . . Stephan, Bound MSS., V, C. H. I. A rather complete digest of the testimony both for and against Stephan in the *Landtag* is contained in Fischer, *op. cit.*, 72—92.

[48] Stübel to Vehse *et al.*, Sept. 12, 1839, Bound MSS., VI, C. H. I.; Lossagung vom Stephanismus, Meurer [?] to C. F. W. Walther, Jan. 27, 1838, MSS., C. H. I.; Lütkemüller, *op. cit.*, 6—8; von Polenz, *op. cit.*, 24, 50; Fischer, *op. cit.*, 48—56.

[49] *Chemnitzer Anzeiger*, Oct. 30, 1838; von Polenz, *op. cit.*, 74; Pleissner, *op. cit.*, 44, 50.

no longer defensible on the basis of the congregation's charter rights. Of the authorities it must be said that their case was more justifiable than their procedure.

The amazing thing about the incident at Nitzschke's is that it was one of the two immediate causes for the emigration of about eight hundred people from Germany. Stephan had mentioned the subject of emigration to a few of his confidants before 1836, but it was not until that year, immediately after the episode just described, that the idea was made more widely known or that any definite action was taken. On February 20, 1836, while the injunction against him was being drafted, Stephan wrote to Löber:

> Our times are becoming constantly graver and more decisive; in the long run things cannot remain as they are now. God will bring about a decision in His Church, whether it is to continue to exist in Europe or to emigrate to North America.[50]

Stephan, however, wished to have a hand in this decision also; so in the spring of that year he called the first formal meetings and summoned the keymen in the movement to come to Dresden for conference.[51]

These meetings are described in detail in Löber's diary. The first took place prior to March 19, 1836, and was attended by teachers and candidates. It was notable for the variety of subjects it took up, considering the fact that Stephan was delivering opinions on all of them, from a model schedule for the school week to the folly of Scheibel's wanting to emigrate to Norway, where all one could do was fish. The theme is constant however: Times are trying. "Without a miracle of God the Lutheran Church will scarcely be able to survive in Europe." The aim of the conference clearly is to get the idea across that emigration to America is the solution to the problem. Although the time is not yet ripe, the faithful must be prepared to seize the opportunity when it presents itself.[52]

The second meeting was called in the middle of April, 1836, and was held on May 3, at Marbach's residence in Dresden. The following men were in attendance: Stephan, Marbach, Vehse, Keyl, Bürger, Löber, the two brothers Welzel, Fürbringer, Brohm, J. F.

---

[50] Stephan to G. H. Löber, Feb. 20, 1836, MS., C. H. I.

[51] Keyl, *op. cit.*, 11.

[52] G. H. Löber, Diary, 1836, pp. 11—15, MS., C. H. I.

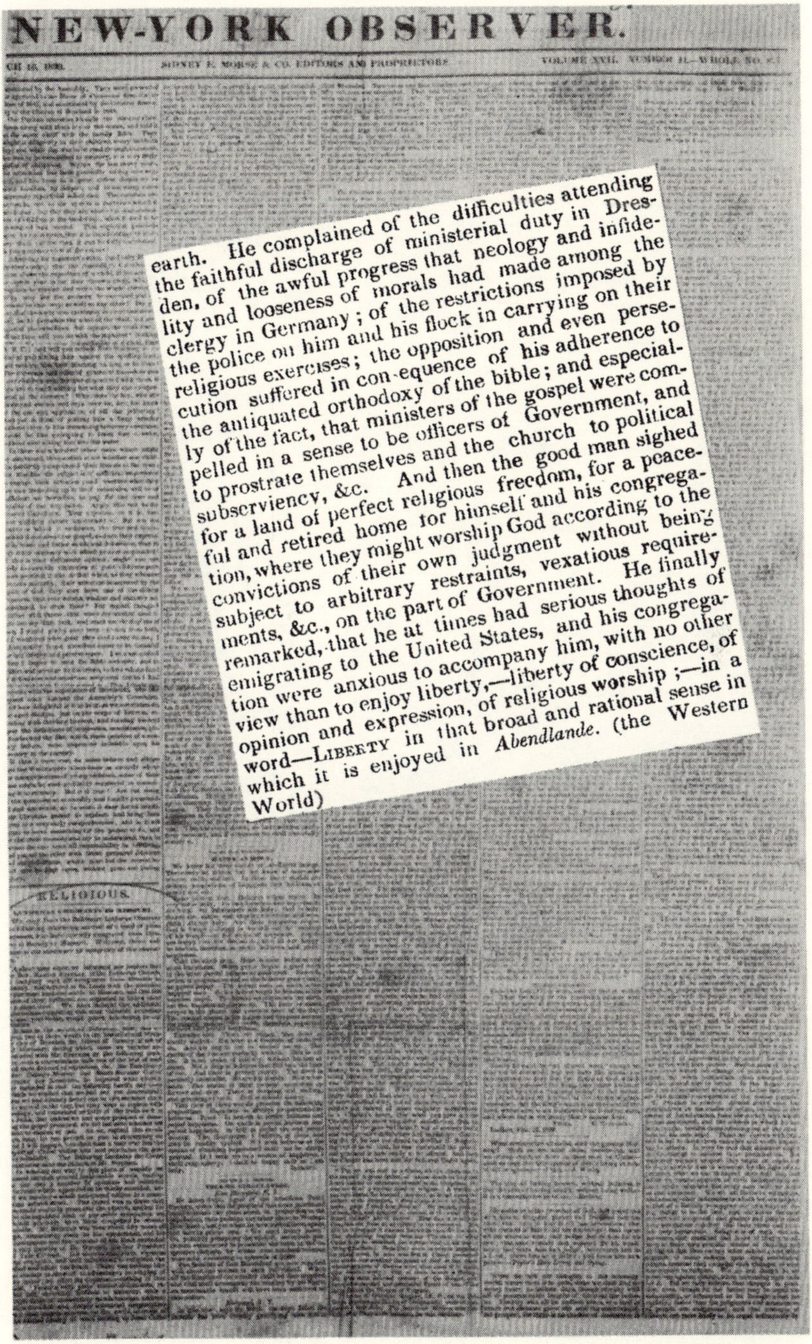

NEW-YORK OBSERVER.

earth. He complained of the difficulties attending the faithful discharge of ministerial duty in Dresden, of the awful progress that neology and infidelity and looseness of morals had made among the clergy in Germany; of the restrictions imposed by the police on him and his flock in carrying on their religious exercises; the opposition and even persecution suffered in con-equence of his adherence to the antiquated orthodoxy of the bible; and especially of the fact, that ministers of the gospel were compelled in a sense to be officers of Government, and to prostrate themselves and the church to political subserviency, &c. And then the good man sighed for a land of perfect religious freedom, for a peaceful and retired home for himself and his congregation, where they might worship God according to the convictions of their own judgment without being subject to arbitrary restraints, vexatious requirements, &c., on the part of Government. He finally remarked, that he at times had serious thoughts of emigrating to the United States, and his congregation were anxious to accompany him, with no other view than to enjoy liberty,—liberty of conscience, of opinion and expression, of religious worship;—in a word—LIBERTY in that broad and rational sense in which it is enjoyed in *Abendlande*. (the Western World)

The Reverend Benjamin Kurtz's report of an 1827 meeting with Stephan in Dresden, reprinted in the New York Observer. *(See page 84)*

PLATE VI

Artist's drawing of the Olbers, *patterned after the painting of that ship by G. H. Hillmer*

PLATE VII

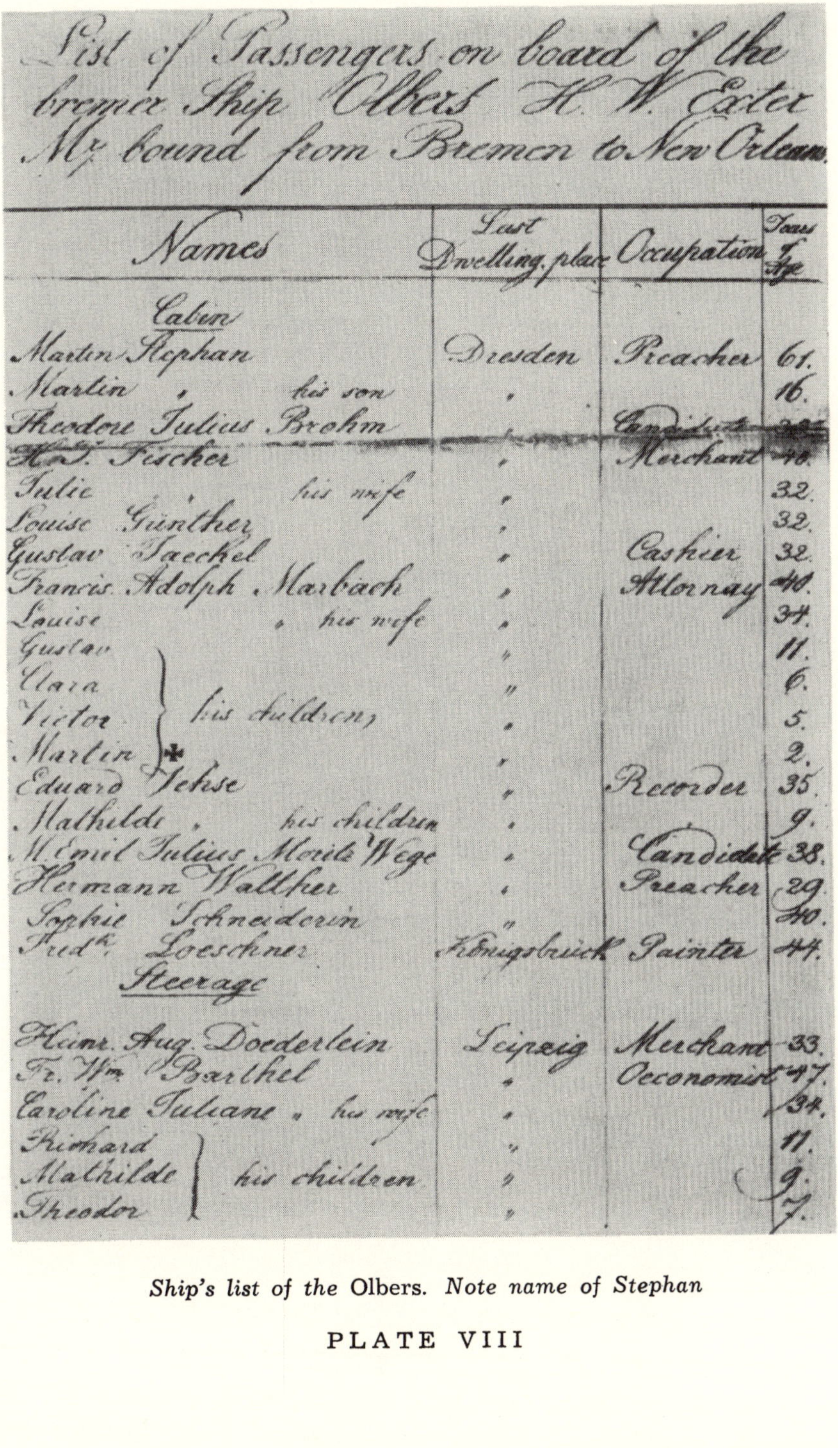

List of Passengers on board of the bremer Ship Olbers H. W. Exter Mr bound from Bremen to New Orleans

Names		Last Dwelling place	Occupation	Years of Age
Cabin				
Martin Stephan		Dresden	Preacher	61.
Martin „	his son	„		16.
Theodore Julius Brohm		„	Candidate	[illegible]
H. F. Fischer		„	Merchant	40.
Julie „	his wife	„		32.
Louise Günther		„		32.
Gustav Jaeckel		„	Cashier	32.
Francis Adolph Marbach		„	Attornay	40.
Louise „	his wife	„		34.
Gustav	his children	„		11.
Clara		„		6.
Victor		„		5.
Martin ✠		„		2.
Eduard Vehse		„	Recorder	35.
Mathilde „	his children	„		9.
M. Emil Julius Moritz Wege		„	Candidate	38.
Hermann Walther		„	Preacher	29.
Sophie Schneiderin		„		40.
Fredk. Loeschner		Königsbrück	Painter	44.
Steerage				
Heinr. Aug. Doederlein		Leipzig	Merchant	33.
Fr. Wm. Barthel		„	Oeconomist	47.
Caroline Juliane „	his wife	„		34.
Richard	his children	„		11.
Mathilde		„		9.
Theodor		„		7.

Ship's list of the Olbers. *Note name of Stephan*

PLATE VIII

Gotthold Heinrich Löber, according to a pencil miniature of 1843 by Gustav Pfau, an artist who was one of the emigrants of 1838

PLATE IX

Bünger, two Delitzsches, Wege, Jäckel, Nitzschke, Teacher Hellwig, Teacher Zöge, and Merchant Schwabe.[53] This assemblage was addressed at considerable length by Pastor Stephan. The approach was the same as that in the previous conference, but the tone was more decided, and the plans were more specific. Löber's notes convey "about" what Stephan said. The burden of his remarks is clear.

> The Church is in greater danger than ever. . . . The occurrences in Dresden prove that everything which is evil succeeds. . . . There has never been a time in the history of the Church like the present. A Luther would be thrown into the Elbe, if he returned. . . . The Church is down to the *punctum saliens*. . . . Pray that God leads His people out of this Sodom and delivers them, and takes His Church to another land, where it can serve His name undisturbed.[54]

But not all went smoothly. Trouble developed when "the chairman of the meeting directed the searching question to his colleagues in office: 'How many souls do you have in your congregations upon whom we can count?' " Bürger tried to answer and became embarrassed because he had placed the number too high. Bürger, it seemed, might be a little lax in dividing the sheep from the goats. Löber was cagier when his turn came to answer. He countered by asking "for more exact marks, wherewith one could tell" which souls were tried and true. A formula was provided for this purpose, but the discussion seems never to have gotten back to the original point: How many? However, other questions regarding emigration were treated at length. Some of their conclusions were startling. As it was against the law in Saxony to encourage emigration, no one was to be urged to go along — not too openly, at least. But anyone "who is established in the faith, and who may be prevented by his relatives (husband, father, etc.) from emigrating, he [sic] must escape; those who are married must, in a case like that, stop sharing bed and board, and then get a divorce on grounds of 'malicious desertion.' " Löber entered this policy pronouncement into his diary without revealing a trace of surprise in his pietistic soul.[55]

Missouri was tentatively but unanimously regarded by those present as the most suitable destination. This attitude was largely

---

53 *Ibid.*, April 13, May 3, 1836.

54 *Ibid.*, May 3, 1836.

55 *Ibid.*

a reflection of their reaction to Duden's account of life there and makes its contribution toward justifying M. L. Hansen's characterization of Duden's work as "the most important piece of literature in the history of German emigration."[56] However, other sources of information were to be sought. The conferees were certain that they did not want to settle near a city, but they did wish to buy land in a well-cultivated and settled area. The Church, they noted, was making great progress in America. Those present were instructed that during the coming year they were to keep themselves in readiness. If one of the pastors had to carry his protest to the point of resignation, all other pastors were to resign in protest as well.[57] At the moment no one was in danger of this, except Stephan.

A "Constitution for the Lutheran Church after It has Safely Landed" was appended to these notes on emigration by Löber. The detail with which even this plan of government was worked out, is evidence that Stephan had been contemplating the matter for some time. The broad outlines of the regulations later found in the Codes, developed during the period of emigration, were laid down here. The founding of a theological seminary was not too large a project, the question of whether women were to knit on Sunday not too small a matter, to be included in this prospectus for Utopia. Most significant, perhaps, is the strongly hierarchical cast given the entire organization. The prospect of establishing an episcopal polity was quite frankly, almost casually, referred to, as though it were understood. There was a clear resolve that the laity was to have nothing to say in making policy and that the clergy was to be a privileged class. As the group would be "the Church," it was even considered possible that they might wish to make an addition to the Symbolical Books of the Lutheran Church.[58] And finally, "regarding the authority of the Church relative to the secular arm, the model of the first four centuries shall be adhered to; that of the German church is to receive little or no consideration."[59]

---

[56] Hansen, *op. cit.*, 149.

[57] G. H. Löber, Diary, May 3, 1836, MS., C.H.I.

[58] This idea was not necessarily original with Stephan. Löber had been thinking along these lines for more than a year. *Ibid.*, Entry at the close of 1834.

[59] *Ibid.*, May 3, 1836.

Definite action was to be deferred until a "sign" should indicate the date for actual departure.[60] Meanwhile, the entire group was alerted, and organizational lines were drawn more closely. Marbach had been in correspondence with Löber since at least January, 1836, had been visited repeatedly by Löber, and now himself went to see the Altenburg pastor in the early summer of 1836, apparently to look over the situation there.[61]

A small group of people, under the leadership of a man named Spröde, did emigrate to the United States in 1836. They had been advised by Stephan not to emigrate yet and above all not to have anything to do with Scheibel. The former they ignored, the latter they observed. Despite their disobedience Stephan "received them into" the Lutheran Church before their departure. They settled in New York and, by keeping in touch with the Dresden pastor, became the outpost of Stephanism in the United States.[62]

But within his immediate following no one made bold to assume the initiative, that is, to discover a "sign." It was well for Stephan that such was the case. Too much enthusiasm at this time might have proved embarrassing to the leader. For when, after a few months of careful surveillance of Stephan's actions, nothing happened, the vigilance of the police began to relax. These months, during which Stephan did not want to give the authorities cause for further complaint, were extremely irksome to the pastor of St. John's; he therefore called the afore-mentioned conference. But when the apparent or actual carelessness of the police subsequently permitted him greater freedom of action, the situation no longer seemed so intolerable. Stephan must have begun to wonder whether it was not possible to get along as before, without taking recourse to the drastic measure of emigration. Certainly, if he was not going to be "persecuted" by the police, he was deprived of the most convenient argument for finding action necessary at this time. A brief truce had set in, but, as Stephan had told Löber, it obviously could not last. Either the police would relax their vigilance completely, and Stephan would regain his former status, or they would have to act again, and the stage would be set all the more thoroughly for Stephan's next move.

---

[60] Keyl, *op. cit.*, 11—12; C. F. W. Walther in Köstering, *Auswanderung*, 12.

[61] G. H. Löber, Diary, Jan. 23—25, April 26, p. 40, 1836, MS., C. H. I.

[62] *Ibid.*, April 27, 1836, and 1836, pp. 40, 50; *Anzeiger des Westens*, Dec. 31, 1842.

The first year and three-quarters after the Nitzschke incident were marked only by the supervision of the police, the Dresden conference, and by the publication of newspaper stories about the alleged excesses at Stephan's meetings.[63] Otherwise conditions seemed to be normal again. Keyl continued his battle with Siebenhaar and Wenzel. C. F. W. Walther even took office at Bräunsdorf, although only after consulting with Stephan on how to avoid possible obstacles, should he decide to emigrate in the near future.[64] Walther then added his contribution to the religious disturbances in the Muldenthal. Löber, after apparently working up considerable enthusiasm for the emigration as a result of the meeting in May, had to discuss it in his diary.[65] No one else seemed to be listening. Stephan, for whom opposition to the authority of the state was supposed to have been "impossible," [66] once more resumed the even tenor of his way, continuing his religio-social, or socio-religious, gatherings in defiance of the court order restraining him.[67] Nothing happened, and it seemed the storm had passed over, as others had before. Consequently the next blow from the authorities was all the more startling when it fell. Why the police delayed action so long as they did is not definitely known, for certainly they would have had as good cause for acting at an earlier date.[68] However, when they did proceed, it was in conjunction with the ecclesiastical authorities and with abruptness and severity.

On the night of November 8, 1837, a meeting was held at the vineyard lodge in the Hoflösnitz. The five Dresdeners present, including Messrs. "Helbig" (probably Teacher Hellwig is meant),

---

[63] Von Karlowitz to the *Kreisdirektion* at Dresden, Oct. 24, 1837, MS., Stephanakten, Landeskirchenamt, Dresden, I, 172.

[64] C. F. W. Walther to Stephan, n. d. [December, 1836], MS., C. H. I. Compare this letter with the description of Walther's "much deliberation and severe conflicts of soul" and his "bleeding heart" on resigning a year and one half later. Dau (ed.), *op. cit.*, 25.

[65] G. H. Löber, Diary, April 27, 1836, and 1836, pp. 40, 42A, MS., C. H. I.

[66] Hennig, "Die Auswanderung Martin Stephans," *Zeitschrift für Kirchengeschichte*, LVIII, 148.

[67] Von Karlowitz to the *Kreisdirektion* at Dresden, Nov. 13, 1837, MS., Stephanakten, Landeskirchenamt, Dresden, II, 1—2; Lütkemüller, *op. cit.*, 52—53.

[68] Von Karlowitz to the *Kreisdirektion* at Dresden, Oct. 24, Nov. 13, 1837, MSS., Stephanakten, Landeskirchenamt, Dresden, I, 172, II, 1—2. Fischer claimed that the attitude of the authorities was the result of a formal promise on Stephan's part that he would observe the restrictions imposed. Fischer, *op. cit.*, 37.

Nitzschke, and Stärtzell (probably Johann August, Jr.), and Louise Günther, had arrived by carriage during the late afternoon or early evening. They then waited for Stephan, who was taking his accustomed stroll toward the same goal in the company of a female companion, probably Sophie Höschel, a domestic employed in the household of the Dresden family von Opel. The police were aware of these plans, and eight gendarmes staged a raid on the place at midnight with considerable bluster. Their move was poorly timed and occurred before Stephan's arrival. The embarrassment of the officers was plain, for there was nothing objectionable going on, and rigid questioning revealed no charges to prefer against anyone present.

The people found at the house were held until five or five-thirty A. M., when Stephan and Sophie approached. Sensing that something was not quite normal, Stephan sent his companion ahead to investigate. She was a match for the police, who met her with a barrage of questions. The officers were about to concede that they had been outmaneuvered, when by accident one of them discovered the pastor of St. John's, whom they did not believe to be in the vicinity, lingering near the house to learn the outcome. A clerk from the Dresden police department either was already present or was summoned, and a hearing was held on the spot. The laymen were escorted back to Dresden by the police after 10 A. M. on November 9. Under threat of being forcibly returned if he did not present himself voluntarily, Stephan (who, for the time being, remained in the lodge with Louise and Sophie) was ordered to come back to the city and appear for a hearing the next day. On the afternoon of the ninth Vehse, Marbach, and Stübel went out to see how Stephan was faring and found him preparing to return.[69]

These events had taken place in the early morning hours of Thursday, November 9, 1837, the very day von Karlowitz's testimony before the Landtag appeared in print. The hearing was to have taken place either on that date or more likely on the next, November 10, depending upon what was meant by the "next" day. The proceedings actually began on the tenth, or at the latest on the

---

[69] Von Karlowitz, to the *Kreisdirektion* at Dresden, Nov. 13, 1837, MS., Stephanakten, Landeskirchenamt, Dresden, II, 1—2; Fischer, *op. cit.*, 50—51; Lütkemüller, *op. cit.*, 52—54; *Leipziger allgemeine Zeitung*, Nov. 22, 1837; Vehse to —, Nov. 16, 1837, MS., C. H. I.

eleventh.[70] On Saturday an order from the *Kreisdirektion* reached Stephan, as a result of which Stephan designated Candidate Klügel as his substitute for preaching the next day, Sunday, November 12. This young man helped to upset a very delicate situation with an impassioned sermon on Matthew, chapter 24, verse 15 and following. On Monday, the thirteenth, the Ministry of Worship issued an order to the *Kreisdirektion* suspending Stephan from the public exercise of his office and (to prevent another of Klügel's homiletical efforts) providing that Pastor Steinert of a Dresden orphanage occupy the pulpit during the vacancy. The Ministry had based its order of suspension upon a report from the *Kreisdirektion* bearing the date November 10 — further evidence that the tenth was the day on which the hearing began.[71]

---

[70] On March 19 von Karlowitz reported to the king that the investigation had been under way for eighteen weeks, *i. e.*, since November 10 or 11, exclusive or inclusive respectively of the day of writing. Von Karlowitz to Fredrick Augustus II, March 19, 1838, MS., Dresdener Hauptstaatsarchiv, Hausarchiv Friedrich August II, No. 151.

[71] Von Karlowitz to the *Kreisdirektion* at Dresden, Nov. 13, 1837, MS., Stephanakten, Landeskichenamt, Dresden, II, 1—2; Vehse to —, Nov. 16, 1838, MS., C. H. I. There has been considerable confusion of chronology in the events of November, 1837. Köstering placed Stephan's suspension into the "late fall of 1838." Köstering, *Keyl,* 48. Hochstetter perpetuated this error. Hochstetter, *op. cit.*, 14. Fischer claimed that the suspension came immediately, on November 9. Fischer, *op. cit.*, 40. See also Mezger (ed.), *op. cit.*, 5. Stephan himself said it occurred on November 11, and Vehse apparently agreed with him. Stephan to Schwabe, March 29, 1838, Bound MSS., VI, C. H. I.; Vehse to —, Nov. 16, 1838, MS., C. H. I. Hennig placed it on November 16, 1837. Hennig, "Die Auswanderung Martin Stephans," *Zeitschrift für Kirchengeschichte,* LVIII. 163. This may be a correct date if it is intended to mean the day on which the *Kreisdirektion* carried out the order of suspension (which had been issued three days earlier by the Ministry of Worship) by formally notifying Stephan. The anonymous writer of Bemerkungen über . . . Stephan, Bound MSS., V, C. H. I., is anything but clear on the time element, yet attempts to make a major point of it. This document makes two claims. First it is charged that the arrest of Stephan was deliberately timed to offset the favorable report of von Karlowitz before the *Landtag.* However, such a line of argument necessitates the assumption of von Karlowitz's co-operation in a scheme whose net result could only have been his embarrassment before the *Landtag* and the public, an inexplicable position for the minister to adopt. Secondly it is charged that the suspension was issued arbitrarily, before the hearing took place, and without any relation to the result of the hearing, but that it was not delivered to Stephan until after the hearing had begun, in order to make it appear that the evidence brought out was damaging to him. However, since the suspension was, by its own statement, based primarily upon Stephan's disregard of the injunction against his meetings, it would not have been surprising if the suspension had preceded the hearing. In fact, it would not have been surprising had the suspension come even before the incident of November 8—9 took place. Neither would a delay of several days in an official document

The hearing of Stephan before Superintendent Heymann was continued on November 15. Stephan was charged with holding conventicles and accused of immoral conduct. Sophie Höschel was also questioned further. While Stephan was at least treated civilly — or "tolerably," as Vehse said — Sophie was subjected to a severe three and one-half hour grilling that finally led her to file several complaints against police officers — of course, to no avail. The line of questioning pursued with her plainly implied the accusation of immorality against Stephan. Soon thereafter Stephan was placed under a virtual house-arrest, which lasted for months.[72] However, other results that might have been expected from the hearing, in the form of some definite conclusion on Stephan's guilt or innocence, were left in suspense, and no further action had been taken even when Stephan left Saxony a year later. As for Nitzschke, this was the second time that he had been found playing a role of great intimacy with Stephan. Since Nitzschke was employed by the government, it was possible for Stephan's influential enemies to bring pressure to bear on the merchant. He presently found that he was to be transferred to Meissen. When he refused to go, he lost his position.[73]

Neither Stephan nor his followers were fully prepared for the shock of his suspension.[74] They had hoped and expected that Stephan's peculiarly independent position at the "Bohemian" congregation, his large personal following, and the lack of any really damaging evidence against him would prevent any action so drastic. It must be admitted that a legal basis, other than his disregard for the injunction of 1836, is hard to find. The authorities protected their position, of course, by not making the order final, merely

---

reaching Stephan be unusual or indicate deliberate, sinister timing. But the very assertion itself, that the hearing followed upon the suspension, is incorrect in view of the dates for the two occurrences here established, no later than November 10 for the former, no earlier than November 13 for the latter. See also Fischer, *op. cit.*, 50—51. Parallel documentation is contained in the Hanewinckel Notes, 52—73, MS., C. H. I.

[72] Vehse to —, Nov. 16, 1837, König. Sächs. Kreis-Direction [(] V. Wintersheim [)] an die Stadtpolizeideputation zu Dresden der Hoeschelin Beschwerde betrf., Dec. 5, 1837, MSS., C. H. I.; Der Sophie Höschelin Vernehmung auf der Superintendur, n. d. [Nov. 15, 1837]. Marbach to Waltz, Jan. 12, 1838. Bound MSS., VI, C. H. I.; Protokolle über die . . . Auswanderung, Feb. 15, 1838, Bound MSS., III, C. H. I.

[73] Lebenslauf des . . . Nitzschke, MS., C. H. I.

[74] Protokolle über die . . . Auswanderung, Feb. 15, 1838, Bound MSS., III, C. H. I.; Marbach to Walz, Jan. 12, 1838, Bound MSS., VI, C. H. I.

issuing a temporary suspension. But surprised or not, Stephan was still capable of exercising his occasionally shrewd judgment. Despite his prompt legal action in the protest of November 21, 1837, he did not deceive himself with any vague hopes of reinstatement.[75] He realized that his career in Germany had come to an end. While he continued to maintain that he was still officially pastor of St. John's, he hastened to develop his plan for the only ready solution to his predicament — emigration. Here was the necessary "sign." As early as November 16, 1837, Vehse wrote: "What we will do, you know. The time cannot yet be definitely set." [76]

If seeking a new field of operations had seemed attractive to Stephan while he was still in full possession of his rights, it must now have seemed imperative.[77] The opposition to him had become so strong that if he persisted in his idiosyncrasies, life would be made difficult for him. By this time his personal ambitions had grown to such proportions that he evidently realized they could never be attained in Saxony. The only alternative, then, was emigration to a country where he would be undisturbed in developing a church that would be officially as well as psychologically under his hierarchical domination. This desire, and his resentment at the restrictions upon his personal and professional activities, are most likely the immediate motives which led to his final decision in calling for a general emigration.[78]

---

75 Bemerkungen über . . . Stephan, Bound MSS., V, C. H. I.; Stephan to Walz, n. d. [Jan. 20, 1838?], Bound MSS., VI, C. H. I.

76 Vehse to —, Nov. 16, 1837, MS., C. H. I. Vehse later claimed that several months intervened between Stephan's suspension and any definite action on the emigration. Vehse, *op. cit.,* 5. Actually less than a month elapsed. Notes on a deliberation between M. F. and J., Dec. 6, 1837, Bound MSS., III, C. H. I. A possible explanation for Vehse's statement may be that he was not drawn into the committee meetings until February 15, 1838. Protokolle über die . . . Auswanderung, Feb. 15, 1838, Bound MSS., III, C. H. I.

77 Lütkemüller, *op. cit.,* 54.

78 E. M. Bürger, Selbstbiographie, 118—119, MS., E. J. Buerger Papers, Ellicottville, N. Y.,; Lossagung vom Stephanismus, Bekenntniss, Marbach, An meine . . . Landsleute, Brohm, Journal of the Voyage on the *Olbers,* and the *Selma* (hereafter cited as Journal), Dec. 15, 1838, MSS., C. H. I. Stübel went so far as to say that in his opinion Stephan sought his own dismissal in order to be free to leave. Stübel to Vehse *et al.,* Sept. 12, 1839, Bound MSS., VI, C. H. I. H. Koepchen makes two claims which conflict with the presentation in the preceding pages: First, that a general decision to emigrate had definitely been reached as early as 1836, and secondly, that this decision resulted from the publication of von Ammon's *Fortbildung des Christentums zur Weltreligion,* a book which deeply shocked the Stephanites. H. Koepchen,

The personal reasons of Stephan were, of course, not advanced in persuading his followers. Many of the latter were made to believe their leader's lament that true Lutheranism was languishing under the despotism and persecution of a state church,[79] and so, under his influence, they followed him. Thus, while religious motives did not always stand alone in the minds of both pastors and laymen of the emigration, it is not necessary to challenge in the case of anyone but Stephan the sincerity of such religious motives as certainly were present. However, the soundness of such motives is open to serious question, and this question was of considerable importance to the emigrants themselves. Their views on it varied from time to time. Just before and during the emigration its leaders pronounced the movement and everything resulting from it good; Saxony, the State Church, and all who opposed the emigration were rotten to the core and had to be abandoned to their inevitable destruction.[80] But in the years just after the emigration all were agreed that it was fundamentally wrong and that its nature and

---

"The Saxon Emigration of 1938, [*sic*] I, Why?," *The Lutheran Witness,* LVII, 94. Neither of these contentions agrees with the facts presented in the preceding and subsequent portions of this study. Furthermore, in regard to the second point, it may be noted that Koepchen's assertion: "This book . . . was decreed to be the guide of the Church of Saxony," leaves open the question of who so "decreed" it; for, whatever von Ammon's position, his book had no official standing. Hennig's presentation of Stephan's motives is equally unconvincing. Hennig found "that the resistance against the 'royal' Saxon State Church was at the same time resistance against police authority," and that "resistance against the government, which bears the sword in God's stead, was impossible for the Lutheran, Stephan. So the only remaining way out was emigration." Hennig, "Die Auswanderung Martin Stephans," *Zeitschrift für Kirchengeschichte,* LVIII, 148. This viewpoint encounters the difficulty of explaining several of Stephan's actions which are in contradiction to it. But even if such an analysis were correct, it would establish only the fact that Stephan had to leave, not explain why he placed himself into such a position that he could do nothing else.

79 Document . . . des Grundsteins . . . St. Louis . . . 22. Juny 1842, Lossagung vom Stephanismus, MSS., C. H. I.

80 Stephan to B. Kurtz, March, 1833, Keyl to —, Sept. 19, 1838, Bound MSS., I, C. H. I.; Stephan to Walz, n. d. [Jan. 20, 1838?], Bound MSS., VI, C. H. I.; Stephan to G. H. Löber, Feb. 20, 1836, C. F. W. Walther to O. H. Walther, May 4, 1840, Lossagung vom Stephanismus, Bekenntniss, Document . . . des Grundsteins . . . St. Louis . . . 22. Juny 1842, Marbach, An meine . . . Landsleute, MSS., C. H. I.; Proceedings, July 30, 1838, Siebenhaar to the *Kreisdirektion,* Aug. 1, 1838, Bound MSS., Acten . . . Pester . . . *C. F. W. Walther,* C. H. I.; Proceedings, 13—17a, Bound MSS., Acten der . . . Superintendur Chemnitz, C. H. I.; O. H. Walther. *op. cit.* 3—16: Brief Outline of the Emigration Code, par. 2, Appendix B; C. F. W. Walther, in Köstering, *Auswanderung,* 10—12; Keyl, *op. cit.,* 12—14. See also the Stephanite conception of the Church and the discussion on that point.

results were highly deplorable.[81] Some maintained this attitude, left the colonies, or even returned to Germany. Others modified their opinion to the extent that they said the emigration was not wrong, but the manner in which it was carried out left a thing or two to be desired.

Chief spokesman for the latter group was C. F. W. Walther, whose revised view has since most frequently been adopted. Briefly stated, it rests on the following points: First, conditions in the Saxon Church were so bad as to justify emigration; secondly, there was no hope etiher that conditions would change for the better in the State Church or that the organization of an independent, "free" church would be permitted. From these premises it is concluded that the simple act of emigration was completely justifiable, even though some of its attendant features may have been unfortunate.[82]

---

[81] Marbach to — ("Hochgeehrter Herr Geheimrat"), May 8, 1840, Marbach to — ("Geehrte Frau Präsidentin"), n. d. [1839—1841], Marbach to Stübel, n. d. [1839—1840], Marbach to Fredrick Augustus II, May 10, 1841, Bound MSS., VI, C. H. I.; O. H. Walther, Predigt bei der von der Gemeinde angeordneten Bussfeier am Schlusse des Kirchenjahres d. 22. Nov. 1840 (hereafter cited as Predigt . . . d. 22. Nov. 1840), Unsigned and undated statement in C. F. W. Walther's hand, probably in preparation for the Altenburg Debate, Lossagung, Bekenntniss, Document . . . des Grundsteins . . . St. Louis . . . 22. Juny 1842, MSS., C. H. I. One of the strongest indictments of the emigration ("Even a heathen would be horrified by it,") is found in C. F. W. Walther to O. H. Walther, May 4, 1840, MS., C. H. I. See also G. H. Löber to G. F. Löber, Dec. 16, 1840, Aug. 26, 1841, in Löber-Eichenberg (ed.), "Ein Briefwechsel," *Mitteilungen . . . Kahla,* VII, 174—179, 184—190; E. M. Bürger, Selbstbiographie, 117, MS., E. J. Buerger Papers, Ellicottville, N. Y.; Bürger, *op. cit.,* 11—12; Vehse, *op. cit.,* 28; Keyl, *op. cit.,* 13—15. Köstering claimed that Keyl later revised his opinion on some points in his confession. This assertion may be true, but when Köstering stated further that the change was a result of the clarification of issues in the Altenburg Debate, he was mistaken by several months. For the Altenburg Debate had already taken place (April, 1841) when Keyl penned his confession (August, 1841). Keyl, *op. cit.,* 18—20; Köstering, *Keyl,* 41—42.

[82] This viewpoint was familiar already in Pleissner, *op. cit.,* 6; Lütkemüller, *op. cit.,* 41; G. H. Löber to relatives in Germany, Sept. 10—30, 1839, in Löber-Eichenberg (ed.), "Ein Briefwechsel," *Mitteilungen . . . Kahla,* VII, 156—162; Nachrichten an unsere Nachkommen, MS., C. H. I. The argument was presented by C. F. W. Walther as the theme virtually throughout the first part of his biography of J. F. Bünger, and it has been liberally adopted since. C. F. W. Walther, *Bünger,* 39—41; Köstering, *Keyl,* 41—46; L. Fürbringer in *Der Lutheraner,* LXXIV, 437; J. T. Müller, "Warum unsere Väter im Jahre 1838 das alte Vaterland verlassen haben," *ibid.,* XCIII, 279—280. This attitude is necessarily approved in some degree by all who allege purely religious motives in the emigration. A viewpoint more nearly approximating that represented in these pages is found in Mezger (ed.), *op. cit.,* 6—7.

On the basis of the facts already presented, the argument is open to several serious objections. In regard to the first point, if conditions in the Saxon Church demanded emigration in 1838, why had they not in years prior to that date? From the standpoint of the orthodoxists conditions were not substantially worse or even essentially different in 1836, 1837, or 1838, from what they had been in 1810, 1825, 1827, 1830, or 1833, as the complaints of Stephan and others in these earlier years have shown. In fact, one of the most drastic changes in the Saxon Church, and one against which the Stephanites rebelled most vigorously, came as early as 1812, with the revision of the *Agenda;* it did not occasion an emigration. In 1823 Stephan plainly asserted that there was no cause for leaving the fatherland, that there was no persecution.[83] In 1833 he admitted that the rights of the Lutheran Church, even as he saw them, were still respected in Saxony.[84] In fact, the assumption that conditions were becoming more intolerable during the decades when the anti-Rationalist movement of the *Erweckung* was in the ascendancy and religious conservatism was on the increase among the masses [85] is, on the face of it, a dubious one that would require the proof it never received. Certainly nothing occurred *in the Church* in 1836 or 1838 to crystallize the decision of Stephan and others. Orthodoxy was no worse off in these years than it had ever been within Stephan's memory. The only thing that changed vitally in the last years in Germany was Stephan's personal position.

Furthermore, whatever conditions were, they cannot be shown to have prompted any of the emigrants of 1838 except Stephan seriously to contemplate emigration prior to 1836. Löber's passing references to it in 1831 and his notes on religious conditions in America are the only indication that he was considering the matter.[86] No plans for emigration came from anyone else in the group but Stephan, even after 1836, and Hennig experienced some difficulty, as late as 1838, in persuading the Muldenthalers of the necessity of leaving.[87] The plan was launched at Stephan's instigation in 1836

---

[83] Stephan, *Herzlicher Zuruf . . . zwei Predigten,* 32.

[84] Stephan to B. Kurtz, March, 1833, Bound MSS., I, C. H. I.

[85] Fischer, *op. cit.,* 96; C. F. W. Walther in Köstering, *Auswanderung,* 4.

[86] G. H. Löber, Diary, Introduction to the year 1831, May 12, 1831, Remarks at close of 1835, MS., C. H. I.

[87] Hennig, "Die Auswanderung Martin Stephans," *Zeitschrift für Kirchengeschichte,* LVIII, 165.

and, because he failed to advance it,[88] lapsed until he revived it in 1837—1838, when he got into personal difficulties.

As early as 1833 some of the students delayed accepting a call into the Saxon Church, yet conscience scruples so serious as that failed to produce an emigration. Apparently C. F. W. Walther was even reassured about the condition of the Church, for he was inducted into office in 1837 after saying in 1833 that if the changes he then feared went into effect, "we could never enter the ministry, at least in Saxony (incl. Schönburg)." [89] While Walther and others were at odds with the authorities, who were plainly unsympathetic to their viewpoint, still others were on the best of terms with their superiors prior to the emigration. Löber, who was offered a more lucrative position if he would stay, admitted outright that he had met with no interference whatever in the discharge of his duties, even according to his own strict conception of them. Löber's objection was solely to "the spirit of the times," which was one of his favorite lamentations. Gruber had just as little cause for complaint on religious grounds.[90]

In summary of the policies and difficulties of all the pastors, the conclusion is justified that they were annoyed rather than "persecuted." Undoubtedly their clashes with the government and with their superiors indicated that their position was being made uncomfortable by men in authority who were opposed to their aims and views. However, it seems equally clear that they were not actually prevented from exercising any of the functions of the ministry which their own Confessions required of them. Therefore, a moral or spiritual *obligation* to emigrate as a matter of conscience

---

[88] E. M. Bürger, Selbstbiographie, 115, MS., E. J. Buerger Papers, Ellicottville, N. Y.; Keyl, *op. cit.*, 11. It was Stephan who insisted in 1831 that obedience to the authorities was no longer necessary, the Leipzigers who said it was. Candidate Kühn to O. Fürbringer, Feb. 29, 1832, MS., C. H. I. L. Fürbringer, however, finds in this lapse of two years between 1836 and 1838 proof that the emigration was "not hasty or rash." L. Fürbringer, "Vor hundert Jahren. Geistlicher Tod und geistliches Leben," *Der Lutheraner*, XCIV, 68.

[89] C. F. W. Walther to O. H. Walther, August, 1833, quoted in M. Günther, *op. cit.*, 15.

[90] *Chemnitzer Anzeiger*, Oct. 30, 1838; *Bedenken der theologischen Facultäten*, 3; The consistory of Saxe-Altenburg to G. H. Löber, Aug. 14, 1838, G. H. Löber to the consistory of Saxe-Altenburg, Aug. 24, 1838, quoted in *ibid.*, 30—35; Duke Joseph of Saxe-Altenburg to G. F. Löber, Sept. 25, 1838, Löber-Eichenberg (ed.), "Ein Briefwechsel," *Mitteilungen . . . Kahla*, VII, 131—133; G. H. Löber, Diary, Introduction to the year 1831, 1836, pp. 2, 12, MS., C. H. I.

cannot be demonstrated, however desirable an escape may have appeared to them.[91] Conditions were not unknown to the pastors of the emigration when they entered the service of the State Church; yet a year or several years later, as the case may be, these conditions, they declared, demanded the abandonment of their posts. The conclusion is therefore inescapable that another factor besides their strong antipathy to the liberalism about them prompted their severance of relations with the State Churches.

The second point, that no change for the better appeared imminent, is irrelevant so far as a motive for the emigration is concerned. For, if the pastors could enter the ministry in the State Church after years of serious consideration of the subject, why could they not continue in its service without such a change taking place? Certainly their acceptance of appointments could not have been predicated upon an expectation that circumstances would improve, when they were constantly insisting that matters were getting worse. The only plausible answer could be that a drastic change for the worse took place within the Church or that a change occurred within them. Neither is demonstrable.

Changes in the Church, or rather the lack of them, have been discussed above. Any new element in the relationship of dissident pastors and the Church must therefore have had its origin in the men and not in the institution. But if the conservatives were consistent, then a change in attitude toward the Church should have been conditioned entirely by changes within that body, for certainly their own doctrinal position was not modified. The absence of such changes should have stabilized, not disturbed, the situation. Yet even if it is assumed that they altered their position irrespective of developments in the Church, no evidence of such a revised position can be found except that they emigrated, and the emigration itself can hardly be considered as evidence in seeking causes for the emigration, unless the position is adopted that the movement was its own cause and provided its own justification.

Furthermore, neither Stephan nor any of the other emigrants ever gave formal notice to the authorities of a change in attitude or demands. L. Fischer asserted that none was given either during the

---

[91] While this conclusion is not based upon any single document or opinion, but upon the entire chain of events and set of circumstances attending the emigration, the same estimate of the situation is found in Marbach, An meine . . . Landsleute, MS., C. H. I.

pastors' tenure of office or even as a courteous word of explanation at the time of their resignation. Keyl for his part admitted the truth of this statement, and later many of the other emigrants accused themselves of not having taken the proper steps to obtain their demands from the authorities.[92] Under these circumstances the fact that no "improvement" in the Saxon Church appeared imminent would scarcely serve as a justification for emigration to men who had become its pastors under almost identical conditions.[93]

The statement that the organization of a "free" church was beyond the realm of possibility is a matter of pure conjecture, for such organization was never attempted by the Stephanites. The conservatives never applied for permission to form a "free" church, nor did they indicate to the government that this was what they sought. Rather, they insisted that the State Church should adopt their viewpoint, minority though they were. The analogy constantly drawn into the argument by the conservatives, at that time and later, as a conclusive demonstration that their alarms were justified and constructive efforts were hopeless, was that of the Prussian State Church, whose Union of 1817 was represented by them as a preview of what was about to occur in Saxony.[94] In the first place, this development and other changes anticipated were "about to" occur for too many years to be impressive as arguments any longer.[95] Secondly, the actual events in Prussia were the best answer to this analogy. For in that kingdom, to which the Saxons pointed in 1838 and from which Grabau and others emigrated in 1839, an independent church was organized with royal sanction in 1841. Responsi-

---

[92] *Ibid.;* Fischer, *op. cit.,* 122—123; Keyl, *op. cit.,* 15; G. H. Löber to the consistory of Saxe-Altenburg, Aug. 8, 1838, quoted in *Bedenken der theologischen Facultäten,* 28—29; O. H. Walther to Superintendent Leo, Aug. 28, 1838, O. H. Walther to the consistory at Glauchau, Aug. 28, 1838, Bound MSS., Acta, die anderweite Besetzung der Stelle eines Pastor vicarius zu Langenchursdorf mit dem Candid. Theol. Heinrich Theodor Füllkrus aus Waldheim betr. Ergangen bei der Ephorie Waldenburg ao. 1838. Litt. LII. No. 11. Rep. II. Vol. Loc. 1. (hereafter cited as Acta . . . der Ephorie Waldenburg), C. H. I.; Bekenntniss, MS., C. H. I.

[93] E. M. Bürger, Selbstbiographie, 117, MS., E. J. Buerger Papers, Ellicottville, N. Y. This fact was at one time admitted even by C. F. W. Walther. C. F. W. Walther to O. H. Walther, May 4, 1840, MS., C. H. I. See also Stübel to Vehse *et al.,* Sept. 12, 1839, Bound MSS., VI, C. H. I.

[94] Stephan to B. Kurtz, March, 1833, Bound MSS., I, C. H. I.; Protokolle über die . . . Auswanderung, April 14, 1838, Bound MSS., III, C. H. I.; Nachrichten an unsere Nachkommen, MS., C. H. I.

[95] At one time C. F. W. Walther recognized the faultiness of this analogy. C. F. W. Walther to O. H. Walther, May 4, 1840, MS., C. H. I.

bility for the fact that a free church was not organized in Saxony until a much later date must be placed in part upon the emigration of the country's most vigorous conservative element. The conservative critics of Stephan at the time pointed out that, while conditions were deplorable, they could not agree that such conditions justified the creation of a division in, or a separation from, the Church and the abandonment of everything for which the battle of the last decades had allegedly been waged.[96]

The existence of the religious motive must surely be recognized. But such an evaluation enjoys perspective only when it is clear that these religious sentiments and the action based upon them resulted from a distortion of the facts. Indeed, it must be admitted that the religion of the emigrants was not, as most of them believed, Lutheranism, which C. F. W. Walther said he desired to save by the emigration,[97] but Stephanism, which produced what the same man called in his own case "an erring conscience."[98] That is to say, the confessional position of Stephan may have been strict enough, sound enough, but that fact, as has been demonstrated, does not solely account for the emigration. Doctrinal disputes created the dissatisfaction which enabled Stephan to make the emigration attractive to his followers; he capitalized upon their natural aversion to "the shallow ethical rationalism of an officious ecclesiastical bureaucracy."[99] But it would be fatuous to claim that confessionalism alone prompted a course of action in 1838 which, on that basis, should logically and chronologically have occurred much sooner or not at all.[100]

The religious factor by itself had for decades been incapable of producing an emigration movement. "Conditions in the

---

96 Stübel to Vehse *et al.*, Sept. 12, 1839, von Uckermann to Marbach, Jan. 9, 1838, Bound MSS., VI, C. H. I.; Keyl, *op. cit.*, 13—14. Rudelbach's opinion is stated in *ibid.*, 1. See also Scheibel, *op. cit.*, 237, 247: Guericke, *Handbuch der Kirchengeschichte*, III, 344.

97 C. F. W. Walther to Sihler, Jan. 2, 1845, in L. Fürbringer (ed.), *op. cit.*, I, 6.

98 C. F. W. Walther, "Reisebericht des Redakteurs," *Der Lutheraner*, VIII, 107. See also Lossagung vom Stephanismus, Marbach, An meine . . . Landsleute, MSS., C. H. I.; *Anzeiger des Westens*, Dec. 31, 1842.

99 Maurer, "Studies in the Sociology of Religion, IV. The Problem of Group Consensus; Founding the Missouri Synod," *American Journal of Sociology*, XXX, 673.

100 C. F. W. Walther in Köstering, *Auswanderung*, 10; Marbach, An meine . . . Landsleute, MS., C. H. I.

Church," which the Stephanites nostalgically deplored, had not led to emigration. "Faithfulness to the Confessions," even as interpreted and volubly averred by them, had not led to emigration. The desire "to save themselves and the Church," which they alleged as their sole aim, had not led to emigration. All these considerations combined had not produced an emigration movement during a period of time when they were more valid than they were in 1838. Something else must finally have been the determining factor in making pastors and people willing, within the space of a few months, to follow a course of action from which they had recoiled for years. This factor was the reaction which Stephan's self-induced and self-styled "martyrdom" called forth in people who had previously fallen under the sway of his dominating personality.[101] The basic reason for the departure of the Stephanites from Germany was not a principle, it was a person — Stephan.

---

[101] E. M. Bürger, Selbstbiographie, 117—121, MS., E. J. Buerger Papers, Ellicottville, N. Y.; Fischer, *op. cit.*, 129—132.

CHAPTER FIVE

PLANNING AN AMERICAN ZION, 1837—1838

ONE OF THE IMPORTANT characteristics of the Stephanite emigration was the care lavished upon its organization.[1] Rarely has a private colonization enterprise of so large a group of people as the Saxons been planned in advance with such complete detail even in a period when careful planning was distinctive of emigration generally.[2] Yet all the arrangements for the departure from Germany, the plans for settlement in the United States, and the actual movement of the people were completed between December, 1837, and November, 1838 — a short period of eleven months.

The best example of careful planning was Stephan's own work in launching the project. After the meeting of 1836 he did not reopen the subject of emigration until December, 1837. Even then he discussed it with only a small number of individuals in Dresden, whose activities in behalf of the venture were controlled by him.[3] Not until these men had worked out a tentative plan in accord with Stephan's wishes was the idea broached in a somewhat wider circle of confidants, who were later to become the directors of the organization.[4] This small coterie, which carried on the preliminary conversations, consisted of three men: Marbach, who from December, 1837, until December, 1838, was Stephan's right-hand man; H. F. Fischer, the Dresden merchant; and Jäckel, henceforth the secretary for all official meetings and transactions. The discussion at

[1] The Codes, Appendix B; E. M. Bürger, Selbstbiographie, 116, MS., E. J. Buerger Papers, Ellicottville, N. Y.; Köstering, *Auswanderung*, 32. This careful organization was what distinguished this plan from similar ones before it that never materialized. Rosenthal, *op. cit.*, 51—56.

[2] Hansen, *op. cit.*, 151.

[3] Notes on a deliberation between M. F. and J., Dec. 6, 1837, Bound MSS., III, C. H. I.

[4] The development of the narrative will bear out this statement, despite the nonchalant remark of C. F. W. Walther: "Since everyone was already prepared for this eventual step, hundreds soon declared their willingness to follow the call." C. F. W. Walther in Köstering, *Auswanderung*, 12—13. Such a portrayal was correct so far as Walther was concerned, but not for "everyone," or even for the majority.

the meeting of these three men on December 6, 1837, gives an indication of the progress which the idea had made. The subject of their deliberation at that time was by no means whether there was to be an emigration, but what the detailed arrangements for it were to be. They decided among themselves upon the general outlines of the movement as Stephan had planned it. Then Stephan himself chose the members of an Advisory Committee (*Berathungscomite*).

Jäckel's "Notes on a deliberation between M. F. and J." of December 6, 1837, show that these three men had arrived at far-reaching conclusions. They were agreed on the destination and mode of travel, the organization of religious affairs of the group, and the financial structure of the proposed company before most other participants were permitted to discuss or approve the measures. According to the "Notes," the plans they developed under the first point were the following: An Emigration Association (*Auswanderungsgesellschaft*) was to be formed, and its members were to proceed by boat from Dresden to Hamburg on the Elbe,[5] except for those who had sufficient means to afford the added expense of traveling by coach or train. From Hamburg the emigrants were to take a chartered vessel to New Orleans, whence they were to continue their journey to St. Louis by steamboat. At the latter place the entire company was to secure shelter and employment while a site was being chosen for a colony in Missouri, Illinois, or Arkansas. The stay in St. Louis promised to be pleasant, for in that city, so they recorded in their minutes, "one can live cheaply if he maintains his own establishment; a whole house can be rented for very little, and foodstuffs are cheap." As a final touch to the rather minute arrangements for travel, it was stated that the emigrants were to be directed to take along eau de Cologne and Rhine wine for seasickness.[6]

On the second point, that of organizing religious affairs, the plans agreed upon on December 6, 1837, were equally detailed. The body of clergymen was to comprise a bishop and nine deacons. The vestments of the old Lutheran Church were to be used, which would distinguish the bishop from his subordinates and vary

[5] Notes on a deliberation between M. F. and J., Dec. 6, 1837, Bound MSS., III, C.H.I. Apparently the large contingent from Saxe-Altenburg and from Prussia, which later left from Halle, on the Saale River, was not yet committed to the plan at this time, so the Saale was not mentioned.

[6] Notes on a deliberation between M. F. and J., Dec. 6, 1837, Bound MSS., III, C.H.I. See also Brief Outline of the Emigration Code, par. 5, Appendix B.

according to the seasons of the year. Materials for the vestments and other supplies, such as altar vessels and sacramental wine, were to be taken along, together with an interesting piece of equipment known as a *Hostienbäckerei,* which consisted of implements for making the host used in the celebration of the Eucharist.[7] It is plain from the discussion of these men that the ecclesiastical structure of the colony was to be strictly hierarchical. The mention of a bishop on this occasion is probably the first official reference to the possibility of establishing an episcopacy among the Stephanites and was the normal outgrowth of planting the idea at the meetings in Dresden the previous year. The matter-of-factness with which the prospective episcopal polity is referred to, eliminates any element of surprise in the later development of the plan.

Financial arrangements were even more carefully worked out at this meeting on December 6, 1837. A common treasury was to be established to finance the emigration, to purchase land in the United States, and to conduct the administrative affairs of the group. The funds were to be contributed by the wealthier emigrants. Some of the money was to be lent to indigent but worthy applicants for admission to the *Gesellschaft,* in order to defray the costs of their transportation. The debtors were to pay no interest on the money advanced until they began earning again. Profits were to accrue to the investors from interest that would eventually be paid by the debtors, from the resale of land that was to be purchased, and from the interest that idle capital would draw from the banks in which it was to be deposited. Provision was already made for the distribution of these anticipated profits. Money and land were to be set aside for a city, a church, and a school. The money was to be placed in the "bank" (as they first called their common treasury), which was to exist as long as might be found necessary. Control over the fund would be exercised by a board chosen by the creditors. Since the planners expected that many of the debtors would not be able to write their own names, provision was also made for witnessing their admission of obligation to the "bank."[8]

---

[7] Notes on a deliberation between M. F. and J., Dec. 6, 1837, Bound MSS., III, C. H. I.

[8] The "bank" system gave rise to rumors that communism was being practiced among the Stephanites. *Chemnitzer Anzeiger,* Nov. 7, 1838. The later development of the idea shows that such rumors were incorrect. Brief Outline of the Emigration Code, pars. 8—9, and Code for the Credit Fund, Appendix B.

An examination of the various Codes under which the emigration was eventually effected will show how closely these first plans formulated by the three men who met on December 6, 1837, were subsequently followed by the other men who acted as leaders of the movement.[9] The deliberations of Marbach, H. F. Fischer, and Jäckel demonstrate the almost farcical character of many of the elaborate meetings held by the Advisory Committee, sessions held ostensibly to decide upon plans. Actually these meetings frequently were not called for the purpose of discussion, but to have a larger and supposedly more representative group adopt measures already decided upon, to assign duties to individuals, and to work out details.

Caution must be exercised in attributing too much originality to the ideas of Marbach, Fischer, and Jäckel, even before the Advisory Committee was formed. Stephan obviously had discussed the possibility of emigration with these men and others. He then took counsel with himself and reached his own decision. Thereafter the only problem was to get someone who would take action for him. The very fact that this triumvirate had been informed of Stephan's plan for emigration before the other members of the committee is an indication that Stephan felt that this was the group he could trust implicitly. His judgment was sound. In the subsequent meetings this small coterie consistently supported the pastor's views. Marbach, the most influential of the three men, constantly referred to what Stephan said and deferred to his wishes with only a single exception.

The first meeting of the larger group of leaders, or Advisory Committee, occurred on December 13, 1837, a week after the "deliberations" and exactly a month after Stephan's suspension.[10] The minutes of this meeting open with the words:

> The present distressed circumstances of the evangelical Lutheran Church and the presumable imminence of the moment when the Church [*die Kirche!*] must leave Europe make it imperative that several of its members, upon whose discretion, silence, and willingness to serve the Lord full reliance may be placed, come together to deliberate jointly on the measures to be taken under these conditions.

---

[9] The Codes, Appendix B.

[10] Protokolle über die . . . Auswanderung, Dec. 13, 1837, Bound MSS., III, C.H.I.

Our revered Herr Pastor Stephan has for the time being appointed the following for this purpose:

1. Herr Lawyer Marbach,
2. " Dr. Stübel,
3. " Candidate Brohm,
4. " Candidate Wälzel [*i. e.*, Welzel],
5. " Merchant Fischer,
6. " Farmer Gube,
7. the Cashier Jäckel (the undersigned),

who have all appeared today to take part in a discussion.

The above named are therefore commissioned to deliberate concerning the arrangements necessary for effecting an emigration and settlement in another quarter of the globe (in North America).[11]

Stephan had appointed Marbach to act as manager of the whole project under Stephan's own direction. For this first meeting Marbach had drafted a prospectus of the contemplated organization and a statement of the principles which were to guide the Advisory Committee. One of these principles emphasized that the members present at the meeting constituted an *advisory* committee, which as yet had no legislative or executive powers. The cardinal principle was: "The entire conduct of business will be carried on in accord with the orders of the Herr Pastor under the direction of Lawyer Marbach.[12] According to the minutes of the first meeting, participation in the deliberations of the committee in no way implied a commitment to emigrate. But the members did obligate themselves to take over such tasks as were assigned to them and pledged their "discretion, silence, zeal, and integrity" in performing them. At this meeting they agreed that all business was to be transacted in a "godly" manner, but they also decided, in more practical vein, that all "Christian admonition" should be eliminated from the dealings of the committee.

According to Marbach's prospectus, the business of the Advisory Committee had been divided into eight classifications and assigned to individual members of the committee. In accordance with this plan, the Advisory Committee entrusted ecclesiastical administration to Jäckel, the secretary of the committee. A separate

---

[11] *Ibid.*

[12] *Ibid.*

division was established for the "care of the person of the Herr Pastor." This important task fell to the lot of the least Stephanistic of the Stephanites on the committee, Dr. Stübel, who eventually remained in Germany. An understanding of his obligations and of the attitude of the members of the committee toward Stephan can be gained through the following extract from the minutes of December 13:

> Consideration of the general welfare of the Church and of the good of our own souls makes this care [of Stephan's person] the subject of highest importance; for every attention must be directed to caring for him who is the Most Reverend Archbishop of the Lutheran Church.
>
> To this department, therefore, is assigned the task of establishing with all possible tact the most effective means for the maintenance and care of the Herr Pastor, establishing a definite set of rules for carrying out those measures, and, as far as possible, applying them now already; it is also to draw up a special set of rules for his care while the Church is on its journey.[13]

Dr. Stübel assumed these exacting duties only after protesting his inability to meet the requirements of the office of protector of the "archbishop."

The Advisory Committee, at its first meeting, left the formulation of "a school and church code [14] for the journey" to Candidates Brohm and Welzel. It decided that there were to be a "library, archives, and chronicles." But since it hoped that Dr. Vehse, who was eminently qualified to head this division, would still be won for the plan of emigration, a provisional arrangement was made which designated Brohm librarian, Stübel archivist, and Welzel chronicler. All matters pertaining to agriculture were entrusted to Gube, who, at that time, was the only farmer on the committee. Merchant Fischer was made responsible for traveling regulations. He was to attend to the necessary commercial transactions, make contracts for the river and ocean vessels that would transport the emigrants and their baggage, assure everyone's prompt arrival, and arrange for crossing state boundaries. Marbach was placed in charge of two

---

[13] *Ibid.*

[14] The German word is *Ordnung,* a term rather pliable in its usage and meaning. It was a favorite with the Stephanites, who employed it freely, especially in compounds. Usually it means a "code" or "constitution," or, less formally, a "set of regulations."

important branches of the committee's activities: the "bank," or common treasury, and the general "emigration code." The purpose of the latter department was to edit and compile all other sets of regulations and codes when the men assigned to them had done the preliminary work. Furthermore, this department (*i. e.,* Marbach) was empowered, at least for the time being, to decide who would be accepted into the *Gesellschaft* and who would be rejected. Admission was to be made difficult, and no one was to be solicited to join.[15] Marbach's tenure of these two positions virtually made him director of the movement.

The structure of the organization as outlined at this first meeting on December 13, 1837, was later modified but never fundamentally altered. The personnel of the Advisory Committee changed from time to time, and the balance between Stephan and the committee, and between the divisions within the committee, varied, but the main features of the plan were permitted to stand. Under the stipulations of this plan the *Auswanderungs-Gesellschaft* was organized, all of its affairs were administered, and the actual movement of people was achieved.[16] The original arrangement remained in effect until the *Gesellschaft* was entirely disrupted in the United States. Even then the outlines of the original structure were clearly reflected in the reorganization which took place. The system was thoroughly hierarchical in both its political and ecclesiastical aspects. The Advisory Committee was developed along the lines of a political cabinet responsible only to the head of the movement, Stephan. The important members of the committee, or cabinet, held portfolios and referred to themselves as department *chefs.*[17] The deliberations of the committee were strictly secret; and while the individual members were at liberty, in organizing their departments, to call upon other trustworthy members of the *Gesellschaft* for assistance, they revealed to their subordinates only what it was necessary for the latter to know in order to carry out specific tasks. The committee was not elective or representative in any way, and the tenure of

---

[15] Protokolle über die . . . Auswanderung, Dec. 13, 1837, Bound MSS., III, C. H. I.; Brief Outline of the Emigration Code, par. 11, Appendix B.

[16] Comparison with the various Codes shows how closely the original plan was followed. The Codes, Appendix B.

[17] Protokolle über die . . . Auswanderung, Dec. 13, 1837, Bound MSS., III, C. H. I.

office of its members depended entirely upon the pleasure of their chief, Stephan, who had appointed them.

Through this Advisory Committee, Stephan accomplished a double purpose: he shifted much of the work and some of the responsibility for the emigration to others, while still retaining complete control. The ecclesiastical and secular affairs of the people who joined him he still dominated in the minutest detail. Marbach practically (for a time, actually) lived with Stephan during the next year, carrying out his policies and following his instructions. In turn, Marbach dominated the committee, both by his control of two of its most important departments and by his chairmanship of the committee itself. Stephan could depend upon Marbach to override any sporadic opposition which might arise. At its first meeting on December 13, 1837, the Advisory Committee established an *Expedition,* or secretariat, with Jäckel at its head. This secretariat became the clearinghouse for all correspondence, issued orders, and performed the indispensable routine work. Again a minor detail shows how thorough was the organization of the committee and how it regarded itself, its functions, and its authority: a certain Klemm, a lackey at the court, was appointed *"Kanzlei-Bothe"* or messenger of the chancellery.[18]

After its organization the Advisory Committee did not meet in plenary session for over two months. Then, on February 15, 1838, it held another session, with only two changes in personnel — Gube was not present, but Vehse had been drawn in.[19] The first question to come before this session was: "Is there anything that remains to be done to maintain ourselves any longer in Europe?" The fact that such an issue could arise at this time, and the treatment it received in the committee meeting, indicate that the spontaneity often claimed for the idea of emigration among the prospective participants did not exist. Not even among Stephan's hand-picked martinets was there consensus on the fundamental issue of whether the step was necessary, and strong handling of the discussion was required. Suggestions by Stübel and Welzel for an appeal to the king or to one of the departments of the government were brusquely overruled by Marbach, despite the fact that in order to attain other objectives more suitable to Stephan this very procedure was fol-

---

18 *Ibid.*

19 *Ibid.,* Feb. 15, 1838.

lowed on several later occasions. The committee obediently reached the conclusion: "All steps have been taken, all possibilities exhausted. Nothing is to be done any more from which a favorable result might be expected." Thereupon the related question was immediately raised: "Shall a passive attitude be adopted, or shall action be taken at once to effect the emigration?"[20]

The discussion of this second point occupied the remainder of the session on February 15 and all of the one on the following day. All the reasons advanced for immediate action concerned themselves with Stephan, and these were the considerations which finally won the day. Proceedings in Stephan's case had been allowed to lapse, but it was reported to the committee that the investigation was now being resumed and that the end was not in sight. The opinion of the Advisory Committee was that the action would be continued intermittently, so long as nothing further was proved against the Bohemian pastor, in order to show he was guilty of something more serious than had thus far been established, and thus retroactively, at least, to justify the action taken against him previously.[21] Stephan was represented to the committee as a persecuted martyr, who was on the verge of starvation and physical breakdown. He was expected to support his wife, eight children, and a grandchild on an income reduced to 400 thaler per year. His health was suffering, for he had been in virtual confinement for three months. Stephan's very life was in danger, it was claimed.[22] The pastor had been convinced of the necessity of emigration for years, Marbach asserted, and now all efforts must be directed toward moving "the Church" from Germany.[23]

Of the Stephanites who formed the committee, Stübel was the most independent. He inquired of Marbach what had become of Stephan's assurances, presumably made in palmier days when the emigration was not so "necessary," that God would show them a solution to their difficulties.[24] Marbach's rejoinder was that

---

20 *Ibid.*

21 *Ibid.;* Bemerkungen über . . . Stephan, Bound MSS., V, C. H. I.

22 Protokolle über die . . . Auswanderung, Feb. 15, 1838, Bound MSS., III, C. H. I.

23 *Ibid.*, Feb. 16, 1838.

24 *Ibid.* See also Stübel to Vehse *et al.*, Sept. 12, 1839, Bound MSS., VI, C. H. I. This letter contains a rather complete and clear statement of Stübel's attitude and is an impressive indictment of the emigration.

preparation for leaving did not preclude the possibility of such deliverance still coming. His real argument, however, was that Stephan had said: "Waiting now is merely wasting time." This statement clinched the case, for on that basis immediate action was endorsed by all but Stübel, who would say only that he would defer to Stephan's viewpoint and not vote against it. However, Marbach informed Stübel that such an attitude was unsatisfactory; whole-hearted agreement was demanded. Stübel was finally prevailed upon to submit; he did not wish to counsel delay if such serious consequences were involved in a situation which had been pictured as so hopeless, for he was told: "The pastor's health and his very life are at stake, and with them the chief means of grace for us." It was then decided, on Stephan's recommendation, to make cautious overtures to the civil authorities, so that their consent to a peaceful departure of the emigrants might be obtained.[25]

Sentiment in favor of immediate preparations for departure received further stimulus at a meeting of the Advisory Committee on February 19, 1838, from a report by Vehse, the newest member of the committee, who enjoyed the confidence of a person represented as being close to the civil authorities investigating Stephan's case. The allegedly authoritative opinion of this unnamed individual was that even if Stephan were fully absolved of the charges still lodged against him, his exoneration would by no means lead to his reinstatement in office. Furthermore, it was quite possible that other criminal suits or disciplinary proceedings might be instituted. Accordingly, the original viewpoint, that further delay was inadvisable and that steps should be taken to assure the safety of Stephan, was strengthened.

The committee adopted the following conditions as the basis on which to negotiate with the officials for permission to emigrate:

I. Free, unobstructed departure in a quiet manner, assured through visas for Pastor Stephan and those who feel in conscience bound to accompany him of their own volition.

II. Retirement with a pension for Pastor Stephan, who has been in office for twenty-eight years, with special consideration for the extraordinary circumstances obtaining and for his large family: a wife and eight children; seven

[25] Protokolle über die . . . Auswanderung, Feb. 16, 1838, Bound MSS., III, C. H. I.

girls [(] among them three deaf-mutes [ )] and one son, [—] the youngest child (a deaf-mute girl) [being only] nine years old.

III. Adequate guarantees of security.

IV. Complete quashing of all proceedings, including the assessment of costs.[26]

Direct discussions with the officials were to be carried on by Marbach and Vehse, who were given complete freedom of action without further report to the committee, provided they acted under instructions from Stephan. Vehse's anonymous friend was to be approached with these conditions and solicited to present them as his own proposals if he approved them.[27] A week later Vehse reported that these negotiations were proceeding satisfactorily.[28] This initial optimism later proved unjustified.

When the committee met on February 27, it devoted most of its time to a discussion of finances, for Marbach had pointed out that funds were becoming indispensable. The plan for the "bank" was reviewed and was left essentially the same as outlined above. At this time the intention seems to have been that only the "bank," or the "Credit Fund" as it now came to be called, was to be permitted to buy land, and that all members of the *Gesellschaft* were to buy only from it.[29] The problem of transferring funds to the United States without loss led Marbach to suggest the creation of a commercial company. The intention was to have this company invest all surplus money in goods of various kinds that might be taken on the ships as freight and then resold on arrival in the United States. He was certain that in this way no loss would be incurred. The advice of the American consul in Dresden later prevented carrying out this plan.

Financial arrangements reached their most embarrassing stage in the more practical question of where the money for the Credit Fund was to be obtained. It became apparent that among the half dozen departmental *chefs* present no more than 4—5,000 thaler were

---

[26] *Ibid.*, Feb. 19, 1838.

[27] *Ibid.*

[28] *Ibid.*, Feb. 27, 1838.

[29] The ultimate plans for the purchase and distribution of land are stated in the Brief Outline of the Emigration Code, pars. 6, 9, Code for the Credit Fund, pars. 2—4, Regulations for Settlement, ch. I, pars. 1—6, Appendix B.

available, that this amount came from only two members of the group, and that the bulk of this modest sum actually belonged to Vehse's nine-year-old daughter. It was further estimated that the farmers who would join could be counted on for about 20,000 thaler. The resulting total, not exceeding 25,000 thaler, did not nearly approach the financial standards that had been set up for the *Gesellschaft.* Originally 100 thaler per person had been considered adequate to cover traveling expenses to St. Louis.[30] Later the committee was to return to this figure. But at the time of this discussion of finances, on February 27, the committee estimated that 300 thaler would be required per person. Although only about one hundred persons were expected to join, such an estimate meant that 30,000 thaler would be necessary for traveling expenses alone. To this sum would have to be added about 35,000 thaler, which would be necessary to carry out their plan of purchasing an entire township. The total of 65,000 thaler was about 40,000 thaler more than the committee could obtain. No solution of the problem seems to have been forthcoming at this time, but Fischer, Vehse, and Jäckel were appointed as administrators of the prospective Credit Fund. The question of whether the further burden of the costs for the Church should be placed upon this fund, already inadequate, gave rise to a dispute which reached no conclusion and was therefore deferred to Stephan for "decision." [31]

By March 2, 1838, a reorganization of the departmental arrangement became necessary; three days later it was completed.[32] Ecclesiastical affairs were taken out of the hands of a layman and given to several of the candidates. Gube had not been present since the first meeting; hence his department was turned over to Jäckel. Stübel, who had been absent for several meetings, was replaced by Vehse. One of the departments was divided into three branches. On March 5, 1838, the assistants to the department *chefs* were also selected. Thus the completed reorganization provided for the following departments and personnel:

---

30 Protokolle über die . . . Auswanderung, Feb. 16, 1838, Bound MSS., III, C. H. I. Mrs. Vehse had died and the orphaned Vehse daughter was now being cared for by Agnes Bünger, who had also nursed the mother in her last illness. L. Fuerbringer, *80 Eventful Years,* 14.

31 *Ibid.,* Feb. 27, 1838.

32 *Ibid.,* March 2, 5, 1838.

Department	Department Head	Assistants
I. Ecclesiastical Affairs	Brohm and Welzel	"The other candidates not included in the committee"
II. Care of Stephan	Vehse	Candidate Bünger and Artist Pfau
III. School and Church	Brohm and Welzel	The other candidates
IV. Travel Bureau	H. F. Fischer	Stärtzell, Nitzschke, and Marbach
V. Traveling Regulations	H. F. Fischer	Stärtzell, Nitzschke, and Marbach
VI. Disciplinary Rules	Vehse	Bünger and Pfau
VII. Agriculture	Jäckel	Gube
VIII. Library, Archives, and Chronicles	Vehse	Brohm and Welzel
IX. Credit Fund	Marbach	Stübel and Brohm
X. General Emigration Code	Marbach	None

Each of the departments was to draw up and submit to the chancellery a code governing that phase of affairs entrusted to it. A draft of each code would then be forwarded to each department for criticism and suggestion. The annotated copies would be returned to the chancellery, which, in turn, would present the net results to a plenary session of the Advisory Committee for further criticism. The final product was to be the Emigration Code, embracing the work of all departments. All members of the *Gesellschaft* were to be required to submit to the Emigration Code *in toto*, including the provision that obedience would be rendered to ordinances not yet passed.[33]

Thus the subject of departmental organization was definitely settled. The only changes made thereafter were in personnel and in the virtual consolidation of several closely related departments. During April the following were added to the committee: Baron

[33] *Ibid.*

von Uckermann, who was anxious to have a hand in drawing up a constitution for the community; Tax Official Barthel, who agreed that "now it was no longer possible to serve God the Lord in the right way in Saxony";[34] and Candidate Fürbringer, who was assigned to work on the Ecclesiastical Code.[35] The two laymen were made corresponding members; the candidate was granted full membership. None of the three lived in Dresden. From time to time, when one of the pastors associated with the movement was in Dresden, he was admitted to the meetings without question; [36] and when it was absolutely necessary, a few of the wealthier laymen were also asked to sit in and approve a major expenditure.[37]

By March, 1838, Stephan was in more serious difficulties than ever. The acrimony of some of his opponents during these months is matched by his own bitterness in describing their activity.[38] On March 10 the consistory decided to deprive him of control over the business affairs of the congregation.[39] Accordingly, on March 15 the superintendent in Dresden directed Stephan to turn over all his papers, primarily his financial accounts, within eight days. On March 20 this order reached Stephan, who filed a protest on March 27, in which he claimed that he was innocent of wrongdoing and declared that he was merely yielding to superior force.[40] While this action was being taken, Vehsé procured an audience with Fredrick Augustus II, in which the representative of the *Gesellschaft* explained the injustice of the prolonged and inconclusive proceedings against Stephan and informed his sovereign of the

[34] *Ibid.*, April 14, 1838. One purpose of von Uckermann's visit to Dresden at this time was to apologize to Stephan for having entertained doubts as to the latter's integrity. Von Uckermann to Marbach, Jan. 9, 1838, Bound MSS., VI, C. H. I.

[35] Protokolle über die . . . Auswanderung, April 25, 1838, Bound MSS., III, C. H. I.

[36] E. M. Bürger and Keyl are examples. *Ibid.*, May 2, June 12, 1838.

[37] *Ibid.*, Sept. 27, 1838. Strange to say, the manuscript for the minutes of this very important meeting, contained in the bound collection constantly cited, is not an original, but a contemporary copy in Jäckel's hand. However, the original, with the authentic signatures is found in Bound MSS., No. 6. Belege zur Cassenführung des Herrn Fischer in Dresden (hereafter cited as Bound MSS., 6), C. H. I. See also Protokolle über die . . . Auswanderung, March 9, 23, 1839, MSS., C. H. I.

[38] Stephan to Schwabe, March 29, 1838, Bound MSS., VI, C. H. I.

[39] Protokolle über die . . . Auswanderung, March 24, 1838, Bound MSS., III, C. H. I.

[40] *Ibid.;* Protest of Stephan to Superintendent Heymann, March 27, 1838, Bound MSS., V, C. H. I.

plan of emigration. Vehse requested the king either to decide the case himself or to bring about a speedy decision on the part of the proper authorities. Very gracious and even friendly, the ruler expressed his personal esteem for Stephan and accepted the written petition presented by Vehse; he observed, however, that he could not take any action himself, since he acted only through his ministers.[41] Thus Vehse's efforts were unavailing; the old days of Anton and von Einsiedel were over. The committee naturally felt that the outcome of Vehse's interview with the king was a vindication of Marbach's insistence that no further effort to effect a *rapprochement* with the authorities be made before resorting to emigration. The king, it was agreed, was impotent, his ministers were hostile, and plans for emigration would have to be accelerated.[42]

In April, 1838, a little specific information concerning the United States also began to reach the committee, whose ideas about this country had heretofore been incorrect or scanty.[43] Prior to April 14 the minutes of its meetings contained little about America aside from assurances that there no longer was any need to be afraid of the Indians,[44] the misconception that living was cheap in St. Louis,[45] and the thumbnail description: "Characterization of an American: A greedy indifferentist." [46] Then, however, the committee learned that living was about as "cheap" in St. Louis as in Dresden and that, since they expected to arrive in winter, the emigrants would have to maintain themselves several months before establishing a settlement. On April 14 the committee came to the following conclusion: "Settlement in Missouri is not yet definitely decided upon. The slave trade there and the prevailing lynch law (the violence of the vulgar rabble) give rise to serious doubts." [47] However, the committee considered Cincinnati "the most beautiful city in America." [48]

---

41 Protokolle über die . . . Auswanderung, March 24, 1838, Bound MSS., III, C. H. I.

42 *Ibid.*

43 This lack of information on the United States was prevalent in Saxony at that time. Rosenthal, *op. cit.*, 43—44.

44 Protokolle über die . . . Auswanderung, Feb. 16, 1838, Bound MSS., III, C. H. I. Some critics of the Stephanites were not as certain as they that Missouri was a safe place. Fischer, *op. cit.*, iv.

45 Notes on a deliberation between M. F. and J., Dec. 6, 1837, Bound MSS., III, C. H. I.

46 Protokolle über die . . . Auswanderung, Feb. 16, 1838, *ibid.*

47 *Ibid.*, April 14, 1838.

48 *Ibid.*, April 25, 1838.

The first direct contact with St. Louis came through Mr. Kimm, a businessman from that city who was visiting his native Dresden during the spring of 1838. Marbach and others consulted with him while he was in Dresden and corresponded with him after he returned to the United States.[49] Kimm gave them considerable help; and it may be fairly surmised that much of the more accurate information reaching the committee at this time originated with him. His firm, Kimm & Tewes, of St. Louis, was of service to the *Gesellschaft* after the Stephanites arrived in the United States; and it was Kimm who recommended the house of Frey & Company, which, for a time, became the commercial agent for the emigrants in New Orleans.[50] Finally, through Kimm they hoped to establish contact with a former Stephanite, Mr. Leonhardt, a smith from Dresden then living on a farm in St. Clair County, Illinois, whom Stephan considered using as an agent in that area.[51]

Kimm left Dresden by May 23, 1838;[52] but even before his departure the committee established contact with another American, Mr. Rivinus, then the United States consul in Dresden.[53] Rivinus was not at all chary with his advice and rudely upset some of the favorite schemes of the committee. He advised that the emigrants take the Hamburg route rather than the one via Bremen and that they travel on "Boston ships" because a more pious spirit prevailed among their crews; furthermore, he counseled decidedly against the trip by water from New Orleans to St. Louis. Marbach's plan of investing the available capital in goods for resale in the United States the consul considered a particularly bad piece of outright speculation liable to result in a loss. With regard to the site for a settlement, Rivinus advised strongly against Missouri because, in his opinion, fever was prevalent there. Only those with the most robust constitutions survived, he asserted; all others rapidly died off. He believed that the best areas for settlement were northern Illinois, Indiana, Ohio, and Michigan, the last being the most de-

---

49 Marbach to Kimm, May 23, 1838, Marbach to Spröde, May 24, 1838, Marbach to Kimm & Tewes, Sept. 14, 1838, Bound MSS., I, C. H. I.

50 Marbach to Kimm, May 23, 1838, *ibid.*

51 Marbach to Spröde, May 24, 1838, *ibid.*; Protokolle über die . . . Auswanderung, April 28, 1838, Bound MSS., III, C. H. I.

52 Marbach to Kimm, May 23, Bound MSS., I, C. H. I.

53 Protokolle über die . . . Auswanderung, May 11, 1838, Bound MSS., III, C. H. I.

sirable. He ruled out Wisconsin because of the danger from the Sioux Indians.[54]

The unfavorable impression of Missouri, created by Rivinus, was dispelled a week later by Kimm, who insisted that Missouri was, as a matter of fact, a very healthful place in which to reside, although he admitted that it would cost a person about three dollars a week to live in St. Louis. (He had certainly not placed the figure too high.) The committee decided that the consul, in making his recommendations, was probably influenced by his government to represent conditions as he had.[55]

The committee established another connection with the United States when it received a letter in April, 1838, from the Mr. Spröde referred to above, then a successful baker in New York City. When Spröde had found that his religious views differed not only from those prevalent in the churches of Germany, but from those in the United States as well, he had founded a small sect which conducted its affairs according to instructions provided by Stephan. A room had been rented for reading services, and a congregation had been founded which attracted a few score people, most of whom had originally come from Berlin. In 1838 this small band of dissenters contemplated moving farther west in a body. Spröde, of course, had been in correspondence with Stephan, although not with the committee, before the spring of 1838 and apparently was also acquainted with Marbach.[56] The Dresden committee welcomed the contact with Spröde for the possible use it might be to them, and presently he was being spoken of as one of them despite the apprehensions of Vehse as to his trustworthiness.[57] Accordingly, when Kimm left Dresden to return to St. Louis, he bore a letter and a set of instructions to Spröde in New York.[58]

---

[54] *Ibid.*

[55] *Ibid.*, May 18, 19, 1838. Michigan was the most popular area for settlement by immigrants from Germany just at this time. Faust, *op. cit.*, I, 464.

[56] Marbach to Spröde, May 24, 1838, Bound MSS., I, C. H. I.; Protokolle über die . . . Auswanderung, April 25, 1838. Bound MSS., III, C. H. I.; G. Günther, *op. cit.*, 37; C. F. W. Walther, *Bünger*, 51—52; *Anzeiger des Westens*, Dec. 31, 1842.

[57] Protokolle über die . . . Auswanderung, April 28, 1838, Bound MSS., III, C. H. I.

[58] *Ibid.*, April 28, May 2, 19, 1838; Marbach to Kimm, May 23, 1838, Marbach to Spröde, May 24, 1838, Stephan and Marbach, Instruction für Spröde und seine Freunde, zum Vorausziehen nach St. Louis im Staate Missouri, n. d. [May 24, 1838] (hereafter cited as Instruction für Spröde), Bound MSS., I, C. H. I.; G. Günther, *op. cit.*, 37.

These communications give a clear idea of the progress which had been made in the emigration arrangements by the spring of 1838. Approximately three hundred emigrants now planned to leave Saxony by way of Hamburg (by October, 1838, at the latest) for settlement in Missouri, Illinois, or Indiana. Details of the movement, according to these communications, were still to be shrouded in secrecy, even to Kimm, so that information on the large number of emigrants and exaggerated ideas about their prosperity would not lead to speculation at their expense in St. Louis or en route. The prospect was held out to Spröde that he might become the "spy in the land of Canaan" for the emigrants. To the instructions drawn up by Stephan, Spröde was to subject himself with "humbleness, simplicity, and care." Such demands, high as they may seem, probably did not appear excessive to people who had assured Stephan of their adherence to him "in need and death."[59]

The thirteen points of Stephan's instructions to Spröde laid the basis for close co-operation between the Saxon and New York groups and for the eventual amalgamation of the latter with the former. Spröde, according to these instructions, was to send two agents ahead to St. Louis to prepare the way for moving the other New Yorkers to the West. This transfer was to be carried out as soon as the advance agents had procured gainful employment for an appreciable number. In any event, the Spröde group was to proceed to St. Louis before the Stephanites arrived. If employment and lodging for so many people could not be found in time to have them all well established in St. Louis when the Stephanites landed there, the New Yorkers might be placed in towns and on farms in the vicinity. However, the two agents, at least, were to remain in the city.

These agents, with the help of the firm of Kimm & Tewes and of Leonhardt, were to inquire about steamboat facilities, lodging, and employment for an additional three hundred people in St. Louis and on neighboring farms, and about the possibilities of purchasing an entire township for the proposed colony. Frequent communication directly between Stephan and Spröde, as long as they were still in Dresden and New York respectively, was provided for. After the end of September, when Stephan no longer

---

[59] Marbach to Kimm, May 23, 1838, Marbach to Spröde, May 24, 1838, Stephan and Marbach, Instruction für Spröde, Bound MSS., I, C.H.I.

expected to be in Dresden and Spröde was no longer to be in New York, contact between the two men was to be maintained through the commercial representatives of the Stephanites, Frey & Company in New Orleans and Kimm & Tewes in St. Louis. In these instructions special care was taken to impress upon Spröde the necessity of having suitable quarters available for Stephan himself, although they were not actually to be rented before Stephan's arrival, just as no contracts of a definite nature were to be made by the New Yorkers on their own authority.[60] Late that summer Spröde made a trip to Germany to confer personally with Stephan and the other leaders.[61]

Even before these instructions were issued, during April, 1838, some money had come in to the committee, and it instructed Vehse to have such funds placed at interest in Leipzig, although H. F. Fischer of Dresden was really to be responsible for them.[62] By this time it was possible for the committee to make a more reliable estimate of the expense of the journey and to outline specific arrangements for the trip, which, in general, were surprisingly similar to those ultimately made. The prices which had been quoted the Advisory Committee for fare from a German port to New Orleans were approximately 45 thaler in gold for a steerage passenger and about 95 to 100 thaler for a cabin passenger. Rates for children were less, and for a larger company, such as the committee was representing, a general reduction was usually given. These rates included all the food except wine.

Inquiries by the committee revealed that the average ship carried 150 to 170 passengers, and a large one perhaps two hundred. Beds for use on board ship had to be taken along by the passengers. A maximum of fifteen cubic feet of baggage per passenger could be shipped without charge. The committee felt that, in order to control the amount of freight that would be taken along, baggage receipts would have to be issued to each individual by the *Gesellschaft*. No agricultural implements were to be transported, the committee decided, for it had learned that those in use in the United States

---

60 *Ibid.;* Marbach to Kimm & Tewes, Sept. 14, 1838, *ibid.*

61 Spröde to Marbach, Oct. 12, 1838, Kimm & Tewes to Marbach, Dec. 10, 1838, *ibid.;* G. Günther, *op. cit.*, 37; *Anzeiger des Westens*, Dec. 31, 1842.

62 Protokolle über die . . . Auswanderung, April 14, 1838, Bound MSS., III, C. H. I.

differed from those employed in Germany.[63] The agricultural department was thus relieved of some of its most important duties, although it was still active in other respects. For instance, correspondence of several months later shows that it was making inquiries about crops which might be suitable in the emigrants' new home.[64]

Meanwhile, approximately at the same time that the first money was coming in, the committee's plan for land purchase was also beginning to take more definite shape. In the committee meetings of March and April the policy was formulated that the proposed *Gesellschaft* was to acquire an entire township of 23,040 acres, in the hope of preserving a degree of political autonomy.[65] The Credit Fund was to offer this land for sale to the members of the *Gesellschaft,* no one of whom was to hold less than thirty nor more than three hundred acres.[66] Consequently the maximum amount of land that might be owned by a group of one hundred (the number anticipated at the time of these arrangements) could not exceed ten thousand acres, and the *Gesellschaft* could look forward to having a considerable portion left for resale at a profit.[67] Later the policy of purchasing an entire township was reaffirmed and the purpose expressed "that, according to the Herr Pastor's plan, a model for ecclesiastical and Christian community relationships might be established in the settlement." [68]

In May Marbach reported cryptically to the Advisory Committee that "someone" was contemplating purchasing a large tract of land close to whatever site would be chosen by the Stephanites, and that the settlement to be established on this additional land

---

63 *Ibid.*

64 Teufel to H. F. Fischer, July 6, 1838, Bound MSS., I, C. H. I.

65 Protokolle über die . . . Auswanderung, March 25, April 14, 1838, Bound MSS., III, C. H. I.; Stephan and Marbach, Instruction für Spröde, Bound MSS., I, C. H. I.; Bekenntniss, MS., C. H. I.; *Chemnitzer Anzeiger,* Oct. 30, 1838. See also Regulations for Settlement, Code for the Civil Community, Appendix B.

66 Protokolle über die . . . Auswanderung, April 14, 1838, Bound MSS., III, C. H. I. These stipulations were later modified. Regulations for Settlement, ch. I, pars. 1—2, Appendix B.

67 Notes on a deliberation between M. F. and J., Dec. 6, 1837, Protokolle über die . . . Auswanderung, Dec. 13, 1837, Bound MSS., III, C. H. I.; Code for the Credit Fund, par. 4, Appendix B.

68 Protokolle über die . . . Auswanderung, May 11, 1838, Bound MSS., III, C. H. I.; Code for the Civil Community, Appendix B.

might then become an affiliate, or branch, of the Stephanite colony.[69] In fact, the leaders of the Stephanites were looking forward to the day when their activity in the United States would broaden out and when the proposed colony would become a nucleus for further colonization by German emigrants, for Stephanite expansion in a spiritual and material way, and for the maintenance of German culture.[70]

In the eyes of the committee primary considerations in the choice of a location for this settlement were to be: climate, healthfulness, fertility of the soil, proximity to a stream and to a larger city, and the topography of the region, which was to resemble that of the Grimma-Rochlitz area in Saxony. With a view to shortening the interim in St. Louis, the committee debated the advisability of sending agents ahead to make inquiries for a location, although such agents were not to conclude a contract.[71] Eventually this plan was not followed, except for the action taken by the New York group.

On May 18, 1838, the Emigration Code was presented to the Advisory Committee in the presence of Stephan and was unanimously adopted.[72] The question of what the Emigration Code was, has never been satisfactorily answered.[73] Some points regarding it are still not quite clear, but a more accurate estimate of its nature can be given now than heretofore. The only available document of this nature is actually headed "Brief Outline of the Emigration Code." [74] The phrasing of the caption could lead to the assumption that there was another document called the "Emigration Code," which was longer and more complete than this one. Actually it is

---

69 *Ibid.* Perhaps Baron von Uckermann was the "someone." See E. L. Krause to Stephan, Oct. 2, 1838, Bound MSS., II, C. H. I.

70 Protokolle über die . . . Auswanderung, April 28, May 11, 1838, Bound MSS., III, C. H. I. See also Regulations for Settlement, ch. I, Code for the Civil Community, Appendix B; Document . . . des Grundsteins . . . St. Louis . . . 22. Juny 1842, MS., C. H. I.; Vehse, *op. cit.,* 33—34.

71 Protokolle über die . . . Auswanderung, April 14, 1838, Bound MSS., III, C. H. I.

72 *Ibid.*, May 18, 1838. The document itself was signed the preceding day. Brief Outline of the Emigration Code, Appendix B. As the preceding pages have shown, the Credit Fund was actually in operation and accepting contributions before this date, not only afterwards, as stated in Th. Gräbner, *op. cit.,* 7.

73 Even Vehse, a member of the committee, was not clear on this point. Vehse, *op. cit.,* 5.

74 Brief Outline of the Emigration Code, Appendix B.

probable that this Brief Outline is the only form in which a comprehensive single code, covering all phases of the emigration, ever existed, for as a document an "Emigration Code" was intended to be no more than an outline. In fact, it would have been absurd to make it more than that, since the detailed codes for the various fields of activity were still being worked out by the individuals designated by the committee.

Other evidence also supports this viewpoint. The drafting of an emigration code was a function of Marbach's department, who made plans and gave directions. The task of developing what Marbach sketched was left to others. Furthermore, the Brief Outline of the Emigration Code was adopted before the other codes. The Code for the Credit Fund, for instance, which was drafted by May 19, 1838, was not adopted until five weeks later, on June 25.[75] One of the detailed codes, that for ecclesiastical organization, apparently was never worked out in full.[76] It seems reasonable to assume that the "Emigration Code," as presented on May 18, 1838, was what its later title indicated, an outline. From this other sets of regulations based upon it were then developed to varying degrees. It seems less likely that individual detailed codes were later separated from a single, all-inclusive code and adopted one by one after the major document had already been approved and had rendered any others unnecessary. Besides, it was simpler to have the people read and sign one brief code which pledged obedience to all others than to have them sign five additional ones separately. Of course, it is doubtful that this signing ever took place, but such was the intention at the time.

The ideas which seem to the writer to be the most acceptable are that all separate sets of regulations were known collectively as the "Emigration Code"; that on the basis of early plans and discussions in the Advisory Committee, Marbach quickly sketched an outline of the fundamentals upon which all regulations were to be

---

[75] Protokolle über die . . . Auswanderung, June 25, 29, 1838, Mound MSS., III, C. H. I. A translation of this code, the "Order of the Treasury of the Lutheran congregation emigrating with Pastor Stephan to the United States of North America," probably made during the course of the suit by Stephan, 1841—1842, bears the date May 19, 1838. Bound MSS., Fasc. IV, No. 4. Gemeinde Verfassungs Sachen (hereafter cited as Bound MSS., IV), C. H. I.

[76] The only form in which this code is known to exist is: "Grundzüge zu einer Kirchenverfassung," supposed to have been written by Stephan quoted in Köstering, *Auswanderung,* 37—38.

based; and that all but one of these, the Ecclesiastical Code, was worked out in full later. In fact, the Brief Outline of the Emigration Code definitely pledges the signers "to subject themselves with Christian sincerity and willingness to the ecclesiastical and civil codes which are to be established." [77] It is worthy of note that the one most urgently needed, the Code for the Credit Fund, is the only detailed code of which there is any definite record of official adoption in the minutes of the Advisory Committee.[78] The reason for the failure to work out the Ecclesiastical Code in detail is most likely that the structure of the Church as Stephan intended it required the establishment of the episcopacy. The adoption of this form of church polity was not achieved until the *Gesellschaft* arrived in St. Louis. All other codes were completed; and the numerous stipulations for the regulation of church affairs which they contain, together with the afore-mentioned sketch by Stephan, make possible a fairly accurate estimate of what the plans for the Church were.[79]

From a comprehensive view of the codes, it is plain that the intention was to found a semiautonomous theocratic community.[80] Power was to be divided largely between the clergy and a privileged wealthy class, with the balance clearly in favor of the former. Furthermore, in the ministerium the final authority was obviously intended to rest with "the primate," or, to give a more literal translation of the term employed, "the first divine." (Stephan had not yet publicly assumed the title of Bishop.) Of interest is the curious mixture of the patriarchal and the progressive. The plan for the city would probably have been an improvement on anything in the field of municipal development in the United States at the time.[81] Nor is there much doubt that Stephan would have seen to its execution. On the other hand, the stipulation that excommunication from the Church entailed loss of political rights and banishment from the colony, deprived the group of any right to claim the intention of

---

[77] Brief Outline of the Emigration Code, par. 3, Appendix B.

[78] Protokolle über die . . . Auswanderung, June 25, 29, 1838, Bound MSS., III, C. H. I.

[79] C. F. W. Walther claimed this code was begun as early as 1836, but agreed that it was never put into final form. C. F. W. Walther in Köstering, *Auswanderung*, 8—9.

[80] This intention was known also in Germany. *Chemnitzer Anzeiger*, Oct. 30, 1838.

[81] Regulations for Settlement, ch. II, "Plan of the City," Appendix B.

practicing the tolerance for which they themselves clamored.[82] Their proposed labor laws, with an eight-hour day, were a hundred years ahead of their time,[83] but a censorship of the press as strict as that for which they provided had probably never been known in American local government.[84] Municipally supported recreation centers, such as they envisioned,[85] were at best a rarity in the United States in 1838; but a solemn pledge of submission to all future legislation, however it might be enacted,[86] was unknown in American history. Generally, however, the codes only carry out in greater detail the principles and practices whose development has been indicated from time to time. The features which have not been discussed are those which belong to the subsequent narrative.

What Stephan — as the chief, if not the sole, architect of the system of the Codes — intended for his followers, required only a slightly greater submissiveness than John Eliot had expected to demand of the Indians two hundred years earlier:

> Before entering upon the new form of government, men would covenant together, confessing "their corruption by nature," acknowledging "the free grace of God, in their redemption" and promising "to give up themselves unto him to be forever his" and to receive from the Lord "both the platform of their Civil Government as it is set down in holy Scripture; and also all their Laws," making the word of God "their only Magna Charta." With such a covenant, and with the word of God to be interpreted only by the rulers, the individual would need a deep and abiding faith in God and in his immediate rulers. But, of course, this is a Christian utopia wherein only Christians might dwell, and Christians according to his [Eliot's — Stephan's?] lights.[87]

---

[82] Code for the Civil Community, pars. 3, 15, *ibid.*

[83] Regulations for Settlement, ch. III, *ibid.*

[84] Code for the Civil Community, par. 13, *ibid.*

[85] Regulations for Settlement, ch. II, par. 3, *ibid.*

[86] Brief Outline of the Emigration Code, par. 3, *ibid.*

[87] Parrington, *American Dreams,* 9.

CHAPTER SIX

ORGANIZATION OF THE "AUSWANDERUNGS-GESELLSCHAFT"

"No hope remains for maintaining the Lutheran Church in our land." [1] Sentiments similar to these had come from Stephan's lips or pen before the committee meeting of May 18, 1838, but never under quite such significant circumstances. The meeting of May 18 was not just another meeting. It was the meeting which marked the end of the period of planning and the beginning of an effort to put these plans into execution. Talk — from the committee, that is — of which Stephan had heard (or read) enough to satisfy him for some time, could now give way to action. Action, it must be admitted, was imperative from Stephan's standpoint, in view of his worsening personal position, which will be described presently. Any further work on "codes," and the like, could be done later; the one that counted had been adopted on this very day. If the committee was left to deliberate, to draft codes, and to find new places in which to settle, there was no telling when or whether they would ever decide the time had come to emigrate. For Stephan the time was now. Someone needed to make decisions. The words quoted were Stephan's way of letting the committee know these facts of committee life. The committee understood.

There was little discussion at this meeting. Instead, there was a lecture by Stephan, using as a point of departure some of the more important subjects included in the Emigration Code, with which he shared the center of the stage on this day. A tirade against conditions in Germany crystallized in the judgment cited above. He then went on to comment on the location for the Stephanite's new home, making no effort to conceal a considerable animosity against the British.[2] He asserted that in England Lutheranism was barely tolerated, that Australia was so wild no one was ever safe

[1] Protokolle über die . . . Auswanderung, May 18, 1838, Bound MSS., III, C. H. I.

[2] This tendency is noted also in Vehse, *op. cit.*, 3.

from the attacks of marauders, and that the entire British Empire was honeycombed with dissatisfaction; in fact, Stephan seems to have considered the British Empire in imminent danger of dissolution. Consideration of the personal and religious liberties enjoyed in the United States seems to have left little doubt in the minds of Stephan and his followers as to their general destination.[3] Vehse gives as another reason for the choice of America the low price of land in the United States; but prices were probably just as attractive in a number of other places.[4]

In the meeting of May 18 Stephan also commented on the question of accepting the "unconverted" into a theocratic community. The plan of accepting dissident religious elements was not clearly stated in the Brief Outline of the Emigration Code and seems to have been rejected in the Code for the Civil Community, but at this time the idea was heartily endorsed by Stephan. The apparent anomaly of admitting into the organization some of the people from whom the emigrants allegedly were trying to escape was explained away by the prospective bishop in a series of similes. The Church, said Stephan, was not only the nurse of the newborn, but also the mother of the unborn. Why this maternal function could not be performed as well in Germany as in the United States he did not disclose, but he did remark with unusual equanimity: "One must accept the Church as it actually is." [5]

In April and May, 1838, legal skirmishes between Stephan and the police continued; so it was decided to engage an attorney for the pastor. Up to this time Marbach had been acting as counsel for Stephan;[6] but the former was now fully occupied with the emigration, and a practicing attorney, preferably a "non-Stephanist," was required.[7] Furthermore, since the early part of 1838 Marbach and other leaders of the emigration were no longer certain that

---

[3] Brief Outline of the Emigration Code, par. 2, Appendix B. "Where else shall we go but to North America?" — Marbach to Walz, Jan. 12, 1838, Bound MSS., VI, C. H. I. See also Hennig, "Die Auswanderung Martin Stephans," *Zeitschrift für Kirchengeschichte,* LVIII, 165—166.

[4] Vehse, *op. cit.,* 3—4.

[5] Protokolle über die . . . Auswanderung, May 18, 1838, Bound MSS., III, C. H. I. See also Brief Outline of the Emigration Code, Code for the Civil Community, Appendix B.

[6] Marbach to Walz, Jan. 12, 1838, Bound MSS., VI, C. H. I.

[7] Protokolle über die . . . Auswanderung, April 25, May 11, 1838, Bound MSS., III, C. H. I.

their mail was uninspected and preferred to receive even their private letters through the offices of the merchant Fischer.[8] Finally, someone with full power of attorney had to be left behind to attend to the joint interests of the *Gesellschaft* as well as to the private affairs of Stephan and his family, whom Stephan apparently had already decided to leave behind. The expenses connected with the pastor's litigation were to be defrayed by the Credit Fund if the consent of the contributors could be obtained, especially that of Baron von Uckermann, who promised and later gave financial support.[9] Consequently a lawyer named Wigard was first requested to take the case;[10] but when for some unstated reason his services were not available, Attorney W. E. Krause was retained.[11]

Krause's first case was a suit by Stephan to retain the rentals from some church property which the pastor had let to two of his friends, Gustav Pfau and the Günther family. Stephan's claim that the income was his "by contract with the congregation" was challenged by the elders, who, during the previous December, had given the tenants notice to move. When Pfau and Günther did not comply, the elders secured an order from the municipal courts that required the property to be vacated in three days.[12] It also fell to Krause's lot to prepare in advance a defense for the pastor against the charges which were certain to result when Stephan resumed his visits to the vineyard (as he deliberately intended to do, in defiance of the order against it), on the grounds that his health demanded it. On April 17, 1838, Stephan's congregation, under the leadership of Precentor Marks, demanded the pastor's complete removal from office on the grounds of alleged financial irregularities.[13]

---

8 Marbach to Walz, Jan. 12, 1838, Stephan to Schwabe, March 29, 1838, Bound MSS., VI, C. H. I.

9 Protokolle über die . . . Auswanderung, May 11, 1838, Bound MSS., III, C. H. I.

10 *Ibid.*, April 25, 1838.

11 *Ibid.*, May 11, 1838.

12 *Ibid.*, April 25, 1838; Petition of Stephan to the Dresden municipal court, April 23, 1838; MS., C. H. I.

13 Protokolle über die . . . Auswanderung, May 11, 1838, Bound MSS., III, C. H. I.; Hennig, "Die Auswanderung Martin Stephans," *Zeitschrift für Kirchengeschichte*, LVIII, 163. On July 5, 1838, these charges were supplemented with further complaints from the congregation against Stephan on grounds of immoral conduct and neglect of official duties. M'Clintock-Strong, *Cyclopedia*, IX, 1008. The feud between Stephan and this element in his congregation is a recurring theme in the documentation contained in the Hanewinckel Notes, MS., C. H. I.

Most of the time in the Advisory Committee's meetings during April and May, 1838, was taken up with wrangling about the ships and the route to be taken. The majority of advisers and correspondents of the committee had warned against chartering a ship, since this procedure required special arrangements and was more expensive than regular travel. But Baron von Uckermann expressed the opinion of the committee when he said that he did not consider it wise to risk the overloading which so frequently occurred on commercial vessels. Two points created most of the difficulty: First, were the emigrants to travel via Hamburg or via Bremen? Secondly, were they to go directly to New Orleans and thence by river to St. Louis, or was it more advisable to go directly to New York and then proceed overland to St. Louis? The pros and cons of these questions were argued at great length and were finally even drawn up into an itemized list, balancing the advantages of Hamburg against those of Bremen.[14] The arguments in favor of Hamburg were rather strong. Hamburg, for instance, offered direct riverboat connection via both the Saale and the Elbe, and required one or two less transfers of passengers and baggage than the Bremen route; Hamburg was the more important port for emigration to the United States at this time; most Hamburg ships went directly to New York, Baltimore, and similar ports on the northern and central Atlantic seaboard, a route which would be cheaper and shorter than the long voyage which would be necessary if the journey were made by way of New Orleans.[15] The only real argument against Hamburg was that some of the leaders had planned on the New Orleans route for a long time and few Hamburg ships went to Gulf ports. Despite the listing of advantages and disadvantages the members of the committee were still undecided; so it was agreed that after the list had been circulated once more and discussed at another meeting,[16] the question was to be submitted to Stephan for decision.[17]

---

[14] Protokolle über die . . . Auswanderung, April 25, 1838, Bound MSS., III, C. H. I.

[15] *Ibid.*, April 28, 1838. Havre was also considered as a port of embarkation, but was rejected because of the expense involved in taking that route. *Ibid.*

[16] *Ibid.*

[17] *Ibid.*, April 25, 1838.

Accordingly Stephan appeared at a meeting of the Advisory Committee for the first time on May 2, 1838.[18] The full extent of Stephan's control over the group is plainly indicated in the course of this session. It seems that the itemized list of considerations and the subsequent discussion on April 28 had clarified the problem in the minds of the committee members, for barely had the meeting opened when they passed a resolution not to take the New Orleans route under any circumstances, whether they went via Bremen or Hamburg.[19] For the reason stated above, such a decision also implied a preference for the latter city as a port of embarkation. Thereupon Stephan took the floor; and before the session was over, the committee, at his insistence, had completely reversed itself and decided to make the trip entirely by water. The arguments Stephan employed to effect this change were primarily two: first, a discrediting of the advice of Spröde, whom Stephan himself had recommended to the committee; and secondly, the plea that he, Stephan, did not wish to travel "a single mile" by land with a company of about three hundred people, including eighty children, because it would be difficult to keep them together on an overland journey, "and he absolutely does not want a separation of the flock, it must remain together." [20]

The wishes of Stephan were also followed in determining the actual itinerary, as well as in all other subjects discussed. Since the committee still planned on leaving from Hamburg, it would be necessary to go via New York, because direct connections between Hamburg and New Orleans did not exist. Though it was frankly agreed in the meeting that the overland journey from New York to St. Louis would have been only about two thirds as expensive as the longer route via New Orleans, the committee nevertheless decided to take a coastwise vessel from New York to New Orleans and then proceed by steamboat up the Mississippi. Everything was done to satisfy Stephan's demand for water transportation and his insistence that "safety and comfort are to be preferred to

---

[18] Probably this and the other meetings in May and June are those referred to by L. Fischer. But when he gives this as the time at which the emigration was decided upon, he is several months late. Fischer, *op. cit.*, 52.

[19] Protokolle über die . . . Auswanderung, May 2, 1838, Bound MSS., III, C. H. I.

[20] *Ibid.*

anything else." [21] Because of the peculiarity of the route, all advice against chartering a ship had to be disregarded. It is obvious that this meeting, which negatived the result of extended and careful deliberation and inquiry, was completely dominated by Stephan. Toward the end of the session there was no longer any discussion; the procedure had degenerated into a mere ratification of a series of so-called resolutions which Stephan had "decided upon." [22] Not until after this meeting were some of the keymen outside of Dresden notified that a definite resolve had been taken to leave. Löber was not certain until May 13 that there would even be an emigration; then Fürbringer brought the news.[23]

The connection of the Saxon emigrants with their agent in Bremen, Otto Hagemann, dated from early June, 1838, and that relationship was to continue intimately for more than a year. Kimm, on his return to St. Louis through Bremen, had advised Hagemann to establish contact with Marbach.[24] At the same time Kimm himself wrote to Marbach and recommended a ship then under construction, the *Olbers,* which, it was then expected, would be completed by the latter part of September. Kimm reported that the *Olbers* could be contracted for through the firm of J. D. Lüdering & Company, ship brokers, whose printed set of conditions for travel he enclosed in his letter to Marbach.[25] Hagemann, too, in a letter to Marbach on June 6, 1838, wrote favorably of the *Olbers,* a three-master represented as capable of carrying three hundred passengers, the exact number planned on at this time. The committee was so impressed with these recommendations that in less than a week it decided to charter the vessel.[26] It is likely that this contact with Bremen shipping interests, established through Kimm, was the final,

---

21 *Ibid.* Stübel and Vehse also commented on Stephan's complete lack of self-sacrifice for the cause he claimed to represent. Stübel to Vehse *et al.,* Sept. 12, 1839, Bound MSS., VI, C. H. I.; Vehse, *op. cit.,* 7.

22 Protokolle über die . . . Auswanderung, May 2, 1838, Bound MSS., III, C. H. I.

23 Excerpts from G. H. Löber's Diary, May 13, 1838, MS., C. H. I.

24 Hagemann to Marbach, June 6, 1838, Bound MSS., I, C. H. I.

25 *Ibid.;* Protokolle über die . . . Auswanderung, June 12, 1838, Bound MSS., III, C. H. I.; "Bedingungen der Ueberfahrt von Bremen nach den Vereinigten Staaten von . . . J. D. Lüdering." Such a set of conditions or terms from a few years before this time has been translated in Bek, "The Followers of Duden," *Missouri Historical Review,* XIV, 42—46.

26 Protokolle über die . . . Auswanderung, June 12, 1838, Bound MSS., III, C. H. I.; Hagemann to Marbach, June 6, 1838, Bound MSS., I, C. H. I.

deciding factor in favor of the Bremen route, since as late as May 24 Hamburg was still Marbach's preference.[27] In view of the fact that conditions for emigrants were very much better in Bremen after 1832 than in most other European ports, the ultimate decision probably was fortunate.[28]

Two agents, Marbach and Fischer, were chosen by the committee to go to Bremen to conclude negotiations and secure a contract after the preliminaries had been arranged by mail.[29] Hagemann, in a letter to Marbach, had mentioned the matter of a cash deposit on the contract, which was to call for a fare of 40 to 42½ thaler per person.[30] However, money was no longer an obstacle to the Stephanites, for the first receipts from the group at large — 4,000 thaler from the Lunzenau-Seelitz contingent — had been sent in by Pastor Bürger.[31] The printed set of conditions which Hagemann had sent did not answer all the questions arising in the committee, so that Marbach made numerous inquiries in his first letter to Hagemann, dated June 14.[32] Besides the normal matters of business which had to be cleared up, Marbach also asked Hagemann whether there would be a ship's doctor aboard and how long a period would be allowed for embarkation; at least a fortnight was requested.[33] The number of emigrants was rising above three hundred, and Hagemann was instructed to keep available another ship that might be chartered for the still indefinite number in excess of three hundred.[34]

Only a few days later, on June 20, Hagemann admitted that the *Olbers* would hold no more than 240 passengers. In reply to the other questions he said that he had another ship in view that would accommodate one hundred and eighty passengers at the same price as that now definitely fixed for the *Olbers* — 42 thaler for

---

27 Marbach to Spröde, May 24, 1838, Bound MSS., I, C. H. I.

28 Wittke, *op. cit.,* 117.

29 Protokolle über die . . . Auswanderung, June 12, 1838, Bound MSS., III, C. H. I.

30 Hagemann to Marbach, June 6, 1838, Bound MSS., I, C. H. I.

31 Protokolle über die . . . Auswanderung, June 12, 1838, Bound MSS., III, C. H. I.

32 Marbach to Hagemann, June 14, 1838, Bound MSS., I, C. H. I.

33 *Ibid.;* Protokolle über die . . . Auswanderung, June 12, 1838, Bound MSS., III, C. H. I.

34 Marbach to Hagemann, June 14, 1838, Bound MSS., I, C. H. I.

steerage passengers and 90 thaler for cabin passengers, with board included in both cases.[35] When the committee learned of these terms, it decided to accept them at once, and instructed Marbach and Fischer to leave for Bremen to close the deal for at least the *Olbers*. The requisite cash was to be taken from the Credit Fund.[36] Marbach thereupon informed Hagemann of the decision to take the *Olbers* and complimented the agent for obtaining terms "so cheap." [37] The committee issued final instructions to Marbach and Fischer as a result of meetings on June 29 and July 2; final important business was transacted at the second of these sessions, the day before the agents left.[38] The committee's disposition of the funds available did not augur well for the economical administration of finances. Passage was to be booked for no fewer than forty cabin passengers, although their fare would total almost half as much as that of the remaining two hundred steerage passengers. Furthermore, the two representatives were given a very generous allowance for expenses.[39]

Marbach and Fischer left Dresden by train at seven o'clock on the evening of July 3, 1838, bound for Leipzig. Two days later they set out from Leipzig for Hamburg by way of Halle and Magdeburg, traveling by post to Magdeburg and leaving for Hamburg by boat on the seventh. They stayed in Hamburg until noon on July 11, when they proceeded to Bremen. They remained there until nine o'clock in the evening of July 16, and then departed for Berlin. A day and a half later they left Berlin on their return trip to Dresden.[40] Upon arriving in Dresden, Marbach learned that one of his children had died during his absence.[41]

---

[35] Hagemann to Marbach, June 20, 1838, *ibid.*

[36] Protokolle über die . . . Auswanderung, June 25, 1838, Bound MSS., III, C. H. I.

[37] Marbach to Hagemann, June 26, 1838, Bound MSS., I, C. H. I.

[38] Protokolle über die . . . Auswanderung, June 29, July 2, 1838, Bound MSS., III, C. H. I.

[39] *Ibid.*, July 2, 1838.

[40] The itinerary can be traced from a collection of receipts for the expenditures made, which are contained in Bound MSS., 6, C. H. I. Expenses for the two men on the trip totaled 179 thaler and 20 groschen. *Ibid.;* Bound MSS., No. 5. Acta, Berechnungen über Reise- Fracht- Elb- Weser- und See-schiff-fahrts- Proviant- Zehrungs- und dergleichen Kosten während und nach der Auswanderung enthaltend (hereafter cited as Bound MSS., 5), C. H. I.

[41] Hagemann to Marbach, Aug. 7, 1838, Bound MSS., I, C. H. I.

The contract for the *Olbers,* dated July 14, 1838,[42] was drawn up and signed by representatives of the various interests concerned: F. and B. Delius, owners of the *Olbers;* the ship brokers, J. D. Lüdering & Company; the commercial agent and Bremen representative of the *Gesellschaft,* Otto Hagemann; and the two deputies of the Advisory Committee, F. A. Marbach and H. F. Fischer. The general terms to which the parties pledged themselves were those in Lüdering's printed set of conditions. Lengthy stipulations were made about the date of sailing, but these became useless when eventually neither party adhered to the terms of the contract. The capacity of the ship, according to the contract, was only two hundred passengers. The fares from Bremen to New Orleans were somewhat reduced from the figures previously agreed upon. The cost for steerage passengers was 40 thaler; for cabin passengers it was 85 thaler if there were no more than nineteen, and 80 thaler if the number reached twenty.[43] The Stephanites had an ample quota of cabin passengers to get the lower rate. The sum of 2,100 thaler was paid as earnest money.[44]

With the chartering of the *Olbers,* the emigration movement reached a definite stage of its development. The closing of a contract for the first ship had a finality about it that did not escape even those who were very close to events. Consequently other preparations were promptly made for the emigration, which were equally decisive. On July 2, 1838, before Marbach and Fischer left Dresden, the Advisory Committee had resolved to send out instructions to the clergymen to ask their respective governments for releases from office. At the same time the pastors were to send to Dresden lists of those people in their congregations who were prospective emigrants together with certain detailed information on each colonist, including a statement of the capital each one possessed.[45] On the same day Fischer made a report which indicated that negotiations were

---

42 Passage Contract for the Olbers, July 14, 1838, MS., C.H.I. The contract was not signed on July 13, nor were five ships hired at this time, as stated in C. F. W. Walther, *Bünger,* 42; Th. Gräbner, *op. cit.,* 3, 7.

43 Passage Contract for the *Olbers,* July 14, 1838, MS., C.H.I.

44 *Ibid.* This figure is substantiated in the Summary of ship contracts MS., C.H.I. Elsewhere it has been given incorrectly as 2,300 thaler. Th. Gräbner, *op. cit.,* 3.

45 Protokolle über die . . . Auswanderung, July 2, 1838, Bound MSS., III, C.H.I.

already under way with the "firm of Weber" in Dresden for chartering one or more Elbe River boats to take the emigrants to Hamburg by water.[46]

But one of the main effects of chartering the *Olbers* was that the movement had to, and was now ready to, come out into the open. Of course, the efforts which had been made to maintain secrecy[47] were not completely successful even before that time. Cartoons of the raid which led to Stephan's suspension from office were on sale throughout Dresden. The city and its vicinity were filled with rumors. Articles on Stephan and the Stephanites had become more numerous ever since the pastor's suspension and were carried by newspapers outside Saxony as well as within the country.[48] Before it all was over, the furore created was so great that a careful student of the European phases of migration to America ventured the opinion: "Few bands of emigrants have ever received the publicity that contemporary observers bestowed upon the Stephanites — followers of Martin Stephan, the religious mystic of Dresden."[49] Difficulties with the law provided sensational news in the latter months, when Stephan for a time was placed under house arrest, with two guards stationed in his room day and night.[50] At approximately the same time open attacks on Stephan began to recur in the press. Lütkemüller began with an article in the *Leipziger allgemeine Zeitung* and continued with the publication of his *Lehren und Umtriebe der Stephanisten.*[51] The Stephanites threatened to institute a lawsuit because of Lütkemüller's attacks.[52]

---

46 *Ibid.*

47 Marbach to Kimm, May 23. 1838, Marbach to Spröde, May 24, 1838, Stephan and Marbach, Instruction für Spröde, I, C. H. I.; Keyl, *op. cit.*, 12.

48 Jäckel to Stephan, Aug. 29, 1838, Bound MSS., I, C. H. I.; Öhrling to G. H. Löber, Sept. 14, 1838, Öhrling to Marbach, Oct. 12, 1838, Bound MSS., II, C. H. I.; Bemerkungen über . . . Stephan, Bound MSS., V, C. H. I.; Walz to Marbach, Dec. 10, 1837, Jan. 3, 1838, Walz to Stephan, Dec. 9, 1837, MSS., C. H. I.; *Leipziger allgemeine Zeitung,* Nov. 22, 1837, July 24, 1838; *Vereinigtes Wochenblatt Rochlitz, Geithain, Geringswalde, Hortha und Waldheim,* Sept. 29, 1838; *Chemnitzer Anzeiger,* Oct. 30, Nov. 7, 1838; Scheibel, *op. cit.*, 247; Lütkemüller, *op. cit.*, 23.

49 Hansen, *op. cit.*, 136.

50 Marbach to O. H. Walther, Oct. 16, 1838, Bound MSS., I, C. H. I.

51 The original essay of Lütkemüller, "Öffentlicher Unfug," is reprinted in his book. Lütkemüller, *op. cit.*, 35—61. This article was supplemented with another in the *Leipziger allagemeine Zeitung,* No. 218, 1838. Lütkemüller, *op. cit.*, 6—7. The book was completed on September 20, 1838. *Ibid.*, 34.

52 *Ibid.*, 6—7, 19—22.

However, contemporary publications did not all oppose the Stephanites. The same paper which printed Lütkemüller's essay, had, as early as November 22, 1837, made an honest attempt to do the movement justice and on July 24, 1838, in an article from its Dresden correspondent, printed the following observations:

> In order to evaluate the motives [of the emigrants] properly, one must, of course, entirely disregard the great mass of those to whom all talk about religious conviction no longer applies, and whose training leads them to consider it an unforgivable folly to make a sacrifice for conviction, most of all the sacrifice of one's very existence and of pecuniary advantage. Similarly, those who place no value on the positive confession of any definite faith will be unable to appreciate this resolve.[53]

To what extent the news traveled by word of mouth is difficult to determine, but an idea can be gained from the experience of Town Councilor Franz Seidel of Wildenfels. Without telling anyone of his decision to emigrate, he went to Dresden for a few days to make arrangements with the leaders of the *Gesellschaft* for his departure. Nevertheless, when he returned home, the news of his plans for emigrating was common property in Wildenfels.[54] According to the Stephanites, their movement was an organized emigration of a large group of people motivated by religious considerations, and as such was a phenomenon which had not appeared in the history of the German states for a hundred years.[55] Wherever this view was shared, the news of the Stephanites' decision to emigrate created a sensation. In fact, at this time emigration from Saxony for any reason was not frequent, and while the movement was on the increase, it still affected only individuals or families and was not organized and carried out by groups or associations.[56] Accordingly, interest in the Stephanite emigration was naturally great simply because it was a novelty; it was strengthened by the economic conditions of the time, which have been described above. Exaggerated rumors about the *Auswanderungs-Gesellschaft* circulated

---

[53] *Leipziger allgemeine Zeitung,* Nov. 22, 1837, July 24, 1838.

[54] Seidel to Marbach, Aug. 17, 1838, Bound MSS., VI, C. H. I.

[55] *Chemnitzer Anzeiger,* Oct. 30, 1838; Marbach to Walz, Jan. 12, 1838, Bound MSS., VI, C. H. I.

[56] Rosenthal, *op. cit.,* 24—26, 33—37; Fischer, *op. cit.,* iii; C. F. W. Walther, *Bünger,* 44; *Bedenken der theologischen Facultäten,* 2; Hennig, "Die Auswanderung Martin Stephans," *Zeitschrift für Kirchengeschichte,* LVIII, 164—165.

in Dresden and spread to other cities and localities. For example, four thousand acres of land were said to have been bought by advance agents; as many as six hundred people were reported enrolled; and the ships were already supposed to be loaded, over three months before the actual emigration.[57]

During more than half a year, from the beginning of the committee meetings to the day on which the *Olbers* was chartered, the number of people on whom the leaders definitely depended as emigrants increased from one hundred to two hundred. And even at the end of that period the maximum considered possible was four hundred.[58] In fact, however, during the nineteen days from August 15 to September 4, 1838, the total soared from a possible four hundred to an actual "over seven hundred."[59] An increase of several hundred would have strained the capacities of the organization even had it occurred over a period of months; but when the addition of three hundred came within a few days, the emigration movement got out of hand, and postponements in the date of sailing, drastic rearrangements, and some confusion resulted. Obviously the imperative necessity was the hiring of more ships; and it is a credit to the leaders in Dresden and their agents in Bremen that by the middle of August arrangements were virtually complete for two more ships, the *Johann Georg* and the *Copernicus,* both large threemasters plying between Bremen and New York, the former having just returned from her maiden voyage. Together with the *Olbers* these ships could accommodate 514 passengers.[60] By October 5, 1838, the chartering of the little emigrant fleet was com-

---

[57] Jäckel to Stephan, Aug. 29, 1838, Marbach to O. H. Walther, Oct. 16, 1838, Bound MSS., I, C. H. I.; *Leipziger allgemeine Zeitung,* July 24, 1838; *Chemnitzer Anzeiger,* Oct. 30, 1838; Pleissner, *op. cit.,* 9; G. Günther, *op. cit.,* 46.

[58] Protokolle über die . . . Auswanderung, Dec. 13, 1837, Bound MSS., III, C. H. I.; Passage Contract for the *Olbers,* July 14, 1838, MS., C. H. I.; Marbach to Hagemann, Aug. 15, 1838, Bound MSS., I, C. H. I.

[59] Marbach to Hagemann, Aug. 15, 1838, Jäckel to G. H. Löber, Sept. 4, 1838, Bound MSS., I, C. H. I. The figure 707 is given in the financial statement of Sept. 4, 1838, Bound MSS., VI, C. H. I.

[60] Sauer to Marbach, Aug. 22, 1838, Marbach to J. D. Lüdering, Aug. 28, 1838, Marbach to Döderlein, Aug. 29, 1838, Hagemann to Marbach, Aug. 29, 1838, Fehrmann to Marbach, Aug. 23, Sept. 2, 1838, Bound MSS., I, C. H. I.; Contract for the *Copernicus,* Sept. 11, 1838 (on the reverse side of a copy of "Bedingungen der Ueberfahrt von . . . J. D. Lüdering"), MS., C. H. I. Although the actual contract for the *Johann Georg* apparently has not been preserved, the date for it is given as Sept. 3, 1838, in the Summary of ship contracts, MS., C. H. I.

pleted with the hiring of the *Republik* and the *Amalia.*[61] The last two ships procured were smaller vessels, carrying 110 and seventy passengers respectively.[62]

On August 23, 1838, Mr. Fehrmann, of Lüdering's in Bremen, asked in perplexity just what the total number of passengers would finally be.[63] Löber, likewise in a quandary, expressed the hope, two days later, that the final arrangements were then being made.[64] One of the reasons that no more definite information could be given these men was that no definite check was possible on some larger bodies of emigrants who were joining the movement just at this time. The most notable of such groups was that under Winter from the Saxon Province of Prussia.[65] Still worse, however, was the insistence of the high command in Dresden that all details of organization and arrangement be referred to the group of leaders living in that city. For instance, all the pastors first had to send in lists of applicants; then, when the applications had been examined and passed upon, the revised lists were sent back to the pastors, who were to notify the fortunate applicants who had been accepted, get the additional information necessary, and send the corrected and completed list back to Dresden.[66] The difficulty was that by the time all this procedure had been followed, a list of new applications often accompanied the "final" list, and it was necessary to begin the process all over again.[67] Some applications came in as late as October and November, 1838.[68]

---

61 Sauer to Marbach, Aug. 22, Oct. 3, 1838, Hagemann to Marbach, Oct. 5, 1838, Fehrmann to Marbach, Oct. 5, 1838, Marbach to J. D. Lüdering, Sept. 15, 1838, Bound MSS., I, C. H. I.

62 Sauer to Marbach, Aug. 22, 1838, Fehrmann to Marbach, Sept. 3, 22, 1838, Jäckel to G. H. Löber, Sept. 4, 1838, *ibid.*

63 Fehrmann to Marbach, Aug. 23, 1838, *ibid.*

64 G. H. Löber to — [H. F. Fischer?], Aug. 25, 1838, *ibid.*

65 Bekenntniss, MS., C. H. I.

66 G. H. Löber to — [H. F. Fischer?], Aug. 25, 1838, Bound MSS., I, C. H. I.; Protokolle über die . . . Auswanderung, June 25, 1838, Bound MSS., III, C. H. I.; A list of emigrants by E. M. Bürger, n. d., a list by G. H. Löber, July 8, 1838, and Anmerkungen to this list of Löber, July 14, 1838, MSS., C. H. I.

67 G. H. Löber to Brohm, Aug. 26, 1838, Jäckel to G. H. Löber, Sept. 4, 18, 27, 1838, G. H. Löber to Jäckel [?], Sept. 9, 1838, Jäckel to O. H. Walther, Sept. 11, 1838, G. H. Löber to —, n. d. [Sept. 11—19, 1838], Keyl to —, Sept. 19, 1838, Bound MSS., I, C. H. I.

68 Keyl to —, Sept. 24, 1838, *ibid.* G. H. Löber resolved to reject all applications as early as September, 1838, but still they continued to come in. As a matter of fact, Löber accepted one family only a few hours before he himself left Eichenberg for Bremen and still later even admitted applicants

Thus it is evident that, while the ability and capacity for work of some of the leaders was tremendous, their insistence on certain "red tape" and their failure to abide by several successive deadlines added to their difficulties and decreased their efficiency considerably. On June 25, 1838, Jäckel had been instructed by the Advisory Committee to make out the first composite list of all the emigrants.[69] How accurate that list was two months later is only a matter of conjecture. However, the delays in sailing were not entirely the fault of the emigrants. The ships were not ready when promised. Most striking was the case of the *Olbers,* still under construction when it was hired. As late as August 7, 1838, the *Olbers* was promised for August 21;[70] by August 21 the date had been advanced to October 3.[71]

Meanwhile a large number of letters and petitions poured into Dresden and flooded the mail of Stephanite pastors in other cities. Some people wrote for the purpose of doing business with the *Auswanderungs-Gesellschaft;*[72] others wanted to give encouragement and advice. Among the latter was the traveler and author Friedrich Bromme, who coupled his sympathies for the "persecution" suffered by the Stephanites with wishes for the success of their venture and an offer of assistance from his friends in the United States. Bromme also included a copy of his "latest little work on America, as evidence of his high regard." [73] But most of the communications contained pleas to be allowed to join the *Gesellschaft.* A number of these frankly stated that they did not wish any religious connection with the Stephanites, but merely wanted to

---

while he was on the way to Bremen and after he had arrived in the port. G. H. Löber to Marbach, Sept. 26, Oct. 21, Nov. 3, 1838, G. H. Löber to Brohm, Oct. 6, 1838, *ibid.* See also M. Niedner to C. F. W. Walther, Oct. 10, 1838, Bound MSS., Invoices, C. H. I.; Fröhlich to Marbach, Oct. 23—24, 1838, MS., C. H. I.

69 Protokolle über die . . . Auswanderung, June 25, 1838, Bound MSS., III, C. H .I.

70 Hagemann to Marbach, Aug. 7, 1838, Bound MSS., I, C. H. I.

71 Sauer to Marbach, Aug. 22, 1838, *ibid.*

72 Jäckel to Stephan, Aug. 29, 1838, Ordemann to Stephan, Oct. 20, 1838, *ibid.*

73 Bromme to Stephan, Oct. 6, 1838, *ibid.* The book probably was Bromme's *Missouri und Illinois,* Baltimore, 1835, cited elsewhere in this study. Bromme was naturally interested in the Stephanite movement, since he was an ardent advocate of emigration to America and in 1832 had played a part in originating some abortive plans for founding a colony in Florida. Rosenthal, *op. cit.,* 52.

ORIGINS OF THE SAXON MIGRATION

Localities in Saxony, the Saxon Duchies, and the Saxon Province of Prussia from which the Stephanites left in 1838–1839

Each community here shown was the home of some member(s) of the emigrant group.

All such communities in the area covered by the map are shown except Barthelsdorf and Hafelbach. These two hamlets were in the Saxon Duchies, but their location could not be determined.

The position of Pursten, Zasznitz, Welttheurer, Zetteritz, could not be established beyond question, but is approximately correct as here shown.

PLATE X

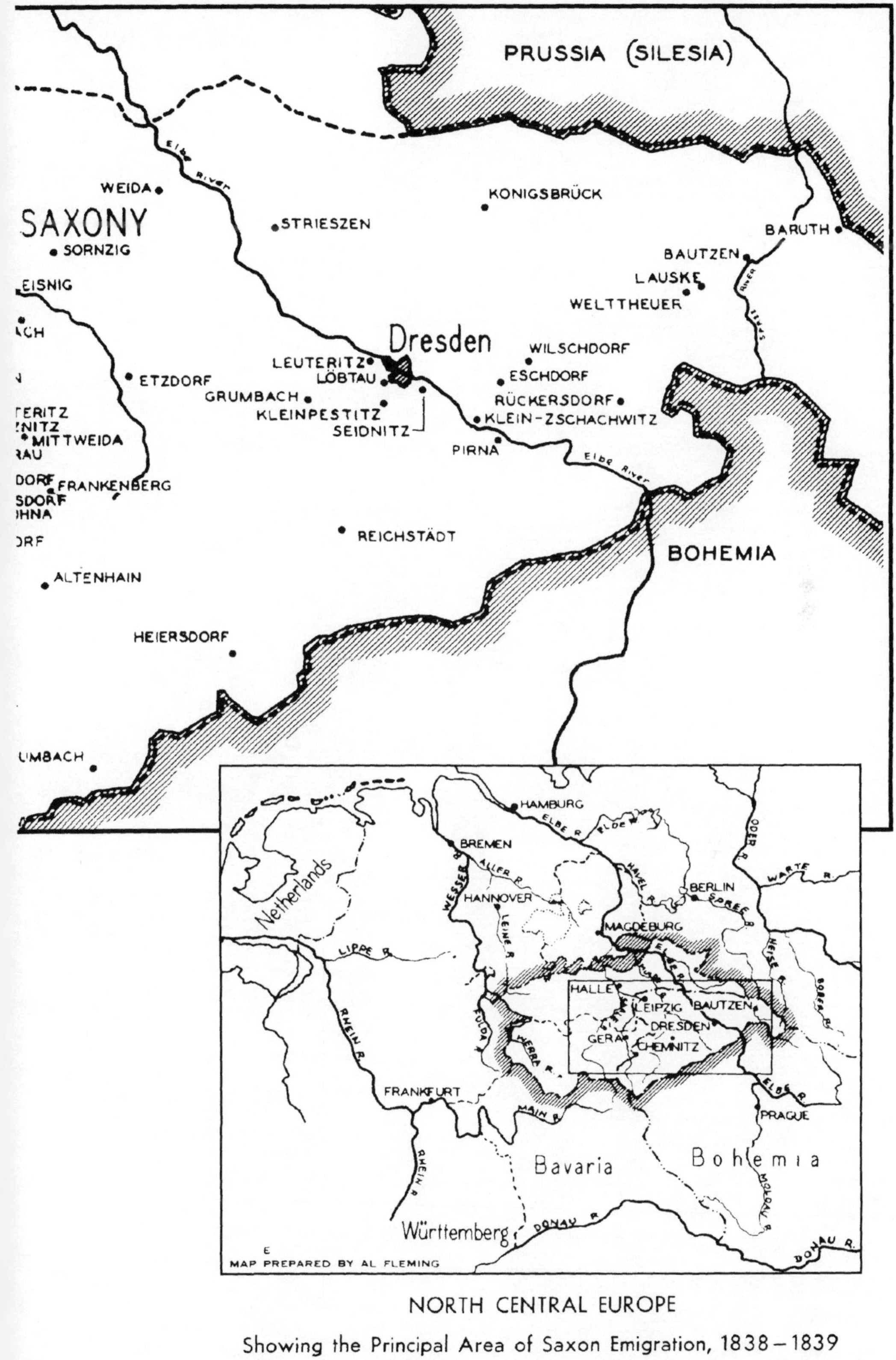

NORTH CENTRAL EUROPE

Showing the Principal Area of Saxon Emigration, 1838–1839

travel with the group.[74] In addition, the usual number of parasites, speculators, social misfits, and cranks put in their applications.[75]

However, by far the greatest number of applicants asserted that their motives in seeking association with the group of emigrants were purely religious.[76] How sincere their claims were is hard to judge. If these people permitted themselves to be moved by the Stephanite argument, then, of course, they were in earnest. From the beginning, although in flagrant violation of the rule set up by Stephan that no one was to be urged to go along, Stephan himself and the leaders of the emigration, clerical and lay alike, relentlessly hammered at the idea that since they were *the* Church the issue in the emigration was a choice between salvation and damnation. In effect, they told the people: "You are at perfect liberty to be damned if you like. We shall not urge you to escape, but damned you will be if you stay." [77] When pronouncements carrying such an implication came from the lips of pastors and trusted friends, the effect could not fail to be at least disturbing. The people who were convinced of what the emigrants told them, then wrote piteous, heart-rending, and sometimes subservient letters to Stephan, pleading to be taken along.[78] Families were frequently disrupted; par-

---

[74] Seidel to Marbach, Aug. 17, 1838, Bound MSS., VI, C. H. I.; Dr. Wenzel to Stephan, Aug. 10, 1838, MS., C. H. I.

[75] — to Stephan, July 19, 1838, von Wolffersdorf to Stephan, July 20, 1838, Ernestine Anders to Stephan, Aug. 26, 1838, Schulze to Stephan, Oct. 25, 1838, Israel to Stephan, Sept. 28, Oct. 25, 1838, Bound MSS., II, C. H. I.; F. E. Schneider to Vehse, Sept. 3, 1838, MS., C. H. I.; *Politische Weltschau* (a supplement to the *Sächsische Dorfzeitung*), July 26, 1839; Pleissner, *op. cit.*, 6—7.

[76] Wesser to Stephan, July 12, 1838, Weber to Stephan, n. d., Quellmalz to Stephan, Aug. 3, 1838, Öhrling to Marbach, Oct. 12, 1838, Schulze to Stephan, Oct. 25, 1838, Israel to Stephan, Sept. 28, Oct. 25, 1838, Bound MSS., II, C. H. I.; *Leipziger allgemeine Zeitung,* July 24, 1838. The consistory of Saxe-Altenburg admitted that religious motivation predominated among those leaving from that country. *Bedenken der theologischen Facultäten,* 24—25.

[77] This attitude of the Stephanites has been discussed above, and the references there cited apply in their entirety. By way of illustration the glaring example of Amalia Quellmalz may be cited here. Jäckel to Stephan, Aug. 29, 1838, Bound MSS., I, C. H. I. Agnes Bünger's son, L. Fürbringer, relates that his mother's question to her brother: "Fredrick, must we really leave our beautiful country and emigrate to the wilds of America and live among Indians?" was answered: "Well, if you want to go down with this country like Sodom and Gomorrah, then stay here." L. Fuerbringer, *80 Eventful Years,* 208.

[78] An entire collection of these is contained in Bound MSS., II, C. H. I. See also Amalia Quellmalz to Stephan, Sept. 6, 1838, Bound MSS., VI, C. H. I.; G. H. Löber to Marbach, Nov. 3, 1838, Bound MSS., I, C. H. I.

ents left their children, children their parents, and divorce and simple desertion by either husband or wife were not uncommon. The strife, heartache, and trouble of all kinds, engendered especially by the religious cast of the movement, are incapable of accurate measurement.[79] Stephan's tortuous mental processes and customary inability to see the relationship between his actions and their consequences enabled him to maintain: "I have called upon nobody to take part in this emigration." [80] Perhaps this monstrous self-deception is the best single example of how far Stephan finally succeeded in removing himself from reality. But if the remorse subsequently experienced by the other pastors for their role in this drama is any indication, then there was too often a strong element of unnecessary tragedy in its closing scenes.

A fanaticism [81] pervaded the group that led its members into gross inconsistencies with their highly moral principles. The authorities were glibly lied to and cheerfully deceived.[82] For instance, it was regarded as a special act of gracious Providence that a number of young girls, some of them in male disguise, succeeded in escaping from their homes against the wishes of their parents and their governments, crossing several boundaries which lay between them and the coast without benefit of visas, and finally reaching

---

79 "But with me the situation is very bad, for my parents as well as my sister are against it [the emigration]. They consider me very simple and even want to draw me away from the true religion. . . . I must therefore abandon everything if I go, since my father wants to disinherit me completely. . . ." — Wesser to Stephan, July 12, 1838, Bound MSS., II, C. H. I. Dr. F. E. Schneider reported to Vehse that "through the Spirit of God" he had persuaded his twenty-one-year-old daughter to break her engagement and resolve to accompany the other members of her family to America. F. E. Schneider to Vehse, Sept. 3, 1838, MS., C. H. I. See also G. H. W. Walther to his children who emigrated [Hermann, Ferdinand, and Amalia], Sept. 9, 1839, Bound MSS., Invoices, C. H. I.; C. F. W. Walther to O. H. Walther, May 4, 1840, MS., C. H. I.; Marbach to Stübel, n. d. [1839—1840], Bound MSS., VI, C. H. I.; Proceedings, 13—17a, Bound MSS., Acten der . . . Superintendur Chemnitz, C. H. I.; The consistory of Saxe-Altenburg to Superintendent Hezekiel, Oct. 9, 1838, quoted in *Bedenken der theologischen Facultäten*, 54; *ibid.*, 3—4, 46—52, 59.

80 Stephan to Flügel, Oct. 12, 1841, MS., C. H. I. A detailed refutation of the obviously false is hardly necessary at this point. It is interesting to speculate, however, on what Stephan thought he was doing at the meeting in Dresden in 1836. G. H. Löber, Diary, May 3, 1836, MS., C. H. I.

81 The term is not too strong, for the emigrants later applied it to themselves. Bekenntniss, MS., C. H. I.; *Anzeiger des Westens*, Dec. 31, 1842.

82 Bekenntniss, MS., C. H. I.

Bremen in time to be taken along.[83] J. F. Bünger exulted discreetly in his diary that the human "contrabrand" on the river boat under his direction was not discovered. Among this "contrabrand" was a minor.[84] O. H. Walther, one of the gentlest of souls, but one of the most ardent Stephanites, took it upon himself to arrange for the departure of two minors over whom he did not have full authority; thus he, together with his brother Ferdinand, set in motion a chain of circumstances that will be described more fully later.

In many cases there is no substantial basis on which to challenge the sincerity of the religious considerations advanced by those participating in the emigration, although the soundness of the argument underlying this attitude is open to question, as has been brought out above. The difficulty of conclusively disproving any motive claimed by the persons involved in an action, and a predisposition on the part of most writers to surround the Saxons with an aura of martyrdom, have encouraged virtual unanimity in pronouncing this movement purely religious, or largely so, and in ignoring or denying that any economic urge might have been at work.[85] The latter viewpoint has at times been reinforced with a reference to what is called the comparative wealth of this group of emigrants from Germany. Of course, fantastic stories were circulating about the financial resources of the Stephanites in Ger-

---

83 Nachrichten an unsere Nachkommen, MS., C. H. I.; C. F. W. Walther in Köstering, *Auswanderung,* 13—14. A notice of the escape of Julius Biltz, thirteen years old, and of a Martin girl [Christiane Wilhelmine?], from the homes of their guardian and father respectively, together with an order for their apprehension and that of the persons instrumental in their escape, was dated October 28, 1838, and inserted by the court at Mittel-Frohna into the *Chemnitzer Anzeiger* (Oct. 30, 1838). Biltz was a half brother of Louise Völker. He later rose to prominence as a clergyman in the Missouri Synod. For a sketch of his life see "C. H. D.," "Franz Julius Biltz," *Der Lutheraner,* LXV, 292—293.

84 J. F. Bünger, Diarium, Oct. 22, 1838, MS., L. Fürbringer Papers, St. Louis.

85 Nachrichten an unsere Nachkommen, MS., C. H. I.; Kirchen-Buch von Frohna, Perry County, Missouri (hereafter cited as Kirchen-Buch von Frohna), MS., Concordia Church Records, Frohna, Mo.; "G. G.," in *Lehre und Wehre,* XLVII, 147—148; Behnken, "Zum neuen Jahr," *Der Lutheraner,* XCIV, 1; Bauer, "America One Hundred Years Ago," *Lutheran Witness,* LVII, 9; H. Koepchen, "The Saxon Emigration of 1838," *ibid.,* 140; P. Kretzmann, "The Saxon Immigration to Missouri, 1838—1839," *Missouri Historical Review,* XXXIII, 157—158, 165; Vehse, *op. cit.,* 33; A. L. Gräbner, *"Bis hieher." Kurzgefasste Geschichte der Missouri-Synode* (hereafter cited as *"Bis hieher"*), 5; Faust, *op. cit.,* I, 448, II, 412.

many prior to their departure. But examples of equally unreliable assertions in what should have been more reliable quarters can be found at a very early date, and these exaggerations have persistently been repeated since that time. For instance, Vehse, who was in a position to know better, generalized that emigration meant a step downward in the economic scale for the majority of the Stephanites.[86] However, if a generalization must be made, it would have to be just the opposite of that.

There is no reason to assume that the Saxon emigrants were fortuitously immune to the economic disturbances described above. The dislocation in industrial life previously described affected a large portion of the Stephanites. Of weavers alone there were forty-nine in the entire group of colonists, forty of whom were among the 612 people on the four ships which brought the main contingent.[87] Their financial circumstances could, on the average, certainly not have been good. During the period of poor wages that accompanied the Saxon industrial revolution, the year 1836, for example, is known as one of comparatively high wages in the weaving industry for the area from which the Saxon emigrants came. Yet even in this relatively prosperous year a master craftsman earned only 6 to 8 thaler a week and a journeyman 4 to 6.[88] The severe agricultural depression discussed above was also significant for the emigrants of 1838—1839, since forty-eight of them were engaged in agricultural pursuits.[89] In addition, as was customary in Saxony, many of the craftsmen, especially the weavers, were also engaged in small-scale farming. Among the 326 colonists whose vocations are known (exclusive of the women whose occupations are listed), 30 per cent were divided almost equally between agriculture and the weaving trade, and 51 per cent were employed in all other crafts combined.[90] Thus farmers and craftsmen comprised

---

[86] Vehse, *op. cit.*, 33. See also von Polenz, *op. cit.*, 76; Polack, *The Building of a Great Church* (hereafter cited as *Building a Church*), 38; Hanser, *op. cit.*, 3.

[87] Table IV, Appendix A.

[88] Hiersemann, *Chronik der Kirchengemeinden Niederfrohna und Mittelfrohna mit Fichtigsthal*, 7.

[89] Table IV, Appendix A. This figure becomes even more telling when it is noted that not one in this classification is listed for the New York group and that all but five (additions in St. Louis: four; *Amalia* group: one) of the forty-eight were among the 612 in the main detachment of Saxons. *Ibid.*

[90] Table IV, Appendix A.

more than four fifths of the total occupational listing of the emigrants. When further allowances are made for day laborers and personal servants and for the lower brackets in some of the other classifications, it becomes obvious that the great bulk of the Stephanites could not have been wealthy.

On the basis of the same figures it becomes equally plain that not many of the Saxon emigrants came from the professional class. Despite frequent incorrect listing or disproportionate emphasis upon the admittedly large number of clergymen and persons of similar education and standing,[91] the average socio-occupational level in the *Gesellschaft* was in direct proportion to the economic — that is, it was low. Clergymen, candidates, teachers, lawyers, physicians, students, and government officials (the precise figures for which can be found in Table IV, Occupations of the Colonists) contributed only about 11 per cent of the total.[92] The overwhelming majority of the emigrants, coming as they did from a strictly class society, was sacrificing no more in social standing or occupational rating than in economic position.

As a matter of fact, it is evident that not even the Saxons could or did ignore the less lofty aspects of the question of emigration. The pleas of applicants for spiritual relief were frequently coupled with an appeal for financial assistance.[93] Stephan and others assured prospective emigrants of material prosperity in a religious community under an episcopal government.[94] Finally, most of the emigrants had so few worldly possessions that they could hardly have made their economic position much worse. Sixty-eight per cent of the personal accounts kept by the Credit Fund showed a

---

[91] Nachrichten an unsere Nachkommen, Document . . . des Grundsteins . . . St. Louis . . . 22. Juny 1842, MSS., C.H.I.; C. F. W. Walther, *Bünger*, 42; Schieferdecker, *op. cit.*, 8; J. F. Bünger, "Ehrengedächtniss des . . . Brohm," *Der Lutheraner*, XXXVII, 189; Fritz, "Die Hundertjahrfeier der sächsischen Einwanderung," *ibid.*, XCIII, 262—263; Stellhorn, "The Saxon Centennial and the Schools," *Lutheran School Journal*, LXXIV, 296.

[92] Table IV, Appendix A.

[93] Wesser to Stephan, July 12, 1838, Schulze to Stephan, Oct. 25, 1838, Israel to Stephan, Oct. 25, 1838, Bound MSS., II, C.H.I.; Ferdinand and Henriette Römer to Stephan, n.d. [Oct. 1—15, 1838?], G. H. Löber to Jäckel, Sept. 9, 1838, Bound MSS., I, C.H.I.

[94] E. M. Bürger, Selbstbiographie, 118, MS., E. J. Buerger Papers, Ellicottville, N. Y.; Bekenntniss, Marbach, An meine . . . Landsleute, MSS., C.H.I.; Keyl, *op. cit.*, 13. Keyl's biographer ignored this portion of Keyl's confession when he stated: "They [the emigrants] did not seek worldly goods." Köstering, *Keyl*, 45—46.

deficit by the middle of June, 1839, when a detailed accounting was made. Since the amount charged each person for expenses was in the majority of cases well under 100 thaler, it is obvious that the capital of most of the emigrants was meager indeed. Furthermore, 61 per cent of the overdrawn accounts, or 42 per cent of the total, show that the persons had no money whatever, or at least paid none of it into the Credit Fund, from which they drew funds for their passage and their support for half a year.[95]

If we distinguish with Fairchild between "predisposing" and "immediate" causes for emigration,[96] then the economic condition of most of the Stephanites was at least not so favorable as to act as a deterrent to their religious enthusiasm for leaving Saxony. Some of the emigrants were frank enough to admit that economic motives, and even simple speculation, had played a part. Pastor Gruber, in his petition to his consistory for release from office, admitted the economic motive as the reason for his desire to emigrate.[97] Just fifty years after the emigration Pastor E. M. Bürger wrote: "The enticing aspects of the temporal advantages to be found in America, of which we had read and heard, may also at the same time have blinded our eyes." [98] And Michael Bock, in an official hearing during his wife's suit against him for divorce, declared that he was motivated solely by the fact that he was not able to make a living in

---

95 List of Saxon Emigrants 1838, MS., C. H. I. (The title of this manuscript is a misnomer, for actually it is the financial account book of the Credit Fund and the *Gesellschaft* from June 6, 1839, to 1847. It is not a list of the emigrants, but of those who had individual accounts with the Credit Fund.) The figures are given above in the form of percentages in order to emphasize the proportion and to avoid confusion concerning the manner of listing several accounts which were later transferred and could thus affect the numerical totals, if the information were given in that form, but which are not numerous enough to change percentages. The actual number of accounts in each classification, arrived at by examining the List of Saxon Emigrants and used in computing the above percentages, are: Total number of personal accounts, 258; those with a credit balance June 6, 1839, eighty-two; accounts overdrawn on that date, 176; and those who made no contribution whatever, 108. For the status on June 11, 1842, of the accounts to which advances had been made, see: A. List of Debtors and Expenses for which Martin Stephan is answerable to the Cash of the German emigrants, Wittenberg (hereafter cited as List of Debtors), June 11, 1842, MS., C. H. I.

96 Fairchild, *op. cit.*, 144.

97 The consistory of Saxe-Altenburg to Duke Joseph, Sept. 4, 1838, quoted in *Bedenken der theologischen Facultäten*, 41—42.

98 E. M. Bürger, Selbstbiographie, 118, MS., E. J. Buerger Papers, Ellicottville, N. Y.

Germany, and that his leaving had nothing to do with his religious views.[99]

The candidates, furthermore, hoped to play far more important roles in the United States than had fallen to their lot in Germany. Stübel asserted that the attitude of the candidates was one of the reasons he began to doubt the soundness of the entire movement and eventually withdrew from it.[100] A sweeping indictment of the motives of all the candidates would probably be an injustice — but only to some of them. The very handsome salaries which the *Gesellschaft,* numbering less than seven hundred souls, was to pay its spiritual leaders, who at one time included a "bishop," six clergymen, eighteen candidates, and four teachers,[101] must have seemed rather attractive to some of the prospective beneficiaries. Pastors were to receive 300 thaler per month, and candidates and teachers, 150 thaler; but it was pointed out to them that these salaries were only an eventual goal, for during the emigration, when funds were low, they would have to be satisfied with the simple necessities.[102]

When the petitions began to arrive in Dresden in greater numbers, serious problems arose as to who was to be admitted to the *Gesellschaft* and who rejected. On this question a sharp division of opinion occurred in the Advisory Committee,[103] and later between two factions among the leaders. This phase of arrangements provides the only clear instance in which Marbach seriously differed with Stephan prior to the embarkation at Bremen. The one party, headed by Vehse and Marbach, was of the opinion that no one was to be taken along who could not pay the estimated 100 thaler for his fare. The aim of such a policy would have been to keep as large

---

[99] Proceedings of the consistory of Saxe-Altenburg, Sept. 25, 1838, quoted in *Bedenken der theologischen Facultäten,* 48. See also Stübel to Vehse *et al.,* Sept. 12, 1839, Bound MSS., VI, C. H. I.; Bekenntniss, MS., C. H. I.; Döderlein to F. W. Barthel, Sept. 9, 1839, Bound MSS., Aa. No. 13. Acta, die Assecuranz der Effecten und Contracten des Schiffs "Amalia" s. w. d. a. betr. (hereafter cited as Bound MSS., 13), C. H. I.; Christiane Löber to relatives in Germany, Dec. 4, 1839, in Löber-Eichenberg (ed.), "Ein Briefwechsel," *Mitteilungen . . . Kahla,* VII, 162—167; E. M. Bürger, *op. cit.,* 23; Keyl, *op. cit.*. 13; Pleissner, *op. cit.,* 6—7.

[100] Stübel to Vehse *et al.,* Sept. 12, 1839, Bound MSS., VI, C. H. I.

[101] Marbach to Kimm & Tewes, Sept. 14, 1838, Bound MSS., I, C. H. I.

[102] Marbach to O. H. Walther, Oct. 16, 1838, *ibid.*

[103] Marbach, An meine . . . Landsleute, MS., C. H. I.; Protokolle über die . . . Auswanderung, March 5, 1838, Bound MSS., III, C. H. I.

a reserve as possible in the Credit Fund for the purchase of land and the establishment of a colony. The allocation of funds that these men and most of the committee favored was 50 per cent for the expenses of settlement, 10 per cent for the church, 10 per cent for general expenses, and only 30 per cent for the cost of transportation.[104]

Marbach pointed out that, at least from his point of view, the *Gesellschaft* was not a charitable organization, but a colonization enterprise and, to that extent, a business venture. To Döderlein he wrote: "The Credit Fund does not exist for the purpose of equipping poor people for the journey, as the Code for the Credit Fund will show." [105] Vehse agreed with his brother-in-law and emphasized that the indigent whose desires and convictions remained unaltered might be allowed to come a year or two later, when the colony would presumably be established firmly enough to care for them.[106] In the committee meeting Marbach plainly stated that he considered indefensible the use of common funds for the purpose of taking along those unable to pay, and that if this practice were continued, he would refuse to accept responsibility for its consequences. To this Stephan replied that he himself would assume the responsibility.[107]

The other party, headed by Stephan, wished to take along all the people whose fare it was financially feasible to pay, who held the correct doctrinal viewpoint, who subjected themselves to Stephan's authority and to the Emigration Code, and who contributed the amount they promised, however small it was.[108] Stephan's opinion, of course, prevailed. It must be admitted that his attitude, if carried out to its logical conclusion, would at least have been in harmony with his doctrine of doom for Germany and salvation through emigration; some sympathy would have been displayed for the harrowed spirits who subscribed to this principle but had no money

---

[104] Protokolle über die . . . Auswanderung, Sept. 20, 1838, Bound MSS., III, C. H. I.

[105] Marbach to Döderlein, Aug. 30, 1838, Gönner to Stephan, Oct. 10, 1838, Bound MSS., I, C. H. I.; Marbach, An meine . . . Landsleute, MS., C. H. I.

[106] Vehse, *op. cit.*, 5—6.

[107] Marbach, An meine . . . Landsleute, MS., C. H. I.

[108] *Ibid.*; G. H. Löber to —, Aug. 25, 1838, G. H. Löber to Brohm, Aug. 26, 1838, Jäckel to G. H. Löber, Sept. 4, 1838, Bound MSS., I, C. H. I.; Jäckel to Schulze, Oct. 27, 1838, Bound MSS., II, C. H. I.

for their fare.[109] What men like Vehse and Marbach thought, who were willing to condemn people but not to help them, is less understandable. But whatever the differing viewpoints on this issue, it was obvious that a considerable outlay of cash was required to combat the kind of spiritual danger to which the Stephanites felt they were exposed.

However, Stephan did not pursue his principle in this regard consistently. The result was that where Marbach and Vehse would have permitted a mandatory financial requirement to determine admission or rejection on an impersonal basis, Stephan permitted the highly subjective factor of whether he considered an individual desirable or not to decide the question on a personal basis. The latitude allowed by the phrasing of the Code for the Credit Fund enabled him to find in it the exact opposite of what Marbach had, to justify his own policies on the basis of this same document, to set up the principles of qualification, and to determine arbitrarily the manner of their application.[110] If Stephan disapproved of an individual, it was easy to eliminate him for the lack of ready cash or of the proper religious viewpoint. On the other hand, when Stephan approved, money was apparently not an obstacle, as is shown by the large number of those who were taken along in spite of the fact that they had not a cent to their name and that they consequently became a total financial liability to the organization.[111]

If the leaders of the emigration were not clear on what the Emigration and Credit Fund Codes meant, neither were the people who joined the *Gesellschaft.* New members did not even sign their names to a copy of the Brief Outline of the Emigration Code, as

---

109 Weber to Stephan, n. d. [Aug., 1838?], Quellmalz to Stephan, Aug. 3, 1838, Öhrling to Marbach, Oct. 12, 1838, Bound MSS., II, C. H. I.; Ferdinand and Henriette Römer to Stephan, n. d. [Oct. 1—15, 1838?], Bound MSS., I, C. H. I.

110 Code for the Credit Fund, par. 2, Appendix B; Marbach, An meine . . . Landsleute, MS., C. H. I.; Protokolle über die . . . Auswanderung, Sept. 20, 1838, Bound MSS., III, C. H. I.; Jäckel to Schulze, Oct. 27, 1838, Bound MSS., II, C. H. I.; Zöge to F. W. Barthel, Sept. 1, 1838, Jäckel to O. H. Walther, Sept. 11, 1838, Jäckel to G. H. Löber, Sept. 27, 1838, G. H. Löber to Brohm, Aug. 26, 1838, Bound MSS., I, C. H. I.

111 Caroline Dittrich to Marbach, Aug. 28, 1838, Marbach, An meine . . . Landsleute, MSS., C. H. I., Ferdinand and Henriette Römer to Stephan, n. d. [Oct. 1—15, 1838?], Bound MSS., I, C. H. I. Of interest in this connection are the penciled notations usually found on the letters of application, especially those in Bound MSS., II, C. H. I. See also List of Saxon Emigrants 1838, MS., C. H. I.; Keyl, *op. cit.,* 15.

had originally been planned, nor to the Code for the Credit Fund, as a portion of the larger "Emigration Code"; much less could they have been aware of how and by whom these codes were to be interpreted. Instead, recruits for the *Gesellschaft* signed a pledge which was drawn up ostensibly to accompany the codes. The standard form for this pledge was the following:

> The undersigned herewith declare that they agree in every particular to the accompanying Emigration Code. They have understood this Emigration Code perfectly throughout and have carefully considered it point for point. They declare further that they are not under the delusion that through their subscription they are acquiring the right to be transported to America at the expense of others.[112]
>
> [The signatures follow.]

It is worth noting that this pledge does not specifically state that each signer *read* any one of the codes. This fact gives room for the suspicion that many of the applicants did not even see these instruments. For if they had, it would have been quite as simple to have them sign a copy of the Brief Outline of the Emigration Code as to have them sign such a pledge. Furthermore, what, precisely, was meant by the term "Emigration Code," referred to in the pledge, is, as pointed out before, by no méans clear. If the Brief Outline was meant, then again the only reason why the applicants could not sign it, as the last paragraph of this document said they should, was because they were not actually shown a copy. It cannot be proved that such tactics were followed, but, it is difficult to account for the necessity for such a pledge on any basis other than that suggested.

The very fact that the last sentence of the pledge had to be included is an eloquent commentary on the attitude of many of the emigrants, or at least of the applicants. Unfortunately for the future of the Credit Fund, with Stephan the sole arbiter of the acceptability of petitioners, the clause was meaningless. About 33,530 thaler, or nearly 30 per cent of the total cash resources of the *Gesellschaft,* were advanced to its indigent members. Less than half this sum was ever paid back.[113]

---

[112] Pledges to the Emigration Code, I—V, MSS., C. H. I.

[113] Epitome from the Cash-Account of the Saxon emigrants; established under the direction of Martin Stephan (hereafter cited as Epitome from the Cash-Account), June 11, 1842, List of Debtors, June 11, 1842, MSS., C. H. I.

It is plain from the foregoing that finances played an important part in the affairs of the emigrants. On February 27, 1838, the Credit Fund was only an idea, and the directors of the movement ruefully had to admit that there was little they were capable of doing to give it some substance. But although the fund started slowly, it gained gratifying momentum. Early in June, 1838, the first contributions had come in. The Code for the Credit Fund was adopted by the Advisory Committee on June 25, and at the same time, at Stephan's suggestion, a vital change was made in the financial structure of the organization.[114] Heretofore receipts for payments into the Credit Fund had been issued in such a form that the sum clearly was only on deposit and that control over its disposition was retained by the contributor. Now a different type of receipt was introduced. The new instrument was issued not only to the new contributors, but also to those who already held the first form, which they were now obliged to turn in. The new receipt placed the money at Stephan's disposal until such time as the Code for the Credit Fund should become fully effective, an event which never fully materialized, largely because Stephan, although very anxious to secure the adoption of the new receipt, was very reluctant to put the Credit Fund on an independent, operating basis.[115] Thus the entire financial structure of the *Gesellschaft* remained dependent upon Stephan, a fact whose implications Marbach, at least, clearly recognized and appreciated.[116]

The form of these receipts, as taken from the copy which circulated among the members of the committee and was approved and initialed by them, was the following:

Form of the receipt.

	The undersigned herewith certify and attest that N. N. in N. today (or. . . . .) paid the sum of N.
M.	*Thaler* — — into the Credit Fund mentioned in par. — of the

---

114 Protokolle über die . . . Auswanderung, Feb. 27, June 12, 25, 1838, Bound MSS., III, C. H. I.

115 *Ibid.*, June 25, 29, 1838; Marbach, An meine . . . Landsleute, MS., C. H. I.; Vehse, *op. cit.*, 6—7.

116 Marbach to O. H. Walther, Oct. 16, 1838, Bound MSS., I, C. H. I.; Marbach to Von Langenn [?], Oct. 16, 1838, Bound MSS., V, C. H. I.; Marbach, An meine . . . Landsleute, MS., C. H. I.; Vehse, *op. cit.*, 6—7.

V.	Emigration Code, with the declaration that these moneys may be administered and expended according
F.	to the regulation of the Code for the Credit Fund and, so long as this Code is not yet in operation,
W.	at the order of Herr Pastor Martin Stephan.
B.	Dresden, ... (Leipzig, ...)

Circulated (by Herr Lawyer Marbach)
27/6/38 to Herr Merchant Fischer,
28/6/ " " " Dr. Vehse,
" " Cand. Welzel,
" " Cand. Brohm,
returned to
Jäckel.[117]

The inadvisability of such an arrangement increased in proportion to the size of the Credit Fund and the seriousness of Stephan's personal difficulties.

By July, 1838, the Credit Fund had grown so large that the *Olbers* could be chartered with ease, and Marbach and Fischer could spend almost 180 thaler traveling in style for sixteen days. By September 4, 1838, the total on deposit was officially placed at 123,987 thaler.[118] This sum, therefore, is the one that has been used most frequently as representing the high point of the Credit Fund's resources.[119] Many other estimates have ranged upward from this

---

117 Quittungs-Formular, MS., C. H. I. A specimen of this later type of receipt, as made out to J. G. Pietsch and signed by Vehse, Jäckel, and H. F. Fischer, has been preserved, MS., C. H. I. Pietsch was one of the few who succeeded in securing repayment with interest, April 5, 1839, *Ibid.* Stephan, nevertheless, found it possible to insist even after the complete financial arrangements had become common knowledge: "I was not a member of this [financial] committee, nor did I have anything to do with this [Credit] Fund." Stephan to Flügel, Oct. 12, 1841, MS., C. H. I.

118 Financial Statement of Sept. 4, 1838, Bound MSS., VI, C. H. I.

119 C. F. W. Walther in Köstering, *Auswanderung,* 13; Hochstetter, *op. cit.,* 4; Th. Bünger, "Etliche Züge aus der Geschichte der Missouri-Synode," *Synodal-Bericht des Iowa-Districts . . . 1901,* p. 21; Mezger (ed.), *op. cit.,* 6; Dau (ed.) *op. cit.,* 9; Gruber, *op. cit.,* 29; "E. E.," "Unsere lutherische Kirche in St. Louis," *Der Lutheraner,* LXXXII, 160; Polack, *Walther,* 40; P. E. Kretzmann, "The Saxon Immigration to Missouri, 1838—1839," *The Missouri Historical Review,* XXXIII, 160.

figure. Vehse gave the maximum as "almost" 125,000 thaler, and in this particular he was followed by Köstering.[120] Later writers have raised the total still higher, to 130,000,[121] 135,000 thaler,[122] \$120,000 (*i. e.,* 174,960 thaler),[123] or even \$125,000 (*i. e.,* 182,250 thaler).[124] Occasionally somewhat more conservative figures have been used, such as Hengstenberg's 120,000 thaler.[125] Sometimes the total has also been given as 124,000 thaler.[126]

None of these figures is correct, however, and even the lowest of them is too high if it is intended to reflect the resources actually at the disposal of the *Gesellschaft.* The financial statement of September 4, 1838, is probably only an estimate of the receipts anticipated, just as the number for the membership of the *Gesellschaft* and its geographical distribution, given in that same statement, are not accurate either. The total of the sums entered in the book of contributions of the *Gesellschaft* never rose higher than 121,161 thaler, 5 groschen, and 10 pfennig, recorded on June 6, 1839. A still higher previous total of 121,900 thaler, 23 groschen on January 24, 1839, included a sum of 4,000 thaler which was really not a part of the Credit Fund and later had to be deducted from the total. This process, of course, affected all previous totals. There must have been other such temporary deposits which resulted in misleading totals. For according to a financial statement of February 2, 1839, signed by F. W. Barthel, the treasurer of the *Gesellschaft,* the total receipts up to that date were 117,382 thaler, 2 groschen, and 6 pfennig.[127]

---

120 Vehse, *op. cit.,* 7; Köstering, *Auswanderung,* 32.

121 Rosenthal, *op. cit.,* 69.

122 G. Günther, *op. cit.,* 109.

123 A. L. Graebner in Hyde-Conard, *Encyclopedia of the History of St. Louis,* III, 1326—1330; Breckenridge, *William Clark Breckenridge,* 206; Culmer, *A New History of Missouri,* 252.

124 *History of Southeast Missouri,* 256; Mauelshagen, *American Lutheranism Surrenders to Forces of Conservatism,* 84.

125 Hengstenberg, "Der Pastor Stephan," *Evangelische Kirchen-Zeitung,* XXVI, 258. See also *Hundertjährige Gedächtniss-Feier der Sächsischen Einwanderung 1839—1939* (hereafter cited as *Gedächtniss-Feier ... 1839—1939*), p. 5.

126 A. L. Gräbner, *"Bis hieher,"* 5; *Celebrating the 100th Anniversary of the Saxon Immigration 1839—1939* (hereafter cited as *Anniversary . . . 1839—1939*), p. 5.

127 Erinnerungen zu der über der Verwaltung der Gemeinde-Credit-Casse bis mit Schluss des Jahres 1838. geführten Rechnungen (hereafter cited as Verwaltung der . . . Credit-Casse bis mit Schluss . . . 1838), MS., C. H. I.

The maximum actually attained by the Credit Fund was $80,604.81¼. At the rate of exchange the Saxons were using, 1 thaler and 11 groschen (or 1.458 thaler) to the American dollar, this meant that the peak of the *Gesellschaft's* financial resources was 117,521 thaler, 19 groschen, and 8 pfennig.[128] Unfortunately the closest previous estimate, 117,244 thaler, which is stated to amount to $80,900.74 [?], cannot be checked against the figure here established as the correct one, since the writer in that case failed to give any source as authority for his assertion.[129]

Theoretically contributions to the Credit Fund were entirely voluntary,[130] but every effort was made to have the emigrants pay into the general treasury as much as possible above their actual expenses. Therefore an attempt was made to ascertain each emigrant's total capital, and then to require him to pay that sum into the fund, instead of merely the equivalent of his anticipated expenses. Later, men who were in a position to know admitted that these methods, and even outright deception, had been used in order to increase the size of contributions.[131] It was permitted to make these contributions in two ways: conditionally, that is, with a definite time limit set for the period of deposit in the Credit Fund; or unconditionally, that is, subject only to the regulations of the Code for the Credit Fund.[132] The latter method was preferred, and its use was encouraged by the leaders.[133] Some agent of the Advisory Committee, usually the nearest pastor, collected the contribution of the

---

128 Epitome from the Cash-Account, June 11, 1842, MS., C. H. I.

129 "W. K." [William Koepchen?], "Die Väter und Gründer unserer Synode," *Der Lutheraner*, LXXVIII, 77. See also H. Koepchen, "The Saxon Emigration of 1938 [*sic*], I, Why?" *Lutheran Witness*, LVII, 94. Henry Koepchen has reference to his father's "monumental work on the Saxon emigration of 1838 (in MS.)," which, the present writer was informed in 1938, is not available outside the Koepchen family.

130 Code for the Credit Fund, par. 1, Brief Outline of the Emigration Code, par. 9, Appendix B; Stephan to Flügel, Oct. 12, 1841, MS., C. H. I.

131 Protokolle über die . . . Auswanderung, July 2, 1838, Bound MSS., III, C. H. I.; Vehse-H. F. Fischer-Jäckel, Protestationsschrift, 88, Bound MSS., Fasciculus, die von Herrn Dr. Vehse und 2. Genossen eingegebene Protestation gegen das Stephansche System des Kirchen-Regiments betr. (hereafter cited as Protestation), C. H. I.; Döderlein to F. W. Barthel, Sept. 9, 1839, Bound MSS., 13, C. H. I.

132 Code for the Credit Fund, par. 2, Appendix B.

133 Marbach [?] to Pastor —, n. d. [August, 1838?], Bound MSS., I, C. H. I.; Financial Statement of March 14, 1839, MS., C. H. I.

prospective colonist by contacting him personally wherever he happened to be living.[134] Money was then forwarded to Dresden or Leipzig, frequently to the latter place by way of Dresden. Funds were eventually placed at interest in the Leipzig banks by the representatives of the committee in that city, Barthel or Döderlein, although the money remained under the control of the directors in Dresden.[135]

After a person had made his contribution and had been accepted, he was certain of at least one thing — his passage to the United States. Whether his deposit had been great or small or nothing at all, he was provided with transportation from his own home in Germany to St. Louis; and all his expenses were paid — fare, duties, freight, meals, and lodging en route. Whatever was left in the Credit Fund when all expenses had been met, formed the reserve, and the individual contributors who had deposited more than had been spent for them became the creditors of this fund.[136] Actually, of course, this credit did them no good, because they were unable to claim it for a period of five years, during which common resources, including the land, were pledged as security for the expenditures of the *Gesellschaft.*[137]

Not only could the creditors not touch their remaining resources, but these resources were probably far less than the creditors themselves suspected. Much of their surplus had been used to transport the penniless and poor, and the fact that these persons now "owed" the Credit Fund a considerable sum was small consolation. As late as June 11, 1842, when many of the more conscientious or more fortunate debtors had paid back all or a part of their obligations to the Credit Fund, there were still eighty-four

---

134 G. H. Löber to —, n. d. [Sept. 11—19, 1838], G. H. Löber to — [H. F. Fischer?], Aug. 25, 1838, G. H. Löber to Jäckel, Sept. 9, 1838, Jäckel to G. H. Löber, Sept. 4, 1838, Bound MSS., I, C. H. I.; Protokolle über die . . . Auswanderung, June 12, 1838, Bound MSS., III, C. H. I.

135 Marbach to Döderlein, Aug. 29, 1838, F. W. Barthel to Marbach, Oct. 8, 1838, Bound MSS., I, C. H. I.; Statement of interest by F. W. Barthel, Sept. 14, 1838, MS., C. H. I. Vehse and H. F. Fischer were responsible for receipts in Dresden. Stephan to Flügel, Oct. 12, 1841, MS., C. H. I.

136 The theory of the system is stated in the Code for the Credit Fund, Appendix B. The practical application can be observed in any of the personal accounts in List of Saxon Emigrants 1838, MS., C. H. I.

137 Brief Outline of the Emigration Code, par. 7, Code for the Civil Community, par. 15, Appendix B.

delinquent personal accounts, the total loss on which amounted to \$13,477.06¼.[138] Other "Purposes of the Credit Fund" are listed in the Code and need not be repeated here.[139] Obviously so long as this financial arrangement was in effect, the fortunes of the "creditors" fluctuated in direct proportion to the degree of discretion shown by the leaders; that is to say, these fortunes declined, for "expenditures" and "cash advances" were elastic cost items, and economy was not one of the virtues of Stephan and his aids.

Because of the highly centralized financial structure of the organization, as well as because of Stephan's domination of the entire movement, the final word on expenditures rested with him. But Stephan was generous and allowed his confidants considerable latitude in drawing on the money at his disposal as they saw fit. Thus the irregular practice began, and continued for almost a year, of permitting those within the inner circle (such as the lay leaders in Dresden and Leipzig, the pastors, and the candidates) to write out drafts on the Credit Fund to someone else or even to themselves, although in the latter case it was usually done on the authority of another person.[140] It seems that only in a single case one of the men failed to take this precaution.[141] Sometimes the authority of Stephan was referred to in these drafts, sometimes not. Although there was as yet no indication of personal dishonesty, adoption of this procedure meant that those on the "inside" got what they wanted — or at least what they thought they needed — for themselves and their friends, whether either party had any money or not; whereas others were hard pressed for the bare necessities, especially when their contributions were not large enough to cover their expenses.

Already some questionable "expenditures" had been authorized, which reduced the reserve capital even beyond the point to which it was brought by the payment of transportation for the in-

---

[138] List of Debtors, June 11, 1842, MS., C. H. I.

[139] Code for the Credit Fund, par. 2, Appendix B.

[140] Several specimens of such drafts are contained in Bound MSS., 6, C. H. I. Specific examples are those issued to Gönner, Jan. 15, Feb. 26, April 10, 1839, to C. F. W. Walther, Oct. 15, 1838, to J. F. Bünger, Nov. 11, 1838, to Döderlein, Nov. 13, 1838, and still others to Fröhlich, O. H. Walther, C. F. W. Walther, F. W. Barthel, Schuster, Zöge, Josing, Quellmalz, C. A. Schnabel, and men in a similar position, MSS., C. H. I.

[141] O. H. Walther to the creditors of the fund, Oct. 6, 1840, MS., C. H. I.

digent. The latter, by the way, included such individuals as a reformed drunkard who hadn't touched a drop "for a quarter of a year," but had no money with which to pay for his fare.[142] Stephan himself was enjoying the benefits of an outright grant of 1,500 thaler. Ostensibly this sum had been allowed him by the *Gesellschaft;* actually authorization came only from the committee which executed this generous gesture in order to enable Stephan to pay his expenses and to demonstrate the gratitude of "all Lutheran congregations toward their bishop, toward the regent of the Church." [143] But Stephan's current obligations, such as the lawyer's fees mentioned above, were even then being borne by the Credit Fund. Before leaving Germany, Stephan had accepted no less than 400 thaler in cash, paid out in 100-thaler installments on September 29, October 11, 18 (or 19), and 22, 1838. To this sum must be added 500 thaler (513 according to some sources) for bail he had to put up before being allowed to leave Saxony; 300 thaler paid to Lawyer Krause on October 19, 1838; and numerous other expenditures for transportation to Bremen, for fare on the *Olbers,* for the purchase of many personal items, and for similar expenses.

Altogether Stephan's total disbursements from the Credit Fund for his own purposes were over 2,650 thaler by November 12, 1838. Even if the 1,500 thaler are regarded as legitimately his (which is open to some ethical objections at least), and even if the 598 thaler which he had paid into the Credit Fund are taken into consideration, Stephan, before leaving Germany, had nevertheless spent, above his total assets, more than 500 thaler of the emigrants' money — money which he had no prospect of ever repaying, except by getting more from these same people. Actually, however, his position was much worse, for with the possible exception of the 400 thaler just referred to, he was not officially drawing upon the money which had been granted him, but left this sum nominally intact until several months later, when he insisted that it be paid him in full in cash. Consequently the indebtedness of the "regent

---

142 G. H. Löber to Jäckel, Sept. 9, 1838, Jäckel to G. H. Löber, Sept. 18, 1838, Bound MSS., I, C. H. I.

143 Protokolle über die . . . Auswanderung, Sept. 27, 1838, Bound MSS., III, C. H. I. This manuscript is a copy. The original grant, bearing the signatures of the men present at that meeting of the committee, is contained in Bound MSS., 6, C. H. I.

of the church" was in reality in excess of 1,600 thaler at the very least.[144]

Some of the candidates and a few laymen were not only given their fare from the Credit Fund, but had their necessary clothing, equipment, debts, and other expenses paid from it as well.[145] One of the most long-suffering funds was that designated for the "church." To its account, among other things, were charged: salaries and equipment for pastors, candidates, and teachers; a large library; expensive ecclesiastical vestments; a carriage for the "regent of the church"; supplies of sacramental wine; altar vessels; a library of sacred music; a complete set of instruments for a full orchestra; several organs; and a set of bells.[146] A tragic irony made the most of these unnecessary supplies not only an extravagance, but a total loss, for many of them were shipped on the *Amalia* and went down with that vessel.

Finally, also the joint expenses of the *Gesellschaft* as a body had to be defrayed from the dwindling fund. The conduct of the administrative affairs of the organization and traveling expenses for its officials and leaders (exclusive of Stephan) easily accounted for 500 thaler. The *Gesellschaft* also had attorney's fees to pay; Lawyer Krause received 25 thaler on July 6, and 75 thaler on September 10, 1838, which apparently were not part of the payment for services rendered Stephan. The printing bills of the *Gesellschaft* were not negligible either, since they included such items as 900 copies of *Luther's Catechism* and 1,700 copies of some poems by O. H. Walther. The cost of secretarial work and various miscel-

---

144 Martin Stephan in Acct. with the Cash of the Saxon Emigrants, June 11, 1842 (hereafter cited as Stephan . . . Acct.; this is a financial statement evidently drawn up in connection with the suit brought by Stephan, and contains the same information as a German manuscript: Berechnung der . . . Credit Casse für Rechnung des . . . Martin Stephan), Financial statement by F. W. Barthel on Stephan's grant of 1,500 thaler, Feb. 14, 1839, Account of Martin Stephan in List of Saxon Emigrants 1838, MSS., C. H. I.; Receipts signed by Stephan, Oct. 18, 22, 1838, Receipts signed by W. E. Krause, Oct. 29, 24—30, 1838, Bound MSS., 6, C. H. I.

145 Protokolle über die . . . Auswanderung, Sept. 20, 1838, Bound MSS., III, C. H. I.; Gönner to Stephan, Oct. 10, 1838, Zöge to F. W. Barthel, Sept. 1, 1838, Fröhlich to Marbach, Oct. 26, 28, 1838, Bound MSS., I, C. H. I.; Draft in favor of Fröhlich, Oct. 6, 1838, MS., C. H. I.; J. F. Bünger, Diarium, Oct. 26, 1838, MS., L. Fürbringer Papers, St. Louis.

146 Account of *Kirche und Schule* in List of Saxon Emigrants 1838, MS., C. H. I. Bills or receipts for most of the individual items mentioned are contained in Bound MSS., 6, C. H. I. All others are among the unclassified MSS., C. H. I.

laneous expenses created a further drain upon the resources of the group. The aggregate of all types of insurance carried by the emigrants occasioned another considerable bill. For example, the insurance on the cash which the *Gesellschaft* carried to the United States amounted to 1,609 thaler for the ocean voyage alone; and the baggage on a single vessel, the *Olbers,* which carried comparatively more passengers and less freight than the other ships, was insured for 20,000 thaler.[147] All costs connected with the transportation of baggage were, of course, divided among the members of the *Gesellschaft;* but since no one was paying any more money for such charges after his initial contribution, the result was that the actual costs were being met from the Credit Fund in any event.

Of the maximum of 117,521 thaler ($80,604.81¼) in the Credit Fund, 85,831 thaler was spent prior to the arrival of the emigrants in St. Louis. However, transportation of the people and their effects, while naturally one of the largest single items of expense, was by no means the only important one. The exact cost of getting everyone to Bremen cannot be determined, although it must have been considerable. The costs of the transfer from New Orleans to St. Louis will be discussed later. But for the longest and most expensive leg of the journey, from Bremen to New Orleans, accurate figures are available. The sums spent for each of the five ships' companies, including all incidentals, such as insurance and other costs borne jointly for the voyage, were: *Olbers,* 11,011 thaler; *Copernicus,* 8,599 thaler; *Johann Georg,* 6,881 thaler; *Republik,* 5,558 thaler; and *Amalia,* 3,071 thaler. These figures, it will be noted, yield a total of only 35,120 thaler, or about 40 per cent of all expenditures made prior to the arrival of the emigrants in St. Louis. Some of these sums are given with slight variations in other sources than those cited here, but never with a discrepancy large enough seriously to affect the proportion.[148]

---

[147] *Conto des Regie-Aufwands* in List of Saxon Emigrants 1838, Printer's bill, Nov. 14, 1838, Stephan . . . Acct., MSS., C. H. I.; Receipts signed by W. E. Krause, July 6, Sept. 10, 1838, Printer's contract, Oct. 15, 1838, Insurance policies, Bound MSS., 6, C. H. I.; Itemized statement of the freight on the *Olbers,* Bound MSS., No. 10. Passagier-Listen und Passagier-Güter von den Seeschiffen (hereafter cited as Bound MSS., 10), C. H. I.; Accounts of the *Olbers, Copernicus, Johann Georg, Republik,* and *Amalia,* Bound MSS., 5, C. H. I.

[148] Epitome from the Cash-Account, June 11, 1842, MS., C. H. I.; Accounts of the *Olbers, Copernicus, Johann Georg, Republik,* and *Amalia,* Bound MSS., 5, C. H. I.

Consequently it is apparent that there was a tremendous outlay of the *Gesellschaft's* money for non-essentials. The leaders of the Stephanite emigration seem to have had a distinct gift for collecting funds, but much less for administering them. Money was spent freely and irresponsibly from the Credit Fund; yet it is doubtful that any one of the emigrants knew exactly what the status of this fund was when they left Germany or how much their departure had already cost them. A reliable financial statement for that day has not been found and probably does not exist. Later, during the journey and in St. Louis, the immigrants took inventory — to their dismay.[149]

---

[149] Financial Statement of March 14, 1839, Epitome from the Cash-Account, July 11, 1842, Verwaltung der . . . Credit-Casse bis mit Schluss . . . 1838, MSS., C. H. I.

CHAPTER SEVEN

PARTING AND DEPARTING

By the beginning of September, 1838, most of the applicants who were to be taken along had been informed of their good fortune. Then their troubles began in earnest. All of them had been given reason to expect that they would be leaving promptly. Most of them were ready to do so. Some, because of distinctly embarrassing relationships to family, friends, or authorities, felt an acute necessity for doing so. Therefore the financial arrangements just described, coupled with the frequent delays which occurred, added painfully to the mental strain and physical hardship of the rank and file of the *Gesellschaft* and made the plight of many of the emigrants during the last months a pitiful one. A majority did not even have the minimum amount which was required to pay for their expenses. Still fewer had such sums in cash; so businesses were sold, farms disposed of, family estates settled prematurely, and homesteads offered for a song in order to obtain the funds necessary to get from "this charnel house" to "Canaan." [1] Then, when a few hundred thaler or less had been acquired and resignations from positions had already become effective, long delays in sailing forced the people to live off their meager capital for weeks while awaiting word to set out for Bremen.[2]

It is little wonder that some of them became resentful. At least one man wrote to the high command in Dresden, including "Pastor Stäphan, the father of many children," that action was imperative. He declared that the period of waiting, the pressure from friends and relatives, and perhaps the thought of subjecting a son less than three years old to the rigors of a two-month voyage were weaken-

---

[1] Ernestine Anders to Stephan, Aug. 26, 1838, Wesser to Stephan, July 12, 1838, Bound MSS., II, C.H.I.; Seidel to Marbach, Aug. 17, 1838, Bound MSS., VI, C.H.I.; G. H. Löber to Brohm, Aug. 26, 1838, Bound MSS., I, C.H.I.; F. E. Schneider to Vehse, Sept. 3, 1838, MS., C.H.I.; *Leipziger allgemeine Zeitung*, July 24, 1838.

[2] G. H. Löber to —, n.d. [Sept. 11—19, 1938], Bound MSS., I, C.H.I. In this letter Löber reported that 120 people were ready to leave.

ing his wife's determination to leave. He and his family were living as frugally as possible in one room of their former home.[3] Another man wrote that he and his wife were forced to sell their small weaving trade to the "merchants" rather than to a private individual, and that consequently its price was beaten down by at least one third of its actual worth, from 200 to 133 thaler. Of that sum they had to pay 77 thaler to creditors; then repeated delays, lasting six weeks, forced them to use more of their cash for living expenses. Somehow the man and his wife managed to exist on 1 thaler per week; with the result that in the end they had 50 thaler left. Both these people were extremely anxious to go along, but now their only hope of obtaining more money was to borrow it from the man's father.[4] A brief, penciled note on the letter, in another hand, reads: "100 thaler to be paid." [5] And paid they were.[6]

Meanwhile, the idea of formally establishing a hierarchy was growing apace. Those in the inner circle, of course, had had ample opportunity to accustom themselves to the idea, since it had been formally presented to them at the meeting in 1836.[7] But now other members of the *Gesellschaft* and the entire committee made direct references to Stephan as the "bishop." [8] While the various Codes constantly refer to him as the clergyman who is first in rank (*der erste Geistliche*) and studiously avoid use of the term "bishop," they nevertheless endow him with episcopal powers and thus justify the conclusion that to them *der erste Geistliche* was indeed a "bishop," or, a "primate." The Codes, in fact, show the trend at a glance, for from them it is apparent that the "ministerium" was to have a hand in practically all affairs of the emigrants, not only while en route, but also after the colony had been founded, settled, and organized as a modified theocracy.[9] These facts and the spirit

---

[3] J. Domschke to the committee, Oct. 19, 1838, F. W. Barthel to Marbach, Oct. 6, 1838, Bound MSS., I, C. H. I.

[4] Ferdinand and Henriette Römer to Stephan, n. d. [Oct. 1—15, 1838], Bound MSS., I, C. H. I.

[5] *Ibid.*

[6] Account of F. Römer in List of Saxon Emigrants 1838, MS., C. H. I.

[7] G. H. Löber, Diary, May 3, 1836, MS., C. H. I.

[8] Notes on a deliberation between M. F. and J., Dec. 6, 1837, Protokolle über die . . . Auswanderung, Dec. 13, 1837, Sept. 27, 1838, Bound MSS., III, C. H. I.; O. H. Walther to — [Marbach?], Oct. 25, 1838, J. F. Bünger to Marbach, Dec. 11, 1838, MSS., C. H. I.

[9] The Codes, Appendix B.

pervading Stephan, the other leaders, and even some of the rank and file, were so definitely hierarchical as to cause some of the best men among the Stephanites to sever their connections with the group just before its departure.[10]

It is hard to escape the conclusion that before leaving Germany, Stephan and the majority of pastors, candidates, and lay leaders were clearly committed to the plan of introducing the episcopal polity.[11] The special ecclesiastical courts which were to be established in the colony are evidences that the clergy were to become a privileged class.[12] This impression is strengthened by the fact that they evidently expected to be supported irrespective of their services. How a group of six or seven hundred people could absorb with profit the full-time ministrations of about twenty clergymen and teachers (twenty-nine according to their own figures) is something of a puzzle. Yet all of them did expect to be paid by the *Gesellschaft,* and the anticipated salaries, which have been quoted above, show that it was to be share and share alike among them — that is, all were supposed to receive full wages. The preponderance of the clergy, especially of the candidates, in the organization was pronounced and did not escape Stephan, who used it to full advantage in the administration of the *Gesellschaft,* in formulating his plans for the colony, and in working toward his elevation to the episcopacy. For the inducements, actual and prospective, which Stephan held out to the candidates, assured him of their unqualified allegiance; and there is frequent testimony to the fact that the candidates as a group distinguished themselves in their subservience

---

[10] Stübel and Delitzsch are examples.

[11] O. H. Walther to G. H. Löber, Keyl, E. M. Bürger, and C. F. W. Walther, n. d. [Feb. 19—22, 1839], Document . . . des Grundsteins . . . St. Louis . . . 22. Juny 1842, Lossagung vom Stephanismus, Bekenntniss, MSS., C. H. I.; Keyl, *op. cit.,* 13; C. F. W. Walther in Köstering, *Auswanderung,* 16—17. Both the events and the statements at the time Stephan was given the office bear out such a conclusion. Even L. Fischer, an opponent of the Stephanites, was acquainted with the plan and must have known of it before the emigrants left Germany. Fischer, *op. cit.,* viii, 71, 133—135. Stephan wrote: "Our church polity, like that of the Swedish Lutheran Church, was to be an episcopal polity. This was the common desire of the entire company." Stephan to Flügel, Oct. 12, 1841, MS., C. H. I. Contrast with these references Hennig's assertion: "St. [Stephan] had absolutely no hierarchical designs." Hennig, "Die Auswanderung Martin Stephans," *Zeitschrift für Kirchengeschichte,* LVIII, 145. See also G. H. Löber, Diary, May 3, 1836, MS., C. H. I.

[12] Code for the Civil Community, par. 10, Appendix B.

to him.[13] If any further support was needed, Stephan could always depend upon those emigrants who were indebted to him for the very privilege of going along, to render perhaps a mercenary but not ineffective loyalty.[14] The foundation on which these hierarchical plans were based was the same set of peculiar Stephanite pretensions described before as fundamental for the entire structure of the *Gesellschaft,* namely, that the Church in Germany was facing extinction, that after the departure of the emigrants it would cease to exist, and that the Stephanites were, indeed, *the* Church. To Stephan and those who bore his name there was nothing unnatural about recognizing that the founder of the *Gesellschaft* was its ecclesiastical overlord.

A rather unique position, somewhere betwixt clergy and laity, was occupied by Marbach. Next to Stephan, Marbach was the most important of the leaders. In influence outside the *Gesellschaft* as well as in talent he ranked second to none. During the final months in Germany, when Stephan was under surveillance or arrest, Marbach, as occasion demanded, assumed almost sole control of the direction of affairs and rendered the movement valuable service.[15] Stübel claimed that without Marbach the emigration would have been impossible, and there is ample reason for agreeing with him.[16]

Just what schemes were crossing through Marbach's ambitious brain is not known, but he later admitted that he expected to play a great role in the New World.[17] No doubt Stephan, writing while in exile from the colonies during 1841, was a trifle acidulous in his judgment when he said of Marbach: "He was full of shady business deals." But there may be some truth to Stephan's claim that Marbach "would have liked to get some factory workers from the group [of emigrants] in order to rebuild his shattered fortunes." [18] The man had a touch of the fanatic about him. When this characteristic was conveniently blended with his really deep religious feeling, his great energy, and his ability, the force generated was considerable.

---

13 Lossagung vom Stephanismus, Bekenntniss, Brohm, Journal, Dec. 31, 1838, Jan. 28, 29, Feb. 3, 1839, MSS., C. H. I.; Stübel to Vehse, *et al.*, Sept. 12, 1839, Bound MSS., VI, C. H. I.; Vehse, *op. cit.*, 2, 5—7.

14 Vehse, *op. cit.*, 5—7.

15 Marbach to O. H. Walther, Oct. 16, 1838, Bound MSS., I, C. H. I.

16 Stübel to Vehse *et al.*, Sept. 12, 1839, Bound MSS., VI, C. H. I.

17 Marbach to — ("Hochgeehrter Herr Geheimrath"), May 8, 1840, *ibid.*

18 Stephan to Flügel, Oct. 12, 1841, MS., C. H. I.

Marbach would brook opposition from no one except Stephan. The death of two of his children, just before the departure from Germany and on the journey, failed to shake his determination. The desperate objections of his wife to the entire idea of emigration led him to see in her a tool of Satan.[19] Marbach became virtually a one-man clearinghouse for every administrative detail of the now far-flung organization. His will to rule was almost unchecked for a time, with the result that he became somewhat arrogant, as illustrated by his rather reckless remarks about the insignificance of Duke Joseph of Saxe-Altenburg.[20] However, when Marbach began to treat not only laymen, but pastors and candidates in somewhat cavalier fashion, and refused them some of the things they wanted, he made a serious tactical mistake and promptly became the object of criticism.[21]

During the final months, evidences of strain became apparent throughout the organization; then Marbach drove onward with redoubled efforts to hasten the emigration.[22] The pressure of working and of waiting was beginning to tell; nerves became frayed and tempers short. Löber complained of being "unstrung" and asked that one of the candidates from Dresden be assigned to help him.[23] Apparently Fürbringer, who was in Eichenberg at the time, was unacceptable to Löber, who expressed some resentment against what he described as Fürbringer's "irascible and belligerent" conduct, which, he said, gave rise to heated arguments between the two men.[24] Keyl was the object of thinly veiled accusations of embezzlement by the Dresdeners. The mediation of O. H. Walther

---

19 "She [Marbach's wife] strenuously resists the Holy Ghost through a highly sinful and false skepticism. . . . I learn something daily of the verse: *Because thou hast hearkened unto the voice of thy wife . . .*" — Marbach to von Uckermann, Dec. 27, 1837, Bound MSS., VI, C. H. I. See also Marbach to Stübel, n. d. [1839—1840], *ibid.;* Brohm, Journal, Jan. 1, 2, 13, 1839, MS., C. H. I.

20 Marbach to G. H. Löber, Aug. 15, 1838, Bound MSS., I, C. H. I.

21 O. H. Walther to — [Marbach?], Oct. 25, 1838, Brohm, Journal, 1, 2, 13, 1839, MSS., C. H. I.; Marbach to O. H. Walther, Oct. 16, 1838, Marbach to Döderlein, Oct. 21, 1838, Gönner to Stephan, Oct. 10, 1838, Bound MSS., I, C. H. I.

22 Marbach to O. H. Walther, Oct. 16, 1838, Bound MSS., I, C. H. I.; O. H. Walther to — [Marbach?], Oct. 21, 1838, MS., C. H. I.; J. F. Bünger, Diarium, Nov. 8, 1838, MS., L. Fürbringer Papers, St. Louis.

23 G. H. Löber to —, n. d. [Sept. 11—19, 1838], G. H. Löber to Marbach, Oct. 5, 1838, Bound MSS., I, C. H. I.

24 G. H. Löber to Stephan, Nov. 7, 1838, *ibid.* Löber had complained of this from the beginning of his association with Fürbringer, G. H. Löber, Diary, Oct. 10, 1831, MS., C. H. I.

was necessary to restore friendly relations.[25] Some people mistrusted Lawyer Krause and censured the leaders for entrusting money to him.[26] Bürger did not prove tractable enough; and again the elder Walther had to step in to convince Bürger of his obligations and the Dresden directors of his docility.[27] Stübel, who had not attended meetings of the Advisory Committee since March 24, finally withdrew from the emigration entirely, because he could not concur in the Stephanite attitude toward Stephan and, to use Stübel's phrase, "find the image of God Himself" in the Dresden pastor. Stübel considered much of the religiosity surrounding the movement sacrilegious.[28] He did, however, maintain contact with some of the emigrants and seems even to have given the movement some financial support.[29] By October it was clear that refusal to submit to Stephan, disagreement on the necessity for emigration, and several theological differences had eliminated Delitzsch, von Uckermann, Stübel, the Leipzig student Otto Rudel, and others, although these men who stayed behind continued their close association with like-minded conservatives.[30]

Into the uncongenial atmosphere of the last troubled months in Germany the old philippics between the Stephanites and their opponents, especially the liberalistic church element, were projected with renewed vigor.[31] The treatment of religious questions by both parties under prevailing circumstances was not productive of much good. Certainly no conclusion was reached. The vituperation by the Stephanites of everything connected with the State

---

25 O. H. Walther to — [Marbach?], Oct. 25, 1838, MS., C. H. I.

26 J. F. Bünger to Marbach, Oct. 22, 1838, Bound MSS., I, C. H. I.; Stephan . . . Acct., MS., C. H. I.

27 O. H. Walther to — [Marbach?], Oct. 21, 1838, MS., C. H. I.

28 Stübel to Vehse *et al.*, Sept. 12, 1839, Bound MSS., VI, C. H. I.

29 Account of Stübel in List of Saxon Emigrants 1838, MS., C. H. I.

30 Fröhlich to Marbach, Oct. 23—24, 1838, Delitzsch to F. W. Barthel, Dec. 8, 1839, MSS., C. H. I.; E. L. Krause to Stephan, Oct. 2, 1838, Bound MSS., II, C. H. I.; Marbach to Döderlein, Oct. 21, 1838, Bound MSS., I, C. H. I.; Stübel to Vehse *et al.*, Sept. 12, 1839, Rudel to —, May 2, 1838, Bound MSS., VI, C. H. I.; J. F. Bünger, Diarium, Oct. 2, 4, 1838, MS., L. Fürbringer Papers, St. Louis. L. Fischer stated that three candidates were expelled from the ranks of the Stephanites in 1838. Fischer, *op. cit.*, 61. Rudel had been intimately associated with the Stephanites since at least 1836. G. H. Löber, Diary, 1836, p. 50, MS., C. H. I.

31 *Chemnitzer Anzeiger,* Oct. 30, Nov. 7, 1838. From these issues it is apparent that the quarrel was being renewed also in the *Allgemeiner Anzeiger der Deutschen.* See also Fischer, *op. cit.,* 72—91.

Church and of all opposed to Stephan, which has been described above, was matched by the tirades of the opposition, who showed a complete lack of understanding for the confessional convictions which animated many of the emigrants. Yet, even relatively conservative elements in the Church found the sweeping denunciations by Stephan and his followers, both in word and in the unmistakably damning act of emigration, far too extreme.

As late as May, 1838, Rudelbach defended Stephan publicly. But on September 13 of that year nine members of the Muldenthal Pastoral Conference, erstwhile friends of most of the emigrating pastors, came out with a signed statement on the emigration, Rudelbach's name heading the list. In this declaration he and his associates did not repudiate conservatism, but rather the charge that their defense of conservative views, similar to Stephan's, had led to the emigration. Furthermore, they denounced the extremism of the Stephanites and their categorical condemnation of almost everything in sight. The statement received wide publicity, for instance, in the *Leipziger allgemeine Zeitung,* September 30, 1838, and in Harless' *Zeitschrift für Protestantismus und Kirche,* October 21, 1838.[32] At times much has been made of the fact that later Rudelbach also left Saxony as a protest against religious conditions. This step is regarded by some as a belated indorsement — even if only through the implication of the action — of the emigration. Yet in order to draw such a conclusion, it is necessary to ignore the fact (which some of those who follow this line of reasoning have also been obliged to admit) that Rudelbach was confronted with a fundamentally different problem.[33]

Another expression of opinion among the conservatives who did not join the emigration was von Uckermann's apt remark: "May God grant you [Marbach, Vehse, and the Stephanites in general] together with the firm, fine faith you have — also the second heavenly gift, without which one cannot be saved — Christian love." [34] Scheibel also remained in Germany. The Silesian conservatives as a group, following Scheibel's lead, kept aloof from the

---

[32] This statement is quoted in full in Fischer, *op. cit.,* 200—204; "Nachrichten," *Evangelische Kirchen-Zeitung,* XXIII, 676—678.

[33] C. F. W. Walther, *Bünger,* 41; Köstering, *Keyl,* 52—53. See also Brohm, "Mittheilungen aus Sachsen," *Der Lutheraner,* II, 91; "G. G.," in *Lehre und Wehre,* XLVII, 147—148.

[34] Von Uckermann to Marbach, Jan. 9, 1838, Bound MSS., VI, C.H.I.

emigration, although other Prussians, especially those from the Saxon province of Prussia, contributed an appreciable number of emigrants. Scheibel found Stephanism "the most tragic phenomenon" in the contemporary history of the Saxon Church.[35] Even the farewell sermons of the departing pastors were polemical and categorically condemned conditions existing in the Church, as well as everyone — liberalist and conservative alike — who bore them more patiently than did the Stephanites themselves. Bürger preached on Micah 2:10 ff., and the claim is made that this passage was written on the doors of the manse on the day he left. During his farewell sermon C. F. W. Walther held forth in such a legalistic manner that some people ran out of the church in terror and tears.[36]

As the final date for departure drew near, opposition to the movement stiffened considerably. Just before, and even after, the Stephanites sailed, newspapers in Germany were carrying articles on emigration so frequently and with such a decided note of alarm that even English newspapers in St. Louis took cognizance of the fact.[37] In Saxony many such articles during 1838 and 1839 were markedly unfavorable to the United States and admittedly tried to discourage emigration. They reported that there was practically no emigration from England to the United States; that many former emigrants from Britain were now returning home because of poverty, unemployment, an oversupply of labor in every field of work, and internal political unrest in the United States; and that the one indispensable requisite for success in America was a great deal of capital.[38]

While the movement in general met with increased opposition in the form of propaganda, the pastors were confronted with actual obstacles placed in the way of their departure. They had all handed in their resignations or asked for their releases, in accordance with the instructions of the Advisory Committee,[39] but peaceful dismis-

---

35 Scheibel, *op. cit.*, 245—247.

36 Fischer, *op. cit.*, 71; Pleissner, *op. cit.*, 65—66, 84—85; Lütkemüller, *op. cit.*, 118; M. Günther, *op. cit.*, 33.

37 *St. Louis New Era*, May 5, 1840, July 7, 1842; *Anzeiger des Westens*, April 18, June 22, Aug. 15, 1843, March 9, 1846; *Daily Missouri Republican*, Feb. 10, 1845, Aug. 7, 1846; *St. Louis American*, March 12, 1845.

38 *Chemnitzer Anzeiger*, Oct. 30, 1838; G. F. Löber to G. H. Löber, July 8, 1838, May 29, 1839, in Löber-Eichenberg (ed.), "Ein Briefwechsel," *Mitteilungen . . . Kahla*, 129—130, 149.

39 Protokolle über die . . . Auswanderung, July 2, 1838, Bound MSS., III, C.H.I.

sal was not always granted. In fact, Bürger and O. H. Walther are the only ones who seem to have had no trouble. The latter resigned on August 28, 1838, effective September 29; his release was granted within a week.[40] Keyl, on the other hand, had become involved in another charge of holding conventicles; so his resignation of August 16, 1838, also effective September 29, was not acted upon, and his passport, applied for on September 7, was held up pending the outcome of the action against him.[41] Proceedings against Keyl were finally dropped only on the day before he sailed for the United States, after he had left Nieder-Frohna and after his father-in-law, G. H. W. Walther, had agreed to pay some of the costs of the case.[42] C. F. W. Walther was in trouble because of his methods, or at least his alleged methods, of persuading people to go along, and was formally charged with breaking up several families.[43] Apparently he was eventually granted a formal release by the consistory.[44]

Löber and Gruber, after repeated appeals to their consistory, were refused both their releases and their passports.[45] Finally both the pastors and the consistory referred the matter to Duke Joseph, with no better results for the pastors.[46] Löber was pursued by the fear that the question would not be settled in time for him to go

---

40 O. H. Walther to Superintendent Leo, Aug. 28, 1838, O. H. Walther to the consistory at Glauchau, Aug. 28, 1838, The consistory at Glauchau to Superintendent Leo, Sept. 3, 1838, Superintendent Leo to O. H. Walther, Sept. 7, 1838, Bound MSS., Acta . . . der Ephorie Waldenburg, C. H. I.

41 G. H. Löber to —, n. d. [Sept. 11—19, 1838], Bound MSS., I, C. H. I.; Proceedings and correspondence, Aug. 26, Sept. 10, 24, 1838, Bound MSS., Acta Ephoralia . . . Keyl betreffend, C. H. I.; Hennig, "Die Auswanderung Martin Stephans," *Zeitschrift für Kirchengeschichte*, LVIII, 161.

42 The court at Nieder-Frohna to Siebenhaar, Nov. 2, 1838, Bound MSS., Acta Ephoralia . . . Keyl betreffend, C. H. I.

43 Proceedings and correspondence, July 30, Aug. 1, 1838, Bound MSS., Acten . . . Pester . . . *C. F. W. Walther*, C. H. I.

44 *Anzeiger des Westens*, Dec. 31, 1842.

45 Bekenntniss, MS., C. H. I.; G. H. Löber to the consistory of Saxe-Altenburg, Aug. 8, 24, 1838, The consistory of Saxe-Altenburg to Duke Joseph, Sept. 4, 1838, in *Bedenken der theologischen Facultäten*, 28—29, 32—46; G. H. Löber to Jäckel, Sept. 9, 1838, Bound MSS., I, C. H. I.; Duke Joseph to G. F. Löber, Sept. 25, 1838, in Löber-Eichenberg (ed.), "Ein Briefwechsel," *Mitteilungen . . . Kahla*, VII, 131—133.

46 Duke Joseph to G. F. Löber, Sept. 25, 1838, G. H. Löber to G. F. Löber, Sept. 26, 1838, in Löber-Eichenberg (ed.), "Ein Briefwechsel," *Mitteilungen . . . Kahla*, VII, 131—135; The consistory of Saxe-Altenburg to G. H. Löber, Aug. 14, 1838, The consistory of Saxe-Altenburg to Duke Joseph, Sept. 4, 1838, quoted in *Bedenken der theologischen Facultäten*, 30—32, 35—46; G. H. Löber to Jäckel, Sept. 19, 24, 1838, G. H. Löber to Marbach, Sept. 26, 1838, Bound MSS., I, C. H. I.

along and wrote anxious letters to Dresden asking what he should do.[47] His real mistake, of course, was that he had made definite arrangements to go before he had secured permission. The advice Löber received from Marbach and Stephan was that which he eventually followed, namely, to announce his resignation, regardless of the attitude of the consistory or the Duke, and to leave.[48] While Löber at one time claimed that he had been granted both his release and a passport,[49] actually, at the time of his departure, he had the sanction of neither church nor civil authorities, nor of his elder brother, Friedemann, who was patron of the parish Pastor Löber was serving. The only passport G. H. Löber possessed was an invalid one, made out for him without authorization by his younger brother, August, the judge.[50] Gruber's ill health, which had threatened to prevent his departure, improved sufficiently so that he could report to Dresden in September that he and his family were "ready to go." [51] Parental displeasure, however, cut off all hope of financial support for Gruber and made it impossible for him to leave at this time. Löber condemned the elder Gruber's "hard-heartedness" severely.[52]

Less attention was focused on the laymen, but even they had their troubles. In Saxe-Altenburg there was open disapproval of the emigration by the government, but no active measures were taken against the movement, and, with the exception of a few isolated cases, passports were granted. Even when such official sanction was withheld, no effort was made to stop the emigrants either at the borders of their own country or of those through which they

---

47 G. H. Löber to Jäckel, Sept. 9, 19, 24, 1838, G. H. Löber to Marbach, Sept. 26, 1838, Bound MSS., I, C. H. I.

48 Marbach to G. H. Löber, Aug. 15, 1838, G. H. Löber to Marbach, Oct. 5, 1838, *ibid.*

49 G. H. Löber to —, n. d. [Sept. 11—19, 1838], *ibid.*

50 G. H. Löber to Jäckel, Sept. 19, 1838, G. H. Löber to Marbach, Oct. 5, 21, 1838, G. H. Löber to Brohm, Oct. 6, 1838, Bound MSS., I, C. H. I.; Duke Joseph to G. F. Löber, Sept. 25, 1838, G. H. Löber to G. F. Löber, July 5, Sept. 26, Oct. 19, 1838, G. F. Löber to G. H. Löber, July 8, Oct. 14, 1838, in Löber-Eichenberg (ed.), "Ein Briefwechsel," *Mitteilungen . . . Kahla,* VII, 128—129, 131—140. Pastor Löber's brothers never had shared his religious zealotry. G. H. Löber, Diary, Dec. 6, 1831, Feb. 4, 1836, MS., C. H. I.

51 G. H. Löber to Jäckel, Sept. 19, 1838, Bound MSS., I, C. H. I.

52 G. H. Löber to —, Aug. 25, 1838, G. H. Löber to Jäckel, Sept. 9, 1938, *ibid.* Löber had been critical of the elder Gruber and his habits for years. G. H. Löber, Diary, Dec. 13, 1831, MS., C. H. I.

had to pass.[53] In royal Saxony, however, it was extremely difficult for some members of the *Gesellschaft* to secure passports. Approval could be and was withheld, for example, because of failure to have rendered military service, because of the laws governing emigration, or merely because of the caprice or animosity of local officials. Opposition was so pronounced, and delays were so protracted, that the problem of securing permission to leave the country became a matter of general concern to the emigrants. Failure to solve this problem in time was one of the reasons for the delay in sailing.[54] In Saxony the emigrants applied for passports in a body, but did not receive them as a group.[55]

Discrimination against anyone associated too closely with Stephan was open and frank. Passports were refused some of the men for no other reason than that they appeared as witnesses in court to testify in Stephan's defense, although there was not the suspicion of a charge against these men themselves.[56] Some of those who wished to emigrate avoided the problem by leaving the country secretly without official permission, either by simply slipping across the border unnoticed or by resorting to disguises and similar subterfuges.[57] Such a solution was not possible on a large scale, however; so the intervention of several high government officials and even of the king himself was sought. The pressure these men brought to bear on their subordinates eventually produced a sudden surge of amiability in granting passports and dispensing with formalities.[58] It is worth noting, perhaps, that the attitude of the government in this case was not prompted solely by opposition to the Stephanites, as the latter seemed to think, but was part of a

---

[53] O. H. Walther to — [Marbach?], Oct. 21, 25, 1838, MSS., C. H. I.; *Chemnitzer Anzeiger*, Oct. 30, 1838; Pleissner, *op. cit.*, 25.

[54] Jäckel to G. H. Löber, Sept. 18, 1838, Bound MSS., I, C. H. I.; J. F. Bünger, Diarium, Oct. 1—3, 6—8, 16, 17, 20, 21, 1838, MS., L. Fürbringer Papers, St. Louis. A copy of such a passport, as issued to Pastor E. M. Bürger and his family, Aug. 25, 1838, has been preserved, MS., C. H. I.

[55] Jäckel to Stephan, Aug. 29, 1838, Bound MSS., I, C. H. I.

[56] Jäckel to G. H. Löber, Sept. 18, 1838, *ibid.*

[57] Bekenntniss, MS., C. H. I.; J. F. Bünger, Diarium, Oct. 22, 1838, MS., L. Fürbringer Papers, St. Louis; G. H. Löber to G. F. Löber, Oct. 19, 1838, in Löber-Eichenberg (ed.), "Ein Briefwechsel," *Mitteilungen . . . Kahla*, VII, 138.

[58] G. H. Löber to G. F. Löber, Nov. 6, 1838, in Löber-Eichenberg (ed.), "Ein Briefwechsel," *Mitteilungen . . . Kahla*, VII, 142—143; Jäckel to Stephan, Aug. 29, 1838, Marbach to Döderlein, Oct. 21, 1838, F. W. Barthel to Marbach, Oct. 8, 1838, Bound MSS., I, C. H. I.; J. F. Bünger, Diarium, Oct. 7, 8, 1838, MS., L. Fürbringer Papers, St. Louis.

broader policy against emigration.[59] But L. Fischer's assertion that the government was tolerant or even obliging in its contacts with departing Stephanites can refer only to the very last weeks.[60]

Any doubt which may have lingered in Stephan's mind in 1837 as to the desirability of emigration was removed by the events of the following year. The unexpected response to the launching of his plan early in 1838 would probably have made withdrawal highly embarrassing for him. This circumstance alone was probably sufficient to assure that there would be an emigration. But Stephan's difficulties with the authorities in 1838 placed all thought of remaining in Germany in his former capacity beyond the realm of possibility.[61] Several brushes with the law following his suspension have already been noted, but they were bagatelles, both in nature and results, compared with later developments. By the summer of 1838 it became doubtful that the Bohemian pastor, who had leisurely debated with himself for years whether he should leave, would be permitted to do so. Panic then gripped Stephan; he asserted that he *must* get out of Germany by the fall of 1838.[62]

Yet even under these circumstances Stephan's effrontery was not appreciably lessened. That he defied the order against his meetings at the Hoflösnitz has already been mentioned. Then in May he had the temerity to request the very authorities whom he considered responsible for his "oppression" to grant him a subsidy from the trust fund of the "Bohemian" congregation, because his salary had been reduced since his suspension.[63] The tactlessness of this maneuver was exceeded in another petition to the same agency the following month, when he asked for money from the identical source to finance his enjoyment of a "cure" at the baths at Radeberg, near Liegau, where he had been accustomed to go almost annually since 1831 or 1832.[64] Whether the Ministry of Worship decided to pay for this junket is not clear, but in any event Stephan did go

---

59 For a discussion of the laws prevalent in the thirties see Rosenthal, *op. cit.*, 17, 40—43.

60 Fischer, *op. cit.*, 69.

61 *Ibid.*, 52.

62 Stephan and Marbach, Instruction für Spröde, Bound MSS., I, C. H. I.

63 Stephan to the Ministry of Worship, May 7 [9?], 1838, MS., C. H. I.

64 Stephan to the Ministry of Worship, June 26, 1838, Bekenntnis der Louise Guenther, MSS., C. H. I.

to Liegau as usual in 1838 and there continued his private gatherings in mixed company.[65]

It seems that by August, 1838, most of the proceedings in which Stephan was involved had been concluded, but by the middle of the month he was summoned from Liegau to Dresden for a continuation of his investigation.[66] On September 1 Stephan was back in Liegau once more, and on that date the Dresden officials made an unsuccessful attempt to link him with the case of Mathilda Welzel, an unwed mother, the sister of Candidate Welzel. Superintendent Heymann and Registrar Günz conducted the hearing, in which Mathilda Welzel was closely questioned about her personal history, the nature of her association with Stephan, her attendance at his meetings, her participation in his nocturnal excursions, her movements between Dresden and Liegau, and similar things. However, Fräulein Welzel absolved Stephan of any complicity in her affairs and named another man as the father of her child. Her father, her brother, and her aunt were also questioned.[67] That night, for no discernible purpose, Stephan's quarters at Bad Radeberg were raided by a detachment of gendarmes. Again the law drew a blank. The prospective bishop was found alone in his room, asleep in bed.[68] It is related that on another occasion a similar visit by the police in the dead of night brought out only the fact that Stephan had departed for Dresden with two female companions, leaving two other women behind to receive the gendarmerie.[69]

In October, 1838, Stephan again was placed into a critical position when a servant girl charged him with improper conduct and his congregation lodged formal complaint against him on the grounds of immoral personal life, frequent neglect of pastoral duties, and embezzlement. Accordingly, Stephan was once more summoned from Liegau to appear in Dresden on October 16. Although he returned a day ahead of time, an officer was sent by the Dresden authorities

---

65 Deposition of Karoline Reihsner, Oct. 16, 1838, Bound MSS., V, C. H. I.; Fischer, *op. cit.*, 52. Numerous letters both to Marbach and to Stephan are addressed to Liegau in 1838, Bound MSS., I, C. H. I. Vehse was also there for a time, it appears. F. E. Schneider to Vehse, Sept. 3, 1838, MS., C. H. I.

66 The Superintendent and the Court of the Second Judicial District, Dresden, to Stephan, Aug. 10, 1838, Bound MSS., 6, C. H. I.

67 An account by one of the Welzel brothers of the hearing his sister had before Superintendent Heymann, Sept. 1, 1838, Bound MSS., VI, C. H. I.

68 Jäckel to G. H. Löber, Sept. 4, 1838, Bound MSS., I, C. H. I.

69 Gruber, *op. cit.*, 29.

to escort him back to the capital. When the officials learned of Stephan's return, he was placed under house arrest, a virtual prisoner under guard of two police officers stationed in his home day and night. This type of custody continued until he was released for the emigration.[70] The flourish with which these and other actions by representatives of the government were carried out suggested the methods of a press agent rather than the prelude to dignified judicial proceedings. The net result was to give unwelcome publicity to a cause that could profit only by getting less of it. Absurd speculations and rumors circulated among the Dresden populace, rumors encouraged, if not in some instances even instigated, by members of the city's police force.[71] Bitter protests were made by Lawyer Krause, who finally requested a change of venue. The request was not granted.[72]

Stephan's supporters were incensed at the manner in which the case against him was conducted. They charged that the protracted investigations were never brought to a conclusion because nothing could be proved against Stephan, that continuing such sterile efforts could have only the one purpose of discrediting him before the public, and that the entire action could not be justified as even quasi-judicial procedure.[73] The complaints concerning the delays in the investigation were at least partly answered by von Karlowitz in a report to the king. The minister pointed out that

---

[70] Marbach to O. H. Walther, Oct. 16, 1838, Bound MSS., I, C. H. I.; Appeal of Stephan to Fredrick Augustus II, Oct. 20, 1838, Complaint of W. E. Krause to the High Court of Appeals at Dresden, Oct. 16, 1838, Supplement to the Complaint of W. E. Krause to the High Court of Appeals at Dresden, Oct. 16, 1838, Deposition of Karoline Reihsner (submitted together with the Supplement of Krause's Complaint), Oct. 16, 1838, Bound MSS., V, C. H. I.; J. F. Bünger, Diarium, Oct. 15, 18, 1838, MS., L. Fürbringer Papers, St. Louis; Lütkemüller, *op. cit.*, 24—25; Fischer, *op. cit.*, 53—54.

[71] Jäckel to G. H. Löber, Sept. 4, 1838, Bound MSS., I, C. H. I.; Complaint of W. E. Krause to the High Court of Appeals at Dresden, Oct. 16, 1838, Supplement to the Complaint of W. E. Krause to the High Court of Appeals at Dresden, Oct. 16, 1838, Deposition of Karoline Reihsner, Oct. 16, 1838, Bound MSS., V, C. H. I.

[72] Supplement to the Complaint of W. E. Krause to the High Court of Appeals at Dresden, Oct. 16, 1838, Bound MSS., V, C. H. I.

[73] Complaint of W. E. Krause to the High Court of Appeals at Dresden, Oct. 16, 1838, Supplement to the Complaint of W. E. Krause to the High Court of Appeals at Dresden, Oct. 16, 1838, Deposition of Karoline Reihsner, Oct. 16, 1838, Bemerkungen über . . . Stephan, *ibid.;* Protokolle über die . . . Auswanderung, Feb. 15, March 24, 1838, Bound MSS., III, C. H. I.; An account by one of the Welzel brothers of the hearing his sister had before Superintendent Heymann, Sept. 1, 1838, Bound MSS., VI, C. H. I.

one of the chief reasons for postponements was the habit Stephan had of appealing each point through all possible courts.[74] This charge was true in at least one known case. The order for the transfer of the records of St. John's issued on March 10, 1838, and appealed by Stephan, was not fully complied with until the following August 6.[75]

Finally the conviction grew among the Stephanites that the action against their leader would be deliberately prolonged in order to prevent his departure, or at least to delay it so long that his followers would have the alternative of abandoning him in Germany or seeing the entire plan shattered. Neither the morale nor the finances of the group could stand the strain of further discredit to Stephan or of a longer period of waiting.[76] The alarm of the Stephanites during these last weeks was especially acute among the people who were already in Bremen. O. H. Walther, their spokesman, piously exclaimed: "We now have no other wish but this: May God soon bring our crown [Stephan] and its pearls [the other leaders still in Dresden] from Dresden to us." [77] When the news of Stephan's final arrest reached them, these emigrants, many of whom were poverty-stricken themselves, collected the sum of 500 thaler, which was given to Stephan for defraying his increased legal and traveling expenses.[78] G. H. Löber made a separate gift to Stephan,[79] and Keyl did likewise.[80] But even such financial sacrifices could not in themselves assure Stephan's release without the proper legal action.

To prevent complete failure, recourse was finally taken to in tercession with the Minister of Justice and other influential persons,[81] and on Ocotber 20, as a last resort, another petition was

---

[74] Von Karlowitz to Fredrick Augustus II, March 19, 1838, MS., Dresdener Hauptstaatsarchiv, Hausarchiv Friedrich August II, No. 151.

[75] Receipt for the books of St. John's, July 23, Aug. 6, 1838, MS., C. H. I.

[76] Appeal of Stephan to Fredrick Augustus II, Oct. 20, 1838, Marbach to von Könneritz, Oct. 16, 17, 1838, Marbach to von Langenn, Oct. 16, 19, 1838, Bound MSS., V, C. H. I.; Marbach to O. H. Walther, Oct. 16, 1838, G. H. Löber to Brohm, Oct. 16, 1838, Bound MSS., I, C. H. I.

[77] O. H. Walther to — [Marbach?], Oct. 26, 1838, Bound MSS., I, C. H. I.

[78] O. H. Walther to —[Marbach?], Oct. 21, 1838, MS., C. H. I.

[79] *Ibid.*

[80] Draft on Keyl's account, Oct. 30, 1838, MS., C. H. I.

[81] Marbach to O. H. Walther, Oct. 16, 1838, Bound MSS., I, C. H. I.; Marbach to von Könneritz, Oct. 16, 17, 1838, Marbach to von Langenn, Oct. 16, 19, 1838, Bound MSS., V, C. H. I.

addressed directly to the king.[82] In this appeal to his sovereign, Stephan resigned from office, requested the quashing of all proceedings against him, and asked for full liberty to leave. Moreover, he blandly recommended to royal mercy his wife and the seven children whom he was leaving behind.[83] The abandonment of his family apparently did not cause Stephan any serious scruples, although he seems to have had a vague idea of having others of his children besides Martin, Jr., follow him at a future date.[84] The government was gracious enough to give Stephan's family some support after he left.[85]

The plea to Fredrick Augustus was answered within five days, and Stephan, for whom the Credit Fund had put up 500 thaler bail — the exact amount of the purse made up by his followers in Bremen — was given permission to leave provided he forfeited this bail as security for the congregation of St. John. He set out for Bremerhaven almost at once, that is, on the night of October 27—28, 1838, only a matter of hours before the last major detachment of emigrants succeeded in leaving Dresden by boat.[86] Traveling posthaste in his private carriage with a valet and a maid, Stephan arrived in Bremen on November 4, the day after the first two ships had set sail; he remained there until November 14, and on the evening of that day reached Bremerhaven.[87]

---

[82] Appeal of Stephan to Fredrick Augustus II, Oct. 20, 1838, Bound MSS., V, C. H. I.; Marbach to O. H. Walther, Oct. 21, 1838, Bound MSS., I, C. H. I. In one place the assertion has been made that Stephan's wife also appealed to the king for the release of her husband. Neve-Allbeck, *History of the Lutheran Church in America,* 88.

[83] Appeal of Stephan to Fredrick Augustus II, Oct. 20, 1838, Bound MSS., V, C. H. I.

[84] The passengers of the *Olbers* to Capt. H. W. Exter, Jan. 19, 1839, Bound MSS., I, C. H. I.; Stephan to Flügel, Oct. 12, 1841, MS., C. H. I.

[85] Von Polenz, *op. cit.,* 74.

[86] Stephan . . . Acct., MS., C. H. I. Hennig says that the proceedings against Stephan were dropped on Oct. 25, while J. Gruber placed it on Oct. 24. Hennig, "Die Auswanderung Martin Stephans," *Zeitschrift für Kirchengeschichte,* LVIII, 163—164; Gruber, *op. cit.,* 30. The article on "Stephan" in Herzog-Plitt, *Real-Encyklopädie,* XIV, 673, states the crown acted on Oct. 23. Fischer claimed that Stephan left Dresden on Oct. 30, while another writer placed the departure as early as Oct. 20 — the latter, of course, an obviously impossible date. Fischer, *op. cit.,* 54; "E. E.," "Unsere lutherische Kirche in St. Louis," *Der Lutheraner,* LXXXII, 160.

[87] G. H. Löber to G. F. Löber, Nov. 6, 1838, in Löber-Eichenberg (ed.), "Ein Briefwechsel," *Mitteilungen . . . Kahla,* VII, 142—143; Vehse, *op. cit.,* 7—8; G. Günther, *op. cit.,* 2. M. L. Hansen's view of the incident through European eyes led him to report that "a swift dash overland brought him

It does not seem to have occurred to Stephan that he might wish to stay for the very purpose of seeing through to a conclusion the proceedings he was so anxious to escape. Instead, he dramatized the incident in his own mind with remarks such as: "Had the justice of the King of Saxony not snatched me from the hands of my powerful enemies, I should not have been able to emigrate." [88]

Notwithstanding the circumstances which have been related here, Stephan claimed that "the emigration now proceeded quickly and quietly." [89] Hennig denies "that Stephan fled . . . before an imminent catastrophe"; any charges involving his morals are written off as so much "Dresden gossip"; and Stephan's real mistake is regarded by his apologist as "a lack of caution." [90] Yet permitting Stephan to leave was perhaps the most generous action taken by the Saxon government in all its dealings with him. At the same time, this step was the most unfortunate. The release of Stephan at this time enabled him to maintain his leadership in the *Gesellschaft* and rendered impossible any legal decision in his case, which would have been given eventually, no matter how long delayed, had he been obliged to remain. The result was that final judgment was deferred until Stephan was in the United States, where the circumstances were even less favorable for arriving at an impartial verdict than they had been in Saxony.

While these final skirmishes in Stephan's personal vendetta with Saxon bureaucracy were being fought by his paladins, the ranks of his followers were helplessly converging on, or expensively marking time in, what all of them hoped would eventually be their port of embarkation. The majority of the emigrants had been enrolled by early September, 1838. Orders then had been sent out to the pastors to have their people ready for departure by September 29, although the last of the five ships was not chartered until October 5.[91] Even before that date detachments of people

---

[Stephan] to his awaiting people — all of which added a touch of the dramatic to the episode and served to heighten the interest with which journalists viewed it." Hansen, *op. cit.*, 137.

88 Stephan to Flügel, Oct. 12, 1841, MS., C. H. I.

89 *Ibid.*

90 Hennig, "Die Auswanderung Martin Stephans," *Zeitschrift für Kirchengeschichte*, LVIII, 163—164.

91 Jäckel to O. H. Walther, Sept. 11, 1838, Jäckel to E. M. Bürger, n. d. [Sept. 11, 1838], Jäckel to C. F. W. Walther, n. d. [Sept. 11, 1838], Bound MSS., I, C. H. I.

began to move toward Bremen, the first families arriving there on October 3.[92] However, because of numerous delays in sailing, the first ships did not leave until exactly one month later, and the last ones not until almost seven weeks after the vanguard made its appearance in Bremen.

The general plan for moving the emigrants was simple and sound. First they were concentrated in small groups drawn from restricted areas; then they were moved in a body to a rendezvous with other groups at some larger city; from these cities they were then taken to Bremen in convenient detachments.[93] The two most important of these larger cities used as rendezvous were Dresden and Halle. There river boats had been chartered which took the great majority of the emigrants directly down the Saale and Elbe to Hamburg. The average cost of transporting a person from Dresden to Hamburg, the greater distance, on these chartered boats was from 5 to 6 thaler.[94] In Hamburg the travelers either debarked, traveled overland to Bremen, and then took another boat to Bremerhaven, or they went overland directly to Bremerhaven.[95] The number of emigrants who left from Dresden and from Halle was nearly equal, with Halle perhaps holding a slight advantage, since 350 are supposed to have left from there.[96] The entire number from either one of these cities could not have been taken on a single boat, even if that arrangement had been desirable, for the facilities on German river boats at that time were not comparable to those

---

[92] Winter to F. W. Barthel, Sept. 29, 1838 (Letter I), Hagemann to Marbach, Oct. 5, 1838, Fehrmann to Marbach, Oct. 5, 1838, Bound MSS., I, C. H. I.; *Vereinigtes Wochenblatt Rochlitz, Geithain, Geringswalde, Hortha und Waldheim,* Sept. 29, 1838.

[93] *Vereinigtes Wochenblatt Rochlitz, Geithain, Geringswalde, Hortha und Waldheim,* Sept. 29, 1838; J. G. Hoffmann to H. F. Fischer, Sept. 26, 1838, Bound MSS., I, C. H. I. (This Hoffmann is evidently one of those who eventually went along, but since his name does not agree exactly with any of those in the lists, it can only be surmised that he is either Gottfried Benjamin or Christian Gottlob Hoffmann.) Numerous other letters in this same collection of manuscripts also show this to have been the arrangement.

[94] Protokolle über die . . . Auswanderung, July 2, 1838, Bound MSS., III, C. H. I.; A contract between H. F. Fischer and Carl Nettelbeck, Oct. 20, 1838, MS., C. H. I.

[95] O. H. Walther to — [Marbach], Oct. 21, 1838, MS., C. H. I.; J. F. Bünger, Diarium, Nov. 2, 3, 1838, MS., L. Fürbringer Papers, St. Louis; J. K. A. Höhne and J. G. Höhne to their brother, Sept. 26, 1841, quoted in *Die Ameise,* Jan. 7, 1842.

[96] Zöge to Winter, Sept. 1, 1838, Bound MSS., I, C. H. I.

on vessels in the United States.[97] Each emigrant was provided with the following standard identification form:

> Bearer of this, N. N., has been accepted by Pastor Stephan as a member of the Association emigrating with him to North America.
>
> Date. Seal. Signature.[98]

In charge of each detachment of emigrants was a representative of the Advisory Committee in Dresden, frequently a pastor or a candidate. He was entrusted with the necessary funds for all his people and had to render an itemized account of his expenditures. Just what the amount of such expenditures was is not as unclear for any stage of the journey as it is for the time before arrival in Bremen. But Keyl's group, for example, which left from Halle and comprised perhaps a hundred persons, had spent a total of 853 thaler of common funds before they reached Bremen.[99] Other groups, of course, which had to travel farther, spent proportionately more, as did also the more important persons in the *Gesellschaft,* most of whom did not use the slow (and inexpensive) river transportation. Moreover, the figure for Keyl's group includes only the costs incurred for his people while en route, not their living expenses before and after the journey from their homes to Bremen.

Not even an incomplete list of these groups, their leaders, and their movements exists, and it is difficult to compile one that is even coherent, since too much of the information must be gleaned not from actual records, but from chance remarks in letters. However, the following dates and facts have been established:

September 19 — 120 of Löber's people were ready to leave.

September 20 — Winter and his group were supposed to leave.

September 26 — A group left Rochlitz.

September 28 — Bürger was advanced 1,796 thaler.

September 29 — Bürger left for Bremen. Keyl was advanced 1,591 thaler (probably indicating that he and his people left the next day).

October 3 — Geyer was advanced 600 thaler.

---

97 Lenz, *Reise nach St. Louis am Mississippi,* 27—30; Vehse, *op. cit.,* 11.

98 Jäckel to G. H. Löber, Sept. 27, 1838, Bound MSS., I, C. H. I.

99 Account H. Bound MSS., No. 8 Miscellanea enthaltend Abschriften von Subrepartitions-Tabellen sub A. — D. G. H. I. (hereafter cited as Bound MSS., 8), C. H. I.

October 4 — Geyer left with his group of sixty on the Elbe. No doubt it is the departure of this contingent which inspired the painting at the Leipzig fair, to which M. L. Hansen referred.[100]

October 8 — Keyl and his group left Magdeburg.

October 10 — Bürger and his group arrived in Magdeburg. Forty people from the Burgstädt-Lunzenau area arrived in Bremen.

October 11 — Fürbringer and his group left Halle, three days late.

October 14 — Bürger's group arrived in Hamburg. A detachment of Löber's people failed to arrive in Bremen as scheduled. C. F. W. Walther was advanced 1,200 thaler.

October 16 — Löber and his family arrived in Bremen. Some people from Paitzdorf, Dresden, Frankenberg, and the Muldenthal arrived in Bremen.

October 17 — Stärtzell [J. A., Jr.?] was advanced 1,000 thaler.

October 18 — Stärtzell and his group left Dresden by boat.

October 20 — Bünger and his group of forty-four left Dresden on the *Amerikaner* at twelve-thirty in the afternoon.

October 21 — Fürbringer's group failed to arrive in Bremen as scheduled.

October 25 — By this time Keyl's group had arrived in Bremen.

October 26 — A detachment of twenty people arrived in Bremen.

October 28 — The last major detachment of Dresdeners left by boat.

November 5 — The last group of Leipzigers left.

November 7 — Bünger arrived in Bremen.

November 10 — The last detachment of Dresdeners arrived in Bremen.[101]

---

100 Hansen, *op. cit.*, 137.

101 Almost all the letters for September and October, 1838, in Bound MSS., I, C. H. I., deal either directly or indirectly with these movements and the preparations necessary for them, hence they are not cited separately. In addition the following references are of value: O. H. Walther to — [Marbach?], Oct. 21, 25, 1838, MSS., C. H. I.; J. F. Bünger, Diarium, Oct. 18, 20, Nov. 7, 10, 11, 1838, MS., L. Fürbringer Papers, St. Louis; *Vereinigtes Wochenblatt Rochlitz,*

When the emigrants arrived in Hamburg or Bremen, they were met by a member of the "Harbor Commission." O. H. Walther, who headed the commission, was to look after the interests of the emigrants, provide lodging and meals for them, and act as the personal representative of Stephan and Marbach.[102] In addition, he conducted all business of the *Gesellschaft* which needed personal attention; convinced the authorities in Bremen and Hamburg that passports were unnecessary; acted as liaison man between the Dresden directors, their commercial agents in Bremen, and the colonists who were arriving; and convinced the people in Bremen that conditions were not as desperate as the Dresden newspaper accounts might lead them to believe.[103]

It also fell to Walther's lot, while in Bremen and Hamburg, to represent the Saxons in their first direct contact with the Prussian emigrants who were to follow them to the United States in 1839. E. L. Krause, the pastor of a group of "Old-Lutheran" dissenters from the vicinity of Breslau, was in Bremen with two deputies from his congregation. Previously, during the first days of October, at the suggestion of von Uckermann, Krause had written to Stephan, asking that Krause's four hundred Silesian farmers be incorporated into the Stephanite *Gesellschaft*. The Prussians had little or no money, but they wished to share in the land which Krause understood the Saxons had already bought or would buy. Eventually the land granted the Silesians would be paid for, Stephan was assured.[104] O. H. Walther reported that his meeting with Krause had left a favorable impression with him except for one important point of difference, namely, polity. Walther could not agree with the Prussians on the relation of laymen to synod or consistory. This disagreement at so early a date is significant in view of later developments within both groups and the controversy which arose between

---

Geithain, Geringswalde, Hortha und Waldheim, Sept. 29, 1838; *Chemnitzer Anzeiger,* Oct. 30, 1838; Receipt signed by E. M. Bürger for draft on the Credit Fund, Sept. 28, 1838, Receipt signed by Keyl for draft on the Credit Fund, Sept. 29, 1838, Draft on the Credit Fund for C. F. W. Walther, Oct. 14, 1838, MSS., C. H. I.; Draft on the Credit Fund for Geyer, Oct. 3, 1838, Draft on the Credit Fund for Stärtzell [J. A., Jr.?], Oct. 17, 1838, Bound MSS., 6, C. H. I.; Fischer, *op. cit.,* 70; Vehse, *op. cit.,* 8; Bürger, *op. cit.,* 12.

102 Marbach to Lüdering, Sept. 15, 1838, Bound MSS., I, C. H. I.

103 G. H. Löber to Marbach, Oct. 5, 1838, G. H. Löber to Brohm, Oct. 6, 1838, Marbach to O. H. Walther, Oct. 16, 1838, *ibid.*

104 O. H. Walther to Stephan, Oct. 11, 1838, *ibid.;* E. L. Krause to Stephan, Oct. 2, 1838, Bound MSS., II, C. H. I.

them. A note of unconscious irony was injected into Walther's report when, in connection with this question of polity, the blight of both groups, Walther extolled the good fortune of the Saxons in having Stephan as their "spiritual father." [105]

Hermann Walther had received orders to be in Bremen by October 6, 1838. As it developed, even this date was three days after the first arrivals reached the city. Actually, however, he did not leave Leipzig for Hamburg until two days after the day on which he was supposed to have arrived, and passed through Hamburg on his way to Bremen on October 9.[106] Böhlau, the other member of the commission, arrived before O. H. Walther [107] and was active as the latter's assistant during the ensuing weeks, while the head of the commission hurried back and forth between Hamburg and Bremen, meeting arrivals and supervising their transfer, quartering, and embarkation.[108] At some time during these final months O. H. Walther found time to write four *Exulanten-Lieder,* or Songs of the Exiles, in which he pictured the "martyrdom" of the Stephanites with morbid sentimentality and represented the emigration as the work of God. Seventeen hundred copies of these songs were printed at the expense of the Credit Fund.[109]

By the end of October, 1838, the great majority of the emigrants had arrived in Bremen.[110] On November 3 their exodus from Germany began with the departure of two ships; the other three followed within fifteen days. The order in which the ships left is the following: The *Copernicus,* November 3, 1838; the *Johann Georg,* a few hours later on the same day; the *Republik,* November 12,

---

[105] O. H. Walther to Stephan, Oct. 11, 1838, Bound MSS., I, C. H. I.; O. H. Walther to — [Marbach?], Oct. 21—22, 1838, MS., C. H. I.

[106] Marbach to Lüdering, Sept. 15, 1838, F. W. Barthel to Marbach, Oct. 8, 1838, O. H. Walther to Stephan, Oct. 11, 1838, Böhlau to Marbach, Oct. 13, 1838, Bound MSS., I, C. H. I.

[107] O. H. Walther to Stephan, Oct. 11, 1838, Böhlau to Marbach, Oct. 13, 1838, G. H. Löber to Brohm, Oct. 16, 1838, *ibid.*

[108] *Ibid.;* O. H. Walther to — [Marbach?], Oct. 21—22, 25, 1838, MSS., C. H. I.

[109] The full title was: *Exulanten-Lieder auf dem Meere. Eine kleine Beisteuer zum geistlichen Schiffsvorrath der um ihres allerheiligsten Glaubens willen mit dem treuen Knecht Gottes und Zeugen der Wahrheit, Martin Stephan, aus Sachsen nach Nordamerika fliehenden apostolisch-lutherischen Gemeinde, den 31. October 1838.* See also Printer's bill, Nov. 14, 1838, O. H. Walther to — [Marbach?], Oct. 21—22, 1838, MSS., C. H. I.

[110] O. H. Walther to — [Marbach?], Oct. 26, 1838, Bound MSS., I, C. H. I.

1838; the *Olbers,* November 18, 1838, between the hours of 10 A. M. and noon; and the *Amalia,* on the same day, several hours later.[111]

The selection of personnel to sail on the various ships had been made in Dresden, but circumstances forced O. H. Walther to change these arrangements in some cases, although it disturbed him to do so without the sanction of the high command in Dresden.[112] According to the stipulations of the Code, the group of emigrants on each ship was to be headed by a pastor.[113] Stephan, O. H. Walther, Marbach, and other important personages were assigned to the *Olbers,* the newest and largest of the vessels. Stephan and Marbach had provided that Löber was to take charge of the very first ship which left, in order to get him out of the country as soon as possible and at any rate before Duke Joseph could intervene.[114] But the duke took no active measures against Löber's violation of the law and of the duke's expressed command, and Pastor Löber assured his brother Friedemann that even if the duke did so, he (the pastor) would be smuggled out of Germany like "countless others" in a similar predicament.[115] Despite these plans and the urgency of the situation, Löber and his people were late in arriving. It was therefore decided to let Bürger and his contingent, who were ready and waiting, take the first ship, the *Copernicus.*[116] Keyl had

---

[111] O. H. Walther to G. H. W. Walther, Nov. 8, 1838, Brohm, Journal, Nov. 18, 1838, MSS., C. H. I.; J. F. Bünger, Diarium, Nov. 18, 1838, MS., L. Fürbringer Papers, St. Louis; G. H. Löber to relatives and friends in Germany, Jan. 15, 1839, in Löber-Eichenberg (ed.), "Ein Briefwechsel," *Mitteilungen . . . Kahla,* VII, 143; C. F. W. Walther in Köstering, *Auswanderung,* 14—15. There is rather general agreement on these dates for sailing, but some discrepancies do occur. O. H. Walther said that the *Copernicus* reached "the open sea" as early as October 26. O. H. Walther to — [Marbach?], Oct. 26, 1838, Bound MSS., I, C. H. I. This remark may have meant simply that the ship left the harbor but was detained by adverse winds and did not actually leave the shores of Germany for several days. The date of sailing for the last two ships is given as both November 17 and November 19 instead of November 18 in C. F. W. Walther, *Bünger,* 50; Fischer, *op. cit.,* 70. See also Hansen, *op. cit.,* 137. One source has the ships leaving already in October. Nachrichten an unsere Nachkommen, MS., C. H. I. The most glaring but (in view of his age) excusable mistake was made by the eighty-three-year-old Bürger, who wrote that six ships left in November and December of 1839 and that the *Copernicus* arrived in this country on December 31, 1839. E. M. Bürger, *Selbstbiographie,* MS., E. J. Buerger Papers, Ellicottville, N. Y.

[112] O. H. Walther to — [Marbach?], Oct. 26, 1838, Bound MSS., I, C. H. I.

[113] Traveling Regulations, par. 3, Appendix B.

[114] G. H. Löber to Marbach, Oct. 21, 1838, Bound MSS., I, C. H. I.

[115] G. H. Löber to G. F. Löber, Oct. 19, 1838, in Löber-Eichenberg (ed.), "Ein Briefwechsel," *Mitteilungen . . . Kahla,* VII, 138.

[116] G. H. Löber to Marbach, Oct. 21, 1838, Bound MSS., I, C. H. I.

not yet arrived in Bremen on the day he was expected, but was there by the time his ship, the *Johann Georg,* was ready, on November 2. Löber expected to leave on November 7, but did not get away until five days later, and Fürbringer, who arrived too late to leave with either of the first two vessels, had to go with him after all.[117]

C. F. W. Walther's plans for sailing were also changed at the last minute as a result of the difficulty, alluded to above, involving the Schubert children. The story is sufficiently interesting and important to justify the telling, for, directly or indirectly, most of the leaders of the emigration were involved, and it therefore gives an indication of the temper of the movement. Furthermore, the spinning of a number of apocryphal yarns about the incident has even led to some confusion about the chronology of the emigration, and clarification of the entire matter seems desirable.[118]

The Walther brothers, Ferdinand and Hermann, with the full knowledge and consent of their parents and the connivance of Magistrate Piether of Waldenburg, decided to take along to the United States the orphaned children of their eldest sister, Mrs. Schubert, who has already been referred to. The children, Marie and Theodor, age fifteen and ten years respectively, had been under the care of their relatives, although legally the guardianship belonged to a Mr. Engel of Waldenburg. Another sister of the Walther brothers, Konstantine, was married to a man named Engel. Whether there is any connection between these two Engels is not known.[119] The Walther brothers took the first illegal step of transporting the minors out of the country, but from Mühlau on the children were entrusted to the care of Widow Bünger, mother of

---

117 G. H. Löber to Marbach, Nov. 3, 1838, *ibid.;* G. H. Löber to G. F. Löber, Nov. 6, 1838, in Löber-Eichenberg (ed.), "Ein Briefwechsel," *Mitteilungen . . . Kahla,* VII, 142—143.

118 The most lucid, frank, and — so far as it goes — complete statement of what went on is contained in a letter from Hermann Walther to his father on November 8, 1838. The first draft of this letter, with numerous corrections by the writer and bearing his own signature, is still extant. O. H. Walther to G. H. Walther, Nov. 8, 1838, MS., C. H. I. Also of value are the entries in J. F. Bünger, Diarium, November 7—December 21, 1838, MS., L. Fürbringer Papers, St. Louis. Except where otherwise indicated, all facts here stated on the Walther-Schubert-Bünger episode are taken from these two sources. See also C. F. W. Walther in Köstering, *Auswanderung,* 14; C. F. W. Walther, *Bünger,* 50—51. The elisions in these two versions by Walther are significant.

119 C. F. W. Walther to Emilie Bünger-Walther, May 26, 1860, in L. Fürbringer (ed.), *op. cit.,* I, 146.

the candidate J. F. Bünger, who got the children to Bremen safely. Meanwhile Mr. Engel had forced Mr. Piether to issue warrants for the arrest of Mrs. Bünger and for the return of the children to Saxony. Accordingly, upon her arrival in Bremen on November 4, Mrs. Bünger was promptly placed under arrest, but the children were concealed from the Bremen officials, who carried out their orders in a halfhearted fashion. On the previous day C. F. W. Walther had fled the country on the *Johann Georg,* and was "thus entirely out of danger of yet being apprehended," as his brother Hermann wrote to their father. Löber phrased it thus: "He [God] has now also guided hither . . . our friend N. N. [C. F. W. Walther], who today sailed out of the harbor on the *Johann Georg* and is now probably on the high seas, together with the *Copernicus.*" [120]

It is on this point, the departure of C. F. W. Walther, that fancy has at times run wild. Martin Günther, in his biography of C. F. W. Walther, said:

> [Walther] was supposed to go on the *Amalia;* but — O wonderful dispensation of God! — when he arrives in Bremen, he is no longer admitted. On the ship *Johann Georg,* to which he then goes, there is no room either [!]; so a young man [a footnote implies it was Gönner] offers to make room for him and goes on another ship, while Walther remains under his [Gönner's] name.[121]

Janzow, another of Walther's biographers, gave a different version of the story. He erroneously stated that the *Amalia* left before the *Johann Georg* and that Walther, "not arriving in time" to take the former vessel, sailed on the *Johann Georg.*[122] J. A. Friedrich, in *Ebenezer,* gave the following explanation:

> He [C. F. W. Walther] had been booked to sail on the ship *Amalia;* but when he arrived in Bremen, he was refused passage on that vessel and was forced to take the *Johann Georg.* The *Amalia* never reached port, and nothing was ever heard of her again. Truly, "God moves in a mysterious way His wonders to perform." [123]

If C. F. W. Walther was ever "booked to sail on the ship *Amalia,*" there was no possible reason for his not finding "room"

---

[120] G. H. Löber to Marbach, Nov. 3, 1838, Bound MSS., I, C. H. I.

[121] M. Günther, *op. cit.,* 33. A very similar version is contained in Wegener, *Memorial Sketch of Dr. C. F. W. Walther,* 8.

[122] Janzow, *Life of Rev. Prof. C. F. W. Walther, D. D.,* 21.

[123] Dau (ed.), *op. cit.,* 26.

or being "refused," because only fifty-eight or fifty-nine of the seventy places on the *Amalia* were ever taken. But it is rather unlikely that any portion of the *Amalia* phase of the legend is true. C. F. W. Walther was probably supposed to go on the *Olbers* with his brother and Stephan. As late as October 29 E. F. A. Fröhlich was scheduled to go on the *Johann Georg*. Between that date and November 3 he was shifted to the *Olbers,* on which he finally sailed. It was Fröhlich's place which C. F. W. Walther took, and Fröhlich was transferred not to the *Amalia,* but to the *Olbers*.[124] That Walther sailed under an assumed name, as Günther implies, is doubtful but possible. At any rate, his right name was used at the port of entry, New Orleans.[125] Finally, Walther could not have missed the *Amalia,* which sailed a fortnight after his departure on the *Johann Georg*. His brother stated the reason for a change correctly when he wrote of the danger of Ferdinand's arrest. By the maneuver C. F. W. Walther was spirited out of the country fifteen days sooner than if he had waited for the *Olbers* (or, for that matter, the *Amalia*), as originally planned.

When J. F. Bünger arrived in Bremen on November 7, he learned that his mother was in jail in Bremerhaven, that there was every prospect that she would remain there until she surrendered the children, and that whoever had them refused to give them up. The children's uncle, O. H. Walther, claimed in a letter to his father that he thought they had sailed on the "*Johann Georg* or on some other ship." If this report was not studied mendacity, then he, as director in chief of operations in Bremen, was shrewdly ill-informed on a matter that should have been of vital interest to him personally and about which he should have been the first to know officially. The only "other ship" which had sailed was the *Copernicus,* and there was never any thought of placing the fugitives on it. The fact of the matter is that at least part of the time they were in Löber's care[126] and part of the time in that of Hermann

---

[124] Compare the passenger lists of the *Olbers, Johann Georg,* and *Amalia,* Bound MSS., I, C. H. I., with Report of . . . Passengers . . . Johann Georg . . . New Orleans, and List of Passengers . . . Olbers . . . New Orleans, MSS., C. H. I.

[125] Report of . . . Passengers . . . Johann Georg . . . New Orleans, MS., C. H. I.

[126] Itemized list of expenditures for the *Republik* group, made out and signed by G. H. Löber, April 11, 1839, Bound MSS., 5, C. H. I.

Walther himself.[127] An attempt was made to take them along on the *Republik,* but at the eleventh hour they were quickly sent back to Bremen.[128] They finally sailed on the *Olbers,* on November 18, with O. H. Walther.[129] Three days later a warrant for Hermann Walther's arrest reached Bremen from Saxony.[130]

As a comfort to Mrs. Bünger, the innocent victim of what O. H. Walther, her future son-in-law, called her "good-natured and unsuspecting desire to oblige," Stephan issued an order for J. F. Bünger to remain in Germany with his mother. A daughter, Agnes, later Hermann Walther's wife, also stayed. However, the profound sympathy which both Stephan and O. H. Walther professed for the unfortunate woman, six of whose children had already left or were leaving for the United States, did not prompt them to set her free by surrendering the Schubert children. Similarly, when she had eluded her guards and her escape was all but assured, they did not permit her to come aboard the *Olbers* for fear, they said, of compromising all on board. Finally, on December 11, when the authorities in Bremen realized that the Schubert children had escaped, when the case had been appealed to the Ministry of Justice in Dresden, and when considerable pressure had been exerted from several directions, Mrs. Bünger was released. She and her son then promptly filed claim for damages through Lawyer Krause in Dresden, who was still representing the Stephanites and attending to their remaining affairs. Mrs. Bünger, her two children, and a fellow emigrant, a Mr. Kohtz, took the ship *Constitution* to New York and arrived in "the American Zion" on February 18, 1839.[131] The Büngers reached Missouri a few months later with the Spröde group.

By November 18, 1838, all the Stephanite emigrants had taken

---

[127] Apparent from O. H. Walther's hotel bill, Nov. 14, 1838, MS., C. H. I.

[128] Itemized list of expenditures for the *Republik* group, made out and signed by G. H. Löber, April 11, 1839, Bound MSS., 5, C. H. I.

[129] List of Passengers . . . Olbers . . . New Orleans, MS., C. H. I.

[130] Fehrmann to Marbach, Nov. 21, 1838, Hagemann to Marbach, Nov. 28, 1838, Bound MSS., 13, C. H. I.; J. F. Bünger, Diarium, Nov. 21, 1838, MS., L. Fürbringer Papers, St. Louis.

[131] Fehrmann to Marbach, Nov. 21, 1838, Hagemann to Marbach, Nov. 28, 1838, Sauer to Marbach, Nov. 28, 1838, Bound MSS., 13, C. H. I.; Sauer to Marbach, July 1, 1839, Bound MSS., Invoices, C. H. I.; C. F. W. Walther to Güldemeister, n. d., Bound MSS., I, C. H. I.; J. F. Bünger, Diarium, Nov. 8, 13, 19, 22, Dec. 11, 1838, Feb. 18, 1839, MS., L. Fürbringer Papers, St. Louis; Sauer to Marbach, Dec. 12, 1838, J. F. Bünger to Marbach, Dec. 11, 1838, Hagemann to Marbach, Dec. 11, 1838, MSS., C. H. I.

their place among the 9,312 who left Bremen in 1838 on their way to the United States.[132] It had been the hope of the Stephanites from the very beginning that the movement would not be confined to a single emigration, but that people would follow them in numbers during succeeding years. This hope was still cherished at the time the *Gesellschaft* left Germany, and there were, in fact, many Stephanite sympathizers who intended to follow the first detachment at a later date.[133] The only appreciable number who did so, were those who arrived with Gruber the next year. For the sake of completeness all groups have been incorporated into Tables I—IV, which are based on the lists of colonists given in Appendix A. The totals here given differ materially from those frequently cited in the past. The entire number of emigrants has been loosely stated as having been anything from 553 to "over 800," or, if the later additions are included, "not quite 1,000 persons."[134] By sheer chance three of the various figures which have been given coincide with numbers which are correct for certain combinations of ships and groups at a specific time. But they either are not the correct number for the classification of emigrants which they claim to represent, or they are arrived at on the basis of composite errors which accidentally yield a correct total.[135] It is plain that such statements are not based upon complete examination of the available sources, yet the figures are often intended to be no more than estimates, and as such some of them come fairly close.

When specific figures for the separate ships are given, the results are equally unsatisfactory. Some of the discrepancies have been compiled by P. E. Kretzmann in *The Missouri Historical Review,* where, among some correct figures, the number 123 is given

---

[132] F. Münch, *Der Staat Missouri; ein Handbuch für deutsche Auswanderer,* 104.

[133] Stübel to Vehse *et al.*, Sept. 12, 1839, Bound MSS., VI, C. H. I.; Hagemann to Marbach, Dec. 11, 1838, MS., C. H. I.; *Chemnitzer Anzeiger,* Oct. 30, 1838; Fischer, *op. cit.,* 71; Pleissner, *op. cit.,* 51, 93.

[134] The following numbers were noted in the course of this study: 553, "about 600," "over 600," 609, 650, 665, 668, 674, 675, 700, "over 700," 707, 750, "about 750," 770, 800, "about 800," "over 800," "not quite 1000."

[135] "W. K." [William Koepchen?], "Die Väter und Gründer unserer Synode," *Der Lutheraner,* LXXVIII, 77; P. E. Kretzmann, "The Saxon Immigration to Missouri, 1838—1839," *Missouri Historical Review,* XXXIII, 161; H. Koepchen, "The Saxon Emigration of 1938 [*sic*], I, Why?" *Lutheran Witness,* LVII, 94. Compare, however, with the figure here given by H. Koepchen the totals for the individual ships given by this same writer later in this same series of articles. H. Koepchen, "The Emigration, 1838," *ibid.,* 141.

for the company on the *Copernicus,* which actually carried 177.[136] Although Kretzmann does not indicate his authority beyond saying that the figure is "based apparently on reliable sources," it is likely that this error for the *Copernicus* originated with an article by L. Fürbringer in *Der Lutheraner.* However, the numbers for the separate ships and the total for all ships in the Fürbringer article are not correct; nor do they, as is claimed, agree with the ships' manifests.[137] Furthermore, even though they did agree with the manifests, they still would not necessarily be correct; for in one instance, the declaration by Captain Haesloop of the *Copernicus,* the sworn statement by the captain of the number of his passengers (178) does not tally with the number of individual names which are listed in the accompanying manifest (177).[138] Other errors quoted by Kretzmann are: 130, 138, or 141 on the *Johann Georg;* 178 on the *Copernicus;* 113 on the *Republik;* 184 on the *Olbers;* eight as having died en route; and one as having been born. Some of these inaccuracies are taken from a list printed in the *Concordia Historical Institute Quarterly,* but this list does not claim to be, and is not in fact, a compilation of "the passenger lists preserved at the Port of New Orleans," as Kretzmann surmises. A comparison will show that they differ.[139]

The actual number of Stephanites who left on the five ships in

---

136 P. E. Kretzmann, "The Saxon Immigration to Missouri, 1838—1839," *Missouri Historical Review,* XXXIII, 161. See also the compilations of previous mistakes, together with new incorrect assumptions in Stellhorn, "The Saxon Centennial and the Schools," *Lutheran School Journal,* LXXIV, 255, 295—296, 343; Burgdorf, "Centennial Corrigenda," *Concordia Historical Institute Quarterly,* XII, 34—36.

137 L. Fürbringer, "Aus vergilbten Papieren," *Der Lutheraner,* XCIV, 157; List of Passengers . . . Olbers . . . New Orleans, List . . . of . . . passengers . . . Copernicus . . . New Orleans, List of Passengers . . . Republik . . . New Orleans, Report of . . . Passengers . . . Johann Georg . . . New Orleans, MSS., C. H. I.

138 List . . . of . . . passengers . . . Copernicus . . . New Orleans, MS., C. H. I.

139 *Ibid.;* List of Passengers . . . Olbers . . . New Orleans, List of Passengers . . . Republik . . . New Orleans, Report of . . . Passengers . . . Johann Georg . . . New Orleans, MSS., C. H. I.; W. G. Polack, "Members of the Saxon Immigration," *Concordia Historical Institute Quarterly,* XI, 33—47; P. E. Kretzmann, "The Saxon Immigration to Missouri, 1838—1839," *Missouri Historical Review,* XXXIII, 161. In other places the number of passengers on the *Olbers* has been placed as high as 195, that on the *Amalia* as high as sixty or more and as low as fifty-three or even fifty. Th. Gräbner, *op. cit.,* 9; Lossagung vom Stephanismus, Brohm, Journal, Nov. 18, 1838, MSS., C. H. I.; Polack, *Walther,* 30.

1838 was 665. Accurate figures for other points of time and with the proper allowances for births, deaths, and defections from the ranks can be found in the appended Lists and Tables.[140] In only one case, that of the *Amalia,* were any non-Stephanite passengers permitted to go along on ships chartered by the *Gesellschaft.* This vessel carried at least two persons (C. A. Schützler and G. Ries) whose names do not appear in the majority of the lists, since they had not formally joined the group.[141]

The location of the places of residence from which the members of the *Gesellschaft* came, accounts readily for the designation "the Saxons."[142] Among the 612 emigrants who arrived on the four ships in 1838 and in the early part of 1839, the predominance of persons from the Kingdom of Saxony is pronounced; and if those are added who came from the Saxon duchies and the Saxon province of Prussia, almost all of the 612 are accounted for. The importance of Table III, however, is the revision it makes in figures heretofore accepted for the distribution of the emigrants among the localities within these areas. The "over 700" emigrants frequently spoken of are usually divided as follows: From Dresden, 240; Leipzig, 31; Keyl's parish, 109; Bürger's, 84; Löber's, 108; Gruber's, 48; O. H. Walther's, 16; and C. F. W. Walther's, 19. These numbers total only 655, and not "over 700"; nor do they distribute the emigrants correctly. There were not 200 from Dresden even in the entire group of 916, much less in that of 612. Still more surprising is the total of 109 given for Keyl's parish, more than double the actual number from both of the Frohnas; or the 108 for Löber's parish, when there was not that number from all the Saxon duchies; or the 84 for Bürger's, who had only 18 from Lunzenau-Seelitz. The reason for these inaccuracies is that the totals given were never checked against the lists which exist, but were taken from the single statement of September 4, 1838, which gives, in addition to the figures just stated, further classifications that total 707. This docu-

---

[140] Appendix A.

[141] These two names are found in a number of places, most recently in W. G. Polack, "Members of the Saxon Immigration," *Concordia Historical Institute Quarterly,* XI, 47. C. F. W. Walther in Köstering, *Auswanderung,* 14, claimed that three persons on the *Amalia* were not members of the *Gesellschaft.* If this was true, then one of them is unknown, for Eichler, sometimes listed as one of the non-members or entirely omitted, was a member of the *Gesellschaft.*

[142] Table III, Appendix A.

ment was probably not intended to be an accurate statement. It very likely gave the geographic distribution according to the centers through which the Dresden committee was operating, according to the points of rendezvous for the gathering of the colonists, and according to the localities where the lieutenants resided who were to lead these people to Bremen. Employing such designations as Keyl's "parish" was easy for Stephanites, who had a rather elastic conception of what a parish was.[143]

The final blast from the arsenal of Stephanite polemics in Germany was their *Lebewohl der aus Sachsen nach Nord-Amerika ziehenden altlutherischen Gemeinde.* This *Farewell* is dated November 18, 1838, the day that the *Olbers* and the *Amalia* left Bremerhaven. Like the *Songs of the Exiles,* it is pervaded by a spirit of martyrdom and reiterates the claim of the emigrants that they were being forced to leave for conscience' sake. Under the guise of a friendly adieu, Stephan managed to have the "last word" in the literary feud from which he had withdrawn years ago, for by the time the *Farewell* appeared in a Saxon paper, the *Leipziger allgemeine Zeitung* of December 3, 1838, Stephan and his followers were on the high seas, bound for "Canaan." [144]

---

143 Financial statement of Sept. 4, 1838, Bound MSS., VI, C. H. I. These figures have been adopted in many later accounts: C. F. W. Walther in Köstering, *Auswanderung,* 13; Köstering, *Keyl,* 49; Dau (ed.), *op. cit.,* 7; *History of Southeast Missouri,* 256; Burgdorf, "Centennial Corrigenda," *Concordia Historical Institute Quarterly,* XII, 34. Cf. Table III, Appendix A.

144 A copy of this document in Jäckel's hand, perhaps the original draft dictated to him by Stephan, dated November 18, 1838, is preserved. Ein Lebewohl der aus Sachsen nach Nord-Amerika ziehenden altlutherischen Gemeinde, Nov. 18, 1838 (hereafter cited as Lebewohl), Bound MSS., Invoices, C. H. I. Another copy is found in Bound MSS., I, C. H. I. The Lebewohl was reprinted in Saxon papers (*e. g., Dresdener Anzeiger,* Dec. 11, 1838), and is found as well in some of the contemporary books. G. Günther, *op. cit.,* 3—4; Fischer, *op. cit.,* 210—211.

CHAPTER EIGHT

THE VOYAGE FROM BREMERHAVEN TO ST. LOUIS, 1838–1839

THE TRAVELING REGULATIONS of the *Gesellschaft* had stipulated that a journal of the entire voyage was to be kept on each ship.[1] Furthermore, one of the departments of the Advisory Committee had been designated to take charge of the "library, archives, and chronicles." But if a systematic log of the journey was kept by each group, these records apparently have not been preserved. In fact, the only reference to any contemporary work by the *Gesellschaft* on its own history is a chance remark, attributed to Stephan during his stay in St. Louis, to the effect that he desired such a history compiled. Nothing seems to have materialized from this wish at the time.[2] Consequently, the facts about the next period in the development of Stephanism, especially those about the voyage, must be gleaned from notes kept by individuals.[3]

Of the four ships which brought the Saxons to New Orleans in 1838 and 1839, the *Copernicus* made the voyage in the shortest time, fifty-nine days. The *Republik crossed* in sixty-two days, the *Johann Georg* and the *Olbers* in sixty-four.[4] (In 1842 the *Olbers* crossed in fifty days, and in 1847 in forty-three; by 1844 the *Copernicus* had reduced its time to fifty-three days.) [5] Concerning the voyage of the first two ships to leave Bremerhaven, the *Copernicus* and the *Johann Georg*, there is little detailed information. The 440-ton

---

[1] Traveling Regulations, par. 17, Appendix B.

[2] G. Günther, *op. cit.*, 87.

[3] An account of this period is also given in P. E. Kretzmann, "The Voyage of the Saxons," *Concordia Theological Monthly*, IX, 347—357.

[4] The dates for departure from Bremen and arrival in New Orleans are given in Dau (ed.), *op. cit.*, 11; C. F. W. Walther in Köstering, *Auswanderung*, 14—15. Obviously none of the ships made the trip in forty-two days, as stated in Köstering, "Kurzer Abriss des Lebens und Wirkens des seligen P. Adolf Wilhelm Bergt," *Der Lutheraner*, XL, 357. The chronology of the immigration period is often very confused (January—May, 1839), for instance, in M. Günther, *op. cit.*, 33; Wegener, *op. cit.*, 9; and throughout G. Günther's anonymous account.

[5] *Anzeiger des Westens*, Dec. 29, 1842, Jan. 4, 1845; *Täglicher Anzeiger des Westens*, June 7, 1847.

Copernicus left Bremerhaven on November 3, 1838, and reached New Orleans on December 31. However, since Captain Haesloop did not have sufficient time to file his declaration with the collector of the port on that day, the ship's arrival was not officially recorded until January 2, 1839.[6] For reasons of economy, the stay in New Orleans of each group of emigrants was to be as brief as possible,[7] and this injunction was followed by all the pastors but Stephan.

On January 19, 1839, the first of the Stephanites, led by Bürger, reached St. Louis on the river steamer *Rienzi.*[8] Upon their arrival they found the public expecting them. As early as December, 1838, news of the coming of the Stephanites had preceded them to Missouri; at the same time the immigration of several thousand other Germans had been announced for the immediate future.[9] The *Anzeiger des Westens,* under the editorship of Wilhelm Weber quickly becoming the most influential German journal in the Missippi Valley, on December 1, 1838, had reported:

> We have received letters from Bremen wherein it is mentioned that a party consisting of 700 persons are in Bremerhaven ready to emigrate to the United States. They are Lutherans, styling themselves "the old Lutheran Congregation," who have left their native country, Saxony, on account of religious intolerance and intend to settle in one of the Western States. They are an industrious set of people and are said to be in possession of rising [sic] half a million of dollars. — The party consists principally of farmers and mechanics, including sixteen ministers of the gospel and four schoolmasters.[10]

The actual arrival of the *Rienzi* group in St. Louis was described as follows by the *Missouri Argus* on Monday, January 21, 1839:

---

[6] List . . . of . . . passengers . . . Copernicus . . . New Orleans, MS., C. H. I.

[7] Vehse to K. W. Welzel, Jan. 30, 1839, MS., C. H. I.

[8] Bürger, *op. cit.,* 12; Schieferdecker, *op. cit.,* 9; Dau (ed.), *op. cit.,* 11. In all these references and in many other places the date is given as January 18. Contemporary newspaper accounts give January 19. At times it has been represented as though the entire number of immigrants arrived at the same time, either on January 18 or 19, or on February 19. Some portrayals even create the impression that there was a general rendezvous in New Orleans. C. F. W. Walther in Köstering, *Auswanderung,* 15; Hanser, *op. cit.,* 3; Krauss, *Lebensbilder aus der Geschichte der christlichen Kirche,* 716; Mezger (ed.), *op. cit.,* 7; Th. Bünger, "Etliche Züge aus der Geschichte der Missouri-Synode," *Synodal-Bericht des Iowa-Districts . . . 1901,* p. 22; Polack, *Building a Church,* 40; *Gedächtniss-Feier . . . 1839—1939,* p. 5.

[9] Kimm & Tewes to Marbach, Dec. 10, 1838, Bound MSS., I, C. H. I.

[10] Quoted in the *Daily Missouri Republican,* Jan. 30, 1839.

> About two hundred and fifty German immigrants from the neighborhood of Dresden, kingdom of Saxony, arrived here on the 19th, on the steamer Rienzi, from New Orleans. Of these thirty were cabin passengers, most of whom we understand are wealthy. They advocate the Lutheran doctrine in its original purity, — styling themselves Stephanites, from the name of the clergyman, Mr. Stephan, who accompanies them.
>
> It is their intention to purchase land and settle in a body in this State. They expect soon to be joined in their new home by six hundred more of their countrymen of the same religious persuasion.[11]

With no more accurate information to guide them than these exaggerated statements, St. Louisans began to dispense advice. On the same day on which the foregoing article appeared in the *Missouri Argus,* the *Daily Evening Gazette* reprinted the *Argus* item and added:

> We advise this colony to purchase out the MORMONS. They have choice lands and improvements in Caldwell county, which would easily accommodate the comers, and could no doubt be bought cheap. The Mormons have probably discovered that they cannot stay in the upper country and will be glad to sell. The Mormons would thus be accommodated and relieved while their improvements would be saved from waste.[12]

In its next issue the *Gazette* carried the following response from a contributor:

> Mr. Editor: You advise the Germans recently arrived here to go to Caldwell county and buy out the Mormons. Would the *Stephanites* fare better than the *Mormonites?*
>
> Yours, Q.
>
> [Comment of *Gazette*:] We hope so. Indeed we cannot suppose that any sect could make themselves so obnoxious as the Mormonites. The Germans have never been disturbed here — and, with their peaceable behavior and industrious habits — it is not to be believed that they ever will be.[13]

---

11 *Missouri Argus,* Jan. 21, 1839.

12 *Daily Evening Gazette,* Jan. 21, 1839.

13 *Ibid.,* Jan. 22, 1839. The Mormon troubles of the times, referred to in these quotations, are beyond the scope of this discussion. However, especially vivid articles are contained in the *Täglicher Anzeiger des Westens,* April 10, 16, 18, 21, 24, 28, May 1, 4, 5, 6, 1846; *Daily Missouri Republican,* May 6, 13, 30, June 15, Aug. 9, Sept. 1, 2, 7, 14, 15, 16, 17, 19, 23, 1846. See also Williams-Shoemaker, *Missouri Mother of the West,* I, 520—547; Culmer, *op. cit.,* 193—216.

Although Bürger received unexpected counsel in St. Louis, he did not find the New York group there nor the accommodations they were to have provided. As previously related, Spröde had been in Germany in the summer and fall of 1838. On returning to New York, he found that his group had been augmented by the addition of a teacher, Müller, and a pastor, Maximilian Örtel. The latter was acquainted with Stephan and Scheibel in Germany, and had arrived in New York at the end of September, 1837, as an emissary of the *Barmer Missionsgesellschaft.* After working independently of Spröde for about a year, Örtel severed his connections with the society which had sent him and joined the group under Spröde.[14] Whether Spröde was unimpressed by what he had seen of the Stephanites and their organization or whether he was acting under orders of Stephan is not clear, but in either case he did not risk his own and his people's fortunes by following the original plan of preceding the Saxons to the West.

Even the plan of sending agents ahead was carried out only halfheartedly and aimlessly. For the mission to St. Louis the New Yorkers selected Ferdinand Rudloff (one of the older members of the group and a business partner of Spröde in his New York bakery) and the two newcomers, Örtel and Müller, the latter because he could speak English.[15] The trio left New York on December 21, 1838, about three or four months later than they should have left. They intended to travel by canal and river boats, but weather conditions forced them to resort to the stagecoach. As a result of this change in plans, the three travelers arrived on the Illinois bank of the frozen and impassable Mississippi, opposite St. Louis, by 6 P. M., January 3, 1839.[16] Since the three had only $16 left of their original fund of $250, they visited Leonhardt in St. Clair County, Illinois, who, as far as can be determined, had done nothing to justify the hopes of the Stephanites for assistance

---

[14] C. F. Rudloff to Marbach, Jan. 7, 1839, Bound MSS., I, C. H. I.; G. H. Löber to relatives in Germany, Jan. 30, 1839, in Löber-Eichenberg (ed.), "Ein Briefwechsel," *Mitteilungen . . . Kahla,* VII, 148; *Anzeiger des Westens,* Dec. 31, 1842; Rathermann, "Professor Maximilian Oertel," *Der Deutsche Pionier,* XV, 58—61. These facts should correct the impression that Örtel was one of the prime movers in the New York group, as it is represented in G. Günther, *op. cit.,* 37.

[15] C. F. Rudloff to Marbach, Jan. 7, 1839, Bound MSS., I, C. H. I. Even the corrected account is incorrect in G. Günther, *op. cit.,* 37.

[16] C. F. Rudloff to Marbach, Jan. 7, 1839, Bound MSS., I, C. H. I.

from him.[17] Leonhardt's hospitality relieved them of financial embarrassment for four days; then, on January 7, Rudloff succeeded in crossing the river to St. Louis and immediately sought out the offices of Kimm & Tewes, located at Number 3, Second Street, on the corner of Market Street.[18] When Rudloff failed to find a letter waiting for him, as he had expected, he wrote to Marbach on that same day and had the letter forwarded by Kimm & Tewes. Rudloff was soon joined by his companions, and then all three of them apparently sat down to await the arrival of the Saxons.[19] Thus Bürger, and later Löber, found their "agents" when they reached St. Louis.[20]

The *Johann Georg* reached New Orleans, after a stormy passage, on January 5, 1839, five days later than its companion ship, the *Copernicus;* Captain Hermann Hohorst filed his manifest on the same day.[21] Keyl and his traveling companions on the *Johann Georg* must have left New Orleans within a week, since they were no longer there when Löber's group arrived on January 12.[22] The company on the *Johann Georg,* transported from New Orleans to St. Louis at a total cost of $1,997.95½, or 2,913 thaler,[23] reached its destination on January 24. The statement has usually been made that the steamboat *Clyde,* which was used for the river journey, arrived in St. Louis on February 9,[24] but an examination of documents shows this date to be incorrect, inasmuch as the following assumptions would be necessary: That it took the *Clyde* twenty-nine days to make the run from New Orleans to St. Louis; that the Löber group, although it left New Orleans five days after the *Clyde,* reached St. Louis ten days earlier; that the arrival of

---

17 *Ibid.*

18 C. F. Rudloff to Marbach, Jan. 7, 1839, Kimm & Tewes to Marbach, Dec. 10, 1838, *ibid.*

19 C. F. Rudloff to Marbach, Jan. 7, 1839, *ibid.;* Schieferdecker, *op. cit.,* 9.

20 G. H. Löber to relatives in Germany, Jan. 30, 1839, in Löber-Eichenberg (ed.), "Ein Briefwechsel," *Mitteilungen . . . Kahla,* VII, 148; Schieferdecker, *op. cit.,* 9—10.

21 Report of . . . *Passengers* . . . Johann Georg . . . New Orleans, MS., C. H. I.

22 G. H. Löber to relatives and friends in Germany, Jan. 15, 1839, in Löber-Eichenberg (ed.), "Ein Briefwechsel," *Mitteilungen . . . Kahla,* VII, 146.

23 Itemized account for the *Clyde,* MS., C. H. I.

24 Köstering, *Keyl,* 53; M. Günther, *op. cit.,* 33; Dau (ed.), *op. cit.,* 11. The date January 30 is given by P. E. Kretzmann, "The Saxon Immigration to Missouri, 1838—1839," *Missouri Historical Review,* XXXIII, 161.

two detachments was reported in St. Louis when only one had reached that city; that in their letters both Löber and Winter ignored the presence of the *Johann Georg* people in New Orleans; and, most unlikely of all, that the *Clyde* had returned to New Orleans ten days before it arrived in St. Louis![25] The implausibility of the previous assumptions proves in a negative way that the date was not February 9; newspaper items contain evidence that the correct date was January 24. On January 25, 1839, the *Daily Missouri Republican* made the following statements: "From New Orleans. — The *Clyde* arrived last night from New Orleans, 12 days out." "One hundred and sixty-six German emigrants arrived in the *Clyde* last night."[26] If the *Republican's* figures were correct, not all the people on the *Clyde* were Saxons.[27] Then, on January 26, 1839, the *Anzeiger des Westens* contained this item:

> We must announce to our readers the arrival of the first two shiploads of Stephanites — together about 300 persons. Among their number are men of mature years who lived in very good circumstances in their homeland — men whom only the misrepresentation on the part of their parsons that if they should die in Europe, they could not be saved, could mislead into taking the unusual step of emigrating at such an advanced age, and into taking the still more dangerous one of investing their entire capital in the nebulous project of a communal settlement. As matters now stand, the intellectual [spiritual?] and secular affairs of the community rest almost without any control in the hands of the clergy, who enjoy unqualified authority and obedience in their sect.[28]

The third group of Stephanites to reach the United States arrived at New Orleans on January 12, 1839, on the *Republik*. There are several fairly complete accounts of the journey made by this company: that of Pastor Löber, who was in charge; that of his assistant, Candidate Fürbringer; and that of Teacher Win-

---

[25] G. H. Löber to relatives and friends in Germany, Jan. 15, 30, 1839, in Löber-Eichenberg (ed.), "Ein Briefwechsel," *Mitteilungen . . . Kahla,* VII, 146—147; O. Fürbringer to Stephan, Jan. 15, 1839, Bound MSS., I, C. H. I.; Winter to Guericke *et al.*, April 28, 1841, *Zeitschrift für die gesammte lutherische Theologie und Kirche,* II, No. 3, pp. 116—132; Vehse to K. W. Welzel, Jan. 30, 1839, MS., C. H. I.; *Anzeiger des Westens,* Jan. 26, 1839, quoted in G. Günther, *op. cit.,* 38—39.

[26] *Daily Missouri Republican,* Jan. 25, 1839.

[27] See Table I, Appendix A.

[28] *Anzeiger des Westens,* Jan. 26, 1839, quoted in G. Günther, *op. cit.,* 38—39.

ter.[29] The *Republik* left Bremerhaven on November 12, at 5 A. M., and a week later passed through the English Channel in thirty hours.[30] For several weeks thereafter, especially off the coast of Spain, the vessel encountered moderate storms, which prostrated most of its passengers with seasickness. Then, after entering the warmer zones, the ship met with calm weather for the balance of the journey.[31] When the passengers were sufficiently recovered to take inventory of their surroundings, they found life comparatively pleasant. Despite some inconveniences, such as rather cramped quarters, the fare at sea, and the somewhat unpalatable drinking water, which had been drawn from the Weser, Löber offered the significant opinion that most of the emigrants, even those in steerage, were in better circumstances on board ship than they had been at home.[32] Throughout the journey Löber directed all the business affairs of the people on his ship and also conducted services and administered Communion regularly.[33]

On December 16, 1838, the *Republik* passed the Canary Islands and on the next day entered the tropics. Thereafter the temperature, which the German emigrants found insufferably hot, caused the pitch and calking of the ship to melt and forced its passengers to seek relief from the stifling atmosphere of steerage compartments by sleeping on the open deck. On December 18 the *Republik* encountered a Swedish man-of-war, which stopped her only for identification; and on December 27 she was challenged by what Winter called a "pirate" ship, but again, after questioning, was permitted to proceed. On December 31, 1838, the ship came within sight of Santo Domingo, while January 2, 1839, found the voyagers enchanted by a view of the hills of "fertile Cuba." [34] By

---

[29] G. H. Löber to relatives and friends in Germany, Jan. 15, 30, 1839, in Löber-Eichenberg (ed.), "Ein Briefwechsel," *Mitteilungen . . . Kahla*, VII, 143—148; O. Fürbringer to Stephan, Jan. 15, 1839, Bound MSS., I, C. H. I.; Winter to Guericke *et al.*, April 28, 1841, *Zeitschrift für die gesammte lutherische Theologie und Kirche*, II, No. 3, pp. 116—132.

[30] Winter to Guericke *et al.*, April 28, 1841, *Zeitschrift für die gesammte lutherische Theologie und Kirche*, II, No. 3, pp. 116—132.

[31] *Ibid.;* G. H. Löber to relatives and friends in Germany, Jan. 15, 1839, in Löber-Eichenberg (ed.), "Ein Briefwechsel," *Mitteilungen . . . Kahla*, VII, 144. See also Gebauer, *op. cit.*, 265-270.

[32] G. H. Löber to relatives and friends in Germany, Jan. 15, 1839, in Löber-Eichenberg (ed.), "Ein Briefwechsel," *Mitteilungen . . . Kahla*, VII, 144.

[33] Winter to Guericke *et al.*, April 28, 1841, *Zeitschrift für die gesammte lutherische Theologie und Kirche*, II, No. 3, pp. 116—132.

[34] *Ibid.;* G. H. Löber to relatives and friends in Germany, Jan. 15, 1839, in Löber-Eichenberg (ed.), "Ein Briefwechsel," *Mitteilungen . . . Kahla*, VII, 145.

January 6 the *Republik* was sailing in the Gulf of Mexico, where the remains of Friedrich Gottlieb Müller were buried. Despite the fact that many persons were sick, Müller's death from a cold on January 6 was the only loss of life during the voyage of the *Republik*.[35]

On January 11 the Saxons were only four miles from the mouth of the Mississippi River and noted that it did not, as their geographies had told them in Germany, "pour into the Gulf of Mexico with a great roar."[36] The coast line of the United States appeared to them low, swampy, and unattractive, and harbored (so they reported to Germany) many crocodiles.[37] At one o'clock on the afternoon of the eleventh a pilot came aboard, affording the immigrants their first glimpse of an American. Later, on the same day, the steamboat *Hudson* came alongside and in twenty-five hours had towed the *Republik* and "4 other big ships" to the port of New Orleans, where they arrived between 7:30 and 8 P. M. on Saturday, January 12, 1839, exactly two months after the *Republik* had left Bremerhaven.[38] The lateness of the hour prevented Captain D. Steenken from filing his manifest until Monday, January 14.[39] When Löber and his party arrived, the Stephanites on the *Copernicus* and *Johann Georg* had already come and gone, while neither the *Olbers* nor the *Amalia* had yet put into port.[40]

New Orleans made a variety of interesting impressions upon the immigrants during the four days they spent there. They noticed especially the melting-pot atmosphere of the place, where drunken Indians wrapped in blankets ran around, with rifles slung over their shoulders, where the blacks outnumbered the whites, and where people of all nations intermingled. Winter, repelled by the scene he so graphically described, asserted that when these con-

---

[35] *Ibid.;* O. Fürbringer to Stephan, Jan. 15, 1839, Bound MSS., I, C. H. I.; G. H. Löber, Diary, Jan. 6, 1839, MS., C. H. I. Löber here gave the cause of death as typhoid fever, but it is doubtful that this is correct.

[36] Winter to Guericke *et al.*, April 28, 1841, *Zeitschrift für die gesammte lutherische Theologie und Kirche,* II, No. 3, pp. 116—132.

[37] *Ibid.*

[38] *Ibid.;* G. H. Löber to relatives and friends in Germany, Jan. 15, 1839, in Löber-Eichenberg (ed.), "Ein Briefwechsel," *Mitteilungen . . . Kahla,* VII, 145; O. Fürbringer to Stephan, Jan. 15, 1839, Bound MSS., I, C. H. I.

[39] List of Passengers . . . Republik . . . New Orleans, MS., C. H. I.

[40] G. H. Löber to relatives and friends in Germany, Jan. 15, 1839, in Löber-Eichenberg (ed.), "Ein Briefwechsel," *Mitteilungen . . . Kahla,* VII, 145.

ditions were combined with an unhealthful climate and the high price of many commodities, it was impossible to enjoy a single moment in New Orleans.[41] Löber agreed with Winter, at least in some respects:

> The enormous number of ships which lie in port here, the great number of steamboats that roar back and forth with a great din, the colossal warehouses and countless streets of this city, but even more the dense crowds of black and white people which one sees here, the very great variety of fruits which are offered for sale in large quantities, all of these things provide much for the eye to see; but the misery of the unfortunate slaves and the coarseness of the many strangers fill the heart with sorrow and pain.[42]

Fürbringer, who was assigned the task of reporting to Stephan on the progress of the journey, described the United States as "the land of religious and certainly also of civil liberty." [43]

Business arrangements in New Orleans were complicated somewhat by the immigrants' disregard of Kurtz's advice to learn some English. Although they were therefore forced to turn to others for assistance, Löber apparently did not employ the services of Frey and Company, whom the Stephanites had expected to use as their agents, or, if he did, he failed to mention it. Instead, the pastor spoke highly of John J. Vles, the Saxon consul in New Orleans and head of John J. (F?) Vles and Company, who was helpful and courteous. Vles assisted Löber in a number of ways, such as exchanging money advantageously for the immigrants, and was prepared to serve the other Saxons when they arrived. Shipbroker Ernst, Löber judged, was indispensable but somewhat forward.[44]

In New Orleans the newcomers were greeted with tales of the inconsiderateness and brutality of steamboat captains. When ice prevented further progress of the boats up the river, the officers

---

[41] *Ibid.;* Winter to Guericke *et al.*, April 28, 1841, *Zeitschrift für die gesammte lutherische Theologie und Kirche.* II, No. 3, pp. 116—132; O. Fürbringer to Stephan, Jan. 15, 1839, Bound MSS., I, C. H. I.

[42] G. H. Löber to relatives and friends in Germany, Jan. 15, 1839, in Löber-Eichenberg (ed.), "Ein Briefwechsel," *Mitteilungen . . . Kahla,* VII, 145.

[43] O. Fürbringer to Stephan, Jan. 15, 1839, Bound MSS., I, C. H. I.

[44] *Ibid.;* G. H. Löber to relatives and friends in Germany, Jan. 15, 1839, in Löber-Eichenberg (ed.), "Ein Briefwechsel," *Mitteilungen . . . Kahla,* VII, 146; Vehse to K. W. Welzel, Jan. 30, 1839, MS., C. H. I.

allegedly set their passengers ashore unceremoniously in the most inhospitable places, thereby subjecting them to severe privations.[45] Despite occasional optimistic reassurances,[46] there was considerable truth to these stories. The *Olbers-Selma* group had some experience with these conditions, which will be described later. At least two boats used by the Saxons in 1839, the *Selma* and the *Rienzi,* were lost a few years later while bringing immigrants up the river.[47] The steamboat captains were often a rough, brawling lot, and their crews were seldom better. Theft on the boats was frequent. When the *Selma* was destroyed, hundreds of German immigrants were left stranded or injured, and their property became the prey of looters. Relief for such unfortunate travelers, if they ever did reach St. Louis, was entirely voluntary and unorganized; hence it was rather sporadic no matter how sincere. The German Immigration Society of St. Louis was not founded until 1847.[48]

The intense rivalry of the steamboat captains led to frequent races. On these occasions it was not unusual for the boilers of the vessels to be heated until the wooden hulls were scorched. Such irresponsibility and carelessness naturally caused numerous accidents, often fatal to some of the passengers.[49] The practice of racing the boats did have the effect, of course, of shortening the time for the trip from New Orleans to St. Louis from a record of four days, twenty hours, and forty-five minutes in 1842 to one of three days and twenty-three hours in 1844.[50] A desire for speed,

---

45 O. Fürbringer to Stephan, Jan. 15, 1839, Bound MSS., I, C. H. I.

46 J. Hall, *Notes on the Western States,* 242 (hereafter cited as *Western States*).

47 *St. Louis New Era,* April 1, 1840; *Daily Evening Gazette,* March 31, 1840; *Daily Missouri Republican,* March 24, April 1, 1840, Nov. 30, 1844.

48 *Daily Missouri Republican,* Jan. 1, 6, 1840, May 22, Aug. 24, 1844, March 29, 1845; *Daily Evening Gazette,* March 31, 1840; *Anzeiger des Westens,* Jan. 14, 1842, Aug. 5, Sept. 14, 30, 1843, March 27, June 12, 1845, Jan. 5, 1846; *St. Louis New Era,* April 1, 1840, Feb. 20, 1845; *Missouri Reporter,* March 21, 1845; *Weekly Reveille,* Feb. 24, 1845; Lenz, *op. cit.,* 36; Kargau, *St. Louis in früheren Jahren,* 280—281.

49 Lenz, *op. cit.,* 27—30. The *Daily Commercial Bulletin* (Nov. 17, 1840) reported twenty-five persons killed in a steamboat accident; the *Anzeiger des Westens,* fifty-five on July 6, 1842, eighty on November 2, 1844, and thirty-one on December 24, 1844; the *Daily Missouri Republican,* fifty on December 30, 1844; the *Daily Morning Missourian,* twenty on November 1, 1845.

50 *Anzeiger des Westens,* May 28, 1842; *St. Louis New Era,* June 12, 15, 1843; *Daily Missouri Republican,* May 8, June 25, 1844.

while an important factor leading to accidents, was not the only one, and numerous mishaps were caused also by the many "snakes," or sunken logs, in the river. In 1839 there were forty or forty-one accidents to boats on the Mississippi and its tributaries. At least twenty-three of the vessels involved were total wrecks, and the combined loss for all accidents totaled not less than a million dollars in property and forty-six lives. Thirteen of these boats, totaling 2,127 tons, were among the forty-five vessels owned in St. Louis in that year. From 1830 to 1840 one hundred and five vessels were lost on the Mississippi by explosion and fire; 835 persons lost their lives in these accidents, and 296 were injured. By 1842 the number of boats lost annually had risen to sixty-eight.[51]

Nevertheless, the *Republik* passengers engaged the steamer *Knickerbocker* to take them to St. Louis, where they hoped to arrive in fourteen days. The *Knickerbocker,* according to Löber, was a fine new boat with a good captain, who agreed to transport the entire company of 110 people for $1,400 — "Spanish dollars," as Löber wrote. The boat left New Orleans on January 16, 1839.[52] On the trip up the Mississippi only the cabin passengers had their meals served; all the others, known as "deck passengers," had to provide and prepare their own meals from provisions purchased in New Orleans. In the case of the Stephanites on the *Republik,* their supplies included those remaining from the trip across the ocean, which Captain Steenken had sold to them very cheaply or had given to them outright.[53] Löber found the mode of travel on the

[51] *Daily Commercial Bulletin,* April 12, 1840; *St. Louis New Era,* Aug. 18, 1840, March 5, 1845; Allen, *The Commerce and Navigation of the Valley of the Mississippi,* 10; *Proceedings of the St. Louis Chamber of Commerce,* 25, 33—35. See also Williams-Shoemaker, *op. cit.,* I, 186—187.

[52] G. H. Löber to relatives and friends in Germany, Jan. 15, 30, 1839, in Löber-Eichenberg (ed.), "Ein Briefwechsel," *Mitteilungen . . . Kahla,* VII, 145, 147; O. Fürbringer to Stephan, Jan. 15, 1839, Bound MSS., I, C. H. I.; Winter to Guericke *et al.,* April 28, 1841, *Zeitschrift für die gesammte lutherische Theologie und Kirche,* II, No. 3, pp. 116—132. Variations in the rate of exchange, in the terminology employed, and in the methods of listing expenses make an absolutely accurate statement of the expenses on the *Knickerbocker* impossible. However, the cost for fares of the group from New Orleans to St. Louis was about 1,490 thaler and for insurance 563 thaler. These two items total approximately the $1,400 mentioned by Löber. Besides, 217 thaler spent for other expenses bring the total to about 2,270 thaler, according to two itemized accounts for expenses of the *Knickerbocker,* MSS., C. H. I.

[53] G. H. Löber to relatives and friends in Germany, Jan. 30, 1839, in Löber-Eichenberg (ed.), "Ein Briefwechsel," *Mitteilungen . . . Kahla,* VII, 147.

"five hundred" [54] steamers plying the river even more hazardous than the ocean voyage in a sailing vessel, mainly because of the dangers referred to above. Evidence of his incipient Americanization is provided by the fact that he had already learned to rely upon Congressional action to bring about the improvement of conditions which everyone desired and expected.[55]

The *Knickerbocker* reached Vicksburg, Mississippi, on Saturday, January 19, 1839, and remained there about twenty-four hours. On Sunday the first ice was encountered on the Mississippi, and on the following Wednesday the steamer arrived at Memphis. There it took a barge in tow; and although its boilers were taxed, the *Knickerbocker's* progress was slow because of the additional load, the ice in the river, and the many stops each day to take on firewood. If a deck passenger helped in loading fuel, $2.00 was deducted from the fare for his trip to St. Louis. The last day of the week, January 26, found the immigrants at New Madrid, Missouri, and one more day brought them to the mouth of the Ohio River. Two days later, near Hamburg, Illinois, it was necessary to halt for repairs, because the barge had sprung a leak from bumping into some obstruction in the water. On January 30, 1839, at 3 P. M., the *Knickerbocker* landed its passengers at St. Louis. It was high time, in view of the poor health of the passengers. Fürbringer had optimistically reported to Stephan from New Orleans that those who had become sick while crossing the ocean were much better. Winter, however, recorded that the physical condition of the travelers grew steadily worse as the journey proceeded. The latter judgment seems the more correct one, for when the immigrants reached St. Louis, many of them were dangerously ill. In St. Louis the *Republik-Knickerbocker* passengers were greeted by the *Copernicus* and *Johann Georg* contingents, which had preceded them, and by the New York emissaries.[56]

---

[54] *Ibid.;* Vehse, *op. cit.,* 10—11. The number is a gross exaggeration.

[55] G. H. Löber to relatives in Germany, Jan. 30, 1839, in Löber-Eichenberg (ed.), "Ein Briefwechsel," *Mitteilungen . . . Kahla,* VII, 147.

[56] *Ibid.,* 147—148; Christiane Löber to relatives in Germany, Dec. 4, 1839, *ibid.,* 166; G. H. Löber, Diary, Jan. 30, 1839, MS., C. H. I.; O. Fürbringer to Stephan, Jan. 15, 1839, Bound MSS., I, C. H. I.; Winter to Guericke *et al.,* April 28, 1841, *Zeitschrift für die gesammte lutherische Theologie und Kirche,* II, No. 3, pp. 116—132. The date February 5, 1839, has also been given for the arrival of the *Knickerbocker.* P. E. Kretzmann, "The Saxon Immigration to Missouri, 1838—1839," *Missouri Historical Review,* XXXIII, 161.

The majority of the immigrants had now arrived; only the *Olbers* and *Amalia* passengers were as yet not accounted for. But the former vessel bore Stephan, O. H. Walther, all the important lay members of the Advisory Committee, and a number of the candidates and teachers, and the organization of the *Gesellschaft* was such that all authority and initiative was vested in this group. Accordingly, there was little for the Stephanites in St. Louis to do but settle down to an indefinite and costly period of expectant inactivity.

The *Olbers* and the *Amalia* left Bremerhaven within a few hours of each other about midday on Sunday, November 18, 1838. The *Olbers* passed through the English Channel in forty hours between November 20 and 22. Even before the *Olbers* reached the channel, it had encountered storms; these continued from November 19, the second day out, until December 8. They were especially severe in the Bay of Biscay from November 23 to 29 and really violent from the 25th to the 28th. All trunks and chests were blocked into place, and the hatches were nailed shut to prevent the waves that swept over the deck from filling the vessel. Water poured into the dining room and some of the cabins nevertheless. Most of the passengers were ill, and some, like Stephan, afraid. Even some of the sailors became sick. During the first of these storms, on November 20, two-year-old Martin Marbach died of "apoplexy." [57]

By the time the *Olbers* encountered the "Passatwinde" (Levanter), on December 17, life was returning to normal for most of the passengers, but two days later E. W. Zeibig, not yet two years old, died of "teething." [58] School was begun on December 12 and thereafter was held almost daily by one of the candidates. There were frequent church services and devotions, conducted on deck when the weather permitted. Yet Stephan seldom preached,

---

[57] J. K. A. Höhne and J. G. Höhne to their brother, Sept. 26, 1841, in *Die Ameise*, Jan. 7, 1842; Brohm, Journal, Nov. 18—29, 1838, List of Passengers . . . Olbers . . . New Orleans, Vehse to K. W. Welzel, Jan. 30, 1839, MSS., C. H. I.; Passenger list of the *Olbers*, Bound MSS., I, C. H. I.; Vehse, *op. cit.*, 8—9; G. Günther, *op. cit.*, 5—6, 10.

[58] Vehse to K. W. Welzel, Jan. 30, 1839, List of Passengers . . . Olbers . . . New Orleans, Brohm, Journal, Nov. 30—Dec. 19, 1838, MSS., C. H. I.; Passenger list of the *Olbers*, Bound MSS., I, C. H. I.; Vehse, *op. cit.*, 9; G. Günther, *op. cit.*, 13.

leaving the pastoral duties largely to O. H. Walther.[59] On the day before Christmas the *Olbers* entered the tropics and thereafter had smooth sailing. Puerto Rico was sighted on January 4, 1839, Santo Domingo on January 6, and Cuba on January 10; by January 13 Cuba was out of sight. Like their compatriots who had preceded them, the travelers on the *Olbers* expressed admiration for the beauty of the islands, echoed their amazement at the wonders of marine life, and voiced similar complaints about the excessive heat, which made them, too, move their sleeping quarters to the deck for a time to escape the oppressive atmosphere of the steerage.[60]

On January 14, 1839, just after entering the Gulf of Mexico, the Stephanites took a step of far-reaching consequence, which will be discussed more fully later but which must not pass entirely unnoticed at this point. On that date they made Stephan their bishop and endowed him with a liberal grant of power to carry out the functions of his office.[61] The very next day a meeting was held that was really nothing else than a continuation of the sessions of the Advisory Committee in Germany. But the group was now called together by Stephan on his new authority, as the opening words of the minutes indicate: "At the command of His Reverence, the Herr Bishop, the undersigned are to deliberate concerning the steps to be taken on arrival in New Orleans. . . ."[62] Those who signed the proceedings for that day were: O. H. Walther, Marbach, Vehse, Wege, Brohm, H. F. Fischer, Barthel, Gube, C. G. Hofmann, and Jäckel.

At this meeting it was decided that when the *Olbers* docked at New Orleans, Marbach was to attend to paying the duty on the baggage. Because there was good reason to suspect that a considerable number of faulty declarations had been made on the freight, Marbach's task promised to present some difficulties, and Barthel

---

59 Brohm, Journal, Nov. 20, 22, 26, Dec. 19, 26, 27, 1838, Jan. 13, 1839, MS., C.H.I.; Vehse, *op. cit.*, 8—9; G. Günther, *op. cit.*, 10—12.

60 J. K. A. Höhne and J. G. Höhne to their brother, Sept. 26, 1841, *Die Ameise*, Jan. 7, 10, 1842; Brohm, Journal, Dec. 28, 1838, Jan. 7, 8, 10, 13, 1839, MS., C. H. I.; Vehse, *op. cit.*, 9; G. Günther, *op. cit.*, 18—19.

61 Stephan's Investiture, MS., C.H.I. This document has been translated and is quoted in full below. See also Brohm, Journal, Jan. 14—15, 1839, MS., C.H.I.; Vehse, *op. cit.*, 9—10; G. Günther, *op. cit.*, 19—21.

62 Protokolle über die . . . Auswanderung, Jan. 15, 1839, Bound MSS., III, C.H.I. See also Brohm, Journal, Jan. 15, 1839, MS., C.H.I.

and Nitzschke were assigned to him as assistants. The chartering of the river steamer was left to O. H. Walther and H. F. Fischer, who received instructions on what the stipulations of the contract were to be. The transfer of freight was made the responsibility of Vehse and Wege. But the elaborate organization of four departments set up for this purpose was rendered utterly useless by the dispatch with which the stevedores performed this routine task in New Orleans. A committee was also appointed to attend to the purchase of supplies. The membership of this committee included Louise Günther, who was named in order to care "especially for the needs of the Herr Bishop." Thus Louise Günther probably became the only woman in the history of the Saxons honored with an appointment to an official committee. It was also arranged that the candidates should remain free from other duties so that they might devote themselves to accompanying and providing companionship for the Herr Bishop, while Klemm and Gräber were assigned to his personal service. Finally, Stephan seems to have anticipated some desertions when the group reached New Orleans, for H. F. Fischer, the bookkeeper, was ordered to be certain to obtain personal notes securing the indebtedness of those who had drawn from the Credit Fund. Apparently the intention was to remove any possible inclination to leave the boat as soon as it docked.[63]

The *Olbers* reached the delta of the Mississippi on January 18, and a pilot came aboard the next day. While being towed toward the New Orleans dock by the *Hudson,* the *Olbers* stuck fast in a shallow place and was pulled off by the *Hudson* and the *Tiger* with difficulty only after 20,000 of the bricks it was carrying had been transferred from stern to bow.[64] On the same day, while the passengers were still on board the *Olbers,* they addressed a letter of thanks to Captain H. W. Exter, commending him for his conduct and praising the accommodations of the ship in every detail. This letter contains one of the very few indications given by Stephan that he ever considered the possibility of bringing to the United States other members of his family besides the one son who was

---

[63] *Ibid.;* G. Günther, *op. cit.,* 25.

[64] J. A. K. Höhne and J. G. Höhne to their brother, Sept. 26, 1841, in *Die Ameise,* Jan. 10, 1842; Vehse to K. W. Welzel, Jan. 30, 1839, Brohm, Journal, Jan. 19, 1839, MSS., C. H. I.; G. Günther, *op. cit.,* 21—23.

with him. To Captain Exter he wrote: "Should you, on a future voyage to New Orleans, have on board the children of the first undersigned [Stephan] or the brethren in the faith who will follow us, then we request that you show them the same kindness and attention that you have shown us." [65]

On Sunday, January 20, 1839, at 4 P. M., the *Olbers* dropped anchor among five hundred other ships at the New Orleans docks and immediately became the center of interest for a great number of Germans in the city who expected news from their native land. The next day Captain Exter filed his manifest and paid the registration fee of $22.37¾ for his ship and its passengers to the "Mayoralty" of New Orleans.[66] The leaders of the *Olbers* group, after being taken in (without serious consequences) by a petty swindler who impersonated a customs official, secured the services of a Mr. Suffert (?), who procured a "good" inspector. As a result the immigrants had only a few trunks opened and paid no duty at all. Suffert was helpful in other ways as well, and Vles, too, made good his promise to look after them. Stephan and his aides left word for the *Amalia* contingent to enlist the services of Vles, and instructed them to declare their baggage as personal effects and church property.[67] The immigrants were permitted to go ashore on January 21, and although they were certain that New Orleans was not as pleasant a city as Dresden, they found it rather cosmopolitan. The slave market was particularly offensive to the German immigrants, and the population of the city in general appeared to them "demoralized." [68] Three days after the *Olbers* had arrived in port, while the Saxons were still living on board

[65] The passengers of the *Olbers* to Captain Exter, Jan. 19, 1839, Bound MSS., I, C. H. I.

[66] List of Passengers . . . Olbers . . . New Orleans, Receipt for the registration fee of the *Olbers*, Jan. 21, 1839, Brohm, Journal, Jan. 20, 1839, MSS., C. H. I.; J. A. K. Höhne and J. G. Höhne to their brother, Sept. 26, 1841, in *Die Ameise*, Jan. 10, 1842; Vehse, *op. cit.*, 10. The date for the arrival of the *Olbers* is incorrect as stated by G. Günther, who claims January 26, and Fischer, who adopts the date January 17, reported in the *Leipziger allgemeine Zeitung*, March 3, 1839. G. Günther, *op. cit.*, 23; Fischer, *op. cit.*, 71. Rosenthal even claims that "several months" elapsed between the arrival of the first and the last ship. Rosenthal, *op. cit.*, 69.

[67] Vehse to K. W. Welzel, Jan. 30, 1839, MS., C. H. I.; G. Günther, *op. cit.*, 24.

[68] J. A. K. Höhne and J. G. Höhne to their brother, Sept. 26, 1841, in *Die Ameise*, Jan. 10, 1842; Brohm, Journal, Jan. 21, 1839, MS., C. H. I.; G. Günther, *op. cit.*, 23.

the ship, a daughter was born to Christiane Henriette Niemann, wife of a Dresden shoemaker.[69]

The *Olbers* group remained in New Orleans and took in the sights of the city for ten rather costly days. The reasons for the delay are nowhere clearly stated, and it seems likely that, had he wished to do so, Stephan could have left for St. Louis sooner than he did. One might surmise that this detachment intended to rendezvous with the passengers of the *Amalia* in order to travel to St. Louis together with them. But such an arrangement seems never to have been a part of the plan. When the contract for the *Selma,* a 355-ton steamboat built in Pittsburgh in 1835, was signed, only three days after the arrival of the *Olbers* in New Orleans, no provision was made for the passengers of the *Amalia.*[70] Neither was departure delayed until the leaders became convinced that the *Amalia* never would arrive, for while some anxiety was felt for the smallest of the five ships, they had not yet given her up for lost. In fact, on January 30, Vehse, under orders from Stephan, wrote out a lengthy set of instructions to Welzel, the candidate who was in charge of the *Amalia* group. In these instructions Vehse seems to have been more concerned about assuring Welzel that "our most reverend *Bishop* (you are now to call him that), praise and thanks to God, is well," than he was about how the *Amalia* had fared.[71] It seems plain that Stephan, and probably the lesser luminaries as well, were not too anxious to leave New Orleans, regardless of any consideration involving the *Amalia.*

The instructions to Welzel were based upon the circumstances encountered by the immigrants in New Orleans, and, with the exception of the economy measures enjoined upon Welzel, the advice given him obviously reflects the experiences of the *Olbers* group. Vehse's letter also contained practical information on purchasing the supplies needed for the trip to St. Louis. The prices for some of the commodities were as follows: Coffee, 3½ cents a pound; butter, 24 to 32½ cents; tea, 37½ cents; sugar, 7 cents; rice, 5½ cents; flour, $8.50 a barrel; beer, $10 a keg; wine, $25 a cask. The wine the immigrants were to use for preventing illness by mixing it with the river water which they would have to drink on their

[69] G. Günther, *op. cit.,* 24.
[70] Contract for the *Selma,* Jan. 23, 1839, Bound MSS., I, C. H. I.
[71] Vehse to K. W. Welzel, Jan. 30, 1839, MS., C. H. I.

way up the Mississippi. Most of the provisions the *Olbers* group had were bought at Schneider's store and in the wine and liquor shops opposite it in St. Louis Street, and Welzel was advised to make his purchases there also. Copies of the instructions were left with Vles, Suffert, and Captain Hohorst of the *Johann Georg,* which was still in port, but Welzel never appeared to claim any of them.[72]

In the purchase of supplies for the river journey "Dem. Louise Günther" justified the confidence that had been placed in her. A partial list of provisions bought the last day in New Orleans included a variety of items especially for Stephan, such as coconuts, oranges, and eight hams. The bill for that day's shopping was over $220, of which $48.45¼ was spent for the cabin passengers, although they were to have their meals furnished on the ship. But these luxuries did not include the eighty dollars' worth of wine purchased by Marbach through Vles & Company on January 23, or the sixty-four thalers' (about $44.00) worth purchased especially for Stephan on January 30, or the special sofa and other furniture for the Bishop's comfort which were acquired in New Orleans.[73] Of course, not all the blame for such extravagances at the expense of the Credit Fund can be laid at Stephan's door. It seems a safe assumption that Vehse, who emphasized these expenditures in his condemnation of Stephan, and others of the clerical and lay leaders assisted in disposing of the eight hams, which the Bishop could hardly have consumed alone.[74] However, it is true that Stephan was primarily responsible, and on February 11, 1839, the itemized list of his personal expenses in New Orleans and up to that date on the river trip, which was made out by the treasurer, Barthel, totaled no less than $180.56¼.[75]

As previously stated, the *Selma* had been contracted for on January 23. The agreement was signed for the colonists by their committee appointed on the *Olbers,* consisting of O. H. Walther and

---

[72] *Ibid.* Compare with Protokolle über die . . . Auswanderung, Jan. 15, 1839, Bound MSS., III, C. H. I.

[73] Bill of sale to Marbach from Vles & Co., Jan. 23, 1839, List of supplies purchased in New Orleans for the *Selma* group, Jan. 31, 1839, Notes by Jäckel on contributions to cover the purchase of the sofa, April 10, 1839, and Stephan . . . Acct., MSS., C. H. I.; Vehse, *op. cit.,* 10—11; G. Günther, *op. cit.,* 25.

[74] Vehse, *op. cit.,* 11.

[75] Statement of Stephan's account, Feb. 11, 1839, MS., C. H. I.

H. F. Fischer, and by Jäckel, and for the contractor by Captain J. Blood of the *Selma* and his agent, Hodgeman.[76] Obligations and stipulations were stated in great detail, as was usual in the transactions of the Saxons, and, just as customarily, were not kept. At the time the contract was signed, the Stephanites still expected all the 179 Saxons to go to St. Louis.[77] But by the time of the departure eight people had left the *Gesellschaft,* namely, the family of Dr. Schnabel and Rosalie Hermann.[78]

A child born on the day the contract was signed need not be included, as it died two days later, on January 25; there were, then, 171 persons to be provided for. Of this total, sixty-two were cabin passengers and were transported to St. Louis at a cost of 2,741½ thaler, or about 44 thaler a person. The remaining 109 persons were deck passengers, whose fare was about one half the price of that for the cabin passengers, that is 1,457½ thaler, or about 13 thaler each. Thus the total fare on the *Selma* was over 4,000 thaler; the addition of freight charges brought it to $3,000, or about 4,374 thaler; and still other expenses yielded a total of 4,829 thaler.[79] The *Amalia* group was expected to get along on considerably less. Welzel was told he might spend 40 thaler each for a very few cabin passengers and 7 thaler each for the deck passengers; furthermore, he was to exchange only as much of the 2,700 thaler which the *Amalia* carried as was absolutely necessary.[80]

On the *Selma* the deck passengers as usual had to prepare their own meals; so it was stipulated in the contract that hot water had to be provided three times daily. Only a four-day supply of bread could be provided for; after that was used up, the travelers had to be content with hardtack. However, enough fresh vegetables to last for the entire trip could be taken along and were

---

76 Contract for the *Selma,* Jan. 23, 1839, Bound MSS., I, C. H. I. Invoice for the baggage of the *Olbers* passengers, Jan. 28, 1839, MS., C. H. I.

77 Contract for the *Selma,* Jan. 23, 1839, Bound MSS., I, C. H. I.

78 Rosalie Hermann left the *Gesellschaft* on January 26, 1839, and the Schnabel family on January 31, 1839. Notes in Jäckel's hand on the Passenger list of the *Olbers,* Bound MSS., I, C. H. I.; G. Günther, *op. cit.,* 25—26.

79 Financial statement for the *Selma,* signed by F. W. Barthel, April 6, 1839, Bound MSS., 5, C. H. I.; Financial statement for the *Selma,* Brohm, Journal, Jan. 23, 25, 1839, MSS., C. H. I.; Contract for the *Selma,* Jan. 23, 1839, Bound MSS., I, C. H. I. The contract called for payment of $3,000, but according to its terms $60 was deducted because the *Selma* was one day late in taking on the immigrants.

80 Vehse to K. W. Welzel, Jan. 30, 1839, MS., C. H. I.

procured in New Orleans. The baggage of the immigrants was insured for the river trip at the same rate as had prevailed on the ocean voyage, 1⅛ per cent of its declared value, and the insurance on specie cost ¾ per cent. The *Olbers* company took out two policies, one with the Ocean Insurance Company, the other with the Mississippi Marine & Fire Insurance Company, both of New Orleans. The terms in the two policies were identical. The goods on the *Selma* were insured for $7,000; at 1⅛ per cent, the cost of this item was $78.75. The insurance on the $12,000 specie amounted to $90. Thus the total cost of each policy, after a charge of two dollars was added for the policy itself, was $170.75. Welzel was instructed to take out only one policy, with the Mississippi Insurance Company, on Canal and Royal Streets. A duplicate of the policy was to be left with Vles & Company, who would send it on to St. Louis.[81]

When the *Olbers* group arrived in New Orleans, a letter from Kimm & Tewes in St. Louis was waiting for them. Kimm informed them of what they must have known, that he had been unable to deliver Stephan's and Marbach's letter to Spröde in New York because the latter had returned to Germany. Neither had Kimm at the time of writing been able to locate Leonhardt in Illinois (although Örtel, Rudloff, and Müller had been able to do so); hence that contact had also failed, according to Kimm. No trouble was anticipated by Kimm & Tewes in finding lodging in St. Louis for the single people, but they feared the problem of finding houses for the families would cause some difficulty. Again Kimm suggested that the Saxons not discuss their problems with others, but rather send several agents ahead to make arrangements.[82] He had evidently made an honest effort in behalf of his clients to get reliable information on possible sites for a settlement. His remarks on this point are given below. In New Orleans the leaders also received the afore-mentioned letter from Ferdinand Rudloff. In this letter Rudloff reported the events which had taken place in New York and St. Louis, as related above, and asked the Saxons, who were already hard pressed for money, to supply him with funds. He also volunteered some singularly unreliable information

[81] *Ibid.;* Policy issued to the *Selma* passengers by the Ocean Insurance Company of New Orleans, Policy issued to the *Selma* passengers by the Mississippi Marine and Fire Insurance Company of New Orleans, MSS., C. H. I.

[82] Kimm & Tewes to Marbach, Dec. 10, 1838, Bound MSS., I, C. H. I.

on several matters of interest to the immigrants, especially when he announced that there would be ample housing to accommodate them in St. Louis.[83]

On Saturday, January 26, one day later than had been specified, the *Selma* came alongside the *Olbers*. The immigrants transferred directly from the ocean to the river vessel, or, as Vehse phrased it, they exchanged "the modest environment of our German ship for the splendid one of the *Selma,* one of the larger of those mighty American water palaces, 500 of which ply up and down the Mississippi, and in comparison with which the European river steamers appear like a mere dot on the 'i.'" The transfer of the 328 separate pieces of freight was completed two days later.[84] Since two of the steamboats which had taken Stephanites up the river to St. Louis had returned to New Orleans by January 30, the *Olbers* group could leave with the assurance that most of those who had preceded them had arrived safely.[85] Just before their departure, when the boat already had steam up, the leaders of the *Gesellschaft* were served with papers in a civil suit brought by Dr. Schnabel, who, although he and his entire family had been transported free of charge, sought payment for his services as ship's doctor on the ocean voyage. The court had accepted the case, and the *Gesellschaft* had to pay his fee of $700 or post double that amount as bond. The latter was done to avoid delay at this juncture. Marbach later fought the case from St. Louis, but lost it at the end of June, 1839.[86]

On January 31, the day after Vehse's letter to Welzel had been written, the *Selma* left New Orleans with the *Olbers* contingent.[87] The 1,250 miles to St. Louis were frequently negotiated

---

[83] C. F. Rudloff to Marbach, Jan. 7, 1839, Bound MSS., I, C. H. I.

[84] Vehse, *op. cit.,* 10—11; Invoice for the baggage of the *Olbers* passengers, Jan. 28, 1839, Brohm, Journal, Jan. 26—28, 1839, MSS., C. H. I.; G. Günther, *op. cit.,* 25.

[85] Vehse to K. W. Welzel, Jan. 30, 1839, MS., C. H. I.

[86] G. Günther, *op. cit.,* 25—26; Brohm, Journal, Jan. 30, 1839, MS., C. H. I.; Dresel, "Texanisches Tagebuch," *Deutsch-Amerikanische Geschichtsblätter,* XX—XXI, 382—84. The discomfiture of the Stephanites is portrayed in this account with a *Kleinmalerei* that took in everything from the expression on Stephan's face to the posture of the nut-cracking constable. Although done with gusto rather than with objectivity, the description of conditions by Dresel substantially corroborates the other reports.

[87] J. A. K. Höhne and J. G. Höhne to their brother, Sept. 26, 1841, in *Die Ameise,* Jan. 10, 1842; Vehse, *op. cit.,* 11.

by the "tremendously speedy" American boats in eight days under favorable circumstances, and even in 1839 they occasionally took as little as five days. However, the low stage of the water at this time of the year impeded progress up the Mississippi, causing frequent interruptions in the journey, and during the latter half of the voyage ice in the river became a real hazard. In addition, there was the constant danger of "snakes" to worry the passengers. Nevertheless, while eight days of travel still found the *Selma* far from St. Louis, satisfactory headway was made for more than a week. The immigrants reached Natchez on February 2, Vicksburg on February 3, the Arkansas border by February 4, Memphis on February 6, the Missouri border by February 8, New Madrid, Missouri, on February 9, and the mouth of the Ohio by February 10.

At the confluence of the Ohio and Mississippi Rivers the most serious difficulties were encountered, and although by far the greater part of the journey had been completed in eleven days, it took the *Selma* almost exactly again as long to make the rest of the trip, or three weeks for the entire distance.[88] The principal reason for this delay was that at the bar of the Ohio River the *Selma,* along with two other boats, the *Majestic* and the *St. Louis,* was held up by low water for several days. During this time the ship's company went ashore and were shown the vicinity by a Negro guide, who was provided by the owner of a neighboring plantation. The immigrants reciprocated for this kindness by helping the farmer clear some of his land, through the simple expedient of setting afire the virgin forest covering it.

On February 13, 1839, while the *Selma* was still unable to proceed, Marbach and Candidates Fröhlich and Klügel went ahead to St. Louis in a smaller boat, the *Brazil,* to rent quarters for the company. The next day another attempt was made to move the *Selma.* After proceeding five miles, she again ran aground on a sand bar, injuring one of the hands and throwing overboard Rudolph Barthel, who was promptly rescued. The captain now left the boat and took a smaller craft to St. Louis, where he intended to hire several vessels of lighter draft to come and pull the *Selma* off. But on February 16 the crew got tired of waiting and, to the horror

---

[88] Brohm, Journal, Feb. 2—10, 1839, MS., C. H. I.; J. A. K. Höhne and J. G. Höhne to their brother, Sept. 26, 1841, *Die Ameise,* Jan. 10, 1842; Vehse, *op. cit.,* 11; G. Günther *op. cit.,* 25—26.

of their passengers, decided to make an attempt to "roll" the ship over the bar. The ensuing maneuver explains some of the numerous accidents to the boats at that time. The boilers were overheated to a dangerous point, pressure was brought up, and everything movable, including the passengers, was rolled or herded from one quarter of the deck to the other to relieve the pressure on whatever side happened to be stuck most firmly. Thus, to the hurrahs of the crew, the *Selma* was virtually rolled, or walked, over the bar, and the journey to St. Louis could continue.[89]

While the Selma was stuck on the sand bar, and on the day it was finally released, two events occurred which further strengthened Stephan's position as leader of the *Gesellschaft.* On February 14 a statement was made out by Barthel and Jäckel on the status of the Bishop's account, consisting of the 1,500 thaler which had been granted him by the Advisory Committee. Since most of Stephan's expenses, including even lawyer's fees and the like, had been paid with *Gesellschaft* funds, this private account was still practically intact. Barthel, the treasurer, had raised mild objections when the expenditures had been incurred. But now he was persuaded — Vehse says he was browbeaten with outrageous treatment — to sign over the 1,500 thaler to Stephan not as an expense account, but as an outright gift to do with as he liked.[90] Two days later, on February 16, the people were persuaded to make a second declaration regarding Stephan's elevation to the episcopacy. In this document, later called the "Pledge of Subjection to Stephan," the Bishop's followers confirmed his hold on the office and reinforced his authority with a solemn assurance of obedience to him.[91] Further details of this important document are given in a subsequent chapter.

Three days after the *Selma* was set afloat, on February 19, 1839, just after noon on a clear, mild day, the steamboat reached

[89] Brohm, Journal, Feb. 10—14, 1839, MS., C. H. I.; G. Günther, *op. cit.,* 26—30.

[90] Vehse, *op cit.,* 11; Statement of Stephan's account, Feb. 14, 1839, MS., C. H. I. See also Brohm, Journal, Feb. 9, 1839, MS., C. H. I.

[91] Pledge of Subjection to Stephan, *Selma,* Feb. 16, 1839. (This document is included in translation below.) Nachrichten an unsere Nachkommen, MSS., C. H. I.; Vehse, *op. cit.,* 11. The date on the document itself shows that it was not "drawn up and signed by all passengers" on February 5, as stated in Burgdorf, "Corrections of, and Additions to, Saxon Centennial Calendar, 1839," *Concordia Historical Institute Quarterly,* XII, 13.

St. Louis, and the *Olbers-Selma* passengers were reunited with their fellow immigrants of the three detachments which had preceded them.[92] The arrival of the most important contingent of the Stephanites was announced in both the *Daily Missouri Republican* and the *Daily Evening Gazette.* The former, on the next morning, contained the usual notice of a steamboat arrival, given in the customary form: "Arrived. Steamer Selma, [Captain] Blood, from New Orleans. — Consignee . . . One hundred and eighty German passengers. Two births on the passage." [93] Elsewhere in the columns of this same issue the *Daily Missouri Republican* published this item, which had appeared in the *Daily Evening Gazette* of the preceding evening:

> MORE EMIGRANTS. — *One hundred and eighty* Saxons, from Dresden and the neighborhood came here by the *Selma,* this evening. They were part of a company of *seven hundred* Germans, who recently arrived at New Orleans, by the *Olbers,* from Bremen.
>
> They are Lutherans accompanied by a Bishop and priests; and look like the material of good citizens. They will settle either in Missouri or Illinois.[94]

---

[92] J. A. K. Höhne and J. G. Höhne to their brother, Sept. 26, 1841, *Die Ameise,* Jan. 10, 1842; Winter to Guericke *et al.*, April 28, 1841, *Zeitschrift für die gesammte lutherische Theologie und Kirche,* II, No. 3, pp. 116—132; Vehse, *op. cit.*, 12; G. Günther, *op. cit.*, 31. On this period see also Polack, "The Arrival of the Saxons in St. Louis," *Concordia Theological Monthly,* IX, 905—908. Different dates have been given also for this event, *e. g.*, Feb. 18, Schnake, "Die Einwanderung der 'Sachsen,'" *Der Deutsche Pionier,* VI, 157. Some of the strangest ideas on the journey are to be found in "Missouri History not found in Textbooks," *Missouri Historical Review,* XXIV, 618.

[93] *Daily Missouri Republican,* Feb. 20, 1839.

[94] *Daily Evening Gazette,* Feb. 19, 1839.

CHAPTER NINE

THE SAXONS AND THEIR NEW HOME

IT HAS BECOME CUSTOMARY in accounts of the Stephanite emigration or in references to it, to deposit the Saxons virtually in a vacuum. Economic questions are usually disposed of by saying that the Stephanites were originally well-to-do, that they became poor because Stephan squandered all their money, but that thrift and hard work eventually enabled them to attain financial independence. St. Louis, more often than not, is accorded little attention beyond stating its population, with varying degrees of inaccuracy. Perry County is described briefly as picturesque, not exceptionally productive, and generally rather primitive. Remarks on the relation of the Saxons to other groups of Germans, particularly those in Missouri, seldom go beyond an uncomplimentary reference to the *Anzeiger des Westens* and perhaps an allusion to the fact that the churches established by the Saxons grew rapidly because of the large German element in the West. The political situation is almost completely ignored. Educational conditions, bad enough in fact, are sometimes pictured as even worse than they actually were, by way of heightening the contrast with the constructive work of the immigrants. Even the exclusively religious stamp frequently placed upon the Stephanite movement has not made it seem worth while to state what was actually encountered in this field, except to emphasize that the German Lutherans were poorly served.

Notable exceptions to these generalizations are the studies by H. H. Maurer in the *American Journal of Sociology* [1] and, to a lesser degree, the monograph of Carl Mauelshagen, *American Lutheranism Surrenders to Forces of Conservatism.* However, worthy as these efforts are in their limited fields — the one strictly sociological, the other strictly ecclesiastical — both suffer severely from the same deficiencies as earlier writings on the subject, namely, a lack

---

[1] Maurer, "Studies in the Sociology of Religion," and "The Political Attitudes of the Lutheran Parish in America. A Study in Religious Sectionalism," *American Journal of Sociology,* XXX, 665—682, XXXI, 39—57, 485—506, XXXIII, 568—585.

of factual accuracy in the story of the Saxons themselves, and the absence of a broader background against which the emigration can be viewed. On the other hand, Carl Mundinger's treatment of polity in the Missouri Synod contains a plethora of historical incident concerning the Stephanites. Yet even in this work the attempt is made to answer at least one of the questions it raises: "What effect did the new environment have upon the church polity of the immigrants?" [2] while making only incidental references to the milieu in which this development took place. Accordingly, both at this point and throughout the rest of this study considerable attention will be devoted to the environment into which the immigrants had projected themselves.

The view of St. Louis which first presented itself to the Saxons and most other immigrants was appropriately that of the river front. The river was the largest single determining factor in the life of the community whose history was closely linked with the stream since the day on which Laclede chose the site. After the arrival of the steamboat *General Pike* in 1817,[3] the city became constantly more dependent upon the Mississippi, not only for the stream of immigrants which stimulated the growth of St. Louis, but also for the rapid and economical transportation of the imports and exports of the city itself and the hinterland that was commercially dependent upon it and for which the Mound City was a vast depot of supplies. St. Louisans not only lived on the Mississippi, but largely by it as well.

The figures on river traffic as given in the daily papers vary so widely that it is difficult to rely completely on any of them. But it does seem clear that the volume of such traffic increased tremendously during the years which form the setting for the settlement of the Saxons. The 1,476 (or 1,589) steamboat arrivals at the port of St. Louis in 1839 rose to 2,000 or more (2,105) by 1844. In 1845 as many as 2,613 arrivals were claimed; they brought the total value of the city's river trade up to $50,000,000 for that year.[4] Of a total of 285 boats, aggregating 49,800 tons, which plied the Mississippi in 1839, forty-five (8,025 tons) were owned by St. Louis in-

---

[2] Mundinger, *Government in the Missouri Synod,* p. XIII.

[3] Keemle, *The St. Louis Directory for the Years 1838—9,* p. iv; Williams-Shoemaker, *op. cit.,* I, 185.

[4] *Daily Evening Gazette,* Jan. 8, 9, 1841; *Anzeiger des Westens,* Jan. 6, 1846; Stevens, *St. Louis the Fourth City 1764—1909,* p. 347.

terests. Two years later the tonnage of St. Louis-owned vessels (eighty-one) was 13,862, and by 1846 it was 18,905 (or 20,420). These figures from contemporary newspapers, whether entirely accurate or not, nevertheless indicate an increase that put St. Louis in second place as a commercial center among the river towns, being outranked only by New Orleans.[5] The total number of boats on the river increased from 285 in 1839 to 371 in 1841, and to 672 by 1843. The total tonnage on the Mississippi waterways in June, 1845, is given as 159,713.[6] At times in 1847 as many as eighty steamboats were tied up at St. Louis at one time.[7]

With such facts beginning to unfold before them, the citizens of St. Louis were to be excused for their firm belief that their destinies rose and fell with the river's stages and the traffic upon its waters. But had figures such as those above left any doubt in their minds, the comparative ease, speed, and comfort of travel on the Mississippi would have convinced the most obdurate skeptic that not even the railroads, creeping westward across the face of the land, could compete with the Father of Waters as a means of transportation. At a time when prolonged delays in the overland delivery of mails were chronic, the river boats by contrast seemed to afford an ideal means of communication, and by 1843 mail service on them was begun. As remarked above, by 1844 the time for the run between New Orleans and St. Louis had been cut to less than four days, whereas two years later the time required to cover the distance between St. Louis and Washington, D. C., was still 6¼ days by overland mail.[8]

The city itself was an irregular, sprawling, ill-planned collection of rather unattractive houses of widely varying ages, of empty lots, and of filthy, crooked streets.[9] Arends, viewing St. Louis the year before the Saxons arrived, declared: "There can hardly be another city of so peculiar appearance on earth." [10] While his de-

---

[5] *Täglicher Anzeiger des Westens,* April 29, 1846; *Weekly Reveille,* May 4, 1846; *Proceedings of the St. Louis Chamber of Commerce,* 25; Allen, *op. cit.,* 6.

[6] *Daily Evening Gazette,* Oct. 18, 19, 1841; Allen, *op. cit.,* 6.

[7] *Täglicher Anzeiger des Westens,* July 29, 1847.

[8] *Anzeiger des Westens,* Nov. 20, 1841, Dec. 15, 1842, Jan. 19, Feb. 25, April 13, 20, 1843, Jan. 26, 1844, July 12, Dec. 18, 1845, March 6, 1846.

[9] Arends, *Schilderung des Mississippi-thales,* 296; Dana (ed.), *The United States Illustrated . . . The West,* 122; Flagg, *The Far West,* I, 117.

[10] Arends, *op. cit.,* 296.

scription is probably an exaggeration, Dana characterized St. Louis of 1836 as "emphatically only a little *French* City," and, quoting his own notes taken in that year, spoke of "a cheerful village air, a certain rus in urbe." [11] In 1839 St. Louis was seventy-five years old; it had been an incorporated city since 1822.[12] In 1830 the population of St. Louis was 6,694; in 1838 and 1839 it was variously estimated from as low as 10,000 to as high as 20,000; in 1837 it was actually 14,253; and in 1840 it reached 16,469.[13] "Then the city proper only extended westward as far as Seventh Street. Beyond that line there were some scattering residences, gutters, and prairie. . . . To the north the city extended to Middle [Biddle] street, and to the south, just below the Convent of the Sacred Heart." [14]

While St. Louis was no longer, strictly speaking, a frontier town, its aspect gave evidence that it had recently been one, for as late as 1847 not all of its log cabins had been replaced, and during the decade of the forties Indians from farther east still filed through its streets on their westward retreat from the white man.[15] Economically St. Louis was vitally interested in the West. Through the city, or from points in the State which were its economic tributaries, caravans were moving to California, Oregon, and Texas. St. Louis newspapers told of events and movements along the Santa Fe Trail, of its dangers, and of the high financial returns of its trade, which employed 1,200 people and was estimated to be worth from $596,900 to $2,000,000 to the city annually during these years.[16] Sutter advertised for the experienced workers he needed in New Helvetia, California, in the columns of the *Anzeiger*.[17] Trade with

---

[11] Dana (ed.), *op. cit.*, 122.

[12] Keemle, *The St. Louis Directory, for the Years 1838—9*, p. vii.

[13] *The Sixth Census of the United States: 1840*, p. 413; *Annual Review . . . From the Missouri Republican*, Jan. 10, 1854, pp. 8—9; *Daily Missouri Republican*, March 14, 1845; Keemle, *The St. Louis Directory, for the Years 1838—9*, p. 56; G. Günther, *op. cit.*, 32; Polàck, *Walther*, 36.

[14] Edwards-Hopewell, *Edwards's Great West and her Commercial Metropolis*, 336.

[15] *Anzeiger des Westens*, Jan. 15, 1842; *Täglicher Anzeiger des Westens*, June 3, Oct. 21, 1846; *St. Louis Daily New Era*, March 3, 1847.

[16] *Anzeiger des Westens*, March 14, 20, April 13, 20, 29, May 4, 13, 27, July 8, Aug. 12, 29, Sept. 2, 9, 1843, Nov. 20, 1844, Jan. 9, 11, 14, Feb. 11, May 27, Sept. 23, 1845, March 19, 1846; *Täglicher Anzeiger des Westens*, June 19, Aug. 24, 1846; *Daily Missouri Republican*, June 10, 1844, Jan. 3, 4, 6, 7, 1845, May 9, 1846; *St. Louis New Era*, May 25, 26, 1843, April 14, 1844; *Missouri Reporter*, May 19, 1846; *Daily People's Organ*, Jan. 15, 1844.

[17] *Anzeiger des Westens*, Sept. 20, 1845.

the Indians brought $1,250,000 a year into St. Louis coffers, while the fur trade, parent of St. Louis, still netted worth-while returns, reaching its greatest development between 1807 and 1843. The value of buffalo skins handled in the single year 1846 alone was estimated at nearly $500,000.[18] Partly because of these contacts with the frontier, St. Louis was a boom town and on the threshold of a spectacular expansion. The Saxons themselves remarked how important commerce and manufacture were to St. Louis at the time of their arrival in 1839.[19] The city early showed a diversity of industry and by 1847 was doing a thriving business in such varying fields as lumbering, slaughtering, and milling, in the manufacture of glass, and in its hemp factories and iron foundries.[20]

Probably the best single index of the development of St. Louis during the forties is a simple statement of the population figures. When the decade began, St. Louis already had something of which to boast in its 2½-fold increase in size since 1830 (from 6,694 to 16,469). But this was literally "only the beginning." The population rose to 19,063 in 1841, to 28,357 in 1843, to 34,140 in 1844, to 36,000 in 1845, to 47,863 in 1847, and to 77,860 in 1850.[21] There was little doubt in the minds of St. Louisans that theirs was not only one of the two fastest-growing cities in the country, but that St. Louis would presently outstrip Boston and any other challenger for first place, a conviction that left the citizens of the "Metropolis of the West" mildly surprised but undaunted by their own greatness. Thus it is not startling to find the St. Louis *Daily Commercial Bul-*

---

18 *Ibid.*, March 19, 1846; *Missouri Reporter*, June 23, 1843; *Daily Missouri Republican*, Oct. 9, 1845, April 1, 1847; Williams-Shoemaker, *op. cit.*, I, 142—143.

19 Winter to Guericke *et al.*, April 28, 1841, *Zeitschrift für die gesammte lutherische Theologie und Kirche*, II, No. 3, pp. 116—132; Vehse, *op. cit.*, 30—33.

20 *Anzeiger des Westens*, Aug. 28, 1845; *Daily Missouri Republican*, Feb. 9, 1847; *St. Louis Daily New Era*, Jan. 20, May 1, June 10, 1846; *St. Louis Daily Union*, Jan. 6, 25, 1847.

21 *The Seventh Census of the United States: 1850*, p. 662; *St. Louis New Era*, June 2, 1841, March 3, 1843, March 4, 1845; *St. Louis Daily New Era*, Feb. 25, 1847; *Daily Evening Gazette*, March 3, 1843, Nov. 15, 1844; *Daily Missouri Republican*, Nov. 15, 1844, March 4, 25, 1845, March 1, 3, 1847; *Anzeiger des Westens*, Nov. 14, 1844; *St. Louis Daily Union*, Feb. 26, 1847; *Die Deutsche Tribüne*, Feb. 26, 1847; Taylor-Crooks, *Sketch Book of St. Louis*, 16. There is considerable variation in the figures given in these sources, but inasmuch as many of them are estimates, the discrepancies are not important. However, Schneider does not even agree with the census of 1850. Schneider, *op. cit.*, 422.

letin stating, in 1840: "St. Louis is destined to be the centre of American civilization and refinement," [22] or the St. Louis *Weekly Reveille* six years later envisioning St. Louis as the national capitol within two decades.[23] But it is indicative of the prestige of the Mound City that even one of its rival's newspapers, the *New Orleans Bulletin,* in 1843 said: "We have always been of the opinion that St. Louis is destined to become the most important inland city in the world." [24]

The Stephanites could hardly have improved the timing of their appearance in St. Louis history had they had the perspective of their children or grandchildren. The stage of development which the city had attained at this time provided the Saxons with an economic and social background that contributed greatly to their personal material success and to their strong growth as a religious body. This background was in no small part the outgrowth of specific local circumstances. For example, the significance of the Mississippi for industrial and commercial St. Louis has already been emphasized. But of equal importance was the steady stream if immigrants which was pouring into the city. For this current and impending growth the community also had the river to thank. To most groups of colonists, of course, other immigrants, particularly immigrants to a city, would have represented only so many economic competitors. But for the Saxons the circumstances they encountered merely enhanced the prospects for the unfolding of their primary mission in the religious and educational fields.

Yet larger population, increased trade, and the greater opportunity in every field of endeavor which these spelled for the newcomer to St. Louis — all these conditions were not caused entirely by the peculiar advantages of the city's location. Rather, these circumstances themselves were in turn partly the result of forces in American history so vast, so fundamental, that in comparison with them the growth of a city, no matter how rapid or relatively important, was only an incident. Prominent among these larger factors which determined the opportuneness of the Saxon immigration were westward expansion, "manifest destiny," "Jacksonian democracy,"

---

[22] *Daily Commercial Bulletin,* April 15, 1840.

[23] *Weekly Reveille,* Feb. 9, 1846.

[24] Quoted in the *Daily Evening Gazette,* Julv 1, 1843.

the beginning of the industrial and the imminence of the agricultural revolution in the United States.[25]

Not only were the year 1839 and the St. Louis area well suited to the Saxons; the Saxons were also well suited to the needs of the time and the place. Of all the immigrants who came to St. Louis, few were basically as well prepared as the Saxons to fit themselves into the social structure of which they were to become a part. It is obvious, of course, that they had a few ideas about their environment and the part they expected to play in it which bordered on the absurd. But in this respect they were not very different from almost all other immigrants. On the other hand, the social composition of the group was in nearly perfect alignment with the needs that were being created by the development of the city and its surrounding territory.

The observation has repeatedly been made that a considerable number of the Saxons were farmers, but that the majority were craftsmen and professional men. Comparison reveals that this occupational distribution varies notably from the usual pattern among other immigrants of that time. Over the three-year period from 1838 through 1840 the records of immigration through the Port of New Orleans always show the classification of "merchants" having a substantial plurality, with farmers and "mechanics," or craftsmen, invariably occupying the next two places.[26] In the cases of the Saxons, however, the craftsmen not only were the largest single group, but out of a total occupational listing of 355 (including women) they numbered no less than 217, or 61 per cent. Agricultural occupations, which were a large factor among immigrants as a whole, accounted for only 14 per cent among the Saxons, little more than the professions, which constituted fully 11 per cent. There were only nine merchants among the Stephanites — no more than 3 per cent of the total.[27]

The preponderance of the craftsmen among the Stephanites augured well for their economic future. In St. Louis of 1840 com-

[25] These factors are discussed in a series of articles by W. G. Bauer, "America One Hundred Years Ago," "How Providence Made Ready a Home for Our Pioneers," "1839 and a Land of New Opportunities," "Crisis — 1837," and "Democracy Welcomes the Pioneers," *Lutheran Witness,* LVII, 9, 38—40, 74—76, 121—122, 154—155.

[26] *House Docs.,* 25 Cong., 3 Sess., No. 210, pp. 26—29; *Senate Docs.* 26 Cong., 1 Sess., No. 594, pp. 22—25; *ibid.,* 2 Sess., No. 206, pp. 24—27.

[27] Table IV, Appendix A.

merce provided employment for 845 persons (21 per cent), manufacture and trade for 2,012 (51 per cent), navigation for 891 (23 per cent), and the professions for 188 (5 per cent). By 1847 the listing was: mechanics 4,657 (52 per cent), laborers 2,345 (26 per cent), merchants 708 (8 per cent), and the professions 539 (6 per cent).[28] While the variation in designations between these two years prevents an accurate comparison, the general pattern of the city's occupational development seems readily traceable. The emergence of a clear-cut distinction between "mechanics" and "laborers" is significant, as is the high percentage of the former by 1847. Simultaneously, it is plain, commerce and trade did not keep pace, in providing employment, with the industrial development of the community. The somewhat indistinct but high figures of 1840 for these classifications had shrunk to a well-defined but unimpressive "merchants, 8 per cent" by 1847.

However these statistics may be interpreted otherwise, they demonstrate that in 1847 more St. Louisans, actually and proportionately, were at the workbench and in the factory than there had been in 1840, while fewer of them, proportionately at least, were making their living as shopkeepers, fur traders, and merchants. Meanwhile the professions were doing little more than holding their own. Much more than in the case of other immigrants, therefore, the proportion of occupations among the Saxons was in line with the future development of their new home. They had the type of skilled worker who was sorely needed and usually unavailable in a rapidly developing West; they had farmers, almost all of whom knew a trade, and craftsmen, almost all of whom were used to doing a little farming; and they had proportionately twice as many professional men as the city at large could boast during a time when this class of citizen could scarcely have been a glut on the labor market. The addition of an occupational group so well suited to the needs of the community as were the Saxons, was undoubtedly an asset to St. Louis and Missouri in 1839.

Other sociological characteristics of the Saxons and the groups associated with them have not always been interpreted as reliably as those just discussed.[29] Consequently, in order to provide accurate

---

28 *The Sixth Census of the United States: 1840,* p. 413; *St. Louis Daily New Era,* March 3, 1847.

29 Fischer, *op. cit.,* 69—70; C. F. W. Walther, *Bünger,* 42; Dau (ed.), *op. cit.,* 7.

information on as many factors as possible, the age, place of residence in Germany, and occupation of each immigrant are given in the appended lists of the various detachments whenever such information was available.[30] For that portion of the immigrants on whom most attention is focused — the 612 on the four ships which arrived early in 1839 — the information is virtually complete. A summary of these statistics is contained in the accompanying Tables I to IV.[31]

Again it becomes apparent that the Saxon group had a distinctly different social texture from that of other German immigrants of the day. One outstanding difference was the greater proportion of women among the Saxons. While the ratio of females to males was forty-five to fifty-five among the Stephanites,[32] among all other German immigrants arriving in New Orleans from 1838 to 1840 only 35 per cent were females.[33] Yet the proportion of women immigrants was usually greater among the Germans than among other nationality groups.[34] The 45 per cent of the Saxons therefore looms even larger in comparison with immigrants as a whole. It accounts in part for the fact that intermarriage was possible to a sufficient extent to assure the homogeneity of the group for some time to come.

Other notable facts about the Stephanites are that, coming from a nation known for its family life and for its immigration by families, the number of unmarried adults, most of whom were young, was large, and the size of the average family was relatively small.[35] Little wonder that the Germans were described as bringing "a host of children," [36] when, for example, according to a St. Louis newspaper of 1841, in a single detachment of 338 German immigrants 129 were children under four years of age! [37] In this class of immigrants, families of three or four children, such as the Saxons averaged at the time of their arrival, were not considered large.

---

[30] Lists I—V, Appendix A.

[31] Tables I—IV, *ibid.*

[32] Table II, *ibid.*

[33] *House Docs.*, 25 Cong., 3 Sess., No. 210, pp. 26—29; *Senate Docs.*, 26. Cong., 1 Sess., No. 594, pp. 22—25; *ibid.*, 2 Sess., No. 206, pp. 24—27.

[34] Mayo-Smith, *Emigration and Immigration*, 50.

[35] Table II, Appendix A.

[36] *Daily Misouri Republican*, Jan. 7, 1847.

[37] *St. Louis New Era*, June 28, 1841.

Yet despite the fact that there were comparatively few children among the Saxons, the average age of this immigrant group was strikingly low — only about twenty-five years.[38] The religious cast of the movement with its appeal to the youthful and with Stephan's ability to impress particularly this age group may account for the presence of an unusual number of young adults, both married and unmarried, who lowered the average age to what it might have been if there had been larger families. This combination of factors meant that the families in many cases had not yet attained their full size; that there was likely to be a high proportion of marriages in a few years; that the supply of marriageable women was far higher than in most groups; and that these factors would make possible both a high incidence of intermarriage within the group and even some growth through marriage into it. Here were the elements of unusual strength in the future of the movement.

The question in 1839, however, was whether the movement had a future. There were those who did not think so, who did not wish it to succeed, and who were in a position to express their opposition with telling effect. Neither they nor their Stephanite victims could or would engage in a dispassionate appraisal of the Saxon immigrants' relationship to their environment. Hence neither group faced the necessity of modifying its emotional reaction to the phenomenon appearing on the scene. These reactions ranged from hatred of religious orthodoxy and clericalism on the one hand to glorification of separatistic confessionalism and a hierarchical leadership on the other. Instead, they faced each other with uncompromising hostility. In the ensuing struggle the Saxons' opponents enjoyed the initial advantage of being able to influence public opinion against them, ably assisted by the Stephanites themselves, who seemed for a time to have a genius for doing the wrong thing at the worst time. The result was just what was to be expected. Even the Saxons saw the light. In 1842, when the colony in St. Louis began the erection of a church, they deposited in the cornerstone of the building a brief account of the immigration up to that time. In this document they stated that one of three great difficulties they had encountered was adverse public opinion.[39] The disrepute

---

[38] Table II, Appendix A.

[39] Document . . . des Grundsteins . . . St. Louis . . . 22. Juny 1842, MS., C. H. I.

in which the Saxons still found themselves more than three years after their arrival was, of course, partially a result of the later developments in Stephan's personal history. But even aside from this factor, the public relations of the group were seriously impaired shortly after their arrival by unfavorable notices of their activities and direct attacks upon them in the press. With newspapers probably the single most important agency for exerting social and political influence, their attitude was important to any body of immigrants. But in the case of the Stephanites the newspapers had an additional significance because of the peculiar nature of their movement, the consequent importance for them of public opinion, and the unusual interest displayed in them by the press. A closer look at the press in the area of their activity is therefore in order.

The principal English newspapers in St. Louis during the period covered in this discussion were: the *Daily Missouri Republican*, the *Evening Gazette (Daily Gazette, Daily Evening Gazette)*, the *Daily Commercial Bulletin*, the *Daily Pennant*, the *Missouri Argus* (absorbed by the *Missouri Reporter)*, the *St. Louis New Era (St. Louis Daily New Era)*, the *Missouri Reporter*, the *People's Organ (Daily People's Organ, People's Daily Organ)*, the *Native American Bulletin* (merged with the *Old School Democrat and St. Louis Herald)*, the *Old School Democrat and St. Louis Herald (St. Louis Democrat)*, the *Daily Missourian (Daily Morning Missourian)*, the *Weekly Reveille*, the *St. Louis American (St. Louis Daily American)*, and the *St. Louis Daily Union* (a merger of the *Missouri Reporter* and the *Daily Morning Missourian)*. However, there was also a steady stream of more transient sheets pouring from St. Louis presses. Thus during these same years brief life was enjoyed by the *St. Louis Herald*, the *St. Louis Ledger*, the *Picket Guard*, the *Missouri Standard*, the *Ariel* (absorbed by the *St. Louis Transcript)*, the *Mill Boy*, the *Slasher*, the *St. Louis Transcript* (successor to the *Ariel)*, the *Sun*, and the *Morning Post*. Besides the English newspapers a number also appeared in the German language, primarily the *Anzeiger des Westens* (1835; *Täglicher Anzeiger des Westens*, beginning in 1846), and *Die Deutsche Tribüne* (1844), but also supplemented at various times by several short-lived efforts: the first *Tribüne* (1838), *Der Missouri Demokrat* (begun in February, 1843), *Die Wage (Die Waage?)*, and the *National Zeitung*. Even two French newspapers appeared for a time, although the original French settlers and their descendants constituted a steadily diminishing percentage of the total population as the other language groups were growing at a much more rapid rate. Both of these papers, *Le Telegraphie* and the French edition of the *Daily Pennant,* appeared in 1840; they do not seem to have survived long.

Brevity of life did not distinguish the French papers from most of the others. Some, like the *Picket Guard* (August 18 to October 8, 1842), appeared for only a few weeks; others for several months, a year, or perhaps two. Even though only three of the twenty-four English, six German, and two French newspapers mentioned *(i. e.,* the *Daily Missouri Republican,* the *Anzeiger des Westens,* and the *Daily Evening Gazette)* were published throughout the years 1838—1847, the total number published at any time during this period was still large enough to assure a varied fare for the St. Louis public. Seven papers greeted the Saxons in 1839. The number rose to eleven in 1840 and to sixteen by 1844, another election year, when three others, whose dates of publication are not entirely clear, were perhaps still in publication, bringing the possible total for the latter year to nineteen. Most of these papers appeared daily, others one, two, or three times a week. Some of them, like the *Anzeiger,* changed the frequency of their publication several times during the years under discussion. Still others, like the political supplements of the larger papers, the *Mill Boy* and the *Slasher,* had no regular dates of issue, but appeared sporadically only so long as they served their purpose, which was usually until after an election. Finally, a number of the larger newspapers also published editions which appeared once, twice, or three times a week, in addition to their daily issues.[40]

---

[40] *Evening Gazette,* July 11, 1838; *Daily Evening Gazette,* April 10, 1840, Feb. 7, 1843, June 1, Aug. 29, Nov. 9, 1844; *People's Organ,* Jan. 31, May 9, 1842, May 15, 1844; *Daily People's Organ,* Oct. 8, 1842, Feb. 8, May 10, June 8, 1843, Feb. 24, March 27, April 6, 1844; *People's Daily Organ,* May 16, 1846; *St. Louis New Era,* April 1, 11, 1840, Dec. 11, 1841, March 14, 1845, *St. Louis Daily New Era,* Dec. 15, 1846, May 31, 1847; *Anzeiger des Westens,* Dec. 29, 1841, Oct. 18, 29, 1842, May 4, Sept. 23, 1843, April 3, 1845, Jan. 5, 1846; *Täglicher Anzeiger des Westens,* July 22, 1847; *Missouri Reporter,* Jan. 4, Feb. 9, June 7, 1843, Aug. 15, 1846; *St. Louis Daily Union,* Aug. 17, 1846, March 19, May 31, 1847; *St. Louis American,* Sept. 8, 29, Dec. 7, 1845; *Weekly Reveille,* Oct. 6, 1845, May 17, June 28, 1847; *Native American Bulletin,* Jan. 3, Aug. 19, Nov. 22, 1842; *Old School Democrat and St. Louis Herald,* March 2, June 7, 1843; *St. Louis Democrat,* Sept. 2, 1844; *Daily Missouri Republican,* March 26, 1845; *Missouri Argus,* Dec. 15, 1841; *Daily Commercial Bulletin,* Jan. 1, Oct. 27, 1840; *Daily Missourian,* Oct. 21, 1844; *Daily Morning Missourian,* Oct. 7, 1845, July 28, 1846;

Besides the thirty-two papers mentioned many other publications were appearing in the city. Generalization about these is even more difficult than about the newspapers, their issuance often even less regular. The one thing they did have in common was that their primary purpose was not the conveying of news, but the representation of the viewpoint of some particular group or person. In the course of this study the following were noted among English-language publications of this type: the *Saturday News (Missouri Saturday News)*, a literary magazine; the *St. Louis Washingtonian*, organ of the temperance movement; the *St. Louis Pilot*, devoted to the cause of Ireland and sponsored by the local Irish element; the *St. Louis Magnet*, a pseudo-scientific journal, and the *Missouri Medical and Surgical Journal*.[41]

The Germans were represented also in this class of publications with four periodicals defending various degrees of religious, social, and political radicalism. Three of the four were edited at times from 1842 to 1847 by Heinrich Koch, the city's number one German rabble rouser; they were the *Antipfaff*, the *Vorwärts*, and *Der Reformer*. The other was *Der Freisinnige*.[42] Fifteen of the thirty-eight newspapers and magazines appearing in Missouri in 1843 were published in St. Louis.[43] A year and a half later the total for St. Louis was twenty-seven, ranging from daily to monthly publications, and it is doubtful that *Der Lutheraner* of the Saxons, then only about one month old, was included in this figure.[44]

With newspapers virtually the only source of information on daily events, it is obvious that they were of great importance to the life of the community and commanded a tremendous amount of attention. Yet even when that fact is taken into consideration,

---

Daily Pennant, April 1, Aug. 19, 1840; *The Slasher*, April 27, 1844; *Die Deutsche Tribüne*, July 15, 1844, May 13, 1847; *Mill Boy*, Feb. 10, 1844, Jan. 21, 1845. See also Green, *St. Louis Directory . . . 1845*, p. xxxiv; Keemle, *The St. Louis Directory, for the Years 1838—9*, p. 52; Skillman, *The Western Metropolis; or St. Louis in 1846*, p. 106.

41 *Daily Evening Gazette*, March 21, 1840; *Missouri Argus*, Sept. 8, 1840; *Native American Bulletin*, April 21, 1842; *Weekly Reveille*, April 28, 1845; *St. Louis Magnet*, May 1, 1845; *Missouri Medical and Surgical Journal*, I, No. 1 (1845).

42 *Anzeiger des Westens*, April 14, 1842, Jan. 31, 1843, May 6, 13, 1845; *Täglicher Anzeiger des Westens*, Dec. 16, 1846, May 20, 1847; *Die Deutsche Tribüne*, May 13, 1845, Jan. 3, 1847.

43 *Daily Evening Gazette*, Feb. 6, 1843.

44 *People's Organ*, Oct. 8, 1844.

their circulation figures are surprising. In 1842 the total circulation of all English-language newspapers was 4,324.[45] In 1847 the *St. Louis Daily Union* alone claimed a daily circulation of 13,000 and contested similar claims on the part of the *Daily Missouri Republican*,[46] while even the neutral *Weekly Reveille* asserted that the total combined daily circulation of German and English newspapers was over 100,000, or an average of two papers per day for every man, woman, and child in the city! [47] However, the picture is not yet quite complete. Since exchange newspapers served in lieu of press associations for national and international news, there was a tremendous demand also for newspapers from other cities. In the single month of October, 1845, the St. Louis post office received 30,202 of them, about 8,000 more than the number of letters.[48] Leading newspapers maintained free reading rooms, where large numbers of the latest exchange papers and magazines were available for the use of the public.[49]

The fourth estate was in a brawling, violent stage of its development. Wordy feuds between two newspapers were frequent.[50] For example, in October, 1838, when the *Missouri Argus* was waging an editorial war with the *Daily Missouri Republican*, the former referred to the *Republican*, that is, to its editor, as "the whipped blackguard of the *Republican*," compared it (him) to "a yelping cur that comes in our way," and, within twenty-four hours, broke a resolve to treat the *Republican* with "silent contempt" in order to rise to new metaphoric heights by designating the rival editor as "the filthy skunk of the *Republican*." [51] Matters became more serious when physical violence was introduced. Such fracases ran the whole gamut, from a common brawl between A. B. Chambers, editor of the *Daily Missouri Republican*, and Joseph Ellis of the *Old School Democrat* over an allegedly libelous article in the latter paper, to a duel with rifles between Chambers

---

[45] *Ibid.*, May 9, 1842.

[46] *St. Louis Daily Union*, March 17, 19, 1847.

[47] *Weekly Reveille*, May 17, 1847.

[48] *Daily Missouri Republican*, Nov. 4, 1845.

[49] *Daily Commercial Bulletin*, July 4, 1840; *Daily Evening Gazette*, Sept. 20, Oct. 11, 1841; *St. Louis Daily New Era*, Jan. 3, 1846.

[50] *Daily People's Organ*, Oct. 28, 1842; *Täglicher Anzeiger des Westens*, Jan. 8, 1847; *St. Louis Daily Union*, March 19, 1847; *Die Deutsche Tribüne*, April 7, 1847.

[51] *Missouri Argus*, Oct. 5, 12. 13, 1838.

and T. B. Hudson, an attorney and candidate for the legislature, over an article in the *Republican.*[52] The most tragic case was that which led to the fatal bludgeoning of Andrew Jackson Davis, proprietor of the *Missouri Argus,* by a political enemy, W. P. Darnes, who had been attacked in the *Argus.*[53] Results quite so drastic never befell the Saxons, but relations with the press were of importance for their development, and the enmity of several publishers, specifically among the Germans, did them great harm during their first years in Missouri.

The disapprobation of the Stephanites by the *Anzeiger des Westens* was mildly indicated already in the article of January 26, 1839, cited above. However, the language employed was still courteous, and it might have been better had Editor Weber's quick temper not been aroused by a rebuttal. Yet, on February 9, two weeks after the appearance of this first item, and more than a week after the *Republik* group had also reached St. Louis, the following rejoinder to the comment of the *Anzeiger* was printed on its pages:

> Mr. Editor!
>
> In the second-last issue of the *Anzeiger* the Stephanite *Gesellschaft* is referred to in a manner which is offensive to the respect and consideration due the unfortunate and persecuted. Such a reception the group could hardly expect from a German and in a land whose first settlers were religious refugees. The cardinal principle of our Constitution is liberty of religion and conscience for everyone. The respect due this principle alone should already have prevented you from giving so unfriendly a reception to compatriots from the old homeland. We are not in harmony with the arrivals in regard to religious opinions and sentiment, but are of the opinion that one must respect their opinions in the same degree as one demands respect for his own.
>
> In behalf of several Germans in St. Louis
>
> *S*[54]

The two quotations from the *Anzeiger* which have been cited were the opening blows in a journalistic free-for-all, which began with the article in the issue of January 26 and lasted until at least

[52] *Daily Commercial Bulletin,* July 17, 1840; *Anzeiger des Westens,* June 10, 1843.

[53] *Missouri Argus,* June 2, 4, 5, 6, 8, 9, 1840; *Daily Commercial Bulletin,* June 2, 1840.

[54] *Anzeiger des Westens,* Feb. 9, 1839, quoted in G. Günther, *op. cit.,* 39.

St. Louis, Mo.

BOUNDARY OF 1841

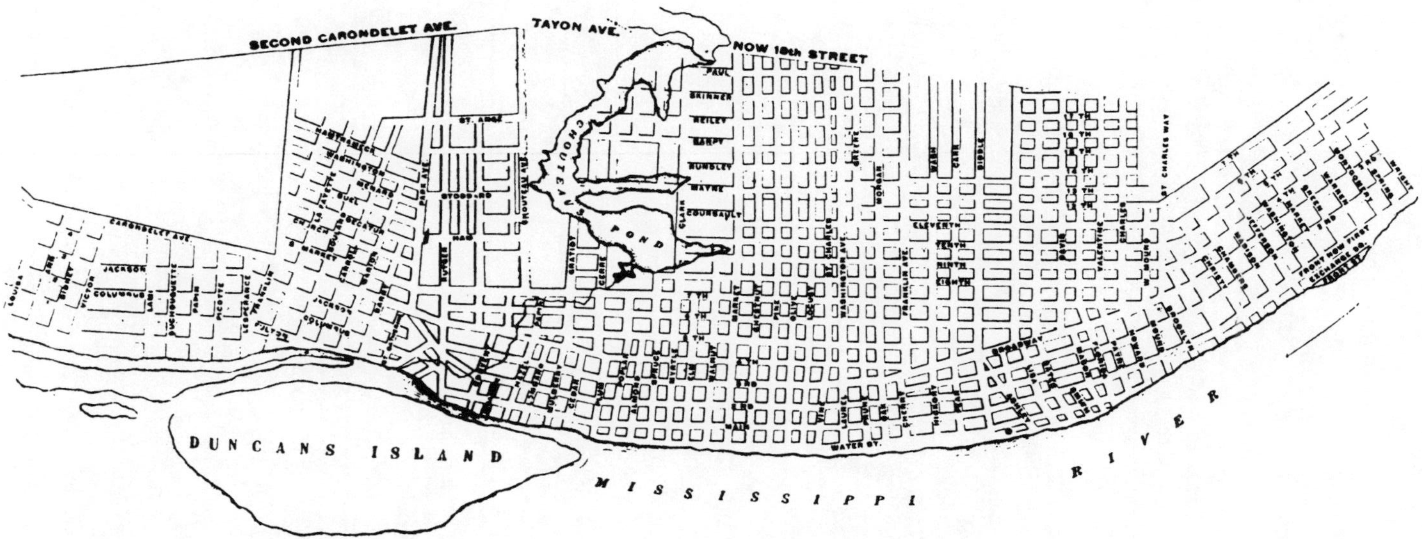

ACT OF LEGISLATURE, FEB. 15th, 1841

POPULATION 16,469

4.78 SQUARE MILES

PLATE XI

View of St. Louis, Missouri, about 1840

PLATE XII

View of Front Street, St. Louis, Missouri, in 1840. Looking north from Walnut Street

PLATE XIII

The Saxons landing at St. Louis. In the center group Pastor Löber is conferring with Dr. Marbach and an unidentified man. In the group of clergymen are Pastor E. M. Bürger (left), Pastor C. F. W. Walther, Candidate O. Fürbringer, and, supposedly, Candidate J. F. Bünger. In the group of men and women the man wearing the stove-pipe hat is Pastor E. G. W. Keyl, and the woman next to him is his wife. Stevedores are removing the baggage from the Selma. *Painting by G. H. Hillmer and F. Nuderscher*

PLATE XIV

the end of June, 1839.[55] The examples given thus far are some of the most tempered and well-considered of the numerous opinions expressed in the columns of the *Anzeiger* during the succeeding months. These two items also laid down the main lines of attack and defense in the ensuing quarrel. After a blast against "S" and the Saxons in the same issue of February 9,[56] the *Anzeiger,* obviously hostile to the Stephanites because of their religious conservatism and their hierarchical system of church polity, remained editorially in the background for some time and, with a gesture of impartiality, printed both charge and countercharge. The editor could well afford to pursue this policy, since his standpoint was strongly, and even at times scurrilously, represented by the prolific and poisonous pen of Heinrich Koch. It would have been a simple matter to eliminate some of Koch's shrill invective (which, to say the least, was in poor taste) without detracting from the substance of his argument. Instead, the *Anzeiger* cheerfully printed all, and, on occasion, supplemented Koch's remarks with some of its own. On the other side, the Stephanites themselves and several interested and distinterested people entered the lists for a desultory defense against what one of them called Koch's "barking."

The plea of the *Anzeiger* and of Koch was that they were not attacking the people in the *Gesellschaft,* for whom they professed nothing but the kindliest feelings; their criticism, they averred, was directed against the clergymen, whose dupes the people were alleged to be and to whom the people were in "slavery." The *Anzeiger* adopted this approach as early as February 9 in an explanatory editorial accompanying the letter of "S," just cited, and insisted that it "owed" such a presentation of the case to its readers and to the rank and file of the Stephanites.[57] The latter, at least "those among the *Gesellschaft* whose energy was not yet completely undermined by the priestly influence and smothered by priestly domination," were called upon to throw off their "chains." The unnecessarily offensive phrasing of the *Anzeiger's* remarks and

---

[55] *Ibid.,* June 29, 1839, quoted in G. Günther, *op. cit.,* 118—122.

[56] *Ibid.,* Feb. 9, 1839, quoted in G. Günther, *op. cit.,* 39—42.

[57] *Ibid.* The fact that Vehse in this case adopted the viewpoint of the *Anzeiger* can best be explained by pointing out that he, too, was engaged in an anticlerical campaign (although of a very different nature) at the time he wrote his book. Vehse, *op. cit.,* 34.

its attack upon the influence of the clergymen, not only in secular affairs, but also upon the religious life of the immigrants, belied its claims that it intended to allow the newcomers complete religious freedom. A distinction between the religious and the secular functions of the clergy in Stephanism could easily have been made; the latter might then, under certain conditions, have become the newspaper's legitimate concern, whereas the former certainly was not. If the *Anzeiger* "did not have the remotest idea of attacking the religious views or the freedom of conscience" of the Stephanites, it would scarcely have been necessary to describe them as "those who do not understand the distinction between papism and religion." [58]

The unfavorable reception accorded the Saxons by the German newspaper and an element of the German population was supposed to have been provoked in part by the tactlessness of the immigrants themselves. Pastor "Berger" [Bürger?], for instance, was said to have warned the immigrants against having any contact with the residents of St. Louis.[59] The element of truth in the story is probably that Bürger cautioned the Stephanites against being victimized by the petty criminals in the city who preyed on immigrants. If he did so, the advice was sound, for with the increase in river traffic, thieves and swindlers had attached themselves to the city like leeches. These facts were the subject of frequent comment in the St. Louis press. It is unlikely that Bürger gave a general description of St. Louisans as "deceitful and immoral," as G. Günther claims, although it is possible that such a version of the incident circulated among the public. Günther does not enhance the credibility of his story by representing Bürger's alleged remark, supposed to have been made at the time the *Selma* docked on February 19, 1839, as the motive for an attack in the *Anzeiger* on February 16, three days earlier.[60] Furthermore, this is the only actual incident cited and seems to have found absolutely no echo in the English press, some portions of which would have been at least as ready to seize upon such an indiscretion, or even a rumor of it, as was the *Anzeiger*.

---

[58] *Anzeiger des Westens,* Feb. 9, 1839, quoted in G. Günther, *op. cit.,* 39—42.

[59] *Ibid.,* 45—46; Vehse, *op. cit.,* 34.

[60] G. Günther, *op. cit.,* 45—46.

Heinrich Koch had begun his literary demagoguery in the *Anzeiger* of February 16, 1839, before Stephan, now bishop, and his group arrived. In this article Koch related the details of an interview between himself and a Stephanite. There was a great deal of common sense in what Koch told the young man; for instance, he asserted that clearing a wilderness bore little resemblance to taking up residence in "Canaan," that the clergymen leaders of the group showed little understanding of the conditions they would encounter, and that the newcomer would be much better off practicing his shoemaker trade in St. Louis than in the hinterland to which the *Gesellschaft* contemplated going. However, Koch's other remarks, presented by the *Anzeiger* for public approbation and amusement, constituted the bulk of the article, and they were a vicious and indiscriminate attack upon the leaders of the group and its religious tenets.

According to Koch, the "parsons" did not even have the will to direct the affairs of their people in the latter's own interest, but sought only their money and their services. Furthermore, Koch found the man's statement of his religious beliefs an evidence that he was "mentally ill" and — echoes of Saxony! — "a mystic." Held up to scorn were not only the immigrant's Stephanite peculiarities, but his Christianity. In this endeavor Koch was aided by the man's horrified announcement that "the devil was speaking through him" (Koch). The St. Louis pamphleteer subjected the entire incident to public ridicule and climaxed the narrative, rather partial to himself, with a poetic effort of seven stanzas, the burden of which was stated in the concluding sentence of the article: "Let him call me the devil; I should rather be called that than be one of their little priests."[61] The same issue of the *Anzeiger* carried as a reprint from a German publication a sketch of Stephan's life by Lütkemüller.[62]

The bitter disappointment of the Stephanites at this development can readily be imagined. Emigration had not provided them with any easy immunity against opposition. True, they were "free," as they had always insisted they would be free in America, to hold whatever views they liked. But this was a freedom enjoyed also by others, and with it went another freedom, that of expression,

---

[61] *Anzeiger des Westens,* Feb. 16, 1839, quoted in *ibid.,* 42—45.

[62] *Ibid.,* 45.

practiced with an abandon to which they were surely not accustomed and for which they were ill prepared. If the Saxons had expected to escape from the milieu of nineteenth-century liberalism by coming to the United States, they merely exchanged it for the atmosphere of an earlier phase of the *Aufklärung*. The fact that the attitude with which they were confronted was an eighteenth-century variety of bourgeois Rationalistic *Freigeister*-ism which was becoming outdated even in their native land, made it no easier to bear. If they had hoped to rid themselves of the restraints of a government which prescribed the liturgy they were to use, they had also sacrificed the protection of a government which had legislated against personal criticism of a clergyman in the public press. Here they were to be exposed to criticism uninhibited in method and brutal in intent. And it was to be directed at them from a quarter from which they had least reason to expect it — other German immigrants. Any effort fully to understand this phase of the Stephanite story requires an examination of the source of this criticism.

CHAPTER TEN

THE FORERUNNERS OF THE FORTY-EIGHTERS IN THE WEST

WHEN THE SAXONS ARRIVED, St. Louis had a population composed of many nationalities. As a result, the city bore a more cosmopolitan aspect than the rather provincial hamlets from which most of the immigrants came. The original French settlers, although still a population group to be reckoned with, were even then a minority and were declining in importance; their numbers were virtually static, while other nationality groups were growing rapidly. The largest single segment of the population was the Anglo-American element, composed of United States citizens and immigrants from England. There seems to be some doubt, however, that even they were a clear majority. In addition to these groups there were those of Irish, German, Dutch, Swiss, Scotch, Polish, Bohemian, and Jewish descent.[1]

Of the immigrant groups just mentioned, the Irish and German were easily the largest and most important. During the later thirties a flood of Irish immigrants had greatly increased the proportion for that nationality group and continued to do so beyond the period covered in this discussion. In St. Louis the Irish were the only group of foreign-born citizens which displayed a class and nationality consciousness comparable to that of the other large body of immigrants, the Germans. The Irish organized for the purpose of taking part in local civic affairs, for promoting Irish independence, and for furthering relief work in Ireland. For a time they even published a newspaper devoted to the cause of Irish liberty.[2] However, the largest single group of immigrants during the period of the later thirties and the forties was that of which the Stephanites were a part, the Germans. The necessary statistics on their coming

---

[1] G. H. Löber to relatives in Germany, Jan. 30, 1839, in Löber-Eichenberg (ed.), "Ein Briefwechsel," *Mitteilungen . . . Kahla,* VII, 147—148; Lenz, *op. cit.,* 52, 54; Kargau, *op. cit.,* 279; G. Günther, *op. cit.,* 32.

[2] *Anzeiger des Westens,* Jan. 30, 1841, March 9, 1842; *Missouri Reporter,* June 19, 1843; *Daily Evening Gazette,* July 15, 1843; *St. Louis New Era,* Jan. 24, 1845; *Weekly Reveille,* April 28, 1845.

have been given in another connection. Their status in, and influence upon, the community would be of importance in any discussion of St. Louis at this time, and are, of course, of even more than ordinary significance for this study.

Germany's chief contribution to the conquest of the New World has correctly been described as that of sending not a few great men, but many good men. However, the difficulty of determining the extent of such a contribution and of evaluating its importance is in direct ratio to the truth of the observation. For the task of portraying the history of the commoner and of gauging the significance of influences exerted only by infiltration from one mass of people to another has appeared less attractive than that of recounting the achievements of eminent individuals and more tedious even than reciting statistics about the mass.[3] Thus, grasping at the obvious or the easy has led to two types of overemphasis. The one stresses the cultural influence of outstanding immigrants who bore the stamp of religious or political liberalism, such as the *Dreissiger* and *Achtundvierziger*. This approach directs attention to individual writers or statesmen like Friedrich Münch[4] and Karl Schurz. The other attributes weight to bulk and points to the swarms of newcomers after the Civil War. This approach specializes in the events of the eighties, when, in that one decade, 1,452,870 arrivals from Germany were reported and when the single year 1882 brought 250,630 German immigrants to the shores of the United States.[5]

Fortunately the effect of either approach is correct in one particular: it concentrates attention primarily upon the period after 1830. Certainly the German immigration of the seventeenth, eighteenth, and early nineteenth centuries was numerically negligible by comparison with the immigration of the middle and latter nineteenth century. And it is also true that, while this earlier group had a potentially greater cultural influence, these potentialities were never fully realized. In all but the fewest cases the amal-

---

[3] Stephenson, *op. cit.*, 4, 7.

[4] For an extended treatment of Friedrich Münch, see J. T. Muench, "A Sketch of the Life and Work of Friedrich Muench," *Missouri Historical Society Collections*, III, 132—144; Bek, "The Followers of Duden," *Missouri Historical Review*, XVIII, 415—437, 562—584, XIX, 114—129, 338—352.

[5] Stephenson, *op. cit.*, 42; Ferenczi-Willcox, *op. cit.*, 386.

gamation of these people with other nationality groups was more complete and self-effacing than that of the generations who followed them, and their distinctive characteristics were less clearly defined and maintained.[6] Both the biographer and the statistician will find less to interest them before 1830 than after that year.

Yet even when the genius of the German contribution to American life is sought in its proper milieu, improper focus is none the less certain to produce distortion. On misplacing emphasis upon a few particular individuals or upon certain types of individuals this entire study is, in a way, an extended commentary. Only a few general observations need be made at this point. When social and cultural influences are given their due, it is usually the politically active Forty-Eighters who are recalled. More recently their revolutionary forebears, the *Dreissiger,* who appeared in America as "Latin Farmers" or as business and professional men and who had made significant contributions before the Forty-Eighters came, have been accorded honorable mention.[7] The volubility of both the Forty-Eighters and the *Dreissiger* has gained for them a recognition some of which, for the sake of correct proportion, should have been reserved for other groups that were certainly on a level with them culturally and far ahead of them in the permanent influence they exerted. Particularly is this the case with the Saxons. It is doubtful that many immigrant groups of similar size excelled them in general educational standards, in cultural attainments, and in the ability of their outstanding individuals. In long-range significance the Saxons undoubtedly overshadowed many elements which have received more of the plaudits. For, as H. H. Maurer has pointed out, "No second generation was born to the Forty-Eighters, their rationalism is forgotten, but fundamentalism has been fruitful as the Lutherans have multiplied." [8]

This power of the Saxons and similar groups of the thirties and forties — for it is of them that Maurer is speaking — to perpetuate their cultural-social influences is a power not inherent in

---

[6] Stephenson, *op. cit.,* 43; Erhorn, *Die deutsche Einwanderung der Dreissiger und Achtundvierziger in die Vereinigten Staaten und ihre Stellung zur nordamerikanischen Politik,* 15—25.

[7] Erhorn, *op. cit.,* 31—32; Wittke, "The German Forty-Eighters in America," *The American Historical Review,* LIII, 714.

[8] Maurer, "Studies in the Sociology of Religion," *American Journal of Sociology,* XXX, 670

their more vociferous fellow immigrants.[9] It is lent further importance by the fact that when the greater mass of Germans did follow in the decades after 1850, their characteristics did not qualify them as successors to ebullient revolutionaries, but rather made for a social integration with their more solidly constructive predecessors and with the institutions which the latter had founded. In support of this viewpoint Carl Mauelshagen declared: "In spite of the prominence accorded the German political refugees, the more conservative Catholic and Lutheran immigrants, who outnumbered the 'Fortyeighters' by about two to one in the fifties, have made permanent contributions to the religious life of America."[10] Mauelshagen might have added two further facts which will become at least partially apparent in the rest of this study, namely, that such contributions were by no means confined to "religious life," and that they were built upon the foundations laid by the immigrants of the thirties and forties. A similar evaluation led M. L. Hansen to preface his narrative of the Stephanite movement — in a chapter on "Pioneers of the Great Migration" — with the observation that groups like the Saxons enjoy the distinction of being the vanguard of the larger immigration which was to follow.[11]

The second approach described above, which devotes a greater share of attention to the body of German immigration as such, is equally likely to produce misconceptions. For, although based upon reliable statistics, it concentrates upon the years showing the largest figures for German immigration. It is, of course, indisputable that many more Germans arrived in the latter decades of the nineteenth century than at any other time. But the volume of this immigration has been emphasized at the expense of weighing both its numbers and its influence with an exact sense of proportion.

The truly phenomenal increase in German immigration *in relation to the existing population* occurred not during the latter nine-

---

[9] Wittke, "The German Forty-Eighters in America," *American Historical Review*, LIII, 721.

[10] Mauelshagen, *op. cit.*, 7. For a treatment and evaluation of immigrant groups diametrically different from Maurer's and Mauelshagen's see, for example, Hawgood, *The Tragedy of German-America*, especially the interpretation underlying Chapter V, or, more pointedly, pp. 203—204. Most of the distortions referred to above are to be found in Hawgood's work, reinforced by the author's peculiar errors of omission in research and commission in the conclusions he draws.

[11] Hansen, *op. cit.*, 136.

teenth century, but just before that century reached the halfway mark, that is, from 1830 to 1850. German mass immigration, as it is usually thought of, began with the first of those two years. During the decade preceding 1830 only 6,761 German immigrants arrived.[12] This was an unimpressive total compared with that amassed during the next ten years. From 1830 to 1840 twenty-two to twenty-three times as many (152,454) German immigrants came to the United States. During the forties even the latter figure was increased by 280 per cent, and German immigration for that decade reached the figure of 434,626.[13] Thus even if the tremendous increase from the 1820's to the 1830's is disregarded because it marked the beginnings of the trend and would naturally offer a striking contrast, the fact still remains that the remarkable growth of German immigration in the forties eclipses that in the second half of the century. The rate of increase which the forties show plainly could not continue. Had it done so, the eighties would have deluged the country with a host of about 27 million persons from Germany alone, instead of about one eighteenth of that number. In fact, from the fifties through the eighties, a period of forty years, the rise in the rate of German immigration was little more (340 per cent) than it was in the previous ten years (280 per cent). That is to say, the foreign-born German population was swelled about four times as rapidly in the decade preceding 1850 as in the four decades which followed that date.

The importance of the immigration before 1850 becomes still more evident in view of the fact that it occurred at a time when the total population of the United States was much smaller and in a greater state of flux, geographically, politically, and culturally, than toward the close of the century. After 1850, when the country's population was rising tremendously, the ratio, although not the number, of German additions to it was declining. The reactions of contemporary Americans reflected this fact. It was not the million and a half immigrants of the 1880's who were faced with the challenge of Native Americanism, but the proportionately more formidable half million of the 1840's.

Similarly the 600,000 Germans who reached the United States

---

12 Faust, *op. cit.*, I, 582.

13 Young, *Special Report on Immigration to the House of Representatives*, in *House Ex. Docs.*, 42 Cong., 1 Sess., No. 1, p. xi.

from 1830 to 1850 had a greater opportunity to exert an influence upon their new environment than the millions who arrived later. Turner as historian of the frontier and Faust as specialist in the German element agree in assigning greater influence to the earlier immigration.[14] Theirs was the influence of the pioneer, not only in helping to people the Middle West, to claim its vast areas of fertile plains, and to found its nascent industries, but also in establishing schools and churches, foreign-language periodicals and societies, political clubs, and other social and cultural agencies. As indicated before, these facts generally apply with special force to the West, where population was sparse and any addition to it was of relatively greater potential importance.

The large-scale settlement of Germans in the St. Louis area began in 1832, when a group from Berlin chose the vicinity of St. Charles, Missouri, as its home.[15] German immigration to Missouri gained momentum with organization of the Giessen *Gesellschaft,* which, in 1834, sent its colonists to found what was intended to be an embryonic German state. Another group of major importance was that sponsored by the German Settlement Society of Philadelphia, which, from 1838 to 1839, founded the German community at Hermann, Missouri. The next organized movement, and the last in this decade, was that of the Saxons, whose arrival followed closely upon the founding of the settlement at Hermann.[16] Meanwhile the infiltration of German immigrants singly or by families had been making steady gains. By 1835 the proportion of German-speaking residents of St. Louis warranted the publication of the *Anzeiger des Westens,* the first German-language newspaper west of the Mississippi River. And three years later an attempt, ultimately successful, to maintain a second German newspaper, the first *Tribüne,* seemed justified. By 1840 there were demands on two English-language journals to supplement the services of the

---

14 Faust, *op. cit.,* I, 585.

15 *St. Louis Daily American,* April 7, 1847.

16 W. Breckenridge to Ruth Crawford, Oct. 1, 1915, quoted in Breckenridge, *op. cit.,* 204. On the Giessen *Gesellschaft,* next to the Saxons the most important of these movements in Missouri, see Körner, *Das deutsche Element in den Vereinigten Staaten von Nordamerika, 1818—1848,* pp. 300—322, and Bek, *The German Settlement Society of Philadelphia and Its Colony, Hermann, Missouri.*

Anzeiger by issuing editions in German.[17] One of these papers, the *Daily Commercial Bulletin,* declared: "Ere long our country will be Germanized." [18]

This prediction, hyperbolic as it was, bade fair to become a reality in the case of St. Louis. By 1840 the German population of the city was estimated to be from one fourth to one third of the total,[19] and seven years later the Germans, spreading out into both North and South St. Louis, had become the strongest single group of immigrants, if not the largest single element, in the city. According to one source, the German population of St. Louis was about 30.7 per cent of the total in 1850.[20] Such figures, of course, depend upon the interpretation of the classification "German." If it is understood to include only those who, as immigrants, had previously been German citizens, then the German element is not shown in its full strength. For their children were numerous, and their group consciousness was generally rather lively for a generation or more. In any event, it is clear that in the face of a four- or fivefold increase in the population of St. Louis from 1840 to 1850, the Germans at least held their own, while comparable groups, such as the Irish, were left far behind, constituting, according to the source just cited, only 14 or 15 per cent. Meanwhile English immigrants amounted to a mere 3 to 4 per cent of the whole.[21]

Like other immigrants, the Germans were sometimes destitute when they reached their destination. However, as likely as not their condition was the result of some misfortune, such as a steamboat disaster, rather than an indication of their true economic status or potentialities. In general, the financial standing of German immigrants does not seem to have been low; instead, it appears to have compared favorably with that of other national groups. In 1844, for instance, the average amount of money brought into the country by each German immigrant was about 170 thaler.[22] In comparison with such a figure the Saxons, despite everything that

---

[17] *Daily Commercial Bulletin,* Aug. 14, 1840; *Daily Evening Gazette,* July 10, 1840.

[18] *Daily Commercial Bulletin,* Aug. 6, 1840.

[19] Vehse, *op. cit.,* 30; Schneider, *op. cit.,* 98. Schneider, who presents the larger of these two estimates, is quoting Georg Engelmann.

[20] Schneider, *op. cit.,* 422, quoting Hyde-Conard, *op. cit.,* II, 890.

[21] *Ibid.*

[22] *Daily Missouri Republican,* May 10, 1845.

has been said about their financial strength, were not especially wealthy. Originally the Stephanites had about 190 thaler each, on the average. But they brought nothing like that amount into the country, for most of it had been used by the time they reached St. Louis. Three years after their arrival the Saxons officially stated that when they came the majority were almost penniless.[23]

In fact, the Germans were considered a desirable addition to the population and were heartily welcomed to St. Louis, not only by the militantly pro-German *Anzeiger,* but also by most English newspapers and a majority of the residents, for the very reason that they were regarded as one of the chief causes for the commercial and economic growth of the city.[24] It was also recognized that they were, by and large, a stabilizing social and civic element. They seem to have been one of the most law-abiding groups among the immigrants and in this respect certainly had a far better record than the other large foreign-born element, the Irish, as statistics in even the semi-Nativist press showed.[25] Especially the Saxons distinguished themselves on this score, and partly for that reason, as well as others, they enjoyed complete freedom from attack or criticism on the part of the English-language press or the English-speaking populace.

Unlike the Saxons, however, other elements among the Germans engaged in sporadic battles with the Irish and in brawls at amusement parks or similar resorts. At Camp Spring, for example, numerous "balls" were held, which were usually sponsored by the management or by one of the German military companies. On these occasions disorder frequently accompanied the principal forms of entertainment, dancing and drinking.[26] Of course, not all the Germans, probably not even a majority, were involved in these affairs, but unfortunately some of those who considered themselves leaders and who too often stepped before the public in that capacity, were

---

[23] Document . . . des Grundsteins . . . St. Louis . . . 22. Juny 1842, MS., C. H. I.

[24] *Daily Commercial Bulletin,* Aug. 26, 1840; *Daily Evening Gazette,* Jan. 21, March 5, 1839, July 10, Sept. 21, 1840; *Missouri Argus,* Nov. 24, Dec. 10, 1840; *St. Louis New Era,* April 5, 1840; *Daily Missouri Republican,* May 10, 1845; *Missouri Reporter,* April 14, 1845. See also G. Günther, *op. cit.,* 32.

[25] St. Louis Daily New Era, Sept. 23, 1846; *Die Deutsche Tribüne,* Aug. 1, Sept. 5, 22, Nov. 10, 1846.

[26] *Anzeiger des Westens,* Feb. 19, 1842, Sept. 12, 1843; *Täglicher Anzeiger des Westens,* Nov. 20, 1846.

the worst offenders. Because of the civic prominence of this group, their lack of decorum stigmatized the rest of the city's German population.

At the same time some characteristics common to all groups of Germans engendered further unfavorable public opinion. Indeed, in view of a certain group temperament and attitude, it is surprising that the Germans as a whole retained as much good will as they did. For with their ability to avoid brushes with the law the peacefulness of these people came to an abrupt end. Among themselves they were the most quarrelsome, contentious, and annoying group of citizens in St. Louis, not even excepting the proverbially belligerent Irish. It seemed that the Germans were chronically engaged in physical encounters or in literary bickering in the newspapers, some of which will presently become apparent.[27] Even the *Anzeiger des Westens* deplored as one of the chief failings of the Germans their quarrelsomeness and their proneness to vent their differences in the public press.[28] This was a sound observation, no matter how strange its setting in the *Anzeiger*.

But the cardinal civic and social failings of virtually all groups of Germans were undoubtedly their clannishness and the tenacity with which they clung to their Germanism.[29] The wholly understandable and unobjectionable desire on their part, not to lose their cultural heritage from the Old World, often deteriorated into a refusal to merge this heritage with the cultural environment of the New World, or even into an effort to impose it upon their new neighbors. The most flagrant manifestation of this characteristic of the Germans was the frequent recurrence of hopes for founding a German state in the United States. Plans for such a project and, at various times, some real attempts to put them into execution were directed toward Wisconsin, Texas, and Missouri.[30] That the aim of the Giessen *Gesellschaft* was a similar one has been

---

27 *Daily Pennant*, Sept. 15, 1840; *St. Louis New Era*, Sept. 26, 1843; *Anzeiger des Westens*, Sept. 28, 1843; *Weekly Reveille*, Dec. 30, 1844.

28 *Täglicher Anzeiger des Westens*, Oct. 2, 1846. See also *Anzeiger des Westens*, Oct. 29, 1842; *Die Deutsche Tribüne*, Aug. 28, 1844; *St. Louis New Era*, May 21, 23, 1844; *Daily Missouri Republican*, May 21, 29, 1844.

29 Fairchild, *op. cit.*, 72; "Einleitung," *Das Westland*, I, 8; *St. Louis New Era*, Jan. 15, March 22, 1845; *St. Louis Daily New Era*, March 19, 1846; *St. Louis American*, Nov. 12, 1845, Oct. 5, 1846; Wittke, *op. cit.*, 211—212.

30 Faust, *op. cit.*, I, 473. See also "Einleitung," *Das Westland*, I, 8; Körner, *op. cit.*, 300; Fairchild, *op. cit.*, 72; Stevens, *Centennial History of Missouri*, I, 317.

noted above. Friedrich Münch, one of the leading spirits of this enterprise, had not entirely abandoned the idea as late as 1866.[31] Of course the more realistic immigrants, even at the time of the Stephanites, realized the impracticability of these dreams of a German political entity in this country, notwithstanding its undeniable attractions for a sentimentally patriotic and increasingly nationalistic people.

The dual question of the desirability and the nature of political action by the Germans as a unit was one over which they divided so sharply that the major groups of German immigrants can be distinguished from each other on this point alone. One thing was plain, of course, namely, that this was a problem which confronted them with a difficult and sometimes drastic decision. All Germans intelligent enough to give the matter some thought realized that their position was approximately as described by Irmgard Erhorn:

> German immigrants have always faced the bitter necessity of either standing up for their individuality, and thus being united — thereby, however, exposing themselves politically to a vote of non-confidence from Anglo-Americans — or surrendering their individuality, assimilating themselves, and then participating only as a unit of German derivation in American politics of a purely Anglo-Saxon character.[32]

The *Burschenschaftler* immigrants (1800—1830) wanted to play a more aggressive role than their eighteenth-century predecessors in this country, whom they saw disappearing before their very eyes, or who, with a few exceptions, had already disappeared. It was the avowed purpose of the pre-*Dreissiger* of the 1800's not to lose their identity, and hence they attempted to preserve at least certain features of their German heritage by establishing their own schools, by fostering the study and use of the German language, and through similar methods.[33]

The *Dreissiger,* who had left chiefly for political reasons, were in varying proportions both nationalist and liberal in their attitude.[34] In view of their comparatively high caliber they could probably have served as a nucleus around which all German Amer-

---

[31] Münch, *Der Staat Missouri; ein Handbuch für deutsche Auswandrer,* 11.
[32] Erhorn, *op. cit.,* 11.
[33] *Ibid.,* 15, 25.
[34] *Ibid.,* 16.

icans who desired could have welded themselves into a powerful unit. However, the *Dreissiger* were not agreed among themselves or with the *Burschenschaftler* on the fundamental strategy for attaining such an end. Some felt their action should be openly and frankly political. The extreme of this viewpoint was, of course, the talk about founding a German state. Others recognized such a plan as fantastic and felt their purpose could be served best by emphasizing the cultural contribution which they were in a position to make. These moderates advocated participating in politics only as the expediency of circumstances in each locality might indicate, and even then not on a separate German-party basis, but only on a balance-of-power basis within the structure of the extant parties, in order to counteract the influences of Nativism and other movements detrimental to the interests of the German element.[35]

In the West, where the proportion of the indigenous population to the German immigrants was comparatively far smaller and the pressure of the former upon the latter far less than in the East, the foundation for a German party on a national scale could conceivably have been laid with some success. However, the same factors which made such action more possible made it seem less necessary to the men who were in a position to take the initiative. The result was that while the most prominent Germans in the West were of the *Dreissiger,* and while the ablest *Dreissiger* were those in Missouri and southern Illinois, the apparent paradox nevertheless developed that the western Germans, with the exception of Münch and a few others, generally adopted the moderate position, and the extreme nationalists were deprived of adequate leadership.[36] For instance, Wilhelm Weber, for all his loud Germanism, reported rather than supported the plans for a German state in the West.[37] Gustav Körner, who has been called "the most important representative of the immigration of the thirties,"[38] threw himself wholeheartedly into the politics of an already established party.

The Forty-Eighters, too, experienced the twin drive of liberalism and nationalism. In fact, judging from the most recent ap-

---

[35] *Ibid.,* 25—31.

[36] *Ibid.,* 17, 22, 29.

[37] Schneider, *op. cit.,* 26.

[38] Erhorn, *op. cit.,* 13.

praisal of this group by an authority on their history, it seems fair to say that they had enough liberalism to make it necessary for them to leave Germany, and enough nationalism to make them wish they could go back.[39] But while "many Forty-Eighters honestly believed that they had a 'cultural mission' to perform in their adopted fatherland,"[40] their principal significance was not the preservation of group influence along the lines of either cultural or political Germanism, but rather the advancement of their ideals, sometimes "radical" for the times, within the existing political organism.[41] Thus the moderate *Dreissiger* were in fact the spiritual forebears of the Forty-Eighters, and at the risk of oversimplification it may be said that despite a difference of emphasis between these two groups, their effect upon practical politics was very similar. Internal differences of opinion on methods and objectives and the impracticability of execution prevented action on a national scale. A German party never arose. Political and cultural activities of the Germans almost invariably became a series of local movements which sooner or later contracted encephalitis.[42]

But before, during, and after the appearance of all the groups mentioned thus far, there was a constant and ever more numerous immigration of another — and we may say more representative — type of German. Such people did not come to found a new Germany or to remake American politics, but to find a new home, to escape from economic want, from rigid social stratification, from the oppressiveness of continental militarism, or from interference in religion by the state. They also clung too tenaciously to some of their traditions, but the same might be said of almost all large groups of immigrants. And eventually they adapted themselves. In the ultimate analysis it was only they who achieved the aims for which they came.

The correctness of these observations accounts for the tone of pique which creeps into remarks on the subject by a student from National Socialist Germany. Irmgard Erhorn laments that "both the *Dreissiger* and the *Achtundvierziger* — in spite of their ideal-

---

39 Wittke, "The German Forty-Eighters in America," *American Historical Review*," LIII, 725.

40 *Ibid.*, 714.

41 Erhorn, *op. cit.*, 16, 31.

42 *Ibid.*, 15—16.

istic, although often confused and contradictory aspirations — did not prove equal to the task of fulfilling their German mission" because they did not "have a class of leaders capable of resisting the influence of assimilation." [43] With a similar note of frustration she delivers the dictum: "In general, however, the German immigrant remained politically passive." [44]

For many Germans the idea of a separate state found at least partial expression in the advancement of German *Kultur* or in the establishment of communities that were largely, sometimes almost exclusively, populated by Germans. Scores of such settlements were being founded in the Middle West at this time. Besides such well-known Missouri colonies as Hermann and the Saxon communities in Perry County, German centers were being established elsewhere in the State as well as in Illinois, Wisconsin, Iowa, Tennessee, Texas, and even in the far West.[45] In many of these localities the Germans were in virtual control of the community; where they conld not be, they frequently developed a group life that served both as the means and as an added incentive for retaining their national identity. This development had taken place in St. Louis. Even before the Forty-Eighters had come as the heralds of a still more numerous German immigration to this city, A. V. Holfern found the characteristics and foibles of the Germans in St. Louis, their lively tavern life, and their beer-drinking, periodical-publishing, self-styled literati a rich field for entertaining and informative, if exaggerated, satire.[46]

At first the attitude of the other population groups was rather tolerant. By and large, the German aliens were not asked to give up their language and customs, but it was expected of them that, if they wished to maintain these things, they would acquire, in

---

[43] *Ibid.*, 9.

[44] *Ibid.*, 12.

[45] *Anzeiger des Westens*, Jan. 15, 1842; Feb. 9, April 13, Aug. 13, 17, 1843, Jan. 7, July 3, 29, 1845; *Die Deutsche Tribüne*, Aug. 1, Nov. 23, 1844, March 20, April 22, May 11, June 12, 25, Sept. 16, 1845; *Daily Evening Gazette*, April 13, 1843; *Daily Missouri Republican*, Sept. 12, 1844, July 2, 1845; *St. Louis New Era*, Jan. 4, 1845; *St. Louis American*, March 12, 1845; Maurer, "The Earlier German Nationalism in America," *American Journal of Sociology*, XXII, 519—521.

[46] Holfern, "Die Deutschen in St. Louis," in *Die Deutsche Tribüne*, March 14—25, 1847. For another informal and vivid description of German life in St. Louis at a somewhat later date, see Gruber, *op. cit.*, 2—6.

addition, the language and the political and social habits of their American neighbors. In other words, the feeling prevailed that they should make an effort to adjust themselves, not to withdraw into community or cultural isolation.[47] Yet such separate identity was the very object for which many of the Germans were striving, for they believed this to be the only means of preserving Continental traditions in the vast crucible of a national melting pot. Both the aim itself and the devices used to attain it soon exposed the Germans to charges of improper segregation. And indeed, a certain clannishness on the part of the Germans showed itself in numerous ways, often inconsequential in themselves, but a potent force in the aggregate. One example of many which could be cited was their *Vereinsmeierei.* The Germans were joiners and everywhere displayed a tendency to band into societies, preferably with bombastic or lurid names or with a military flair.

> In the foreign countries where the German consciously fostered his national heritage, there the *Vereinsmeierei* of the inter-confessional bowling alley, the Turner club, and the singing society took it under their wing; German genius took refuge in German geniality. The props of Germanism were the beer-barrel and skat.[48]

In St. Louis this proclivity manifested itself not only in the existence of special lodges for the Germans and in the founding of various nondescript societies, but especially in the formation of a number of German military companies, which by 1843 included the Rangers, the Artillery, the Fusileers, the Infantry, and the Dragoons.[49] Even more general was the love of the Germans for their language, an attachment that prompted them to adopt in their meetings sententious resolutions like the following: "To base American nationality on the British language is a thoughtless, mistaken notion." [50] This feeling for the language, coupled with a profound admiration for German educational methods, led to the establishment of German schools.

The element among the Germans which has just been de-

---

[47] *Daily Evening Gazette,* March 5, 19, 1839.

[48] Amrhein, *Die deutsche Schule im Auslande,* 36.

[49] *Anzeiger des Westens,* Feb. 23, July 23, Aug. 11, Dec. 7, 1842, Jan. 12, 21, May 27, July 22, 29, 1843.

[50] *Täglicher Anzeiger des Westens,* May 30, 1846; *Die Deutsche Tribüne,* June 2, 1846. See also *Daily Evening Gazette,* March 5, 19, 1839.

scribed, was composed in St. Louis largely of the arrivals of the earlier thirties. For a time a number of men in the group formed a clique which tried to, and in most cases did, control and give expression to the social and political life of the Germans in the city.[51] Almost all the prominent members of this group came into direct contact with the Saxons at some time during the first years that the latter were in the State. Consequently the individuals constituting this cabal merit at least brief mention.

Heinrich Bimpage was the founder of the *Anzeiger des Westens,* which first appeared on October 31, 1835. Since the previous year he had also been running an Intelligence and Commission Office, which specialized in land deals. By the time the Saxons reached St. Louis, Bimpage had disposed of his interest in the *Anzeiger* and was devoting all his energies to his other enterprises.[52]

Wilhelm Weber, a native of the duchy of Altenburg, had taken refuge in the United States during the early thirties as a political fugitive from Leipzig, where he had divided his time between his studies and the revolutions of the years immediately preceding his flight. His chief claim to lasting importance and his significance for this study lie in the fact that he was at various times editor and publisher of the *Anzeiger des Westens,* and for years its guiding spirit.[53] Weber was, with one exception, the most arrogant of the group. Also interested in the *Anzeiger* as editors and publishers at various times during the period under discussion were Wilhelm Palm, a machine manufacturer,[54] and Theodor Olshausen, a St. Louis publisher.

Friedrich Kretzschmar was a prominent politician of this circle of German leaders, a justice of the peace, and a captain of one of the German military companies. He enjoyed considerable prominence, popularity, and confidence among the Germans. Kretzschmar's chief failing in the eyes of the *Anzeiger* and those who supported it was that he was not a Democrat. Consequently, he did not always get along well with the dominant element of the clique,

---

51 *Daily Missouri Republican,* May 21, 29, 1844; *Daily People's Organ,* April 11, 14, 1843.

52 Körner, *op. cit.,* 317. His real name was Bimbach. Stephan to Flügel, Oct. 12, 1841, MS., C. H. I.

53 Körner, *op. cit.,* 318.

54 Kargau, *op. cit.,* 215.

which invariably centered around the *Anzeiger.*[55] He was frequently employed by the Saxons as translator or legal counsel and was highly thought of by them.[56]

Georg Engelmann, well known for his scientific observations and his interest in education, was perhaps the only real intellectual in this array of immigrant leaders and can be classed with them only during the earlier years of the period. Later, when the constant bickering among these men became offensive to him, he had fewer contacts with them. The Kayser brothers, Alexander (an attorney) and Heinrich (eleven times city engineer between the years 1839 and 1855), were prominent in the St. Louis German community.[57] Other names which are frequently connected with the activities of the Germans in St. Louis during the thirties and forties are E. K. Angelrodt, Prussian consul in St. Louis; Kribben; Fischer; and Koch.[58]

Some of these men had enjoyed at least a taste of university training in Germany, and a few probably had completed their course of study. Such educational opportunities were not common in the West of 1840. Perhaps it was their advantage in this respect which gave some of them such an exaggerated conception of their intellectualism that it could find adequate expression only in open contempt for all who did not agree with them, German or American. At any rate, many of this class were, as Schneider has remarked, "arrogantly proud" of their erudition and culture and looked down upon their fellow immigrants from Germany, some of whom no doubt were dirty and ill-mannered.[59] But it would create a false impression to draw such a comparison without adding that some of those very immigrants whom the Webers and Kochs despised most fervently were far better educated than they; that not all educated Germans outside the ranks of this group shared their contempt for the less fortunate; and that the manners of some of the "uneducated" immigrants frequently compared favorably with

---

[55] *St. Louis New Era,* May 21, 1844; *Daily Missouri Republican,* Jan. 31, May 21, 1844; *Daily Evening Gazette,* Jan. 22, 1839.

[56] *Anzeiger des Westens,* Feb. 17, 1840, Feb. 21, April 25, June 6, 15, Nov. 1, 1842.

[57] *German Engineers of Early St. Louis,* 3, 16—27.

[58] Most of these men, as well as those mentioned just above, are discussed in greater detail in Körner, *op. cit.,* 307—323.

[59] Schneider, *op. cit.,* 28—29.

those of the leading element. The activities of this fraternity which grouped itself around the *Anzeiger* varied from providing relief for destitute German immigrants to herding German voters to the polls; from baiting the Saxons to making war on the Nativists; and from urging the attainment of American citizenship upon German immigrants to raising funds for political agitation in Germany.[60] Common to almost all members of the group was a rather laborious attempt to assert an "enlightened" liberalism that they too often did not practice.[61]

As has been indicated, the *Anzeiger* was the unofficial organ of this group until its members fell out among themselves in 1843. Almost at the same time the *Daily Missouri Republican* founded the *Anzeiger's* first successful rival, *Die Deutsche Tribüne* (1844). The *Anzeiger* was one of the best-known newspapers in the West and one of the most prominent German papers in the country. It must be credited with doing valuable pioneer work in journalism, as the first German newspaper west of the Mississippi River; with staunchly defending the Germans as a group at all times; and with filling a real need in the life of the community and the much wider area which it served outside the city and State. While its style of German at times left something to be desired, its news coverage was as good as that of the average English newspaper. However, during the years covered in this study, its editorial policy, determined primarily by Weber and to a lesser degree by Palm and Olshausen, was frequently tactless, sometimes outrageous; and its readiness to print any contribution, no matter how ill-mannered or scurrilous, gave evidence of an unfortunate lack of discrimination. In a day when personal attacks in the press might go to almost any length, the *Anzeiger* nevertheless succeeded in drawing down on its head not infrequent libel suits.[62]

The *Anzeiger* was at all times unreasoningly and violently anticlerical and saw in even the simplest church organization an

---

60 *Daily Commercial Bulletin*, Dec. 1, 1840; *Anzeiger des Westens*, Jan. 5, Feb. 23, June 17, July 7, 16, Aug. 6, Oct. 20, 1842, Sept. 28, 1843, Oct. 11, 1845; *Täglicher Anzeiger des Westens*, Aug. 4, Dec. 15, 1846; *Die Deutsche Tribüne*, Dec. 10, 20, 24, 29, 1846; *Daily Missouri Republican*, May 21, 29, 1844; Erhorn, *op. cit.*, 31—32.

61 *Anzeiger des Westens*, Sept. 25, 1845.

62 *Anzeiger des Westens*, July 18, 1843, Oct. 2, 1845; *Daily People's Organ*, Sept. 23, 1843; *St. Louis New Era*, March 18, 1845; *Daily Missouri Republican*, March 14, 1845.

attempt at hierarchical domination.[63] Any opportunity to attack the clergy was pursued with vigor, if not with venom.[64] The *Anzeiger's* policy was uniformly that of supporting those who opposed the churches, and it did not hesitate itself to attack religious beliefs as such.[65] "The *Anzeiger des Westens* zealously assumed the role of watchdog over religious affairs. Such a paper would have found its match in Germany, but on the Missouri frontier it had the field to itself, and the liberalism it expressed became increasingly vicious and intolerant." [66] If Körner — and those who echoed his encomiums — could bring themselves to say that Weber "avoided extremes" and "always controlled his pen" and could laud his "rare lenience of judgment," [67] it is to be hoped that they did not read the paper Weber edited. However, a reaction against these tendencies of the *Anzeiger* set in during the fifties.[68]

There was, indeed, a considerable section of the German press in the country which made a practice of attacks upon almost all established churches. The *Wahrheitsverbreiter* of Baltimore (1840 to 1841) and Mühl's *Photophilus* or *Lichtfreund* (1840 ff.) of Cincinnati, for which Olshausen was the St. Louis agent, are examples of what Schneider has called the "loud-mouthed rationalistic press." Later (1843) Mühl transferred his activities to the German colony at Hermann, Missouri, where he edited the *Hermanner Wochenblatt* and published a number of religio-philosophical works.[69] The Germans in St. Louis were offered books "For Rationalists," as the German book concerns advertised them in the *Anzeiger*.[70] Rationalism was sponsored in lectures by Samuel Ludvigh, editor

---

63 *Anzeiger des Westens,* Sept. 25, 1845; Schneider, *op. cit.,* 33—34.

64 *Anzeiger des Westens,* March 16, June 27, Aug. 19, 26, 1843, Oct. 31, Nov. 5, Dec. 21, 31, 1844, April 15, 17, 1845; *Täglicher Anzeiger des Westens,* May 3, July 1, 1846.

65 *Anzeiger des Westens,* Jan. 26, March 3, 1842, March 18, April 27, 1843.

66 Schneider, *op. cit.,* 33. However, compare *ibid.,* 30.

67 Körner, *op. cit.,* 320; Scharf, *History of St. Louis City and County,* I, 933. See also Schnake, "Geschichte der deutschen Bevölkerung und der deutschen Presse von St. Louis und Umgegend," *Der Deutsche Pionier,* III, 229—234.

68 Schneider, *op. cit.,* 195.

69 *Anzeiger des Westens,* Dec. 8, 15, 1841, April 23, 1842, April 27, Aug. 31, 1843, May 15, June 19, 26, 1845. See also Schneider, *op. cit.,* 123; Bek, *op. cit.,* 169.

70 *Anzeiger des Westens,* Dec. 8, 1841.

of the *Fackel,* and by others,[71] and for a time was advocated in St. Louis in the *Freisinniger,* published by G. Scho and F. Volland from December, 1846, to May, 1847, when it collapsed because of financial difficulties.[72] A favorite device of all such publications was to overemphasize as much as possible any publicity which was adverse to clergymen and churches of every denomination.[73]

It is not necessary to agree fully with the generalization of P. F. Douglass, that the German secular press as a whole was anti-Christian, to appreciate the fact that his appraisal is at least strongly indicative of the true circumstances.[74] On the basis of careful research, others have also described both the *Dreissiger* and the Forty-Eighters as generally antiecclesiastical and have ascribed to them concerted "rationalistic propaganda." [75] Any characterization of the German immigrants of those years as "almost without exception of the Lutheran faith," [76] obviously cannot include the men here being discussed.

The extremes of the *Anzeiger* and other German publications were eclipsed and almost made to appear temperate by comparison with the literary activity of Heinrich Koch, the stormy petrel of the vociferous coterie of St. Louis Germans repeatedly mentioned above. This watchmaker-writer intensified all the *Anzeiger's* violence and embellished it with improprieties of his own creation. For several years Koch got along very well with Weber and his friends, and efforts were made to maintain a working agreement even after an acrimonious quarrel among the Germans about their military companies in 1843.[77] The *Anzeiger's* columns were always open to Koch; the newspaper heralded the appearance of his antireligious *Antipfaff* ("a rude and turbulent journal" which appeared in April, 1842), commented favorably upon it, and acted

---

71 *Ibid.,* Sept. 21, 23, 28, Oct. 3, 1843, Feb. 8, 1845; *St. Louis Daily New Era,* March 3, 1846.

72 *Täglicher Anzeiger des Westens,* Dec. 16, 1846, May 20, 1847.

73 This is apparent from even a casual perusal of the *Anzeiger,* and finds its practical illustration in the history of the Saxons. See also Schneider, *op. cit.,* 199.

74 P. F. Douglass, *The Story of German Methodism,* 57.

75 Schneider, *op. cit.,* 33. See also Maurer, "Studies in the Sociology of Religion," *American Journal of Sociology,* XXX, 544—545.

76 W. Breckenridge to Ruth Crawford, Oct. 1, 1915, quoted in Breckenridge, *op. cit.,* 204.

77 *Anzeiger des Westens,* July 8, 11, 13, 15, Aug. 18, 1843.

as its agent; it praised, at least for a time, Koch's socialistic *Vorwärts;* and it did not react unfavorably to his communistic *Reformer.*[78]

But even as early as 1843 the *Anzeiger* found Koch a little too vitriolic, and the first indication appeared that they were later to come to a parting of the ways. For a brief period the *Anzeiger* was calling Koch's writings "ravings," and the *Anzeiger's* current competitor, the *Demokrat,* served as Koch's instrument of attack upon the former.[79] By 1845 the *Antipfaff* again seems to have been in somewhat better favor with the *Anzeiger.*[80] But at the same time biting articles against Koch personally, found their way into the newspaper, a thing which seldom happened in earlier years.[81] Eventually the *Anzeiger* even attacked Koch and his friends editorially, saying that "respect for the public has long ago made it our rule not to enter any public controversy with them." [82]

The *Tribüne* tried for a time after its establishment in 1844 to keep up with the battles constantly raging around Koch and his various publications, some of which appeared concurrently.[83] Finally, however, when Koch's rant developed unmistakably cloacal characteristics, the *Tribüne* also became disgusted with him [84] and decided to be very chary of its contacts with someone who, by 1845—46, had aroused almost the entire German population against himself, including most of the members of the ruling junto of Germans. For Koch respected no one's feelings nor the privacy of another person's affairs. He could get along with no one, and his venomous pen and violent temper were doubly dangerous because they were coupled with an utter lack of self-restraint.

Among Koch's antagonists were Friedrich Kretzschmar and Christian Kribben; they were joined by numerous other people, such as the contributor to the *Tribüne* who said that Koch must

---

78 *Ibid.,* April 14, 21, 1842, Jan. 31, 1843, May 6, 13, 1845; Schneider, *op. cit.,* 127. See also *Die Deutsche Tribüne,* May 13, 1845, Jan. 3, 1847.

79 *Anzeiger des Westens,* Aug. 8, 10, 1843.

80 *Ibid.,* May 6, 1845. See also *Die Deutsche Tribüne,* April 1, 1845.

81 *Anzeiger des Westens,* July 19, 1845; *Täglicher Anzeiger des Westens,* Jan. 28, 1847.

82 *Anzeiger des Westens,* Jan. 13, 1846. See also *Die Deutsche Tribüne,* Jan. 10, 13, 1846.

83 *Die Deutsche Tribüne,* Jan. 12, 18, May 13, 30, June 6, 8, 10, 11, 14, 15, 22, 24, July 10, 11, 1845.

84 *Ibid.,* July 15, 1845.

have been "stung by a tarantula"; [85] or a certain Bernhardt Müller, who added a new refinement to the perpetual polemics fathered by Koch when he issued a denial of an attack by Koch before it even appeared in the *Vorwärts;* [86] or Matthias Kraft, who issued a biweekly German publication specifically for the purpose of combating the *Antipfaff.*[87] On the day after the Bernhardt Müller article appeared, the *Tribüne* announced it could no longer accept articles against Koch, for they were becoming too numerous for the space available in its columns.[88] However, less than a month later the *Tribüne* was in the midst of another quarrel involving the bellicose pamphleteer and thereafter again took cognizance of him.[89]

Koch finally became the president and one of the prime movers in a German Rationalistic society which, when it was organized early in 1846, was at first interested in Socialism.[90] Before the end of the year the organization, under the leadership of its president, was frankly calling itself Communistic. The Communist movement was rather strong at this time and for the next few years,[91] and Franksen and Wesselhöft, the German bookstore then on South Second Street between Myrtle and Spruce Streets, obligingly provided appropriate Communist literature.[92] Koch's political theorizings were interrupted by his participation in the Mexican War. Shortly after his return to St. Louis his openly contemptuous treatment of the flag of his company of volunteers brought down upon him the ire of almost the entire German portion of the populace,[93] and drew sharp comment also from the English press.[94] Before a

---

85 *Ibid.*, July 9, 1845. See also *ibid.*, March 29, July 20, 1846; *Anzeiger des Westens*, June 9, 11, Aug. 20, Nov. 22, 24, 1842, Jan. 14, April 18, July 22, 1843, April 2, 1845; *Daily People's Organ*, April 11, 14, 1843.

86 *Die Deutsche Tribüne*, July 16, 1845.

87 *St. Louis New Era*, March 15, 27, 1845.

88 *Die Deutsche Tribüne*, July 17, 1845.

89 *Ibid.*, Aug. 12, 19, 1845.

90 *Anzeiger des Westens*, Dec. 2, 1845, Feb. 6, 1846; *St. Louis Daily New Era*, March 19, 1846.

91 C. F. W. Walther to O. Fürbringer, Feb. 17, 1847, in L. Fürbringer (ed.), *op. cit.*, I, 37.

92 *Täglicher Anzeiger des Westens*, April 23, Oct. 31, 1846; *Die Deutsche Tribüne*, Aug. 25, 1844, March 15, April 2, Sept. 20, Nov. 1, 11, 1846.

93 *Die Deutsche Tribüne*, May 12, 14, 15, June 30, Sept. 9, 11, 13, 26, 1846, Jan. 6, 8, 10, 1847; *Täglicher Anzeiger des Westens*, Jan. 5, 6, 7, 9, 11, 13, 14, 1847.

94 *Daily Missouri Republican*, Sept. 11, 1846, Jan. 9, 1847; *St. Louis American*, Sept. 10, 16, 17, 1846; *St. Louis Daily New Era*, Sept. 12, 1846; *St. Louis Daily Union*, Sept. 19, 1846.

year had passed, Koch was forced out of the office he held with the Communists. The society split into factions, and another undeclared war of contributed articles and editorials had broken out, both in the *Anzeiger* and the *Tribüne*.[95] Undaunted by the storm crackling around him, Koch launched a fresh journalistic venture, the afore-mentioned *Der Reformer*.[96] Opposition also to this new publication was prompt, and its success was doubtful.[97] The watchmaker did not add to his popularity by publicly striking a woman, a performance which cost him $35.00 in court.[98] Koch, to sum matters up, was congenitally unfit for an even relatively peaceful gregarious society. This unadmirable character, whom Scharf pungently described as a "born agitator," [99] finally transferred the scene of his activities to Communia, a Communistic settlement in Clayton County, Iowa. But he did not find utopia here either. He quarreled with the enlightened as he had with the benighted, and moved on, in the pursuit of happiness, to Dubuque, where he engaged in politics, land deals, and government contracts.[100]

With personalities like Koch and Weber in control of the avenues of expression for Germans in St. Louis, it is not surprising that the great number of their more quiet, less discourteous countrymen, who stolidly went their law-abiding, thrifty, conservative way, were scarcely heard from. Other persons had little opportunity to impress any, not even the most desirable, qualities of their character upon German organizations of which the Weber-Koch cabal or its individual members were in control. It must be remarked that those who opposed the dominant group did at times raise a feeble voice. And eventually their growth in numbers turned public opinion against the Koch type of individual and forced the *Anzeiger* to come of age and adopt a modicum of dignity. But for a decade or more the screechings of Koch and the ridicule of Weber deprived most people of any desire to outshout the former or to debase their argument to the level of the latter. "Innocents

---

[95] *Täglicher Anzeiger des Westens,* March 22, 23, 25, 31, April 1, May 6, July 27, 1847; *Die Deutsche Tribüne,* Dec. 16, 18, 1846, March 30, April 14, 1847.

[96] *Die Deutsche Tribüne,* Dec. 29, 1847; *Täglicher Anzeiger des Westens,* Jan. 4, 1847.

[97] *Täglicher Anzeiger des Westens,* Feb. 26, March 16, 1847.

[98] *Ibid.,* July 27, 1847.

[99] Scharf, *op. cit.,* I, 939. See also Schneider, *op. cit.,* 127.

[100] Faust, *op. cit.,* I, 462; Scharf, *op. cit.,* I, 939; Wittke, *op. cit.,* 357.

abroad" like the Saxons, no matter how richly they deserved a considered criticism, were utterly unaware of the hornets' nest their very presence was stirring. And of course they were at a serious disadvantage in defending themselves because they would not match the ranting of their antagonists.

It cannot be emphasized too strongly that the attitudes and viewpoints of the *Anzeiger* and its controlling group, or — still worse — of Koch, were anything but representative of the Germans who arrived, unheralded, between the influx of revolutionaries in the early thirties and in forty-eight. Nevertheless, it is equally true that precisely such an impression was frequently created. The people who, during this period before 1848, were to make real contributions to the life of the city were rarely heard from in the daily press. Examples of this type of immigrant are the Saxons in education and religion, Georg Engelmann in education and science, Alexander Kayser in engineering, and Adolphus Meier in industry.[101] Two of those mentioned, Engelmann and Kayser, originally belonged to the group of Weber and Koch, but had progressively less to do with it after the beginning of the forties. Both Engelmann and the Saxons found it expedient to establish their own organs for the expression of their views, the former in *Das Westland,*[102] the latter in *Der Lutheraner.* Moreover, it was during these years that "the original start in the wholesale grocery business, the flour milling, the grain, produce, and commission branches were made by the German settlers."[103] The commanding position of the Germans in many fields was admitted even by the anti-German press. But these achievements of the majority did not engage a fraction of the attention commanded by the continual displays of rudeness by the minority.

Most Germans were members of the Democratic Party. When they arrived as immigrants, they naturally were drawn into the orbit of the party from whose masthead flew the banner of "Western" and of "Jacksonian democracy," which was, at least nominally, the champion of the common man. Important for this trend was the added circumstance that Native Americanism found

---

[101] *St. Louis New Era,* July 11, Aug. 24, 1844; *Daily Missouri Republican,* March 15, 21, 1845.

[102] This publication is discussed in Schneider, *op. cit.,* 30—31.

[103] Crawford, *op. cit.,* 10.

a foothold first among the Whigs. Later, however, as the assimilation of the immigrant progressed and his wealth increased, he himself frequently went over to the Whigs. Such a change was facilitated by the fact that the Democratic Party was strongest in the South and represented its interests, whereas the Germans were concentrated more heavily in other areas, and even when they did settle in the Southern and border States, did not as a group belong to the slave-holding class.[104] But in 1840 the majority of Germans was still in the Democratic fold, and, according to the violently partisan views of the *Anzeiger,* scarcely had a right to be elsewhere. This paper jubilantly claimed in 1845 that four fifths of the Germans in the West and two thirds of those in the East were Democrats.[105]

The political enthusiasm of the *Anzeiger* and of the small clique of Germans who were "leading" their fellow immigrants finally brought about an attempt on their part to control the German vote and to deliver it faithfully at the polls. This practice and other improprieties of the *Anzeiger* finally drew the fire not only of the leading Whig newspaper in the city, the *Daily Missouri Republican,* but of a number of others as well.[106] Resentment at seeing the German immigrant capture elections was at least as old as Benjamin Franklin's complaint that "they come in droves and carry all before them."[107] His method for coping with the situation by founding a newspaper which would appeal to them in their language still seemed the most effective one a hundred years later. The political tactics of the *Anzeiger* led directly to the founding of its only successful rival during these years, *Die Deutsche Tribüne,* which was established in 1844 by the *Daily Missouri Republican* as a counterpoise to the *Anzeiger.* After the presidential campaign of that year the *Tribüne* succeeded in maintaining itself and justifying its existence by attaining independence of its parent paper. For a time the newcomer in the field even seriously threatened the position of the *Anzeiger,* which became a daily paper only after the *Tribüne* had shown the way in this respect. Thus, after

---

104 Erhorn, *op. cit.,* 13, 17—18, 21—22.

105 *Anzeiger des Westens,* Jan. 23, 1845.

106 *Daily Evening Gazette,* March 19, 1839; Daily People's Organ, April 15, 1843; *Daily Missouri Republican,* May 21, 29, 1844; *St. Louis New Era,* May 21, 23, 1844.

107 Quoted in Wittke, *op. cit.,* 87.

1844, two of the fifty or sixty German newspapers in the country appeared in St. Louis.[108] The fact that a Whig paper was as successful as the *Tribüne* leads to the conclusion that at least politically there was considerable dissatisfaction with the *Anzeiger.* For this dissatisfaction there seems to have been ample cause.

Although one of the most conservative newspapers in the city, the *Daily Missouri Republican* expressed itself concerning the *Anzeiger* and its editor in a manner which cannot be attributed entirely to the *Republican's* Whig sympathies, and still less to an antipathy for the Germans, toward whom, as a group, this paper was consistently cordial. A particularly discourteous outburst by the *Anzeiger,* in reference to an incident involving Captain Kretzschmar, occasioned this comment in the *Republican:*

> The tone of the writer for the German paper will surprise, if it does not excite, many of our citizens. There is an unwarrantable and insulting tone in reference to the Whig citizens of Missouri, which will not be very well relished in this community — at the same time that the particular objects of denunciation are attacked with a rancour which ought not to be tolerated, come from what quarter it may. . . .
>
> The malevolent disposition and vindictive feelings of the demagogues who busy themselves continually in attempts to stir up strife, and to array one class of our citizens against another, received a rebuke which can, it seems, find no other vent than an incendiary press, and hence the publication to which Capt. K. [F. Kretzschmar] refers. It may suit the purpose of desperate men to attempt to dictate a course of conduct for our citizens, but the time is coming when their efforts will be properly appreciated by their own countrymen, and when they will be abandoned to the contempt of every good citizen. If they are wise, they will adopt a new line of conduct, and commend themselves to the public confidence, by a decent respect for the institutions, the laws and the people of the State, and not by personal abuse of those who entertain different political opinions from themselves, and more liberal notions of what is due to propriety and to each other.[109]

About a week later the *Republican* described the *Anzeiger* as

> . . . a German paper issued in this city, which few of them take, and a still less number read . . . in which each party is,

[108] *Anzeiger des Westens,* Dec. 6, 1842; *Daily Evening Gazette,* Feb. 9, 1843.
[109] *Daily Missouri Republican,* May 21, 1844.

> in turn, abused and misrepresented. So far as we are concerned, coarse language is employed to intimate a denial of the facts stated, at the same time that the writer admits their correctness, but gives different, and ridiculous, reasons for the line of conduct pursued by him (Capt. K.) and his associates. We do not think it worth while to follow this editor — whose "sick bed" does not seem to have improved his manners or his morals.
>
> . . . We cannot forbear expressing the opinion that this conduct is significant of what may be expected hereafter, whenever any German dares to think or act for himself. . . . Capt. Kretzschmar is to be hunted down and sacrificed, because he will not submit to the dictation of a clique, who have, until now, attempted to control German people: and when they are likely to fail to do so any longer — when their influence is waning, and the Germans will not reply upon appeals to past prejudices — they think it necessary to make demonstrations which will silence the revolt. "Shoot the deserters!" is the maxim upon which they purpose to act, but we are mistaken if our German fellow citizens are to be deterred, by any such measures, from exercising freedom of thought and freedom of action, on all subjects, political or otherwise, which may be submitted to them.[110]

The *Daily People's Organ* lost patience even sooner. This paper, which on October 18, 1842, had called Palm, then editor of the *Anzeiger,* "cool-headed, sober-minded, intellectual," was so incensed by the attempt of the *Anzeiger* at political domination that on December 30 of the same year it exclaimed: "Thank God there are few such Germans in Missouri as Wm. Palm." [111] The *Anzeiger's* handling of a notorious case involving morals charges against an Evangelical pastor named Heyer prompted the *Daily People's Organ* to comment not upon the accused, but upon the *Anzeiger's* editorial writer: "We are astonished to learn that there lives among us a man capable of writing such an effusion." [112]

The tendency on the part of many Germans toward segregation and the unnecessarily unfavorable impression created by a few of their number at length led to a natural feeling of resentment among the other nationality groups, especially the English-speaking portion of the population. Several instances in which these

---

[110] *Ibid.,* May 29, 1844.

[111] *Daily People's Organ,* Oct. 18, Dec. 30, 1842. See also *ibid.,* Aug. 18, Dec. 9, 12, 1842, April 14, 1843; *Anzeiger des Westens,* April 15, 1843.

[112] *Daily People's Organ,* April 11, 1843.

German characteristics led to censure in the English press have been noted. But the most violent form of such criticism was that which found expression in the Native American Party and which thereby threw the whole question of immigration and the status of aliens into the political arena. The party attained national prominence about 1835 and was formally organized in St. Louis by 1840.[113] The same year, however, also witnessed the first of many protest meetings against the movement.[114]

The motive forces behind Nativism were primarily opposition to all immigrants, especially to their participation in politics, and enmity toward the Roman Catholic Church. Only the first part of this double program is of direct interest here. Native Americanism was well represented in almost all cities of the West where the German population was large or Roman Catholicism was strong. In St. Louis, where both of these conditions prevailed, Nativism made a powerful bid for political supremacy and became the important political issue of the day.[115] In the mayoralty election of 1842 the Nativists were defeated by a Democratic candidate who enjoyed the support of a coalition of Irish, German, and English voters; in 1844 they lost to the Whig candidate. Nevertheless, the Nativists grew in strength so that by 1846 they virtually controlled the city administration.[116]

It is easy to criticize the Native American Party for its rather naive notion that American birth — removal by one generation from European shores — conferred an innate emotional and intellectual fitness for United States citizenship. The extremes of the party's claims and of the language used to justify its fundamental premises were plainly wrong. Yet the plea of the Nativists was lent an appeal of which it could have been deprived had the immigrants, in St. Louis specifically the Germans, revised some of their habits and attitudes. With the *Anzeiger's* arrogant hyperconsciousness of ethnic distinctions and its militant effort to control the German vote

---

113 *Daily Commercial Bulletin,* Dec. 1, 1840; *Daily Evening Gazette,* Dec. 3, 1840. See also Fairchild, *op. cit.,* 70; Monroe, *Founding of the American Public School System,* 223—224. For the constitution and by-laws of the party, see *Native American Bulletin,* Jan. 3, 1842.

114 Erhorn, *op. cit.,* 22.

115 *St. Louis American,* Sept. 28, 1846.

116 *People's Organ,* April 4, 1842, Aug. 8, 1844; *Anzeiger des Westens,* April 10, 1845; *St. Louis Daily New Era,* April 7, 8, 1846; *St. Louis American,* Aug. 8, 1846.

constantly before the public, it was not difficult to make the Native American argument sound like a plausible one.

As the Nativists grew in numbers, they became bolder in their claims and demands. An active campaign was under way to lengthen the term of residence in the United States which would be required of immigrants before granting them citizenship, some Nativists insisting on as much as twenty-one years.[117] Such a program was merely the concrete manifestation of a general antialien feeling among Nativists, based upon the party's claim that "the American is a mortal in every way superior, as a man, to a foreigner, no matter of what country he comes from,"[118] and its complaint that "Americans do not rule America."[119] In St. Louis, where "alien" and "foreigner" were coming to mean each year a few thousand more Germans, or "Dutch," the feeling against them ran high, and the Nativists attempted to stir up anti-German sentiment even among the immigrants, notably the Irish.[120] In Philadelphia, on the other hand, the Irish themselves were the objects of rioting and bloodshed.[121] But in St. Louis, notwithstanding occasional tirades in the press against the inhabitants of the British Isles,[122] the Irish, by way of contrast with the Germans, became objects of commiseration, almost admiration. For — so ran the lugubrious lament — "The Irish are passing away from our sight, before the strong blasts of Dutch competition. Six Dutchmen can live, where *one* Irishman would starve."[123]

Less than two months later the same newspaper stated in a series of editorials entitled "The Crisis":

> Where again are our Irish, diggers and hodmen, who, with all their faults, are a noble, generous-hearted nation? They, too, are mostly gone! . . . a Dutchman was preferred — he did his day's work a few bits less, and got the pay. The old citizen, whether mechanic, laborer, or otherwise, deeply humbled and no little mortified, had to leave. . . . Hundreds more will have to go. . . . From every description of business

---

117 *St. Louis New Era*, March 31, 1842; *Anzeiger des Westens*, Nov. 23, 1844.

118 *St. Louis Daily American*, March 16, 1847.

119 *St. Louis American*, July 14, 1846. See also *ibid.*, July 28, 1846.

120 *Daily Missouri Republican*, Feb. 23, 1847.

121 *People's Organ*, May 18, July 17, 1844.

122 *St. Louis Daily American*, March 15, 1847.

123 *Ibid.*, Feb. 19, 1847.

or trade, the Dutch are ruining our occupation. . . . Mr. Keyser [H. Kayser], our late City Engineer, was complained of for employing the Dutch in his department. He very promptly answered, there were none else to be had. They are gone!

. . . ninety-nine out of every hundred doing the work of the city in this department — all Dutch . . . our scavengers, pavers, graders, masons of all sorts, smiths of every grade, brewers, bakers, tailors and house builders. And where is the hotel, tavern, or boarding house that is not full of Dutch, in the character of cooks, butlers, &. They are everywhere and at everything in and around the town, and in every hole and corner in the town. If a hole is to be dug, or a wheel turned, there you find a Dutchman. Pass Market street, and eighteen out of twenty you meet are Dutch. The lower end of the city formerly called Frenchtown, now more emphatically *Dutch town* — we say that they have nearly monopolized every branch of industry, to the exclusion of our own citizens, who aided in the growth and prosperity of the city.[124]

The position occupied by the Germans in the professional life of St. Louis during the forties is indicated by an explanation, given at a much later date, of the frequent drafting of Heinrich Kayser as city engineer, with the words: ". . . as we had, at that time, no American engineers or good schools of technology, it was natural that foreigners should be called into service." [125]

The character as well as the number of German immigrants was cause for alarm to the Nativists and led them to exclaim:

"They come! they come!" The pauper, the lazaroni, the criminal, the fugitive from justice, and the convicted felon. A few, a very few, are of a better class.[126]. . . A large portion . . . have been turned out of the *prisons* in Germany, and sent here by the *public authorities* . . . 60,000 more of the same *foreign infusion* will be landed in New Orleans within the next *thirty days.* And still they come — the Hun, the Goth — the Visagoth [sic], the serf, hordes of culprits and vagabonds! Will the country bear this foul insult? [127]

Descriptions of the German immigrants as "offscourings" of Europe, "most filthy and inferior beings," [128] and as a "moral and

---

124 *Ibid.*, April 7, 1847.

125 *German Engineers of Early St. Louis*, 2.

126 *St. Louis Daily American*, Feb. 6, 1847.

127 *St. Louis American*, Dec. 24, 1845.

128 *St. Louis Daily American*, Jan. 9, 1847.

political pestilence"[129] were climaxed with diatribes such as the following:

> This Bremen hive seems in no danger of being emptied of its *serf* and *pauper hordes.* They come in swarms, like Egypt's locusts — but the locusts change their character — annually; the Germans never. Once a Dutchman, always a Dutchman. They seldom acquire the language, customs, or habits of the people, among whom they settle — but adhere to their own cherished habits, feelings, and prejudices. Centuries have not changed their character in New York and Pennsylvania.[130]

To the Nativists the language which the aliens brought with them was no more welcome than the immigrants themselves. The *St. Louis American* even saw a threat to its diet in the speaking of German. It queried indignantly:

> Is our native tongue to be given up and exchanged for the euphoneous [*sic*] Dutch? Are our laws to be kept in that language? The modest assurance of these new comers will speedily require us to abandon our mother tongue and speak nothing but Dutch — and feed in Dutch, upon sour kraut. Could you stand it?[131]

As these quotations show, when the Nativists had finished dissecting the immigrant, there was little good left about him.[132] He was impoverished, worked for less, drove down wages, and lowered the standard of living. He came from the lowest class of society; he was a jailbird. He continued to speak "Dutch" and was clannish. Still worse, however, he sometimes voted illegally; and when he voted, legally or otherwise, he somehow seemed to vote the wrong way, that is, against the "Natives," with surprising regularity. In fact, he was an undemocratic individual, unsuited for absorption into the United States, incapable of understanding American politics, and certainly unfit to hold public office. For, according to Nativist dogma, "An European education, in a great measure, disqualifies a man for the proper discharge of his duties as an Amer-

---

[129] *St. Louis Daily New Era,* Aug. 13, 1846.

[130] *St. Louis American,* Dec. 15, 1845. See also *ibid.,* Dec. 24, 1845.

[131] *Ibid.,* July 21, 1846.

[132] *Native American Bulletin,* May 14, June 7, 1842; *St. Louis New Era,* Jan. 13, 15, March 22, 1845; *Anzeiger des Westens,* Aug. 14, Sept. 6, 1845; *St. Louis American,* Jan. 7, 8, 14, Feb. 6, March 3, Oct. 5, 1846; *St. Louis Daily New Era,* Jan. 5, Feb. 5, March 17, May 6, June 27, 1846.

ican citizen."[133] As likely as not the German was not merely German, but a combination of the twin evils: German *and* Roman Catholic. In Cincinnati the undesirable characteristics of the German, as the Nativists saw them, were summed up tersely and trenchantly in the succinct campaign slogan: "Damn the Dutch."[134]

Fortunate though it was for the Saxons from the economic standpoint that they came to Missouri when they did, it was nevertheless unfortunate that they came at a time when the Nativists were beginning intensive activity in this area and when the arrival of several hundred immigrants became a matter of political concern. The Saxons as a body avoided politics meticulously. But it is misleading to state this fact without qualifying it at once by pointing out that, although involuntarily, they were a part of an explosive political issue. Furthermore, such unwelcome significance attached to them at a time when politics was of considerable importance in the life of the average man, even as it was the chief concern of most newspapers.

This was a day when the press often showed little restraint, and virtually none was imposed by the agencies of law. A political *faux pas* was almost as likely to result in a duel or a clubbing as in a defeat at the polls. Political campaigns could easily climax in rioting,[135] and political feeling could be perverted into the hate expressed by these bitter toasts allegedly used at an Indiana political rally held on the Fourth of July:

> Here's to General Harrison — may his days be few in the land, and his wife a widow, and his children motherless, and all their prosperity [sic], and may they be cast into some desert place, and may they beg for their living all the days of their lives.
>
> Here's to General Harrison, Hull, Burr, and their mothers, and their posterity, all be crammed with Hell and Damnation, thunder bollts thicken them, and a streak of lightening to mix it, and an earthquake to cram it down their God damned throats.[136]

The contest among all parties for the votes of the Germans

---

133 *St. Louis Daily New Era,* July 10, 1846.

134 *Anzeiger des Westens,* Oct. 22, 1844.

135 *Anzeiger des Westens,* June 24, 1842; *St. Louis New Era,* April 2, 1844.

136 *Daily Evening Gazette,* Aug. 18, 1840, quoting the *Daily Commercial Bulletin,* which had taken it from the *Madisonian.*

began at an early date, and before long charges of voting irregularities were being made.[137] The formation of the Nativist Party, which cut across existing party lines by drawing its membership from both Whigs and Democrats, as well as the factional split within the major parties themselves, produced new alignments that operated under the names of Natives, Whigs, Hard Democrats, Soft Democrats, Old School Democrats, Locofocos, Bentonites, anti-Bentonites, and others. The political situation finally became so confused that no one was very sure where he stood, and even the contemporary newspapers found that the repeated fragmentation of recognized parties had produced conditions that bordered on the ludicrous.[138]

The majority of the newspapers continued their friendly attitude toward the Germans, gave anti-Nativist meetings generous publicity, often actively opposed the Native party, and deplored the mixing of politics and religion, especially when some clergymen in certain of the English Protestant denominations openly espoused this plank of Nativism.[139] But other papers, led by the *Native American Bulletin* and the *St. Louis American,* were violently anti-German. Still others, which had been fairly neutral at first, became so disgusted with "the flaming patriots who come over from Europe to set this country upon end, but have little idea of the operation of a complicated constitutional republic," [140] that they went over to the Nativist camp.[141]

The Stephanites, too, had far-reaching plans which provided, if not for the founding of a state, then at least for as large a degree of political autonomy as possible. The question presents itself how

---

137 *Daily Commercial Bulletin,* Aug. 3, 1840; *Anzeiger des Westens,* Dec. 6, 8, 10, 13, 1842.

138 *Old School Democrat and St. Louis Herald,* April 1, 1843; *Daily Missouri Republican,* Jan. 11, 1846. See also Culmer, *op. cit.,* 217—243, 273—300.

139 *Daily Pennant,* May 11, 12, 13, 1840; *Daily Evening Gazette,* Dec. 11, 1840, Sept.—Oct., 1841; *Daily Commercial Bulletin,* Dec. 12, 1840; *Missouri Argus,* Jan. 28, 29, Feb. 20, May 29, June 1, 1841; *Missouri Reporter,* Sept. 2, 1843; *People's Organ,* Dec. 7, 1844; *Daily Missouri Republican,* April 1, 1845; Feb. 20, March 20, 21, 24, 26, 1846; *Die Deutsche Tribüne,* July 15, Aug. 1, 10, Sept. 25, 1844; *Anzeiger des Westens,* Nov. 23, Dec. 5, 1844, Jan. 14, Sept. 6, 1845; *St. Louis Daily Union,* Sept. 7, 10, 1846, Feb. 13, 1847; *Daily Morning Missourian,* March 11, April 3, 9, 1846; *Weekly Reveille,* March 2, 1846.

140 *St. Louis New Era,* Jan. 11, 1845.

141 *Native American Bulletin,* April 1, 2, May 14, June 7, 1842; *St. Louis American,* March 3, 12, April 14, July 28, Sept. 28, 1846; *St. Louis New Era,* Jan. 10, 1843, Jan. 2, 4, 15, 16, 17, 23, Feb. 8, Sept. 23, 29, 1845.

they escaped the wrath of the Nativist press, when its venom flowed as freely as it did. For they did escape. In fact, during the formative years none of the English-language newspapers in St. Louis — let it be said to their credit and in testimony to the fundamental worth of the Saxons — published a single editorial attacking them, although other immigrants were viciously criticized. The answer to the question of the Saxons' relationship to the English press is simply that they, unlike the noisier among their fellow immigrants, did not create a problem if one did not make a problem of them. Thus even their plans for settlement — and this point cannot be emphasized too strongly — were merely the means to an ulterior and entirely non-political end, namely, freedom of action in religious matters.

Autonomy was not a desideratum to the Stephanites because they wanted to Germanize or to liberalize the United States. They had no idea of doing the latter. The former appealed to them only insofar as they felt it necessary to retain their language, maintain the identity of their religious traditions, and concentrate their economic strength, in order to serve the spiritual needs of the vast numbers of German immigrants in the West. The desire for founding a German community which would be also politically under their control was simply based on the hope that this measure would provide an additional bulwark against interference with their religious beliefs and practices. The Saxons realized their error within six months after their arrival. Furthermore, they soon understood that the plan was not only impossible of execution, but, in view of their modified objectives after the abandonment of Stephanism, also unnecessary in the United States. A similar scheme was never revived among them, although Münch and other German nationalists clung to this idea for decades.

But before the Saxons were to learn the lesson of these six months, many bitter experiences lay before them. Some of these experiences resulted from their own follies. One of the greatest of these was their submission to Stephan, which they were about to make complete and formal.

CHAPTER ELEVEN

ESTABLISHING THE EPISCOPACY

THE DUBIOUS ATTENTIONS which the *Anzeiger* had showered upon the Stephanites thus far, had all preceded the arrival of the *Selma* group. In view of the inoffensive demeanor of the Saxons up to that time, Weber's lack of manners seemed all the more objectionable. But when Stephan himself appeared upon the St. Louis scene on February 19 as a bishop and put on the airs of an unapproachable prelate, the criticism of the *Anzeiger* and the invectives of a Koch, whatever the public may have thought of them originally, were lent some plausibility. As soon as the *Selma* arrived at St. Louis, its decks swarmed with people. St. Louisans were there because this practice was customary in the United States, the Stephanites because they themselves were anxious to see their Bishop, the news of Stephan's elevation to this office having preceded him to St. Louis.[1] However, both the curious and the faithful were disappointed. Stephan was suffering from a throat ailment and could speak very little. Accordingly he remained in his cabin until evening and emerged only at dusk to be driven to his elaborately furnished quarters. Stephan's private rooms, which had been procured for him at a reputed cost of $20.00 monthly, constituted one of the three apartments in the home of Dr. White, between Second and Third Streets.[2] Apparently the rest of the dwelling had also been rented by the Stephanites.

During his first few weeks in St. Louis, Stephan continued to suffer from an infection of the throat, and presumably for this reason was attended only by O. W. Walther and did not preach or appear in public except on the rarest occasions. But even after he was well again, most of his time was spent in splendid seclusion in his handsomely appointed quarters, where the pastors and lay

[1] *Anzeiger des Westens*, Feb. 16. 1839, quoted in G. Günther, *op. cit.*, 31; Vehse, *op. cit.*, 12—13; Schieferdecker, *op. cit.*, 10. However, the people had not yet ratified the election, as Günther pictures it.

[2] G. Günther, *op. cit.*, 31, 35; Vehse, *op. cit.*, 12—13.

leaders were permitted to see him, but to which the people did not have access.[3] He was soon restored to health by Dr. Gempp of St. Louis, a very capable man who had formerly been personal physician to the Prince of Reuss-Lobenstein-Ebersdorf. Gempp was by no means a member of the Stephanite group, as has been claimed,[4] but he now promptly struck up a friendship with Vehse.[5]

The first concern of Stephan, upon his arrival in St. Louis, was to effect the ratification by the other immigrants of his elevation to the episcopacy.[6] Ever since the departure from Germany the hierarchical tendency had become clearer and stronger, not only in Stephan, but in the entire governing coterie, which included all of the pastors, the candidates, and the committee members. Evidence of the obvious intention to make Stephan bishop, which became manifest even before the departure from Germany, has been discussed above. What was said there is borne out by developments during the journey and immediately afterwards.

Although the different groups of emigrants on the several ships were frequently referred to by the Saxons themselves as "congregations," they were not such in the true sense of the term. The clergymen who served them were not, properly speaking, their pastors; they had not received a call from these people and presumably held their "office" only on the strength of appointment by Stephan.[7] The mere fact that each one of the ships was placed under the sole authority of a clergyman, who provided not only spiritual, but financial and administrative leadership as well, is significant enough in itself.[8] The arbitrariness with which some of these men, whose business acumen was questionable, handled financial affairs, and the harshness with which they exercised their administrative powers, further demonstrated that they had a rather glorified conception of their position. Bürger, always one of the frankest of the pastors,

---

[3] G. Günther, *op. cit.*, 34.

[4] *Anniversary . . . 1839—1939*, p. 4; P. Kretzmann, "The Saxon Immigration to Missouri, 1838—1839," *Missouri Historical Review*, XXXIII, 159.

[5] G. Günther, *op. cit.*, 53.

[6] Vehse, *op. cit.*, 13.

[7] Winter to Guericke *et al.*, April 28, 1841, *Zeitschrift für die gesammte lutherische Theologie und Kirche*, II, No. 3, pp. 116—132; Bekenntniss, MS., C.H.I.

[8] Bürger, *op. cit.*, 12. As has been indicated above, all financial accounts for the various ships were kept by the pastors, with the possible exception of the *Olbers* and the *Selma*, on which the treasurer, Barthel, was traveling.

admitted that he had antagonized many of the people on board ship with actions that were downright tyrannical, and pleaded as his only excuse the great strain placed upon him by his work. On the *Clyde,* Keyl is supposed to have struck a young man who suspected Stephan of immorality.[9]

What appeared as tendencies on the other ships, became policies on the *Olbers,* where Stephan himself was in charge, always docilely assisted by O. H. Walther. According to the Traveling Regulations, only the chosen few of his confidants were permitted to come into his presence without being granted express permission.[10] Brohm's diary indicates that this regulation was observed. Stephan's fellow passengers asserted that he seldom showed himself or preached, and that when he did, his sermons were of mediocre caliber, delivered in a mood and with the language of a vengeful representative of the Almighty Himself.[11] In private, however, there was nothing divine about Stephan's utterances. His secretary, Brohm, entered Stephan's remarks in his diary with such perfect composure that there is no indication of surprise or resentment. If his obedient mind was tempted to opposition, he does not reveal it. When Stephan castigated his lack of spirituality, Brohm humbly accepted the chastisement without a whimper even in the privacy of his journal, merely regretting that he could not more nearly achieve the frame of mind which Stephan desired.[12] There is, therefore, no reason to doubt the literal accuracy of Brohm's account.

On November 25, 1838, Brohm wrote: "The steerage passengers sinned in that, because of their gluttony, they spent the greater part of Sunday in making dumplings, causing serious concern to the Herr Pastor over the spiritual condition which this indicated."[13] The following day, and perhaps as a sequel to the previous day's events, there were complaints about the food in steerage, but these were characterized by Brohm as "sinful." [14] On December 9, 1838, the secretary recorded: "A sharp sermon of admonition. Among other

---

9 Köstering, *Keyl,* 54; E. M. Bürger, Selbstbiographie, 130, MS., E. J. Buerger Papers, Ellicottville, N. Y.; Bürger, *op. cit.,* 12.

10 Traveling Regulations, Appendix B.

11 Vehse, *op. cit.,* 8—9; G. Günther, *op. cit.,* 9, 11, 13; J. A. K. Höhne and J. G. Höhne to their brother, Sept. 26, 1841, in *Die Ameise,* Jan. 10, 1842.

12 Brohm, Journal, Dec. 31, 1838, Jan. 24, 28, 29, 1839, MS., C. H. I.

13 *Ibid.,* Nov. 25, 1838.

14 *Ibid.,* Nov. 26, 1838.

things the Herr Pastor said: 'I have been bitterly deceived by you.'"[15] Four days later Stephan complained about what he felt was the sad spiritual condition of his followers, finding the number of upright small indeed and little zeal to build the Church. In fact, he said, the majority of his followers would go back to Germany if a passing ship offered them the opportunity and if they were not prevented by "circumstances [financial?] and shame."[16] On December 15 Stephan again reproached his people. Most of them, he found, were interested more in eating and drinking than in heavenly treasures. Stephan despaired, so he said, of ever making of them what he called a really Christian congregation and asserted that the majority despised God's Word. He hoped, however, that those on the other ships were not in such a sorry spiritual state. In any event, he consoled himself, he did not rely upon men, and had the confidence that God would build His Church in America, where "a whole people waits for God's Word."[17]

New Year's Eve, 1838, Stephan delivered a long harangue to a group of his intimates, weeping profusely meanwhile. The reading of Joshua 22 and the injunction to all those present to commit this chapter of Scripture to memory were merely a beginning. Only a direct quotation of Stephan's scarcely coherent pronouncements on this occasion, as reported by Brohm, can do justice to the outburst:

> You are young. I have little to seek in this world any more, but I do wish that the evening of my life might be more quiet than was the day. I ask little for myself, but of you I ask much. I must concern myself with lice and bedbugs — tormented and downtrodden man that I am — must concern myself with chamber pots. At the close of the year I assure you I am weary. I do not desire to lead the *Gesellschaft,* I seek nothing for myself. An old man like me, sixty years of age, ought not to be caused so much worry and trouble. Would to God some one else would lead you, I should be the first

[15] *Ibid.,* Dec. 9, 1838.

[16] *Ibid.,* Dec. 13, 1838. The enchantment which the distance of two and one-half years lent to Stephan's view enabled him to claim that at this time he enjoyed the love, respect, and confidence of the entire group of emigrants, and that only Marbach and a few others gave evidence of an "underhanded hostility" toward him. Stephan to Flügel, Oct. 12, 1841, MS., C. H. I.

[17] Brohm, Journal, Dec. 15, 1838, MS., C. H. I.

> to extend my hand to him — but so long as I am the one to do it, I demand obedience. When I frequently told you that I should rather be a bee master, I was in dead earnest. But if I am to act as your leader, then follow me, otherwise I will not lead you! Otherwise I will not lead you! Remember this, so that later on you do not say: He is a hard man. I have forsaken my children, I would also forsake you, although I love you. Do you want that to happen? I was not obliged to go along to America. I have no temporal aims, I do not wish to rule, but also do not wish to permit another to rule. You are all young men — P. [Pastor] Walther, Marbach, Vehse, Brohm, Fröhlich, Klügel, Jäckel — I am telling you my sentiments. Hereafter make no more trouble for me, for I bear the marks of the Lord Jesus on my body.[18]

From the foregoing it is apparent that Stephan's harsh and domineering ways became more pronounced on the *Olbers*. There such restraint as he had still felt in Dresden disappeared, and his desire for self-indulgence and for authority was given full rein.[19] This tendency showed itself in many small ways, from obtaining through Captain Exter a corner on all provisions for cabin passengers to taking along on shipboard, where space was extremely limited, the coach which had been purchased for his precipitate retreat from the Saxon capital, and which he was in reality supposed to have sold in Bremen, in order to recover a little cash for the Credit Fund.[20] Such petty tyranny and inconsiderateness were matched by the impropriety of his expenditures, some of which have been described above and more of which will be mentioned presently. Criticism of Stephan's financial policies was not entirely lacking, and Vehse claims protests were made on board the *Olbers*, but that Stephan overrode all objections with a great show of authority.[21] Just how it would have been possible for Stephan to do this had the committee offered any determined opposition, Vehse fails to reveal.

As a matter of equal importance with the creation of the episcopacy itself, Vehse mentions another development aboard the *Olbers*, namely, that Stephan effected the fall of his "legal counsel,"

---

18 *Ibid.*, Dec. 31, 1838. See also *ibid.*, Jan. 1, 24, 28, 1839.

19 Nachrichten an unsere Nachkommen, MS., C. H. I.; G. Günther, *op. cit.*, 9, 11, 13; C. F. W. Walther in Köstering, *Auswanderung*, 15—16.

20 Vehse, *op. cit.*, 9; G. Günther, *op. cit.*, 7—9.

21 Vehse, *op. cit.*, 7.

that is, Vehse's brother-in-law, Marbach. The story, according to Vehse, is that Marbach had threatened to bring about a division between ecclesiastical and secular power, but that Stephan succeeded in discrediting Marbach and defeating his plan before the people.[22] Actually, this is another way of saying that the majority of the small group of leaders who were controlling the affairs of the *Gesellschaft* adhered to Stephan and failed to support Marbach. "The people" had next to nothing to say about what was going on. Marbach's version of the affair was that he warned Stephan on the *Olbers* because of the older man's stubbornness and injustice, that he himself threatened to quit Stephan's services, and that for these various acts of insubordination he was placed under a virtual "ban" by the Bishop.[23]

The statements of Marbach and Vehse regarding these events seem to be essentially true. Brohm's diary, while it is none too specific on the actual issues involved, does reveal that a bitter battle developed between Marbach and Stephan, in which the latter did not hesitate to bring into play the full force of his position as leader of the group, as pastor, and as Marbach's personal spiritual adviser, in order relentlessly to beat the man down. The constant recurrence of remarks by Stephan regarding his powers, the fact that while he claimed he did not want authority he would nevertheless let no one else exercise any, and his repeated demands for obedience so long as he was in charge, indicate the undercurrent of tension on these points.

The matter came out into the open on January 1, 1839, a day which Brohm called "the most remarkable one of my life." By then Marbach had already lost. His self-assurance was gone, for Stephan had convinced him, at least temporarily, that his opposition was sinful. At any rate, that is the admission which Marbach is supposed to have made to Stephan's secretary.[24] But Stephan nevertheless spared no effort to render Marbach completely harmless and to keep him in a position in which he could do nothing else but heed Stephan's bidding. The ensuing mental, spiritual, and emotional bludgeoning which was administered to Marbach is as revolt-

---

22 *Ibid.*, 9.

23 Marbach to Stübel, n. d. [Nov.—Dec., 1839], Bound MSS., VI, C. H. I.; Marbach, An meine Landsleute, MS., C. H. I.

24 Brohm, Journal, Jan. 1, 1839, MS., C H. I.

ing in its heartlessness as it was effective in its thoroughness. Stephan spoke openly against Marbach to the other leaders, clerical and lay, all of whom had been Marbach's friends heretofore, and succeeded in turning all of them against him. Confidence in Marbach was destroyed, his position was undermined, and he was completely isolated. Stephan concentrated on the theme that Marbach was in a state of "slavery to his wife, love of the world, ambition, lovelessness." [25] These ideas were implanted especially in O. H. Walther, the candidates, and the laymen of the inner circle. Stephan told them Marbach's worst temptation was his wife, whose Christianity Stephan questioned. As for Marbach himself, Stephan stated that he would not claim outright that Marbach wished to seize power for himself, but neither was he certain Marbach did not wish to do so.[26]

Within less than two weeks, that is, a day or two before Stephan was elevated to the episcopacy, he had succeeded in bringing the Marbach family to such a pass that Mrs. Marbach was illegally detained in her cabin under virtual "arrest," and her husband could do no more about it than discuss the matter with Stephan's secretary.[27] If any evidence is required to demonstrate Stephan's unscrupulousness in using his powers and his opportunities as leader of the movement, this case provides it. It must be remembered that the Marbachs were already under a severe strain as a result of the loss of their son during the early part of the voyage, and Mrs. Marbach was expecting another child.[28] To administer spiritual and emotional lashings at such a time, instead of dispensing comfort, and to climax this brutality by even confining her physically — these tactics constituted a stroke of cruelty which the Marbachs had little reason to expect from the man who was supposed to be their spiritual adviser. It must have been almost equally shocking to them to learn that men who were pastors, or candidates of the ministry, or their close personal friends, not only passively lent themselves to Stephan's designs, but were even induced by him to take an active part in persecuting the Marbachs, as when some of them assisted in subjecting the former first lieutenant of the

---

[25] *Ibid.*

[26] *Ibid.*, Jan. 2, 1839.

[27] *Ibid.*, Jan. 13, 1839.

[28] G. H. Löber, Diary, April 7, 1839, MS., C. H. I.

Gesellschaft to a veritable grilling.[29] In some cases, of course, these men may have excused themselves in their own minds by recalling Marbach's manner of dealing with them formerly, which had been brusque. But Brohm, for instance, felt no personal resentment or animosity against Marbach and merely did what Stephan wanted him to do, remarking at the same time that he, Brohm himself, "had to accuse myself of blindness and dullness in the Marbach matter." [30] This state of affairs was allowed to continue even during the stay in New Orleans and on the steamboat *Selma*.

It was not until the immigrants were on the river voyage that Marbach began to strike back at his tormentor. On February 3, 1839, he mentioned his distrust of Stephan to Brohm. This interview between Marbach and Brohm gives rise to the rather interesting surmise that Brohm himself may have begun by this time to have his misgivings about his employer. For it is amazing to note that when Brohm learned of the trouble with Marbach on January 1, 1839, he was so surprised that the day was "the most remarkable in his life," but the voicing of suspicions against the Bishop himself, on February 3, does not seem to have shocked him in the least and did not create so much as a ripple on the now placid surface of Brohm's diary.[31] The account by Brohm, contemporary with events and substantially corroborating Vehse's and Marbach's assertions of what went on, removes any doubt that these occurrences took place.

Where both Vehse and Marbach were wrong, however, was in trying to give the impression that they — especially Marbach — were motivated solely by the difference between their and Stephan's ideological concepts of church and *Gesellschaft* polity. It must never be forgotten, in examining most accounts of what happened during these fateful months, that they were written after the great debacle and the deposing of Stephan. Only a few months before, Marbach had been one of the principal figures in drawing up the codes and had worked in conformity with them until the group left Germany. That this man now suddenly felt severe pangs of conscience about the division of temporal and spiritual power, of which there is scarcely even a fundamental concept in the codes, borders on the

---

29 Brohm, Journal, Jan. 28—30, Feb. 4, 9, 1839, MS., C. H. I.

30 *Ibid.*, Jan. 29, 1839.

31 *Ibid.*, Feb. 3, 1839.

incredible. Furthermore, if Marbach, Vehse, and others who protested against the tendencies they noticed, had really possessed a firm conviction that the difference was one in principle, they could not and should not have compromised or yielded on this principle as they did. The most plausible interpretation of the quarrel between Marbach and Stephan, therefore, is not that Marbach at this time objected very strongly to the episcopacy as an institution, not even as an institution combining spiritual and secular power, such as the *Gesellschaft*. Rather Marbach and those who later claimed they agreed with him objected to the exercise of secular powers by Stephan because they felt, correctly, that he was using them in a manner which was leading the *Gesellschaft* along the road to ruin.

If this interpretation is correct, then the incident between Marbach and Stephan can hardly be viewed in any other light than that it was a challenge by Marbach of Stephan's domination of the group, which Stephan effectively quelled. The motives of the two men varied considerably, of course, but their aim was a single one. Stephan was demonstrating daily by word and act the double fact that he possessed an ambition to establish unbounded control over every phase of *Gesellschaft* activity, and on the other hand that he was entirely unfitted for such a role. The tirade on December 31, 1838, not only showed little judgment, foresight, and knowledge of human nature, but lacked even recognition of, and adherence to, facts, while at the same time it placed in doubt the man's emotional stability. In fact, even through a welter of pious phrases it is apparent that the very things were true which Stephan was denying most frequently and emphatically, when he claimed that he was not seeking his own interests and did not wish to lead the *Gesellschaft*. In short, Stephan was determined to establish himself as the sole authority, and Marbach was determined to frustrate this plan. The reasons for the conduct of both men are not hard to find.

Stephan realized that emphasis and interests within the group were being, and would be still more, altered by changing circumstances. The aura of martyrdom, which he had used to such good advantage, would not be as effective in the New World as in the Old. Indeed, in view of Stephan's assurances that in the United States there was complete freedom, the continuance of an appeal to the sympathies of his followers on the plea that he was being persecuted would no longer be possible without bringing him into contradiction with himself. Hence the establishment of the episcopacy, which he had desired even before embarkation, became an immediate necessity, not only to assure his present control of both the temporal and spiritual affairs of the *Gesellschaft,* but also to prevent any possible challenges to his authority, such as that made by Marbach. These considerations also account for Stephan's precipitate haste in pushing forward with the "election" on board the *Olbers,* before the entire body of immigrants could reassemble in St. Louis. By this stratagem he had assured himself of the adherence of the largest single group of Stephanites, the *Olbers* company, and of the *Gesellschaft's* most influential members, before all were reunited and opposition could be organized.

Marbach also recognized that the balance of power was shifting. Perhaps he would not have been averse to capitalizing upon this fact by placing larger control into his own hands, no matter what the circumstances. But that surmise is not necessary in view of the way events were actually developing. The tendencies which Stephan was displaying in word and action were justification enough for opposing him and attempting to curtail his influence. If Marbach's conduct required an excuse, Stephan had certainly provided it. The autocratic power and abject obedience which Stephan demanded were not an inherent part of the episcopacy. However well it may have fitted in with Marbach's personal aspirations, his opposition to Stephan was probably based fundamentally upon his recognition of the fact that Stephan was not fit to direct the secular affairs of the immigration and that someone else would have to take over, then or later. That Marbach decided this change should be effected immediately, and that the power to be relinquished by Stephan should pass into Marbach's own hands, were probably both wise, even if not modest or selfless, decisions. Unfortunately he could not carry them to a successful conclusion.

The clash between Marbach and Stephan was heightened by several other factors. Each had used the other for his own ends. Stephan had capitalized upon Marbach's organizing ability, Marbach upon the drawing power and authority of Stephan's name. Their talents had complemented each other. Indeed, until the shores of Germany had receded into the distance, the two men had been indispensable to each other. But at the same moment each also became an obstacle to the other, and each then simultaneously experienced an urge to possess greater control over the project, wishing to relegate the other to a position of distinctly secondary importance: Stephan by taking over everything, Marbach by taking over the secular administration of the *Gesellschaft,* which he fully realized would be relatively more important than the ecclesiastical during the time the colonies were being established. Then the primary concern of the immigrants would be survival and not revival. In fact, the very continuance of the ministry would depend upon the ability of the colonists to eke out a living. The character of the *Gesellschaft,* the areas of control, and the techniques of administration were changing.

In the contest that followed Marbach lost, and the spoils went to the victor. Marbach, who was not asking for everything, would quite probably have been willing to work out an amicable readjustment. However, Stephan, sensing his temporary advantage, forced a test of strength, and Marbach accepted the gage. In the kind of struggle that ensued, it is to Marbach's credit that he lost. Nevertheless, he was still fundamentally the realist and had foresight enough not to make ultimate victory impossible. Marbach, it will be noted, did not drive his opposition so far as to make it impossible for him to continue as a member of the *Gesellschaft.* Instead he came to heel, salvaged as much as possible of his influence, and, by taking orders from Stephan instead of giving them to others for a time, succeeded in remaining close to the nerve center of the organization. The day of final reckoning was postponed.

Stephan's next tactic was to secure formal recognition of the absolute control which he now in reality enjoyed. Accordingly O. H. Walther, Stephan's faithful *famulus,* was instigated to draw up the following document:

[STEPHAN'S INVESTITURE]

Right Reverend Sir,

Beloved Father in Christ:

Your Reverence has, according to the gracious council of God, remained standing as the last, unshakable pillar on the ruins of the now devastated Lutheran Church in Germany, to which all those have clung in the name of the Lord who have still earnestly cared for the right way to salvation, the true Church, and its holy Confessions. Among these there were also 5 servants of God's Word, by whom you were loved and honored as spiritual father, and approached for counsel and judgment in all important matters which pertained to their own welfare or that of their congregations. Accordingly, you have already for a long time occupied the position of a bishop and performed episcopal functions among us. However, this has become even more apparent since the plan, considered according to God's Word, of transplanting the Lutheran Church from Germany to the United States has been put into execution. You have been recognized by all individual congregations and congregation members as the father of all, as highest shepherd of souls, and as leader; without the name of a bishop you have exercised the office of bishop with paternal kindness, firmness, justice, care, and wisdom. Now that you are about to step on the soil of America, it becomes urgently necessary that this inner, tacit choice receive external and public expression. We have been instructed by you in many things, and from this instruction an abiding conviction has resulted in us that an episcopal form of polity, in accord with the Word of God, with the old Apostolic Church, and with our Symbolical Writings, is indispensable. Such a form of polity, in which a greater or smaller number of clergymen are subordinated to a bishop in the government of the Church and form a council with him and under his leadership, is therefore our joint, fervent, and earnest desire. It is also our abiding conviction that the real purpose of our emigration, as it is expressed in Par. 2 of our Emigration Code, can be attained only under a free episcopal form of polity.

In consequence of all this, therefore, we approach you with the reverent, urgent plea: Accept, Reverend Father, also for the future the office of bishop among us, bestowed upon you by God, and grant that we may now already express with this name our unqualified confidence in your fatherly love and pastoral faithfulness toward us, and the assurance of our sincere, complete, and childlike obedience toward you.

We are doing this at the same time in the name of the 4 clergymen who, together with their congregations, have preceded us, in the firm confidence that they fully agree with us in this matter and that we are only expressing what we already heard from them and what you, Right Reverend Sir, if it pleases God, will shortly hear from them personally.

May Jesus Christ, the chief Bishop of all souls, who has bought His Church with His own blood, hear our prayer for you and permit you, as our leader on the way to eternity, to hold the bishop's staff among us until the most distant limit of your — God grant it — very high old age, for our spiritual and temporal welfare, for the building of the ruined Lutheran Zion, for the blessing of all Christendom, and to the glory of the Triune God, to whom alone be praise and honor in the Church which is in Christ Jesus.

On board the *Olbers,* January 14, in the year of grace 1839.

Otto Hermann Walther, formerly pastor vic. at Langenchursd. in the Principal. of Schönburg, for himself and in the name of his Lutheran brethren in office

Gotthold Heinrich Löber, formerly pastor at Eichenberg in the Duchy of Altenburg

Ernst Gerhard Wilhelm Keyl, formerly pastor at Niederfrohna in Saxony

Carl Ferdinand Wilhelm Walther, pastor at Breunsdorf in Saxony.[32]

[A duplicate of the document, marked "Copy" and written in O. H. Walther's hand, includes in addition to the names above, the following:]

M. Emil Julius Moritz Wege, Cand. rev. min.
Gottlieb Klügel, Cand. rev. min.
Johann Jacob Gönner, Cand. theol.
Theodor Julius Brohm, Cand. rev. min.
Friedrich August Ernst Fröhlich, Cand. theol.

Dr. Carl Eduard Vehse,
Franz Adolph Marbach,
Heinrich Ferdinand Fischer, [Johann Höhne, Sr.]
Gustav Jäckel,
Johann Georg Gube,
Friedrich Wilhelm Barthel,
Christian Gottlob Hoffmann,
Gustav Pfau,
Johann Gottlieb Hellwig,
Johann August Stärtzell,
August Friedrich Häcker,
Carl Julius Otto Nitzschke,

as the deputies for signing elected by majority vote of the congregation on the Olbers.[33]

---

32 Stephan's Investiture, MS., C. H. I. See also Nachrichten an unsere Nachkommen, O. H. Walther to G. W. Löber, Keyl, E. M. Bürger, and C. F. W. Walther, n. d. [Feb. 19—24, 1839], MSS., C. H. I.; G. Günther, *op. cit.*, 21.

33 Günther gave the names of the deputies as found on the manuscript copy cited, except that for the name of H. F. Fischer he substituted that of the elder Johann Höhne, as indicated in the translation here given. In this instance Günther is in all probability correct, for H. F. Fischer is the one man who, according to other evidence, is not supposed to have signed these documents.

Before dinner on the day the document was signed, Stephan explained privately to Vehse that it was necessary for the former to be bishop before landing in America. Stephan is supposed to have given as a reason for immediate action that it would add to the prestige of the group to have someone with the rank of bishop at its head by the time it landed in St. Louis. If Stephan actually entertained such a thought, it is an eloquent testimony to his ignorance of conditions and attitudes in the West.[34]

After dinner O. H. Walther preached a sermon in which, through a peculiar process of dialectics, the alleged "servitude" of the Church in Germany was presented as motivation for subjecting it to an episcopal form of polity in the United States and in which the desirability of electing Stephan to the office of bishop was emphasized. While this may have appeared a normal step to those who were aware of the plans for formally establishing a hierarchy, Vehse reported that the people did not know what to make of this singular concatenation of events. It is easy to believe that Vehse was right. Nevertheless, on the next morning, that is on the fifteenth, the people elected twelve deputies, among them Vehse and Marbach. By the afternoon of that day the deputies returned the document, already signed.[35] Stephan coyly feigned a sudden and inexplicable detachment from these developments and claimed that after years of "unspeakable suffering" he longed only for rest and quiet; he made a pretense of harboring a preference for being only "adviser" to the bishop, but was prevailed upon, for the sake of the Church and his petitioners, to accept the office of bishop, although he did so with a show of reluctance. However, the newly elected Bishop now appeared satisfied, said all would be well, and only hoped that his office would not be made unduly difficult for him by the stubbornness and ignorance of the people.[36]

Matters seemed to have progressed, in the main, according to

---

[34] Vehse, *op. cit.*, 10. See also C. F. W. Walther in Köstering, *Auswanderung*, 16; Schieferdecker, *op. cit.*, 10—11; Köstering, *Keyl*, 54.

[35] Vehse, *op. cit.*, 10; O. H. Walther to G. H. Löber, Keyl, E. M. Bürger, and C. F. W. Walther, n. d. [Feb. 19—24, 1839]. MS., C. H. I.; G. Günther, *op. cit.*, 19—21. The sequence of events from January 14 to 16, as related by Günther, is somewhat different. However, he is frequently inaccurate in his chronology. There is agreement on the essential facts.

[36] *Ibid.*; Stephan to Flügel, Oct. 12, 1841, MS., C. H. I.; C. F. W. Walther in Köstering, *Auswanderung*, 16; Köstering, *Keyl*, 54; Schieferdecker, *op. cit.*, 10—11.

Stephan's desires until the *Selma* was under way for St.Louis. Then the Bishop evidently noticed some dissatisfaction among his people, and the objections of Barthel and others to his expenditures also caused him some alarm. Accordingly, on the evening of February 9, 1839, Stephan lectured for several hours on the errors of Marbach and Barthel. The Bishop deplored the fact that the opposition these two men were offering him not only was not prevented by his more faithful followers, but even affected their attitude toward him unfavorably.[37] Despite this damaging admission — or perhaps because of it — a reaffirmation of Stephan's authority was secured. On February 16, 1839, just a few days after the transfer of the 1,500 thaler, and three days before the *Selma's* arrival in St. Louis, a "Pledge of Subjection" was extracted from the group.

The declaration, again not drawn up on the initiative of the people, but on that of Stephan, O. H. Walther, and their confidants, was preceded by a homiletic tirade from O. H. Walther, which was delivered to all adult members of the ship's company as they were standing in the "men's lounge." In the sermon the people were told that if they did not wish to follow Stephan on the terms now proposed, they should forthwith leave the *Gesellschaft* and, if necessary, the pastors would support the Bishop with their own hands. According to the description of Vehse, the people were stupefied at being thundered at in this fashion. They submitted, and the declaration, pledging obedience to Stephan in all spiritual and *temporal* matters, was signed in the form of an oath by all adult members of the *Gesellschaft* save one.[38] The lone independent was not Vehse or Marbach, who claimed to have been protesting, not Barthel, who was named as a recalcitrant by Stephan, nor least of all O. H. Walther, but Heinrich Ferdinand Fischer.[39]

Vehse related how, while conversing with Stephan in the ladies' lounge on the evening of the sixteenth, he expressed to the Bishop some compunctions about the sweeping nature of the submission being exacted from the people, but went on to maintain that he was reassured by the Bishop's assertion that when they reached St. Louis,

---

[37] Vehse, *op. cit.*, 11; G. Günther, *op. cit.*, 28—29, 32; Brohm, Journal, Feb. 9, 1839, MS., C. H. I.

[38] Vehse, *op. cit.*, 11—12; Nachrichten an unsere Nachkommen, MS., C. H. I.

[39] Vehse, *op. cit.*, 12; Gruber, *op. cit.*, 32.

he would turn over the management of all financial and other secular affairs to the deputies of the people.[40] If Vehse was actually deceived by such promises, then he was more gullible than one with Vehse's excellent opportunities for observing the trends in the *Gesellschaft* need have been. Vehse himself said he realized that considerable concentration of authority was necessary to direct the founding of a colony efficiently, and was temporarily reassured, but that thereafter relations between him and his chief were strained.[41]

The document, described by Bürger as a "hellish decretal," was the following:

PLEDGE OF SUBJECTION
TO STEPHAN

In the name
of the Triune God.

The lamentable spiritual state of a large part of the congregation which emigrated with us — which state has become manifest during our whole journey and has grown ever more pronounced — has filled us with deep sorrow. The sins which hold sway among us and which especially cause us distress are: great indifference to God's Word and despising of the holy office of the ministry, in particular a damnable spirit of mistrust and dissatisfaction toward our Right Reverend Bishop, which has frequently found expression in shocking insolence, utter lack of all Christian love of one's fellow man; on the other hand, a morbid tendency toward slandering, vengefulness, envy and ill will, hypocrisy and disobedience to the orders given by His Reverence, heathenish unbelief and worldly-mindedness, and all in all such behavior as brings shame and discredit upon the Christian name.

If we consider that we are supposed to be a congregation which wished to emigrate for the sake of the pure, Apostolic-Lutheran faith, and had [have] given the definite promise to serve God in pure faith and a godly life, we feel constrained all the more to make the following declaration in writing, lest we, through sinful silence and indifference, become partakers in all the afore-mentioned sins, and in order that our deeply distressed pastor and Bishop may know what he has in us and what he may expect of us.

Above all, we affirm and testify before the countenance

---

[40] Vehse, *op. cit.*, 12.

[41] *Ibid.*, 12, 14.

of the omniscient God, in agreement with the truth, that we have complete and firm confidence in the wisdom, experience, faithfulness, and well-meaning fatherly love of our Very Reverend Bishop; and we abhor all distrustful, suspicious statements and thoughts, in which he is accused of injustice, harshness, aggrandizement, selfishness, carelessness in the administration of our temporal goods, etc.

We reaffirm with sincere heart that we are determined to adhere steadfastly and firmly to God's Word and the pure old-Lutheran confession of faith. We further declare that we are determined to hold fast with heart and soul, to keep most faithfully, and to live, suffer, and die under the episcopal method of church polity, with the introduction of which among us a beginning has already been made and which, when established according to the Word of God, has been used by the Apostolic Church, has been recognized by the true Church at all times, has been retained by the Lutheran Church of Sweden until this very day, and is in accord with the Symbolical Writings of the Lutheran Church.

Further, we solemnly pledge ourselves, as we have already promised by signing the Emigration Code, par. 3, to submit with Christian willingness and sincerity to the ordinances, decrees, and measures of His Reverence in respect to both ecclesiastical and community affairs, and not to regard them as an irksome yoke, but as the means of promoting our temporal and eternal welfare.

We repeat and reaffirm the promise, given in par. 7 of the Emigration Code, to contribute according to ability toward erecting and maintaining church and school, both with financial support and also other, personal service; likewise we shall also, in conjunction with the other congregations, provide with Christian willingness and without murmuring for the maintenance of our Bishop and our other clergymen and schoolteachers as much as the present circumstances permit, in order also thereby to give evidence of our obedience to God's commandments, our due thankfulness, and our deep appreciation of the spiritual gifts bestowed upon us through the holy office of the ministry.

Because of the numerous calumnies which our revered Bishop as well as his spiritual assistants have had to experience from various quarters, we feel obliged to make the declaration that we will always treat him with due respect and will in the future tolerate no calumny, regardless of its source, remembering the words of our Lord Jesus Christ: Whosoever heareth you heareth Me, and whosoever despiseth you despiseth Me, and 1 Tim. 5:17: Let the elders that rule well be counted worthy of double honor. As often as we are in need of a reprimand or a correction because of any kind of mistake, we will accept it willingly and thankfully, whether it come directly from the Bishop or through an authorized intermediary, and will altogether conduct ourselves in a sincere, honest, and obedient manner toward our pastors, bearing in mind the word of God: "Obey them that have the rule over you, and submit yourselves, for they watch for your souls as they that must give account, that they may do it with joy and not with grief; for that is unprofitable for you."

Should malicious persons attempt to sow the seeds of dissatisfaction and dissension among us or to form factions, we will earnestly and vigorously oppose them and promptly report them according to the explicit command of God 2 Thess. 3:14: "And if any man obey not our word by this epistle, note that man, and have no company with him, that he may be ashamed," and 1 Cor. 5:13: "Therefore put away from among yourselves that wicked person."

The preceding declaration and vow we have well understood and made voluntarily, without persuasion and haste, after mature consideration, and have signed it with our own hands in the presence of the likewise subscribed witnesses, and we intend to keep it faithfully and honestly; so help us God through Jesus Christ. Amen.

To the foregoing declaration I feel bound to add also the following:

I, too, have been permitted to join the *Gesellschaft* which has emigrated with His Reverence Herr Bishop Martin Stephan, only on the condition, and after making the oral and written promise, that I would be obedient to His Reverence and to all ordinances made by him, and altogether would live and conduct myself as it becomes a member of the *Gesellschaft* which emigrated for the sake of its most holy faith. However, I have not faithfully and honestly kept this promise and have frequently betrayed the confidence placed in me. I also have participated to a greater or lesser degree in the grievous sins named in the previous declaration. I should have to recognize it as a just and well-deserved measure if I were completely excluded from the Christian community. But I confess that I am heartily sorry for these my transgressions, and approach His Reverence with the humble and urgent plea to tolerate me in his *Gesellschaft* still in the future. I renew the promise that I will in true repentance, with the assistance of the Holy Ghost, recognize the sins I have committed ever more thoroughly and abstain from them, and in future conduct myself toward God's Word, toward His servants, and toward the entire Christian congregation as it becomes a true Christian.

However, if I should again break my word and agreement, which God forbid, and my complete expulsion from the *Gesellschaft* be demanded by our Very Reverend Bishop, then I hereby obligate myself forthwith and without protest to leave the *Gesellschaft* after settlement of my secular obligations or after providing adequate security for them. Under these obligations is to be understood the repayment of each and every sum advanced to me for equipment for the journey and the transportation to America of my person and my respective family and relatives as well as of my and their effects, likewise of all other sums advanced in connection with the emigration and the settlement, especially also the obligation expressly assumed in par. 7 of the Emigration Code of jointly raising the church and community expenses for five years in proportion to financial circumstances.

This confession, well understood and voluntarily made by me, is my true, unfeigned sentiment, and I intend, with the help of God, faithfully to keep the accompanying vow. This I attest before God and in the presence of the other subscribed witnesses by the signature of my name; so help me God through Jesus Christ, Amen.

On board the steamboat *Selma,* Febr. 16, 1839.

Otto Hermann Walther, P. Vic.
M. Emil Julius Moritz Wege as
Theodor Julius Brohm, Cand. rev. min. witnesses

Johann Samuel Günther
Christiane Theresia Tirmenstein
Johann Andreas Gottfried Estel
Ernst Lebrecht Krause
Auguste Wilhelmine Pötzsch
Ernestine Emilie Pötzsch [42]

As observed before, the news of the action taken by the *Olbers-Selma* group in "electing" Stephan bishop had preceded the *Selma* to St. Louis. It was probably borne by Marbach when he left the *Selma* on February 13. O. H. Walther had written a letter to the clergymen in St. Louis on February 5, in which this event was undoubtedly discussed.[43] No effective opposition appears to have been

---

[42] Pledge of Subjection to Stephan, *Selma,* Feb. 16, 1839, MS., C. H. I The first two thirds of this declaration (to the first "Amen") is contained in Vehse, *op. cit.,* 159—163.

[43] Brohm, Journal, Feb. 5, 1839, MS., C. H. I.

offered, or even contemplated. In fact, the very persons who might have been expected to recognize the dangers inherent in the arrangement — the pastors — were already committed to the plan.[44] These men, who were the only possible nuclei of effective resistance, not only entertained no thought of counteracting the propaganda now launched in favor of the episcopacy, but actively engaged in it. They were somewhat surprised and estranged that the action had been taken without them, before the rendezvous in St. Louis,[45] but this circumstance did not materially change the scheme of things as it had been visualized in Germany.

O. H. Walther, Stephan's constant proxy in these maneuvers, compensated for the Bishop's inactivity during the first few days in St. Louis with a burst of apparent initiative. After arriving in St. Louis, Walther addressed a second formal statement to his colleagues, Löber, Keyl, Bürger, and his brother, Ferdinand Walther, in which he sought to justify the premature action on the *Olbers*, to which he had been party, and urged them to express their assent, which he had already assumed.[46] His letter was a combination of pious phrases and fulsome flattery of Stephan, the real import of which was: Stephan is now Bishop, and you are expected to go through with our plan. He began his letter with a lengthy preamble devoted largely to giving thanks for the *Gesellschaft's* good fortune in having Stephan as its leader. Next he gave an account of the developments while en route, describing them as the fulfillment of "the wish which we have cherished for years." Along with this letter Walther sent a copy of the *Olbers* document. He did not state his reasons for taking action independently and at the time when he did, except to remark that it was done "for several important causes" and "in the knowledge of your complete agreement with me." He did not so much as mention the declaration of submission on the *Selma*. Perhaps even O. H. Walther realized that the extremes of this document were not necessarily a part of the episcopacy and could hardly be demanded of others. But Stephan's vicar did call upon the other pastors and their "congregations" to

44 Stephan's Investiture, MS., C. H. I.

45 G. H. Löber, Diary, Entry for period between June and December, 1840, MS., C. H. I.

46 O. H. Walther to G. H. Löber, Keyl, E. M. Bürger, and C. F. W. Walther, n. d. [Feb. 19—24, 1839], MS., C. H. I.

fall in line and add their approval of the episcopacy to that of the *Olbers* group.[47]

The four other clergymen — Löber, Keyl, Bürger, and Ferdinand Walther — responded nobly to O. H. Walther's appeal. February 24 was a Sunday. Unleashing a barrage of sermons to their people on the question of the episcopacy and the necessity for electing Stephan, they upbraided the people for their thanklessness and sinfulness, reproved their disobedience to Stephan and the other pastors, and held forth on Stephan's great saintliness, great service to the *Gesellschaft,* and his eminent qualifications for the office. The pastors expressed discouragement in extremely harsh terms; leaving the *Gesellschaft* they denounced as a great wrong. From their remarks it was easy to reach the conclusion that some of the people were not even Christians.[48] Only one example of such an address is still extant, and it appears to be in C. F. W. Walther's handwriting. Its closing words are: "I will now read to you . . . ," and then there evidently followed one of the various documents the people were expected to sign, although in this case the specific document was not included in the manuscript.[49]

The results of this campaign by the clergymen were prompt and gratifying. On the same day, less than a week after Stephan's arrival, the pastors drew up a new document in their own behalf and that of their "congregations," as they were still in the habit of calling the various sections of the *Gesellschaft* grouped under individual clergymen on the journey. Each of these "congregations" had elected four deputies, who then, together with the pastors, signed the instrument in the name of the people whom they represented, and the result was the following Confirmation of Stephan's Investiture, which was formally presented to the Bishop on February 26, 1839:[50]

---

[47] *Ibid.;* Stephan to Flügel, Oct. 12, 1841, MS., C. H. I.

[48] Bekenntniss, Lossagung vom Stephanismus, Bürger to the immigrants in St. Louis, June 29, 1840, Keyl to the immigrants in St. Louis, July 1, 1840, MSS., C. H. I.; Winter to Guericke et al., April 28, 1841, *Zeitschrift für die gesammte lutherische Theologie und Kirche,* II, No. 3, pp. 116—132; Bürger, *op. cit.,* 13; Keyl, *op. cit.,* 17; Vehse, *op. cit.,* 13; Schieferdecker, *op. cit.,* 10—11.

[49] Address in support of Stephan's elevation to the episcopacy [by C. F. W. Walther], MS., C. H. I. The contents make the purpose and date of the address unmistakable. It was written from February 19 to 24, 1839, by one of the pastors, apparently C. F. W. Walther, although he himself was not in charge of one of the vessels, because of the necessity for his departure on his brother-in-law's ship.

[50] G. H. Löber, Diary, Feb. 24, 1839, MS., C. H. I.; Vehse, *op. cit.,* 13.

[CONFIRMATION OF STEPHAN'S INVESTITURE]

Right Reverend Sir,
Beloved Father in Christ!

Your Esteemed Reverence has on the ship *Olbers* graciously accepted a petition drawn up under date of the 14th of last month, in which you are unanimously and fervently requested, in the first place, by Pastor Vic. Walther, and at the same time, in the name of us four clergymen here subscribed, and also with the concurring signature of five candidates and twelve deputies of the congregation on that ship, to take over in the name of God the office of our first Apostolic-Lutheran Bishop under the episcopal church constitution so desirable for us and about to be re-instituted.

We could not but with the most cheerful consent of our hearts read the faithful copy given us of this petition to Your Esteemed Reverence, about the well-considered contents of which there has — thank God! — for some time already been no doubt among our confraternity.

Indeed, the more we ourselves, through the grace of God, now for a number of years have enjoyed the good fortune of being dissuaded by you, Right Reverend Father, from false religious beliefs and of being instructed from the correct understanding of the Gospel how we should behave ourselves in the house of God, which is the Church of the living God, the pillar and ground of the truth [1 Tim. 3:15], the more we have come to the conviction that our own welfare as well as the welfare of the congregations that have emigrated with us can be promoted only in the manner of the early Christian Church, with a well-ordered episcopal form of polity.

And the more we have come to know of your doctrine, your method, your intention, your faith, your long-suffering, your love, your patience, your persecution, and your tribulations, the more we cannot but give thanks that the gracious and merciful God has kept you for His Church until now, and that your paternal, faithful care for the reflorescence of this dear Church did not permit you to refuse at this perilous time the episcopal office offered to you.

True, after the many storms of your hitherto arduous life we should gladly have seen you spared so grave a burden of office and should have heartily wished for you a period of rest and tranquility free from care; but to whom could the powerful Bishop's staff then have been given at the present time?

Therefore we will at least take all the more care that

the burden of your high office, which includes so many duties, will not be made greater or heavier through any fault of ours.

Therefore, also we and the three candidates subscribing with us herewith promise solemnly and before God that we will at all times and with unqualified confidence follow your further paternal leadership, for which we plead, as well as comply with childlike, willing obedience with your episcopal ordinances in all things.

Our congregations have been instructed in this ecclesiastical matter by us, the subscribed clergymen, and they have given their cheerful consent to the proposed episcopal form of polity as well as to the selection made by us, which they have herewith expressed through the twelve deputies also subscribed.

May the God of all comfort and all help, Who has delivered you from such great tribulation, protected you on the waves of the sea, and kept you until now, also in the future be your shield and your great reward, and increase your health and strength, that you may for a long time still be a light and exercise influence among us!

May He permit you to see the happiness of Zion and peace in its walls! May He bless your going out and your coming in until [you reach] those mansions of eternal peace, where you will one day shine in heaven's radiance! Amen.

St. Louis, February 24, 1839.

Gotthold Heinrich Löber, formerly pastor
in Eichenberg in the Duchy of S. Altenburg.
Ernst Gerhard Wilhelm Keyl, formerly pastor
in Niederfrohna in the Kingdom of Saxony.
Ernst Moritz Bürger, formerly pastor
in Lunzenau in the Kingdom of Saxony.
Carl Ferdinand Wilhelm Walther, formerly pastor
at Breunsdorf in Saxony.

Ottomar Fürbringer, Cand. Minist. D.
Carl Ludwig Geyer, Cand. Theol.
Georg Albert Schieferdecker, Cand. Theol.

Johann Friedrich Ferdinand Winter, schoolteacher.
Johann Christian Friedrich Müller of Planena
Johann Bernhard Schmidt of Cahla.
Johann Gottfried Otto of Jenalöbnitz.

Johann Gottlieb Palisch of Löbtau
Christian Friedrich Hoffman of Frankenberg
Johann Gottfried Heinig of Nieder Frohna.
Johann Christian Grafe of Dresden

George Klügel of Paitzdorf
Christian Gottfried Müller of Piesern
Johann Christian Poppitz of Pürsten
Christian Gottfried Schlimpert of Bernsdorf
as deputies for signing elected by majority vote by the three congregations on the ships *Republik, Johann Georg,* and *Copernicus.*[51]

But the end was not yet. As on the *Olbers* and the *Selma,* so also in St. Louis the desired results were brought about by degrees. Neither the simple fact of his followers' approval of him as bishop nor the fawning phraseology of the St. Louis document satisfied Stephan's lust for power. Furthermore — and this was a more realistic consideration — while the people in St. Louis had agreed to the episcopacy, they had not yet been placed in the same position of dependence upon Stephan as the signers of the *Selma* document.[52] However, this objective was also attained with at least the majority when further declarations were signed in St. Louis. Three such documents are extant, one for the *Copernicus* group, under Bürger, and two others for the company on the *Johann Georg,* under Keyl.[53] Of the latter, one was signed by Keyl, Geyer, Schieferdecker, and all the adults on the *Johann Georg;* the other, by Keyl, Fröhlich, Geyer, and seven of the people. The second statement was identical with the first, except for additions in a very similar vein at the end of the original text, which increased its

---

51 Confirmation of Stephan's Investiture, Feb. 24, 1839, G. H. Löber, Diary, Feb. 24, 1839, MSS., C. H. I.

52 Vehse, *op. cit.,* 13, stated that the Confirmation of Stephan's Investiture expressed agreement with both the *Olbers* and *Selma* declarations. An examination of the text will show that the Pledge of Subjection on the *Selma* is not mentioned.

53 Pledge of subjection to Stephan by the *Johann Georg* group, I, II, Pledge of subjection to Stephan by the *Copernicus* group, MSS., C. H. I. As stated above, there were two such pledges for the *Johann Georg,* which are distinguished for the purpose of reference with the Roman numerals "I" and "II," of which II is the longer and more complete. None of these pledges are dated, but that of the *Copernicus* group states that it was drawn up in February, 1839, and presumably all of them were adopted before the end of that month. See also Keyl, *op. cit.,* 17.

length by about one third. The declaration of the *Copernicus* people was signed by Bürger, Geyer, Schieferdecker, and all the adults in that group.

The three St. Louis declarations were almost alike except for the greater length of the one *Johann Georg* document. They vary little from the Pledge of Subjection on the *Selma* except that the preambles are slightly different and that they are slightly longer; the body of the statements in some parts is identical with the Pledge on the *Selma,* in others merely similar. In all of these declarations, what was left of the individual and collective dignity of the *Gesellschaft* is presented to its idolized Bishop as a literary votive offering in a series of degrading self-recriminations by the immigrants and of extended panegyrics to Stephan.[54] "They pledged their riches and their freedom of action for the assurance that in the person of their leader the *ecclesia repraesentativa* was with them."[55]

In the past there has been some confusion as to who signed these various documents, a confusion which is aggravated by a frequent failure to distinguish between the Investiture, the Confirmation of the Investiture, and the various Declarations of Subjection. It may have been noted that Löber's group has not been mentioned as having signed a supplementary declaration, after the Confirmation of the Investiture. There is, however, no reason to believe that the *Republik* people and their pastor did not do so, and, as far as is known, no such claim has ever been made, not even by the people involved. All that can be said is that the document could not be located in the course of this investigation. There is only one clue as to what became of the declaration presumably made by the *Republik* group. In 1842 Spröde declared that at that time he had in his possession a copy of one of these declarations with more than a hundred signatures.[56] Those among the Saxons who were opposing Spröde did not challenge his statement; so it probably was true. Accordingly it seems probable that the document in Spröde's hands was that of the *Republik* passengers; and this conclusion would also account for the fact that just this declaration is the one which is missing from the Concordia Historical Institute col-

---

54 *Ibid.*

55 Maurer, "Studies in the Sociology of Religion," *American Journal of Sociology,* XXX, 674.

56 *Anzeiger des Westens,* Dec. 20, 1842.

lection, for no item that had found its way into Spröde's possession is likely ever to have been returned to the Saxons or their descendants. This view of events is supported by the final coincidence that Spröde claimed a hundred signatures on the statement he had, and the number of people on the *Republik* was only a little in excess of a hundred.

Frequent discussions regarding C. F. W. Walther's role in these developments lend interest to the question of his part in the establishment of the episcopacy. Attempts by Walther's admirers to separate him from the commonalty and picture him as the great independent have often been made, from the days of Köstering and Hochstetter to those of O. Hattstädt and Stellhorn.[57] Köstering appealed to tradition, Hochstetter, Hattstädt, and others, relied upon Köstering or upon their own fatuous assertions. Just what the claim is — that he signed the one document or that he signed neither — is not always clear. The primary purpose appears to be to absolve Walther of any connection with this episode, and this purpose can best be accomplished by not-too-specific phrases, such as: Walther "never subscribed to Stephan's hierarchical designs."[58] Walther himself stimulated some of these conjectures by claiming that he did not sign "the Pledge of Subjection," a somewhat equivocal term inasmuch as there were several of them.[59] One indisputable fact remains — C. F. W. Walther did sign the document cited above as the Confirmation of Stephan's Investiture.[60] This act alone is sufficient to deprive him of any serious claim to a special independence of Stephan or to a clarity of perception not enjoyed by the others. His spirited defense of Stephan to both von Einsiedel and Meurer

---

57 Köstering, *Auswanderung*, 38—39; Hochstetter, *op. cit.*, 20—21, 72; Hattstädt, "Vor hundert Jahren, 5, Die Rettung," *Der Lutheraner*, XCIV, 163; Stellhorn, "The Saxon Centennial and the Schools," *Lutheran School Journal*, LXXIV, 345, quoting Th. Bünger, "Etliche Züge aus der Geschichte der Missouri-Synode," *Synodal-Bericht des Iowa-Districts . . . 1901*, pp. 22—23. See also A. L. Gräbner, *Half a Century*, 12; Wolf, *Die Lutheraner in Amerika*, 373; Steffens, *Doctor Carl Ferdinand Wilhelm Walther*, 115.

58 Dallmann-Dau-Engelder, *Walther and the Church*, vi.

59 C. F. W. Walther, "Antwort auf die neueste Vertheidigung der Union," *Der Lutheraner*, I, 80.

60 Walther's signature would suggest this. But, in addition, G. H. Löber, who was there and admitted signing it himself, said Walther did so. G. H. Löber, Diary, Feb. 24, 1839, MS., C. H. I. See also Stephan to Flügel, Oct. 12, 1841, MS., C. H. I.

also shows that his relationship with Stephan did not differ essentially from that of the other pastors.[61]

In the face of C. F. W. Walther's pledge of obedience to Stephan "in all things," any claims of "independence" on his part can rest only upon the fact that a supplementary declaration bearing his signature cannot be found. On the same basis, Löber and all his people would have to be excused, but this idea has never gained any prevalence. The fact that Walther signed neither of the *Johann Georg* statements is not conclusive, for the division into groups is not strictly followed in this signing. Both Schieferdecker, who was on the *Copernicus* and the *Rienzi,* and Fröhlich, who was on the *Olbers* and the *Selma,* signed one of the *Johann Georg* documents. Meanwhile, Heinrich Ferdinand Fischer, who if anyone deserved the plaudits accorded Walther, is all but ignored by the admirers of the latter. Fischer's history does not embellish the Walther myth. But what seems to escape the authors of this version is the fact that any effort to represent Walther as feeling a peculiar aversion for the servility of the *Gesellschaft* can, if successful, merely afford proof that he violated his conscience more ruthlessly than the rest, or that he disliked the phraseology of the Pledges more than that of the Confirmation of the Investiture, which he did sign.

In any case, however, the emphasis upon Walther at this point is misplaced. It was not yet his day. The Bishop was now in complete control of the group.

---

[61] C. F. W. Walther to von Einsiedel, Feb. 3, 1838, Meurer [?] to C. F. W. Walther, Jan. 27, 1838, MSS., C. H. I.

CHAPTER TWELVE

FIRST CONTACTS WITH RELIGIOUS CONDITIONS IN THE WEST

UP TO THIS TIME the various groups of Saxons had never held a joint service. It was plain that this would be impossible until a place had been found where all the people could assemble. The immigrants accordingly were confronted with the alternative of attempting to rent a hall or of securing permission from one of the other congregations in the city to use its building. The former expedient proved impracticable; only the second remained. This dilemma for the first time brought the Saxons face to face with the circumstances of their religious environment. In view of the strongly religious cast of the movement, it is surprising that the Stephanites had not made a greater effort to find out what conditions they were likely to encounter in the church life of St. Louis. But while they may have considered such information unnecessary, a brief description of the religious community in which the Saxons now found themselves, especially in so far as it affected the Germans, is indispensable for this study. The fact that the future development of the Saxon group lay largely in the ecclesiastical field adds to the importance of the religious environment in which this development took place.

Religious conditions in the West were in a somewhat confused and rather primitive state. The oldest church body was the Roman Catholic, firmly entrenched since its privileged Spanish days and assured of considerable numerical strength by virtue of the French and Spanish populations. Next in point of importance were the Episcopal, Baptist, Methodist, and Presbyterian churches, all of which were already well represented in the area before the Saxons arrived. Besides, there were numerous smaller religious organizations in the area, almost all of which were established in St. Louis by 1847. A listing of the denominations, other than the Saxons, represented in St. Louis will not only give a picture of the situation in that city, but more generally of conditions in the West as well.

The churches in St. Louis before 1847 were the following:[1] The *Roman Catholic* Church, active since 1770, one congregation, the Cathedral, in 1839, six congregations in 1847; the *Protestant Episcopal* Church, since 1825, one congregation, Christ Church, in 1839 (dedicated February 17 of that year), four in 1847; the *Methodist* Church (Methodist Episcopal, Methodist Protestant, African Methodist, German Methodist), since 1807, two congregations in 1839, at least twelve in 1847; the *Presbyterian* Church (Northern and Southern Presbyterian, Associated Reformed Presbyterian), since 1817, two congregations in 1839, at least eight in 1847; the *Baptist* Church (Northern, Colored, Southern), active since 1798, organized since 1818, two congregations in 1839, five or six in 1847; the *German Protestant* Church, discussed at greater length below, which began as a single group, but by 1847 had branched out into an independent Protestant congregation and two Evangelical congregations; the *Jewish* synagog, since 1839, with two congregations in 1847;[2] and the Unitarians, Universalists, "Holland Reformed," "Swiss Reformed," an unidentified "German Church," Christian Disciples (Campbellites), the "New Church" or Swedenborgians, Millerites, Mormons, Free German Catholic (*Rongianer*), and Bethel Church, an interdenominational religious society founded to

---

1 The following general references may be listed at this point to prevent repetition: Scharf, *op. cit.*, II, 1649—1659, 1670—1679, 1682—1695, 1702—1707; Keemle, *St. Louis Directory, for the Year 1838—9*, pp. 59—61; Keemle, *The St. Louis Directory, for the Year 1840—1*, pp. 73—74; Green, *St. Louis Directory . . . 1845*, xxxi—xxxii; *Green's St. Louis Directory, for 1847*, p. 11 (hereafter cited as *St. Louis Directory . . . 1847*); Skillman, *op. cit.*, 104; *St. Louis New Era*, Dec. 24, 1841; *Daily Evening Gazette*, March 5, 12, April 9, 30, May 14, June 4, 1842; *Anzeiger des Westens*, Jan. 18, 1845; *People's Organ*, May 14, 1842; *St. Louis American*, Oct. 6, 1845; *Daily Morning Missourian*, Oct. 7, 1845.

2 *Missouri Argus*, April 14, 1840; *Missouri Reporter*, April 15, July 7, Aug. 3, 1843; *Daily Pennant*, April 13, 1840; *Daily Morning Missourian*, Nov. 14, 1845; *Native American Bulletin*, May 11, 1842; *St. Louis American*, Dec. 2, 1845; *Weekly Reveille*, Sept. 29, 1845, Jan. 5, Dec. 21, 1846; *Die Deutsche Tribüne*, Sept. 17, Oct. 2, 1844; *Anzeiger des Westens*, Dec. 25, 1841, Jan. 10, June 24, 1843; *People's Organ*, May 11, 1842, July 12, Aug. 14, Dec. 31, 1844; *Daily People's Organ*, April 16, 1844; *St. Louis New Era*, Dec. 24, 1841, Aug. 6, 1842, April 24, June 24, 1843, April 16, Oct. 1, Dec. 31, 1844; *St. Louis Daily New Era*, July 3, 1846; *Daily Missouri Republican*, Feb. 16, 18, 1839, March 18, April 16, July 12, Dec. 28, 1844, Feb. 8, May 22, July 9, Nov. 14, 1845, Jan. 7, Feb. 5, July 1, 4, Nov. 2, 17, 1846, Feb. 7, 1847; *Daily Evening Gazette*, Feb. 18, April 11, 1839, April 28, Oct. 12, 1840, Feb. 1, 1841, March 3, May 3, 11, 1842, Jan. 21, July 5, Sept. 9, Dec. 2, 1843, April 15, Sept. 14, 1844; Scharf, *op. cit.*, II, 1713—1732; *Annual Review . . . From the Missouri Republican, January 10, 1854*, p. 8; *Catholic Cabinet and Chronicle of Religious Intelligence*, I, 573; Kargau, *op. cit.*, 279.

serve the transient population that was brought to St. Louis by the river traffic.[3]

Sects were flourishing, especially in the West; Peck listed in addition to the bodies just named: Tunkers, Shakers, United Brethren in Christ, and Quakers.[4] Of the "German Lutherans" Peck had this to say: "We have no data to give the statistics of this denomination. There is a Synod in Ohio, another in Western Pennsylvania, and perhaps others. There are probably 50 or 60 ministers in the West, and 150 congregations."[5] The only organization which was even nominally Lutheran and laid claim to serving the Central States was the Synod of the West. This body was organized in 1834 and was represented, prior to the time the Saxons came, in Indiana, Illinois, Tennessee, Kentucky, and Missouri. In 1840 or 1841 it became affiliated with the General Synod (Lutheran).[6] Although the Synod of the West was in the best position to do something for the German Lutherans, it never proved equal to the demands of conditions confronting it.

Work had been begun among the Germans in St. Louis by emissaries of the Basel[7] and Barmen[8] Mission Societies before 1840. But the only German church in the city when the Saxons arrived was a Protestant congregation that was an American counterpart of the German "Union." Religious meetings had been held as early as 1832, and a congregation was organized in 1834 by a Pastor Korndörffer. There was a brief interim during which Johann Büttner and Johann Kopf carried on as pastors. Beginning with 1836, the congregation was served by the Rev. G. W. Wall. Until

---

[3] *St. Louis New Era,* June 30, Dec. 24, 1841, Sept. 10, 1842, March 27, 29, 30, 1843, Jan. 21, 1845; *Daily Evening Gazette,* June 17, 1841, March 5, 12, June 4, 1842, Dec. 2, 1843, May 31, 1844; *Anzeiger des Westens,* March 30, 1843, Jan. 18, Oct. 30, 1845; *Täglicher Anzeiger des Westens,* July 10, 19, Aug. 5, Sept. 5, 1846, May 6, 1847; *Weekly Reveille,* Oct. 13, 1845; *Die Deutsche Tribüne,* May 8, 1847; *People's Organ,* March 31, April 3, 1842; *Daily People's Organ,* Dec. 8, 11, 1843; *St. Louis Democrat,* June 1, 1844; *Daily Missouri Republican,* Nov. 25, 1839; *St. Louis Daily Union,* April 8, 1847; *Missouri Argus,* April 16, 1841; Scharf, *op. cit.,* II, 1738—1743.

[4] Peck, *A New Guide for Emigrants to the West,* 352—362. See also Arends, *op. cit.,* 216—218; Britton, "Pioneer Life in Southwest Missouri," *Missouri Historical Review,* XVI, 282—283; *Die Deutsche Tribüne,* May 2, 1845.

[5] Peck, *op. cit.,* 356.

[6] Schneider, *op. cit.,* 66; Fuerbringer-Engelder-Kretzmann (eds.), *op. cit.,* 281.

[7] Schneider, *op. cit.,* 47—53.

[8] *Ibid.,* 53—58, 84—96.

1839 these people worshiped in the Methodist church at Fourth and Washington Streets, and from 1839 to 1840 in the Presbyterian church at Fourth and Chestnut Streets. In the latter year, on August 9, they dedicated the church at Seventh and Clark Streets known as the German Protestant Church of the Holy Ghost, which had been under construction when the Saxons arrived.[9]

The unionistic principles of the congregation caused it to adopt a rather unfriendly attitude toward the conservative Saxons and at the same time led to its own eventual dismemberment. Wall himself was sufficiently evangelical to be called "Pietistic." But meanwhile the congregation's policy of following the practices of the German state churches, made all who had been members of these churches in the homeland feel that they were entitled to join here. As the membership of a German state church frequently included virtually everyone in the country who was not an avowed Roman Catholic, many who became members of Holy Ghost Church were doubtful assets to any congregation. Contemporary critics complained that "they gather everything about them that is called Protestant," and even present-day observers have adjudged the composite character of the group "ultra-liberal." [10] Trouble between Pastor Wall and a congregation composed of such elements was inevitable. Actual battle was precipitated by the organization of the *Kirchenverein des Westens.*

By 1842 factions in the congregation were engaged in open warfare. Heinrich Koch was accepted as a member admittedly for the purpose of combating Pastor Wall.[11] The *Anzeiger* of June 11, 1842, carried a notice, signed by "many members," which called for a meeting of the dissatisfied elements of the congregation, and eleven days later the summons to those interested in the "welfare" of the church was repeated. Almost exactly a year later, during June, 1843, the *Anzeiger* carried announcements by the congregation, or its remnants, that the pastorate would be vacant on July 1 and that applications for the position would be considered. While such

---

9 *Ibid.*, 74—75, 91—93; Kargau, *op. cit.*, 265—266, 272. On the beginning of work by the Evangelicals in the St. Louis area, especially under Hermann Garlichs, see Bek, "The Followers of Duden," *Missouri Historical Review*, XVIII, 36—54.

10 C. F. W. Walther to Sihler, Jan. 2, 1845, in L. Fürbringer (ed.), *op. cit.*, I, 13; Schneider, *op. cit.*, 93, 197—198, 238—240.

11 Schneider, *op. cit.*, 126—129.

items were appearing, the resignation of Pastor Wall was announced by the *Anzeiger* with a wretched pun that insinuated a connection between him and an unpleasant episode involving the Evangelical Pastor Heyer.[12]

Wall had been forced out, and a portion of the congregation went with him. This group for a time held services in Benton School House, on Sixth Street between Locust and St. Charles Streets. Then, in 1845, they divided into two congregations, with separate buildings, separate names (St. Marcus in South St. Louis, St. Peter's in North St. Louis), and an annual change of pastors (Caviezell, Riess, Baltzer). By 1848 these two churches had achieved organizations completely independent of each other, and one of them (St. Marcus) was again rent by a division which resulted in the founding of yet another congregation, St. Paul's.[13] Meanwhile, the residue of the parent organization of them all, Holy Ghost Church, retained the building and the name and became an independent Protestant group. The Rev. F. Picker succeeded Rev. Wall as pastor of this congregation after the office had been filled for only a few months by a Pastor Detharding. By 1846 the process had begun all over again. Picker was in trouble, meetings were called by a new faction in the congregation, opposed to him, and he called opposition meetings. However, Picker proved more durable than his predecessors. Despite dissension and division he lasted until 1855. Then he, too, was removed.[14] Another German Protestant church with which the Saxons came into contact directly was that of the Rev. E. L. Nollau in Gravois Settlement (Mehlville, Missouri).[15]

Church life in the West at this time found an outlet for much of its energy and a stimulus to many of its endeavors in the numerous auxiliary organizations and activities connected more or less directly with the established church bodies. Such organizations, for instance, were the Missouri Sunday School Union, the Missouri

---

12 *Anzeiger des Westens*, June 11, 22, 1842, June 15, 24, 27, 1843. On Heyer, see also Schneider, *op. cit.*, 121—126.

13 Kargau, *op. cit.*, 265—266, 272; Schneider, *op. cit.*, 164—166. Slightly varying information on these congregations is given in Devoy, *A History of the City of St. Louis and Vicinity*, 178; Hyde-Conard, *op. cit.*, IV, 2389.

14 *Anzeiger des Westens*, Jan. 20, Feb. 4, 1846; *Die Deutsche Tribüne*, July 23, 1845; Kargau, *op. cit.*, 266—268; Schneider, *op. cit.*, 129.

15 *Anzeiger des Westens*, March 20, 1846; Kargau, *op. cit.*, 272.

Tract Society, and the Missouri Bible Society.[16] Camp meetings, revivals, and the employment of "Holy Roller" methods were common not only among the smaller nondescript sects, but also among the larger church bodies, such as the Methodists, Baptists, and Presbyterians.[17] Schneider describes the men and the preaching even in the Evangelical *Kirchenverein* as revivalistic.[18] Sunday "blue laws" and Sabbath observance were generally sponsored by the churches and supported by the English press, but the *Anzeiger* was militantly opposed to them.[19]

The Missouri Temperance Society was organized in 1832, and the local chapter in St. Louis was founded at the First Presbyterian Church on February 5, 1839.[20] The movement was rather strong at this time. By 1842 St. Louis had three societies, which for a time published a paper.[21] The temperance movement was at least unopposed by all English-language newspapers, although the sincere support of some of the editors is not beyond question. But the *Anzeiger* minced no words in treating the movement with unconcealed disgust.

Lodges flourished in St. Louis during these years. The Masons had begun to give some evidence of their presence as early as 1807 to 1809, were formally organized by July 24, 1820, and had founded six separate lodges in St. Louis by 1842.[22] In that same year, the even more active Odd Fellows, who were organized since 1834, had seven lodges in the city, one a special "Germania" lodge for the

---

16 Keemle, *The St. Louis Directory, for the Year 1840—1,* pp. 74—78.

17 *People's Organ,* Feb. 3, March 3, 1842; *Daily People's Organ,* March 25, 1843, Jan. 31, 1844; *Daily Evening Gazette,* Feb. 16, 1843; *St. Louis New Era,* Jan. 24, 1845; *Daily Missouri Republican,* Sept. 2, 1846; *Anzeiger des Westens,* Sept. 23, 1845; Nov. 14, 1844; *Die Deutsche Tribüne,* Nov. 22, 1844, May 18, Oct. 24, 1845; Britton, "Pioneer Life in Southwest Missouri," *Missouri Historical Review,* XVI, 282.

18 Schneider, *op. cit.,* 215—217, 271—275.

19 *Daily Commercial Bulletin,* Sept. 12, 1840; *People's Organ,* Feb. 11, 1842; *Daily Missouri Republican,* Dec. 5, 1846; *Anzeiger des Westens,* Sept. 18, 1845; *Täglicher Anzeiger des Westens,* Sept. 9, 1846.

20 *Daily Evening Gazette,* Feb. 6, 1839; Shoemaker, "Six Periods of Missouri History," *Missouri Historical Review,* IX, 232.

21 *The St. Louis Directory, for the year 1842,* p. x.

22 *Daily Missouri Republican,* Sept. 30, 1843, Feb. 21, 1844; *The St. Louis Directory, for the year 1842,* p. x; Keemle, *The St. Louis Directory, for the Years 1840—1,* p. 79; Kuhn, *Centennial History of The Grand Lodge, Free and Accepted Ancient Masons of Missouri,* ii; Denslow, *A History of Royal Arch Masonry in the State of Missouri,* I, 7; Shoemaker, "Six Periods of Missouri History," *Missouri Historical Review,* IX, 232.

Germans. In 1845—1846 they put up a spacious hall which attracted wide attention in the city and was used freely by some of the churches.[23] Both of these orders were on friendly terms with some of the Protestant denominations, notably the Methodists, and were permitted to take part in their services.[24] However, some opposition was beginning to develop among the more conservative Protestant churches in St. Louis, mainly the Episcopalian, and at times the secret orders became a political issue.[25]

All denominations were expanding their operations in the West by 1839, and in St. Louis churches were built by the dozen in the period between that date and 1847, as the previous listing shows.[26] The oldest denominations enjoyed the largest gains, especially the Roman Catholics, the Presbyterians, and the Methodists. The Roman Catholics were so active that they gave rise to a society organized especially to counteract their influence.[27] The Baptists also were extremely aggressive, but their activity was most effective in rural Missouri. Baptist work among the Germans did not begin until 1847.[28] The building programs which these churches felt were necessary to serve their increased membership, were frequently financed by solicitation of funds from people in the city at large, regardless of denominational lines, a practice followed by the congregations in the *Kirchenverein* and later adopted also by the Sax-

---

[23] *Anzeiger des Westens*, Aug. 31, 1842, April 25, July 22, Aug. 22, 1843, Dec. 3, 1844, April 24, 1845; *Täglicher Anzeiger des Westens*, Oct. 28, 1846; *Daily Missouri Republican*, April 23, 28, 1845, Oct. 20, 1846; *St. Louis Daily New Era*, Oct. 21, 1846; *Weekly Reveille*, Nov. 2, 1846; *The St. Louis Directory, for the year 1842*, p. xi; Keemle, *The St. Louis Directory, for the Year 1840—1*, p. 79; Shoemaker, "Six Periods of Missouri History," *Missouri Historical Review*, IX, 232.

[24] *Missouri Argus*, Jan. 4, 1841, May 11, 1842; *Daily Evening Gazette*, Feb. 2, 1841; *Missouri Reporter*, April 6, 1843; *Daily Missouri Republican*, Oct. 20, 1846; *St. Louis Daily New Era*, Jan. 1, Oct. 21, 1846.

[25] *Missouri Argus*, Aug. 28, 1841; *Daily Evening Gazette*, Oct. 18, 1843; *Daily Missouri Republican*, Sept. 20, 1844, April 13, 1846; *St. Louis Democrat*, March 12, 1844; *Die Deutsche Tribüne*, May 28, 1845; *St. Louis Daily New Era*, April 13, 16, 17, 20, 1846.

[26] *Daily Missouri Republican*, April 11, 1839; Arends, *op. cit.*, 218. Varying figures on the strength of the principal denominations at this time are given in the following: *Die Deutsche Tribüne*, Oct. 24, 1844, Nov. 27, 1845; *Weekly Reveille*, Aug. 12, 1844; *Daily Missouri Republican*, Aug. 7, 1844, Oct. 18, 1845; *Daily Evening Gazette*, July 27, 1843; *St. Louis Daily Union*, May 26, 1847; Bromme, *op. cit.*, 42; Arends, *op. cit.*, 276—277, Peck, *op. cit.*, 352—362.

[27] Schneider, *op. cit.*, 84—90.

[28] R. S. Douglass, *History of Missouri Baptists*, 123; Yeaman, *History of the Missouri Baptist General Association*, 90; Schneider, *op. cit.*, 381.

ons.[29] The religious bodies which were better established and were drawing their membership from the comparatively well-to-do, assured themselves of a very handsome revenue by selling pews in their churches at an average of $500 each. In this manner Christ Church raised the sum of $31,236.50 in 1839. The same policy was followed by the Presbyterians and the Roman Catholics.[30] This method of defraying expenses was so common that the Episcopalians received special commendation when, in 1840, they erected a "free" church (St. Paul's) in St. Louis; for, as the *Gazette* remarked, "Even in the more favored portions of our country, but few, very few Free Churches are to be found." [31]

Another favorite method of obtaining funds for churches or charities was the presentation of entertainments. Concerts vied with "fairs," suppers, and lectures for the attention of the members and the general public. In the absence of many entertainment attractions which were to offer competition only at a later day, these events were usually well patronized. This phase of church activity was carried to the point where it savored strongly of commercialism, with profits running as high as $1,400 at a single "orphans' fair." [32] The prevalence and importance of the socio-commercial enterprises of some churches are graphically described by one writer in these words:

> Those old churches were the scene of many curious life dramas, and what labor and self-sacrifice — mostly of women — they represented! Their foundations were laid in egg-money, their shingles were ice-cream saucers, the "main edifice" was the result of festivals, socials, oyster suppers, chicken-pie dinners, concerts, and those humble forerunners of the movies, tableaux, not to forget Rebecca at the lemonade well, the post office and gypsy fortune-teller. The debt — there was always a debt, it is fair to say — was substantially reduced at times by some brother, who was unwilling to have all his religion in his wife's name.[33]

---

[29] *Daily Evening Gazette*, Sept. 13, 1843; Schneider, *op. cit.*, 228—231.

[30] *Daily Evening Gazette*, Feb. 19, 20, 1839, Oct. 10, 1840, April 19, 1843 *Missouri Reporter*, Feb. 19, 1839, April 20, 1843.

[31] *Daily Evening Gazette*, April 28, 1840.

[32] *Daily Missouri Republican*, May 3, July 20, Dec. 4, 14, 16, 18, 20, 21, 28, 1844, Jan. 8, Dec. 29, 1845, May 13, June 19, 25, Oct. 19, 23, 1846, Feb. 4, 1847; *Missouri Reporter*, June 23, 1843; *St. Louis New Era*, Oct. 3, 1843; Schneider, *op. cit.*, 231.

[33] Owens, "Social Customs and Usages in Missouri During the last Century," *Missouri Historical Review*, XV, 186—187.

Usually the newspapers were generous with their support of ventures which promised to aid the churches financially, but occasionally the business aspect of these pious promotions went too far even for the press, and open disapproval was expressed.[34] The *Weekly Reveille,* not too reverent itself, printed the following poem, contributed by one of its readers, as a reflection of the overemphasis on extraneous interests in the churches of the day:

Going to Church

'Tis true, 'tis pity; and pity 'tis, 'tis true.
Some go to church just for a walk,
Some go there to laugh and talk;
Some go there the time to spend,
Some go there to meet a friend;
Some go to learn the parson's name,
Some go there to wound his fame;
Some go there for speculation,
Some go there for observation;
Some go there to doze and nod,
But few go there to worship God! [35]

Editorial or poetic wrist slapping, of course, did not seriously impede the activities of the growing church bodies.

Probably the most serious single blow to the prestige of the Protestant Church during the years under discussion was the division caused in many of its most powerful denominations by the slavery issue. In Missouri the internal quarrels among the Methodists, Baptists, and Presbyterians attracted attention. The Methodists staged the most spectacular fight. Bishop Soule claimed that for a time the Methodist Church was actually losing ground as a result of the battle over slavery.[36] Most of the Missouri churches, of course, went with the Southern factions in their denominations. This tendency on their part was merely a reflection of the attitude prevalent in St. Louis at this time, when slavery was either vigorously defended or at least generally accepted. Not a single St. Louis newspaper came out unequivocally against slavery during this period, although the *Daily People's Organ* was bold enough to insist

---

[34] *Daily People's Organ,* Sept. 3, 1843; *Anzeiger des Westens,* Sept. 12, 1843.

[35] *Weekly Reveille,* March 16, 1846.

[36] *Daily Missouri Republican,* May 3, Sept. 12, 29, Oct. 14, 1845; *Weekly Reveille,* May 15, 19, 1845; *Missouri Reporter,* Feb. 11, May 5, 1845; *St. Louis Daily New Era,* March 4, 7, 13, 1846; *Die Deutsche Tribüne,* Sept. 16, 1845.

that the Union must be preserved.[37] *The Catholic Cabinet, and Chronicle of Religious Intelligence* asserted: "There is no danger, no possibility on our own principles, that the Catholic theology should ever be tinctured with the fanaticism of abolition." [38]

The observation of Arends in 1838, concurred in by Münch two decades later, was that generally preachers in the Western States were poorly educated.[39] In the case of Münch, of course, the generalization was partly the result of his simply ignoring denominations that did not suit his fancy. As late as 1859 he wrote as though he did not know of the existence of Concordia Seminary. However, the condition he described did exist, especially in the late thirties and early forties. Many localities had no preachers whatever. In other places diminutive hamlets were served only by lay preachers, either because of a lack of clergymen, or because of a lack of funds to support them, or because the religious beliefs of some of the multitude of sects in the Mississippi Valley disapproved of an established clergy. These lay preachers frequently supported themselves in whole or in part with other employment. When not even this kind of service was available, the community might depend upon the infrequent and irregular appearance of some itinerant evangelist or circuit rider. Under these circumstances there frequently was no church building in the community, and meetings were held in private homes.[40]

Such ministers as there were, regardless of their educational equipment, came and went in a bewildering procession. Even in urban centers like St. Louis, where the caliber of the men was probably above the average, changes were made almost annually at some churches. A Baptist church in St. Louis had at least seven known ministers from 1839 to 1847, and the First Methodist Church in the city boasted an array of eight for the same period of time.[41] The frequent change of pastors at the Evangelical churches in

---

[37] *Daily People's Organ*, Jan. 22, 1843.

[38] *The Catholic Cabinet, and Chronicle of Religious Intelligence,* I, 570, quoting from the *U. S. Catholic Miscellany.*

[39] Arends, *op. cit.*, 276; F. Münch, *Der Staat Missouri, geschildert mit besonderer Rücksicht auf teutsche Einwanderung*, 164.

[40] Eliot, *A manual of prayer for public and private worship; with a collection of hymns,* iv; Arends, *op. cit.*, 217; Britton, "Pioneer Life in Southwest Missouri," *Missouri Historical Review*, XVI, 277—279.

[41] Scharf, *op. cit.*, II, 1675, 1692.

St. Louis has just been described.[42] While this practice would have been of doubtful value at any time, it was clearly unfortunate during these years and in a section of the country in which the Church needed to demonstrate its stability in order to win respect.

The prestige of the clergy suffered also for other reasons. Some clergymen in almost all denominations had no compunctions about entering the political arena. Although they were severely censured for this in the secular press, they were not greatly deterred. It may even be said that at times they seemed to make no attempt at maintaining a clear distinction between the religious and political fields.[43] Finally, quarreling within congregations themselves was not infrequent, and, as likely as not, took the form of bickering in the newspapers or of locking a church against one faction of its membership by another, or of personal violence against the minister.[44]

Religious life among the German immigrants was at a low ebb in the forties.[45] One reason for this condition was indicated by Münch, who, in 1859, could still say that "educated" Germans did not take part in church life.[46] This remark was Münch's highly inaccurate way of making a fundamentally accurate observation. Many of the immigrants of the thirties (the decade in which Münch entered the country) and of the forties, who enjoyed an educational training above that of the average immigrant, were militantly or passively opposed to the established church organizations. This attitude has been described in part above in connection with the *Anzeiger des Westens,* and Bek comments on the many "freethinkers" in the large German settlement at Hermann, Missouri.[47]

---

[42] See also Schneider, *op. cit.,* 137.

[43] *Missouri Argus,* May 18, 20, 21, 24, 26, 27, 31, Oct. 14, 16, 1841; *St. Louis New Era,* Oct. 31, 1841; *Daily Evening Gazette,* Oct. 31, Nov. 9, 1841; *Native American Bulletin,* March 17, 1842; *Daily Missouri Republican,* Jan. 9, 1844; *Missouri Reporter,* April 1, 1843; *Anzeiger des Westens,* Oct. 17, 1844; *St. Louis American,* Feb. 20, 21, 23, 25, 26, Nov. 2, 1846.

[44] *Anzeiger des Westens,* Nov. 26, Dec. 22, 1842, Jan. 26, March 23, April 20, Sept. 9, 1843, April 22, 1845; *Daily Missouri Republican,* April 19, 21, Sept. 12, 1845; *Daily People's Organ,* Jan. 4, Dec. 25, 26, 1843, Jan. 1, 1844; *St. Louis New Era,* Aug. 5, 1843; *Die Deutsche Tribüne,* Dec. 25, 1845. See also Schneider, *op. cit.,* 32—40, 124.

[45] F. Wyneken to his mother, Jan. 29, 1840, in *Der Lutheraner,* LIV, 3—4, 10—11; C. F. W. Walther, "'Die Noth der deutschen Lutheraner in Nordamerika,'" *ibid.,* I, 31-32; Fricke to Sihler, Dec. 20, 1847, MS., C. H. I.; Grabau, *Lebenslauf des Ehrwürdigen J. An. A. Grabau,* 45.

[46] F. Münch, *op. cit.,* 164.

[47] Bek, *op. cit.,* 157.

The colonies of Germans in Missouri, established by the time the Saxons arrived, had largely been founded by this class of immigrants. Here was to be found that stratum of "self-righteous, non-churchgoing" Germans which was composed largely of Rationalists, social reformers of anticlerical bent, and those among the other elements who, for one reason or another, followed them. These were the places where coarse ridicule was encouraged; where "sacred rites were rudely satirized"; where a dog could be baptized, or a beer keg dragged into the pulpit; where self-styled "liberals" deliberately planned the destruction of churches in order to force out the pastors currently serving them, so that these pastors could be replaced with men (e. g., F. Münch) less objectionable to those engineering the change; and where violence against the reverent was not unknown.[48] Under such circumstances it was no more than natural that the antireligious attitude among the "upper" classes should be reflected among the average immigrants as well in the form of a gross materialism.[49] The general characterization of the German element as "unchurchly" is hardly too severe.[50]

Nevertheless, there were large numbers of German immigrants who would have continued their church affiliations in the United States had the opportunity been given them. But these people, especially in the West, usually went entirely unserved. Left to their own devices, often ignored by the established churches, frequently lacking in the religious leadership that might have been supplied by their disinterested "educated" countrymen, these German immigrants could see to it themselves how they might organize their religious life. The result was that they either drifted away from the church entirely or at best were gathered into the fold of the Methodists or some other normally English denomination, which was not properly equipped to give them the necessary attention, but which at least thought enough of them to attempt serving them in the German language.

Preachers for German congregations were scarce, and if the educational level of the average clergyman was low, qualified German ministers were still fewer, so that congregations were fre-

---

[48] Schneider, *op. cit.*, 120, 124, 194—197. See also Maurer, "Studies in the Sociology of Religion," *American Journal of Sociology*, XXX, 544—545.

[49] Schneider, *op. cit.*, 32—40.

[50] Neve-Allbeck, *op. cit.*, 88.

quently victimized by impostors. Churches therefore advertised quite openly in the press, inviting one and all to apply for vacant pastorates. As likely as not the qualifications included that the prospective preacher should or should not be a "Rationalist," depending upon the predilections of the congregation employing him. Frequently he was required to teach school, preferably in German. Schneider remarks on the fact that the two oldest Evangelical congregations in Missouri (at Femme Osage and at St. Charles) were started by an "unordained gentleman farmer," Hermann Garlichs, in 1834—1835. Often the pastor sought by independent churches was specifically not to be a member of any organized church body or synod; sometimes he was not even to be ordained.[51]

The last two qualifications are indicative of a common attitude toward the clergy in the West at this time. The line of the frontier moving across the face of the country never in its progress marked a high degree of organized religious life. But at a time when Nativism was focusing attention upon the Roman Catholic hierarchy, anticlericalism was running especially high. Bishop Kemper of Christ Church was attacked in the press as "undemocratic" because of such practices as changing vestments during the course of a service, and the Presbyterians vigorously attacked the theory of the episcopal succession in the newspapers.[52]

The prejudice against church organizations was even stronger among the Germans than in other elements of the population. The parson-baiting tactics of the *Anzeiger* and of Koch have been mentioned above. Of these two the *Anzeiger* was, of course, the more dangerous to the churches, since its attacks were not as crude as those of the *Antipfaff*. Yet the sentiments and purposes of both on this score were very similar. The *Anzeiger* reveled in publicity unfavorable to the ministers, and although it seemed to think it had a special judicial function, it made no attempt at impartiality, even during the course of a legal trial. The pastor who was put on the stand by Weber or his contributors was put in the pillory

---

[51] *Anzeiger des Westens*, Aug. 6, 1842, March 2, 1844, Feb. 13, 1845; *Täglicher Anzeiger des Westens*, June 29, Aug. 14, 1846, March 2, 1847; Schneider, *op. cit.*, 32—40, 59, 109—110, 122, 135—136, 198—200. On religious conditions among the Germans, see also the series of articles reprinted from the *Hamburger Literarische und Kritische Blätter* in the *Anzeiger des Westens*, July 11, 13, 15, 1843; Dau (ed.), *op. cit.*, 46, 54—58.

[52] *Daily Evening Gazette*, April 13, 14, 15, 1840; *St. Louis New Era*, Aug. 5, 1843.

as well; he had already lost his case. Few things quite so aroused the anti-church element among the Germans as the mere mention of ecclesiastical organization, whether clerical or lay, whether a synod or a conference. To them it was all sinister, all hierarchical.[53] These attitudes and the policy of the *Anzeiger* in such matters can best be illustrated by an example.

In 1840 the Evangelical pastors Wall, Nollau, Garlichs, and four others, mostly in the immediate vicinity of St. Louis, attempted to organize under the name of *Kirchenverein des Westens.* This body has sometimes incorrectly been called *Synode des Westens* and confused with the Synod of the West, referred to previously. Although Pastors Heyer and Garlichs did join the Synod of the West for a short time, this body did not, as already indicated, fill their requirements. In fact, the Synod was so little interested in keeping its members in Missouri that it advised them rather to join Lutheran or Reformed organizations in their vicinity. Generally the Evangelical pastors in the St. Louis area had little inclination to associate themselves with the Synod of the West.

Accordingly the idea of founding a *Kirchenverein des Westens* was projected at a meeting in Gravois Settlement on October 15, 1840. Formal organization took place May 3, 1841. The new church body was not a synod, but a conference of "ordained pastors, lay delegates, and advisory members." [54] This action was at best a feeble attempt to bring a measure of order into the disorganized religious life of this section. It is claiming too much to say: "Utterly independent of any ecclesiastical connections in Europe or in America, the *Kirchenverein des Westens* was born — the indigenous product of socio-religious conditions prevailing in the West." [55] The *Kirchenverein* pastors almost all had strong connections with persons or organizations in Germany, and very definite support had come to some of them from American sources in the Eastern United

---

[53] *Anzeiger des Westens,* April 15, 18, 20, May 2, 6, 23, 25, 27, 30, June 1, 3, Aug. 3, 1843, Dec. 16, 1845; C. F. W. Walther to Sihler, Jan. 2, 1845, in L. Fürbringer (ed.), *op. cit.,* I, 8—9; Schneider, *op. cit.,* 33—34, 82, 113—126. See also *Old School Democrat and St. Louis Herald,* May 22, 1843; *Daily People's Organ,* April 11, 14, May 23, 1843; *Daily Evening Gazette,* April 21, 1843.

[54] Schneider, *op. cit.,* 67—68, 108,—109, 112. See also C. F. W. Walther, "Die evangelische Kirche in Nord-America," *Der Lutheraner,* I, 42—44, 45—47, 50—52, 56; Bek, "The Followers of Duden," *Missouri Historical Review,* XVIII, 46—51.

[55] Schneider, *op. cit.,* 106.

States. The entire trend of the *Kirchenverein* was to reconstruct in America a counterpart of the German Union, with its erasure of denominational lines between Lutheran and Reformed bodies. Yet it is true that the *Kirchenverein* was designed to meet local conditions and that any organization was preferable to the prevailing chaos.

The storm that was called forth among those Germans opposed to the organization of the *Kirchenverein* — any *Kirchenverein* — spent itself to a great extent on the pages of the *Anzeiger des Westens,* whose reputed editorial self-control seems to have forsaken it on this as on many other occasions. In April of 1842 the *Anzeiger* issued the clarion call: "Attention, countrymen! — 'The Evil Seven' are reaching out for the local German Protestant church, which they intend to shove into the synodical bag, together with the congregation." [56] The *Anzeiger's* attitude apparently had not relaxed by 1844, when it commented upon the withdrawal of five congregations from a synod in Pennsylvania by saying that they "wished to save themselves from the claws of priestly domination in time, before it should cost the blood of [some] citizens." [57]

Language became even more colorful when the *Anzeiger* accepted contributions on the subject from Mühl,[58] from Münch (writing as "Photophilus" or "Non-Partisan"),[59] from a number of anonymities,[60] and from Koch. The latter outdid himself and the other opponents of "the Evil Seven." The assertion that "where there is much religion, there is little civic virtue," was merely the introduction to the following characterization: "A parson occupies a place among humanity similar to that occupied among the animals by one which does not till the soil, like the ox, does not carry loads, like the ass, does not bark at thieves, like the dog, but which, like the tiger, tears and devours everything about it." [61] A show of impartiality was maintained in the *Anzeiger* by printing also some replies to this concerted attack,[62] but the language of both the

---

[56] *Anzeiger des Westens,* April 28, 1842.

[57] *Ibid.*, Nov. 9, 1844. See also *ibid.*, April 30, May 26, Aug. 6, 1842, May 25, 1843.

[58] *Ibid.*, Dec. 15, 1841, March 5, 1842.

[59] *Ibid.*, Aug. 20, 1842, Jan. 7, 1843.

[60] *Ibid.*, March 9, 10, 12, April 23, May 26, June 29, July 2, 1842.

[61] *Ibid.*, Nov. 24, 1842. See also *ibid.*, Dec. 22, 1841, June 8, Aug. 3, 1842.

[62] *Ibid.*, Jan. 26, June 1, July 7, 28, 30, Aug. 24, Sept. 1, 1842.

editors of the *Anzeiger* and the other opponents of the *Kirchenverein* was such that the pastors, with the exception of one diffident attempt by Pastor Garlichs, chose not to enter the fray.[63] The controversy over the *Kirchenverein* helped to break up Wall's congregation.[64] When the Saxons, both during Stephan's tenure of office and thereafter, thought that an episcopal polity would give them standing in the community, impress their new environment favorably, and provide an ideal church organization for a new Zion in the West, they merely demonstrated their innocence of any knowledge of actual conditions and of the temper of the people.

The presssure of attacks from without and the weaknesses of organization and personnel within combined to allow the *Kirchenverein* only a very troubled existence at first. Within the first three years two members had to be asked by the body to resign. By 1844 the association consisted of only six members. Within six years five of the eight charter members had withdrawn. Heyer had joined the Presbyterians by 1845. Garlichs eventually became a member of the Synod of Pennsylvania and the New York Ministerium. However, replacements were relatively easy to get. Thirty pastors were admitted during the first decade of the *Kirchenverein's* existence, and by 1850 it had churches in Missouri, Illinois, Indiana, Iowa, and Louisiana.[65]

From the foregoing it is apparent that there was no lack of religious activity in St. Louis when the Saxons arrived. On the contrary, the competition was already rather keen, notwithstanding a widespread spirit of unionism that embraced all denominations except the Roman Catholics and, after 1839, the Lutherans.[66] Therefore, Marbach, who was appointed to make the arrangements for the Saxons' first service in St. Louis, did not face an easy task. The German congregation, for instance, which might have been expected to be the most obliging to the immigrants, adopted a hostile attitude. Not to be discouraged, Marbach approached also the Episcopal congregation in St. Louis and petitioned for the use of its new church, dedicated as recently as February 17, 1839, and probably the finest

---

63 *Ibid.*, June 15, 1842.

64 *Ibid.*, Nov. 24, 26, Dec. 3, 6, 1842, Jan. 24, 1843.

65 Schneider, *op. cit.*, 135—137, 141, 161. On the later expansion of the *Kirchenverein*, see *ibid.*, 164—193.

66 *Anzeiger des Westens*, July 10, Oct. 30, 1845; *Die Deutsche Tribüne*, July 10, 19, Aug. 5, 1846; *Daily Missouri Republican*, Nov. 25, 1839.

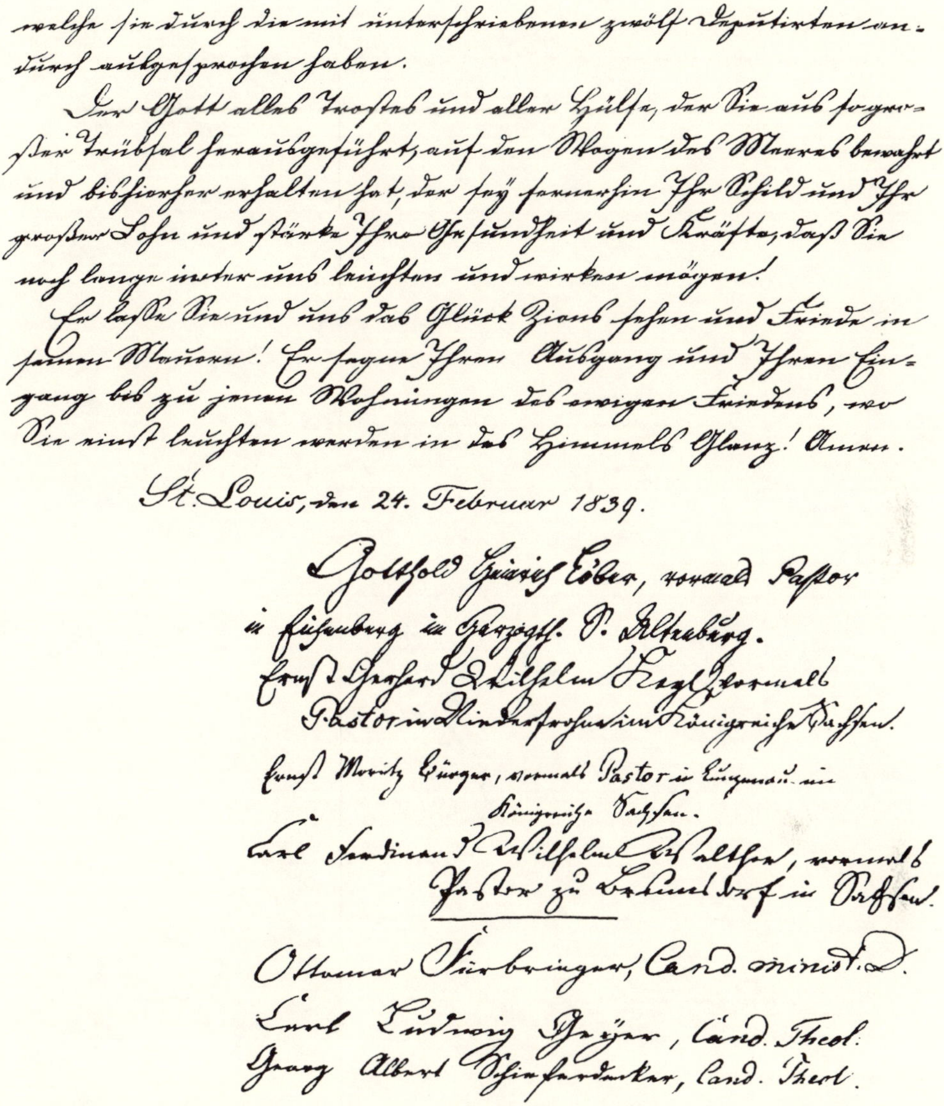
welche Sie durch die mit unterschriebenen zwölf Deputirten an-
durch ausgesprochen haben.

Der Gott alles Trostes und aller Hülfe, der Sie aus so gro-
ßer Trübsal herausgeführt, auf den Wogen des Meeres bewahrt
und bisher erhalten hat, der sey fernerhin Ihr Schild und Ihr
großer Lohn und stärke Ihre Gesundheit und Kräfte, daß Sie
noch lange unter uns leuchten und wirken mögen!

Er lasse Sie und uns das Glück Zions sehen und Friede in
seinen Mauern! Er segne Ihren Ausgang und Ihren Ein-
gang bis zu jenen Wohnungen des ewigen Friedens, wo
Sie einst leuchten werden in des Himmels Glanz! Amen.

St. Louis, den 24. Februar 1839.

Gotthold Heinrich Löber, vormals Pastor
in Eichenberg im Herzogth. S. Altenburg.
Ernst Gerhard Wilhelm Keyl, vormals
Pastor in Niederfrohna im Königreiche Sachsen.
Ernst Moritz Bürger, vormals Pastor in Lunzenau im
Königreiche Sachsen.
Carl Ferdinand Wilhelm Walther, vormals
Pastor zu Bräunsdorf in Sachsen.
Ottomar Fürbringer, Cand. minist. D.
Carl Ludwig Geyer, Cand. Theol.
Georg Albert Schieferdecker, Cand. Theol.

Signatures on the "Confirmation of Stephan's Investiture." Note signature of of C. F. W. Walther. (See pages 299—301)

PLATE XV

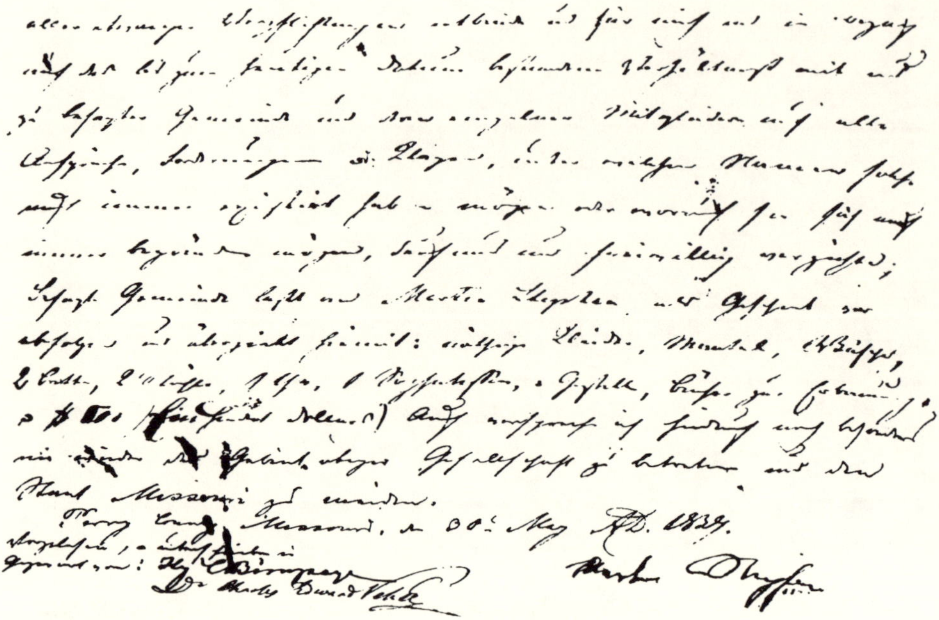

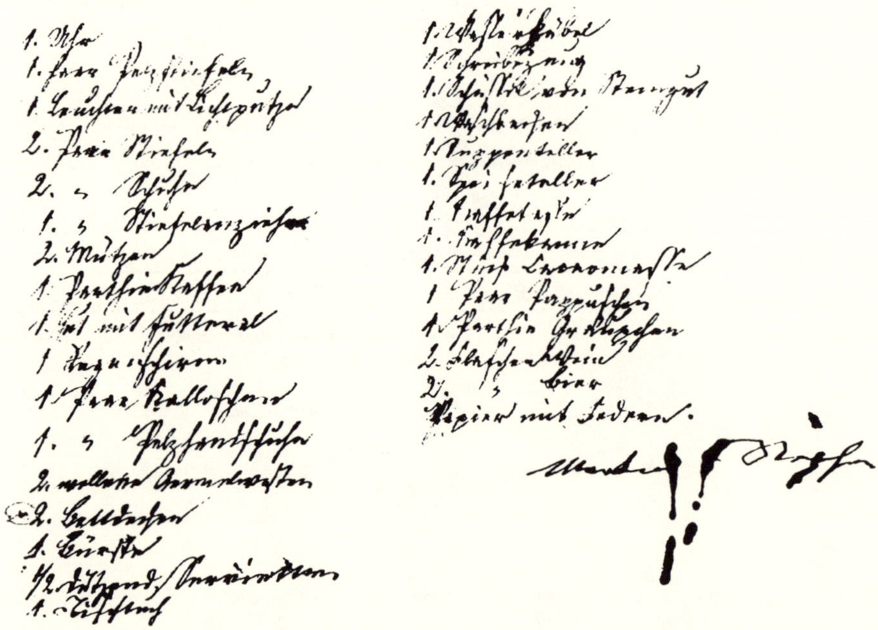

Stephan's signatures on the documents separating him from the Gesellschaft: *Above, the renunciation of claims; below, the list of effects Stephan was permitted to keep. (See pages 420—422)*

PLATE XVI

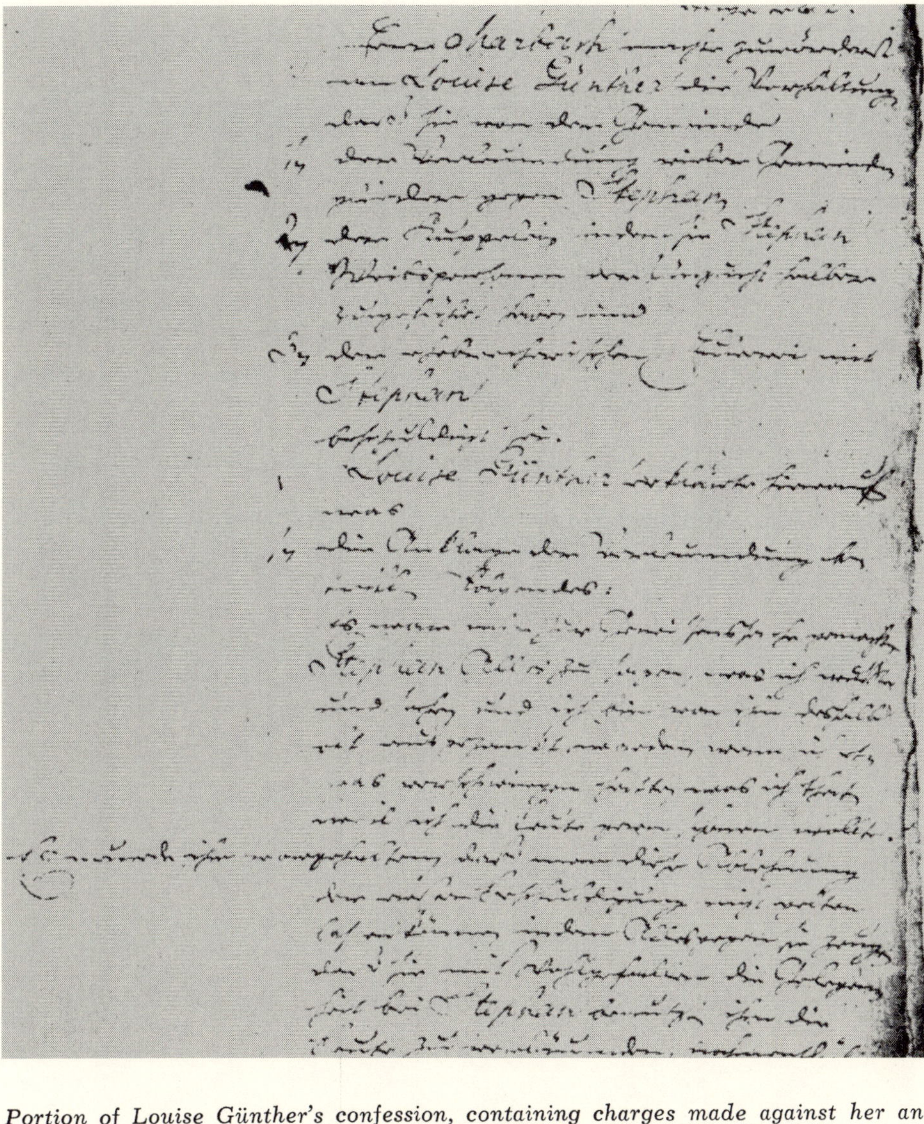

Portion of Louise Günther's confession, containing charges made against her and Stephan by the leaders of the Gesellschaft. *(See pages 426, 427)*

PLATE XVII

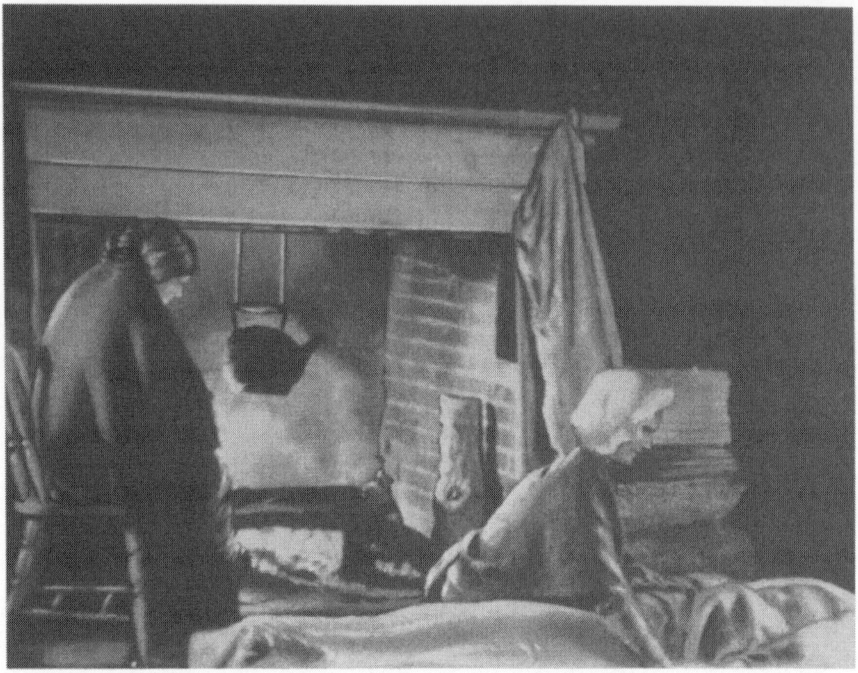

Sickbed scene from centennial film Call of the Cross, *1938*
(See pages 331, 450)

PLATE XVIII

Protestant house of worship in the city.[67] The request was granted by the vestry and announced to his congregation by Bishop Kemper in an oft-quoted statement that constituted one of the most cordial welcomes extended to the Saxons anywhere,[68] not even excepting the *New York Observer's* "Welcome, thrice welcome to our shores are all emigrants of this character." [69]

Two circumstances should not go unmentioned in connection with this action of the Episcopalians. First, the kindness of the congregation, while commendable even under favorable conditions, was especially noteworthy in view of the fact that at this time the Saxons were by no means enjoying an untarnished reputation. The derogatory comments of and in the *Anzeiger* had begun, and, as just mentioned, Holy Ghost Congregation, composed of their own compatriots from overseas, had no use for these conservatives, nor any thought of extending a similar courtesy as was sought from the English congregation. Secondly, the benefactions of Christ Church were coupled with a remarkable patience. For approximately three and one-half years, until the immigrants had succeeded in erecting their own place of worship, the use of Christ Church was extended to them by this same congregation, often at the cost of serious inconvenience to the latter. On the ultimate significance of this action, W. B. Stevens expressed himself as follows:

> The act of church hospitality on the part of Christ Church was fraught with great consequence, material as well as spiritual, to St. Louis. It added to and helped to assimilate one of the most desirable elements of the population. It helped to make the city not only nationally but internationally the capital of a powerful religious organization. A college, a theological seminary, a publishing house, a hospital were established.[70]

Accordingly, on March 3, 1839, the entire *Gesellschaft* assembled for the first time in St. Louis in Christ Church to hear the newly

---

[67] G. Günther, *op. cit.*, 49.

[68] Nachrichten an unsere Nachkommen, Announcement by Bishop Kemper granting use of Christ Church to the Saxons, MSS., C. H. I. The text of this announcement is quoted in Scharf, *op. cit.*, II, 1735; Stevens, *St. Louis the Fourth City* 1764—1909, I, 729—730; Schuyler, *Historical Discourses*, 27; Schneider, *op. cit.*, 103; *Der Lutheraner*, LXXIV, 437; P. Kretzmann, "The *Saxon Immigration to Missouri*, 1838—1839," *Missouri Historical Review*, XXXIII, 162—163.

[69] *New York Observer*, March 16, 1839.

[70] Stevens, *Centennial History of Missouri*, 316.

elected Bishop who, thanks to his suspension from office in Saxony and the journey of several months, had not officiated at a public service for sixteen months. Besides the Saxons a considerable number of visitors from the St. Louis public, primarily representing the German element, also were present.[71] The notices in the English press continued to be uniformly favorable. Two days after this memorable service both the *Daily Missouri Republican* and the *Daily Evening Gazette* carried a brief report of the event and reiterated their welcome to the Saxons in these words:

> Christ's Church, in this city, was appropriated in the afternoon of Sunday last, to the use of a Lutheran Congregation, recently from Saxony. They are a part of a colony of seven hundred — more than one half of whom are yet to arrive — at the head of which is a Bishop, Priests, etc. This is the first time for three months that they have been able to join in the worship of their church, and the ceremonies are said to have been deeply interesting.[72]
>
> On Sunday afternoon last, a very novel and interesting spectacle was witnessed by the assembling together of the large number of *German Lutherans,* who have lately arrived here.
>
> The use of CHRIST CHURCH being kindly granted them by the Wordens [*sic*] and Vestry, they held their services in that spacious building, commencing at 2 o'clock. They are attended by a Bishop and several Priests; and their service, which is liturgical and in their native tongue, was both solemn and interesting.
>
> Having left their native land for conscience's sake — being persecuted by the Government, on account of their religious opinions — they have come among us; and it is well that they should be allowed the privilege of worshipping God agreeably to the dictates of their own consciences.
>
> A more respectable and intelligent looking body of foreigners, I venture to say, has never before been seen in this part of the country. — Throughout the service, which was

---

[71] G. H. Löber, Diary, March 3, 1839, MS., C. H. I.; Winter to Guericke *et al.*, April 28, 1841, *Zeitschrift für die gesammte lutherische Theologie und Kirche*, II, No. 3, pp. 116—132; G. Günther, *op. cit.*, 49. Communion services, attended by virtually the entire congregation, were held later that same week. G. H. Löber, Diary, March 6, 7, 1839, MS., C. H. I.

[72] *Daily Missouri Republican,* March 5, 1839. The incorrect figure on expected arrivals shows how exaggerated ideas of their numbers became current. The *New York Observer* of March 16, 1839, said that only 250 had arrived on that date and 600 more were expected.

> quite protracted, they maintained a deportment, tending to inspire a confidence in the reality of their professions and the worth of their characters.[73]

Despite these evidences of cordiality, Stephan's oratorical efforts on this occasion were a rather dismal failure. That he would be unsuccessful in making a favorable impression upon Koch and his kind was probably to be expected. But he also disappointed some of his own people. In the succeeding months Stephan preached only infrequently. When he did take the pulpit, his discourses continued to be liberally interspersed with rantings at his own followers. The Bishop claimed his people doubted, even slandered him, and he asserted that, while he was used to bearing trials, he could not tolerate such degradation of his office.[74] However, usually the pastors took turns in preaching, thereby relieving Stephan of his homiletic duties and the people of the necessity of listening to his diatribes. Strangely enough, neither these outbursts nor even the offering of prayers for Stephan and his "divinely appointed task of the emigration," could dissuade the interested citizens of St. Louis from continuing to attend these services which were held in the basement of Christ Church.[75]

One admirer even became lyric under the stimulus of his Christian fraternalism and a dedication to religious tolerance which the subject of his efforts can hardly be said to have shared. And if the facts were not quite accurate, the spirit was liberal, the sentiment was true, and the vision was more prophetic than either he or the Saxons were to realize for many a year. The Missouri muse had written thus:

> Mr. Editor: — The following lines were suggested by seeing the numerous body of German emigrants engaged in worship, in Christ Church.
>
> Brothers in heart and hand,
> Welcome to this our land!
> Welcome where freedom *fills* her vast abode!
> Accepted as the hymn of praise to God!
> For o'er the troubled deep

---

[73] *Daily Evening Gazette*, March 5, 1839.

[74] J. K. A. Höhne and J. G. Höhne to their brother, Sept. 26, 1841, quoted in *Die Ameise*, Jan. 10, 1842.

[75] Winter to Guericke *et al.*, April 28, 1841, *Zeitschrift für die gesammte lutherische Theologie und Kirche*, II, No. 3, pp. 116—132.

From scenes of early love, from joys and tears,
From homes still hallowed by the love of years,
　　Ye turned away to weep!
　　Yet in high purpose strong.
E'en from the graves of buried sires ye turned
And on strange altars pour the hearts that burned,
　　And chant the holy song!
　　Here can ye rest in peace!
　　Here may your sorrows cease!
No tyrant dare uplift the avenging rod!
No priesthood dictate how to worship God!
Welcome to prairies green, to woods and streams
Fairer than ever blest your brightest dreams.

IONE

St. Louis, March 6th, 1839.[76]

---

[76] *Daily Evening Gazette,* March 7, 1839.

CHAPTER THIRTEEN

PROBLEMS OF COMMUNAL LIVING IN ST. LOUIS

WHILE STEPHAN was holding his episcopal court and living in style, the rank and file of the Stephanites were eking out a rather miserable existence. For a few days after the *Selma* had arrived, the weather was pleasant and the temperature mild. Then it became bitterly cold, snow fell, and the immigrants began to suffer real hardships.[1] The causes for their sufferings were many: the economic conditions of the time and resulting high prices; the inadequate housing facilities of St. Louis and its poor health conditions; the sickness rampant among the Saxons when they arrived and the fact that the financial resources of the *Gesellschaft* were rapidly ebbing; and finally, inexperienced leadership.

When the Saxons arrived, St. Louis, the West, and in fact the entire country were still in the throes of the depression which followed upon the heels of the Panic of 1837.[2] Everyone, including the immigrants, agreed that times were hard and prices high. Slogans were as prevalent as a century later. The *Daily Pennant's* diagnosis of the economic ills of the day described as the worst of them: *"Confidence is destroyed."*[3] So far as the monetary situation was concerned, this lack of confidence was justified. Illinois money was worth about 50 cents on the dollar in March, 1842. Three months later, St. Louis notes, usually comparatively sound, were passing at a 10- to 15-per-cent discount, and in October were down to 60 cents. Under such sharp declines the laboring class suffered most acutely.[4] Indiana accepted coonskins in payment of taxes, and the *Anzeiger des Westens,* which considered pelts much sounder exchange than bank notes, accepted furs in payment for its sub-

---

[1] Winter to Guericke *et al.*, April 28, 1841, *Zeitschrift für die gesammte lutherische Theologie und Kirche,* II, No. 3, pp. 116—132; J. K. A. Höhne and J. G. Höhne to their brother, Sept. 26, 1841, quoted in *Die Ameise,* Jan. 10, 1842.

[2] Bauer, "Crisis — 1837," *Lutheran Witness,* LVII, 121—122.

[3] *Daily Pennant,* May 28, 1840.

[4] *Anzeiger des Westens,* March 3, June 1, Oct. 18, 1842.

scriptions.[5] The confusion in the field of finance caused not only chaos in the business world, but actual privation among the poorer and middle classes.

Prices on commodities in St. Louis fluctuated more with the seasons than from year to year. Because of different conditions of supply and demand, the cost of these items in comparison with each other was very different than it is today. Manufactured articles, such as clothes, were especially expensive, and half boots sold normally at $5.00 to $9.00.[6] Potatoes brought $3.00 a bushel, green apples $2.50, and flour $4.50 a barrel. But mutton and veal were 6 to 8 cents a pound, beef only 5 to 6 cents, and butter 9 to 12 cents, while eggs sold for 8 cents a dozen and milk for 6½ cents a quart.[7] If Günther can be relied upon, some of these prices seem to have been somewhat different in 1839,[8] but those given here are average for the period of the next few years. According to the standards of that day such prices were not unusually low, and if the immigrant had been under the impression — as the Saxons were at one time — that he could live inexpensively in St. Louis, he was soon disillusioned. Interest rates in St. Louis, normally 10 per cent, were among the highest in the country. In New York they were only 5 per cent.[9] Returns on some investments were fantastically high. The St. Louis Insurance Company, for instance, declared dividends of 10 per cent for a three-month period in 1845.[10]

The Stephanites had been warned that St. Louis did not offer adequate housing facilities. Of course, the arrival of only some six hundred Saxons over a period of more than a month can scarcely have caused "considerable commotion" [11] in a city whose population was frequently augmented by more than 10 per cent in a few days and which absorbed as many as 1,526 travelers and immigrants in a single day by 1844.[12] Nevertheless, the Saxons soon

---

5 *Ibid.*, Jan. 9, Feb. 23, 1842.

6 Winter to Guericke *et al.*, April 28, 1841, *Zeitschrift für die gesammte lutherische Theologie und Kirche*, II, No. 3, pp. 116—132.

7 *Anzeiger des Westens*, Nov. 2, 1844; *Daily Evening Gazette*, June 8, 1844.

8 G. Günther, *op. cit.*, 33—34.

9 *Daily Missouri Republican*, July 10, 1846.

10 *Ibid.*, Sept. 4, 1845.

11 P. Kretzmann, "The Saxon Immigration to Missouri, 1838—1839," *Missouri Historical Review*, XXXIII, 162.

12 *St. Louis New Era*, April 20, 1844.

found that the warning had not been without foundation. As early as 1838 the immigrant and transient population of St. Louis kept the city in a chronic state of overpopulation with its attendant evils.[13] Thousands came each month, at times each week, either to stay or to use the city as a temporary base before penetrating into the plains and prairies of the Midwest for the conquest of vast uninhabited areas in a half-dozen neighboring States and Territories. The majority of these immigrants, especially after 1840, came via New Orleans. But considerable numbers also reached St. Louis after traveling overland or on river boats from the Eastern seaboard States. Thus in 1844, seven or eight thousand of the immigrants that arrived in St. Louis had come by way of New York.[14] On Löber's first day in St. Louis he wrote that in this city there was "a veritable confluence of emigrants, so that from Pittsburgh alone 15 boats are still expected this week, wherefore lodging was rather expensive." [15]

St. Louis' hotels, of which there were nine as early at 1838,[16] and its numerous boardinghouses were usually filled to overflowing.[17] In 1839 the cost of a room was $5.00 to $7.00 weekly,[18] a considerable drain on the resources of the average immigrant if he was unable to secure employment for several weeks, or even months. But housing facilities were scarcely adequate and comparatively high-priced even for the stationary population. Lyford in 1837 generalized on his travels: "Board at hotels is from $2.00 to $2.50 per day — and the farther west a person travels, the more indifferent I have found them." [19] Stevens quotes an opinion by the Rev. Dr. Humphrey from his *Letters by the Way* that applies directly to St. Louis in 1839:

> Rents are enormously high, higher than in any Eastern city, not excepting New York itself, and I believe higher than anywhere else on the continent of America. For a handsome two-

---

[13] Keemle, *The St. Louis Directory, for the Years 1838—9,* v; Kargau, *op. cit.,* 22.

[14] *Anzeiger des Westens*, March 20, 1845.

[15] G. H. Löber to relatives in Germany, Jan. 30, 1839, in Löber-Eichenberg (ed.), "Ein Briefwechsel," *Mitteilungen . . . Kahla,* VII, 147—148.

[16] Keemle, *The St. Louis Directory, for the Years 1838—9*, p. 67.

[17] *People's Organ*, June 11, 1842; *Daily People's Organ,* June 18, July 21, 1842; *Daily Evening Gazette*, July 1, 1843.

[18] Winter to Guericke *et al.*, April 28, 1841, *Zeitschrift für die gesammte lutherische Theologie und Kirche,* II, No. 3, pp. 116—132.

[19] Lyford, *The Western Address Directory,* 400.

> story brick house with one parlor in front, you would have to pay seven or eight hundred dollars per annum.[20]

Throughout the period from 1838 to 1847 house rents continued to range from $350 to over $500 a year and were constantly complained of as high or as "still higher than in any other town in the union." [21]

Under such circumstances returns on real estate investments ranged from 8 or 10 per cent to as high as 20 or even 40 per cent.[22] Landlords could well afford a "war against babies," by which the *Weekly Reveille* meant refusal to accept as tenants families with children.[23] Although some land was deliberately held for speculation,[24] most owners of real estate preferred to capitalize upon the situation and garner the attractive returns land was bringing. Prices ranged from $52 per foot of frontage on Third Street, between Mulberry and Lombard, in 1841, or $55 on Walnut, between Second and Third Streets, in 1844, to $400 per foot on Water Street in 1840, and $33 per foot for a one-year lease on Fourth Street property in 1846.[25] The highest price for several years was reported in 1847, when lots on Front Street, facing the river, sold for $500 per foot. During the same year, however, lots outside the city limits were still selling for $5 to $60 per foot, depending on the location.[26]

Building activity bordered on the phenomenal for a city the size of St. Louis. The general trend of residential construction was northward from the city, while South St. Louis, the original home of the French settlers, was, by 1839, the coming industrial section.[27] In both 1844 and 1845 about 1,200 houses were built in

---

[20] W. Stevens (comp.), *The Building of St. Louis*, 43.

[21] *Daily Evening Gazette*, Jan. 23, 1840. See also *Missouri Argus*, Nov. 9, 16, 1838; *People's Organ*, June 11, 1842; *Daily Missouri Republican*, April 11, July 9, Sept. 10, 1844; *St. Louis New Era*, April 20, 1843, Jan. 25, 1845; *St. Louis Daily New Era*, Jan. 6, March 10, 1846; Winter to Guericke *et al.*, April 28, 1841, *Zeitschrift für die gesammte lutherische Theologie und Kirche*, II, No. 3, pp. 116—132.

[22] *Evening Gazette*, July 20, 1838; *Daily Missouri Republican*, April 11, 1844.

[23] *Weekly Reveille*, Nov. 24, 1845.

[24] *St. Louis New Era*, Jan. 28, 1845.

[25] *Ibid.*, Sept. 23, 1840, Aug. 28, 1841, April 24, 1844; *St. Louis Daily New Era*, March 7, 1846.

[26] *St. Louis Business Directory, for 1847*, p. 97.

[27] *Weekly Reveille*, Oct. 27, 1845; *Anzeiger des Westens*, Feb. 27, 1845; Flagg, *op. cit.*, I, 117; Keemle, *The St. Louis Directory, for the Years 1838—9*, vi; Stevens (comp.), *The Building of St. Louis*, 43.

St. Louis, half of them constructed of brick. About 42,000,000 bricks were used in St. Louis annually at that time, many of them produced in the thirty St. Louis brickyards.[28] Estimates of the number of new buildings constructed the next year, 1846, ran as high as 1,700 or even two thousand.[29] By 1847 more of the city's 6,641 buildings were of brick than of any other material. The majority were two-story structures, some three- and four-story.[30] The assessed valuation of property in the city rose from $8,682,506 in 1840 to $11,721,425 in 1843, and from that figure to $13,900,000 in 1844, and $15,055,720 in 1846.[31]

The Saxons were confronted by the housing problem immediately upon arrival. In an effort to meet the difficulty as economically as possible, the immigrants rented houses into which both the married and unmarried were grouped, in order to avoid the high prices for individual room rents or for separate houses for each family. The exact arrangements as to numbers, sex, marital status, and age are known in only a very few cases, particularly as the costs of board and lodging were defrayed from the common treasury. Later the costs for these items were apportioned to individuals,[32] but at this time the cost for rent and food was defrayed from the dwindling Credit Fund. If it is remembered that all persons involved were single and included members of the highly respected clergy, it may be indicative of the conditions to remark that one house on Broadway Street, rented for $25 a month from Charles R. Anderson, was occupied by seven adults and one child, namely: "P. Walther" (in all probability C. F. W. Walther), Örtel, Brohm, Schütz, Vehse, Jäckel, Mathilde Schütz, and Mathilde Vehse.[33] Less-distinguished persons did not fare nearly so well.

According to members of the Advisory Committee, the Credit Fund had to meet a monthly bill of about $1,500 for board and

---

28 *Daily Missouri Republican*, Sept. 10, 1844, Feb. 25, Oct. 24, 1845; *Weekly Reveille*, Jan. 27, 1845; *Missouri Reporter*, July 28, 1845.

29 *Anzeiger des Westens*, Jan. 6, 1846; *St. Louis Daily New Era*, Sept. 30, 1846; *St. Louis Daily Union*, Dec. 16, 1846.

30 *St. Louis Daily New Era*, March 3, 1847.

31 *Anzeiger des Westens*, May 30, 1843; *Missouri Reporter*, May 29, 1843; *Annual Review . . . From the Missouri Republican, January 10, 1854*, pp. 8—9; Taylor-Crooks, *op. cit.*, 16.

32 Rent receipt, Charles R. Anderson to Örtel, April 13, 1839, MS., C. H. I.

33 *Ibid.*

lodging.[34] In its anemic condition such a drain did the treasury of the Saxons no good, and yet the figure is startlingly low. It is about as easy to understand how six hundred people could subsist on $1,500 as it is to imagine how the Credit Fund could afford such a sum. The only relief came from the small wages that members of the *Gesellschaft* paid into the treasury when they were fortunate enough to get a few odd jobs. This amount, for various reasons, can never have been very high.

Exactly what proportion of the $1,500 was expended for either lodging or food is not known. G. Günther claimed that the bill for rentals was "5—600 Dollars" monthly and that six to eight single people or several families occupied the same quarters.[35] Either Günther was, contrary to his usual custom, indulging in an understatement, or his figures indicate that barely $1.00 a month per person was used for rentals. This average, of course, seems microscopic. The minimum monthly rental for even a modest house was, as stated above, $25 or more. The appropriation of the *Gesellschaft,* according to Günther, would have procured only twenty-four such houses, each of which would then have had to accommodate twenty-five people. This figure constitutes a serious conflict with his other statements. However, an assignment of eight people to each house would have meant that an average of only $7.50 monthly could have been spent for the individual residence rented. The inadequacy of this amount, under prevailing conditions, is obvious.

The difficulty is that even Günther's low estimate of the expenditure for rental leaves only about $1.50 a month for food per person. It is necessary to accept the figure of $600 for lodging or to assume that the average immigrant was allowed less than 5 cents a day for food. Either assumption is equally incredible, although one of them must be true. In general, a comparison of the prevailing prices given above on both housing and food with what was spent by the Saxons makes it clear that they were miserably fed and probably even more poorly housed. Little wonder that to his followers — even the more favored — the $20-a-month apartment of the Bishop appeared sumptuous and his bill of fare represented extravagance! From any viewpoint, provisions for the physical well-

[34] Minutes of a meeting between Vehse, Jäckel, and Stephan, March 14, 1839, MS., C. H. I.

[35] G. Günther, *op. cit.,* 32.

being of the members of the *Gesellschaft* were inadequate. This inference is substantiated by the immigrants themselves, who reported that many of them were living in poorly constructed board houses which offered little protection against the cold.[36] Less was said by the Stephanites about the food they were given, but this became the subject of public debate in the press.

It is also reasonable to suppose that even such shelters as the *Gesellschaft* provided were not properly heated. The high price and scarcity of fuel was a constant source of annoyance and hardship to the people of St. Louis, and must have been a more serious problem for the immigrant. The papers charged that fuel was maintained at what they considered its exorbitant price level partly by poor transportation facilities, but mainly by collusion between dealers and producers.[37] Wood usually sold at $6.00 to $8.00 a cord.[38] Coal might sell for 15 cents a bushel, but could range upward to 18, 20, 25, 37½, or even 50 cents a bushel.[39] As a last resort, despite its abundance in the immediate vicinity, e. g., in the southern Illinois coal fields, fuel was shipped in from considerable distances on river boats.[40] Meanwhile, however, the immigrant, like the native St. Louisan, paid the price or froze — often the latter.

Other factors were equally dangerous to the Saxons from the standpoint of health. Despite intermittent attempts by St. Louis papers to deny conditions,[41] they usually had to admit that the community deserved its reputation as one of the most unhealthful cities in the world.[42] The death rate for the decade of the forties was approximately one in 23,[43] while in New Orleans it was only one in 54, in Charleston one in 52.18, in Boston one in 44.1, in

---

[36] Winter to Guericke *et al.*, April 28, 1841, *Zeitschrift für die gesammte lutherische Theologie und Kirche*, II, No. 3, pp. 116—132.

[37] *Daily Missouri Republican*, Dec. 3, 1845, Oct. 21, 1846; *St. Louis Daily New Era*, Oct. 2, 4, 13, 1846.

[38] *Daily Missouri Republican*, Dec. 3, 1845; *Täglicher Anzeiger des Westens*, March 12, 1847; Lenz, *op. cit.*, 45.

[39] *Daily Missouri Republican*, Oct. 21, 1846; *St. Louis Daily Union*, Dec. 3, 1845, Oct. 28, 1846, March 3, 11, 1847; *Täglicher Anzeiger des Westens*, March 3, 1847; G. Günther, *op. cit.*, 34.

[40] *Täglicher Anzeiger das Westens*, May 1, 1846.

[41] *Daily Missouri Republican*, Aug. 16, Sept. 6, 1844.

[42] *St. Louis New Era*, March 23, 1844; *Daily Missouri Republican*, July 17, 1844; *Weekly Reveille*, June 23, 1845; G. Günther, *op. cit.*, 34.

[43] *Weekly Reveille*, June 23, 1845; *St. Louis Daily Union*, Feb. 8, 1846; Moore, *Vital Statistics of St. Louis since 1840*, pp. 301—317.

Chicago one in 41.08.[44] Especially among the children the toll was appalling. Twenty-five per cent of them died in their first year, 40 per cent by the fifth year.[45] Frequently children under seven years of age formed more than half of the city's high total of deaths for a year! [46] Sometimes a majority of the deaths occurred among children up to only five years of age.[47] In fact, during the warmer months of the year children less than five years old usually accounted for at least 50 per cent of the death rate, often more.[48] The prevalence of disease and death was attributed in part to the large transient population of the city, and the figures for 1844—1845 seem partly to bear out this claim.[49]

Until 1846 the only hospital in the city was that on Spruce Street between Third and Fourth Streets, conducted by a Catholic order, the Sisters of Charity. Although $12,000 to $15,000 annually was paid these Sisters of Charity by the city to take care of all its patients, the service rendered was still far from adequate.[50] Finally the city decided to build a hospital, which was opened on August 20, 1846, and completed the following year.[51] Charitable institutions, in fact, were few. One Catholic and several Protestant orphans' societies before 1847 maintained homes, and there were several "Benevolent Associations." [52] A county poor farm, moved to the

---

[44] *St. Louis Daily Union,* Feb. 8, 1846.

[45] *Täglicher Anzeiger des Westens,* Sept. 9, 1846.

[46] *St. Louis New Era,* March 23, 1844; *Täglicher Anzeiger des Westens,* July 24, 1847; Green, *St. Louis Directory . . . 1845,* xxii—xxiv.

[47] Mitchell, "Disease Statistics of St. Louis for 1845," *Missouri Medical and Surgical Journal,* I, 269.

[48] *Anzeiger des Westens,* July 27, Aug. 19, 26, Sept. 2, 9, 1843; *Missouri Reporter,* Aug. 3, 1843; *Daily Missouri Republican,* July 9, 1845; *Die Deutsche Tribüne,* Aug. 1, 1845.

[49] *Daily Missouri Republican,* June 11, 1845; *St. Louis American,* Sept. 5, 1846; *St. Louis Daily New Era,* Sept. 7, 1846; *St. Louis Daily Union,* March 12, 1847.

[50] *Anzeiger des Westens,* Aug. 9, 1845; Skillman, *op. cit.,* 86; Keemle, *The St. Louis Directory, for the Years 1838-9,* p. 61.

[51] *Anzeiger des Westens,* Aug. 9, 1845; *Daily Missouri Republican,* Oct. 3, 1845; *St. Louis Daily New Era,* Aug. 19, 1846; *Täglicher Anzeiger des Westens,* Aug. 20, 1846; *Annual Review . . . From the Missouri Republican, January 10, 1854,* p. 10.

[52] *Daily Evening Gazette,* May 31, 1841; *Daily Missouri Republican,* June 24, 1845; *The St. Louis Directory, for the year 1842,* ix; Keemle, *The St. Louis Directory, for the Years 1838—9,* pp. 60—61; Keemle, *The St. Louis Directory, for the Year 1840—1,* p. 75; Mangold, "Social Reforms in Missouri 1820—1920," *Missouri Historical Review,* XV, 207.

buildings of former Kemper College during this period, was also in operation.

As a breeder of disease, probably few things in St. Louis surpassed the city's streets. Like a number of other matters mentioned, the streets were a perpetual source of complaint in the newspapers, as well they might be. Unpaved for the greater part, their surface seemed always to be either quagmires or lanes of choking dust; the repository for most of the city's garbage, and yet without sewage facilities or sidewalks, they were strong contributors to the high St. Louis death rate.[53] In 1845, when the city ordinance was passed banning pigs from the streets, the *Anzeiger des Westens* remarked that the best part of the city health department was being abolished.[54]

Under such circumstances it was only to be expected that although vaccination was practiced, epidemics of smallpox as well as epidemics of influenza, cholera, fever — especially in the warmer months — and other diseases would be common.[55] The simplest principles of sanitation were unknown or ignored. Cellars were permitted to remain filled with stagnant water almost indefinitely. Dead dogs and other animals were left lying in the streets or were thrown into a pit in Lucas Grove, to fill the air with their stench. The decaying carcass of a horse or some other animal might occasionally be left lying in Franklin Avenue. The final touch to this picture is provided by the fact that these streets were innocent of the convenience of an omnibus, until hourly service between Market Street and the Arsenal was begun in 1844.[56]

The results of these conditions for the immigrants were summed up by John Hogan in his *Thoughts about St. Louis* with the words:

> . . . the great influx of foreigners, who came here, many of them diseased, all of them unacclimated, subject to great

---

53 *Daily Commercial Bulletin*, June 25, 1840; *Daily Evening Gazette*, Dec. 2, 1841; *Daily People's Organ*, Aug. 13, 1842, April 16, 1844; *Anzeiger des Westens*, Aug. 17, 1843; *St. Louis New Era*, Feb. 28, 1844; *Daily Missouri Republican*, Aug. 17, 1844; *St. Louis Daily New Era*, Jan. 24, 26, July 1, 1846; *Weekly Reveille*, June 29, 1846; *Missouri Reporter*, Aug. 15, 1846.

54 *Anzeiger des Westens*, May 3, 1845.

55 *Ibid.*, March 19, Aug. 6, 1842, Feb. 11, July 15, Aug. 17, 1843, Dec. 25, 1845; *Daily People's Organ*, Jan. 15, 1844.

56 *Daily Missouri Republican*, Aug. 17, 1844; *St. Louis New Era*, June 17, 1843, May 30, June 20, 1844; *St. Louis Daily New Era*, April 22, June 4, 1846; *Anzeiger des Westens*, Jan. 7, March 11, 1845; *Annual Review . . . From the Missouri Republican, January 10, 1854*, p. 19.

> changes in water, in food, in habits, must necessarily produce among them great suffering, eventuating, in many cases, in death. . . .
>
> It is not to be forgotten, either, that in consequence of the great scarcity of houses, the apparent inability to supply the demand, very often the newly arrived emigrants are huddled together in rooms too small for the accommodation of one-fifth of the number; and such places became, in consequence, the nurseries of disease and death. . . .[57]

Hogan might well have been speaking of the Saxons. As noted before, many were ill when they arrived in St. Louis. Now, as a result of the change in climate, the severe weather conditions they happened to encounter, poor living conditions, and improper municipal health protection, many more became sick. Numbers of them died during the very first months in this country, while they were still in St. Louis. Twenty people whom Winter knew personally died shortly after their arrival.[58] On the number of deaths during this period neither this figure nor any other that could be arrived at in the course of this study is accurate; but it is indicative. An estimate can be made on the basis of data supplied by Löber. In reporting to his family in Germany, he mentioned eight people who had died before May 30.[59] However, in doing so, he apparently was mentioning only those who would be known to his relatives. His diary yields the names of eleven in his group who died between February 22 and April 30, 1839.[60] If Löber's experience is at all representative of the general mortality rate among the other groups of Saxons in St. Louis, then sixty-five or seventy of them must have died within three or four months of landing in the Missouri city, for the *Republik* carried approximately one sixth of the Stephanites who reached their destination.

In view of the rumblings of discontent which he had heard, Stephan probably feared that if some of his people had good positions when the time should come for moving the *Gesellschaft,* they might not be inclined to follow him into the wilderness. Accord-

[57] Hogan, *Thoughts about the City of St. Louis,* 22.

[58] Winter to Guericke *et al.,* April 28, 1841, *Zeitschrift für die gesammte lutherische Theologie und Kirche,* II, No. 3, pp. 116—132.

[59] G. H. Löber to relatives in Germany, Sept. 10, 30, 1839, in Löber-Eichenberg (ed.), "Ein Briefwechsel," *Mitteilungen . . . Kahla,* VII, 159.

[60] G. H. Löber, Diary, Feb. 22, 27, 28, March 23, 29, 31, April 1, 2, 7, 9, 10, 1839, MS., C. H. I.

ingly he decreed that no one should be permitted to accept work in St. Louis which bound him for more than a single day.[61] Such a policy reduced all members of the *Gesellschaft* virtually to the level of day laborers and considerably decreased their opportunity for employment as well as their potential earning capacity at a time when they sorely needed further funds. The result was that the Stephanites were even more ready than the average immigrant to take any kind of job they could get, and thereby they drew down upon themselves some rather unfavorable publicity. The plans which had been made for lodging and hiring out some of the Saxons in the environs of the city were carried out only on a small scale. Hierarchical supervision had to be maintained also over these people, so Pastor Bürger, currently in disfavor with Stephan, was removed by being placed in charge of this company.[62]

The Stephanites had given as one of their reasons for leaving Saxony their dissatisfaction with the educational policies which the Saxon government had sought to impose upon them. It is therefore of interest to note what they did with the unrestricted freedom which they enjoyed in building their own system. They began promptly enough. It is apparent from Bünger's diary that at least religious instruction was given already on the river boats in Germany as soon as the exodus began.[63] Provisions had been made in the Codes for strict supervision of the children and for daily teaching on board the ocean vessels.[64] These plans were at least partially put into effect. However, all such arrangements were makshifts that constituted little more than a demonstration of sincere purpose.

The real opportunity for formulating educational policies and placing them into operation in an actual system did not exist until the immigrants had reached Missouri. Then, however, they were virtually untrammeled in applying their ideas. That is to say, internal difficulties within the group, such as their financial circumstances, of course placed serious limitations upon their activities;

---

61 G. Günther, *op. cit.,* 89.

62 E. M. Bürger, Selbstbiographie, 124, MS., E. J. Buerger Papers, Ellicottville, N. Y.

63 J. F. Bünger, Diarium, Oct. 23—27, 1838, MS., L. Fürbringer Papers, St. Louis.

64 Traveling Regulations, Appendix B.

but there was no external interference, since private educational facilities in the West offered no formidable competition and State regulation in Missouri was virtually non-existent. These conditions encountered by the Saxons naturally influenced the development of the school system set up by them; and as this is one of their lasting contributions, the factors affecting it must be examined in some detail.

Public concern with education was in its embryonic stages in Missouri, and in the West generally, in 1839. In St. Louis a school board had been organized as early as 1833, but did not really function until 1838. An approach to an adequate system for the State was not made until the following year with the passage of the Geyer Act.[65] Public school instruction was inaugurated in St. Louis on April 2, 1838, and the next winter, when the Saxons arrived, only about 250 of the 2,800 children of elementary school age in the city attended the two public schools, that were functioning with a staff of four teachers.[66] By 1844 the number of pupils in the public schools had risen to seven hundred, but in view of the increase in population during this period it is doubtful that this figure represented any proportionate gain.[67] Despite the charge of $2.50 per quarter for most pupils even in the public schools until 1843, and notwithstanding the fact that the schools had extensive property holdings in St. Louis, the city school board was constantly in financial difficulties, and was frequently under fire from the newspapers.[68] The board paid its teachers salaries ranging from $300 to $800 a year.[69] The length of the school day varied from six

---

[65] Stevens, *St. Louis The Fourth City 1764—1909*, I, 882; Phillips, "A Century of Education in Missouri," *Missouri Historical Review*, XV, 300. See also Williams-Shoemaker, *op. cit.*, I, 290—300.

[66] Keemle, *The St. Louis Directory, for the Years 1838—9*, vii; *Daily Commercial Bulletin*, March 11, 1840; Lange, "Facts Concerning One Hundred Years of Progress in the Public Schools of St. Louis 1838—1938," *Public School Messenger*, XXXV, No. 5, p. 10.

[67] *St. Louis New Era*, March 16, 1844.

[68] *Anzeiger des Westens*, Dec. 15, 1841, Dec. 31, 1842; *Daily People's Organ*, May 18, 1843; *Daily Missouri Republican*, May 25, 1843; Lange, "Facts Concerning One Hundred Years of Progress in the Public Schools of St. Louis 1838—1938," *Public School Messenger*, XXXV, No. 5, pp. 18, 20.

[69] *St. Louis New Era*, March 16, 1844; *Die Deutsche Tribüne*, July 19, 1844. See also Lange, "Facts Concerning One Hundred Years of Progress in the Public Schools of St. Louis 1838—1938," *Public School Messenger*, XXXV, No. 5, pp. 11, 20—21.

hours in the fall and winter months to seven hours in the spring and summer.[70]

By 1846 the number of schools in St. Louis had increased to four,[71] but the lack of general interest in education was still marked. Alphonso Wetmore in 1837 optimistically declared: "It cannot be pretended that there exists a human being in the state, who is insensible to the advantages of education."[72] But the *Platte Eagle,* six years later, observed more realistically: "A most culpable apathy exists among the farmers of Upper Missouri, and we suspect in other sections of the State, as to the mental improvement of their children."[73] By 1847 only fifty-seven of the State's ninety-seven counties had applied for State grants available to them for their schools, if any.[74]

Under these circumstances Missouri's position in the literacy ratings of the States naturally was not high. In 1842 Missouri stood as low as nineteenth among the twenty-six States. Actual figures are probably only partially reliable estimates. But in that same year it was said that one in sixteen white persons in the State over twenty or twenty-one years of age was unable to read or write. By 1846 Missouri had improved its position slightly, occupying eighteenth place. Inexplicably its ratio of illiterates over twenty-one years old is supposed to have risen, at the same time, to one in seven.[75]

Fortunately attendance at the public schools was greatly exceeded during this period by enrollment in private schools, which had provided the only means of instruction before 1838. An accurate distinction between elementary and secondary schools, between high schools, colleges, and universities, is almost impossible and frequently perhaps did not really exist. There was a considerable number of such independent schools in the St. Louis area. Some

---

[70] Lange, "Facts Concerning One Hundred Years of Progress in the Public Schools of St. Louis, 1838—1938," *Public School Messenger,* XXXV, No. 5, p. 12.

[71] Skillman, *op. cit.,* 93. See also Green, *St. Louis Directory . . . 1845,* xxviii.

[72] Wetmore (comp.), *Gazetteer of the State of Missouri,* 17.

[73] Quoted in the *Daily Evening Gazette,* March 14, 1843. See also *Daily Missouri Republican,* Feb. 13, 1844.

[74] *Daily Missouri Republican,* Jan. 8, 1847.

[75] *St. Louis New Era,* Sept. 27, 1842; *Daily Evening Gazette,* July 20, 1843; *Täglicher Anzeiger des Westens,* June 10, 1846.

were strictly private ventures, with a very elastic curriculum, and were conducted by individuals, such as those of Messrs. Palos, Aikers, W. Brown, J. Deslisle, J. S. Muzzy, S. A. Holmes, M. Butler, J. Durkan, A. J. Dorn, and J. V. Shields, and Mr. and Mrs. Bonfils. Others were small colleges or universities of a more formal nature, often operated by churches or associations, like St. Louis University (Roman Catholic), O'Fallon University, Franklin Institute, Oakfield Institute, Oakly Seminary, Shurtleff College (Baptist), Kemper College (Episcopalian), Menard Academy, McKendree (McKendre) College (Methodist), St. Charles College (Methodist), Marion College (Presbyterian), and the Masonic College. In addition there were a few professional schools. Those which were noted in contemporary newspapers can be grouped as follows: two commercial schools, Mr. Jones' and Mr. Ligget's; three medical schools, those of Dr. C. Ruge (Washington, Mo.), of Kemper College, and of St. Louis University; and, after 1841, one law school at St. Louis University. Theological schools were rare. According to one survey there were only thirty-nine in the entire United States, of which few were in the West. In Missouri the Roman Catholics had one at St. Mary's (Perry County). The Protestants of the State relied upon private instruction by some enterprising clergyman or upon the theological course offered at several of their colleges (e. g., Marion and Shurtleff), but were beginning to think seriously of founding schools for training their ministers.[76]

Tuition at these colleges, which often included board and room, naturally varied greatly. Oakly Seminary charged $100.00 a year, Kemper College, $150.00, Ruge's Medical School $200.00, St. Louis University $200.00 in 1840 and $130.00 in 1842.[77] Nevertheless, practically all of them had financial difficulties; and some which had the support of large church bodies, like Kemper, McKendree,

---

[76] *Daily Commercial Bulletin*, Feb. 28, June 15, Aug. 3, 13, 14, Sept. 5, 24, 1840; *Missouri Argus*, May 10, 1839, Nov. 2, 1841; *People's Organ*, Feb. 20, March 9, 1842; *Native American Bulletin*, March 24, 1842; *St. Louis New Era*, Sept. 1, 1843; *Daily Missouri Republican*, Feb. 25, March 4, 1840, Jan. 19, Feb. 10, 15, 20, March 1, 5, Aug. 24, 1844, Dec. 8, 1845, March 12, 1846; *St. Louis Democrat*, Feb. 26, 1844; *St. Louis American*, Dec. 8, 1845; *Anzeiger des Westens*, Nov. 28, 1844; *Täglicher Anzeiger des Westens*, Feb. 1, March 8, 1847; *St. Louis Daily Union*, Oct. 15, 1846; Skillman, *op. cit.*, 118; Green, *St. Louis Directory . . . 1845*, xvii; Peck, *op. cit.*, 338—339.

[77] *Daily Commercial Bulletin*, Sept. 5, 1840; *Daily Missouri Republican*, Feb. 9, 1844, Aug. 22, 1845; *Catalogue of the Officers and Students of the St. Louis University, (Missouri) 1839—40*, p. 15 (hereafter cited as *Catalogue . . . St. Louis University*); *ibid.*, 1841—1842, p. 3.

Marion, and Shurtleff Colleges, even had to close temporarily or permanently.[78] When Kemper College was abandoned and sold to the county as a poor farm, its medical school was taken over by the University of Missouri and incorporated into the latter's medical department.[79] The medical schools were not in great favor with the public. That of St. Louis University drew the ire of the citizens with the aroma it created and with its reputation for dissection, which on at least one occasion caused rioting and subsequent legal action.[80]

St. Louis University was one of the oldest of these schools. It was founded in 1828; began sessions on November 2, 1829, received its charter on December 28, 1832, and graduated its first class two years later. Although the school's enrollment was 135 by 1836 and 172 by 1840, it graduated only twelve students during the first ten years of its existence.[81] The University of Missouri was not founded until the year the Saxons arrived in St. Louis. In five years it had an enrollment of 780, attracted no doubt in part by its low tuition charge of $30.00 a year. But its faculty consisted of only five men.[82] Wetmore's *Gazetteer of the State of Missouri* was probably correct in lamenting: ". . . the opinion . . . prevails extensively that common school education is sufficient for all the sober purposes of life." [83]

There were pleas for coeducation, coupled with attacks on the alleged futility of much of the schooling that young women were receiving.[84] But in 1844, when Oberlin University (founded in

---

78 *Daily Missouri Republican*, March 1, 1844, Oct. 25, Nov. 6, Dec. 8, 1845; Peck, *op. cit.*, 338—339.

79 *Daily Missouri Republican*, Feb. 5, March 2, 1846.

80 *Ibid.*, Feb. 27, 28, 29, May 16, 1844; *St. Louis Democrat*, Feb. 26, 1844; *Daily Evening Gazette*, Feb. 26, 27, 1844.

81 *Memorial Volume of the Diamond Jubilee of St. Louis University*, 52—53, 55—56; *Catalogue . . . St. Louis University*, 1835—1836, p. 6; *Catalogue . . . St. Louis University*, 1839—1840, p. 8; Shoemaker, "Six Periods of Missouri History," *Missouri Historical Review*, IX, 231; Hill, *Historical Sketch of the St. Louis University*, 40, 43. See also Garraghan, "The Beginnings of St. Louis University," *St. Louis Catholic Historical Review*, I, 98—107; Stevens, *St. Louis The Fourth City, 1764—1909*, I, 882.

82 *St. Louis New Era*, Aug. 23, 1844; *Daily Missouri Republican*, Aug. 28, 1845.

83 Wetmore, *op. cit.*, 18.

84 *Daily Pennant*, May 5, 6, 1840; *Daily Evening Gazette*, Jan. 8, 1843; *Daily People's Organ*, Dec. 9, 1843; *Daily Missouri Republican*, Aug. 4, 1845; *St. Louis Daily New Era*, April 15, 1846.

1833) could already boast of an enrollment of 188 women in its student body of 480, strict separation of boys and girls was still observed even in the elementary public schools of St. Louis.[85] The city had only one school which could lay claim to being coeducational, that of Spencer Smith and his wife.[86] However, there were a number of English girls' schools in the city and vicinity, such as those conducted by Mrs. Macaulay, P. Mauro and his daughters, Mrs. Wyman, the Misses Shaw, the Misses Johnson and the Conway, Lindenwood, and Monticello Seminaries.[87] There was also at least one German school for girls in St. Louis, operated by a Mrs. Scheidler.[88]

In addition to the educational agencies mentioned there were numerous private teachers and tutors. The private schools retained their popularity long after public schools had been established, and the transition to the latter was gradual. In 1841, when the public schools had been in operation three years, there were seven hundred children of elementary-school age in private schools, only 350 in the public schools.[89] In 1840 the United States census did not rate a single school in St. Louis as a college or university, and of 173 such schools in the entire country only two were in St. Louis County. The ten "academies or grammar schools" in the city had 577 students, while an even smaller number, 467, were in the "primary or common schools." [90] The best university in the Mississippi Valley, at least in the opinion of Arends, was Transylvania, at Lexington, Kentucky.[91]

This somewhat dismal picture was brightened very little by a self-conscious effort in some quarters to raise the cultural level of the community. Numerous "lectures" and "debates" were held by local civic leaders, preachers, doctors, or itinerant intelligentsia

---

85 *St. Louis New Era*, Nov. 9, 1844; Lange, "Facts Concerning One Hundred Years of Progress in the Public Schools of St. Louis 1838—1938," *Public School Messenger*, XXXV, No. 5, pp. 11—12, 15; Monroe, *op. cit.*, 474—475.

86 Skillman, *op. cit.*, 93.

87 *Ibid.*; *Missouri Argus*, Aug. 3, 1840, Jan. 5, 1841; *Daily Commercial Bulletin*, April 1, Aug. 4, 1840; *Daily Missouri Republican*, Feb. 6, Aug. 24, 1844; Green, *St. Louis Directory . . . 1845*, xvii.

88 *Anzeiger des Westens*, Dec. 22, 1842.

89 Campbell (ed.), *Campbell's Gazetteer of Missouri*, 543.

90 *The Sixth Census of the United States: 1840*, pp. 413, 475.

91 Arends, *op. cit.*, 220—221.

who claimed for themselves various titles and degrees. Such events were patronized well enough to encourage their frequent presentation, often by, or at least in, the churches. The subjects discussed were varied: anthropology, philology, psychology, anatomy, politics, literature, drama, history, geology, mineralogy, chemistry, education, "Neurology," "Phrenology," "Mesmerism," "Animal-Magnetism," "Phreno-Mnemotechny," and occasionally a topic so daring as "Vice" or so subtle as "Responsibility; or, Young Men 'not their own.' "[92] Although the admission fee to these lectures was sometimes as much as $2.00, their actual worth was not always regarded highly. The *Daily Evening Gazette* exclaimed: " 'Popular lectures!' What are *they* but popular failures. . . ."[93] A recent writer has expressed the more favorable estimate: "The lyceum platform . . . became a powerful factor in political discussion, in social improvement, and in intellectual advance."[94] A part of the audience was almost certain to get full value; the ladies were usually admitted free of charge.

As a partial substitute for the lack of a public library, lending libraries were maintained for both the English and the German population. Furthermore, private libraries were founded by interested groups such as the Mercantile Library Association of St. Louis or the association of Germans in St. Clair County, Illinois.[95] Reading rooms filled with exchange publications were maintained for the general public by some of the local journals and together with generous patronage by the public of these newspapers themselves, were a supplement to the educational agencies mentioned.

Educational activity among the German element of St. Louis followed the same line of cleavage as that which divided the German element generally into the afore-mentioned groups of nationalists, revolutionaries, and antireligionists on the one hand, and the

---

92 *Daily Commercial Bulletin*, July 8, 21, Oct. 5, 1840; *Daily Pennant*, Oct. 7, 1840; *Daily Missouri Republican*, Feb. 1, 3, 15, 24, Nov. 12, Dec. 3, 16, 1844, Jan. 28, Feb. 11, March 8, 29, April 7, May 5, Oct. 15, 1845; *Weekly Reveille*, Jan. 13, March 10, April 7, 14, Dec. 9, 1845; *St. Louis New Era*, Jan. 4, 1845; *Anzeiger des Westens*, Feb. 12, 1846; *People's Daily Organ*, April 29, 1846.

93 *Daily Evening Gazette*, Nov. 8, 1844.

94 Monroe, *op. cit.*, 268.

95 *Anzeiger des Westens*, March 19, 1842, April 6, 1843, Dec. 25, 1845, Feb. 23, 1846; *Daily Missouri Republican*, Feb. 3, Dec. 13, 1844, Feb. 23, April 11, Dec. 3, 1846; *St. Louis New Era*, Feb. 13, 1844, Feb. 7, March 29, 1845.

nonpolitical, conservative, and religious groups on the other. Even before the period immediately under discussion the former element among the Germans in St. Louis was attempting to maintain a secular elementary school through the medium of the "German School Association," of which F. Kretzschmar was president and Wilhelm Weber was secretary for a number of years. Instruction seems to have begun as early as November, 1836. Then, in 1837, the "St. Louis German Academy" was founded by a group of over a hundred subscribers drawn largely from this Association. Their school began operation on February 6, 1838, and the society was incorporated just at the time the Saxons arrived, namely, on February 13, 1839.[96]

The project seems never to have flourished. Only fifty-one of the 138 children who had attended the school during the course of 1841 were still enrolled at the beginning of 1842. By this time the membership of the Association had gone down from a high of 137 to seventy-nine. Despite these discouraging conditions there was talk of erecting a new building.[97] Tuition of $1.00 a month was charged for each child, and in 1841, for instance, only seven of the fifty-one children with which the year closed were "free" pupils.[98] But this revenue evidently was not sufficient, and the Association was in frequent if not perpetual financial straits. During 1842 the aggregate enrollment went down to 108 and the number of pupils at the close of the year to forty. In spite of an increase of ten in the membership of the Association for this year it owed Teacher Weyse $268.69 in back salary, $150.00 of which he canceled.[99] Further ambitious planning, entirely out of keeping with the lack of progress shown by the school and the organization supporting it, and fervid articles and editorials in the *Anzeiger* failed to overcome a pronounced lack of general interest in the venture.[100] Consequently the school closed its doors by 1846.[101]

---

[96] *Anzeiger des Westens*, Jan. 5, 1842; *The St. Louis Directory, for the year 1842,* vii; Keemle, *The St. Louis Directory, for the Year 1840—1,* p. 79; Arends, *op. cit.*, 305; Schneider, *op. cit.*, 31. See also Bek, "The Followers of Duden," *Missouri Historical Review*, XVI, 119—126.

[97] *Anzeiger des Westens*, Jan. 5, 1842.

[98] *Ibid.*, Jan. 5, 1842, March 4, 1843.

[99] *Ibid.*, Jan. 5, 1842, Feb. 23, 1843.

[100] *Ibid.*, May 20, June 24, Aug. 17, 24, Sept. 30, 1843.

[101] *Ibid.*, Feb. 14, 1846.

Like the English-speaking population, the Germans were served by numerous private teachers. Representative names for the years immediately following 1839 were: W. Decker, R. Wollkoff, G. W. Pötter, Teofilo Schmidti, F. Steines, J. Eickoff, C. F. Flamm, M. Ruppelius, E. Mundy, F. Bry, E. Robyn, J. Fey, M. Kraft, and G. Scho.[102] Candidate Schieferdecker of the Saxons also joined this group a year and a half after his arrival, when he advertised these unusual educational wares:

> Teacher of German and other Languages
>
> Having made literature the business of my life I recommend myself to the inhabitants of this city for a teacher of German, Latin, Greek, and Hebrew Languages. Persons who should regard this, are assured to receive, under a moderate expense, a solid and perfect information of said languages, and are kindly requested to apply to
>
> G. A. Schuferdecker [sic],
>
> Poplar street, No. 14, between 1st and 2nd streets, in the home of the Rev. O. H. Walther.[103]

At the time the Saxons entered the picture there was comparatively little religious education in the city. Instruction in the English Protestant churches does not seem to have progressed much beyond the Sunday school stage, although at least the Episcopalians and the Evangelicals did have confirmation, which perhaps predicated some additional religious training.[104] Despite the existence of several convent schools, there seems to be no evidence of an attempt by the Roman Catholics to establish a parish-school system prior to the initiative taken by the German Protestants.

Holy Ghost Church maintained a parish school which had been founded as early as 1835. After 1843 this school was continued in the basement of the church, but it did not survive many years. An attempt at organizing a "high" school for Holy Ghost Church failed utterly, despite editorial support from the *Anzeiger*. When

---

102 *Ibid.*, Jan. 12, April 7, Aug. 24, Oct. 18, 1842, July 11, 20, Sept. 2, 1843, March 22, Sept. 4, Oct. 4, 1845, Feb. 18, 21, 1846; *Täglicher Anzeiger des Westens*, Oct. 18, 1846, May 21, 1847. The Steines family, of some importance in the history of the Germans in Missouri, is discussed at length in Bek, "The Followers of Duden," *Missouri Historical Review*, XIV, 29—73, 217—232, 436—458, XV, 519—544, 660—699, XVI, 119—132.

103 *Daily Evening Gazette*, Aug. 17, 1840.

104 *Missouri Argus*, April 21, 1840; *Anzeiger des Westens*, Dec. 25, 1841, Jan. 10, 1843. See also Arends, *op. cit.*, 219.

Pastor Wall was forced to leave this congregation, he again organized a parish school with the group loyal to him. By 1845 there were schools for both the North and South St. Louis Evangelical congregations, at Eleventh and Biddle and Ninth and Geyer Streets respectively. However, the success of these schools is questionable. Since they were organized primarily to preserve the German language, the congregations failed to see their potential value as spiritual agencies and found them an unwelcome and unnecessary financial burden. The progress of these institutions was further impeded by the fact that their teachers "came and went like in a dovecote." The parish schools of the *Kirchenverein* were admittedly in poor condition, especially during the first decade of its existence. There was a serious dearth of professionally trained teachers, an abundance of impostors, and the duties of conducting the school usually fell upon the ministers, whose qualifications as teachers often were not on a par even with their limited pastoral abilities.[105]

One of the first concerns of the Saxons upon arrival in St. Louis was to establish a school. Already during the first days of March, 1839, a house on First Street was rented for $12.00 a month as a school building.[106] This fact renders unlikely the claim that the first Saxon school was held in the basement of Christ Church.[107] Other temporary schools were organized by the immigrants in various sections of the city.[108] Winter is known to have been one of the several teachers who were active in St. Louis before going to Perry County in May of 1839.[109]

In these initial stages of the Saxons' educational work there was no equipment save that which the immigrants had brought along, and the teachers struggled with the most adverse circumstances. By the end of March they had succeeded in securing the very modest appropriation of $40.00 for supplies, such as tables

---

105 Kargau, *op. cit.*, 270—271; Schneider, *op. cit.*, 31, 279—287. See also *Anzeiger des Westens*, May 5, Dec. 1, 1842, Aug. 3, 23, Sept. 8, 1844, March 20, 29, 30, Dec. 13, 1845, Feb. 6, 1846; *Täglicher Anzeiger des Westens*, July 26, 1847; *Die Deutsche Tribüne*, July 23, Dec. 25, 1845, Jan. 6, July 22, Aug. 27, 1846.

106 Receipt for rent on school building, March 4 to April 4, 1839, MS., C. H. I.

107 Stellhorn, "The Saxon Centennial and the Schools," *Lutheran School Journal*, LXXIV, 344—345.

108 Schieferdecker, *op. cit.*, 11.

109 Winter to Guericke *et al.*, April 28, 1841, *Zeitschrift für die gesammte lutherische Theologie und Kirche*, II, No. 3, pp. 116—132; Köstering, "Johann Friedrich Winter," *Der Lutheraner*, XXX, 36.

and benches.[110] Even then the task of the teachers must have been a difficult one, and they earned the $25.00 paid them. No mention is made of the purchase of books for the school at this time. The only books purchased were for the general library of the Saxons and consisted of such unjuvenile items as a *Statutes and Gazetteer of Missouri,* which Vehse acquired for $9.00.[111]

Attempts by the Saxons to reintroduce regular school and church work were seriously impeded by their public embarrassment over the controversy centering about them in the *Anzeiger.* On March 2, the day before the first service was held in Christ Church, an appeal had been made in the *Anzeiger* for a public declaration by the immigrants. The writer, who signed himself "Ein Toleranter," repudiated, for himself and for that segment of the public which he claimed to represent, both the opinion of Koch and the manner in which it was stated in his condemnation of the Stephanites on February 16. The contributor on March 2 called for religious tolerance and for a fair and objective examination of the group, its organization, and its beliefs. These factors could best be judged, the writer asserted, if Stephan himself, as leader of the movement, preached in public and gave people the opportunity to form an unbiased opinion. For this purpose the correspondent was certain that merely for the asking any place of worship in the city would be placed at the disposal of the Saxons by its congregation.[112] Such an assumption was far too optimistic. The "German Protestant" church of Pastor Wall, for instance, which "Ein Toleranter" specifically suggested, would not have been available, since it was not dedicated until several months later and, as already noted, its leading members were strongly opposed to the Stephanites. In view of the fact that only twenty-four hours intervened between the time at which this article appeared and the time at which the service was conducted, it is unlikely that the latter was a result of the former, as has been asserted.[113] But that such an appeal even appeared is indicative of the interest that was centering in the Saxons at the time.

---

110 Draft on the Credit Fund for school supplies, March 30, 1839, MS., C. H. I.

111 Bill for books, March 2, 1839, MS., C. H. I.

112 *Anzeiger des Westens,* March 2, 1839, quoted in G. Günther, *op. cit.,* 47—49.

113 G. Günther, *op. cit.,* 49.

Stephan's sermon seems to have accomplished little more, however, than to serve as ammunition for Koch's campaign. In the issue of the *Anzeiger* which appeared on March 9 he ridiculed the writer who had called for a service and asserted that he found Stephan neither a brilliant nor even an enthusiastic speaker, but rather a mediocre one. Koch not only claimed that Stephan compared himself to the patriarch Abraham, but found "laughable" the fact that a prayer for the American government was included in the liturgy used by the Stephanites. Finally Koch, of all people, had the temerity to accuse Stephan of hasty and unsound judgment because of the latter's "slanders" against the government in Germany, and prophetically remarked that Stephan was not yet acquainted with what he might encounter here.[114]

The strange spectacle therefore began to present itself of the Saxons being attacked even in America for their opposition to German governments from which they felt they had to flee. However, the paradox is not complete until one recalls that the attack made upon them came from men who themselves had to flee from these same governments, which they on other occasions roundly denounced, and whose overthrow they actively helped to promote. The essence of the matter was that the opponents of the Saxons expected them to be judged, and to judge them, on very different standards from those which these opponents wished to have applied to themselves; that what was fair for the one was not fair for the other; and that in the eyes of Koch, Weber, and their ilk the Saxons were damned, no matter what they did.

Koch, moreover, in the same article renewed his vituperation of the leaders of the emigration, especially the clergymen, as exploiters of the people. Koch's own character as well as his extreme bitterness against this particular group again showed through every line of his sensational, incendiary article. Specifically Koch charged: that while the clergymen lived in comfort, the people permitted themselves to be "hired out" for 25 cents a day; that even these "small wages were conscientiously carried back by the people to those who hired them out"; that the people were kept in such a condition that "they begged for bread from compassionate people"; that "whole families are living on old meat, no longer salable in

---

[114] *Anzeiger des Westens,* March 9, 1839, quoted in *ibid.,* 50—53.

the market; and that women are harnessed to carts in order to haul [them] through the streets in quadruped company, to the horror and pity of the public." [115]

A week later Dr. Gempp replied to this blast with an article in the *Anzeiger* of March 16. Gempp took Koch to task for his "intolerance" and, on the strength of his close relation with the Stephanites as physician of the *Gesellschaft,* denied or greatly modified each of the allegations of Koch. People were not "hired out" in the sense that Koch had implied. When the pastors heard of opportunities for work, they referred prospective employers to those immigrants whom the pastors knew to be qualified. Certain of the people had worked for 25 cents a day, a wage equivalent to the best that some of them could get in Germany. Often this was all that was offered. Others, however, were being paid 50 cents or more daily. When such people took the money to the pastors, it was for deposit in the Credit Fund or for paying their fare, which in many cases had been advanced by the *Gesellschaft.* The entire arrangement, Gempp contended, was a laudable display of willingness to work and to pay off debts.

Begging, if it occurred at all, was done either by penniless members of the group who had secured free passage from the Credit Fund and then severed their connections with the Stephanites to avoid paying back their fare, or by persons who used the name of the Saxons. The story about the meat, Gempp, as physician for the group, denied categorically. That some of the Saxons, both men and women, had moved some of their goods through the streets in carts when sufficient draft animals were not available, Gempp made no effort to deny. But he did remark that it was not unusual in Europe for women to join in such work and that the newcomers were not yet acquainted with American customs. Gempp concluded his reply to Koch with an ill-advised insinuation that Koch was exposing himself to a slander suit.[116]

In the same issue of the *Anzeiger* in which Dr. Gempp took up the cudgels, the Stephanites also made their literary debut with a "Reply to Friendly and Unfriendly Reception," dated March 9

---

115 *Ibid.*, 51.

116 *Anzeiger des Westens*, March 16, 1839 (the article is dated March 13, 1839), quoted in *ibid.*, 55—59.

and purporting to come from the entire *Gesellschaft*.[117] Despite some flamboyant phrasemaking and a dramatic reiteration of persecution and martyrdom in Germany, there was nevertheless a sincere undercurrent of sound thought. Although the Saxons reasserted their Lutheranism emphatically and aggressively, they pledged themselves to respect the religious beliefs of others and renounced any proselyting. However, they requested the same courtesies for themselves. They pledged allegiance to their new home, obedience and loyalty to its government, and their lives and property for its defense.[118]

Neither Gempp's nor the Stephanites' articles satisfied Koch. The former received his reply in the issue of March 23, the latter theirs on April 6.[119] The article against Gempp succeeded in reaching a new low mark in this literary quarrel. An arresting statement, in view of Koch's character and later history, was his assertion: "I wish to avoid for the future every personal war of the pen, which I hate." [120] This resolve was taken under inauspicious circumstances. In the same contribution Koch devoted much space to an elaborately sarcastic personal attack upon the physician and observed "the absence of the language of an educated man in the entire article of Mr. Gempp, in which clear reason and a delicate feeling in expression and judgment are entirely lacking." [121]

The examination of a series of points in the controversy then culminated in a vicious attack upon the Saxons for accepting low wages. Koch did not hesitate to threaten a lynching of both the laborers and those who, according to him, were still "hiring them out." Koch, of course, claimed that this would be a spontaneous and understandable, if not justifiable, expression of the resentment which he claimed already existed, primarily among the German but also among the American and Irish laborers in the city.[122] There is not a shred of supporting evidence for Koch's alarms in the contemporary English newspapers, which would have been quick to seize on even the rumors of a lynching. The remarks of Koch seem

---

117 *Anzeiger des Westens*, March 16, 1839, quoted in *ibid.*, 65—69.

118 *Ibid.*

119 *Anzeiger des Westens*, March 23, April 6, 1839, quoted in *ibid.*, 60—65, 69—73.

120 *Anzeiger des Westens*, March 23, 1839, quoted in *ibid.*, 60.

121 *Ibid.*

122 *Ibid.*, 60—65.

to have been an appeal to mob spirit for hatching such a scheme rather than a warning that one already existed. Koch's article was a deplorable piece of demagoguery, which the *Anzeiger* should have been careful not to print.

The inflammatory words of Koch and the alleged undercutting of wages by the Saxons focus attention briefly also upon the labor conditions in St. Louis during these years. Some groups of laborers in the city were organized by 1840. During the next seven years, evidence of further organization, of labor troubles, and of strikes to secure higher wages are frequent among the joiners, carpenters, building trades generally, cobblers, boat hands, and dock workers.[123] Average wages for unskilled laborers were $1.00 a day and board. As a result of fluctuations in the labor supply skilled workers received wages ranging all the way from $1.25 to $3.00 a day; the average was between $1.50 and $2.00.[124]

German and Irish workers were known for working for less than others. This circumstance was the result of a fact well understood and frequently noted by American newspapers, namely, that wages in European countries were lower than in America.[125] But standards nowhere were high. Farm hands in the West received about $2.50 to $3.00 a week, and maids "at least 80 Doll. yearly." [126] Such wages prevailed in spite of the fact that personal service was not popular with the element that was attracted to the West, so that there was always a scarcity of this type of worker, and he was well treated.[127]

The other charges which had been discussed by Dr. Gempp were simply repeated and elaborated by Koch. Matters which might normally have been considered the private affairs of the Stephanites, regardless of their truth or untruth, were made subjects of public interest and the particular concern of Heinrich Koch. This trans-

---

123 *Daily Commercial Bulletin*, March 14, 1840; *Missouri Argus*, Feb. 22, 24, 25, 1841; *Daily Missouri Republican*, Sept. 26, 1844; *Daily Evening Gazette*, Aug. 30, 1844; *St. Louis Daily New Era*, April 3, May 1, July 14, 1846; *Anzeiger des Westens*, March 3, 1846; *Täglicher Anzeiger des Westens*, March 25, 1846.

124 *Daily Evening Gazette*, Aug. 30, 1844; Winter to Guericke *et al.*, April 28, 1841, *Zeitschrift für die gesammte lutherische Theologie und Kirche*, II, No. 3, pp. 116—132; G. Günther, *op. cit.*, 34.

125 *St. Louis New Era*, July 12, 1844; *St. Louis American*, Oct. 22, 1845.

126 *St. Louis Daily New Era*, Feb. 3, 1846.

127 *Ibid.*; G. Günther, *op. cit.*, 33.

formation was achieved by asserting that the actions of the Saxons reflected unfavorably upon the entire German element in the city, of which he was the self-appointed spokesman.[128] Rabble-rousing such as that in which Koch indulged had the result that Vehse and one of the candidates were stoned in the street one day[129] and that on another occasion stones were flung through the windows of Stephan's residence.[130] The name of the Stephanites was a byword among the urchins of the city,[131] and when the Saxon Bishop took his walk, he was occasionally followed by people shouting invectives.[132]

After having, as he no doubt believed, disposed of Gempp and anything that the doctor had to say, the St. Louis provocateur, during the next week, composed an essay, with the March 16 statement of the Stephanites themselves as an inspiration. The product was printed a week after the attack on Gempp.[133] In this article, "An Elucidation of the Reply to Friendly and Unfriendly Reception," Koch gave full play to his passionately anticlerical and antireligious feeling. There is no need for disagreeing with the writer because he placed into question the Stephanite assertions that they were driven from Saxony, or when he criticized sweeping denunciations of people and conditions in Germany, or when he found the submissiveness and self-recrimination of the Saxons repellent.[134] Their defense of even the extremes of their system and the reassertion of their martyrdom in their first public statement had testified again to the thorough Stephanism of the *Gesellschaft* and the apparently incurable fixation of its members that they were being persecuted.

Yet how all this was any of Koch's concern, what portion of it was a public and what a private affair of the Stephanites, and what good purpose was served by unnecessarily re-creating the quarrels of Germany, where a State-Church system made them inevitable, in America, where separation of Church and State made them avoidable, seems not to have occurred to either Koch or Weber.

---

128 *Anzeiger des Westens,* March 23, 1839, quoted in G. Günther, *op. cit.,* 65—69.

129 *Ibid.,* 46.

130 *Ibid.,* 53.

131 *Ibid.,* 46.

132 *Ibid.,* 86.

133 *Anzeiger des Westens,* April 6, 1839, quoted in *ibid.,* 69—73.

134 *Ibid.*

Furthermore, the ribald manner in which the entire affair was treated in the article reflected discredit not only upon Koch for writing it, but also upon the *Anzeiger* for printing it. Of course, at this time Koch was still a member in good standing of the oligarchy of "prominent" German immigrants who dominated the affairs of their compatriots in the city; consequently, he was given free rein by the *Anzeiger*.

It was a bitter disappointment to the Stephanites to learn that in America they were to fare little better at the hands of the public than in Germany; that freedom of worship in the United States was accompanied by a freedom — and in that day almost a license — of the press. The opposition of the German press helped greatly to put the Saxons on the defensive for several years. Even in 1842 they still felt it necessary to assure their friends at Christ Church, rather pathetically: "We are not a fanatic congregation." [135]

---

[135] C. F. W. Walther and the six "wardens" of the Saxon congregation in St. Louis to Christ Church, Feb. 14, 1842, MS., C. H. I.

CHAPTER FOURTEEN

FOUNDING THE PERRY COUNTY COLONY

THE AFFAIRS of the *Gesellschaft,* meanwhile, were taking a constantly graver turn. Directly or indirectly, most of these developments had to do with the problems of administration under the episcopacy. Once he had succeeded in having himself confirmed as bishop of the group, Stephan was not slow to capitalize upon his conquest. The absolutism of the system constructed by the Codes, consecrated by the documents of investiture, and confirmed by the supplementary declaration, probably has few parallels in the religious or secular history of postcolonial America. Stephan's craving for power, coupled with his extreme hierarchical views and his miscalculation as to how far he could go without reaching the breaking point, were leading him directly into trouble, just as they had in Germany. However, this time he was not heading a group subservient to him in opposition to the government, but was standing alone against his own people, and when the break with them came, it spelled the end of his career.

When the Bishop had desired that documents be signed and representatives elected with whom he might deal, it had been possible to assemble all members of the various groups of emigrants in the several schoolrooms used by them. But now, it seems, Stephan could find no place to conduct similar elections of the people's representatives who could take over the secular affairs of the *Gesellschaft,* as both he himself and the Codes had guaranteed.[1] Accordingly, the Code for the Credit Fund, the one of most pressing importance, was never put into operation.[2] Stephan kept the entire administration of that fund in his own hands until, as he explained, "the land has been bought and we can assemble on our own property undisturbed." [3] The practice now was begun, which was fol-

[1] Vehse, *op. cit.,* 13; Schieferdecker, *op. cit.,* 11.

[2] Vehse, *op. cit.,* 7.

[3] *Ibid.,* 13.

lowed so long as Stephan was in control, that the Bishop issued a "protocol" of his official acts, pronouncements, and orders. When these related to financial affairs, they amounted to a simple draft on the Credit Fund, paid out by the treasurer, merely on the strength of this "protocol."[4] Sometimes, in the case of some of the more important expenditures, Stephan also had the chief contributors to the Credit Fund sign, as in the case where he had 500 "Piasters" made over to himself in St. Louis, for the expense of his episcopal establishment there.[5] The feasibility of merely issuing "Chancellery orders" was introduced into the discussions led by Stephan. The fact is that such orders — whether called by that name or not — were used by him, since his "protocols" amounted to orders. However, these policies were not entirely new, as Vehse represented them.[6] They had been in effect ever since the committee was organized. The fundamental difference was that formerly either the committee members or Stephan indulged in the practice at will. Now Stephan enjoyed the prerogative alone.

These autocratic tendencies in the administration of the *Gesellschaft* were exemplified and strengthened in many other less important, but no less significant, ways. The hierarchical trend in polity was the most noticeable. The preparation of the episcopal regalia, planned since December, 1837, was now begun, despite the fact that some of the material designated for this purpose had been on the *Amalia* and hence was lost. Stephan was to have a bishop's vestments and accompanying paraphernalia, a staff, a cap, and a cross and chain. The staff, a most intricate piece of carving, was later to be gold-plated. The golden chain for the cross was a heavy piece of ornamentation manufactured by a St. Louis goldsmith, who was paid $100 for his work. The pastors were also to have appropriate ecclesiastical vestments, but the full splendor of all these accouterments was not to shine forth until Stephan should be installed as bishop in his own little realm. However, the work was begun, and in part completed, already in St. Louis. Vehse relates with pathos that a part of the cost of the equipment just mentioned was defrayed by obtaining contributions from people in the *Gesellschaft* who donated their jewelry to the cause. The sum thus

---

[4] *Ibid.;* Schieferdecker, *op. cit.*, 11.

[5] Vehse, *op. cit.*, 13—14.

[6] Vehse, *op. cit.*, 13—14, 16.

realized was about $170.[7] Artist Gustav Pfau designed the vestments according to the directions of Candidate Wege. The actual work was done by Tailor Roschke with the assistance of a number of women, some of whom were living in Stephan's home at this time: M. Schütz, N. Geyer, L. Völker, P. Weidlich, S. Höschel, and Mrs. Koch. The money to pay for this work was taken from the Credit Fund.[8]

Plans for an episcopal residence in the prospective colony were drawn up by a St. Louis joiner. Vehse described the building, which he called a "palace," as a very handsome structure with a seventy-foot colonnaded front.[9] The second Roman Catholic church in St. Louis was dedicated at this time. Stephan told his preachers and candidates to go to the services and to observe the proper liturgical procedure for dedicating their proposed church in the new colony.[10] At the "soirees" given by the Bishop, the practice of kissing the Bishop's hand is said to have been introduced. To these affairs the pastors, the candidates, the teachers, and one layman, Stephan's [?] secretary, were admitted.[11] To stimulate a higher appreciation of Stephan, the laudatory article by Kurtz, cited above, was translated into German and read to the people.[12]

Equally typical of his conduct was the resumption of the very habits which had led to his difficulties with the authorities and with some of his own followers in Germany.[13] According to Vehse, "re-

---

[7] Vehse, *op. cit.*, 15; G. Günther, *op. cit.*, 49; Itemized list of articles sold by Jäckel, G. H. Löber, and Wege to Mr. Blancjour, April 27, May 4, 1839, signed by Jäckel, MS., C. H. I.

[8] Draft in favor of Mathilde Schütz, Natalie Geyer, Louise Völker, Pauline Weidlich, Sophie Höschel, and Mrs. Koch, signed by Jäckel and F. W. Barthel, March 11, 1839, Draft in favor of Roschke, signed by Jäckel and F. W. Barthel on order of Stephan, March 11, 1839, MSS., C. H. I.

[9] Vehse, *op. cit.*, 18. There are some very early plans for a board dwelling with dimensions of thirty by forty feet, two floors, eight rooms, a portico, and a colonnade, made by an F. Gottschalk. Whether this was to be Stephan's residence or not, is not clear. The plans do not correspond exactly to Vehse's, but he was inclined to exaggerate. Plans for a house by F. Gottschalk, MS., C. H. I.

[10] Vehse, *op. cit.*, 15—16.

[11] G. Günther, *op. cit.*, 75; Vehse, *op. cit.*, 13. It is not quite clear whom Vehse meant when he spoke of Stephan's secretary. If he meant Brohm, who was actually filling this position, then he was mistaken in calling him a layman, for he was a candidate. If he meant Jäckel, who was a layman, then he is mistaken in calling him Stephan's secretary, for he was secretary of the *Gesellschaft* and the committee.

[12] G. Günther, *op. cit.*, 54—55.

[13] Nachrichten an unsere Nachkommen, MS., C. H. I.

sumption" would be an inaccurate term. Vehse claimed Stephan continued his questionable habits also on board ship, where he shared a cabin with his son. What the latter there observed, allegedly led him to remark to a trusted friend: "My father will meet an evil end, you will find it out in a very short time." [14]

It was only a matter of weeks after arrival in St. Louis before Stephan gradually began again to re-establish the way of life to which he had become accustomed in Germany. The Bishop always had a number of women staying with him at his residence in St. Louis.[15] The brother of one of them has given the names of the most frequent guests as: Louise Völker, Louise Günther, Mrs. Schneider, Pauline Weidlich, and the youthful Marie Schubert, niece of the Walthers. Others came and went.[16] Vehse remarked that Americans, who according to him observed strict decorum in regard to their women, took offense at Stephan's establishment.[17] The nocturnal strolls were also resumed in St. Louis, although it does not seem that even the semblance of a religious gathering was given them here.[18] In general, conditions prevailing in the movement while it was in Germany were duplicated as nearly as possible, with the exception that Stephan felt free to develop them even farther and more openly in America than in Saxony. Whether he would permanently have been unmolested in his practices and way of life in America, is debatable. Internal developments in the group prevented a test.

After Stephan had established control of the various groups in both ecclesiastical and secular affairs, his tendency to domineer was virtually untrammeled, and he gave it full rein. His manner is said to have been extremely brusque and his capricious way of handling his people unduly partial. When his followers came to him, he admitted only those whom he chose to receive. Strangers

---

[14] Vehse, *op. cit.*, 17. Plainly this appraisal of Stephan's conduct by his son would have greater value if it came from another source than Vehse's often biased pen.

[15] *Ibid.*, 14—15.

[16] G. Günther, *op. cit.*, 36. The most scurrilous description of Stephan's household is to be found *ibid.*, 35—37.

[17] Vehse, *op. cit.*, 14—15.

[18] Winter to Guericke *et al.*, April 28, 1841, *Zeitschrift für die gesammte lutherische Theologie und Kirche,* II, No. 3, pp. 116—132; G. Günther, *op. cit.*, 53—54, 86—87.

who became interested in the movement were repelled.[19] Yet he expected no complaint and sought to dominate the lives of his people in even the minutest and most private detail. It will be recalled that Stephan seems even to have had the rather naive idea that he could control his subjects' thoughts; or at least, he made the effort to do so.[20] The poorer people whom he had taken along and the majority of whom were devoted to him, he treated contemptuously.[21] As a result of this kind of administration a depressed feeling is now supposed to have settled over the *Gesellschaft,* according to the assertions of Walther and Köstering.[22] If this portrayal of reactions was more than an afterthought, there still does not seem to have been enough resentment as yet to create any telling opposition to Stephan. At most there were indications that revolt was brewing. Some people had left. More were to do so presently. Criticism had been offered by a number of the leaders, already in Germany and then on the journey. The people had begun to be alarmed over the unnecessary expenditure of money.

The strongest indication that the *Gesellschaft* was in a dangerous mood was that the Bishop himself not only felt the undercurrent of opposition, but considered countermeasures necessary.[23] Even the average man could notice that Stephan's actions had offended some people already on the journey.[24] Of course, claims of opposition to Stephan must be discounted to a certain extent. All the accounts come from people who had an interest in representing themselves and their actions favorably, as did Vehse, in whose work his own vindication is a constant theme. Yet in view of ample supporting testimony, the statements of even such men bear some weight. It seems that during the period in St. Louis, Vehse contributed an innovation to the opposition against Stephan when, for the

---

19 G. Günther, *op. cit.*, 46, 88—89.

20 Pledge of Subjection to Stephan, *Selma*, Feb. 16, 1839, Pledge of Subjection to Stephan by the *Copernicus* group, Pledge of Subjection to Stephan by the *Johann Georg* group, I, II, MSS., C. H. I.

21 G. Günther, *op. cit.*, 9, 46.

22 C. F. W. Walther, "Vorwort der Redaction zum vierzehnten Jahrgang des Lutheraner," *Der Lutheraner*, XIV, 1—2; Köstering, *Keyl*, 53—54.

23 Pledge of Subjection to Stephan, *Selma*, Feb. 16, 1839, Pledge of Subjection to Stephan by the *Copernicus* group, Pledge of Subjection to Stephan by the *Johann Georg* group, I, II, MSS., C. H. I.

24 J. K. A. Höhne and J. G. Höhne to their brother, Sept. 26, 1841, quoted in *Die Ameise*, Jan. 10, 1842.

first time, he shifted the attack from administrative to religious grounds. He charged that the Bishop was acting contrary to Lutheran Confessions when he excluded from the *Gesellschaft* and from the right to hold property in the colony all who did not subscribe to the episcopacy, and again when he demanded obedience in secular affairs.[25] However, in both instances Stephan repelled the attack readily when supported by the clergy.[26]

But not even the loyalty of the clergy could stand the strain which Stephan placed upon it. The highly touted practical psychology of Stephan seems to have forsaken him utterly, for he did not even have the ordinary common sense not to alienate those who stood closest to him, who shared the limelight of respect and veneration in the hierarchical system, and through whom he might have hoped to perpetuate his influence over his followers, namely, the pastors. These gentlemen had amply demonstrated their readiness to make common cause with Stephan in establishing a thoroughgoing hierarchical system. They had given him the support without which he could not have gained complete control of the group. There is not even any evidence that such support was given reluctantly. Evidently both pastors and candidates were thoroughly impressed with the importance of their clerical positions and definitely committed to upholding the authority of the clergy. Their loyalty to the principle did not waver. Even the removal of Stephan, when it came, by no means spelled the end of the hierarchical system.

Stephan could easily have enjoyed a pre-eminent position as long as it was in the power of the pastors to confer it. But this was not enough to satisfy the constantly more unreasonable demands of the erstwhile Bohemian weaver's apprentice. While the Bishop showed his colleagues some special favors, such as financial remuneration, he also demanded a subservience from them so complete that they were not to tolerate it very long. Keyl did not preach a sermon while in St. Louis which went uncensored by Stephan.[27] Perhaps Bürger was less docile, or perhaps Stephan merely bore a grudge from the previous tilt between the two. At any rate, a relatively harmless remark in one of Bürger's sermons caused Ste-

---

25 Vehse, *op. cit.*, 14, 24.

26 *Ibid.*, 24.

27 Keyl, *op. cit.*, 17.

phan to accuse him of "false doctrine." This charge was amplified by Stephan's assertion that Bürger's wife dominated him and that the resulting marital relation was not what the Bishop thought it ought to be. Bürger was summoned before an ecclesiastical court composed of Stephan and his clerical puppets, called upon to confess, and, when he refused, placed under the ban. Although Bürger was himself a pastor, the spiritual care of his wife was given to "Pastor Walther."[28] In fact, Bürger was deprived entirely of association with both his wife and Stephan. Virtual banishment was achieved by the expedient of placing him in charge of a crew of wood choppers living in an open camp about twenty miles from St. Louis.[29] Bürger gave Stephan virtually all the blame for the outrageous treatment accorded him, but it must not be overlooked that there were other pastors concerned in this action, that one of them, "Pastor Walther," lent himself to its execution very directly, and that Bürger himself submitted to it.

If incidents of this kind could take place among the clergy, it is difficult to tell how far Stephan's interference and domination went in the private and family affairs of his lay followers, who were notoriously on a lower scale in the Stephanite system than were the pastors. What happened in the case of the Marbach family has been described above. Melodramatic charges have even been made that Stephan established a veritable spy system. Thus Candidate Klügel is supposed to have been quartered with C. F. W. Walther in order to observe him and report to Stephan.[30] Actually, however, the two do not seem to have lived together at the time that this espionage is supposed to have taken place. It may be noted further that Hochstetter, who made this claim, based it upon statements in a letter written December 28, 1881, more than forty years later, by J. F. Bünger. But Bünger was still in New York or on the high seas while the Saxons were in St. Louis.[31] It is easier to believe Bürger when he claims that the reading and brooding, for

[28] Probably C. F. W. Walther is meant. As a rule, when their titles were used, O. H. Walther was called *Pastor Vicarius* (abbreviated P. Vic.), because he had been his father's assistant, and C. F. W. Walther was called *Pastor* (abbreviated P.), because he had had full rank as sole clergyman of his parish.

[29] E. M. Bürger, Selbstbiographie, 123—124, MS., E. J. Buerger Papers, Ellicottville, N. Y.; Bürger, *op. cit.*, 13.

[30] Köstering, *Auswanderung*, 21—22; Hochstetter, *op. cit.*, 21.

[31] Hochstetter, *op. cit.*, 21.

which he had ample time while in "exile," led him to become suspicious of Stephan, although he claims that out of loyalty to his oath he tried to combat the feeling.[32] Even if one assumes that the Bürger and Marbach cases were some of the more extreme, Winter seems to have characterized the situation accurately when he expressed himself thus: "It did not take long before he [Stephan] let one or the other among the pastors and candidates feel his power, and worked toward setting the pastors and candidates against one another, so that more than one of them contemplated withdrawing quietly and severing his connection with the *Gesellschaft.*" [33]

Yet the opposition of the clergy does not appear to have been based upon disagreement with Stephan on the principle of the hierarchy, the confusion of secular and religious matters, or the ruthless disregard of individual rights. The composite picture which presents itself is not that of conscientious objectors beginning to have serious doubts about the soundness of Stephan's religious views or the correctness of his extreme hierarchical system, but rather of resentment against affronts to themselves as individuals and of antipathy to the Bishop's person. Any objections in principle should have come at the time when that principle was established, namely, the elevation of Stephan to the episcopacy and the subsequent subjection of the group to his will. At that time the pastors were upholding Stephan's hands. Of course, people can change their minds, but any change of heart later — if it really was a change — would have taken the form of an appeal to the rights of the people, perhaps even an appeal to the people to assert their rights. Of such ideas there was as yet no trace among the clergymen. They were rather engaged in the second phase of the contest begun by Marbach — a jockeying for power and control. They were not at variance with the principle of the hierarchy, but with the practical result that Stephan became *the* hierarchy.

A realization of the actual trend of events gradually began to dawn upon the pastors and candidates during the month in St. Louis. An opportune moment for action had not yet presented itself, but

---

[32] E. M. Bürger, Selbstbiographie, 124, MS., E. J. Buerger Papers, Ellicottville, N. Y.

[33] Winter to Guericke *et al.*, April 28, 1841, *Zeitschrift für die gesammte lutherische Theologie und Kirche,* II, No. 3, pp. 116—132.

it seems safe to say that by the time Stephan turned his back upon them to go to Perry County, not all, and perhaps none, of them could still claim to "abhor all distrustful, suspicious statements and thoughts." [34]

But no matter how hostile the press notices of the Saxons were, or how unfriendly the attitude of Stephan toward strangers, the *Gesellschaft* could at this stage of its development still have enjoyed a large and valuable increase in membership if it had been properly managed. Several Germans in St. Louis, for instance, Mr. Sagner of Dresden, had resolved to join together with their families.[35] Vehse's friend Dr. Gempp had his two sons, the older of whom was two and one-half years old, the younger less than six months, baptized by Stephan on April 23.[36] Presumably Gempp, who was inclined to join the *Gesellschaft* outright, was prevented from doing so only by its economic collapse. Vehse judged correctly that it would have been a great asset to secure the adherence of Gempp, and in view of the sickness which ravaged the colonists, the services of a competent medical man were an urgent necessity.[37] Vehse again scored a point when he stressed the fact that because of Gempp's respected position among the Germans of the city his joining would not only have encouraged others, but would in itself have enhanced the credit-rating of the organization. And credit was indispensable for starting the colony.[38]

While a number of people for various reasons did enter into closer relations with the *Gesellschaft* during this time, such connections usually did not prove permanent after collapse of the venture.[39] However, about twenty persons did formally join the group. Their names are given in "List III. Additions in St. Louis." [40] The great majority of these recruits was made up by four families

---

[34] Pledge of Subjection to Stephan, *Selma*, Feb. 16, 1839, Pledge of Subjection to Stephan by the *Copernicus* group, Pledge of Subjection to Stephan by the *Johann Georg* group, I, II, MSS., C. H. I.

[35] Vehse, *op. cit.*, 36; G. Günther, *op. cit.*, 47.

[36] G. H. Löber, Diary, April 23, 1839, MS., C. H. I.; G. Günther, *op. cit.*, 75. Official acts were performed also for people named Weuler, Querl, and Ostmann. G. H. Löber, Diary, Feb. 25, April 1, 1839, MS., C. H. I.

[37] Vehse, *op. cit.*, 36.

[38] *Ibid.*

[39] "Hamilton, N.," "Jäger, Gottfried," "Jäger, Christina," "Leonhard aus St. Clair," and "Slaughter," in List of Saxon Immigrants 1838, MS., C. H. I.

[40] See Appendix A.

from Hanover, who on March 17 put in their application for acceptance, "if possible," into the "apostolic-Lutheran *Gesellschaft*." These people pledged obedience to the "Emigration Code" (probably the Brief Outline of the Emigration Code), the Code for the Credit Fund, and the "Episcopal Constitution." Their signed petition, witnessed by Löber, bears a penciled note stating that "His Reverence" had given his approval.[41] The combined contributions to the Credit Fund made by these families on the day of their application totaled $560.[42]

Unfavorable publicity, Stephan's brusqueness, and, most of all, the uncertain future of the movement combined to keep down the number of new adherents.[43] Moreover, the *Gesellschaft* was also showing some numerical losses to counterbalance its modest gains. While references to the people who left the *Gesellschaft* in St. Louis are not infrequent, their names and number are difficult to determine, as they are usually listed with those who left both earlier and later. Among those who did leave while the group was in St. Louis were Lieutenant Schlegel and Dr. Schneider. The departure of the latter left Dr. Gempp serving the medical needs of the *Gesellschaft* alone. Anyone leaving was roundly condemned as irreligious in a public statement issued by the *Gesellschaft*.[44]

The financial loss was probably felt more keenly by the *Gesellschaft* than the numerical decrease or the alleged faithlessness of its erstwhile members. Schlegel's departure reduced the Credit Fund by $207.87½, the sum which was still due him after the necessary deductions for fare and other expenses had been made. Schlegel, in turn, renounced all claims on the *Gesellschaft* in a properly notarized transaction between himself and F. W. Barthel,

---

[41] Application of Timken, Böschen, Grother, and Holschen for admission to the *Gesellschaft*, March 17, 1839, MS., C. H. I.

[42] List of additions in St. Louis, signed by G. H. Löber, March 17, 1839, Bound MSS., 10, C. H. I.; Notation by Jäckel, March 17, 1839, on Minutes of a meeting between Vehse, Jäckel, and Stephan, March 14, 1839, MS., C. H. I. Slightly different figures are given in G. H. Löber, Diary, March 17, 1839, MS., C. H. I.

[43] Stephan's version was that the movement was gaining the respect and confidence of the Americans, and that this so aroused the envy of his opponents within the *Gesellschaft* that they resolved upon his destruction. Stephan to Flügel, Oct. 12, 1841, MS., C. H. I.

[44] *Anzeiger des Westens*, March 16, 1839, quoted in G. Günther, *op. cit.*, 65—69. See also Pledge of Subjection to Stephan, *Selma*, Feb. 16, 1839, Pledge of Subjection to Stephan by the *Copernicus* group, Pledge of Subjection to Stephan by the *Johann Georg* group, I, II, MSS., C. H. I.

acting as treasurer of the group, on March 12, 1839.[45] Two days later, when Dr. Schneider and his family left, the Credit Fund became poorer by $2,600.00.[46] Since the transfer of this sum overpaid his account with the Credit Fund, it may be assumed that he demanded compensation for his professional services, perhaps under threat of suit, as Dr. Schnabel had done. Certainly the *Gesellschaft* did not recognize the doctor's demands as just, for its records carried the account showing a deficit of $783.40.[47] Further shrinkage of the Credit Fund resulted from the fact that certain wealthier members of the group were permitted to withdraw from the Fund, before its collapse, sizable sums which had been deposited only temporarily. Thus Pastor Keyl was paid $858.00, and Mrs. Johanne Sophie Schneider $819.00.[48] Johann Gottlieb Pietsch received payment of at least a part of his contribution, with interest, on April 5, 1839.[49] Total "Advanced money and reimbursements to particular members" in St. Louis was $5,645.50.[50]

The largest single numerical loss to the *Gesellschaft* was that which resulted from the sinking of the *Amalia*. In May the hopes of the Stephanites were suddenly and unexpectedly raised that the *Amalia* had not fallen prey to the waves. It appears that some rumor or communication had reached them of sufficient credibility to cause Vehse to write to Welzel again on May 10, 1839, this time instructing him to proceed directly to Perry County, where land had by then been purchased.[51] This letter, sent in care of Vles in New Orleans,[52] was, of course, never delivered to its addressee. The *Amalia* had disappeared without leaving a single trace. The tragedy made a deep impression on many of the Stephanites and cast a pall over the first months in their new home. There was also a considerable financial loss involved, not only because of the money which

---

45 Financial statement closing Schlegel's account, March 12, 1839, MS., C. H. I.

46 Minutes of a meeting between Vehse, Jäckel, and Stephan, March 14, 1839, MS., C. H. I.

47 List of Saxon Emigrants, 1838, MS., C. H. I.

48 Minutes of a meeting between Vehse, Jäckel, and Stephan, March 14, 1839, MS., C. H. I.

49 Financial statement closing Pietsch's account, April 5, 1839, signed by Vehse, H. F. Fischer, and Jäckel, MS., C. H. I.

50 Epitome from the Cash-account, June 11, 1842, MS., C. H. I.

51 Vehse to K. W. Welzel, May 10, 1839, MS., C. H. I.

52 Vehse to Vles, May 10, 1839, MS., C. H. I.

K. W. Welzel was carrying, but even more because of the large amount of goods, belonging to the *Gesellschaft,* which had been shipped on this vessel. This event and the other transactions just mentioned again bring to the fore the subject — ever present in the story of the Saxons — of finances.

There is virtual unanimity in accounts of the immigration on at least one point, namely, that Stephan's expenditures upon himself and his mismanagement of common funds were especially objectionable during the period in St. Louis.[53] The Bishop had evidently decided that his days of "persecution" were over, and that he was to live on a scale and in a style befitting his position. Thus the Credit Fund was exposed to the caprices of a vain old man, whose sense of responsibility had not been strengthened by attaining absolute power simultaneously with his arrival in "the land of freedom." Only actual examples can do justice to Stephan's performance.

The coach in which Stephan had effected his retreat from Dresden had by now become a notorious piece of equipment. After being freighted all the way to St. Louis it was found inappropriate for his needs and sold — at a loss of 200 thaler — so that a light carriage could be purchased.[54] The episcopal residence in St. Louis was a considerable expense in itself, but Stephan's personal needs constituted an even larger item. The fact that several women were always living in the same establishment at the cost of additional rental that was higher than the average, and that Stephan frequently entertained the elite of the *Gesellschaft,* mainly the actual and prospective clerics, did not reduce the bill.[55] The requirements of the Bishop for quantities of the best and most expensive wines

---

[53] Winter to Guericke *et al.*, April 28, 1841, *Zeitschrift für die gesammte lutherische Theologie und Kirche*, II, No. 3, pp. 116—132; J. K. A. Höhne, and J. G. Höhne to their brother, Sept. 26, 1841, quoted in *Die Ameise*, Jan. 10, 1842; Nachrichten an unsere Nachkommen, MS., C. H. I.; Vehse, *op. cit.*, 7, 14, 16, 35; Schieferdecker, *op. cit.*, 12; G. Günther, *op. cit.*, 74.

[54] Stephan . . . Acct., MS., C. H. I.; Vehse, *op. cit.*, 14; Günther, *op. cit.*, 55.

[55] Vehse, *op. cit.*, 14—16; G. Günther, *op. cit.*, 75. Vehse's Pollyannish assurance that expensive delicacies were concealed from him in the Stephan apartment for fear of Vehse's censure, is not very convincing. Stephan feared no one in the *Gesellschaft* at this time. If Vehse was indeed the watchdog of the Stephanite treasury, he had more than enough to occupy his attention besides the item of food.

surprised even his American dealer, Vehse asserted.[56] The commemoration of Stephan's thirtieth anniversary in office, April 3, 1839, was the occasion for a private celebration of the chosen, and in the jubilarian's estimation justified his order for two kegs of beer at $7.00 each.[57] A tailor's bill for Stephan decreased the Credit Fund, from which all of these expenses mentioned were met, by another $31.50.[58]

Yet such expenditures were important from the financial viewpoint only as indicative of a trend. Compared with some other spending that was going on during the period in St. Louis, they were picayune. There was, for instance, an item of $400.00 paid out to O. H. Walther by Böhlau from the Credit Fund on Stephan's order. Later, when a general accounting was made, Walther was billed for this amount but protested, saying he was willing to assert on oath that he did not use it himself. While he admitted that he was legally liable for the sum, he begged to be excused from paying it. On the basis of this simple assertion and plea the creditors of the Credit Fund were kind enough to cancel the obligation, despite the fact that Walther did not do them the courtesy of stating clearly what happened to the money.[59] In general, the system of making cash advances to anyone with sufficiently good standing to rate authorization from Stephan, was continued also after the journey.[60]

The largest item of expense of this kind was the payment of "salaries" to the Bishop, clergy, candidates, and teachers in St. Louis. When the original plans had been drawn, Marbach had been willing for the emigrants to support these men. Yet even when the *Gesellschaft* was still on comparatively firm financial ground, he had in-

---

[56] Vehse, *op. cit.*, 16.

[57] Draft by Stephan on the Credit Fund for beer, April 4, 1839, signed by Jäckel and F. W. Barthel, G. H. Löber, Diary, April 3, 1839, MSS., C. H. I.; G. Günther, *op. cit.*, 75. It is interesting to note the different tone prevailing in Stephan's account of this occasion. Stephan to Flügel, Oct. 12, 1841, MS., C. H. I.

[58] Draft on the Credit Fund for Stephan's tailor's bill, March 5, 1839, MS., C. H. I.

[59] O. H. Walther to the creditors of the fund, Oct. 6, 1840, List of Saxon Emigrants 1838, MSS., C. H. I.

[60] Draft authorized by Stephan in favor of Teacher Müller (New York group) to purchase clothes, signed by Jäckel and F. W. Barthel, March 2, 1839, Draft in favor of Teacher Müller (New York group), signed by Jäckel, April 8, 1839, Draft in favor of Gönner, authorized by Stephan, Feb. 26, 1839, Draft in favor of Gönner, signed by Jäckel, April 10, 1839, MSS., C. H. I.

sisted on deferring the matter until the colonies should be well established. For a time his influence prevailed. But now Marbach's star had been dimmed, the hierarchy was in complete control, and the people were held to their ill-advised promise to support the battalion of clergymen and near-clergymen accompanying the immigrants.[61] Consequently, despite the desperate financial condition of the *Gesellschaft,* "salaries" were paid and, it must be remarked, accepted by men, most of whom were already in debt to the Credit Fund.

Stephan was given first consideration; he received $500.00. This sum was secured on the pretext that since leaving Bremen he had used his private funds (consisting of money given him by his followers) for the general purposes of the *Gesellschaft.* The transaction took place as the result of a meeting of the Advisory Committee, as constituted since the episcopacy had been introduced. The weird procedure in this case illustrates how affairs were now being conducted. The minutes reveal that the reason just given for considering an appropriation in Stephan's favor was stated. Then the actual grant was made forthwith. However, in doing this the action was not taken by the entire committee, but only by the clergymen, all five of whom (Löber, Keyl, Bürger, and the two Walthers) affixed their signatures to the minutes. Thereupon the protocol continued with a statement that since the pastors had served the *Gesellschaft* so well and had followed Stephan's example, they should receive $100.00 each. This portion was signed by Vehse, Gube, Schlimpert, Palish, George Klügel, Sr., and Häcker.

A supplement to these minutes, signed by Jäckel, the secretary, indicated that Stephan's presence was not even required to put the deal over, but that the minutes were then read to him on the same day for his approval. Approve he certainly did. Not only that, but he remarked that he had expected such action from them and was gratified that it had now been taken, not because he desired anything for himself, but because he desired that his spiritual charges should abound in good works, particularly in gifts, since "the Lord loveth a cheerful giver." The news of their action, he went on to say, consequently was "refreshing" to him because it again raised

[61] Pledge of Subjection to Stephan, *Selma,* Feb. 16, 1839, Pledge of Subjection to Stephan by the *Copernicus* group, Pledge of Subjection to Stephan by the *Johann Georg* group, I, II, MSS., C. H. I.

his hopes as to their spiritual condition.[62] No time was lost in carrying these "good works" through to a successful conclusion. Later on that same day Stephan signed a receipt for $500.00 paid him in cash from the Credit Fund.[63]

Although the Bishop had gone through the formal motions of securing an appropriation for this amount, it is interesting to note that this item does not appear in the later accounting of Stephan's total expenses beginning with the organization of the Credit Fund.[64] What happened to the money, who actually paid it out to him, or how the books were eventually made to balance, is not clear. But the signatures of the clergymen on the minutes make it clear who had an interest in covering up the maneuver, and Stephan's signature on the receipt removes any doubt that he actually received the money. Other cash withdrawals by him in St. Louis total about $400.[65] Vehse stated that 4,000 thaler were spent for the personal expenses of the Bishop in seven months (November, 1838—May, 1839), during three of which he was on board ship or boat.[66] This figure is high enough, but in order to obtain a true picture of how Stephan was exploiting his position, it would be necessary to add the figures given previously for the obligations incurred and benefits accepted by Stephan even before leaving Germany.

But Stephan was not the only one who apparently had deserved well at the hands of the *Gesellschaft.* On March 12, 1839, three days after the grant to the Bishop, the five pastors — Löber, Keyl, Bürger, O. H. Walther, and C. F. W. Walther — were each paid their $100.00.[67] If the impropriety of such transactions under prevailing financial circumstances, or the fatuous character of the homily accompanying the major item of largess to Stephan, struck any of the men involved, they gave no sign thereof. Instead, two weeks later the same group listed above, now functioning as the Advisory Committee, held another meeting, with Vehse acting as

---

62 Protokolle über die . . . Auswanderung, March 9, 1839, MS., C. H. I.

63 Receipt for $500.00 paid Stephan from the Credit Fund and signed by him, March 9, 1839, MS., C. H. I. See also Vehse, *op. cit.,* 13—14.

64 Stephan . . . Acct., MS., C. H. I.

65 *Ibid.*

66 Vehse, *op. cit.,* 16.

67 Receipt signed by Pastors Löber, C. F. W. Walther, O. H. Walther, Keyl, and Bürger, for $100.00 paid each of them from the Credit Fund, March 12, 1839, MS., C. H. I. See also Keyl, *op. cit.,* 16.

secretary in the absence of Jäckel. On this occasion $30.00 was voted to Candidates Wege, Fröhlich, Klügel, Fürbringer, Geyer, and Schieferdecker; $25.00 to Teachers Helbig (Hellwig), Winter, and Koch; and $50.00 to Jäckel; $100.00 to Barthel; and $25.00 to Böhlau.[68] On March 26 Böhlau's compensation was increased to $30.00.[69] The following day the payments to the candidates and teachers were made, and receipts were signed by them. It developed that Brohm had been overlooked in the original distribution, but he received the same share as the other candidates.[70] Receipts indicating that payment was ever made to any of the laymen were not discovered during the course of this study.

Thus, during the month of March a total of $785.00 was paid out in benefits to the clergy, candidates, and teachers. Vehse substantiated the fact that these payments were made, and mentioned the promise, which was also set forth in the minutes, that these men were to be paid more when times would be better.[71] It is noteworthy that the former stalwarts of the *Gesellschaft,* Marbach, Vehse, and H. F. Fischer, were in such disfavor that they were ignored in this dispensation, in which even Bürger and Barthel were permitted to participate.

The unnecessary outlay for costly ecclesiastical regalia has been described in the foregoing. Church plate was apparently also of paramount importance, and on February 27, 1839, O. H. Walther was advanced $50.00 to buy some.[72] Again, such ill-advised spending was only a fraction of the total. As early as January 17, 1839, before the *Olbers* even landed in New Orleans, the account of "Church and School" showed a deficit of 5,208 thaler.[73] For this sum, as well as for the original capital with which the account had been credited, the *Gesellschaft* had nothing to show except the

---

68 Protokolle über die . . . Auswanderung, March 23, 1839, MS., C. H. I.

69 *Ibid.*, March 26, 1839.

70 Receipt signed by Candidates Wege, Brohm, Geyer, Schieferdecker, Fröhlich, Fürbringer, and Klügel for $30.00 paid each of them from the Credit Fund, March 27, 1839, Receipt signed by Teachers Hellwig, Koch, and Winter, for $25.00 paid to each of them from the Credit Fund, March 27, 1839, MSS., C. H. I.

71 Protokolle über die . . . Auswanderung, March 26, 1839, MS., C. H. I.; Vehse, *op. cit.*, 14.

72 Draft in favor of O. H. Walther, signed by Jäckel and F. W. Barthel, Feb. 27, 1839, MS., C. H. I.

73 List of Saxon Emigrants 1838, MS., C. H. I.

possession of sundry items without which they could have managed equally well. Even the leaders seem to have considered this state of affairs questionable. So attempts were now made to cover up some of the more injudicious expenditures previously incurred. For instance, contributions were now made by several of the leaders to defray the cost of a rather expensive sofa which had been bought in New Orleans from *Gesellschaft* funds for Stephan's comfort on the *Selma.*[74]

By way of keeping the deficit for ecclesiastical purposes within bounds, the financial jugglers of the *Gesellschaft* began, on January 17, to write off rather large amounts from this fund to individuals in the *Gesellschaft* who were still substantial contributors.[75] It is not recorded, and there is no reason to believe, that these people paid such amounts as further contributions at that time. The process appears to have been simply a transfer of credits from the Credit Fund to the specific account of "Church and School," and what a single account had gained, the whole fund must necessarily have lost. So while the general financial situation was not improved in the least, a handsome sum appeared on the books to balance the expenditures in the ecclesiastical account. By May 11, this process had netted 2,719 thaler, and the deficit of "Church and School" could be reduced by that amount.[76] However, further spending in this department had been going on meanwhile, for an additional $1,133.00 for "Religious and School Purposes" had been withdrawn between February 21 and May 24.[77] Judging from the modest outlay for the educational program described above, one may conclude that the most of this money was spent not for school, but for "religious" purposes. To make matters worse, most of the unnecessary supplies bought in Germany, many of which were for the benefit of "the church," had been loaded on the *Amalia,* and these became a total loss.[78] The importance of the sum involved can be gauged from Vehse's statement that the total cost of an

---

[74] Statement by Jäckel of contributions by O. H. Walther, Vehse, Jäckel, Gube, *et al.*, for payment of a sofa bought for Stephan, April 10, 1838, MS., C. H. I.

[75] List of Saxon Emigrants 1838, MS., C. H. I.

[76] *Ibid.*

[77] Epitome from the Cash-account, June 11, 1842, MS., C. H. I.

[78] Winter to Guericke *et al.*, April 28, 1841, *Zeitschrift für die gesammte lutherische Theologie und Kirche,* II, No. 3, pp. 116—132.

organ, orchestra, library, and similar easily dispensable items was 8,000 thaler.[79]

Unfortunately, it was far easier to exploit these evidences of squandering and financial chicanery after Stephan was no longer present, than it was to take any action on them at the time. No actual curb was placed upon the Bishop, and only one effort seems to have been made during the St. Louis phase of the migration to call the leader's attention to the consequences of his policies. In fact, while some financial reverses, such as the loss of the *Amalia,* could not be concealed, ignorance of the exact status of the Credit Fund, noted above, probably prevailed until March 14, 1839, almost a month after arrival in St. Louis.[80] How true this supposition is becomes evident upon examining the confused statements of the leaders, even of Vehse, who was one of the best informed.

Vehse claimed, for instance, that when the *Olbers* docked, the *Gesellschaft* still had "30,000 Spanish dollars (ca. 45,000 Prussian thaler; the crossing had cost ca. 60,000) of the approximate sum of 125,000 thaler" which, according to him, had originally been in the Credit Fund.[81] However, Vehse's total of the sum spent and the sum on hand does not tally either with his figure (125,000 thaler) nor the correct figure (117,521 thaler) of the capital of the Credit Fund. Furthermore, a later and more reliable financial statement by Barthel places total costs up to arrival in St. Louis at $58,869.[82] Vehse's assertion that total costs up to arrival in New Orleans were 60,000 thaler, or about $40,000, would mean that nearly $19,000 had been spent in getting from New Orleans to St. Louis, an extravagant exaggeration in view of what was actually spent on that leg of the journey.

The figures for costs on the ocean vessels have been given, as well as those for all river boats but the *Rienzi,* for which the exact amount is not available. All these sums, even including a very generous allowance for the trip on the *Rienzi,* total less than 50,000 thaler and thereby show that a large percentage of *Gesellschaft* funds was being dissipated. Comparison of the facts given here

---

79 Vehse, *op. cit.,* 16.

80 Minutes of a meeting between Vehse, Jäckel, and Stephan, March 14, 1839, MS., C. H. I.

81 Vehse, *op. cit.,* 16.

82 Epitome from the Cash-account, June 11, 1842, MS., C. H. I.

with Barthel's figure, stated just above, leads to the conclusion that, by the time the Stephanites reached St. Louis, some $24,000 or $25,000 had been spent for purposes other than transportation and maintenance of the immigrants. Furthermore, the costs on Stephan's ship were always disproportionately high. It is worth noting that in this case, as in others, there was both squandering and a leakage of funds where Stephan was concerned. The costs on the *Olbers* were given above from reliable financial statements as 11,011 thaler and those on the *Selma* as 4,829 thaler. Together these figures total 15,840 thaler. Yet the actual expenditures for the *Olbers-Selma* group were finally determined to have been slightly over 16,308 thaler. There is a difference of about 469 thaler unaccounted for.[83]

The upshot of the matter was that no one, not even Vehse, knew how much had been spent and what remained. His motive for adopting the figures he chose, was probably the desire to clear himself of blame for the failure of the colonization enterprise. His claims as to finances are a springboard for the assertion that the money remaining on arrival in St. Louis was sufficient to establish a comfortable existence.[84] Such a presentation postpones all blame for failure to the period in St. Louis and to the purchase of land. Since developments at this time did not go according to his advice, he — and others — mistakenly felt justified in washing their hands of the entire matter.

However, even Vehse's own figures, inaccurate as they were, belie his claims. If there had been $30,000 left on arrival in New Orleans, it is certain that there must have been some thousands less after the cost of transportation to St. Louis, of a sojourn there, however brief, and of transfer to a new location had been met. Yet the Advisory Committee, of which Vehse himself was a member, had set the minimum purchase price for land, computed at the cheapest rate of $1.25 an acre, at $20,000 to $30,000 exclusive of the cost of necessary supplies, equipment, materials, initial building costs, and the repayment of temporary deposits in the Credit Fund. Plainly, the *Gesellschaft* was bankrupt in effect long before the books began to show it.

Finally, Vehse was, in point of actual fact, somewhat better

---

[83] Account C, Bound MSS., 8, C. H. I.

[84] Vehse, *op. cit.*, 34.

informed than his writings indicate. He was genuinely alarmed, recognized the need for action in this critical state of affairs, and took steps to prevent further waste. This part of his role is to his credit, and he should have emphasized it in his account of events. Instead, he attempted to picture conditions with an optimism strained to the point of inaccuracy. Actually, Vehse's apprehensions were so disturbing to him that they led him to beard the lion in his den. That is to say, together with Jäckel he appeared before Stephan on March 14, 1839, and confronted him with a statement of the financial status of the *Gesellschaft.*[85] Barthel, the treasurer, whose presence might have been expected at such a meeting, apparently was absent.

Barthel's accounts show that on February 21, 1839, the *Gesellschaft* had \$21,735.81¼ left, and that by May 24, further payments of \$1,876.81¼ and "Reimbursements" to the Credit Fund of \$953.75 brought total assets for the period to \$24,566.37½.[86] But by the date on which Vehse and Jäckel conferred with Stephan they had to report that the capital of the Credit Fund, including actual cash on hand and further receipts definitely promised, had already decreased to \$18,657.[87] From this amount a number of important deductions still had to be made, such as \$1,500 monthly for living expenses so long as the *Gesellschaft* remained in St. Louis.[88] Hence it became plain even to Stephan that only about \$10,000, or at most \$12,000, would remain for the purchase of land. Stephan observed that since the terms on all offers of land made up to that time had called for one third cash, the sum on hand for that purpose was too little to permit the consideration of most of these offers.[89] The offers, therefore, must have ranged from \$30,000 upward.

When brought face to face with the unpleasantness of such starkly real details, the Bishop became a rather helpless figure.

---

85 Minutes of a meeting between Vehse, Jäckel, and Stephan, March 14, 1839, MS., C. H. I. In an effort to absolve himself of any blame Stephan wrote, over two years later, that he did "not to this day know either the receipts or the expenditures of this Fund." Stephan to Flügel, Oct. 12, 1841, MS., C. H. I. It is interesting to note that in Stephan's mind such irresponsible ignorance would have been justified — had it been true.

86 Epitome from the Cash-account, June 11, 1842, MS., C. H. I.

87 Minutes of a meeting between Vehse, Jäckel, and Stephan, March 14, 1839, MS., C. H. I.

88 *Ibid.*

89 *Ibid.*

His only contribution toward a solution of the financial problem was the perplexed and futile hope that some members of the *Gesellschaft* who still had money would contribute still more.[90] Only one person is known to have responded to this invitation to involve himself more deeply in the *Gesellschaft's* tangled finances. G. H. Löber recorded that "on March 16 Weber [very likely Johann Christoph Weber of Planena], on his sickbed and in the presence of two witnesses, Dr. Vehse and George Klügel, Sr., bequeathed 1000 thaler for building the church in the future; the document accomplishing this has been placed into the hands of the Herr Bishop." [91] There was only one instance in which the Credit Fund was augmented directly during these months of the episcopacy; that was when Kimm & Tewes notified Vehse and Marbach that the sum of $811.00 had been sent by Vles in New Orleans to Kimm & Tewes on the account of the *Gesellschaft.* Vehse accepted it, in Marbach's absence, on May 6 and acknowledged it to Vles on May 10, 1839; while a notation by Jäckel stated it had been placed with F. W. Barthel into the Credit Fund on May 11. There is no indication of the source of these funds.[92]

Vehse at least recognized his own inability to cope with the situation and suggested securing the advice and services of his new friend, Dr. Gempp. Stephan replied, apparently with some relief, that Gempp was indeed an excellent individual, whose friendship was valuable, and that he should be drawn into their deliberations for consultation.[93] A note in these same minutes, dated the next day, March 15, stated that Gempp had agreed to serve the *Gesellschaft.*[94]

The sudden realization of the sorry plight of the immigrants caused a flurry of activity in the treasurer's office. Itemized accounts were made, and a general inventory was begun, although not

---

[90] *Ibid.*

[91] G. H. Löber, Diary, March 16, 1839, MS., C. H. I.

[92] Kimm & Tewes to Marbach and Vehse, May 6, 1839, Bound MSS., 6, C. H. I.; Vehse to Vles & Company, May 10, 1839, MS., C. H. I. The money may simply have been the balance of a larger sum left on deposit with the New Orleans agents in order to meet obligations of the colonists which they had not discharged while in the city. Perhaps it had even been left there for Welzel's use when the *Amalia* should arrive.

[93] Minutes of a meeting between Vehse, Jäckel, and Stephan, March 14, 1839, MS., C. H. I.

[94] *Ibid.*

actually completed for months. The detailed statement by G. H. Löber for the *Republik* was finished on April 11, almost a month later. That for the *Olbers* was approved as correct by Stephan and signed by Jäckel as late as April 22, 1839. The detailed expense account for the *Selma,* signed by F. W. Barthel, was not ready until April 26, 1839.[95] The general computation of receipts and expenditures of the Credit Fund was made for the date of May 24, 1839,[96] and the balances of the individual accounts were not entered until June 6, 1839.[97] The discussion of finances in the foregoing pages has already touched upon a closely related matter which was also claiming the attention of the *Gesellschaft,* that is, the purchase of land.

The meeting of March 14, just described, was also the occasion for restating the principles which should guide selection of the site for the new colony.[98] The original plans of the committee on this point have been stated above. Now other considerations seem to have motivated Stephan, at least on some points. For these were the criteria he set up on March 14, in the interview with Jäckel and Vehse:

1. One third of the cost was not to exceed $10,000.

2. The site should comprise sufficient farm land to support eight hundred people for the first year.

3. That portion of the land, which would later become the site of the city that was to be founded, might be a few miles from these farms.

4. There must be additional uncleared land in the immediate vicinity purchasable at a later date.

5. The colony must be situated within one day's journey by wagon from St. Louis.

6. The colony should not contain land adjacent to a river navigable by steamboat, but should be on a tributary of such a river or on a highway leading to St. Louis.

---

95 Itemized list of expenditures for the *Republik* group, made out and signed by G. H. Löber, April 11, 1839, Repartitionen den *Olbers* betreff., approved by Stephan, signed by Jäckel, April 22, 1839, Financial statement for the *Selma,* signed by F. W. Barthel, April 26, 1839, Bound MSS., 10, C. H. I.

96 Epitome from the Cash-account, June 11, 1842, MS., C. H. I.

97 List of Saxon Emigrants 1838, MS., C. H. I.

98 Minutes of a meeting between Vehse, Jäckel, and Stephan, March 14, 1839, MS., C. H. I.

7. The location should be healthful, the soil should be of at least medium fertility, and the land should contain a stand of timber sufficient for the building that needed to be done.

8. The *Gesellschaft* must obtain a clear title to the land.[99]

Between the dates of these two partially conflicting statements of factors that were to determine their choice, the leaders had received further advice from Kimm. In the letter directed to Marbach at New Orleans, the St. Louis businessman had pointed out that it would be necessary for the *Gesellschaft* to settle some distance from St. Louis. In the immediate vicinity of the city land was selling at $200.00 an acre, and even ten to twelve miles away it was $8.00 to $12.00 an acre. Kimm furthermore urged the immigrants to locate near a navigable stream, and accordingly suggested they procure land on the upper Missouri or Mississippi Rivers — in Kimm's opinion preferably the latter — where it was still obtainable at $1.25 an acre. A warning was also contained in the letter that the leaders of the Stephanites should personally inspect any contemplated site before the actual purchase of land. It would even be desirable, Kimm suggested, to obtain the opinion of some impartial, competent, and trustworthy third party. For this purpose Kimm & Tewes recommended Mr. Geyer, a young botanist of Dresden, who knew Stephan and who had returned from a United States Government expedition only a few days prior to the date of Kimm's writing.[100] Events reveal how lightly this or any other advice was regarded.

The acquisition of a site for the proposed settlement should have been the primary concern of the *Gesellschaft's* leaders. Stephan's apparent expectation of momentary departure from St. Louis invites the conclusion that purchase of land was, indeed, the first order of business. Yet in point of fact weeks were allowed to slip by before any noticeable activity was developed in this department. Then, on March 9, 1839, a committee, whose duty it was to seek suitable land, was advanced $600.00 for expenses on the order of Stephan.[101] How the members of this group, composed of Gube,

---

[99] *Ibid.*

[100] Kimm & Tewes to Marbach, Dec. 10, 1838, Bound MSS., I, C. H. I. Further reference to Botanist Geyer can be found in Garraghan, "The Beginnings of St. Louis University," *St. Louis Catholic Historical Review*, V, 101.

[101] Draft by Jäckel in favor of the land committee, authorized by Stephan and signed by the committee members, March 9, 1839, MS., C. H. I.

[C. G.?] Schlimpert, and Palisch, were chosen is not clear even in the less restrained accounts, such as Bürger's.[102] But Gube was the committee's most active and influential member, and he was a trusted aid of Stephan. Less than a week later the conversation of Stephan, Vehse, and Jäckel took place, and Gempp was asked for his advice.

Offers were soon made to the Stephanites, for land was still plentiful in the West. Millions of acres of desirable Government land were for sale within reasonable distances at the prevailing low price of $1.25 an acre. During the first three quarters of 1838, Illinois and Missouri were leading all States in the sale of Government land with a turnover of 752,000 acres and 694,000 acres respectively.[103] The following year Missouri actually assumed the leading position and was still third among all States in 1845.[104] As late as 1846 eight thousand acres of privately owned land within 120 miles of St. Louis were offered for sale at $1.25 to $5.00 an acre.[105]

The most attractive of the offers made the Saxons was probably one secured through Gempp. The physician and his friend Vehse advocated the acquisition of the Gratiot estate on the Meramec River, about twelve to fifteen miles from St. Louis. This tract of some fifteen thousand acres was offered to the Stephanites by the Gratiot family through Gempp at what Vehse described as a very attractive price and on very easy terms.[106] Vehse's description, while probably partial, nevertheless leads to the conclusion that the purchase of this site would have been an eminently sound investment. Although his visionary plans for making a health resort of the area, because it contained a few sulphur springs,[107] were a little premature and overdrawn, his other observations are plausible enough. The soil was rich, the region was healthful, and the location, on a stream very near to St. Louis, was almost ideal. Furthermore, some of the land was heavily wooded, and with fuel bringing

---

[102] E. M. Bürger, Selbstbiographie, 122, MS., E. J. Buerger Papers, Ellicottville, N. Y.

[103] *Daily Evening Gazette*, Feb. 17, 1840.

[104] *Anzeiger des Westens*, Sept. 28, 1843, Oct. 16, 1845.

[105] *Die Deutsche Tribüne*, Jan. 28, 1846.

[106] Vehse, *op. cit.*, 34—35.

[107] *Ibid.*, 35.

high prices in St. Louis the settlers would have had an excellent opportunity for realizing a handsome cash return on their investment at once and thus tiding themselves over financially for a time.[108]

Why the Gratiot estate was not purchased is nowhere explained, except as the answer may be found in Vehse's disappointed remark: "But Stephan's mind was fixed on the wilderness." [109] It is likely that there was a large element of truth in this accusation. Both past and future events, both the nature of the location Stephan did not choose and the nature of that which he did choose, show that he wished to build his own little city-state rather than to become a part of a larger metropolis. Some of the actual principles motivating his choice, as well as some of his stated principles which he eventually ignored, tend to bear out the implication contained in Vehse's jibe. Moreover, the reception which Stephan received in St. Louis was not likely to make him any more favorably inclined toward the idea of remaining in that city or its immediate vicinity.[110] An appraisal of the situation of the immigrants after the lapse of a century indicates that the offer of the Gratiot estate was the Stephanites' golden opportunity as well as their leader's last chance to redeem himself and make his movement the success he dreamed it might become. But the purchase was not made, and the plan became merely another in a lengthening series of might-have-beens.

Meanwhile other offers were being made. Several tracts of land that were under consideration during the ensuing weeks are described in an undated statement evidently drawn up during this period.[111] This document shows that even at this time land in Perry County, Missouri, was being investigated. At the unknown date on which the summary of possibilities was made, 544 acres in that county had been offered at the ruinous price of $5,450 or about $10 an acre for the entire tract, of which only 110 acres were under cultivation. There were a few buildings on one of the farms included in this parcel of land, and a six-acre tract, also within the

---

108 *Ibid.*

109 *Ibid.*

110 G. Günther, *op. cit.*, 46.

111 Ueberblick zu erkaufender Ländereien, Bound MSS., VI, C. H. I.

544 acres, contained a sawmill. At the same time some four hundred acres of land at $1.25 an acre could also be bought in the vicinity of the same 544-acre plot. For another 777-acre tract with a few buildings and only a hundred acres in cultivation, about twelve to fifteen miles from this Perry County location, $5,000 was being asked. Some land in Illinois was also being considered. But a site in Missouri was preferred because there the topography more nearly approximated that of their homeland. Besides, the areas in Missouri were less populous and therefore, in the opinion of the leaders, bore promise of greater growth.[112]

The figures just cited as being quoted the Saxons, as well as the two indications in the meeting of March 14, 1839, that most offers were running up to more than $30,000, demonstrate attempts to victimize the immigrants by asking exorbitant prices on small tracts of land or by offering them land at lower prices but in such tremendous stretches that they surpassed even the Advisory Committee's visions and were utterly out of the question for a tragically depleted Credit Fund. The impractical, sentimental attachment to the picturesqueness of parts of the Saxon countryside, that has been noted a number of times as helping to determine a choice of the location for the colony, made it even easier to place the Stephanites at a disadvantage in a land deal. In this respect they were, of course, not unique. Contemporary German observers were struck by two factors in this connection: first, that the "Yankees" generally were known as sharp traders and shrewd investors,[113] and secondly, that the German immigrants, while they were entirely competent to appraise the quality of the soil, nevertheless frequently exercised poor judgment in making land purchases, when, like the Saxons, they were influenced by sentimental considerations.[114]

"The German farmer," observed Wittke, "usually was shrewd in selecting the best farming country available." [115] Not so the Stephanites. It was on impractical grounds, such as topography

---

112 *Ibid.*

113 Lenz, *op. cit.*, 46—48.

114 Zimmerman, "Travel into Missouri in October, 1838," translated by Bek in *Missouri Historical Review*, IX, 37; Schneider, *op. cit.*, 30.

115 Wittke, *op. cit.*, 208.

and the desire to build a "Zion" far removed from the distracting influences of a robust and blustering young West, and by a committee of questionable competence and independence, that the eventual site of the colony was determined. All locations under consideration were inspected by the land committee of three mentioned above, and often reinforced by O. H. Walther, Marbach, and Heinrich Bimpage.[116] The last of these, whose name has occurred before, was engaged as real estate agent and legal representative for the Saxons. In this capacity he played an important part in almost all their affairs for the next few months, the most troubled period in the history of Stephanism. The fact that Bimpage was intimately associated with Wilhelm Weber makes his choice as a confidant of the immigrants a peculiar one, and its undesirable consequences may be seen in the detailed nature of information detrimental to the Saxon cause, which later appeared in Weber's *Anzeiger*.[117] The interests of the *Gesellschaft* at this critical juncture were accordingly placed into the hands of a group of six men, one of whom (Bimpage) was a friend of their most influential opponent, Weber, and three of whom (its most important members, O. H. Walther, Marbach, and Gube) were clearly under the domination of the man who had done more than any other to create the crisis in the affairs of the immigrants, Stephan. The advice of Kimm to rely upon the judgment of impartial persons could scarcely have been more thoroughly disregarded.

The new settlement was finally located in Perry County, Missouri, a little over a hundred miles south of St. Louis on the Mississippi River. Here 4,475.88 acres of privately owned and Government land were acquired in purchases during the months of April and May, 1839. All land was in Gube's name, and he bought much of it himself. Most, if not all, of the Government land was entered in Gube's name, especially in the transactions of April 12 and May 22, 1839.[118] There is considerable confusion on all facts con-

---

116 G. Günther, *op. cit.*, 74.

117 *Ibid.*, 47.

118 Abstract of Original Land Entries in Perry County, Missouri, 126, 128—129, 131—135, MS., Office of the Clerk of the Perry County (Mo.) Court, Perryville, Mo.; Johann Gottlieb Palisch and thirty-eight other plaintiffs vs. Henry C. Bimpage, Circuit Court of Perry County, Mo., exercising chancery jurisdiction, Nov. term, Nov. 29, 1839, Chancery Record, 127, MS., Perry County (Mo.) Circuit Court Records, Perryville, Mo. (hereafter cited

cerning the Saxon land purchase. G. Günther, for instance, pictures it as though the entire deal was completed by April 8, 1839.[119] The actual amount of land acquired has caused even more serious discrepancies and has been described variously as "several thousand," [120] four to five thousand,[121] 4,400,[122] 4,472.66,[123] 4,473,[124] "about 5,000," [125] five thousand,[126] *"circa* 5,600," [127] six thousand,[128] or even ten thousand acres.[129]

The total cost of the purchase was $9,234.25. This figure is arrived at from information contained in the financial account, "List of Saxon Emigrants," where the expenses are itemized as follows: $1,000.00 (1,458.33 thaler) for the landing place bought from Mr. Sullivan, April 12, 1839; $3,200.00 (4,666.67 thaler) for the land

---

as Palisch *et al.* vs. Bimpage); Johann Gottlieb Palisch and thirty-eight other plaintiffs vs. Henry C. Bimpage, Bill in Chancery, No. 28, Circuit Court of Perry County, Mo., exercising chancery jurisdiction, Nov. term, Nov. 29, 1839, MS., Circuit Clerk and Recorder's Vault, Perryville, Mo. (hereafter cited as Palisch *et al.*, vs. Bimpage, Bill in Chancery, No. 28, Circuit Court of Perry County, Mo., Nov. 29, 1839); Exhibit A (Power of attorney, J. G. Gube to J. G. Palisch and C. G. Schlimpert, Aug. 5, 1839 — hereafter cited simply as Exhibit A), *ibid.;* Exhibit A and F (List of Lands entered by Joh. George Gube and claimed by a number of Settlers, styled the german lutheran Congregation — hereafter cited as Exhibit A and F, and to be distinguished from Exhibit A), *ibid.* The only other instance in which the correct figure is given for the amount of land purchased, is *Gedächtniss-Feier . . . 1839—1939,* p. 5.

119 G. Günther, *op. cit.,* 74.

120 J. F. Bünger, "Ehrengedächtniss des seligen Pastors Brohm," *Der Lutheraner,* XXXVII, 189.

121 Vehse, *op. cit.,* 35.

122 Nachrichten an unsere Nachkommen, MS., C.H.I.; A. L. Gräbner, *"Bis hieher,"* 6; Bonnet, "Dr. C. F. W. Walther," *Lutheran Witness,* XXX, 170; Hattstädt, "Vor hundert Jahren, 3, Die Auswanderung," *Der Lutheraner,* XCIV, 132; Rupprecht, "Gotthold Heinrich Loeber," *Concordia Historical Institute Quarterly,* XI, 51. This is the most popular figure and is used by many writers in addition to those cited here.

123 H. Koepchen, "The Saxon Emigration of 1838," *Lutheran Witness,* LVII, 188; P. Kretzmann, "The Saxon Immigration to Missouri, 1838—1839," *Missouri Historical Review,* XXXIII, 164; Stellhorn, "The Saxon Centennial and the Schools," *Lutheran School Journal,* LXXIV, 346.

124 Schneider, *op. cit.,* 103.

125 Fritschel, *Geschichte,* 175.

126 Document . . . des Grundsteins . . . St. Louis . . . 22. Juny 1842, MS., C.H.I.

127 Stephan to Flügel, Oct. 12, 1841, MS., C.H.I.

128 Winter to Guericke *et al.*, April 28, 1841, *Zeitschrift für die gesammte lutherische Theologie und Kirche,* II, No. 3, pp. 116—132; G. Günther, *op. cit.,* 74.

129 *Daily Evening Gazette,* May 3, 1839.

bought from Mr. Lawless,[130] April 30, 1839; and $4,787.00 (6,979.58 thaler) for the land bought by Mr. Gube.[131] To the sum of $8,987.00 (13,104.58 thaler), which these figures yield as the cost of the land proper, must be added $249.00 for expenses connected with inspecting sites, choosing the location, and completing the necessary transactions.[132] Thus the final cost of the entire real estate venture becomes that given above, $9,234.25 (13,466.58 thaler).[133]

This figure differs from any other one given, even that in the "Epitome from the Cash-account of the Saxon emigrants," where an item is listed as: "$8,741.622. Purchase of Land."[134] The figure from the List of Saxon Emigrants was accepted in this study in preference to all others; first, because it is contained in an official documentary record kept by F. W. Barthel and in use from 1839 to 1847, a period of time which would have given him ample opportunity to make a correction, had a mistake occurred; secondly, the account is itemized, which leads to the supposition that it was more carefully and accurately drawn up than a statement of a lump sum. The statement on the matter in the Epitome, given above, is the only other one in the records of the Saxons. The Epitome, however, is reliable only up to May 24, 1839, the date on which the accounts it contains were closed. It is quite likely that land was purchased even after May 24 and that some purchased immediately before May 24 may not have been included in the Epitome's accounting. Gube purchased a large amount of it as late as May 22. In any event, the Epitome probably does not include the expenses of

---

130 Who Lawless was is not clear. The rather spectacular career of Col. Luke E. Lawless, Judge of the Circuit Court, who may have had extensive land holdings in this area, is discussed in Scharf, *op. cit.*, II, 1474; Garraghan, "The Beginnings of St. Louis University," *St. Louis Catholic Historical Review*, I, 92—93. Note also that this Judge Lawless was personally connected with the investigation of the only lynching in the St. Louis area during these years — a matter which was later to become of interest to the Saxons. Dwight L. Dumond, "The Mississippi: Valley of Decision," *Mississippi Valley Historical Review*, XXXVI, 15.

131 "Länderey-Conto" in List of Saxon Emigrants 1838, MS., C. H. I.

132 *Ibid.*

133 According to the rate of exchange employed by the Saxons themselves and used in this study, 1.458 thaler to a dollar, the total in dollars and cents would be $9,236.34. However, in this case, perhaps because of the size of the amount involved, the rate of computation was carried to at least hundred-thousandths: 1.45833. On this basis the result becomes $9,234.23.

134 Epitome from the Cash-account, June 11, 1842, MS., C. H. I.

$249.00 connected with securing the land, since they could scarcely have been known as early as May 24.

In previous narratives the sums involved have been treated with as little consideration as the acreage acquired. One mistake often made is to take the figure of $9,234.25 mentioned above, which already included the $1,000 for the landing place bought from Mr. Sullivan (as the itemized account given there shows), and then *add* to the basic figure the sum of $1,000.00 for the landing place, producing a total of $10,234.25.[135] Elsewhere figures of $10,000 or more than $10,000 are frequently found.[136]

The average price per acre paid by the Saxons accordingly was $2.06. Exactly what portion of the land purchased was private and what Government land is not certain. One reasonable assumption, however, would help to clear up the question considerably. It is based upon two circumstances: first, in the transactions with private individuals Gube does not seem to have acted alone,[137] and secondly, in the itemized account the names of such private individuals with whom the Saxons dealt are given. Therefore it seems likely that when the name of Gube, who is known from other sources to have been a prominent or even the sole purchaser of Government land, is given alone as the buyer accompanied by the name of no seller, this was all Government land, and that the balance was all private land. If such a supposition — and it is only that — is correct, then the $4,787.00 Gube spent would have bought about 3,430 acres of Government land at $1.25 an acre. The remaining 646 acres would then have cost the balance, $4,200.00, or about $6.50 an acre, inclusive of the landing place. It is even possible to surmise that the odd six-acre parcel of land surrounded the landing place and that the full section of 640 acres was bought for the $3,200 remaining after subtracting the purchase price of the land-

---

135 H. Koepchen, "The Saxon Emigration of 1838," *Lutheran Witness*, LVII, 188; P. Kretzmann, "The Saxon Immigration to Missouri, 1838—1839," *Missouri Historical Review*, XXXIII, 164; Stellhorn, "The Saxon Centennial and the Schools," *Lutheran School Journal*, LXXIV, 346.

136 Stephan to Flügel, Oct. 12, 1841, MS., C.H.I.; Vehse, *op. cit.*, 35; Th. Gräbner, *op. cit.*, 16; Hattstädt, "Vor hundert Jahren, 3, Die Auswanderung," *Der Lutheraner*, XCIV, 132.

137 Personal note for $3,200.00, Sullivan to Marbach, May 2, 1839, and transfer of this note, Marbach to O. H. Walther, May 6, 1839, Bound MSS., 6, C.H.I.

ing. This would make an even $5.00 an acre for the whole section and be a more reasonable figure to have spent for such a stretch of land, than the prices originally quoted the Saxons. G. Günther claims the prices varied from $1.00 to $6.00 an acre.[138] The financing of the purchase is even more obscure, but evidently it was for cash, even though that method necessitated securing at least a short term loan of $3,200.00 (the precise amount of the purchase from Lawless) from Mr. Sullivan.[139]

The acquisition of land was again an event worthy of note in the English press. The *Daily Evening Gazette* had the following to say:

> We learn that the company of Lutherans, amounting to some 700 persons, who arrived here a few weeks since have purchased 10,000 acres of choice land in Perry County (Mo.), comprising an excellent landing place on the Mississippi, at the mouth of Brazoe Creek.
>
> This company owns a library of some 20,000 volumes; and intend, shortly, to establish a College. They will form a desirable addition to the population of this State.[140]

The *Cape Girardeau Patriot* wrote:

> We understand that a company of Germans, amounting to 700, have lately settled in Perry county, Missouri, and purchased, in a body, 10,000 acres of land, in what is called Brazoo Bottom, the best part of the county. They are of the Lutheran persuasion, and have a library of 20,000 volumes, and intend shortly to establish a college. The Germans are an honest and industrious people, and a desirable population.[141]

In Perry County the Saxons had not chosen a rapidly growing or otherwise promising area in which to settle. St. Louis was multiplying in size four- to fivefold during the decade of the forties, and the increase even for the State at large, from a population of 383,702 in 1840 to 508,372 in 1844 and to one of 682,044 in 1850, amounted to 77.75 per cent.[142] Perry County, meanwhile, showed a popula-

[138] G. Günther, *op. cit.*, 74.

[139] Personal note for $3,200.00 Sullivan to Marbach, May 2, 1839, and transfer of this note, Marbach to O. H. Walther, May 6, 1839, Bound MSS., 6, C. H. I.

[140] *Daily Evening Gazette*, May 3, 1839.

[141] *Cape Girardeau Patriot* in *Daily Missouri Republican*, May 30, 1839.

[142] *The Sixth Census of the United States: 1840*, p. 417; *ibid.*, 1850, p. 665; *Anzeiger des Westens*, Jan. 30, 1845.

tion of only 5,760 in 1840, of 6,669 (840 of them slaves) in 1844, and of no more than 7,215 in 1850.[143] Perryville, the county seat, was a diminutive hamlet of 219 in 1844 and had even lost in size by 1850, when its population was only 177.[144] The population of southeast Missouri at this time was composed largely of the original French, in settlements such as Ste. Genevieve and Cape Girardeau, and of English-speaking people, either American-born or immigrant Irish, Scotch, or English. There were few Germans in the area before the advent of the Saxons. In Perry County Germans had been a negligible portion of the population, and they had begun to enter Cape Girardeau County in numbers only in 1838.[145]

The general remarks on religious conditions in the West and in Missouri are applicable also to Perry County. The Roman Catholics were rather strong there at an early date, and since 1818 had been maintaining an educational establishment, St. Mary's, then located at Perryville, which included a nunnery, a girls' school, a primary school, a preparatory school, and a seminary for priests. By 1840 St. Mary's had an enrollment of seventy-five.[146] There were no "academies," as the United States census classified schools, in Perry County in 1840. In fact, there were only eight "primary or common schools," all of them private institutions, with a combined enrollment of 169.[147] The Protestant church bodies represented in Perry County were the Baptists, the Presbyterians, the Methodists, and the Lutherans. Of these the Baptists were probably the best established, since they had founded a mission in the Jackson district, Cape Girardeau County, as early as 1807.[148] The Lutherans had been represented in the population of this district during the 1820's and 1830's, especially around Cape Girardeau, but also in Perry County, and had appealed to the Henkels, a prominent family of Lutheran clergymen in North Carolina, to serve them. However,

---

143 *The Sixth Census of the United States: 1840,* p. 409; *ibid.*, 1850, p. 665; *Daily Missouri Republican*, Jan. 4, 1845.

144 *Daily Missouri Republican*, Jan. 4, 1845; *The Seventh Census of the United States: 1850,* p. 661.

145 Faust, *op. cit.*, I, 449.

146 *The Sixth Census of the United States: 1840,* p. 409; Peck, *op. cit.*, 338—339; Wetmore (comp.), *op. cit.*, 145.

147 *The Sixth Census of the United States: 1840,* p. 409.

148 Scharf, *op. cit.*, II, 1670.

no congregation had been organized by the time the Saxons arrived.[149]

Perry County was furthermore a relatively poor region. In 1841, when the State revenue from St. Louis County was $152,478.18, that from Perry County was only $1,303.96.[150] The latter county was overwhelmingly agricultural. While there was much talk of mining, there was actually not a single person in the county engaged in that occupation in 1840. The 1,626 persons employed in agriculture were served by only about 150 in all other vocational classifications.[151] The soil in the county as a whole varied widely in its fertility, and so did that in the section acquired by the Saxon immigrants. Most of the land purchased was of no more than medium quality, and some was unmistakably poor. A few stretches, especially those in the Brazeau River bottom and around the landing place, contained rich soil, but such areas were damp, low-lying, and usually unhealthful. Included in the land procured through Lawless was a small farm that had belonged to a man named Martin. This farm was cleared and tillable, and had some buildings on it. But these buildings were inadequate to house the immigrants and the cultivable land insufficient to support them.

The purchase of land was a step of the most vital importance for the *Gesellschaft* and one of the outstanding failures of its leadership.[152] Had the investment been a wise one, the leaders might yet have redeemed all or most of the blunders they had made in administration, particularly in regard to finances. Later, of course, all blame for this fiasco also was heaped upon Stephan, as stated above, and he was roundly berated for the low status of the treasury, for taking too many poor people along, for unnecessary expenditures, for the costly loss of time in St. Louis, for the choice of a location, for buying on a cash basis — in fine, for everything

---

[149] A. L. Gräbner, "Early Lutheranism in Missouri," *Theological Quarterly,* III, 319—353; O'Malley, "The Centenary of the Foundation of the St. Louis Diocesan Seminary," *St. Louis Catholic Historical Review,* I, 40—49.

[150] *Mill Boy,* Feb. 10, 1844.

[151] *The Sixth Census of the United States: 1840,* p. 409.

[152] The best evidence that this judgment is correct is Stephan's attempt to escape responsibility for the obvious mistakes made. Despite the role he played, as described above, he criticized the purchase on the score of price, location, and quality of soil. He fails to explain how the transaction would have been possible without his co-operation. Stephan to Flügel, Oct. 12, 1841, MS., C. H. I.

Earliest known picture of Carl Ferdinand Wilhelm Walther, 1843, by Gustav Pfau

PLATE XIX

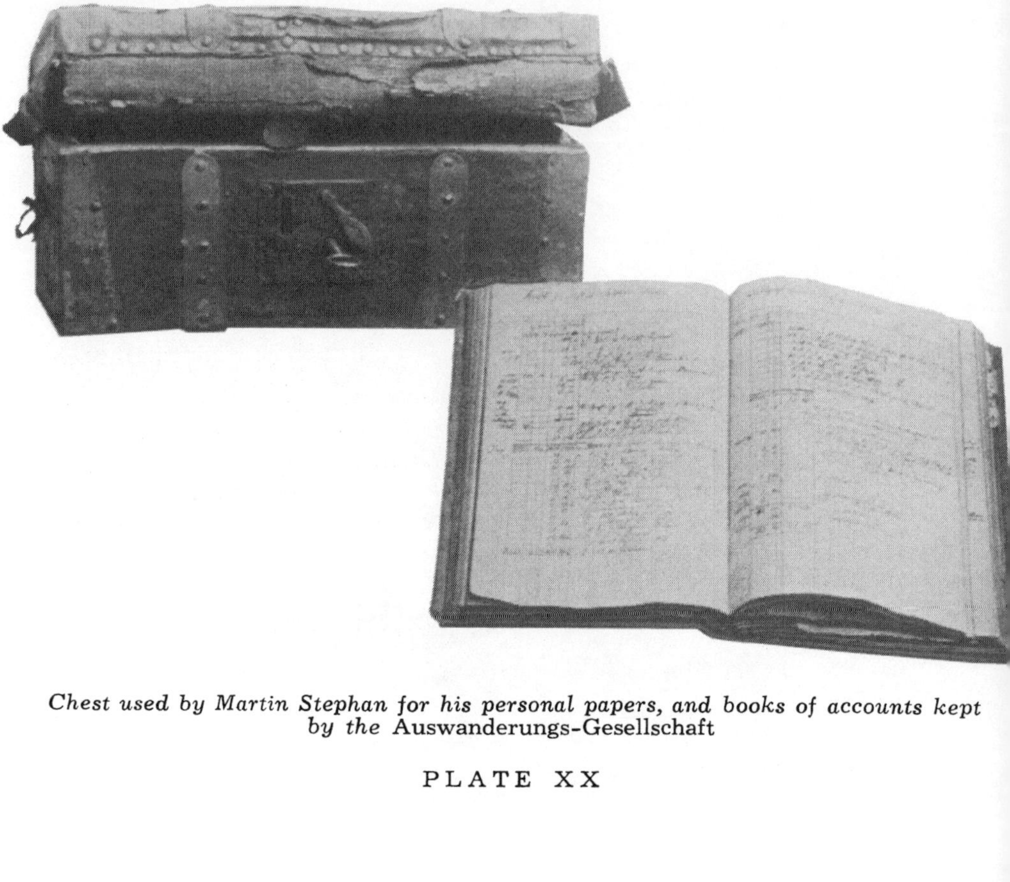

Chest used by Martin Stephan for his personal papers, and books of accounts kept by the Auswanderungs-Gesellschaft

PLATE XX

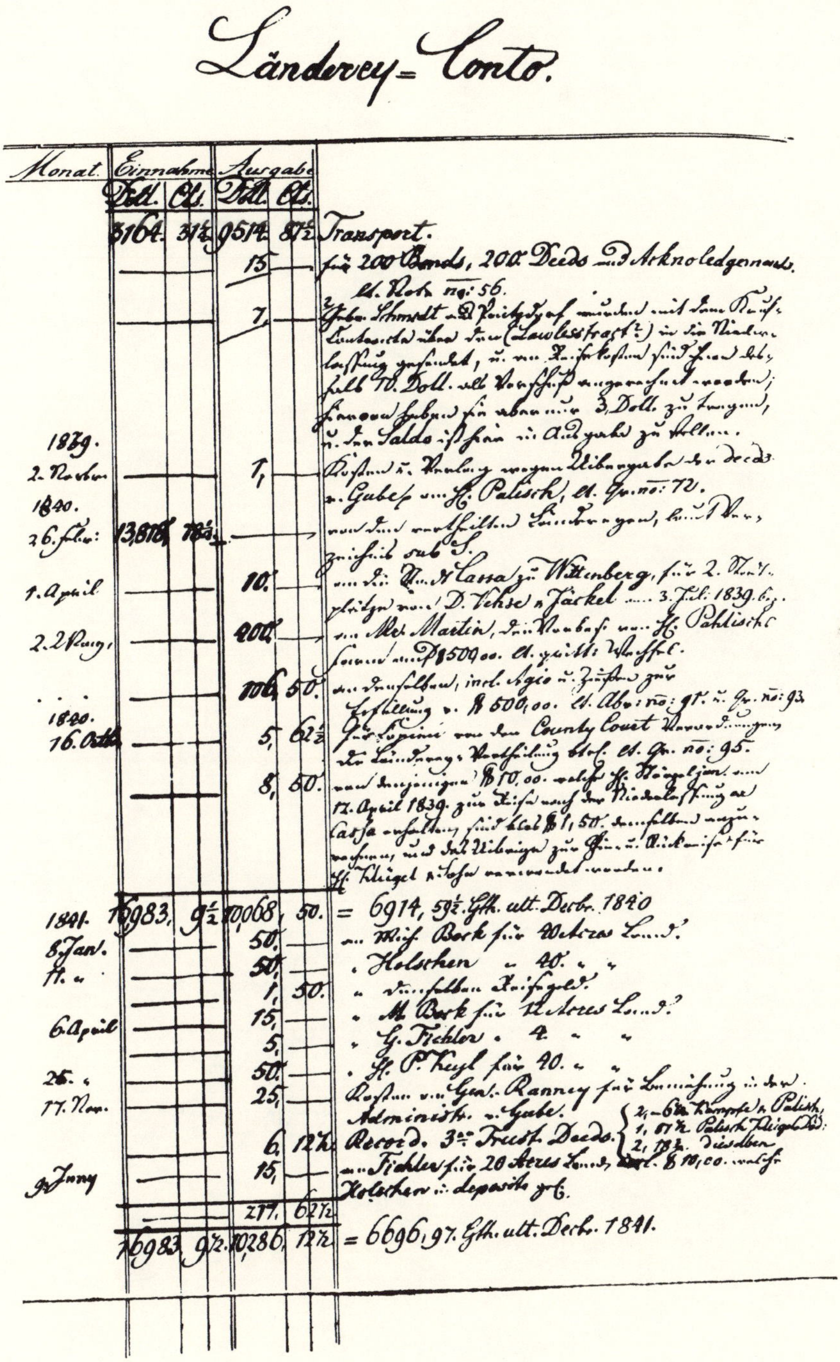

Länderey=Conto.

Monat	Einnahme Doll.	Cts.	Ausgabe Doll.	Cts.	
	3164.	31½	9514.	87½	Transport.
			15		für 200 Bonds, 200 Deeds und Acknoledgements [illegible] no: 56.
			7		[illegible]
1839. 2. Novbr.			1		[illegible] H. Palisch, [illegible] no: 72. [illegible] sub S.
1840. 26. Febr.	13,818	78½			
1. April			10		[illegible] Cassa zu Wittenberg für 2. [illegible] D. Vehse u. Jäckel [illegible] 3. Febr. 1839 [illegible]
2. 2[illegible]			400		[illegible] Mr. Martin, [illegible] H. Pahlisch [illegible] $1500.00 [illegible]
			106	50	[illegible] $500.00. [illegible] no: 91 [illegible] no: 93
1840. 16. Octbr.			5	62½	[illegible] County Court [illegible] no: 95.
			8	50	[illegible] $10.00 [illegible] 12. April 1839 [illegible] $1,50 [illegible]
1841.	16983	9½	10068	50	= 6914, 59½ Gth. ult. Decbr. 1840
8. Jan.			50		[illegible] Bork für 40 Acres Land.
11. "			50		" Holschen " 40. " "
			1	50	" derselben [illegible]
6. April			15		" M. Bork für 12 Acres Land.
			5		" G. Fichler " 4. " "
			50		" H. P. Keyl für 40. "
25. "			25		[illegible] Genl. Ranney für [illegible]
17. Nov.					Administr. [illegible]
			6	12½	Record. 3 Trust Deeds. [illegible]
9 Juny			15		[illegible] Fichler für 20 Acres Land, [illegible] $10,00 [illegible] Holschen [illegible] deposito [illegible]
			217	62½	
	16983	9½	10286	12½	= 6696,97. Gth. ult. Decbr. 1841.

Page from the Book of Accounts

PLATE XXI

Christ Episcopal Church, St. Louis, dedicated February 17, 1839, and used by the Saxons as a place of worship from 1839 to 1842. *(See page 321)*

PLATE XXII

that subsequently proved inadvisable. But all such recriminations unfortunately took the form of second-guessing, and that at a time when Stephan was a convenient scapegoat. While the Bishop's decision undoubtedly carried great weight, those who worked with him, namely, the pastors, the lay leaders, and the land committee, cannot be absolved of all responsibility. The protests, which some of them claimed they made, and which Vehse and Jäckel actually did make, seem always to have taken the form of polite representations made directly to Stephan, who, as they should have known, was not open-minded. All the behind-the-scenes maneuvering of which his lieutenants were capable was of no avail, and they should have known it, and probably did know it. Their only hope for success in combating the prevailing policies, if, indeed, they saw the folly of these policies clearly, lay in a forthright appeal to the people; but this they did not have the courage to make, for fear of incurring Stephan's displeasure.

But now, for better or for worse, the land had been bought, and the problem at hand was to establish a colony upon it. Even before all the land had actually been paid for, crews of workmen had been sent to Perry County to begin the task of making the place habitable.[153] Adolph and Sophie Fischer, for instance, arrived at the colony's landing place on April 11, 1839, to work for four "bits" and three "bits" respectively per day.[154] When Stephan saw that the work of his inexperienced followers in the settlement was progressing too slowly, four American laborers were hired to put up log cabins.[155] E. M. Bürger stated that the necessary buildings were erected before the transfer of any appreciable portion of the people took place,[156] but the later experiences of the colonists do not bear out the claim. In fact, most, if not all, of the buildings fit for use when the first detachment of settlers arrived had already been on the farm land included in the purchase when the tract was acquired.

On April 26, 1839, a month or more before the last of the various land deals had been completed, Stephan left St. Louis on the

---

[153] G. Günther, *op. cit.*, 74.

[154] Bill for services by Adolph and Sophie Fischer, presented March 6, 1840, Bound MSS., 19, C. H. I. One "bit" equaled 12½ cents.

[155] G. Günther, *op. cit.*, 89.

[156] E. M. Bürger, Selbstbiographie, 122, MS., E. J. Buerger Papers, Ellicottville, N. Y.

steamboat *United States* with the first detachment of actual colonists, bound for the site of the settlement.[157] The group accompanying the Bishop was not, as has been asserted, a majority of the immigrants,[158] but rather a relatively small body of people, most of them farmers, with the younger persons predominating. Most of the craftsmen, some of whom had found steady employment, stayed in St. Louis.[159] In fact, most of the people could not go to Perry County, because there was no shelter for them there.[160] Some of the most trusted leaders, such as O. H. Walther, Marbach, Gube, and Nitzschke, either were already in Perry County or now accompanied Stephan. Just who of the clergymen and lay leaders, besides those mentioned, was allowed to go along is not certain. There may also have been some traveling back and forth. Köstering asserted that Keyl went along in April, and P. Kretzmann accepts this statement. But if this is the case, Keyl soon returned, for he is known to have been in St. Louis during the first half of the next month. This much is clear, that most of the leaders at this time remained in St. Louis.[161] Stephan's version of this episode in the story of the Saxons differs so sharply from all others that he shall have to speak for himself: "It was now the common desire of all to move to the new land as soon as possible. . . . But as the land which had been purchased offered neither food nor shelter, I, together with a number of workmen, bent every effort to erect some dwellings as quickly

---

157 Vehse, *op. cit.*, 16. The actual date of departure was April 26, although both this and the following date, April 27, are given in P. Kretzmann, "The Saxon Immigration to Missouri, 1838—1839," *Missouri Historical Review*, XXXIII, 163—164. This same writer describes the period of the transfer to Perry County, largely on the basis of the account in G. Günther's book and in the Löber letters contained in *Mitteilungen . . . Kahla*, in P. Kretzmann, "The Saxons Move to Perry County," *Concordia Theological Monthly*, X, 358—370.

158 Hanser, *op. cit.*, 9; Th. Bünger, "Etliche Züge aus der Geschichte der Missouri-Synode," *Synodal-Bericht des Iowa-Districts . . . 1901*, p. 22.

159 Winter to Guericke *et al.*, April 28, 1841, *Zeitschrift für die gesammte lutherische Theologie und Kirche*, II, No. 3, pp. 116—132; E. M. Bürger, Selbstbiographie, 122, MS., E. J. Buerger Papers, Ellicottville, N. Y.

160 G. Günther, *op. cit.*, 89.

161 Köstering, *Keyl*, 56; P. Kretzmann, "The Saxon Immigration to Missouri, 1838—1839," *Missouri Historical Review*, XXXIII, 163—164. Kretzmann also claims that Brohm went along with Stephan in April, *ibid.* For this information he probably relies upon Hochstetter, *op. cit.*, 403. In any event, it is clear where these men were during the latter part of April and again the latter part of May, for their presence in St. Louis or Perry County is indicated by their signatures in the *Anzeiger des Westens*, April 27, June 1, 1839, quoted in G. Günther, *op. cit.*, 76—78, 94—95.

as possible, so that families with children could be given some shelter."[162]

The truth of the matter unfortunately seems to be, however, that Stephan still had not attained a realization of the crisis in the *Gesellschaft's* financial affairs. On the steamboat his demands for special foods and special service were so unreasonable that later, when another section of the immigrants wished to hire the *United States* to take them to Perry County, its captain quoted them prohibitive prices.[163] When Stephan ordered the supplies sent ahead in anticipation of his arrival, he included a generous stock of fine wines, purchased through Bimpage, for the episcopal residence in Perry County. This residence was a modest board house, on the Martin farm near the landing place, reserved for Stephan's personal use.[164] But the fact remains that this was the best building available, and Vehse does not omit pointing out that Stephan was occupied with plans for a more elaborate residence, even before his people had any kind of permanent shelter.[165] For the church services which were promptly instituted, a large arbor, or tabernacle, was built. Such a temporary shelter, we are told, did not meet with the approval of Stephan, because he considered it too mean a structure for his episcopal ministrations.[166] Be that as it may, Stephan had the satisfaction of knowing that within two weeks of his arrival in Perry County there was a sign at the mouth of the "Obrazo" reading: "Stephan's Landing."[167] Moreover, the outlay of money was not markedly reduced. The total amount spent for supplies, such as, "Cattle, Ploughs, Wagons, Victuals, etc.," even prior to May 24 was $3,271.622.[168]

Köstering, indeed, told appalling tales of Stephan's stupid vanity and gross incompetence in directing operations in Perry County. The charge is made, for instance, that before the people were permitted to build houses or plant crops, they were ordered

---

162 Stephan to Flügel, Oct. 12, 1841, MS., C. H. I.

163 Vehse, *op. cit.*, 16.

164 *Ibid.;* G. Günther, *op. cit.*, 74.

165 Vehse, *op. cit.*, 18. Stephan's version: "I myself, however, had to be satisfied with poor food and shelter," Stephan to Flügel, Oct. 12, 1841, MS., C. H. I.

166 Köstering, *Auswanderung*, 22—23.

167 Vehse to K. W. Welzel, May 10, 1839, MS., C. H. I.

168 Epitome from the Cash-account, June 11, 1842, MS., C. H. I.

to lay out streets and to build bridges over creeks and ravines, at points where they were swept away by the first heavy downpour. In this work, it is furthermore related, the men were forced to do much of the most difficult work themselves in order not to endanger the few available draft animals in the rough terrain. Such work as was done, the story goes, had to wait upon the sanction of Stephan before it could even be begun, for he controlled even the minutest details. The recital is climaxed by the assertion, encountered before, that Stephan was employing a spy system on his people.[169] Unfortunately, however bad Stephan's management may have been, that of his immediate successors in the leadership was little better.

Almost at the exact time that Stephan left for Perry County the journalistic battle flared up gain. The *Anzeiger* on April 20 had carried a reprint of an article by Scheibel in which he repudiated Stephanism and denied having had any part in it. In support of his position he quoted the statement by Rudelbach and other clergymen, referred to above.[170] To the pastors, this action of the *Anzeiger* looked like another attack and promptly drew their fire. The next issue of the *Anzeiger,* which appeared the day after Stephan had left, carried a reply, written by five of the pastors, Löber, Keyl, Örtel, Bürger, and C. F. W. Walther, on April 24.[171] The clergy said in effect that the charges Scheibel had made were lies and that their simple assertion to the contrary should be sufficient to demonstrate the fact. Furthermore, Weber was characterized as "a great admirer of European lies." Therefore, they stated, unless obliged to legally, they, the clergy, would make no further defense in the *Anzeiger.*[172] Weber's extended comments on this somewhat offhand reply to Scheibel added up to just one thing: The simple assertion of these five clergymen was not enough to dispel the cloud under which the Stephanites found themselves both in the Old World and the New.[173]

The lay members of the *Gesellschaft* made their contribution in

---

169 Köstering, *Auswanderung,* 21—22. Stephan: "While I was bending every effort to prepare the area for residence by the congregation, my secret enemies in St. Louis were bending every effort to turn the hearts of the congregation against me," Stephan to Flügel, Oct. 12, 1841, MS., C. H. I.

170 G. Günther, *op. cit.,* 75—76.

171 *Anzeiger des Westens,* April 27, 1839, quoted in *ibid.,* 76—78.

172 *Ibid.*

173 *Ibid.*

the *Anzeiger* of the following week. Under the title of a "Protest," dated April 29, they took exception to the fact that the nature of their religious organization, a private matter, had been made an issue in the public press. A reiteration of the claim that they had been driven from Germany, and that everything unfavorable said about the Stephanites thus far was an assortment of lies, was followed by a defense of, and a pledge of confidence in, their pastors. Finally, the laymen joined the pastors in saying they would make no direct reply to specific charges.[174] This editorial flourish was, so to say, the dying gasp of the episcopacy. The halcyon days of Stephan and Stephanism were over. The next public statement of the immigrants was to sound the disillusioned death knell of many dreams and an ambitious career.

---

174 *Anzeiger des Westens*, May 4, 1839, quoted in *ibid.*, 82—86. The signatures of the twenty-four lay deputies subscribed to this statement are the same as those on Stephan's Investiture and on the Confirmation of Stephan's Investiture, except that the name of Tirmenstein appears in place of that of H. F. Fischer.

CHAPTER FIFTEEN

DISCREDITING STEPHAN'S LEADERSHIP

STEPHAN'S ATTEMPT to take out insurance even against thoughts disloyal to him[1] did not add to his reputation as a shrewd psychologist. Nevertheless, it indicated a shrewd analysis of the fundamental problem confronting his leadership. The Bishop's position rested largely upon the good will and confidence of his followers. By this token, the days of Stephan's rule were numbered already when he left St. Louis. For by that time he had destroyed the favorable attitude of an important segment of the *Gesellschaft,* that is, the majority of the clergy, the candidates, and the lay leaders. Evidences of dissension have been pointed out from time to time in the preceding chapters. Between September, 1838, and May, 1839, Stephan had serious disagreements with, or outright challenges of authority from, Keyl, Bürger, Marbach, Vehse, H. F. Fischer, Barthel, and Nitzschke. But as long as Stephan was on the scene to guide the conduct of affairs and apply the tactic *divide et impera,* it was unlikely that disgruntled individuals would organize into a compact party.

The self-interest of the ruling clique had prevented any one of these incidents from crystallizing into a movement toward effective opposition. Each time the hapless recalcitrant found himself standing alone, and, with the sole exception of H. F. Fischer, he regularly beat a hasty retreat, while the others were making hay in the sunshine of episcopal favor. Neither did any of the dissidents, as has also been noted, have the courage to stake his all upon an open break with Stephan and bring the matter before the people, but, instead, they preferred to remain within the fold upon Stephan's terms. So, each incident had no really constructive effect. The current example at the beginning of May was that of Bürger, who,

[1] Pledge of Subjection to Stephan, *Selma,* Feb. 16, 1839, Pledge of Subjection to Stephan by the *Copernicus* group, Pledge of Subjection to Stephan by the *Johann Georg* group, I, II, MSS., C. H. I.

with the approval of the rest of the clergy, was being subjected to the outrageous treatment described above.

However, in May, 1839, there were two new factors in the situation. First, Stephan either felt secure enough, or saw himself forced by circumstances, to turn his back upon almost all the potential troublemakers at the same time and when they were all together, a thing which had never happened before. When Stephan departed for Perry County, he left behind him a group which included at various times during May: G. H. Löber, Keyl, E. M. Bürger, C. F. W. Walther, Vehse, Jäckel, F. W. Barthel, H. F. Fischer, and presumably a majority of the candidates.[2] Secondly, Stephan's tactics had succeeded in producing antagonism or alarm in a greater number of his lieutenants than at any previous time. In part this attitude was clearly personal, but in part the dissatisfaction which was rife had its roots also in a genuine disagreement on policy and a very real fear that Stephan's administration — or maladministration — would result in disaster. Especially in the matter of finances Stephan appeared to be following an *après-nous-le-dèluge* policy, which alarmed those who still expected to be present *après nous,* or whose sense of responsibility to the people was better developed than that of the Bishop. The gradual development of these misgivings over a period of time has been described in the foregoing. The new element suddenly injected into this situation was the absence of Stephan, which provided opportunity for frequent consultation and the expression of opinion on the part of all the leaders in St. Louis.[3]

Probably this unusual freedom was the special stimulus required to induce a sufficient number of these men to risk their future careers in open opposition to Stephan, by starting a movement to depose him or limit his authority. Certainly dissatisfaction, apprehension, and personal animosity all were present. At this very time, for instance, there was friction even in Perry County. Nitzschke dared to question the propriety of Stephan's conduct and was banished from the presence of the Bishop for this act of insubordination.[4] The opportunity for exchanging views and venting their

---

2 *Anzeiger des Westens,* June 1, 1839, quoted in G. Günther, *op. cit.,* 94—95; Hochstetter, *op. cit.,* 19; Köstering, "Ehrengedächtniss des . . . Schieferdecker," *Der Lutheraner,* XLVIII, 145.

3 G. Günther, *op. cit.,* 90.

4 *Ibid.,* 90—91.

feelings, which the group in St. Louis now enjoyed, merely served to heighten their resentment and give them courage. An understanding of these facts is indispensable for an interpretation of the occurrences in the troubled months and years to follow, for their importance in determining the course of future events will become evident in the subsequent narrative. Any further impetus required was provided by the explosive element of renewed accusations against Stephan's personal life. The repercussions were startling.

The chain of events in the period from May, 1839, to April, 1841, was unwittingly set into motion by Pastor Löber. In the early service held by the immigrants on Rogate Sunday, May 5, 1839, Löber preached what seems to have been a rather searching sermon. Allegedly as a result of Löber's message, two women, each of whom subsequently disclaimed any knowledge of the other's action, came to him at different hours on that same Sunday and made detailed confessions of improper relations with Stephan.[5] During the days immediately following this fateful Sabbath, several other women made similar statements to the clergymen. Some of these confessions, including the two original ones, were outright admissions of adultery, others were accusations that Stephan had unsuccessfully attempted to seduce the women making them. Several of these women were willing to repeat their charges under oath.[6]

---

[5] Winter to Guericke *et al.*, April 28, 1841, *Zeitschrift für die gesammte lutherische Theologie und Kirche*, II, No. 3, pp. 116—132; Lossagung vom Stephanismus, MS., C. H. I.; E. M. Bürger, Selbstbiographie, 125, MS., E. J. Buerger Papers, Ellicottville, N. Y.; G. Günther, *op. cit.*, 91—92; Schieferdecker, *op. cit.*, 13. Vehse claimed the confessions were made on Exaudi Sunday, which would have been May 12, 1839. Vehse, *op. cit.*, 17. However, this date is in conflict not only with all other accounts, but even with direct statements and the chronology of related events given elsewhere in Vehse's own work. *Ibid.*, 17—19, 143.

[6] At least three women are definitely known to have made such statements: Louise Völker, Wilhelmine Hahn, and Sophie Höschel. G. H. Löber, Abkündigungsbuch in Perry County, 1839, July 7, 1839 [*i. e.*, "D. VI p. Trin."], MS., Trinity Church Records, Altenburg, Mo. G. Günther gave the names of Louise Völker, Sophie "Henschel" (or, in another place, "Herschel" — he undoubtedly referred to Sophie Höschel), and a third, not mentioned by Löber, Auguste Pötzsch, all of whom he claimed made full confessions. G. Günther, *op. cit.*, 91, 124. Günther, of course, failed to mention in this connection the admissions made by his sister about a month later. See also Document . . . des . . . Grundsteins . . . St. Louis . . . 22. Juny 1842, MS., C. H. I.; Schieferdecker, *op cit*, 13; Vehse, *op cit.*, 17. According to Vehse, some of these statements were taken down in writing, and he claimed to have seen them. For once Stephan and Vehse agree, although the impression each tries to convey is quite different from that sought by the other. Stephan asserted: "Several lying statements were made in writing, and the documents

No contemporary narrative undertook to explain how this epidemic of confessions came about, that is, whether the pastors sought substantiation for the original accusations made against Stephan, or whether, after the developments began to be whispered about among the Saxons in St. Louis, the power of suggestion or example produced spontaneous results among the other women.

Löber is supposed to have been greatly surprised and probably was deeply shocked by what he heard. He promptly told the story to C. F. W. Walther.[7] Within the next few days the secret was shared with Keyl, and E. M. Bürger, who appears to have returned from "exile" at about this time, was also informed.[8] Thus, for approximately a week the clergymen were the only persons in the group aware of what had taken place. This time was used by the pastors in mapping out their strategy for dealing with the situation. Then, after detailed preparations had been made, the news was broken gradually to the uninitiated. On May 13, the eighth day after the first statements to Löber had been made, Vehse was drawn into the clergy's confidence. On the next day "Stephan's secretary" was informed; no doubt Jäckel, the secretary of the *Gesellschaft*, is meant.[9] Shortly thereafter all real efforts to keep the secret were abandoned, and Löber admitted that he had told people about the matter when asked. He insisted that the information was given out with the express permission of the women involved. In his estimation this circumstance seems to have justified his action.[10]

---

were given to all to read, even to the immature youth." Stephan to Flügel, Oct. 12, 1841, MS., C.H.I. With the exception of the statement by Louise Günther, these documents were not discovered in the course of this investigation. Wilhelmine Hahn was married within a few months to E. M. Grosse. O. H. Walther, Zur Agende Dom. II. p. Trinitatis 1839, ad. Dom. I. p. Epiph. 1841, Oct. 20, 1839 [*i. e.*, "Dom. XXI p. Tr."], MS., L. Fürbringer Papers, St. Louis (hereafter cited as Zur Agende).

[7] E. M. Bürger, Selbstbiographie, 125, MS., E. J. Buerger Papers, Ellicottville, N. Y. Hochstetter presumed, without giving a source, to quote the words exchanged during this highly confidential interview between G. H. Löber and C. F. W. Walther and thereby subjected his entire account to the suspicion of being apocryphal. Hochstetter, *op. cit.*, 19—20.

[8] E. M. Bürger, Selbstbiographie, 125, MS., E. J. Buerger Papers, Ellicottville, N. Y.; Bürger, *op. cit.*, 13. E. M. Bürger's chronology is not entirely correct or consistent in these two accounts, but the general facts of his return and the information given him are in agreement.

[9] Vehse, *op. cit.*, 17; Vehse-H. F. Fischer-Jäckel, "Schluss-Zusatz," in *ibid.*, 143.

[10] G. H. Löber to Nitzschke, Feb. 27, 1845, MS., C.H.I.

The result of this tantalizingly gradual divulgence of the information was to invite rumor, encourage gossip, and heighten interest in the matter, not only among the Stephanites, but throughout the city. During the latter half of May, 1839, a wave of excitement swept the colony of Saxons, and there was much whispering among them.[11] The profound surprise at the revelations which was professed by both clergymen and laymen at this time and later, is a little surprising itself. In view of previous occurrences it is difficult to share A. L. Gräbner's view that the revelations came with utter suddenness.[12] As a matter of fact, no more nor less was known now than had been known several months — and, in fact, several years — before in Saxony. Accusations were made in both places, but a competent investigation had been conducted in neither. Fundamentally the charges made by the women in St. Louis were no different from those made already in Germany, which had not been entirely "malicious talk" and "Dresden gossip," as Hennig has lightly dubbed them,[13] but included specific charges, such as those in the trial of October, 1838, or in Caroline Dittrich's letter to Marbach. The only real difference between the two cases was that prior to this time Stephan's lieutenants had failed to place any credence in the accusations against him, no matter what the circumstances were, whereas this time they believed the worst only too readily.

The very different attitude of the same men on these two occasions is significant and gives a demonstration of their psychological reflexes. In Germany they did not want to believe ill of Stephan because of their high regard for him and their close association with him. Hence they closed their eyes to all evidence and their ears to all "slander" against him and pronounced him an innocent martyr. By the time the St. Louis episode occurred they were rather thoroughly cured of their profound admiration for the Bishop, and anything which promised to discredit him before the people or even to rid them of him entirely was accepted without further scrutiny. Their attitude in Germany had been typified by Keyl's remark noted above, that he did not believe the assertions against Stephan

---

11 E. M. Bürger, Selbstbiographie, 126, MS., E. J. Buerger Papers, Ellicottville, N. Y.; Schieferdecker, *op. cit.*, 13; Document . . . des Grundsteins . . . St. Louis . . . 22. Juny 1842, MS., C. H. I.

12 A. L. Gräbner, *"Bis hieher"*, 6.

13 Hennig, "Die Auswanderung Martin Stephans," *Zeitschrift für Kirchengeschichte*, LVIII, 162—163.

to be true, but that if they were, he was certain Stephan had repented, and all was well. It would have been equally as simple to say and do the same thing in St. Louis. Instead, a policy was adopted which was the complete antithesis of that in Germany. Apparently the feeling now was that the charges were true, but that if they were not, Stephan should be removed anyway, for all was *not* well. A few months earlier the accusers were condemned as slanderers — unheard. Now the accused was condemned as a libertine — also unheard.

That these were actually the reactions among Stephan's followers is further borne out by the fact that although nearly all claimed to be surprised and shocked almost — but, of course, not quite — to the point of incredulity, not a single person seems to have been convinced of the Bishop's innocence. There was reason to expect that someone, anyone, would at least have called for a thorough investigation. There is no known record that anyone did so.[14] Both Köstering and Hochstetter attempted to rationalize these attitudes by asserting that it was a psychological impossibility for the women involved to have made untrue confessions.[15] However, even if such an interpretation of the psychology involved is correct, which is by no means above question, it would have applied with equal force in Germany, where the reaction of Stephan's followers was a very different one.

In fine, all immediately assumed Stephan's guilt, and almost every one of any consequence was anxiously employed in making assertions in some form or other that he — the individual in question — certainly knew nothing of all this in Germany. The practice quickly took hold among both leaders and people, especially the former, of blaming Stephan for everything possible — and impossible — by shouldering upon him responsibility for all the ills that had, did now, and would in the future beset the *Gesellschaft*. Everyone, without exception, of course, claimed that he had been duped. All were now quite clear that they had not *really* approved of the very policies and measures which virtually all had countenanced, voted for, helped to execute, and sealed with their signatures. Later

[14] Nitzschke's attitude in 1845 is the only possible exception, and that was based upon compunctions about the procedure adopted. G. H. Löber to Nitzschke, Feb. 27, 1845, MS., C.H.I. At the time, in 1839, Nitzschke himself was at loggerheads with Stephan.

[15] Köstering, *Auswanderung*, 24; Hochstetter, *op. cit.*, 19.

numerous "confessions" and admissions were made, but at first the tendency was toward an effort to avoid as much blame as possible.

Although everyone connected with the leadership of the *Gesellschaft* saw that he would have to accept at least partial responsibility for the condition of the group's affairs, the initial aim of them all was to reduce such responsibility to a minimum. Vehse's attitude, as revealed in his book on the emigration and shared by most of the lay leaders, was to place the blame upon Stephan, the pastors, the hierarchical system, and false doctrine, in that order. If any responsibility remained, he was willing to share it equally with the rank and file. The pastors had a somewhat different approach, but a very similar idea, of course substituting for themselves in the list of culprits, the laymen, such as Vehse. The people were impartial in their censure of both clergy and laity after Stephan had been given the major responsibility. In some accounts of this period, the effort of the writers to excuse themselves is tempered by their realization that complete self-exculpation might be unconvincing.[16] In later years admirers of some of the leaders showed less insight when they disregarded even the frank admissions of those whom they were trying to canonize.[17]

---

[16] Nachrichten an unsere Nachkommen, Bekenntniss, Lossagung vom Stephanismus, Document . . . des Grundsteins . . . St. Louis . . . 22. Juny 1842, Delitzsch to F. W. Barthel, Dec. 8, 1839, Keyl to the immigrants in St. Louis, July 1, 1840, Lebenslauf des . . . Nitzschke, MSS., C. H. I.; Marbach to Stübel, n. d. [November—December, 1839], Marbach to — ["Hochgeehrter Herr Geheimrath"], May 8, 1840, Bound MSS., VI, C. H. I.; J. K. A. Höhne and J. G. Höhne to their brother, Sept. 26, 1841, quoted in *Die Ameise,* Jan. 10, 1842; Winter to Guericke *et al.,* April 28, 1841, *Zeitschrift für die gesammte lutherische Theologie und Kirche,* II, No. 3, pp. 116—132; Christiane Löber to G. F. Löber, n. d. [September—December, 1839], Christiane Löber to relatives in Germany, Dec. 4, 1839, G. H. Löber to G. F. Löber, Dec. 16, 1840, Aug. 26, 1841, in Löber-Eichenberg (ed.), "Ein Briefwechsel," *Mitteilungen . . . Kahla,* VII, 152—156, 162—167, 174—179, 184—190; C. F. W. Walther to Sihler, Jan. 2, 1845, in L. Fürbringer (ed.), *op. cit.,* I, 6; *Anzeiger des Westens,* Dec. 31, 1842; *ibid.,* June 1, 1839, quoted in G. Günther, *op. cit.,* 93—95; *ibid.,* p. iv; Schieferdecker, *op. cit.,* 16; Bürger, *op. cit.,* 13; Schieferdecker, "Synodalrede," *Verhandlungen des Westlichen Distrikts der . . . Synode von Missouri . . . 1856,* p. 7; J. F. Bünger, "Ehrengedächtniss des . . . Brohm," *Der Lutheraner,* XXXVII, 189; K. Gruber, "Ehrengedächtniss des . . . Gotthold Heinrich Löber," *ibid.,* VI, 146. The attitude described above is frequently found in the presentation of both C. F. W. Walther and Keyl. C. F. W. Walther in Köstering, *Auswanderung,* 1—18; Keyl, *op. cit.,* 3—20.

[17] Köstering, *Keyl,* 41—42. Köstering surpassed himself on another occasion, however, when he discovered that the reason for the failure to perceive the errors of Stephan was the fact that there was a place on the Mississippi so appropriately named as "Devil's Bakeoven." Köstering, *Auswanderung,* 66.

As a result of this general attitude, Stephan was judged without a hearing. It may be argued that the outcome of such a hearing was a foregone conclusion and that subsequently he had the opportunity to express himself, although he denied that he was ever given such an opportunity. But the fact remains that he had been condemned in both the minds and the councils of his followers, especially in the minds of the pastors, before they even saw him or investigated the matter further. That these are the standards of justice which prevailed is evident from the course of action pursued. That Stephan, understandably, resented this procedure, is evident from his indignant narrative of these events.[18]

Within a week after the events of May 5, the pastors had taken it upon themselves to decree Stephan's removal from office. In view of the fact that they felt they had "elected" him,[19] it probably did not appear illogical in their minds to assume the initiative in terminating his tenure of office.[20] Accordingly, the pastors had a complete plan of procedure before they ever mentioned the matter to anyone else, even to Vehse. This plan called for immediate disciplinary action against Stephan in any event, although it was not yet entirely clear to the clergymen whether deposition would be necessary or suspension would suffice. As to procedure, they were sure of the following: First, that whatever was to be done, must be done by them; secondly, that if Stephan were to be excommunicated by them, this action would have to precede his deposition from official position; and, thirdly, that whatever they might do, would then be presented to the people as a *fait accompli,* which the latter might ratify. However, as the pastors still feared Stephan's influence with the people, and as it was essential for them to gain control of the economic affairs of the *Gesellschaft,* an agent was to be sent to Perry County. Such a representative was not to deal with Stephan, but to win over the people who had already been transferred to the site of the colony, the New York group, which was expected to arrive there daily, and the trustees in whose names the deeds to the land were made out. All three of these groups could be gained for the pastors' viewpoint by discrediting Stephan on the

---

18 Stephan to Flügel, Oct. 12, 1841, MS., C. H. I.

19 Confirmation of Stephan's Investiture, MS., C. H. I.

20 *Anzeiger des Westens*, Dec. 20, 1842.

basis of the morals charges with which they had conveniently been provided.[21]

The opportuneness of these charges against Stephan is indeed a striking coincidence. That financial and economic considerations weighed heavily with the pastors is evidenced by their very deliberate effort to win over the trustees and by the fact that Stephan's misapplication of funds was one of the official reasons for which he was finally removed. However, the morals charges were almost indispensable to the group engineering the Bishop's ouster, as a means of undermining his position with the rank and file of his followers. Once confidence in Stephan had been destroyed by accusations which at the same time brought the entire colony into a high state of excitement, it was easy to place all the blame also for the bankruptcy of the *Gesellschaft* at his door.

Had an attempt been made to depose Stephan in a calmer mood, solely on the basis of his inefficient or prodigal administration, the question would most certainly have arisen — or Stephan himself would have raised it — as to who actually authorized the elaborate expenditures and who profited by them? The answer would have been that, as has repeatedly been shown in the preceding narrative, Stephan was by no means solely responsible for the wastefulness which had created for the immigrants their present financial difficulties. Neither was Stephan the only beneficiary of the system. The pastors and lay leaders were far from clear of all blame for the straits in which the colony found itself, for no power could have forced them to approve Stephan's proposed expenditures, and without such approval the expenditures could not have been made. Furthermore, both the leaders and a majority of the entire body of immigrants had reaped the benefits, great or small, of Stephan's financial system. Later both leaders and people were to realize these facts more clearly. But at the moment Stephan was the colonists' scapegoat for all that ailed them individually and collectively. Everyone else had been grossly deceived, he alone was the hoary profligate and trickster.

---

[21] Vehse-H. F. Fischer-Jäckel, "Schluss-Zusatz," in Vehse, *op. cit.*, 143—144; *ibid.*, 18; Winter to Guericke *et al.*, April 28, 1841, *Zeitschrift für die gesammte lutherische Theologie und Kirche,* II, No. 3, pp. 116—132. G. H. Löber to Nitzschke, Feb. 27, 1845, MS., C. H. I.; E. M. Bürger, Selbstbiographie, 126, MS., E. J. Buerger Papers, Ellicottville, N. Y.

The man chosen for the mission to Perry County was C. F. W. Walther. The reasons for this choice are obscure, except for the fact that ever since the day G. H. Löber had confided in him, Walther seems to have been one of the prime movers for drastic action against Stephan. Subsequently it was Walther who pictured the procedure in dealing with Stephan as a necessity.[22] The choice of Walther has been hailed as a tribute to his strength of character, to his independence of thought, to his ability as a leader. A point is made of the circumstance that he was the youngest of the clergymen. The difficulty of the task is stressed, and the fact that he was chosen nevertheless is taken as an indication that his outstanding qualities were generally recognized.[23] However, it is difficult to subscribe to this viewpoint, which is evidently prompted in some cases by an effort to place the later Walther, whom his eulogists knew, into as favorable a light as possible. There is no evidence to support the view that there was, up to this time, anything outstanding about the role played by C. F. W. Walther which might have merited general acclaim and recognition. In fact, he was one of the least important members of the clerical clique. But, however that might be, assigning a man this task was hardly a compliment to him, whoever he was, for he had a rather unsavory duty to perform. The most likely conjecture — and nothing more can be offered on this point — as to why Walther was sent rather than any of the others, is that someone had to do the job, and he was less reluctant than the rest.

Vehse and his sympathizers were quick to discover that the system of the pastors was to decide upon a course of action and then merely inform the laymen of it — to take or leave. The cordial relations between the leading laymen and the clergymen immediately changed when the latter began, collectively, to supplant Stephan in running the *Gesellschaft*.[24] Naturally, the procedure of the clerics called forth resentment in the lay leaders, and in this resentment lay the germ for the bitter and prolonged quarrel which was to follow: first, a personal pique on the part of Vehse and his associates, then a contest for administrative power, next a theological controversy between Vehse and the clergy, and finally a

---

22 C. F. W. Walther, *Bünger*, 53.

23 Vehse, *op. cit.*, 18; Hochstetter, *op. cit.*, 20—21; Steffens, *op. cit.*, 125—129

24 Vehse, *op. cit.*, 35, 38.

bitter multifactional battle that involved each of these factors and all of the immigrants for a period of several years.

However, in May, 1839, it would still have been possible for the clergy and the lay leaders to reach an agreement. The laymen's demands were few. First of all, Vehse, who dwelt on the horribleness of the confessions with an ill-concealed shudder of self-righteous indignation, felt a great personal bitterness against Stephan and demanded his immediate and unceremonious removal. To Vehse, removal meant both Stephan's deposition from office as bishop, clergyman, and head of the *Gesellschaft* and his excommunication by the church — in other words, complete severance of his connections with the colony.[25] Vehse claimed that the first impulse — probably chiefly his own — was to bring Stephan to trial before a court regardless of any action which might be taken by the immigrants as a church. Allegedly on the advice of three of the most prominent citizens of St. Louis, "among whom was the ranking magistrate of the city, Herr D. Lane," they did not take court action. These three individuals are supposed to have advised expelling Stephan from the colony and taking him to the Illinois side of the Mississippi to avoid the scandal and the lynching which would "inevitably" [!] result from legal proceedings.[26]

Another of the St. Louisans consulted appears to have been Mr. Sullivan. He had a far more realistic viewpoint. Apparently Marbach had struck up a friendship with him similar to that between Vehse and Gempp. In view of the loan which was secured, it was a highly useful acquaintanceship. Marbach wrote to him and asked for advice on the proper method of dealing with Stephan. Sullivan, while he duly lamented what had occurred, counseled against a trial, because he considered it purposeless. Court action would merely give avoidable publicity of the most damaging nature, both to the entire movement and to the women involved, without producing any beneficial results. Expulsion, after Stephan had been subjected to a thorough examination and had signed a statement, would serve the purpose quite as well. Stephan could be warned never to return to the colony, or even to Missouri, under threat of instituting suit at any time he would show himself. There was no talk of

---

25 *Ibid.*, 1, 7, 22, 35, 38; Vehse-H. F. Fischer-Jäckel, "Schluss-Zusatz," in *ibid.*, 143.

26 *Ibid.*, 17—18.

lynching in Sullivan's letter, but the idea of banishment to Illinois seems to have had its origin here. Sullivan wrote on May 28, and it is possible that his letter was carried to Marbach by the immigrants who came from St. Louis for the deposition of Stephan. If not, that is to say, if the letter had to go through the regular channels, it could not have arrived in time to influence the counsels in Perry County.[27]

Thus Vehse's story of the advice given the Saxons, while partially true, bears the earmarks of his imaginative dramatization of an incident which struck his fancy. Unfortunately, the tale has subsequently been used in attempts to justify the procedure adopted in dealing with Stephan.[28] Actually, an examination of the facts offers little in the way of justification. The objectionable features of the methods employed for removing Stephan — precipitateness, the arbitrary action taken, the failure to hear Stephan — were unnecessary, whether Stephan were to be brought to trial before a court or not. If "Magistrate Lane" actually advised banishment from Missouri, he was singularly ill-informed on the extent of Stephan's civil and personal liberties, even as an alien. Nor does it seem likely that any responsible official would have told the Saxons that a lynching was "inevitable." There had been no lynching in St. Louis for two years. The one that had occurred in 1837 was for a crime far more heinous than even Vehse's description makes Stephan's. And there was not another for at least a decade, that is, until 1847.[29] As for avoiding scandal, that was hardly possible after using the *Anzeiger* to make a public statement on the matter.[30]

The pastors, at first, however, were not certain that they would either depose Stephan or excommunicate him, and so they refused Vehse's demands. Even after they saw that the vindictiveness of

---

[27] Sullivan to Marbach, May 28, 1839, MS., C. H. I. See also G. H. Löber to Nitzschke, Feb. 27, 1845, MS., C. H. I.

[28] G. H. Löber to Nitzschke, Feb. 27, 1845, MS., C. H. I.

[29] *People's Daily Organ*, March 26, 1846. See also *St. Louis New Era*, April 30, 1841. The present writer failed to note a serious case of lynching except as indicated above, in covering all St. Louis newspapers available for the years 1838—1847.

[30] *Anzeiger des Westens*, June 1, 1839, quoted in G. Günther, *op. cit.*, 93—95. Gotthold Günther asserted that the failure to bring Stephan to trial was prompted by fear on the part of the leaders that he would make revelations implicating some of them. *Ibid.*, 103—105.

Vehse and men like him would make drastic action almost inevitable, they maintained that they alone could excommunicate the Bishop and that this would have to take place before his deposition.[31] The laymen at once recognized this as a highly undemocratic principle, one which they felt to be un-Lutheran from a theological viewpoint, and finally, one which gave every evidence of an attempt to perpetuate the hierarchical authority of the clergy in the Stephanite system.[32] Such an appraisal of the pastors' views led at once to Vehse's second demand, a twofold one: namely, that there be a complete division of secular and clerical authority and functions; and further, that the former be turned over to the laymen, while the latter — with proper safeguards for the rights of the congregation, for which the pastors were displaying little respect — might be retained by the clergy.

This request of Vehse fared no better than the first, and his demands were put off with the simple explanation that the present was a very poor time at which to raise such questions. There was, of course, little that Vehse could do. The clergymen had taken the initiative, and they made the most of their advantage. They naturally had larger personal followings than Vehse did, so that a last-minute appeal by the layman to the people remaining in St. Louis would have been futile. The pastors' plans were made, and they went ahead with them. Vehse had little time to make any. He was informed of the state of affairs only two days before C. F. W. Walther left St. Louis on his mission for the pastors. Jäckel was informed only one day before; and H. F. Fischer, later one of Vehse's chief supporters, was not aware of what was going on until four days after Walther had left.[33] The one attempt of Vehse to take matters into his own hands was his suggestion of bringing legal action against Stephan. If this stroke had been successful, Vehse would certainly have ruined the well-laid plans of the pastors. But the outcome of this effort has already been described, and by the time Vehse and Marbach had final word from their friends in answer to their inquiries it was too late to formulate other countermeasures.

Walther left St. Louis, accompanied by a journeyman weaver

---

[31] Vehse-H. F. Fischer-Jäckel, "Schluss-Zusatz," in Vehse, *op. cit.*, 143.
[32] *Ibid.*, 35.
[33] Vehse-H. F. Fischer-Jäckel, "Schluss-Zusatz," in *ibid.*, 143.

of the Saxon group, on May 15, 1839.[34] Again it was E. M. Bürger who was least inclined to mince words about the nature of Walther's assignment. He wrote: "Every effort now had to be made to render Stephan harmless and to prevent his gaining a following. It was decided to send Pastor Walther to Perry County. And he [Walther] succeeded in persuading all who had already gone there to forsake Stephan before Stephan noticed anything of it." [35] Winter expressed himself somewhat more guardedly in saying: "Some time later Herr Pastor Ferd. Walther was sent to our colony in order to inform several members of our *Gesellschaft* at that place, without, however, saying anything to Stephan about it." [36] What these men described is essentially what happened, as even Stephan agreed, although he does not emphasize Walther's role.[37]

Stephan had decreed that no one was to enter the colony without his express permission, and that the people in St. Louis were not to come at once in a body, but in small detachments. The latter arrangement, incidentally, was a very sound one, since facilities for the entire number could be provided only gradually. C. F. W. Walther, of ocurse, did not have Stephan's approval for his visit; so his welcome from the Bishop was not a hearty one. Hochstetter relates that Walther and his companion arrived in the Perry County colony in the dead of night. The captain of their steamboat had unceremoniously deposited them on the Missouri shore north of the Brazeau although they tried to tell him that he was putting them off on the wrong side of the river. They had been fortunate enough to find a boat in the dark and to row across the swollen Brazeau without mishap, reaching their friends by the light of a campfire which was kept all night near the landing place. Stephan was with the group gathered there, but after according Walther a reception that was anything but cordial, he left abruptly.[38]

When C. F. W. Walther had an interview with Stephan on the next day, he did not confront the Bishop with the charges against him, but reportedly gave as the reason for his own unauthorized

---

34 *Ibid.;* Hochstetter, *op. cit.*, 21.

35 E. M. Bürger, Selbstbiographie, 126, MS., E. J. Buerger Papers, Ellicottville, N. Y.

36 Winter to Guericke *et al.*, April 28, 1841, *Zeitschrift für die gesammte lutherische Theologie und Kirche*, II, No. 3, pp. 116—132.

37 Stephan to Flügel, Oct. 12, 1841, MS., C. H. I.

38 Hochstetter, *op. cit.*, 21—22; Vehse, *op. cit.*, 18.

presence in Perry County that he had been delegated to convey to Stephan the urgent wish of all the immigrants in St. Louis to come to Perry County at once.[39] If these were Walther's representations to Stephan, they simply were not true, for it is also related that he is supposed to have objected to the rule against accepting employment for more than a single day.[40] This was the kind of protest which would come from people who expected to stay in St. Louis, not leave it. Furthermore, between one hundred and two hundred of the Saxons chose to stay in St. Louis at the end of this same month, when the group took matters in its own hands and simply transferred itself to Perry County. But, worse than that, the position was unsound, for there simply were not accommodations for that number of people in Perry County. Stephan took no pains to make his refusal a courteous one, neither did he make any effort to conceal his dislike of anyone who disobeyed his orders — in this case C. F. W. Walther. Thereafter the two men apparently did not get together again during the entire time that Walther was in the colony.

The younger Walther, however, now proceeded to do everything he could to undermine Stephan's authority in many small ways without actually coming out into the open at once. In the services Walther disregarded the order of worship upon which Stephan had heretofore insisted. In going through the colony the agent of the St. Louis group encouraged the people in Perry County to disobey Stephan's orders for the construction of roads and bridges, and rather to devote their time to building dwellings and planting crops — which, of course, was advice both popular and sound. In general, C. F. W. Walther seems to have deliberately conducted himself in such a way as to give the impression, with his studied insubordination, that something was very wrong. Meanwhile he informed the key figures of events and plans in St. Louis.[41]

Several days after Walther arrived in Perry County, the New Yorkers came, over one hundred strong, and with them the three Büngers, who had been separated from the rest of the family by

---

[39] Hochstetter, *op. cit.*, 22—23; Vehse, *op. cit.*, 18.

[40] Hochstetter, *op. cit.*, 22.

[41] E. Bünger, Einiges aus dem Leben unseres theuren unvergesslichen Dr. C. F. W. Walther, MS., C.H.I. (hereafter cited as Aus dem Leben . . . C. F. W. Walther); Hochstetter, *op. cit.*, 23.

the performance of the Walther brothers in the incident involving the Schubert children.[42] The Büngers had booked passage on the *Constitution* the same day that Mrs. Bünger was released in Bremen, December 11, 1839. They had sailed from Bremerhaven in the company of Kohtz, December 19. The American coast was sighted February 18, 1839. With the aid of Kohtz's meager English ("Where is Norfolk Street?"), Spröde was located the following day.[43] His new environment evoked from Bünger the wry comment: "Nothing, nothing but trade. One can notice that he is in America." [44] Letters from St. Louis arrived in New York on February 19, the same day Stephan landed in St. Louis. The New Yorkers were informed in these letters that Bürger, Keyl, C. F. W. Walther, and G. H. Löber had already arrived in St. Louis and that Stephan and O. H. Walther were still in New Orleans on January 30. Bünger answered these communications and reported his arrival to Stephan on February 22.[45]

Sunday, February 24, provided Bünger with his first opportunity to appraise the New York group. Its orthodoxy left nothing to be desired. Evidently Stephanism was Stephanism, even in the "Diaspora." For, while the clergy in St. Louis were spending the day in climaxing their hierarchical *tour de force* by having their people sign the Pledge of Subjection, services in New York were attended by about a hundred persons, who were subjected to another of Spröde's frequent readings of one of Stephan's sermons.[46] The next evening Spröde presided over a meeting of the men of his group. In the absence of definite instructions from Stephan, Spröde advanced his own ideas, which were unopposed, and presumably prepared his hearers for the fact that all or some of them would have to remain in New York because funds for transportation were lacking.[47] On March 1 the New York group was informed by Kimm of St. Louis, who was in New York on business, that Stephan and his company had not yet arrived in St. Louis on February 14.

---

42 E. Bünger, Aus dem Leben . . . C. F. W. Walther, MS., C.H.I.

43 J. F. Bünger, Diarium, Dec. 11, 19, 1838, Feb. 18, 19, 1839, MS., L. Fürbringer Papers, St. Louis.

44 *Ibid.*, Feb. 19, 1839.

45 *Ibid.*, Feb. 19, 22, 1839.

46 *Ibid.*, Feb. 24, March 3, 10, 17, 1839.

47 *Ibid.*, Feb. 25, 1839.

Accordingly, J. F. Bünger wrote another letter to Stephan on March 2,[48] and it became constantly clearer in Bünger's journal that the New York group would not move without instructions from St. Louis. No answer was forthcoming; so the New Yorkers spent several weeks marking time, and Bünger occupied himself with studying English, visiting churches, converting Captain Volkmann of the *Constitution* to Stephanism, and writing letters to Germany.[49]

Finally, on March 18, definite word was received from St. Louis. Four letters arrived on that day — one each from Örtel, C. F. W. Walther, and Ferd. Rudloff, while the fourth presumably came from Stephan.[50] It appeared that a division of opinion had developed among the Saxons in St. Louis on the question of whether or not it was wise to have the New York group come at the present time. After some delay, Stephan had decided the question affirmatively.[51] However, no financial help was promised from the Credit Fund, and it appeared Spröde's people would have to shift for themselves. Two evenings later another meeting of the men was held, and, according to the Stephanite pattern, the Code for the Credit Fund was read, and each one was required to state the amount of his cash resources.[52] Less than a week later, on March 25, a committee was elected to administer the affairs of the Spröde group on about the same basis as the committee of the *Gesellschaft* acted for the Stephanites. Members constituting this executive body for the New York contingent were Spröde, C. Körner, R. Koch, Geisel, Jacob Fischer, Motz, and J. F. Bünger. Meanwhile the *Gesellschaft* in St. Louis had little word from New York other than Kimm's report that the Büngers had arrived.[53]

On March 26 further letters from St. Louis convinced the New York group that it was futile to wait for assistance from the Credit Fund. Accordingly, at a meeting of the New York committee that same evening, the tentative action of the previous evening was con-

48 *Ibid.*, March 1, 2, 1839.

49 *Ibid.*, Feb. 23, March 5, 6, 20, 23, 1839.

50 *Ibid.*, March 18, 1839.

51 C. F. W. Walther, *Bünger*, 52.

52 J. F. Bünger, Diarium, March 18, 20, 1839, MS., L. Fürbringer Papers, St. Louis.

53 *Ibid.*, March 25, 26, 1839.

firmed, namely, that those who could not afford to pay for their own transportation would have to wait for better days. It was deemed inadvisable to deplete the resources of the group as a whole by spreading out their available capital too thinly over a larger number of people through loans for traveling expenses, as the *Gesellschaft* had done. Hope was held out to those without means that if on arrival in St. Louis the New York group would find that funds were at their disposal nevertheless, the money could promptly be made available, and a second contingent could follow the first from the East within four weeks. Geisel was elected as elder of those remaining and was deputized to act as their leader.[54] Eventually, however, he went with the first contingent.

Spröde and Bünger appear to have succeeded in imbuing also the New York group with a thoroughgoing Stephanism. The resolutions of their committee on March 26, for instance, were not put to any kind of vote of the people or even submitted for approval. A meeting of all the men was called for the following evening, March 27, and the resolutions were announced to them without further ado. Opposition was not given an opportunity to arise, since difference of opinion simply was not tolerated. One man made bold to express the opinion that "the Word of God still existed in Germany." Unfortunately he was one of the few who were getting some financial assistance. Upon expressing such heresy he promptly found this assistance withdrawn. This disciplinary measure brought him to terms in twenty-four hours and presumably changed his opinion of religious conditions in the Fatherland. For the edification of the Spröde group, Bünger read to them the "Reply to Friendly and Unfriendly Reception" from the *Anzeiger des Westens* and, on instruction from St. Louis, also had the article reprinted in the New York *Staatszeitung*.[55]

On April 4, 1839, Spröde and Bünger made inquiries of the local German Immigrant Society. On the basis of the information obtained it was decided to leave on April 22, since the Erie Canal would not be open until April 20.[56] This intention was carried out, and on the twenty-second 108 persons began the journey to St. Louis

---

54 *Ibid.*, March 26, 1839.

55 *Ibid.*, March 26, 27, 29, 30. See also *Anzeiger des Westens,* Dec. 31, 1842.

56 J. F. Bünger, Diarium, April 4, 1839, MS., L. Fürbringer Papers, St. Louis.

by steamboat. According to one of their number the itinerary was "Bogibsi . . . Albani . . . Utika . . . Rochester . . . Bufalo . . . Clivland . . . Ackron . . . Cinsinati . . . Louiswill." [57] Spröde and his "New Yorkers" arrived at the landing place in Perry County on the forenoon of Friday, May 17, 1839.[58] Both the number of persons in this group as well as the date of their arrival in Perry County are frequently given with slight variations. Most frequently their number is placed at ninety-five or one hundred,[59] while the time is described as "just after Pentecost" (May 19).[60] The figure on the total, adopted here, is that in the list which Löber prepared in 1844, and no reason has been found to question it. The date, May 17, is that given by a participant in the journey, and also is the one that fits best into the account of C. F. W. Walther's activities during these days.

Everything now seemed to be conspiring against Stephan. The arrival of the New Yorkers is a case in point. They arrived in Perry County just at the time when C. F. W. Walther was there and thus gave him a splendid opportunity to carry out his mission before Stephan could condition their minds against what they were soon to hear. As though that were not enough, it also happened that one of the two leaders of this group, J. F. Bünger, was one of C. F. W. Walther's closest friends. The New Yorkers, accordingly, were won without too much difficulty to become some of Stephan's bitterest

---

[57] Excerpts "from the report of a man who came with the 'New Yorkers,'" in H. Schmidt to Dau, Nov. 22, 1912, MS., C. H. I.

[58] *Ibid.*

[59] Vehse, *op. cit.*, 18; Köstering, *Auswanderung*, 29; Schieferdecker, *op. cit.*, 10; C. F. W. Walther, *Bünger*, 53; Th. Gräbner, *op. cit.*, 22. The figure ninety-five undoubtedly can be traced to Nachrichten an unsere Nachkommen, MS., C. H. I., which gives this as the number of the New York group. However, the list used to arrive at the more accurate figure of 108 was the very one accompanying the Nachrichten, also prepared under the supervision of G. H. Löber. An explanation of the contradiction has never been suggested; and until one can be advanced, it would seem more reasonable to total the list than to accept Löber's statement. Other contemporary sources give one hundred as the number. Stephan to Flügel, Oct. 12, 1841, MS., C. H. I.; J. F. Bünger, Diarium, MS., L. Fürbringer Papers, St. Louis; *Anzeiger des Westens*, Dec. 31, 1842. The *History of Southeast Missouri*, 256, even placed the number as low as seventy-five.

[60] C. F. W. Walther, *Bünger*, 53; M. Günther, *op. cit.*, 34. Schieferdecker compromised by giving May 18 as the time for arrival, Schieferdecker, *op. cit.*, 10; and Stephan supported this version. Stephan to Flügel, Oct. 12, 1841, MS., C. H. I.

opponents in the next few weeks.[61] Walther, of course, immediately instructed J. F. Bünger on the state of affairs but did so in the sleeping quarters of a group of about twenty-five to thirty men, and the fact that it was done in Latin did not prevent others, such as Ernst Bünger, from understanding it. This episode is typical of Walther's methods on his mission. He did not make the mistake of immediately mounting a stump and denouncing Stephan, but gave his information to hand-picked individuals, always with the caution that they were to keep it to themselves for the time being.[62]

The results of Walther's method were as nearly perfect as could be desired. By Pentecost Sunday, May 19, the entire colony was seething with an undercurrent of excitement and curiosity, prompted either by their knowledge of what was going on or their knowledge that something was going on. Stephan was still permitted to preach on that day in spite of the fact that he already stood condemned in the eyes of the leaders who were engineering his dethronement.[63] But Stephan also noticed that something was afoot. He spoke of a conspiracy against him and cautioned Ernst Bünger: "Beware of that Ferd. Walther, that fellow is a fox." [64] Accordingly, when Sunday came, Stephan ordered everyone to appear at the landing place (Wittenberg), where he was to preach. C. F. W. Walther countered by summoning everyone to the other settlement farther inland (Altenburg), where he was to be guest speaker for the day.[65]

The extent to which the campaign against Stephan had progressed can be gauged from the fact that in a group as subservient to a man as the immigrants had been to their Bishop, all but "2 or 3" as Ernst Bünger reported, now nevertheless braved their leader's wrath for the sake of hearing C. F. W. Walther. Even the people from the landing place on the river left Stephan to himself and came to hear what Walther had to say. They were not disappointed. After

---

[61] G. H. Löber to Nitzschke, Feb. 27, 1845, MS., C. H. I.

[62] E. Bünger, Aus dem Leben . . . C. F. W. Walther, MS., C. H. I.

[63] Vehse, *op. cit.*, 18.

[64] E. Bünger, Aus dem Leben . . . C. F. W. Walther, MS., C. H. I.; Vehse, *op. cit.*, 18; G. Günther, *op. cit.*, 103.

[65] E. Bünger, Aus dem Leben . . . C. F. W. Walther, MS., C. H. I.; Hochstetter, *op. cit.*, 23. Hochstetter pictured this incident as having taken place on Pentecost Monday. The eyewitness account of E. Bünger stated it was Sunday. The immigrants probably had services both days, and little importance attaches to this discrepancy.

the regular service, during which Walther preached on John 3:20, he rose to say: "Many of you will have been surprised this morning that I preached in spite of the invitation and against the orders of the man who until now has been beloved and respected by us all, but terrible things have happened, which I shall now communicate to you."[66] The disclosures to which this was the preamble, made everyone very "sorrowful," E. Bünger asserted; yet everyone believed them.[67] Walther's work in Perry County was done for the time being. Stephan's fate was sealed.

---

[66] E. Bünger, Aus dem Leben . . . C. F. W. Walther, MS., C. H. I.; Hochstetter, *op. cit.*, 24.

[67] E. Bünger, Aus dem Leben . . . C. F. W. Walther, MS., C. H. I.

CHAPTER SIXTEEN

STEPHAN'S EXPULSION FROM THE GESELLSCHAFT

WHEN C. F. W. WALTHER returned to St. Louis from Perry County, the stage was set for the denouement of Stephan's career. The precise date of Walther's arrival in St. Louis is not clear, but Vehse and his collaborators said that he was gone a week, which would imply his return to St. Louis on May 22 or May 23.[1] Meanwhile some of the laymen in the city, led by Vehse, were meeting with little success in their further efforts to reach an understanding with the preachers on the division of secular and ecclesiastical powers. A number of preliminary suggestions which the laymen had drawn up as a basis for discussion were rejected, and young Walther on his arrival condemned their insolence with the remark that they were dealing with the pastors "worse than the King of Prussia."[2] However, the report of Walther's success in his mission made possible agreement between the pastors and laymen on at least one point, namely, the decision to make short shrift of Stephan. To this idea, of course, the clergy had never been opposed *per se,* so long as it rested on their authority and the proper preliminary maneuvers took place; these Walther had now executed.

Accordingly, the immigrants resolved to move to Perry County in a body for the ceremony of dethronement. Precisely how many of the Saxons were still in St. Louis at this time is nowhere indicated. Since the day that Stephan left for Perry County, more and more of the colonists had gradually been transferred from St. Louis. But it seems reasonable to assume that in excess of four hundred had not yet seen the site of their new colony. Even now a considerable number decided to remain in the city, at least for a time, and to forgo the satisfaction of witnessing Stephan's actual removal. These

1 Vehse-H. F. Fischer-Jäckel, "Schluss-Zusatz," in Vehse, *op. cit.,* 143.

2 *Ibid.,* 144.

people were mostly the families of craftsmen who had found employment, or who hoped to find it more readily in St. Louis than in the wilderness. It appears that about one hundred to 120 of these Saxons were left behind on this occasion. Some of the others who made the trip returned almost immediately. Since two steamboats had to be chartered to accommodate the passengers, the assumption that the total of those in St. Louis was over four hundred at the time Walther returned seems amply justified.[3] The wisdom of moving two to three hundred[4] more persons to Perry County at this time and in the absence of proper accommodations for them was doubtful, to say the least. Furthermore, their presence was by no means necessary for deposing Stephan, in view of the manner in which this matter was being handled. But removing Stephan did not imply that his plans were to be abandoned, and, as G. Günther pointed out, taking the people to Perry County was the surest way of preventing their leaving the *Gesellschaft* at this juncture.[5]

The events within the *Gesellschaft* were also being rumored about the city. But of the English newspapers the *Daily Evening Gazette* was the only one to take notice of the sensational developments; it did so in these guarded words:

> We have had occasionally insinuated to us the most painful innuendoes in regard to the Colony of German Lutherans, who have made their establishment in the southern section of this State. We wish that the German paper of this city would publish a full and impartial statement of facts, in order that the public mind may be spared from the effects of misrepresentation and abuse.[6]

But already the wish of the *Gazette* was fulfilled. On Monday,

---

[3] Winter to Guericke *et al.*, April 28, 1841, *Zeitschrift für die gesammte lutherische Theologie und Kirche*, II, No. 3, pp. 116—132; Nachrichten an unsere Nachkommen, MS., C. H. I.; Vehse, *op. cit.*, 18—19; Köstering, *Auswanderung*, 21. Stephan's interpretation was that those who did not come along to Perry County were those who refused to declare themselves against Stephan. Stephan to Flügel, Oct. 12, 1841, MS., C. H. I. However, there is little in the subsequent history of the St. Louis group to suggest that they were "pro-Stephanite."

[4] Stephan said the correct figure was 300, Stephan to Flügel, Oct. 12, 1841, MS., C. H. I.

[5] G. Günther, *op. cit.*, 92.

[6] *Daily Evening Gazette*, May 29, 1839.

May 27, before leaving St. Louis, the pastors had drawn up a statement for publication, which appeared in the issue of the *Anzeiger des Westens* on June 1, 1839, and read as follows:

> Explanation
>
> Only a few weeks ago we, the undersigned, felt constrained openly to reject the many evil rumors from Germany which had been directed against our erstwhile Bishop Stephan also at this place. Unfortunately, however, during the past few weeks we have made the discovery that we were the dupes of a deceit so shameful as to fill our hearts with horror and revulsion. Stephan was indeed guilty of the secret sins of immorality, unfaithfulness, and hypocrisy, and it was just to us that the unsolicited confessions were made which exposed him; we have immediately made the necessary communications regarding these confessions also to others.
>
> Since we have in the past defended this man through ignorance and in voluntary allegiance to him, therefore, now that God through His gracious providence has opened our eyes, we publicly renounce the reprobate.
>
> Our hope is that the Lord, who has hitherto so visibly blessed us and the entire congregation of emigrants, will avert all harmful effects of this grievous offense from us and others.
>
> St. Louis, May 27, 1839.
>
> Gotthold Heinrich Löber, Pastor,
> Ernst Gerhard Wilhelm Keyl, Pastor,
> Ernst Moritz Bürger, Pastor
> Carl Ferdinand Wilhelm Walther, Pastor
> (at the same time in the name of their two absent colleagues:)
> Otto Herman Walther, Pastor
> Maximilian Oertel, Pastor.[7]

The other Saxons still in St. Louis were represented by their deputies in making a supplementary declaration, which appeared immediately below that of the pastors. The laymen expressed themselves in these words:

> With reference to the Protest inserted by us into this paper on April 29 of this year, we also declare that, insofar as Stephan's person was concerned, we unwittingly gave false

[7] *Anzeiger des Westens*, June 1, 1839, quoted in G. Günther, *op. cit.*, 93—94; C. F. W. Walther in Köstering, *Auswanderung*, 17—18.

testimony, and hereby formally retract the same. Stephan will immediately be deposed and removed from the settlement which we have purchased in Perry County.

St. Louis, May 27, 1839.

The provisional deputies of the evangelical Lutheran congregation which has immigrated from Germany: Dr. Vehse, Jäckel, Barthel, Hoffmann, Pfau, Hellwig, Häcker, Winter, Müller, Schmidt, Palisch, Hoffmann, Heinig, Gräfe, Poppitz; at the same time in the name of those who have gone ahead to Perry County:

Marbach, Gube, Sörtzel, Nitzschke, Otto, Klügel, Müller, Schlimpert.[8]

The date of publication has occasioned the assertion that this declaration was made as a result of direct dealings with Stephan in Perry County and of his deposition on May 30.[9] It will be noted, however, that the authors were in Perry County at the time of publication, consequently must have drawn up their statement before leaving, as also the actual date of writing, May 27, indicated. The "Explanation" had no relation to what took place in Perry County May 29—30.

Obviously, Stephan's followers were now ready to join in condemning him publicly without any kind of hearing. With agreement on this point, however, harmony among them seems to have ended. The difference of opinion between the pastors and some of the laymen was becoming more acute. Just before departure for Perry County the lay leaders handed a written protest to the clergy which attacked the latter's conception of their position and asserted the principle that expulsion from the church was not a prerogative of the clergy, but was within the power solely of the congregation.[10] This principle was later to be reiterated.[11] Moreover, just before the colonists left St. Louis, Mr. Tennstädt demanded repayment of his investment in the Credit Fund, and when this was refused, he brought suit against the *Gesellschaft,* naming F. W. Barthel and Jäckel, who had signed his receipt. A bond of $1,000 had to be given

---

[8] *Anzeiger des Westens,* June 1, 1839, quoted in G. Günther, *op. cit.,* 94—95.

[9] P. Kretzmann, "The Saxon Immigration to Missouri, 1838—1839," *Missouri Historical Review,* XXXIII, 165; Steffens, *op. cit.,* 134—135.

[10] Vehse-H. F. Fischer-Jäckel, "Schluss-Zusatz," in Vehse, *op.-cit.,* 144.

[11] Vehse-H. F. Fischer-Jäckel, "Protestationsschrift," in *ibid.,* 57—58.

to prevent the arrest of these two men and permit their departure from the city.[12] The eventual result was that Tennstädt was one of the few who was paid in full.[13]

As remarked above, two boats, the *Prairie* and the *Toledo,* were hired for the transfer of the people and their possessions.[14] The *Prairie* arrived at the mouth of the Brazeau at 4 A. M. on May 29.[15] In the light of the customary watch fire at the landing the debarking immigrants saw the woman whom Vehse unchivalrously termed Stephan's "concubine" — no doubt he referred to Louise Günther — on the lookout for them. An attempt was made to seize her, but she fled to Stephan's house near by, and the Bishop himself came to the door. A brief but heated altercation between Vehse and Stephan followed, after which Stephan and Louise withdrew into the house to remain there for the rest of the day. During the greater portion of the twenty-ninth the new arrivals amused themselves as best they could while waiting for the *Toledo* and its passengers. Vehse inspected the settlement on horseback and then loitered around Stephan's house. The *Toledo* did not discharge its passengers at the landing until 5 P. M.[16]

The entire company was now present, and Vehse was all for proceeding to the deposition forthwith. As he naively remarked almost a year later, there was nothing to debate or to discuss, the first and only order of business was to get rid of Stephan. However, the pastors, all of whom were now in Perry County, were a little less precipitate, although hardly more charitable, than Vehse. Their hesitancy was not occasioned by any compunctions about the justice of what they were about to do, but by their indecision as to what the proper formal procedure should be under the circumstances.

---

12 G. Günther, *op. cit.*, 93.

13 List of Saxon Emigrants 1838, MS., C. H. I.

14 Vehse, *op. cit.*, 18; E. M. Bürger, Selbstbiographie, 126, MS., E. J. Buerger Papers, Ellicottville, N. Y.; G. Günther, *op. cit.*, 92, seems to have known of only one vessel. The most complete account of what happened during the next few days is found in Vehse's book. While his treatment is journalistic, his facts are usually correct, and his narrative is corroborated by others in most essentials. Vehse, *op. cit.*, 18—22. See also G. Günther, *op. cit.*, 93—106; Schieferdecker, *op. cit.*, 14. Günther is the least accurate, but, because of his quotations from the *Anzeiger,* often indispensable.

15 Stephan to Flügel, Oct. 12, 1841, MS., C. H. I.; Vehse, *op. cit.*, 18—19. The date could hardly have been May 30, as stated in G. Günther, *op. cit.*, 103.

16 Vehse, *op. cit.*, 19.

In order to decide this question, Marbach was drawn into their deliberations, while the latter's brother-in-law, by now already *persona non grata* with the men of the cloth, chafed at the delay.[17]

Probably during this meeting the letter of Sullivan to Marbach exerted its influence, as well as the advice of "Magistrate Lane" and of the third individual who had been consulted. This third man most likely was Bimpage, their agent, who was also present in the colony at this time and is supposed to have counseled the leaders to take the action they did.[18] Late in the evening a decision was reached. Keyl and Löber called on Stephan in his home, for the first time formally charged him with his misdeeds, and summoned him to a meeting of "the Council" the following day. Stephan, to whom this Council was nothing but the leadership of a rebellious faction, challenged its jurisdiction over him and appealed to the *Gesellschaft* as such. The two preachers withdrew, Gube was placed in charge of Stephan's person, the house was placed under heavy guard, and all parties awaited the next day.[19]

Just how this "Council" came into being, neither Vehse, who repeatedly referred to it, nor anyone else has divulged. Its membership consisted of the men who signed Stephan's Sentence of Deposition. It is possible that purely for the sake of form an election may have been held, although that is nowhere recorded. It is difficult to see how this could have been done, with the groups of the *Gesellschaft* separated from each other for over a month. Nor does there seem to have been a clear definition of the functions and powers of the Council. Its endowment with office and authority seems to have rested largely on its assumption of both. In effect it was heir to the committee of the *Gesellschaft*.

The indistinctness of the origin and scope of the Council were its chief dangers. The theory appears to have been that where secular affairs were concerned its entire membership acted, while when ecclesiastical matters came up, the ministerium alone had jurisdiction. The ministerium, however, was simply the ordained ministers of the group acting as a unit. On those occasions the

---

[17] *Ibid.;* Stephan to Flügel, Oct. 12, 1841, MS., C. H. I.

[18] G. H. Löber to Nitzschke, Feb. 27, 1845, MS., C. H. I.

[19] *Ibid.;* Stephan to Flügel, Oct. 12, 1841, MS., C. H. I.; Vehse, *op. cit.*, 20; G. Günther, *op. cit.*, 104.

laymen were present only by invitation, as Marbach in the case of the meeting on May 29. It was this arrogation of exclusive authority which was at the bottom of Vehse's complaint, as well as the delicate question of why the clergymen should not, by the same token, be excluded from the handling of secular affairs, and the further problem of determining which matters were secular and which ecclesiastical. The deposition of Stephan was a case in point. The pastors claimed that the first action required was a purely ecclesiastical matter, since it involved his excommunication and removal from office. Vehse rightly contended that both of these actions could be taken only by the church, or congregation, as a body. The compromise seems to have been that the ministerium did what little deliberating was necessary, and the entire Council then acted upon the matter. The pastors insisted, furthermore, that they have a majority in this Council.[20]

The next morning, May 30, 1839, the Council held a meeting in which it was first resolved to issue another invitation to Stephan to appear. The Bishop declined emphatically, denying the authority of his self-appointed judges with the words: "I know of no council."[21] The fact that on this particular point Stephan was in all probability in the right, did not save him. Still worse, adopting this position had the practical effect of depriving Stephan of the opportunity for formally replying to the charges against him. Stephan, of course, found no difficulty in asserting: "I was not conscious of having done anything wrong," and then complaining that he had no opportunity to defend himself.[22] But, as several times before, the impartial observer cannot but note that once more Stephan's stubborn insistence on a prerogative seemed more important to him than the greater good of clearing his name — if that was possible — and bringing peace to the church. The Council countered by promptly voting his removal from office and his excommunication. The instrument giving official expression to this action of the Council was then read to the people and ratified by them. Thereupon the Council proceeded to Stephan's residence, where Bimpage, now acting as the legal representative of the Council, read to Stephan the following document:

---

[20] Vehse-H. F. Fischer-Jäckel, "Schluss-Zusatz," in Vehse, *op. cit.,* 144.

[21] G. H. Löber to Nitzschke, Feb. 27, 1845, MS., C. H. I.

[22] Stephan to Flügel, Oct. 12, 1841, MS., C. H. I.

[Sentence of Deposition Pronounced upon Stephan]

After you, Martin Stephan, erstwhile Bishop of the evangelical Lutheran congregation which immigrated to North America from Saxony, have been accused before the subscribed Council of the sins of fornication and adultery, committed repeatedly, and of prodigal maladministration of the property of others, also because you have become guilty of false doctrine, but on the other hand have not recognized the Council legitimately placed over you, have thereby not only evaded the investigation pertaining [to these charges] and yourself forfeited the right of defense, but have also, by rejection of the Council, rejected the Word of God, the church, the office [of the ministry], and all divine order: we hereby declare by virtue of our office

> That you have forfeited not only your investiture with this spiritual office, but also the rights and privileges of a member of the Christian Church, in the name of God the Father, the Son, and the Holy Ghost. Amen.

Enacted in Perry County, at the mouth of the Brazo,
May 30, 1839.

The Council of the evangelical Lutheran congregation settled at that place.

Gotthold Heinrich Löber, Pastor.
Ernst Gerhard Wilhelm Keyl, Pastor.
Ernst Moritz Bürger, Pastor.
Otto Hermann Walther, Past. Vic.
Carl Ferdinand Wilhelm Walther, Pastor.
Johann Jakob Maximilian Oertel, Pastor
Dr. Carl Eduard Vehse
Johann George Gube
Christian Gottfried Schlimpert
Johann Gottlieb Palisch
Johann Friedrich Sproede

Read to the division of the *Gesellschaft* assembled at the Brazo River, and formally and solemnly ratified by it for itself and for the absent members of the *Gesellschaft*.

Enacted as above,

Hy. C. Bimpage, drafted
as recording secretary.

As witnesses
Edward Thierry
Johann Friedrich Gruenhayn [23]

---

[23] Sentence of Deposition Pronounced upon Stephan, MS., C. H. I. The original document, which is in German, bears no title. However, Vehse referred to it as "Stephan's Absetzungs-Urtheil," and quoted it in full. Vehse,

Stephan made a final, futile attempt to present a bold front; he refused to heed the order to vacate his home and leave the colony at once. A bitter dispute ensued between the ex-Bishop and the Council members. A crowd gathered, people began milling about the house and even entering it, until the room in which the tableau was taking place was packed. Vehse, E. M. Bürger, and the elders of the New York group were especially pugnacious in their attitude. The proceedings no longer bore any semblance — if they ever did — to orderly ecclesiastical or civil action. Rather, a mob psychology seemed to be spreading and allegedly the sound of a riding whip striking the boards on the outside of the house penetrated into the room. Stephan capitulated. Later Vehse reported that the Bishop had requested protection "from the common people," that he had preferred to deal with a delegation rather than with the entire group, and that he had expressed a preference for Vehse's services in this capacity. Stephan's rejoinder was that Vehse's "entire conduct was not that of a sane person but that of a crazy person, possessed by the devil." Of Marbach he said that he "was constantly near by, directing everything in a violent rage." All in all, Stephan succeeded in conveying the impression that his feelings toward these two men by 1841 were not yet cordial, though at the time of his deposition he may well have sought help from one of them. However, as Stephan correctly observed when confronting his enemies in Perry County, he was now a prisoner, and regardless of whether he liked it or not, Vehse and Bimpage remained as representatives of the Council and the *Gesellschaft*.[24]

The discredited leader's house, his effects, and his person were now thoroughly searched. The details of procedure supplied by Stephan suggest, even after allowances are made for the Bishop's indignation, that Vehse conducted the search in an unnecessarily

---

op. cit., 166—167. A later typewritten copy is headed: "Absetzungsurkunde Martin Stephans," MS., C. H. I. See also Stephan to Flügel, Oct. 12, 1841, MS., C. H. I.; Vehse, *op. cit.*, 1, 20; Vehse-H. F. Fischer-Jäckel, "Protestationsschrift," "Schluss-Zusatz," *ibid.*, 57, 144. Winter to Guericke *et al.*, April 28, 1841, *Zeitschrift für die gesammte lutherische Theologie und Kirche*, II, No. 3, pp. 116—132; E. M. Bürger, Selbstbiographie, 126—127, MS., E. J. Buerger Papers, Ellicottville, N. Y.; J. K. A. Höhne and J. G. Höhne to their brother, Sept. 26, 1841, quoted in *Die Ameise*, Jan. 10, 1842.

[24] Vehse, *op. cit.*, 20; Stephan to Flügel, Oct. 12, 1841, G. H. Löber to Nitzschke, Feb. 27, 1845, MSS., C. H. I.; G. Günther, *op. cit.*, 103—104. Günther has yet another version on some points.

humiliating manner. A considerable sum in cash and "curiosities of all kinds," as Vehse cryptically remarked, were found. Stephan is supposed to have offered the explanation that the money had been laid aside by him in order to pay Sullivan, his attorney in St. Louis. In view of the fact that Sullivan was also Marbach's adviser and had suggested the action which was being taken, it appears that Stephan's legal counsel was not of the best. The former Bishop had not yet become accustomed to his new status, for he protested petulantly that he was an old man, unable to support himself, and that if he were stripped of all his possessions, he would be destitute. He concluded that some provision would have to be made for him.[25] Stephan's listing of the items "stolen" from him is, of course quite different from any other, just as his conception of which funds belonged to him and how much remained is based on his singular system of accounting and ethics.[26]

Because of discrepancies in the various financial statements, the state of Stephan's account by this time cannot be accurately determined. But one itemized statement drawn up after his departure from the settlement showed a deficit of $1,802.87½ at the very least. Even then, some of his expenditures and withdrawals from the Credit Fund which have been described above were not included in this accounting, and their addition would bring his total liability much higher.[27] However, the immediate object now was to be rid of him, and so the document which was supposed to effect final settlement with Stephan was drawn up. Stephan also was brought to agree to and sign this *cessio bonorum,* which was in effect a renunciation by him of all claims upon the *Gesellschaft* and its individual members, as well as a promise forever to avoid the colony, and, in fact, the State of Missouri. In return for this the colonists paid him $100.00 and permitted him to keep certain personal effects.

---

[25] Stephan to Flügel, Oct. 12, 1841, MS., C. H. I.; Vehse, *op. cit.,* 21. It is interesting to note how the story was improved upon with the telling. Vehse, who was present, said that seven gold pieces were found on Stephan. The *Anzeiger* reported a hundred. *Ibid.* Günther made it 130 or more. G. Günther, *op. cit.,* 104—105.

[26] Stephan to Flügel, Oct. 12, 1841, MS., C. H. I.

[27] Stephan . . . Acct., List of Debtors, June 11, 1842, MSS., C. H. I. Stephan insisted that the *Gesellschaft* owed him or took from him, among other things, about 3,500 thaler, a library of 1,500 volumes, 120 acres of land, and other valuables, such as watches, a silver goblet, and the like. Stephan to Flügel, Oct. 12, 1841, MS., C. H. I.

These were the exact stipulations:

[Stephan's Renunciation of Claims on the *Gesellschaft*]

I underwritten Martin Stephan, formerly bishop of the Lutheran evangelic congregation which has settled on the mouth of Obrazo County of Perry Mo. do certify by these presents, that after the discussions and examinations which took place on this day, and after the account between me and the said congregation has been settled and presented to me, I owe to her so much that I neither now nor ever shall be able to compensate or make amends as for those useless expenses or damages caused by me, as for her other just and moderate demands. Therefore by these presents I do voluntarily cede and give up to the said congregation, namely to her trustees to wit: Johann G. Gube, Christian Gottfried Schlimpert, Johann Gottlieb Pahlisch, all my moveable and unmoveable property of every kind and description: I acknowledge as dissolved all conjunctions with the above said congregations, and release the whole congregation as well as each particular individual of her from all obligations of any kind towards me, and resign voluntarily and throughout, in reference to the connexion I have been till to day with the said congregation and her particular members, to every claims, demands, and suits, under what title they ever might have existed or could arise. The said congregation on the contrary let have to Martin Stephan and delivers to him as a present: the necessary clothing, a cloak, linnen [sic], 2 beds, 2 chairs, 1 clock, 1 Sofa cushion and its frame, books of meditation and 100 (One Hundred) Dollars.

Besides this I promise never to come back to the territory of said company, and to the State of Missouri.

Perry County Mo. 30th of May 1839.

Read to me and underwritten of me and in presence of

Henry C. Bimpage.
Dr. Charles Eduard Vehse [28] Martin Stephan.

---

[28] Stephan's Renunciation of Claims on the *Gesellschaft*, MS., C. H. I. The title is not on the original manuscript, but the instrument is referred to variously as *cessio bonorum* (Vehse, *op. cit.*, 21) and *Stephan's Verzicht* (the latter in a typewritten copy of much later date, C. H. I.). In the Concordia Historical Institute there is the original copy of this Renunciation in German, bearing the original signatures of Stephan, Vehse, and Bimpage, and two contemporary copies, one in German, the other an English translation, which has been quoted above. Presumably this translation was made by Bimpage. A fourth copy is to be found in Bound MSS., VI, C. H. I., and a fifth is the typewritten copy bearing a later writer's title, just referred to. See also Stephan to Flügel, Oct. 12, 1841, MS., C. H. I.

To this renunciation there was then added a list of the items allowed Stephan, headed with the words: "Included the above said things and $100 say One Hundred Dollars I have got besides the following things, to wit: . . ." This list was also signed by the deposed Bishop.[29] By this time the unfortunate man was noticeably affected by the personal catastrophe confronting him, and his signatures on the original German document, both at the close of the renunciation and of the list of effects, are barely legible. It is related that Stephan was now given the choice of going back to Germany, or facing trial, or being transported across the Mississippi River to Illinois. Confronted with these arbitrary alternatives, Stephan is supposed to have chosen the last of them.[30]

The new masters of the situation expected to climax their precipitate action in removing Stephan by putting him out of the colony on that same day. The great number of logs floating down the river made crossing it so hazardous that no one could be found who would venture out in a rowboat that day. At the same time the bitterness of the colonists against their former idol did not permit Stephan to remain in his house any longer. Hence the fallen leader was obliged to spend the night from May 30 to May 31 in a tent near his former residence. Few hearts, it seems, were softened among those who found him bowed over his Bible the following morning. On May 31, at 10:30 A. M., Stephan, stooped over a cane and protesting his innocence with visible emotion, was conducted to the waiting ferry. Not many people were present. Stephan's request had been granted that the crowd be kept away. The ex-Bishop was rowed across the Mississippi River by Bimpage and Teacher Müller of the New York group. Equipped with a spade and an ax, he was set down upon the Illinois side near a curious rock formation that

---

29 Stephan's Renunciation of Claims on the *Gesellschaft*, MS., C. H. I. There is also another unsigned, undated list of Stephan's property before this adjustment was made. List of Stephan's effects, MS., C. H. I. In addition there is a similar list in Bound MSS., No. 3. Verzeichniss von Stephan's, Meisters und Kokuschke's Effecten, C. H. I. (hereafter referred to as Bound MSS., 3). This latter list indicates that before the allowances shown on the Renunciation were made, Stephan turned over all his property to Gube, C. G. Schlimpert, and J. G. Palisch, representatives of the *Gesellschaft*. See also on these proceedings G. H. Löber to Nitzschke, Feb. 27, 1845, MS., C. H. I.; J. K. A. Höhne and J. G. Höhne to their brother, Sept. 26, 1841, quoted in *Die Ameise*, Jan. 10, 1842; E. M. Bürger, Selbstbiographie, 126—127, MS., E. J. Buerger Papers, Ellicottville, N. Y.; Vehse, *op. cit.*, 21.

30 A. L. Gräbner, "*Bis hieher,*" 6.

bore the lurid name of "Devil's Bakeoven." Stephan's reference to his "miserable dwelling" suggests that some provision for quarters had been made for him, either in a house of some sort or with a neighboring family.[31]

Stephan soon took rooms with an American farmer near by and, according to the allegations of his enemies, assured himself of good care by showing the man $700 in cash. A further sum of $400 in Missouri bank notes, which were missing from the Credit Fund, is also supposed to have found its way into Stephan's possession and been taken along by him. How this money escaped scrutiny during the officious and undignified search remains unexplained, unless one wishes to phantasize with Vehse about hollowed canes and buried treasure. The hapless Stephan, of course, pictured himself as almost entirely destitute.[32] Louise Günther was suspected of assisting Stephan to secure this money, but in a confession in which she admitted some other highly damaging things, she specifically denied having had anything to do with these financial irregularities.[33] It would appear, therefore, that if Stephan actually had these amounts, he himself tricked his victims once more even while they were executing their judgment upon him.

Stephan did not relinquish all hopes of re-establishing contact with his former followers. As early as June 12, 1839, he crossed the Mississippi to the Missouri side and wrote a pitiful letter to someone in the colony, describing his plight. He was ill, could not make himself understood (he spoke no English), and required the services of a physician. The ex-Bishop's requests were: that a doctor from the settlement be sent to the ferry, where Stephan promised to remain until 7 P. M.; that the unknown addressee of the letter also come to him; and that he be permitted to see his son Martin, who had remained with the colonists.[34] This incident was one of several

---

[31] Stephan to Flügel, Oct. 12, 1841, MS., C. H. I.; Vehse, *op. cit.*, 21—22; E. M. Bürger, Selbstbiographie, 127, MS., E. J. Buerger Papers, Ellicottville, N. Y.; J. K. A. Höhne and J. G. Höhne to their brother, Sept. 26, 1841, quoted in *Die Ameise*, Jan. 10, 1842; G. Günther, *op. cit.*, 106.

[32] Stephan to Flügel, Oct. 12, 1841, MS., C. H. I.; Vehse, *op. cit.*, 22; G. Günther, *op. cit.*, 105. The sum of $400 has been mentioned above as having mysteriously found its way from the Credit Fund into Stephan's hands. There may be some connection between these identical amounts, although the present writer was not able clearly to establish it.

[33] Bekenntnis der Louise Guenther, MS., C. H. I.

[34] Stephan to —, June 12, 1839, Bound MSS., VI, C. H. I.

occasions on which Stephan came back to the colony, despite his agreement. He also wrote to various of his former adherents a number of times.[35] All such attempts at resuming relationship with the *Gesellschaft* failed, for when Stephan came to Perry County, none of the settlers would have anything to do with him, and when he wrote, his letters went unanswered.[36]

Later that same summer Stephan became seriously ill with fever, and because he wrote to the colony that he was dying, G. H. Löber went to see him.[37] According to Hochstetter, Brohm accompanied Löber on this mission.[38] In spite of repeated attempts no one had yet succeeded in getting from Stephan an admission of the misdeeds with which he was charged. The interview in the summer of 1839, therefore, seems to have been confined almost exclusively to an attempt by Löber to get what was expected to be a deathbed confession. But while, according to Löber's assertion, Stephan made some surprising statements, the exhortations of Löber failed to produce the results most desired. In fact, it appears that Stephan never gave his followers the satisfaction of providing with his own lips or pen the admissions which they might have regarded as vindication of their actions.[39] The fever was not fatal to him on this occasion.

When Stephan saw that he was making no headway against the unrelenting judgment passed upon him by his erstwhile subjects,

---

[35] Vehse, *op. cit.*, 23; *Anzeiger des Westens,* June 29, 1839, quoted in G. Günther, *op. cit.*, 118—122.

[36] Vehse, *op. cit.*, 23.

[37] *Ibid.;* G. H. Löber to Nitzschke, Feb. 27, 1845, Stephan to Flügel, Oct. 12, 1841, MSS., C. H. I. Whether it is this contact or the previous one which is referred to in Stephan's letter of 1841, it is difficult to determine. He added to the list of his needs, however, bread, wine, and the delegation of one of the colonists to act as his servant and nurse.

[38] Hochstetter, *op. cit.*, 25.

[39] *Ibid.;* G. H. Löber to Nitzschke, Feb. 27, 1845, Document . . . des Grundsteins . . . St. Louis . . . 22. Juny 1842, MSS., C. H. I.; Vehse, *op. cit.*, 23; E. M. Bürger, Selbstbiographie, 127, MS., E. J. Buerger Papers, Ellicottville, N. Y.; Winter to Guericke *et al.*, April 28, 1841, *Zeitschrift für die gesammte lutherische Theologie und Kirche*, II, No. 3, pp. 116—132. G. Günther, *op. cit.*, 104—105, claimed that Stephan made a concession to Vehse and Bimpage. This is the only place such a statement is made. Others explicitly asserted the opposite. G. Günther's remark can no doubt be discounted entirely. Vehse failed to make any mention of a confession, and he can be relied upon not to have overlooked an item of such interest. Stephan was in no mood to confess anything to "that God-forsaken congregation." Stephan to Flügel, Oct. 12, 1841, MS., C. H. I.

he changed his tactics. As early as July 1, 1839, he tried to bring suit against the *Gesellschaft*. The question of Stephan's lawsuits in America is one of the most confused in the history of the immigration and has been the subject of numerous inaccurate statements. In 1841 Stephan did actually file two separate actions for recovery of his personal property and for damages. However, his attempt in 1839 was unsuccessful, although the *Anzeiger des Westens* reported that he sued and won the case.[40] Vehse corrected this error as early as 1840, when he related that Stephan tried to take his grievances to court in a three-thousand-dollar damage suit but was rejected ("ist damit abgewiesen geworden").[41] Vehse's phrasing does not indicate whether Stephan could not get a lawyer to handle the case or whether it was thrown out of court, but Stephan himself stated that for lack of money the former was the case.[42]

G. Günther's version was that Stephan filed a suit based upon the fact that some of the land was in his name and that he had been unlawfully deprived of it.[43] Schieferdecker's account has Stephan winning a case on an indefinite date.[44] Hochstetter found that "for the confiscation of his [Stephan's] personal property he later secured redress through legal action."[45] If any kind of suit was filed by Stephan in 1839, a search of the court records in St. Louis and in Perry County by the present writer failed to reveal it. This evidence seems to bear out Stephan's statement that

---

[40] *Anzeiger des Westens*, June 29, 1839, quoted in G. Günther, *op. cit.*, 118—122. On the later suits see Martin Stephan vs. Fredrick William Barthel, Henry C. Bimpage, Gustavus Jaeckel, Ernst Gerhard William Keyl, and Francis Adolphus Marbach (Trover and conversion), Circuit Court of Perry County, Mo., MSS., File No. 600, Circuit Clerk and Recorder's Vault, Perryville, Mo.; Martin Stephan vs. Gotthold Henry Loeber, Ernst Gerhard William Keyl, Ernst Moritz Buerger, Henry Christian Bimpage, Friedrick William Barthel, Francis Adolphus Marbach, John Gottlieb Palish, and Gustavus Jaekel (Trespass vi et armis), Circuit Court of Perry County, Mo., MSS., File No. 601, Circuit Clerk and Recorder's Vault, Perryville, Mo.

[41] Vehse, *op. cit.*, 23. See also Köstering, *Auswanderung*, 25.

[42] Stephan to Flügel, Oct. 12, 1841, MS., C. H. I.

[43] G. Günther, *op. cit.*, 107. It is true that at least 120 acres had been entered in Stephan's name. Abstract of Original Land Entries in Perry County, Missouri, 131 [entries of May 2 and May 14], MS., office of the Clerk of the Perry County (Mo.) Court, Perryville, Mo. That this land was *Gesellschaft* property is doubtful. Stephan, of course, claimed that it was his property, eighty acres of it purchased by him, forty presented to him as a gift from the *Gesellschaft*. Stephan to Flügel, Oct. 12, 1841, MS., C. H. I.

[44] Schieferdecker, *op. cit.*, 14.

[45] Hochstetter, *op. cit.*, 24.

he wished to file suit soon after his ouster but could get no one to take the case. Early in 1841, however, he was successful in getting the matter into court. Gustav Körner of Belleville, referred to above, took the case with little or no retainer as an inducement. Stephan was entirely satisfied with Körner personally and professionally, but lamented the fact that neither he nor Körner had the means to press the suit effectively.[46]

While it had proved impossible to secure an admission of guilt from Stephan in reference to the charges against him, the Council had better success with his maid, Louise Günther. Less than a week after Stephan had been expelled from the Perry County settlement, Louise was subjected to a cross-examination begun on June 4 and completed on June 5, 1839. Marbach, the lawyer, conducted the questioning. The "Protokoll" of these pseudo-judicial, extra-legal proceedings is signed under both dates by Louise Günther herself and by Jäckel, acting as secretary. The three original charges against the "defendant," upon which the examination was based, were: first, slandering many members of the *Gesellschaft* before Stephan; secondly, pandering, inasmuch as she was supposed to have brought other women of the *Gesellschaft* into Stephan's company; and, thirdly, having illicit relations with Stephan." [47]

The first charge Louise admitted with qualifications. She attempted to excuse herself by asserting that frequently she had also defended people before Stephan and that he had succeeded in making her believe that she was in conscience bound to inform on others.

The second charge was denied categorically. When Louise was confronted with the case of Caroline Dittrich, she denied any knowledge of it. All other incidents involving specific people were explained away by her in one fashion or another. Every suspicion that Stephan had associated with other women was repudiated, although the rivalry for Stephan's favor and the resultant bickering among his more intimate female companions, as described by Louise Günther, paralleled the domestic complications in an Oriental seraglio.

To the third charge, Louise Günther pleaded guilty. Her admission, covering incidents over a period of seven or eight years,

---

[46] Stephan to Flügel, Oct. 12, 1841, MS., C.H.I. The case eventually was settled out of court.

[47] Bekenntnis der Louise Guenther, MS., C.H.I.

was qualified only by the complaint that Stephan had represented her part in the affair and her previous perjury about it as a moral duty. This preposterous idea Stephan is supposed to have advanced through misapplication of a number of incidents in religious and secular history and through his familiar complaints about his family and personal life.[48]

Also involved to varying degrees in Louise Günther's statements were Louise Völker, Mrs. (Johanne Sophie) Schneider, Wilhelmine Hahn, Pauline Weidlich, Mrs. — Höhne, Auguste Pötsch, and Sophie Höschel. But an actual accusation against any of these Louise Günther refused to make.[49]

After this confession had been obtained, Vehse and others wished to bring Louise Günther to her father in St. Louis. But continued disagreement between the pastors and the laymen in the Council on the proper method of procedure prevented Vehse from carrying out this plan. Louise saw her opportunity, made her escape from the colony, and promptly followed Stephan to Illinois sixteen days after his removal.

In his declining years Stephan lived a rather quiet and secluded life, plagued by poverty and illness. Despite his lack of knowledge of English, he soon made some friends among the Americans. By 1841 he was living in or near Kaskaskia, Illinois, and preaching in the courthouse there every two weeks. He finally succeeded in organizing a congregation in "Horse Prairie," near Red Bud, Illinois. Louise remained in his employ until his death, on February 22, 1846.[50]

A full evaluation of the case for Stephan cannot be attempted without serious consideration of Louise Günther's confession. In a weird and sometimes deliberately obscured phase of the Saxon emigration, disregard of this document and acceptance of Stephan's quixotic "defense" constitute a greater strain upon the impartial observer's credulity than to take Louise's statements, in view of corroborating testimony and circumstances, at face value. A middle

---

[48] *Ibid.* See also G. H. Löber to Nitzschke, Feb. 27, 1845, MS., C. H. I.

[49] Bekenntnis der Louise Guenther, MS., C. H. I.

[50] Vehse, *op. cit.,* 23; *Anzeiger des Westens,* June 29, 1839, quoted in G. Günther, *op. cit.,* 118—122; Stephan to Flügel, Oct. 12, 1841, MS., C. H. I. At this time Kaskaskia, the first state capital of Illinois, was the county seat of Randolph County. A flood in 1844 led to the removal of the county seat, and by 1910 the Mississippi River had obliterated the town site.

position scarcely seems possible. Surely the value of this confession is considerably enhanced by her action in rejoining him and by the fact that he accepted her. Furthermore, doubts about the reliability of her statements, based perhaps on the suspicion of duress, are reduced to simple caviling for anyone who knows that shortly after Stephan's death Louise sought admission to Trinity Congregation in a petition which, although filled with abject self-recrimination, was supported by a letter from her father.[51] So far as Stephan's relationship at least to Louise Günther is concerned, it is no longer necessary to confine appraisal to such commonplaces as: "Even yet the matter of Stephan's guilt or innocence is in dispute." [52]

The fall of Stephan signaled the beginning of difficult and turbulent times for the Saxons — an interval which, in its various phases and degrees, was to last for almost two years. As the experiences of these months were to exert a lasting influence upon the Saxon colonies in America and upon the character of the institutions which they developed, the period is comparable in importance to that of the actual emigration.

The initial repercussions of the sensational turn which events had taken, were naturally felt in the colonies themselves. Yet it was only a matter of days before the essential facts became generally known, only a matter of weeks before the news had reached the Old World. The responsibility for this development rested, of course, partially with the Saxons themselves but in part also with the *Anzeiger des Westens.* As was to be expected, Weber was psychologically incapable of publishing anything as potentially piquant and racy as the pastors' declaration of May 27 without his own editorial comment, three to four times as long as the declaration itself.[53] A generous portion of triumph for the *Anzeiger* in the "I-told-you-so" vein, and an equal share of invective for Stephan, was followed by the *Anzeiger's* characteristic interference in affairs which neither were in the remotest its concern nor bore any semblance to factual reporting. Upon the pretext that "the public does

---

[51] Louise Günther to Trinity Congregation and J. S. Günther and Louise Günther to Trinity Congregation, n. d. [February—August, 1846], MSS., C. H. I. See also G. H. Löber to Trinity Congregation, Sept. 8, 1846, MS., C. H. I.

[52] Neve-Allbeck, *op. cit.,* 179.

[53] *Anzeiger des Westens,* June 1, 1839, quoted in G. Günther, *op. cit.,* 95—103.

not look upon the matter with indifference, but desires a full presentation of facts and the separation of the guilty from the innocent," the *Anzeiger* laid down a three-point program which it wished to foist upon the immigrants.

> 1. Delivering Stephan to the civil authorities, together with complete statements and testimonies concerning his revolting escapades as well as concerning his illegal depleting of the common fund, in order that he be justly punished according to the law, but the innocent on the contrary be justified.
>
> 2. A necessity for satisfying the public and for making the Emigrant Association secure is: a complete and prompt accounting, and providing security for the property which still remains.
>
> 3. Finally it must and can be demanded with right and justice that those who wish to withdraw from the Association after what has occurred receive prompt repayment of their money which cannot be denied after subtraction only of those sums used for their benefit.[54]

Under the first point Weber permitted himself a scurrilous portrayal of incidents in Stephan's life and the serious charge — unsubstantiated save by calling any alternative "unthinkable" — that those who associated closely with him must have known of Stephan's misdeeds, deliberately suppressed such information, and were accordingly implicated. A flood of unwarranted insinuations and accusations against the leaders, particularly the pastors, almost submerged the very sound observation that since they were willing to share Stephan's authority, they could not escape part of the responsibility for what had occurred, especially in the field of finances. The second point was followed by an attack upon the communal system of the Credit Fund. The third point became a preamble to an attempt at encouraging the members of the *Gesellschaft* to withdraw from it.[55]

The lengthy article was concluded with the assumption that the manner in which the entire matter had been conducted by the pastors, and their removal of another large group of people to Perry County, where there were neither adequate facilities to shelter them nor sufficient cleared land to support them, was prompted by

---

[54] *Ibid.*

[55] *Ibid.*

a desire to prevent people from leaving the *Gesellschaft.* To the *Anzeiger* this meant that the clergy intended to continue the hierarchical system and thereby assure themselves of an opportunity to extend indefinitely their parasitic existence.[56] The "great excitement" spoken of by the *Anzeiger* as prevalent among the population of St. Louis was largely the *Anzeiger's* own responsibility. Had the immigrants been permitted to work out their own problems, they would undoubtedly have fared at least as well as they did after receiving the *Anzeiger's* gratuitous advice. For Weber's counsel was so plainly motivated by hostility to the aims of the Saxons and his demands were so offensively phrased that they were certain to call forth resentment rather than favorable action.

Nevertheless, the Saxons were in an unenviable position. When they learned that the worst of their suspicions about Stephan apparently were confirmed, "some went into the woods, leaned against the trees, and wept aloud." [57] There was considerable confusion among the people. No one knew exactly what his position was, what the status of the *Gesellschaft* was, or what the future was likely to bring. While it was clear to some that there would have to be a certain amount of reorganization, there was also a very natural desire on the part of many to make no more changes than necessary. Consequently both the personnel of the leading group and the actual plans of the *Gesellschaft* remained fairly intact for some time after the deposition of Stephan. Even the hierarchical system remained in force for the first. At this time the expectation of all parties probably was that the removal of Stephan would, with a little retrenchment, solve all of their problems. This hope and the policy it suggested were the natural corollary of the thesis to which apparently everyone was still committed, that Stephan was solely or largely responsible for all their troubles.[58]

---

[56] *Ibid.*

[57] Gruber, *op. cit.,* 35.

[58] Vehse, *op. cit.,* 1, 7, 22, 24, 37; G. Günther, *op. cit.,* 108; Winter to Guericke *et al.,* April 28, 1841, *Zeitschrift für die gesammte lutherische Theologie und Kirche,* II, No. 3, pp. 116—132; E. M. Bürger, Selbstbiographie, 126, MS., E. J. Buerger Papers, Ellicottville, N. Y. Stephan concurred that confusion reigned and that he was made the scapegoat for everything that was wrong. But he lamented that all his excellent arrangements for the welfare of the *Gesellschaft* were abrogated by his "persecution." Stephan to Flügel, Oct. 12, 1841, MS., C. H. I.

Whatever the individual attitude, however, complete dissolution of the *Gesellschaft* at this time was effectively prevented by the fact that strong economic ties bound its members together. An effort had to be made to salvage something from the financial shambles of the Credit Fund.[59] Ethical and theological scruples, which later were to loom so large, seem to have enjoyed little prominence at first. Everyone apparently was satisfied that the arch-sinner had been removed from their midst. The only major development for several months in the ecclesiastical field came already on the day after Stephan's banishment, that is, on June 1, 1839, the same day on which the denunciation of Stephan and Weber's editorial blast appeared in the *Anzeiger*. In reviewing the new order of things, it seems suddenly to have occurred to the clergy for the first time in their careers as impresarios of the immigration that they were occupying a most peculiar position in relation to the various groups of people over whom Stephan had placed them and whom they had been wont glibly to call their "congregations," but with whom they really had no official standing.[60] As Vehse was to point out to them later, they were at this time no pastors at all. They had resigned their positions in Germany and had not been called to office since that time, but had merely been appointed by Stephan.[61] Now that the Bishop had been removed, they were deprived of any basis for such nebulous authority as they had claimed and exercised. A restatement of that authority seemed necessary.

The clergymen were successful in securing confirmation of their positions from the people, apparently without serious protest, although in great haste. On the request of the ministers themselves, "calls" were issued to them orally on June 1, 1839, by the *Gesellschaft* as a body, and they forthwith began serving the several groups of colonists who were to become the nuclei of the various settlements then being formed.[62] Although O. H. Walther began acting as pastor of the St. Louis congregation on June 9, 1839,[63]

---

59 Nachrichten an unsere Nachkommen, MS., C. H. I.; G. Günther, *op. cit.*, 108—109.

60 Keyl, *op. cit.*, 16—18.

61 Vehse-H. F. Fischer-Jäckel, "Schluss-Zusatz," in Vehse, *op. cit.*, 144.

62 Vehse-H. F. Fischer-Jäckel, "Protestationsschrift," in *ibid.*, 58; *Anzeiger des Westens*, June 8, 1839, quoted in G. Günther, *op. cit.*, 110—113; Keyl, *op. cit.*, 17—18; Bekenntniss, MS., C. H. I.

63 O. H. Walther, Zur Agende, MS., L. Fürbringer Papers, St. Louis. The first entry in this manuscript is for "Dom. II p. Trin. 39," *i. e.*, June 9, 1839.

he did not receive a formal, written call from that group for more than a year. The resolution for a written call to him was passed October 19, 1840.[64] The action of the colonists in calling these men, even if only orally, casts some doubt on G. Günther's assertion that already at this time "the unlimited confidence of the members in the pastors, which had held the *Gesellschaft* together, was shaken to its foundation." [65] Later this statement became true.

It is not known that a single voice in the *Gesellschaft* was raised against this irregular procedure at the time. Vehse seems to have stood irresolutely by, only to become, at a later date, the spearhead of an attack upon the system whose salvaging he now was too bewildered to oppose. Spröde also inveighed against this assumption of office — subsequently. Even the pastors had their compunctions, but were careful to express them only in private. Notably, their scruples were based upon nothing more than continued adherence to the hierarchical principles of Stephan with which they were still imbued. According to their theories of the episcopal succession, they believed in the continuance of the ministry only through ordination by a bishop or a similar dignitary. Thus despite their insistence upon a "call" from the people, the clergymen were not convinced in their own minds that this was sufficient. For this reason they considered an appeal for ordination to the Swedish Lutheran Church, to whose episcopal form of polity they had referred admiringly a number of times in their official documents.[66]

However, in the lives of a majority of the Saxons the stark realities of a struggle for their very existence crowded most other considerations into the background during the balance of this year. The matter of most pressing importance was that of finances. Ever since the condition of the Credit Fund had been investigated in St. Louis, it was fairly clear to at least a few people how desperate the actual state of affairs really was. But the group at large had not yet been permitted to share that information fully, nor had a detailed breakdown of general expenses into personal accounts been completed, so that the individual still could not be certain of his exact financial status.

---

[64] Erstes Protokollbuch, Oct. 19, 1840, MS., Trinity Church Records, St. Louis.

[65] G. Günther, *op. cit.*, 108.

[66] Vehse-H. F. Fischer-Jäckel, "Protestationsschrift," in Vehse, *op. cit.*, 111; *Anzeiger des Westens*, Dec. 20, 1842.

Now they were to learn the grim facts. An audit probably had been initiated either when the pastors began handing in their separate accounts for the expenses of the groups of which they were in charge, or when, in St. Louis, they had decided to depose Stephan at the earliest possible date. If, on the other hand, the immigrants waited until after Stephan's expulsion, then the huge task of checking every individual account was completed in the remarkably short time of one week. For by June 6, 1839, all expenses of the *Gesellschaft* since its organization had been itemized and totaled against the name of each individual. The result was the *List of Saxon Emigrants,* which, as has been previously noted, is really a book of personal accounts, containing also a listing of expenses for certain classifications of joint expenses, such as those for church and school, and for land.[67]

At this early date the intention was still that individuals were to pay interest for the sum advanced them by the Credit Fund from the date a month after their arrival in St. Louis, as the Code for the Credit Fund had indicated.[68] Accordingly each debtor was charged with an additional 6 per cent of the amount by which he had overdrawn his account, these charges being computed from April 1, 1839.[69] The debtors were now required to sign this form:

> — Date —
>
> That I owe Mr. Fried. Wilh. Barthel the sum of —— American Dollars and —— Cents, and will pay 6% interest per annum for this sum until it is paid, I herewith witness. I have received full value.
>
> (Signature)[70]

Later the interest accruing under these terms was canceled and only the principal, that is, the actual amount drawn by the individual, was charged to his account.[71] The condition of the Credit Fund, uncovered by the new investigation and revealed in a statement drawn up by F. W. Barthel, was pitiful. On May 24, even before

67 List of Saxon Emigrants 1838, MS., C. H. I.

68 Code for the Credit Fund, par. 4, Appendix B.

69 List of Saxon Emigrants 1838, MS., C. H. I.; F. W. Barthel to K. E. Schuricht, July 24, 1840, Bound MSS., No. 19. Belege zu Vertragen in Credit-Cassen-Angelegenheiten, C. H. I. (hereafter cited as Bound MSS., 19).

70 Form for notes given the Credit Fund, Bound MSS., 19, C. H. I.

71 List of Saxon Emigrants 1838, MS., C. H. I.

the major portion of colonists had left St. Louis, the actual assets of the *Gesellschaft* had been only $2,748.50.[72] By the time more people had been transported, and all of them had lived off the Credit Fund for a few weeks, it must have been completely exhausted.

After having made a major issue of the fact that Stephan had failed to permit the election of a committee for administration of financial affairs, the men now at the helm could hardly afford to pursue the same policy. Consequently, shortly after Stephan's deposition, a "Managing Committee," or Administrative Board, was elected in Perry County. Here, of course, the pastors were present to guide affairs. And here, if they maintained a solid front, they could, according to the Code for the Credit Fund, still remain in virtual control of affairs.[73] Actually the same people as before remained in charge. In the week after Stephan's deposition, Vehse, vice-chairman of this Board, traveled to St. Louis to preside over a meeting of the Saxons who were still in that city. In this meeting, on Thursday evening, June 6, 1839, a committee of six was elected to act for the St. Louis group. However, the understanding was unmistakable that this committee was to be subordinate to the Perry County Board. Furthermore, the system of issuing receipts was changed once more, in such a manner that names of Fund officers no longer appeared on them, as they formerly had. Plainly it was no longer possible to hold any individual for whatever sum might still be due a depositor; legal recourse in securing funds deposited was virtually cut off. The number of creditors who would leave the *Gesellschaft* under such circumstances would be few.[74] Despite certain modifications, continuance of something very much like the existing financial system thus was assured. The meeting in St. Louis, and the reorganization taking place, again struck sparks from the flinty editorial policy of the *Anzeiger* and served as the chief subject of attack in a new article of considerable length.[75]

---

[72] Epitome from the Cash-account, June 11, 1842, MS., C. H. I.

[73] *Anzeiger des Westens*, June 8, 1839, quoted in G. Günther, *op. cit.*, 110—113; Letter of resignation, Vehse-H. F. Fischer-Jäckel to the Administrative Board, June 22, 1839, in Vehse, *op. cit.*, 167—168.

[74] *Anzeiger des Westens*, June 8, 1839, quoted in G. Günther, *op. cit.*, 110—113.

[75] *Ibid.*

Just what the plans of the colonists — or, more accurately speaking, just what the plans of the pastors, who were in control of the colonies — were at this time is not clear. That the clergy actually intended to maintain the episcopacy, as Vehse claimed,[76] is not certain, although, judging from the events related in both the preceding and subsequent narrative, it is likely. What events do plainly show is that the clergy, and with them a majority of the other emigrants, had not yet abandoned their hopes of creating a single autonomous settlement, to be developed along the hierarchical lines laid down in the Codes. The contemplated transfer of the St. Louis group is a case in point. In June of 1839 the Saxons in St. Louis had no idea that they would settle permanently in that city. When they submitted another petition to Christ Church, they requested use of the building for only a few months to meet what they regarded as a temporary emergency, before they would join their brethren in Perry County.[77]

Such plans were doomed to failure. Granted that in Germany some of the skilled workers had also been engaged in agriculture and would not suffer if they now gave all their attention to farming, nevertheless, it should have been evident to their leaders that the percentage of craftsmen in the *Gesellschaft* was out of proportion to the total number of people in the colonies whom they might serve. It should also have been clear that the best thing would be to leave these people, most of whom were even then in St. Louis, in a larger population center, where they could support themselves. These workers themselves were not anxious to become a part of the Perry County colony. They revealed their attitude by remaining in St. Louis at the end of May. Within less than a year they became even more assertive and, to indicate their complete break with the policies of their superiors, "Resolved: that, in order to avoid offending weak spirits which might thereby be prevented from joining our congregation, the words [']Lead us, when Thy time comes['], etc., be omitted in the order of service, since they create the impression that the congregation intends to leave here in the

---

[76] Vehse, *op. cit.*, 24, 35.

[77] The elders of the Saxon congregation in St. Louis to Christ Church, June 13, 1839, MS., C. H. I. See also G. H. Löber to relatives in Germany, Sept. 10—30, 1839, in Löber-Eichenberg (ed.), "Ein Briefwechsel," *Mitteilungen . . . Kahla,* VII, 156—162.

near future." [78] Still later the folly of concentrating the people in Perry County was officially recognized.[79]

It appears that the chief proponents of the plan for bringing the immigrants to Perry County were the pastors. In a theocratic settlement such as was developing, the clergy was almost certain to, and did, exercise a great deal of influence. Some aspects of this clerical authority have already been described. A further step in extending the power of the pastors was taken, soon after Stephan's removal, when they began to act as judges for the colonies also in secular affairs.[80] The disastrous outcome of the first phase of the hierarchical experiment under Stephan, and the fact that they themselves had found it necessary to help terminate it, seem to have carried no lesson to the pastors. However, before the second phase of the system, now under their own leadership, could be fully developed, a storm of controversy broke loose.

In its later stages, this controversy, which lasted from 1839 to 1841, had a strong theological cast. It has, therefore, been easy to represent the subject of the entire struggle as exclusively religious, and ever since the days of the Saxons such a portrayal has found favor.[81] However, it will presently become apparent that initially the issue involved was primarily that of administrative control. A second word of caution is necessary for a correct understanding of this phase of the Saxon movement, and that is a warning against overemphasis — or more frequently underemphasis — of the part played by Vehse. No one who understands Vehse's characteristics, temperament, and personal relationship to other people, especially the pastors, or who appreciates his ability, can fail to recognize that he was a central figure in the movement so long as he was with the immigrants. Yet attempts to discredit and minimize his contribution have frequently been made in either or both of two forms: first, that of stressing the sense of pique, frustration, and resentment which he betrayed in the administrative phase of the quarrel; secondly, that of ignoring as fully as possible his real, individual

---

[78] Erstes Protokollbuch, April 6, 1840, MS., Trinity Church Records, St. Louis.

[79] Document . . . des Grundsteins . . . St. Louis . . . 22. Juny 1842, Bekenntniss, MSS., C. H. I.

[80] Vehse-H. F. Fischer-Jäckel, "Protestationsschrift," in Vehse, *op. cit.*, 64.

[81] Winter to Guericke *et al.*, April 28, 1841, *Zeitschrift für die gesammte lutherische Theologie und Kirche,* II, No. 3, 116—132.

contribution in the theological field. The latter is accomplished by giving much of the credit which should belong to Vehse, to C. F. W. Walther, who almost two years later defended a viewpoint strikingly similar to that expressed in the first instance by none of the clergymen, but by the doctor of laws.[82]

Vehse's name will appear frequently in the next portion of the narrative, but only because he happened to be the leader of one faction. If Vehse had not raised the question of who was to exercise administrative authority, someone else in all probability would have been obliged to do so. And if no one else had been inclined to make an issue of the problem, the development of circumstances would have thrust it forcibly upon the attention of the Saxons. For what was actually wrong with the organization of the *Gesellschaft* after Stephan's deposition, was that its proposed government was an anachronism.[83] It is doubtful that the semiautonomous, theocratic, isolationist ideas for governing the proposed settlement, outlined in the Codes, ever would have worked in the West of mid-nineteenth-century America. But the removal of Stephan also removed any prospect of success which these plans may ever have enjoyed. The scheme of government, with ecclesiastical and secular administration inextricably intertwined, was designed solely for the days when Stephan was still in charge. It was predicated upon the presence of a single omnipotent figure, who controlled all, upon whom all were dependent, and who apportioned authority among his subordinates in both the religious and secular fields as rewards for faithful adherence to him. Stephan had been such a figure. But all that was now past. A new day had dawned.

This fundamental change the pastors failed to recognize. All that they could see was what lay immediately before them, namely, the system of Codes, which still guaranteed to the clergy a commanding position in the settlements. That this system was the one

---

[82] *Ibid.* Winter is a good example, although by no means the most extreme.

[83] Vehse, *op. cit.*, 24. V. L. Parrington, Jr., found even John Eliot's mid-seventeenth-century "Christian Commonwealth" unlikely to succeed unless a complete autocracy could be maintained: "Given the conditions he envisioned, given a body of Christians believing in his beliefs and not zealous enough to question them, such a system might work. It might have worked, for example, with Father Rapp's brow-beaten believers at New Harmony." Parrington, *op. cit.*, 9. If it could have worked with the Stephanites, it could have done so only under Stephan's leadership.

they attempted to perpetuate was indicated [84] when they brusquely refused a division of secular and ecclesiastical authority; when they insisted that it was their right to decide whether or not Stephan was to be excommunicated; when they insisted that excommunication had to precede deposition; when they insisted that they have a majority on the Council which deposed Stephan; when they considered an appeal to the Swedish Church, in order to have a source of authority for their assumption of office, which they could regard as having greater validity than the mere will of their own people, who had already been kind enough to overlook the part of the pastors in the emigration and to extend calls to them; when they arrogated to themselves the position of secular judges; when they proposed to transfer the entire group to Perry County in spite of the economic obstacles; when they lent their leadership to a continuation of all or most of Stephan's original impracticable plans; and finally, when, as will presently become apparent, they opposed a division of the *Gesellschaft's* land.

The pastors apparently felt that the structure of the organization could remain just what it was so long as they acted as a unit. They were "the ministerium" of the Codes, and while there was at the moment no "primate," they were quite capable of performing his functions as a body. If it became necessary or desirable at some future date to have a "primate," it was quite possible to supply one from their own number. These viewpoints were not expressed by the pastors quite so plainly as they are here stated, but as a group the clergy certainly acted upon these premises. Marbach flatly stated: "After the fall of Stephan, the ministerium took his place."[85] The minutes of ministerial meetings illustrate the truth of Marbach's charge.[86] Accordingly, the pastors saw no reason to meet the demands of the laymen, and things continued to move along in their accustomed hierarchical way, with the clergy still protected by an inordinate deference to "the office" of the ministry.[87]

Some of the laymen did recognize the change that had taken place.[88] Furthermore they realized clearly that unless there was a

---

[84] *Ibid.*, 24, 35, 37; *Anzeiger des Westens,* Dec. 20, 1842.

[85] Marbach, An meine . . . Landsleute, MS., C. H. I.

[86] Minutes of the Ministerium of the Saxon Immigrants, Sept. 4, 9, 1839, MSS., C. H. I.

[87] Vehse, *op. cit.*, 24, 35, 37; Bekenntniss, MS., C. H. I.

[88] Vehse, *op. cit.*, 24.

modification of the hierarchical system, their position in the *Gesellschaft* was bound to deteriorate. They had been relegated to a secondary role also when Stephan was in control. But he was only one man and could not do everything, so at least in the administration of secular affairs he had given the lay leaders a role comparable to that of the rest of the clergy excepting himself — if for no other reason than that he was constantly playing off the one faction against the other. The laymen now demanded formal recognition for a similar division of authority into secular and ecclesiastical departments, as had previously obtained informally at Stephan's pleasure. In other words, the laymen were willing to co-operate with the clergymen, and by co-operating to present a solid front to the host of problems pressing in upon them. But what these men refused to do was to become utterly dependent upon the pastors and leave everything in their hands, as these gentlemen evidently seemed to expect.

These demands were not consistent with the former agreement of the laymen (with the possible exception of H. F. Fischer) to the hierarchical system which they were now attempting to abrogate. Similarly these demands were not justified by any greater degree of success on the part of the laymen in the government of the Association up to this point than the pastors had enjoyed. These demands probably were based in part upon a selfish desire of the laymen to regain some of the ground they had lost during the months that the *Gesellschaft* was becoming constantly more hierarchical and upon the added hope of removing control of at least some of the *Gesellschaft's* affairs from the exclusive jurisdiction of the clergy. But even though all these things may be true, the irrefutable logic of changing conditions was nevertheless on the side of the laymen. The plan proposed, of separating church and secular matters, was *per se* a sounder one than the theocratic system. The simple fact, that the only figure who might have made the original plan work — Stephan — was now gone, made some sort of reorganization inevitable. Thus, when the pastors refused to meet even moderate, justifiable demands, they enjoyed only initial success and assured ultimate defeat. Natural developments later forced the pastors not only to countenance, but in some cases even to espouse, the very things which, when proposed by the laymen in May and June, 1839, drew down upon their unanointed heads the damning "Worse than the King of Prussia."

Relations between the laymen, headed by Vehse, and the pastors rapidly grew more strained. When the constructive suggestions of the former for administrative reorganization were simply scrapped by the clergy, Vehse, H. F. Fischer, and Jäckel took what seemed to them the only other course possible and washed their hands of the entire matter. This action could not absolve them from partial responsibility for bringing the Gesellschaft into the straits in which it found itself, but it does absolve them of responsibility for the unnecessary delay, ghastly blundering, and almost criminal short-sightedness which caused much of the human misery in the colony during the ensuing months.

After only three weeks, on June 22, 1839, Vehse, Fischer, and Jäckel resigned from the newly created Administrative Board. The underlying causes for the split have been discussed above. Five specific reasons for their action were given by these three men, who were, respectively, the vice-chairman, the bookkeeper, and the secretary of the Board. The first was the failure of the clerical members of the Board to permit a step which the three officers considered vitally important, the abandonment of the communal system through a division of the land. The pretext for refusal on this occasion, as before, was that this was not an "opportune time." The second was the failure to attend to pressing matters, such as the case of Louise Günther (who, as related, had thereby been permitted to make her escape) or the examination of the notes held by the Credit Fund. Thirdly, the pastors refused to recognize the urgent need for establishing a sound fiscal system. A budget was still lacking, although the support of the colonists during the previous fortnight had used up $500 of the $2,000 cash still remaining in the Credit Fund. As Vehse, Fischer, and Jäckel saw it, "private administration [of property] must begin." Fourthly, the power of the Administrative Board had been left so indefinite that the resigning members felt they could not serve until there was a clear understanding in the matter. Fifthly and lastly, everything seemed to point to the intention of the chairman of the Board to override or remove any objections and exercise unlimited power under the cloak of his clerical office.[89] The chairman's name is not mentioned. Indications point to G. H. Löber.

---

[89] Letter of resignation, Vehse, H. F. Fischer, and Jäckel to the Administrative Board, June 22, 1839, in *ibid.*, 167—168.

If there had been any doubt up to this time as to whether secular or religious factors were basic for the split which occurred in the summer of 1839, this letter should have removed it. It was now amply clear that theological questions, while present, were still of secondary importance in comparison with the administrative. This conclusion is corroborated by two further reasons for their action, which these men gave at a later date. The one was that the pastors arrogated to themselves the position of judges in secular matters, as stated above. The other was that the interpretive alchemy of the clergymen appeared to transform almost everything into a "spiritual" question, which, accordingly, could be decided only by them.[90] The ministers themselves appeared to view their position as patriarchal rather than as pastoral.[91]

The pastors, forgetful of the fact that there was no longer a Stephan available to put down insurrection for his own benefit and that of the clergy in general, evidently made little or no effort to prevent the resignation of three of the Board's most capable men and at first went complacently on as before. The victory of the clergy, apparent or actual, was a costly one. Strictly speaking, it was their last. For a few months, of course, nothing happened. Everyone was more than occupied with the struggle for existence, with planting a meager crop, with putting up the inadequate shelters in which they were to spend the next winter, with caring for the sick and burying the dead, or even with building a "college."

But in early fall, Vehse, Fischer, and Jäckel opened a new phase of the contest, and the pastors suddenly found themselves confronted with tactics similar to those they themselves had employed against Stephan. Defeated in a simple administrative dispute, the pastors had taken recourse to moral questions to bring about Stephan's fall. Similarly the laymen now raised theological questions and brought charges involving the ethics of the pastors. As was pointed out in the case of the pastors, this was not necessarily a conscious or deliberate policy on their part, and it is just as possible to assume the same of the laymen at this point. Vehse, H. F. Fischer, and Jäckel were dissatisfied with the system and their position in it. When, feeling that the system was wrong, they then

---

[90] Vehse-H. F. Fischer-Jäckel, "Protestationsschrift," in *ibid.*, 64; *ibid.*, 36—37.

[91] *Ibid.*, 38.

examined it for error, they found an abundance. The result of their examination was a fundamental challenge of the basis upon which the *Gesellschaft* had been organized and the position of the pastors in it. What began as a question of administrative policy, intensified by personal issues, developed into a full-grown religious controversy which raged until April of 1841.

The prophetic forebodings of L. Fischer and Pleissner were being fulfilled. Both of these men had warned against the hierarchy. Pleissner had cautioned that the idea of the Credit Fund and the policy of having the clergymen handle secular and financial affairs were unsound.[92] Even before the end of June, 1839, his judgment was already so thoroughly vindicated that the very existence of the *Gesellschaft* was menaced. L. Fischer had foretold that the system could not fail to produce factions which would split into episcopal and presbyterial wings once Stephan was no longer at the head.[93] Now L. Fischer's augury of evil was also, for the greater part, to come true. However, before this development took place, a number of other events transpired, which must first be examined.

---

92 Pleissner, *op. cit.*, 7, 84, 90.
93 Fischer, *op. cit.*, 133—135.

CHAPTER SEVENTEEN

RETRENCHMENT AND REAPPRAISAL

THE MAJORITY of the colonists had their first opportunity to look about them, and to appraise the new environment in which they were situated, only after Stephan's expulsion from the *Gesellschaft*. It is helpful for an understanding of the subsequent development of the colonies to take a preliminary glance, even as the Saxons did. Fortunately, a composite picture of the Perry County communities in the summer of 1839 can be drawn from the descriptions of a number of settlers, especially that of Winter, who was the most observant.[1] After August of that year the settlements were put on a different basis of operation, and changes ensued which will be described in another connection.

The stretch of land which had been bought was undulating and heavily wooded. Basically the soil was clayey, but it had been blanketed with humus from the great variety of trees and bushes which formed the virgin growth covering it. The ground was badly run through with tree roots, and clearing it was correspondingly difficult. Stretches of grassland would have provided adequate pasture for livestock even late in the fall. But for the majority of the settlers the possession of cattle represented a degree of wealth they did not attain for several years, although smaller domestic animals were kept. Sheep were as yet not commonly raised in the region. The area seemed especially suited to growing cotton, tobacco, flax, and hemp. A great number of fruits, such as peaches, apples, pears, plums, cherries, and a variety of berries could be grown with little difficulty, or even gathered from the not altogether inhospitable forest.

The forest also provided, besides the cultivable crops, a large and varied supply of game with which the frontiersman could replenish his larder, for instance, deer, rabbits, squirrels, opossums,

[1] Winter to Guericke *et al.*, April 28, 1841, *Zeitschrift für die gesammte lutherische Theologie und Kirche,* II, No. 3, pp. 116—132. See also J. K. A. Höhne and J. G. Höhne to their brother, Sept. 26, 1841, quoted in *Die Ameise,* Jan, 10, 1842; G. Günther, *op. cit.,* 74; Schieferdecker, *op. cit.,* 12.

turkeys, pigeons, geese, partridges, pheasants. The fears of the relatives in the homeland that there was danger from beasts of prey were allayed by the reports they received that the settlers only occasionally saw, and almost never were molested by, wolves, foxes, and bears, which were plentiful enough. Snakes, especially copperheads and rattlesnakes, were encountered frequently, but not one of the settlers became their victim.

On June 1, when the pastors were called, the action had still been taken by the *Gesellschaft* as a unit. But almost simultaneously the colonists proceeded with a rough division of the people into separate settlements. Such communities were, with one exception, nothing more than parishes composed of persons from a particular locality or attached to a particular pastor in Germany, and for most of them the idea of maintaining a church was, for a time, the principal unifying factor. The locality in which a particular group was to settle was determined by lot. Thus six separate hamlets came into existence on the land of the Saxons.[2] The largest settlement was called Altenburg. By comparison with some of the other communities, Altenburg was favorably situated, lying at a sufficient elevation to assure reasonably dry land and a healthful, not too humid atmosphere. The people were a rather heterogeneous group composed of immigrants from Saxe-Altenburg, from the Saxon Province of Prussia, from Dresden and elsewhere in Saxony itself, from Hannover, and from New York. G. H. Löber had been chosen as their pastor when the "calls" were issued on June 1, 1839, and he continued to serve them until his death in 1849.

A small settlement adjacent to Altenburg was founded by people who had been members of Keyl's congregation in Germany. Their origin was reflected in the name Nieder-Frohna. It was an-

---

[2] Winter to Guericke *et al.*, April 28, 1841, *Zeitschrift für die gesammte lutherische Theologie und Kirche*, II, No. 3, pp. 116—132; Christiane Löber to G. F. Löber, n. d. [September—December, 1839], G. H. Löber to relatives in Germany, Sept. 10—30, 1839, in Löber-Eichenberg (ed.), "Ein Briefwechsel," *Mitteilungen . . . Kahla*, VII, 155—156, 158—161; C. F. W. Walther to O. H. Walther, May 4, 1840, Nachrichten an unsere Nachkommen, MSS., C. H. I.; E. M. Bürger, Selbstbiographie, 127—128, MS., E. J. Buerger Papers, Ellicottville, N. Y.; *Anzeiger des Westens*, June 8, 1839, quoted in G. Günther, *op. cit.*, 110—113; Bürger, *op. cit.*, 13—14; Schieferdecker, *op. cit.*, 16; Köstering, *Auswanderung*, 34. The date for the founding of the Perry County settlements is given variously as from 1838 to 1847. R. Douglass, *History of Southeast Missouri*, 271, 479; *History of Southeast Missouri*, 576.

ticipated that this congregation would increase considerably when Gruber arrived, for at this time it was still expected that many people from the Frohnas would be coming with him.

The parish of Dresden was founded by a number of people from Dresden, Saxony, and some of the "Berliner," that is, the New York group. C. F. W. Walther was assigned to this settlement, where O. Fürbringer lived with him, at least until September, 1839. In fact, at first there was a veritable colony of clergymen within this colony. Several of the most habitable dwellings were located in the area of Dresden, and as the pastors naturally enjoyed priority, three of their number who were married lived here with their families until their own houses could be erected. Later the remainder of the New York group founded a branch of the Dresden settlement a short distance away in Cape Girardeau County and called the community Johannisberg. This parish was at first an affiliate of the Dresden congregation and so was served by C. F. W. Walther.

The people from Bürger's congregation in Germany and from that of his father organized a settlement and congregation which they called Seelitz. This group was located in the Brazeau Creek bottoms and nearer to the river than Altenburg. Seelitz land was rich and well watered, but the atmosphere was especially damp and unhealthful. The parish was in charge of Pastor Bürger.

The landing place on the Mississippi was given the name Wittenberg. This settlement constituted the single exception to the generalization that at this early stage the communities were no more than scattered rural parishes. Wittenberg, however, was to become the city to which the immigrants had referred in their Codes, a metropolis which would serve as the trade and population center of the entire colony. For the first no pastor was stationed here, but services were held each Sunday by one of the pastors or candidates, and school was taught daily by Winter or a substitute.[3]

The observation has been made above that the leaders of the *Gesellschaft,* especially the pastors, did not have sufficient perspective to see how decisively conditions affecting the movement had

---

[3] It appears that Keyl served Wittenberg more frequently than the other pastors and candidates. Schieferdecker, *op. cit.,* 16; Köstering, *Auswanderung,* 34.

changed by June, 1839. But worse than that, the resignation of Vehse, H. F. Fischer, and Jäckel, which gave the clergy unquestioned control, made it even more difficult for the latter to appreciate the fact that the project of building a theocratic Zion was doomed. It was, therefore, expecting too much to hope that they would change either their conduct or the *Gesellschaft's* policies. And so virtually the entire *Gesellschaft* — the pastors, the remaining lay leaders, and the majority of the people, who were still accepting the same incompetent leadership — pursued their *fata morgana* of plans which were fantastically ambitious under the circumstances, plans for founding numerous churches, for building a thriving city, for becoming an important center of German immigration, for establishing an academy, and for similar grandiose enterprises. In no case is the self-delusion which nurtured these dreams more clearly illustrated than in that of Wittenberg.

That retrenchment was still far from the minds of the leaders and people in June, 1839, can be seen from Weber's reports in the *Anzeiger*. Wittenberg was to be located in the angle formed by the Brazeau and the Mississippi. Here several hundred building lots were to be laid out in such a way that two outer rows of houses would face the banks of the two streams, and two inner rows of houses, back to back with the others, would face away from creek and river toward the open country beyond. The portion of this open space closest to the angle formed by the rows of houses was to be converted into a market place, which would become the business center of the city. Ecclesiastical and educational buildings were to be grouped about the market place. The more prominent members of the colony and the professional people in general were to occupy these four rows of houses adjacent to the two streams and attractively situated on the bluffs overlooking them. On the lower land, sloping away from the bluffs and the proposed market place, lots were to be laid out for use by the laborers and craftsmen.[4]

The *Anzeiger* was not exaggerating the impracticality of the immigrants. The people themselves, poorly informed at first and not taken into the confidence of their leaders for some time, did not realize how desperate their circumstances were. Therefore,

---

[4] *Anzeiger des Westens*, June 29, 1839, quoted in G. Günther, *op. cit.*, 118—122. See also Document . . . des Grundsteins . . . St. Louis . . . 22. Juny 1842, MS., C. H. I.

when some of them suggested that the sale of lots on the river be thrown open to the public, others, especially some of the New York group, violently opposed this move. The New Yorkers even severed financial connections with the *Gesellschaft,* and withdrew into a separate settlement, although they continued other contacts with the Saxons and worked for them for hire.[5] Possibly it was this incident which led to the establishment of Johannisberg and the maintenance of two separate settlements of New Yorkers in close proximity to each other.

If these were the ideas of the settlers in June, they had not learned to revise their thinking by the fall of the same year. The hope and expectation of all, of course, was that the Saxons remaining in St. Louis would soon earn sufficient money to buy many of these lots and move down to Perry County. G. H. Löber still wrote of this in September, 1839.[6] Despite severe hardships and serious financial difficulties during the intervening months, plans had not been curtailed even by November. At that time the colonists provided

> that all the proceeds of the Sale of the Lots or parcels in said town [Wittenberg], only and forever are laid out for the public improvements of the said town and for the general benefits thereof; particularly for building as soon as possible along the Mississippi River a good and substantial Wharf; to secure the Mouth of Brazeau; to have the Streets of the town levelled and paved; to subscribe a substantial Sum to a bridge to be build [*sic*] over the Brazeau; to erect water works and so forth. — they shall and will make provisions to save one tenth of the proceeds aforesaid for the erection of a lutheran church and a good public school and for the repairing of them; further one tenth of the proceeds aforesaid to assist the establishing of an academy, which shall be forever under the controll of the proper city government; and further one tenth for establishing a profitable manufactory of any kind, agreed upon by the City government: they shall and will make provisions to have laid off a sufficient number of public squares and market places; and to set apart four acres for an asylum for orphants [*sic*], 4 acres for a gravy [*sic*] yard, ten acres for an academy as above mentioned; 2 acres for a hospital, and other small tracts for the general and public welfare if

---

[5] *Ibid.*

[6] G. H. Löber to relatives in Germany, Sept. 10—30, 1839, in Löber-Eichenberg (ed.), "Ein Briefwechsel," *Mitteilungen . . . Kahla,* VII, 156—162.

> required; and do all what is in their power to assist the rise and good management of the said Town of Wittenberg; till the said town of Wittenberg is incorporated according to the laws of the State and proper City government organized.[7]

Chimerical ambitions of this kind had from the first been fair game for Wilhelm Weber's splenetic strictures.[8] However, had he known it or bothered to ascertain it, he could have taken comfort from the fact that few of the plans he most violently denounced were being carried out. True enough, the immigrants were slow to yield even to experience; in theory they clung persistently to their original project. Yet in actual fact, circumstances prohibited so much as an attempt to execute most of such projects during the first year. And if the Saxons did not revise their thinking in accordance with Weber's precepts, that may be the very reason why in later years, retaining the ideals they had brought with them, they accomplished much more than even they originally had hoped, much more than Weber — or they themselves — would have considered possible. Realistic retrenchment would have produced certain immediate advantages in 1839; it would not have provided an incentive for the accomplishments of the future.

Yet even the Saxons were obliged to recognize the compelling demands of the struggle for survival. No experience with the frontier was required to see the dire need for two things: shelter and food. But the heroic efforts of the colonists to meet the emergency were hampered in numerous ways. Ignorance of methods in their new environment led to a waste of effort, and ignorance of conditions led to an insistence upon working at times when excessive heat made their labors worse than a waste. The lack of draught animals forced them to do even the heaviest work themselves, such as clearing land and hauling logs for the cabins. Their meager fund of cash was soon depleted, and then no money was available for even the small outlay that was necessary when they put up their own dwellings, not to speak of hiring more experienced laborers in order to expedite construction. Within two weeks after

---

[7] Exhibit A and F, Palisch *et al.* vs. Bimpage, Circuit Court of Perry County, Mo., exercising chancery jurisdiction, Nov. term, Nov. 29, 1839, MS., Circuit Clerk and Recorder's Vault, Perryville, Mo.

[8] *Anzeiger des Westens,* June 15, 29, 1839, quoted in G. Günther, *op. cit.,* 113—122.

the deposition of Stephan, not a single log cabin had been completed by the Saxons themselves.[9]

The food, bought at first from the funds of the *Gesellschaft* at an average cost of $250 weekly, consisted mainly of bacon and rice, and was carefully rationed to the individual families. Soon, however, the *Gesellschaft* was no longer able to carry the burden of furnishing provisions for its members. Only eighty acres of their land were under cultivation. The result was that undernourishment and finally hunger set in.[10] Starvation was averted for some of the German colonists only by the generous hospitality and frontier neighborliness of the English, Scotch, Irish, and French in the southeastern Missouri area. These people had some difficulty in understanding the Saxon mentality and habits, and freely predicted that the newcomers went to church so much of the time that they would surely starve. But since some of the "natives" were themselves, as the Saxons reported, "good Christians," they put forth their best efforts to prevent the grim eventuality which they had foreseen.[11]

The condition of the people in these colonies was at first a pitiful one. Descriptions vary little except in the extent of their detail and in the variation of their emphasis upon the diverse misfortunes of the Saxons. The pathetically inadequate facilities in the settlements did not provide even all of the women and children with a place in one of the few solidly constructed buildings on the *Gesellschaft's* land. The actual houses were occupied largely by the clerical and lay leaders of the emigration and their families. A majority of the people, composed of almost all the men and some women and children, slept in shacks, or lean-tos, or out in the open. When not even human beings had a roof over their heads, little attention could be devoted to the baggage. Both the emigrants and their possessions were frequently drenched by seasonal spring rains.

A change of seasons offered little relief. Fair weather brought

---

[9] *Ibid.;* Winter to Guericke *et al.,* April 28, 1841, *Zeitschrift für die gesammte lutherische Theologie und Kirche,* II, No. 3, pp. 116—132; Nachrichten an unsere Nachkommen, MS., C. H. I.; E. M. Bürger, Selbstbiographie, 128, MS., E. J. Buerger Papers, Ellicottville, N. Y.; Letter of resignation, Vehse, H. F. Fischer, and Jäckel to the Administrative Board, June 22, 1839, in Vehse, *op. cit.,* 167—168.

[10] *Ibid.*

[11] Christiane Löber to G. F. Löber, n. d. [September—December, 1839] in Löber-Eichenberg (ed.), "Ein Briefwechsel," *Mitteilungen . . . Kahla,* VII, 153; Köstering, *Auswanderung,* 32—33; Köstering, *Keyl,* 60—61.

with it the heat of a Missouri summer, which was as disagreeable and prevented progress quite as effectively as a downpour. Weather and climate were two of the worst enemies of the colonists, forcing frequent suspension of work on land and buildings and exacting their toll in heat prostrations and death among the inexperienced and unacclimatized. Furthermore, the elements aided another of the settlers' foes — sickness. "Fever" of various descriptions was common throughout the settlements but made its greatest inroads in the damp, low-lying, and unhealthful hamlets of Wittenberg on the Mississippi River and Seelitz in the Brazeau bottom. Medicinal supplies and the services of a competent physician were lacking. A tragically large number of the settlers died, sometimes simply for want of proper care or because of failure to take the necessary precautions.[12] Unfortunately almost all these observations regarding the general condition of the colonies in the first months apply in some degree to the period of the first few years, certainly to the period covered in this chapter, that is, to the end of 1841.

Many things could be borne by sheer fortitude and stoicism, but the death toll simply had to be reduced if the colonies were to survive. The two physicians of the *Gesellschaft* had left, and Dr. Gempp had chosen to remain in St. Louis when it became evident that the great debacle was impending. In this emergency Ernst Bünger, the young medical student, was drafted into service as a physician and forthwith began practicing as one. Young Bünger found that the exigencies of the situation more than made up for the lack of a professional reputation, for his services were sought after, even by people like the Löbers; and Pastor Löber correctly remarked that Bünger rapidly acquired a wide experience.[13]

---

[12] G. H. Löber to relatives in Germany, Sept. 10—30, 1839, in Löber-Eichenberg (ed.), "Ein Briefwechsel," *Mitteilungen . . . Kahla*, VII, 156—162; Nachrichten an unsere Nachkommen, C. F. W. Walther to O. H. Walther, May 4, 1840, MSS., C. H. I.; Winter to Guericke *et al.*, April 28, 1841, *Zeitschrift für die gesammte lutherische Theologie und Kirche*, II, No. 3, pp. 116—132; J. K. A. Höhne and J. G. Höhne to their brother, Sept. 26, 1841, quoted in *Die Ameise*, Jan. 10, 1842; E. M. Bürger, Selbstbiographie, 128, 132, MS., E. J. Buerger Papers, Ellicottville, N. Y.; *Anzeiger des Westens*, June 8, 15, 29, 1839, quoted in G. Günther, *op. cit.*, 110—122; Schieferdecker, *op. cit.*, 12; E. M. Bürger, *op. cit.*, 14, 16, 46; K. Gruber, "Ehrengedächtniss des . . . Gotthold Heinrich Löber," *Der Lutheraner*, VI, 146; Köstering, "Johann Friedrich Winter," *ibid.*, XXX, 36; Hengstenberg, "Der Pastor Stephan," *Evangelische Kirchen-Zeitung*, XXVI, 259.

[13] G. H. Löber to relatives in Germany, Sept. 10—30, 1839, April 29, 1840, in Löber-Eichenberg (ed.), "Ein Briefwechsel," *Mitteilungen . . . Kahla*, VII, 156—162, 169—173; C. F. W. Walther, *Bünger*, 54.

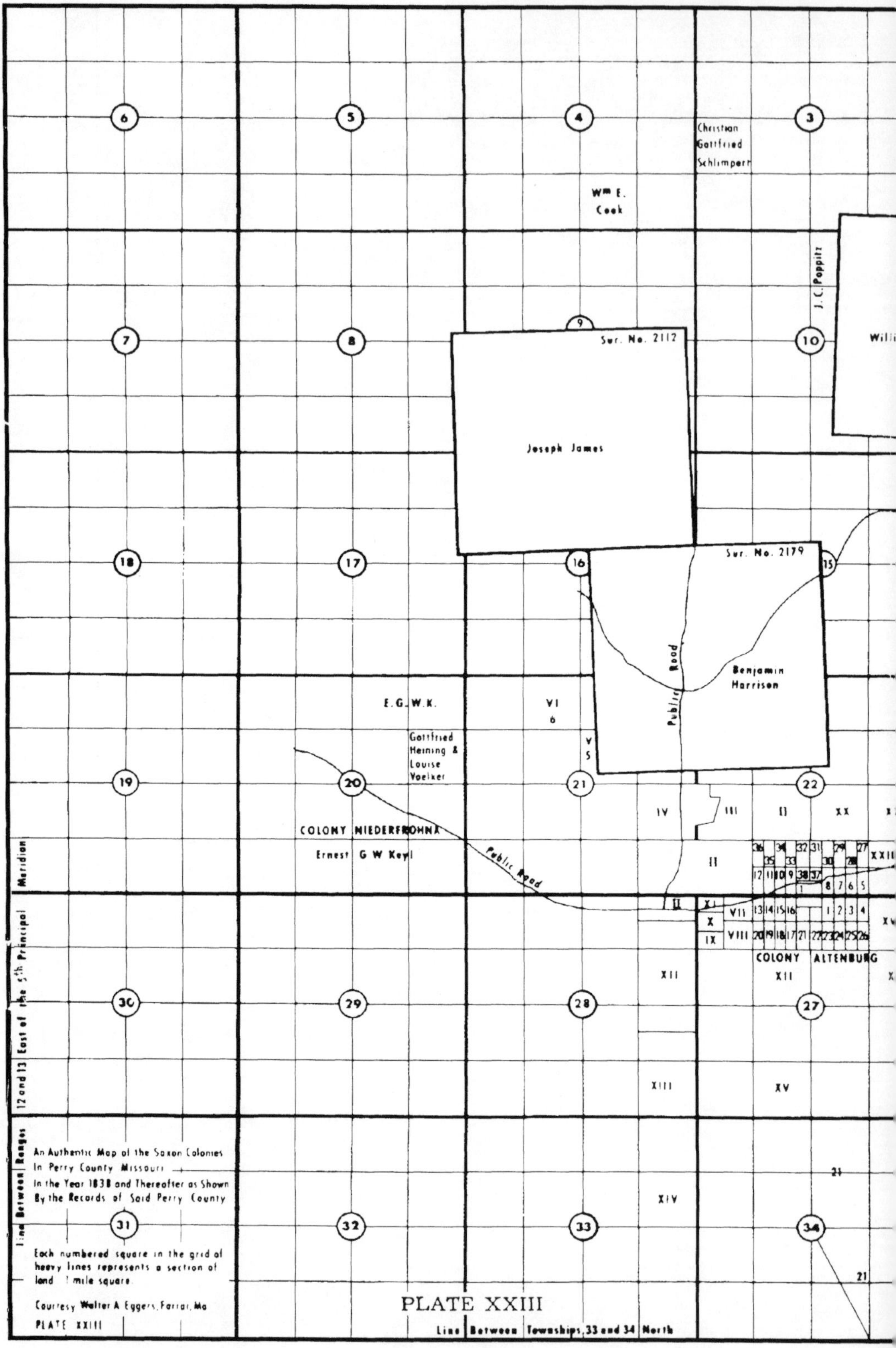
6
5
4
3
Christian Gottfried Schlimpert
Wm E. Cook
J. C. Poppitz
7
8
9
10
Sur. No. 2112
Willi
Joseph James
18
17
16
15
Sur. No. 2179
Public Road
Benjamin Harrison
E. G. W. K.
VI
6
V
5
Gottfried Heining & Louise Voelker
19
20
21
22
IV
III
II
XX
COLONY NIEDERFROHNA
Ernest G W Keyl
Public Road
II
XXII
VII
X
IX
VIII
COLONY ALTENBURG
XII
XII
30
29
28
27
XIII
XV
Meridian
12 and 13 East of the 5th Principal
Line Between Ranges
An Authentic Map of the Saxon Colonies
In Perry County Missouri
In the Year 1838 and Thereafter as Shown
By the Records of Said Perry County
XIV
31
32
33
34
21
21
Each numbered square in the grid of heavy lines represents a section of land 1 mile square
Courtesy Walter A Eggers, Farrar, Mo
PLATE XXIII
Line Between Townships 33 and 34 North

PLATE XXIII

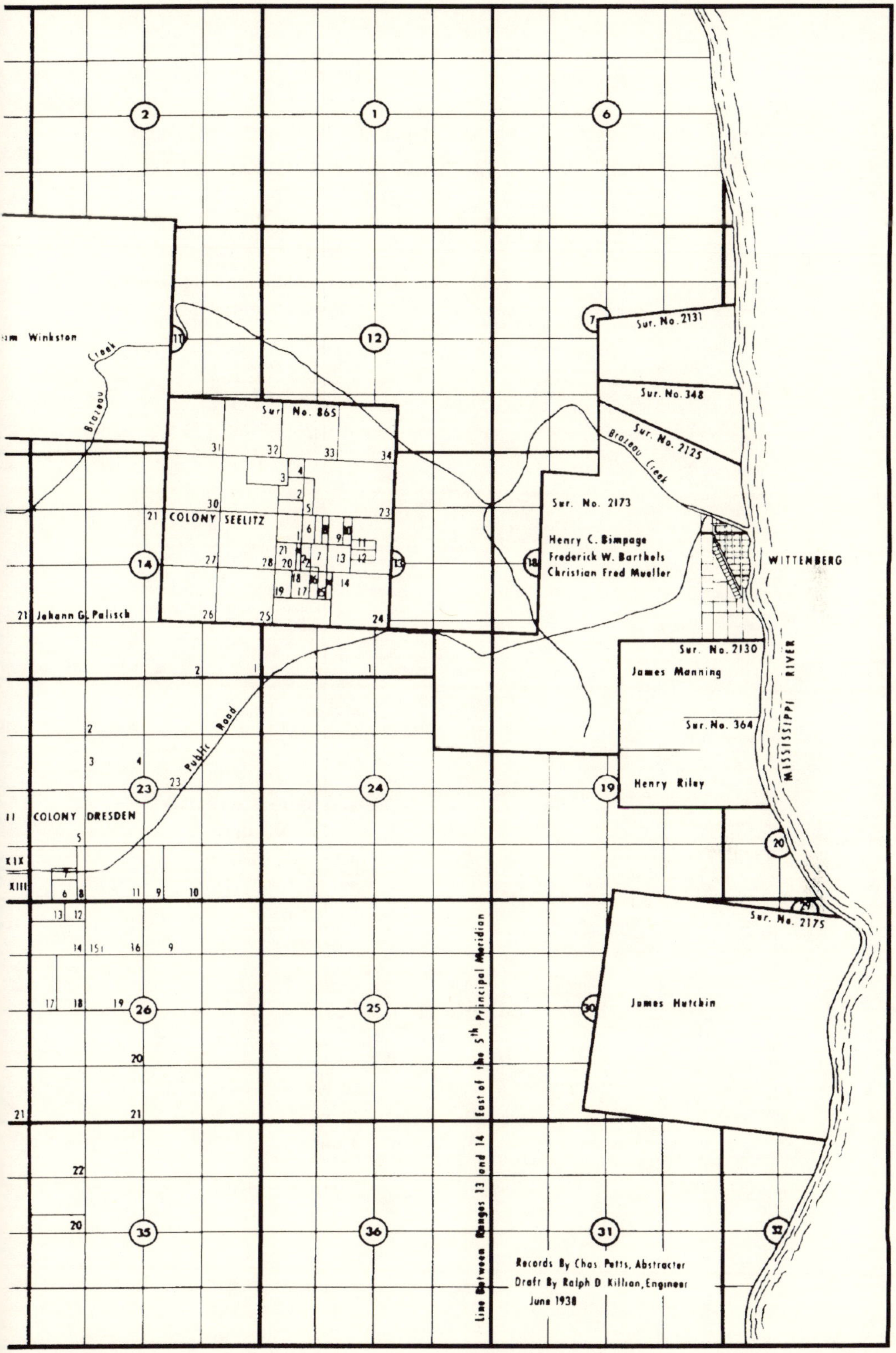

2
1
6
Winkston
Brazeau Creek
12
7
Sur. No. 2131
Sur. No. 348
Sur. No. 865
Sur. No. 2125
Brazeau Creek
COLONY SEELITZ
Sur. No. 2173
Henry C. Bimpage
Frederick W. Barthels
Christian Fred Mueller
14
WITTENBERG
Johann G. Palisch
Sur. No. 2130
James Manning
Public Road
Sur. No. 364
MISSISSIPPI RIVER
23
24
19
Henry Riley
COLONY DRESDEN
20
Sur. No. 2175
26
25
James Hutchin
Line Between Ranges 13 and 14 East of the 5th Principal Meridian
35
36
31
32
Records By Chas Petts, Abstracter
Draft By Ralph D Killian, Engineer
June 1938

TAKEN FROM THE MAP OF THE SAXON COLONIES IN PERRY COUNTY, MISSOURI, 1838 (PLATE XXIII), AND COPIED EXACTLY AS RECORDED BY CHAS. E. PETTS

Owners of Lots in Altenburg

1. Christian Lober — George R. Schmidt
2. Gottlob Schmidt & Bro. — Gottfried Cramer
3. Same
4.
5. George Kluegel — Johann Schmidt
6. Johann Frederick Kopple
7. Rozina Block — Jacob Seible
8. Johann Seible — Conrad Theiz
9. Gottfried Schmidt — Gottfried John
10. Gottfried Cramer — Gottfried Schmidt
11. George Kluegel Sen. — Johann Schmidt
12. Same — These lots for church
13. Jacob Fisher
14. Johann Frederick Fisher
15. Conrad Geisel
16. Gottlob Schmidt & Bro — Gottfried Cramer
17. Johann Christian Daumer — George Burger
18. Frederick Heinig
19. Rozina Goehring
20. Gottfried John
21. Frederick Richter
22.
23. Bernhardt Eisenschmidt
24.
25.
26.
27. Johann Schmidt
28. Gottlob Schmidt & Bro — Gottfried Cramer
29. George Kluegle & Son
30. Johann Gottfried Otto
31. Johann Christian Richter
32. Christian Frederick Mueller
33. Heinrich G. C. Marksworth
34. George Ilgen
35. Wilhelm F. Buck — M. S. Walters
36.
37. Barnhard Schmidt
38. Same
39. George Kluegel, Sr.
40. Same

Owners of Lands

I. Borough of Altenburg
II. Bernhard Schmidt
III. Joh. Gottleib Goethe
IV. Lutze Grother
V. Johanne Holschen
VI. Bock & Fiehler
VII. John Gottfried Otto
VIII. Johanne Bohmin
IX. Fredr. Nieman
X. Michael Nitsche
XI. Sophie Multarin
XII. George Kluegel — Son
XIII. Gottfr. Nonnig
XIV. Nonnig Jr.
XV. Maria D. Weber
XVI. Schmidt & Cramer
XVII. John Carl Wunderlich
XVIII. Christine Loeber
XIX. Geo. Joach Schmidt
XX. Joh. Rosine Hoffman & Barthels
XXI. Johann Schmidt
XXII.

Owners of Lots and Lands in Seelitz

1. Ernst Moritz Buenger
2. Johann C. Hinklemann — Johann C. Poppitz
3. Johanne Sophie Schlimpert
4. Christian Gottfried Schlimpert
5. Johann Christian Kuhnert
6. Johanne Sophie Storlin
7. Johann Gottfried Schubert
8. Gottleib Richter
9. Johann Christian Hinklemann
10. Christian Gottfried Schlimpert
11. Frangott Schlimpert
12. Christian Gottfried Mueller
13. John Adam Kuhn
14. Maria Therese Benedictine
15. Johanne Rosina Leupin
16. Johann Gottleib Dade
17. Gottleib Augustine
18. Gottfried Lorenz
19. Johanna Sophia Storlin
20. Gotthold Darstedt
21. Frederick Engerst
22. Christleib Richter
24. Christian Gottfried Schlimpert
25. John Christian Poppitz
26. Christian Frederick Uhlig
27. J. C. Schlimpert — C. F. Uhlig
28. Johann Adam Kuhn
29. Christian Gottfried Schlimpert
30. Same
31. John Christian Poppitz
32. Same
33. John Christian Poppitz
34. Same

Owners of Lots and Lands in Dresden

1. J. G. Palisch, Geo. Kluegel Sr.
   H. A. Dorderlein
2. Sophia Schnider
3. Heinrich August Dorderlein
4. John Christian Graefe
5. Samuel Gottleib Kaempfe
6. Frederick Buenger
7. Samuel G. Kaempfe, J. G. Palisch
8. Andrew Estel
9. Frederick Spoede
10. J. G. Palisch, Carl G. Zeibig
11. August Frederick Hacker
12. Natalie Geier
13. Christine Bunger — widow
14. Gustav Pfau
15. Johann G. Deishmann, J. G. Palisch
16. Johann Christian Richter
17. Same
18. Samuel G. Kaempfe, J. G. Palisch
19. Louise Marbach — F. A. Marbach
20. Johann August Stevzle
21. Johann Gottleib Palisch
22. Johann G. Hoehne, J. C. A. Hoehne
23. J. G. Palisch, Geo. Kluegel Sr.
   H. A. Dorderlein
24.

Bünger, of course, had no supplies and no money with which to buy them. The Credit Fund had no money to buy supplies for him. The people had no money with which to pay Bünger for his services or the Credit Fund for sums it had advanced. In this dilemma the colonists improvised with some ingenuity. The Credit Fund did have medical supplies, which were accordingly advanced to Bünger and charged against his account to the amount of $194.56¼. Thus, when he attended a creditor, the latter was charged for the services, but without requiring the transfer of any cash. The amount was deducted from the creditor's account and balanced against Bünger's, who thus theoretically had repaid the Credit Fund for the supplies received when the total of deductions from creditors' accounts equaled his indebtedness to the *Gesellschaft*.[14] Other situations were met with similar bookkeeping devices, for there was little cash in circulation in the colony for several years.

There were, therefore, certain obvious advantages in continuing to maintain a Credit Fund. Indeed, the initial effect of Stephan's fall, as has been pointed out, was to strengthen the communal system rather than to weaken it. To Weber of the *Anzeiger* this result was a great annoyance. But the choice at that time was one between complete dissolution (recommended by Weber) and banding together more closely than ever.[15] Under the circumstances the Saxons can be forgiven for not obliging their most indefatigable tormentor. The ties of relationship and friendship, of language and custom, of religion and common adversity, and a hundred other intangible factors all prevented disbanding entirely. As a matter of fact, the group probably became much more compact, as a result of joint experiences in 1839 and the years immediately following, than it would ever have become under more prosperous conditions.

Yet eventually Weber had his way on one point. The force of circumstances compelled the Saxons to modify the system of joint finances and joint property administration or ownership.[16] The lack of ready cash, essential to conducting any kind of business in the

---

[14] List of Saxon Emigrants 1838, MS., C. H. I.; G. H. Löber to relatives in Germany, April 29, 1840, in Löber-Eichenberg (ed.), "Ein Briefwechsel," *Mitteilungen . . . Kahla*, VII, 169—173.

[15] *Anzeiger des Westens*, June 1, 15, 1839, quoted in G. Günther, *op. cit.*, 95—103, 115—118.

[16] Nachrichten an unsere Nachkommen, MS., C. H. I.; Schieferdecker, *op. cit.*, 15.

community, was one of these circumstances. For a time it was advantageous to have a Credit Fund, which permitted bookkeeping maneuvers such as that described in the instance of Ernst Bünger. Gradually it became clear, however, that so long as all the assets of the group were tied up in a common treasury or a common parcel of land, no individual was likely to become solvent until all of them did. This realization called forth an understandable anxiety on the part of the investors, that if the present system were continued and none of the settlers, creditors or debtors, ever attained financial independence, the result would be chaos and economic ruin for all. The practical question of who was to benefit from property held jointly, was another deterrent to continuing the communal system.

On June 7, 1839, the land fund showed a deficit of $9,234.25, the total amount spent for that purpose.[17] This account, therefore, could not extend any credits. Neither was it possible to withdraw more from the balance on hand in the Credit Fund, for this had to be used for the purchase of food — so long as this pitifully small balance was not completely exhausted. The original plan, of reselling to individual colonists enough of the land which had been purchased so that dividends from the profits could be paid to various agencies and to the creditors, was not workable in a colony where common and private capital was almost non-existent. The result of the one attempt to bring new capital into the venture by offering to sell lots in Wittenberg to non-members of the *Gesellschaft* has already been described. There was only one alternative. Some basis for dividing the assets had to be devised eventually if the creditors were ever to realize anything from their investment. The only asset was land, and so the land itself had to be divided. However, months were allowed to elapse before this inescapable step was taken.

Then, in August, 1839, two events occurred which made the division of the land inevitable. On August 5, 1839, Vehse made the first move in his final campaign to change the structure of the *Gesellschaft*. The subsequent course of the controversy will be sketched below. It will suffice to say at this point that although Vehse and his two companions, H. F. Fischer and Jäckel, stood alone at first, it was nevertheless plain that internal quarreling had broken out. The possibility had to be considered seriously that

[17] List of Saxon Emigrants 1838, MS., C. H. I.

the entire venture would be blown into a score of fragments and that reconstruction of the *Gesellschaft* and its Credit Fund might become impossible. The creditors, including one of the pastors, Keyl, could not have failed to see this.

The second occurrence of August, 1839, was undoubtedly the deciding factor in prompting the creditors to act. The deeds for all the land bought jointly through the Credit Fund had been registered in the name of Johann Georg Gube. In August Gube died.[18] This event was a serious blow to the communal system, for it meant that legal measures would have to be taken to transfer title.[19] The legal claims had to be based upon the individual financial contributions, hence only the investors or creditors could act.

Gube, evidently foreseeing his end and the confusion it would cause, had taken steps to prevent these difficulties. On August 5, 1839, the identical day on which Vehse had begun making his final effort, Gube had given his power of attorney to two men, Johann Gottlieb Palisch and Christian Gottfried Schlimpert, to enable them

> . . . to transfer, set over, grant bargain, and sell all those messages and Lands, which I the said Joh. G. Gube have entered and bought since April last and up to this date, in my name but to the only use and benefit and in trust of about fifty two men, members of the German Lutheran Congregation, now settled on the Mouth of Brazo, Perry Co. Mo., who advanced the money for the messages and Lands bought and entered by me and in my name.[20]

This might have been a satisfactory arrangement, had Gube lived long enough so that Palisch and Schlimpert, acting under the power conferred upon them, could have transferred title to the land to their names or those of the individuals concerned. However, this was not done prior to Gube's death, and immediately after that happened, Gube's estate had to go through probate, with all of the land still in his name. The colonists promptly discovered that the

---

18 Palisch *et al.* vs. Bimpage, Bill in Chancery, No. 28, Circuit Court of Perry County, Mo., Nov. 29, 1839, MS., Circuit Clerk and Recorder's Vault, Perryville, Mo. See also G. H. Löber to relatives in Germany, Sept. 10—30, 1839, in Löber-Eichenberg (ed.), "Ein Briefwechsel," *Mitteilungen . . . Kahla,* VII, 156—162.

19 J. K. A. Höhne and J. G. Höhne to their brother, Sept. 26, 1841, quoted in *Die Ameise,* Jan. 10, 1842.

20 Exhibit A, Palisch *et al.* vs. Bimpage, Bill in Chancery, No. 28, Circuit Court of Perry County, Mo., Nov. 29, 1839, MS., Circuit Clerk and Recorder's Vault, Perryville, Mo.

"trustees" whom Gube had designated, Palisch and Schlimpert, had "no legal power to dispose of and sell the . . . Lands,"[21] and were certain to be superseded by the executor or administrator of the Gube estate, whoever he might be. Furthermore, they learned that "the Deeds and Receiver's Certificates of the above-mentioned Lands or messages are partly in the Court of Records in Perryville, partly in the hands of Henry C. Bimpage."[22] Consequently, if the colonists wished to secure title to the land which rightfully belonged to them, the only solution was to take recourse to a suit against Bimpage, whom Gube had evidently designated as executor of his estate.

Accordingly, thirty-nine of the creditors on November 23, 1839, drew up a bill in chancery, which they filed with the Circuit Court of Perry County on November 29, 1839. In this bill the plaintiffs set forth the circumstances of their claim and petitioned the court to appoint Bimpage administrator of the estate, with power to dispose of the land and divide it.[23] The choice of Bimpage probably was dictated by the fact that he knew English, whereas none of the creditors apparently had an adequate command of the language, and by his superior experience, as he was operating a land office in St. Louis.[24] In passing, it may be noted that the action which

---

[21] Palisch *et al.* vs. Bimpage, Bill in Chancery, No. 28, Circuit Court of Perry County, Mo., Nov. 29, 1839, MS., Circuit Clerk and Recorder's Vault, Perryville, Mo.

[22] Exhibit A, *ibid.*

[23] Palisch *et al.* vs. Bimpage, Bill in Chancery, No. 28, Circuit Court of Perry County, Mo., Nov. 29, 1839, MS., Circuit Clerk and Recorder's Vault, Perryville, Mo. The names of the thirty-nine creditors who brought this action, as they appear on the original petition, are the following: "Johann Gottlieb Palisch, Christian Gottfried Schlimpert, Johann Bernhardt Schmidt, Ernst Gerhardt W. Keyl, Aug. Friedrich Doederlein, Aug. Friedrich Häcker, Johann Gottlieb Hoehne, Joh. Carl August Hoehne, Samuel Gottfried Kaempfe, Johann Gottlieb Palitzsch, Gustav Pfau, Joh. Gottlieb Pietsch, Joh. Christian Richter, Sophie Schneider, widow, Johann August Sterzel, Carl Gottlieb Zeibig, Michael Bock, Gottlob Fiehler, Georg Klügel, Sen., Joh. Gottlob Cramer, Gottfried Normig [Nönnig?], Carl Friedrich Richter, Gottlob Schmidt, Gottfried Schmidt, Johann Schmidt, Marie Dorothea Weber, widow, Joh. Carl Wunderlich, Christ Gottlob Hoffmann, Joh. Christ. Hinkelmann, Christian Gottfried Muller, Joh. Christ. Poppitz, Christ. Friedrich Uhlig, Joh. Georg Stiegler, Johann Gottl. Schlimpert, Johann Adam Kühn, Lütje Grother, Johann Holschen, Gottfried Heinig, Louise Voelker, spinster." Since Gube several months earlier had referred to the creditors as "about fifty-two men," it is apparent that not all creditors participated in this action. Some may have been paid off; others were no doubt among those who had left Perry County by this time.

[24] J. K. A. Höhne and J. G. Höhne to their brother, Sept. 26, 1841, quoted in *Die Ameise,* Jan. 10, 1842.

the petitioners now saw themselves forced to take was essentially what Vehse had demanded before Gube's death, when the transaction would have been much simpler and more prompt. Ironically, the creditors included one of the pastors, Keyl, who was even one of the petitioners. Yet in spite of this demonstration that, at the very least, Vehse was not altogether wrong and the pastors had not been altogether right in opposing him. Vehse was during these very days subjected to an attack from the clergymen which was so uncompromising that in a few days he left the colony forever.

On the same day on which the bill was filed, suit was brought by these same thirty-nine creditors against "Hy. C. Bimpage, Administrator of all and singular goods, chattels, rights and credits which were of John George Gube, deceased," and Bimpage voluntarily entered his appearance. The petitioners reviewed the circumstances of their case and restated their desires, as specified in the bill in chancery.[25] They furthermore submitted a plat of the area, a list of the lands, and a plan for its apportionment which had purportedly been agreed upon on November 23, 1839.[26] Actually, the division into settlements and a large number of the allocations to individuals had been made at least several months before. Köstering pictured it as though the division had taken place already at the time the settlements were founded.[27] In view of other circumstances related above, it does not seem likely that the division took place that early. But the records of the Saxons themselves corroborate the general fact that it took place,[28] while a letter by G. H. Löber establishes that division was accomplished by lot and that it had been made already by September, 1839.[29]

The creditors further had decided that one section was to be set aside for development in the town of Wittenberg. The plaintiffs

---

[25] Palisch *et al.* vs. Bimpage, Circuit Court of Perry County, Mo., exercising chancery jurisdiction, November term, Nov. 29, 1839, Chancery Record, 127, MS., Perry County (Mo.) Circuit Court Records, Perryville, Mo.

[26] *Ibid.;* Exhibit D (A plat of the land purchased by the Saxons, hereafter referred to simply as Exhibit D), Palisch *et al.* vs. Bimpage, Circuit Court of Perry County, Mo., exercising chancery jurisdiction, November term, Nov. 29, 1839, MS., Circuit Clerk and Recorder's Vault, Perryville, Mo.

[27] Köstering, *Keyl,* 58.

[28] Nachrichten an unsere Nachkommen, MS., C. H. I.

[29] G. H. Löber to relatives in Germany, Sept. 10—30, in Löber-Eichenberg (ed.), "Ein Briefwechsel," *Mitteilungen . . . Kahla,* VII, 156—162.

petitioned that Bimpage, F. W. Barthel, and "C. F. Muller"[30] be made trustees of this land, with specific instructions as to the uses for which it was intended, some of which have been quoted above. Bimpage was to make the survey and lay out the lots. For this service he was to receive, as partial compensation, twenty of the 640 acres at Wittenberg. This grant was in addition to the six acres which had already been deeded to him by Gube on July 12, 1839, presumably in payment for services up to that date. However, only one of the twenty additional acres he was now to receive might front on the Mississippi River. The three trustees were jointly to make out the deeds to lots in Wittenberg as they were disposed of.[31]

The boundaries of Seelitz and of Nieder-Frohna were given, although in the case of these settlements, the court was informed, "the special partition is not yet agreed upon." For Altenburg and Dresden both the boundaries and the "special partition" could be stated, for these had been fixed and agreed upon after a survey by Bimpage, who had also witnessed the division.[32]

In view of the preliminary agreement among them, the petitioners sought the ratification of the court for their actions thus far, as well as for their plans that the 640 acres be set aside for Wittenberg, that the men they had proposed be appointed trustees for this land, and that the remaining 3,835.88 acres be divided among them as agreed. Finally, they specified that 142 acres were to be set aside as commons. They stipulated, however, that while most of this land could be disposed of according to the pleasure of the majority, forty acres were to be reserved for a church and a "public school . . . for all and every Settler in the said Communities of Seelitz, Dresden, Altenburg, and Niederfrohna, and shall be kept forever as Common Property."[33]

---

30 No doubt Christian Gottfried Müller is meant. His name is given in one list as Christian Friedrich Müller, but in most instances it is Christian Gottfried. Very likely he had three names, Christian Gottfried Friedrich, or Christian Friedrich Gottfried. On the bill in chancery itself, where the style of the case is given and the plaintiffs are listed, his name appears as "Christian Gottfried Muller."

31 Exhibit A and F, Palisch *et al.* vs. Bimpage, Circuit Court of Perry County, Mo., exercising chancery jurisdiction, November term, Nov. 29, 1839, MS., Circuit Clerk and Recorder's Vault, Perryville, Mo.

32 *Ibid.*

33 Exhibit A and F, Palisch *et al.* vs. Bimpage, Circuit Court of Perry County, Mo., exercising chancery jurisdiction, November term, Nov. 29, 1839, MS., Circuit Clerk and Recorder's Vault, Perryville, Mo. See also Chancery Record, 127, MS., Perry County (Mo.) Circuit Court Records, Perryville, Mo.

The court acceded to the petition on all points, and appointed C. G. Schlimpert and E. G. W. Keyl to act jointly with Bimpage as commissioners for laying out the remaining 3,835.88 acres into parcels, as agreed upon. These commissioners were to give deeds for the land to the individual people involved.[34]

In the face of all the difficulties described thus far, organized religious and educational life in the settlements during the summer of 1839 amounted, with one exception, to little more than regular services held under the most primitive conditions.[35] That one exception, however, was a notable one. Lack of funds on the part of the *Gesellschaft* and preoccupation with the problem of eking out a livelihood on the part of the great majority of colonists forced abandonment of the formal plans for establishing a school of higher education on the model of the German *Gymnasium*. But the idea survived among the pastors and candidates. At first, Brohm had offered his services to a Lutheran missionary in Indiana, Wyneken by name. As the latter had temporarily returned to Germany, the letter went unanswered. At this juncture the pastors suggested the establishment of a school.[36] And so it was to be.

Already in the summer of 1839, while people around them were suffering and dying for want of proper food, shelter, and care, a group of three candidates, Brohm, O. Fürbringer, and J. F. Bünger, succeeded in acquiring a few (four or six) acres of land in the settlement of Dresden and joined their efforts to provide a place of instruction for something approximating a *Gymnasium* course. In this venture they enjoyed the active support of the ministers, especially of C. F. W. Walther, who, as pastor in Dresden, was near by. The three candidates did most of the work in erecting the log cabin which was to become the "College." Naturally these men, unaccustomed to manual labor, taxed their strength and experienced considerable difficulty as well as physical discomfort in such work as felling trees, hewing logs, moving them, sawing them, and digging a well. However, they were not to be deterred, and with the encouragement of the pastors and the more practical help of some

---

[34] *Ibid.*

[35] G. H. Löber to relatives in Germany, Sept. 10—30, 1839, in Löber-Eichenberg (ed.), "Ein Briefwechsel," *Mitteilungen . . . Kahla*, VII, 156—162.

[36] J. F. Bünger, "Ehrengedächtniss des . . . Brohm," *Der Lutheraner*, XXXVII, 189.

of the laymen, building progressed, although not as rapidly as had been hoped. Several delays occurred which postponed opening the doors of the proposed school for several months.[37]

Meanwhile, developments in St. Louis at first were hardly more encouraging than those in Perry County. The article in the *Anzeiger des Westens* of June 8, which had reported the meeting of the St. Louis group presided over by Vehse, informed the public with crackling indignation that calls had been issued to O. H. Walther, who was now to serve St. Louis, and to the other clergymen. A new series of attacks was also launched against the leaders, bitterly criticizing their system, or lack of it. These editorial forays continued throughout the month in later issues.[38] The issue of June 8 called a meeting of the citizens of German extraction for the purpose of "helping" the Saxons.[39]

The meeting was held two evenings later in the establishment of Mr. Weinheimer.[40] The proceedings, printed in the *Anzeiger des Westens,* reported that the "large number" of Germans present were presided over by Mr. Kimm and that Mr. Palm (of the *Anzeiger*) acted as secretary. Mr. Theodor Engelmann gave a brief summary of the history of the Stephanites. Mr. Wilhelm Weber (of the *Anzeiger*) moved the appointment of a committee to draw up resolutions, and Mr. Kimm named Messrs. Carstens, Meier, and Engelmann. While the committee was out, the crowd was addressed by Wilhelm Palm, H. Koch, and E. Angelrodt. The committee returned and presented its resolutions, which were adopted. The resolutions stated that:

Whereas those present felt they had a "deep interest" in "everything which is designated German or is spoken of in connection with the German name," and had always striven to bring only honor to that name, therefore they resolved:

---

[37] C. F. W. Walther, *Bünger,* 55—56; Keyl, *op. cit.,* 17—18; J. F. Bünger, "Ehrengedächtniss des . . . Brohm," *Der Lutheraner,* XXXVII, 189; O. Fürbringer to Delitzsch, Sept. 7, 1839, quoted in L. Fürbringer, "Aus vergangenen Tagen und vergilbten Blättern," *ibid.,* LXXXVI, 118; Lochner, "Ottomar Fürbringer," *ibid.* XLIX, 172; Köstering, *Auswanderung,* 67. Such humble beginnings for a theological seminary were not unusual at the time. See Arndt, "The Beginnings of the Theological Seminary of the Ohio Synod," *Concordia Theological Monthly,* I, 621.

[38] *Anzeiger des Westens,* June 8, 15, 29, 1839, quoted in G. Günther, *op. cit.,* 110—115, 118—122.

[39] *Anzeiger des Westens,* June 8, 1839, quoted in *ibid.,* 108.

[40] *Anzeiger des Westens,* June 15, 1839, quoted in *ibid.,* 115—118.

That they took a deep interest in the fortunes of the Saxons.

That these Saxons had been "shamefully deceived and abused" by Stephan and the other clergymen, that "their wives and daughters had been seduced," and they themselves had been "despised, enslaved, and robbed of their possessions."

That the Saxons appeared unable to help themselves.

That it was the duty of those present to "free" them.

That while they by no means wished to interfere with the religious beliefs and ecclesiastical affairs of the *Gesellschaft* or restrict its members in the exercise of their beliefs, they nevertheless expressed their regret that the Saxons continued to keep their leaders.

That, on the other hand, those pledging themselves to this resolution wished to "extend the hand of friendship to all who intend to cast off the shackles of their present dependence," in order to support them as much as possible with word and deed.

That a committee of seven be named to inform the Saxons of these resolutions and to offer them the aid and assistance of the committee.

The men named to serve on this committee were given as: E. Angelrodt, Th. Engelmann, Ben. Sagner, Joh. Humbert, F. Lüdehring, J. Kimm of St. Louis, and Dr. Brühl (later agent for the *Anzeiger* [41]) of Perry County.[42]

This not too subtle attempt by the familiar clique which was trying to run the St. Louis German element to extend their operations into the Saxon *Gesellschaft* for the purpose of destroying it, is described by G. Günther as giving evidence of a "fine characteristic" on the part of the men involved.[43] Actually it was a joining of hands between the *Anzeiger*-Koch cabal and a number of disgruntled individuals, in order to punish those who had not kowtowed to them. The presence of Sagner at the meeting and of the committee is understandable in view of the affront he is supposed to have suffered. Kimm's part in the affair may be explained by the fact that the original plan of using his firm as St. Louis agent for the *Gesellschaft* had not been carried out in full and that many

---

41 *Täglicher Anzeiger des Westens*, April 4, 1846.

42 *Anzeiger des Westens*, June 15, 1839, quoted in G. Günther, *op. cit.*, 115—118.

43 *Ibid.*, 108.

(and the most lucrative) of the Saxons' business transactions were being handled by Bimpage. Whether anything ever came of this meeting is not reported. If actual aid was extended to any of the people who left the *Gesellschaft,* then Weber, with unaccustomed modesty, apparently was silent about it. Other people in St. Louis, however, who did not hold a meeting about it and whose names were not recorded, did materially help the Saxons who remained with the *Gesellschaft,* as the latter gratefully acknowledged.[44]

On June 9, 1839, the Sunday between the meeting of the Saxons on June 6 and that of Weber and his confreres on June 10, O. H. Walther was "installed" as pastor of the St. Louis Saxon congregation. Actually, in view of the manner in which the clergymen were called, this probably means simply that he began acting as its minister. A parish school was established almost at once, and Geyer was hired as its teacher. The arrangement at this time appears to have been that a house was rented on Poplar Street, between Second and Third Streets, and that this house served as parsonage, school, and teacher's residence. O. H. Walther lived in several rooms on the second floor, while the first floor provided the schoolroom in which Geyer also had his living quarters.[45]

The problem of securing a place of worship, however, could not be solved by similar expedients. Therefore, a week after the meeting of organization on June 6, the Saxon congregation in St. Louis petitioned the congregation of Christ Church for a further extension of the privilege of using the basement of that building. The Saxons pointed out that about two hundred of them anticipated being in St. Louis for at least several months. They implied that the reason for remaining in the city was the deposition of Stephan, although a statement to that effect was not made. The congregation apologized for the scandal which had been linked to their name, but claimed that Stephan alone had brought all this shame upon them and that the other clergymen enjoyed the full confidence of their people. The petition specified that services would be held on Sunday from 7 to 9 A. M. and from 1 to 4 P. M., and on Wednesday, probably in the evening, although the hour for this service was not

---

[44] F. W. Barthel, Niemann, and Hoppel to Trinity Congregation, St. Louis, Nov. 8, 1845, MS., C. H. I.

[45] O. H. Walther, Zur Agende, June 9, 1839, MS., L. Fürbringer Papers, St. Louis; Hanser, *op. cit.*, 12—14.

given in the petition.[46] The vestry of Christ Church was keenly aware of the deplorable effect the Stephan incident would have. To Vehse it was characterized by the vestry as a misfortune, "Not only for you, Sir; it's a misfortune for us all, for the whole [of] Christianity." [47] Nevertheless, the request was granted. Thanks to several extensions of the courtesy, the St. Louis Saxons continued to use Christ Church three and one-half years longer.

While these attempts were being made, both in St. Louis and Perry County, to place the two colonies on a secure footing, another major problem had arisen to plague the immigrants. About six weeks after the resignation of Vehse, H. F. Fischer, and Jäckel, and on the same day that Gube executed his power of attorney in anticipation of his death, the opening gun was fired in a new phase of the controversy between the laymen and the pastors. The Association was thereby divided into bitterly warring camps for the next two years. The immediate occasion was a set of six "theses" drawn up by Vehse, which dealt with the office of the ministry.[48] These theses were submitted to O. H. Walther by Vehse alone, on August 5, 1839, when both men were in St. Louis. The statement of Vehse was accompanied by an earnest plea that the pastors give careful consideration to the views expressed.[49]

An accurate chronological account of the controversy from this point until December, 1839, has not been given anywhere in the literature on the Saxon movement. For this reason, the separate steps in the development of opposing viewpoints and the sequence of events reflecting this development, are set down here. It has seemed all the more necessary to do this, since the telescoping of occurrences taking place at significantly different times, and the elision of incidents or documents important for the history of the entire movement, have distorted both the picture as a whole and the role played by individuals. Even the accounts of those who participated in events sometimes merely refer in general terms to a protest by several laymen, or to an attack upon the clergy, and to

---

46 The elders of the Saxon congregation in St. Louis to Christ Church, June 13, 1839, MS., C. H. I. The signatures on the first draft of this letter indicate that the elders at this time were Gottfried Heinig, Niemann, Gräber, and Harnisch.

47 Vehse, *op. cit.*, 23.

48 *Ibid.*, 103—105.

49 *Ibid.*, 106.

a reply by the latter.[50] The erroneous impression is thereby created that there was a simple, clear-cut statement of issues between reasonably well-defined factions. Actually, this was not the case. Later writers have employed hiatus and exaggeration effectively in order to italicize the chronicle in conformity with their bias. For example, even in some fairly extensive treatments of the contest agitating the colonists from 1839 to 1841, there is a tendency to discuss issues not, as would seem natural, at the time they arose, but at the time they were resolved. Perhaps this is only a question of judgment, but it has certain distinctly misleading results. Perhaps it is only an incidental fact — but a fact it is, nevertheless — that this enables the narrator to report, with approbation, C. F. W. Walther's defense by 1841 of principles in the controversy very similar to those he had opposed in 1839, when they came from Vehse's lips.[51]

The original mistake, leading to much of the confusion described, was probably made by Vehse himself in referring to "a Protest," and thus lumping together a number of separate documents written at different times.[52] On one occasion he indicated that this was his rather inaccurate method, and then compounded his error by saying that the separate documents had come out from September to October.[53] The fact of the matter is that different items in the literature of this controversy appeared from August to November. The text of the "Protest," as conceived by Vehse, occupied almost a hundred pages of his book.[54] For the purposes of publication, Vehse even inserted a number of passages into his "Protest" which were not in the original documents. However, he indicated these passages clearly. An early draft of Vehse's Protest exists that is clearer in its division and in its dating of the several original sections which Vehse later combined into a single "Protestationsschrift." [55] When necessary to clear up a point, reference is made in the present study to this manuscript. As a rule, however, the printed form, as it appeared in Vehse's book, is preferable for ref-

---

50 An example is Winter to Guericke *et al.*, April 28, 1841, *Zeitschrift für die gesammte lutherische Theologie und Kirche*, II, No. 3, pp. 116—132.

51 Köstering, *Auswanderung*, 35—42. His plagiarists are recognizable.

52 Vehse, *op. cit.*, 45.

53 *Ibid.*, 24—25.

54 *Ibid.*, 47—142.

55 Bound MSS., Protestation, C. H. I.

erence because of its greater accessibility. The text is not the original in either case.

In the theological sense, the gist of the points made by Vehse in writing to O. H. Walther on August 5 was an assertion of the Lutheran doctrine of the universal priesthood of all believers. However, the practical application of dogma to the central problem of the *Gesellschaft* was made in the crucial sixth thesis: "The office of the ministry is no more than a public service, when something is enjoined upon a person by the whole congregation." [56] O. H. Walther replied to this communication the same day, August 5, professing his own agreement with it and promising to forward the theses to his colleagues in Perry County.[57] Later O. H. Walther told Vehse that the other pastors also subscribed to these theses, but Vehse never received such a declaration from them.[58]

The best that the clergy could offer as a parry was an open letter of September 9, 1839, to the St. Louis congregation from the four pastors in Perry County and from vacillating O. H. Walther, warning the St. Louis group against those "who would unfairly abuse this declaration in order to discredit our office, maliciously sow the seeds of mistrust against us, and bring about dissension and offense in the congregation." [59] There was no effort in this letter to meet the issues raised by Vehse. The writers simply fell back upon the now familiar tactics of the Stephanite system — attempting to override objection by a show of clerical authority couched in pious phrases. A profession of sorrow over the evils which had befallen the immigrants through the actions of the pastors was appended by the latter to this blast against Vehse.[60]

That this salvo, in which no names are mentioned, was actually aimed at the protesting Vehse is apparent from later correspondence. Marbach described the attitude of the pastors toward his brother-

---

56 Vehse, *op. cit.* 105.

57 O. H. Walther to Vehse, Aug. 5, 1839, in *ibid.*, 107.

58 *Ibid.*, 107.

59 *Ibid.*, 108. The text of the letter (G. H. Löber, Keyl, E. M. Bürger, C. F. W. Walther, and O. H. Walther to the Saxon congregation in St. Louis, Sept. 9, 1839) from which the few words given above are taken, is contained in *ibid.*, Appendix E, 169—170. See also Keyl, *op. cit.*, 17—18, where at least one of the pastors specifically admitted that his action on this occasion was not right.

60 G. H. Löber, Keyl, E. M. Bürger, C. F. W. Walther, and O. H. Walther to the Saxon congregation in St. Louis, Sept. 9, 1839, in Vehse, *op. cit.*, 169—170.

in-law by saying that the ministerium "issued an official warning against Dr. Vehse which declared that 'the devil was speaking through him.'"[61] This letter of September 9 had been drawn up at a meeting of the ministerium, which by this time had developed into a body that held formal sessions and kept minutes of its transactions. O. H. Walther was also in Perry County for the session of September 9. The original draft of the letter was a part of the minutes.[62]

Meanwhile Vehse himself had not been idle. H. F. Fischer and Jäckel, who had joined him in resigning on June 22, had been won over to the lone dissident's position; and a more complete statement of their views, embellished with frequent and lengthy quotations, especially from Luther, Spener, and Seckendorf, had been drawn up. This document, the one which ought actually be called "the Protest," was completed and signed by Vehse, H. F. Fischer, and Jäckel, September 19, 1839.[63] A preliminary address to their fellow immigrants made the same request as that directed to the pastors, namely, that careful consideration be given the Protest for the sake of sound doctrine.[64] This plea was followed by a detailed outline of the document being submitted, as laid down in three points, or "chapters":

> I Evidence concerning the rights of the congregation in relation to the clergy in religious and ecclesiastical matters.
>
> II Evidence against the wrong Stephanite system, in which the rights of the congregation are not respected, but suppressed.
>
> III Evidence from Luther and [a statement of] our private opinion on the justifiability of the emigration.[65]

This outline reflects the main subjects of argument.

The original contributions of the writers of the Protest in developing this outline are far fewer and slenderer than the number

---

61 Marbach, An meine . . . Landsleute, MS., C. H. I.; O. H. Walther to Vehse, H. F. Fischer, and Jäckel, Oct. 29, 1839, in Vehse, *op. cit.*, 170.

62 Minutes of the Ministerium of the Saxon Immigrants, Sept. 9, 1839, MS., C. H. I.

63 Bound MSS., Protestation, 1—94, C. H. I. In this manuscript copy it is clearly indicated which was the original document of September 19, "the Protest," and which is a supplement of November 9, 1839. In Vehse's version the distinction is not clear, since he runs both statements together and puts the single date, September 19, 1839, at the end.

64 Vehse, *op. cit.*, 47—49.

65 *Ibid.*, 49—53.

and the bulk of quotations which appear in the text proper. The Protest was reinforced with an "Accompanying Statement" of September 23, 1839, which was addressed "to the Herr Pastors Löber, Keyl, Bürger, and the Walther brothers," which pleaded for an honest examination of the contents of the Protest.[66] It is not clear whether release of the text of September 19 was delayed until the 23d, when the letter to the pastors was written, and both then appeared simultaneously, or whether each of the two was released on the day it is dated.

For over a month there was no formal answer to the representations of Vehse, H. F. Fischer, and Jäckel. Then, on October 29, 1839, O. H. Walther made a written statement to them that the September 9 letter of the clergy (which O. H. Walther had signed, in spite of the fact that at the outset he had professed agreement with Vehse, at least in principle) was indeed directed against Vehse, H. F. Fischer, and Jäckel; but that after their statement of September 19 there could be no thought in his mind of applying to these men the accusations insinuated in the "warning" that had been issued. Walther also stated that he would use his influence with the other pastors to effect a similar declaration by them.[67]

Apparently Walther's influence was not strong enough; for when, by November 9, nothing had been heard from the other clergymen, Vehse, H. F. Fischer, and Jäckel on that date came out with a Supplement to the Protest.[68] On November 14 a "Closing Supplement" was added by the three protesting laymen, which was largely devoted to a critical sketch of the procedure of the pastors in the deposition of Stephan.[69] However, this communication was not immediately delivered to the pastors, and no mention was made of it by them when on November 20 (19?) they finally made their first formal answer to the charges directed against them.[70] The

---

[66] *Ibid.*, 45—47.

[67] O. H. Walther to Vehse, H. F. Fischer, and Jäckel, Oct. 29, 1839, in *ibid.*, 170.

[68] G. H. Löber, Keyl, E. M. Bürger, C. F. W. Walther, and O. H. Walther to Vehse, H. F. Fischer, and Jäckel, Nov. 20, 1839, *ibid.*, 151—153. The letter, as given in Vehse, bears the date of November 20; he repeated it in another place. *Ibid.*, 25. The text of the letter in the manuscript copy gives November 19. Bound MSS., Protestation, C. H. I.

[69] Vehse-H. F. Fischer-Jäckel, "Schluss-Zusatz," in Vehse, *op. cit.*, 142—151.

[70] G. H. Löber, Keyl, E. M. Bürger, O. H. Walther, and C. F. W. Walther to Vehse, H. F. Fischer, and Jäckel, Nov. 20 (19?), 1839, in *ibid.*, 151—153.

statement of the clergy in turn elicited the final reply from Vehse, H. F. Fischer, and Jäckel, a letter of November 23, in which they denied the accusation of deliberate faultfinding made by the pastors and called upon the latter to follow the example of O. H. Walther and to retract such charges, especially those contained in their communication of September 9 to the congregation. Included also was the "Closing Supplement," which had been written on November 14.[71]

Such was the chronology of this phase of the controversy, which at least on the surface — but only on the surface — was a contest between the five pastors and the three laymen. Only three of the nine separate letters and documents just referred to need be examined further: the Protest and its Supplement, of September 19 and November 9 respectively, which may be treated as a unit; and the single answer of the pastors to both of these statements in their reply of November 20 (19?). The nature of the other items is sufficiently clear from the brief remarks above, and the factual data they contain on the immigration have been incorporated into the preceding narrative. No attempt will be made in this study to enter into a critical examination of the theological side of the controversy. However, the positions taken by the various parties at this point and later, cannot be overlooked, because of their importance for the history of the colonies.

The Protest is composed of three positive points with a negative corollary. In its entirety the Protest constitutes a ringing assertion of the rights of the congregation as opposed to synod, episcopacy, a domineering clergy, or any other agency in the Church which would tend to curtail these rights. Hereby the three immigrant Saxon laymen gave strong utterance to a principle which has become generally accepted and firmly established in American Lutheranism and which, when applied as the Saxons interpreted it, has assured the autonomy of the local congregation.

The fundamental approach of the Protest was established in the first of the major points listed above; it is the theological doctrine of the universal priesthood of all believers, which was reinforced with frequent reference to the passage: "Where two or three are gathered together in My name, there am I in the midst of them"

---

71 Vehse, H. F. Fischer, and Jäckel to G. H. Löber, Keyl, E. M. Bürger, O. H. Walther, and C. F. W. Walther, Nov. 23, 1839, in *ibid.*, 153—156.

(Matt. 18:20). The assertion of such a principle under the circumstances prevailing in the Saxon colonies in 1839 naturally gave rise to some critical inferences.

The second point, therefore, was an attack on several people and institutions, which may be described collectively as the Stephanite system. The following were expressly repudiated: the system's hierarchical or "papistic" principle; its episcopal polity, which, it was pointed out, was neither Saxon nor American; the overemphasis of the pastoral office and the glorification of those who held it; the peculiar Stephanite view (as Vehse, H. F. Fischer, and Jäckel interpreted Stephan's theology) that a church, or congregation, could be created only by a properly ordained clergyman, instead of the exact reverse of this view, as held by the signers of the Protest, that the church, or congregation, could at will create the office of the ministry without benefit of ordination by any fixed agency, group, or person; the reliance upon an individual for the interpretation of Scripture, as had been done in the case of Stephan; and the veneration of Stephan's person.

Such a position had as its logical conclusion an attack also upon the pastors. The clergymen were criticized for their association with Stephan, a responsibility which the authors of the Protest shared but which they glossed over. The ministers were further rebuked for their part in attempting to establish the episcopacy; their hierarchical procedure in the deposition of Stephan; their refusal to recognize the rights of the laity at that time or later; their assumption of office in the hasty and high-pressured fashion of June 1, 1839 (at first they apparently had not considered authorization by the people necessary and had acted as pastors without it; subsequently they had placed into question the validity of their "calls" of June 1 by contemplating an appeal for ordination to the Swedish Church, which was episcopal); their refusal to accede to a separation of secular and ecclesiastical affairs and to relinquish their hold upon the former, as typified by their attempt to act as judges; their unwarranted attack upon the three laymen opposing them, in the "warning" of September 9, without answering the questions which had been raised.

The rights and functions of the clergy, as conceived by the protesting laymen, were threefold; first, the office of religious teaching or instruction; secondly, the authority to administer the Sacraments; and, thirdly, the exercise of the Office of the Keys "(in the noncontroversial cases)." The essential demand of Vehse and his companions was that the pastors confine themselves to these functions and relinquish control of secular affairs. The soundness of these demands deserves more attention than the absurdity of some of the laymen's suggestions regarding future practices.

Under the third point, an examination of conditions in Saxony led the authors of the Protest to the conclusion that their situation had been difficult, but that it had not been so serious as to make emigration necessary. Accordingly, they decided that the emigration had not actually been forced upon them. They now believed that previous assertions — that emigration was obligatory and that it was a divinely inspired and directed action — were wrong. In fact, the emigration had been a mistake. Each of the three major points was illustrated with references to events, all of which have been described above.[72] The flat assertion that the emigration was wrong, made even more clearly in portions of Vehse's subsequent book, appears less drastic when it is recalled that he wished to return to Germany, and finally did.[73]

The reply which the pastors made to the Protest and its Supplement of November 9 was probably a stronger argument in support of the charges made against them by the laymen than any which Vehse, H. F. Fischer, and Jäckel themselves had constructed. The pastors continued the practice of "blame Stephan," in which everyone was engaging, including the three recalcitrant laymen. The pastors avowed that they were ashamed of the part they had played, but fell back upon the familiar defense that they had been duped. However, they claimed that from the time of Stephan's fall they had repudiated with abhorrence every vestige of the Stephanite hierarchy. What they had actually done, of course, was to abhor Stephan and preserve the hierarchy. The clergymen did not warm up to their subject properly until they began to censure their accusers for continuing to criticize the action of the clergy after Stephan's fall. As evidence of their good faith, the pastors affirmed that they would correct whatever might be shown to be wrong in the future. In a final gesture of generous renunciation they stated

---

72 Protest and Supplement, Sept. 19, Nov. 9, 1839, in *ibid.*, 54—141.

73 *Ibid.*, 28—33, 178.

that for the sake of peace they would give up the episcopal form of polity.[74]

In quoting this last statement, Vehse aptly remarked in a footnote that it is possible to "give up" only what one has, and the episcopal office was something the ministerium did not have; for the congregations, which alone could confer such office, had not bestowed it upon the pastors, individually or collectively.[75] Apparently the pastors, as the trio of laymen had alleged, still clung to their preference for the episcopal polity and to the idea that it had been transmitted to them by Stephan and that it still existed among them to do with as they liked.

But most damaging to the clergymen was their complete and total silence on every one of the specific incidents — and there were many — named by the laymen, in which the ministerium had exceeded or misused its authority, as well as every case in which the pastors had given evidence of the hierarchical trend which they now attributed solely to Stephan's influence. The fatuous assertion that all these things had vanished into thin air with Stephan's departure was not sufficient to neutralize the force of the specific cases adduced in the Protest and its Supplement. These charges could not simply be brushed aside. The clergymen owed both their opponents and their people either a frank admission of error or a defense worthy of the issues involved.

By the time these exchanges had taken place, that is, by the beginning of December, 1839, the minds of the colonists were considerably agitated by the questions that had been raised. One evidence of the disturbance created has been mentioned above, namely, the fact that the development of the controversy was promptly followed by a division of the land. Another indication was that the St. Louis congregation officially reproved its pastor, O. H. Walther, for his Stephanism, and enjoined upon him adherence to the Bible and the Confessions of the Lutheran Church.[76] However, the Stephanite psychology was still strong. The people generally were slow to follow a line of thought that differed as radically as did the views expressed in the Protest from what had thus far been dinned

---

[74] G. H. Löber, Keyl, E. M. Bürger, C. F. W. Walther, and O. H. Walther to Vehse, H. F. Fischer, and Jäckel, Nov. 20 (19?), 1839, in *ibid.*, 151—153.

[75] *Ibid.*, 153.

[76] Bound MSS., Protestation, C. H. I.

into their ears. With the single exception of the one gesture by the somewhat more independent St. Louis group, the laity at this time was still reluctant to think for itself, much less to state its views openly and boldly.

Accordingly, while Vehse, H. F. Fischer, and Jäckel had some sympathizers, officially they stood entirely alone. E. M. Bürger, later the first of the clergymen to abandon the approved clerical position, was still not prepared to join the dissenting triumvirate.[77] Notwithstanding a recent claim that Marbach participated in the Protest,[78] the evidence does not show that even he, who in succeeding years became spokesman for the opposition to the pastors, as yet shared his brother-in-law's views. Instead, the lawyer remarked rather weakly that Vehse was not entirely clear in his own mind and himself had much to answer for.[79]

This kind of sniping at Vehse's personal part in preceding events seems to have been typical of the attitude toward him. Winter, for instance, commented that the Protest contained error.[80] This, according to Winter's viewpoint, may have been true. But Winter neither stated wherein this error consisted nor made any comment upon those aspects of Vehse's position which Winter himself would have been forced to admit as correct. The teacher then went on to say that Vehse's method of bringing his views before the public aroused the antagonism of the pastors. Yet he did not indicate what was objectionable in Vehse's method, nor explain how any error on Vehse's part, either in substance or method, could justify the action taken by the pastors and their ignoring of legitimate objections to their procedure and position. All that Winter would say, that was not directed against Vehse, was that the pastors did not examine the Protest fairly or carefully.[81]

Vehse, seeing the apparent hopelessness of the situation, gave up in disgust and returned to Germany. This was a plan he had cherished for some time, in fact, almost since his resignation from

---

[77] Bürger, *op. cit.*, 14.

[78] P. Kretzmann, "The Saxon Immigration to Missouri, 1838—1839," *Missouri Historical Review*, XXX, 166.

[79] Marbach to Stübel, n. d. [November—December, 1839], Bound MSS., VI, C. H. I.

[80] Winter to Guericke *et al.*, April 28, 1841, *Zeitschrift für die gesammte lutherische Theologie und Kirche*, II, No. 3, pp. 116—132.

[81] *Ibid.*

the Administrative Board, and for which he had already established contacts in his former home.[82] But his inability to meet a debt of $227.66 to the *Gesellschaft* for his transportation and other expenses had stood in the way of carrying out his intention. Vehse's proposal that he transfer the debt to his brother-in-law's account was considered "ridiculous" by Döderlein, who blocked the move, although Vehse had gotten the consent of several members of the committee of creditors. In view of the fact that Marbach had never contributed a single cent to the *Gesellschaft* and that he already owed a debt of $774.08, which he could not clear, Döderlein was probably justified in his lack of enthusiasm for permitting the lawyer to incur further obligations. Vehse, however, countered by asserting that Mrs. Schneider would assume his debt, which she then actually did.[83] Meanwhile Vehse and Marbach each fell heir to a one-fifth share in an estate of £5,825, left by a London relative, and their immediate financial problems were certain to be solved as soon as they could get the money.[84] Of course, since Vehse had succeeded in arranging the deal with Mrs. Schneider, he was able to leave before the money from the inheritance arrived, while Marbach, for financial and other reasons, remained until 1841.[85]

Vehse accordingly shook the dust of St. Louis from his feet on December 16, 1839, a few days after Gruber's group arrived in Perry County. During Vehse's return voyage to Germany from New Orleans on the *Johann Georg* (still in command of Captain Hohorst), Vehse reworked the Protest, made the additions mentioned before, and wrote the text of *Die Stephan'sche Auswanderung.* The work was finished "on board the *Johann Georg* in the North Sea, off Helgoland, February 21, 1840." An epilogue was added in Dresden, dated April 11, 1840, the same year in which the book appeared.[86]

---

82 Döderlein to F. W. Barthel, Sept. 9, 1839, Bound MSS., 13, C. H. I.; Bach (a London attorney) to Vehse and Marbach, Oct. 18, 1839, Bound MSS., VI, C. H. I. A notation by Marbach on Bach's letter, before forwarding it to Vehse, clearly indicated the latter's intentions.

83 List of Saxon Emigrants 1838, MS., C. H. I.; Döderlein to F. W. Barthel, Sept. 9, 1839, Bound MSS., 13, C. H. I.

84 Bach to Vehse and Marbach, Oct. 18, 1839, Bound MSS., VI, C. H. I.

85 List of Saxon Emigrants 1838, MS., C. H. I. Marbach also realized a considerable sum from the sale of his personal property at auction. Nevertheless, his account was not brought into balance until 1845, four years after he had left.

86 Vehse, *op. cit.*, 25, 42, 183.

Vehse himself stated that his reasons for writing the book were the following: first, to warn the people in the American settlements of the Stephanism still prevalent among them; secondly, to dissuade many people in Germany from following their friends to the United States; thirdly, to vindicate the procedure of the Saxon government against Stephan; fourthly, to correct the wild rumors and misconceptions about events in the colonies; fifthly, to warn other German immigrants in America against falling into sectarianism and unionism. To these purposes might be added those expressed elsewhere in the same work, namely, to reply to some of the works and articles which had appeared in Germany on the subject of the emigration, and to defend himself against certain accusations made against him. Another possible motive, which Vehse did not admit, but which was not entirely unrelated to the third point of his aims, was to regain favor with the Saxon government, whose service he re-entered.[87]

It was obvious that Vehse, H. F. Fischer, and Jäckel had stood alone — not in their disenchantment with Stephanism, but in their ability to see where the root of their problem lay and in the courage of their convictions. The shabby treatment they received from the pastors, the evasion practiced by the ministers in their one meager reply, and the continuance of the system favored by the clergymen, met with not a single formal protest from the other colonists. Criticism of Vehse was easy, criticism of the pastors called for more independence of spirit than most as yet possessed. Opposition to the clergymen and their supporters was to become general, but not until later.

---

[87] *Ibid.*, 25—26, 29, 39, 173—181. Stephan seized upon Vehse's partisanship as an opportunity to characterize him as an unabashed liar. Stephan to Flügel, Oct. 12, 1841, MS, C. H. I. Comments on the quality of Vehse's reporting have been made above, wherever required. L. Fuerbringer joined those who have a tendency to discount Vehse's contribution, basing his opinion on the questionable quality of Vehse's historical writing. L. Fuerbringer, *Persons and Events,* 86. However, note Fuerbringer's very different appraisal of M. Günther's popular biography of Walther. L. Fuerbringer, *80 Eventful Years,* 119.

CHAPTER EIGHTEEN

DISORGANIZATION AND REORGANIZATION

THUS FAR little reference has been made to the effect which developments in the Stephanite *Gesellschaft* had produced in Germany. Since the movement was of significance to the Old World as well as the New, a glance backward is in order. Furthermore, a rather large group of the Saxons had yet to make the journey when the organization began to disintegrate, and a few words must be devoted to them. That the Saxon emigration was no seven-day wonder is demonstrated by the permanent concern called forth by the movement in the immigrants' former home. Significant developments occurred already before the first word of the arrival of the emigrants got back to Germany on February 15.[1]

In Saxe-Altenburg excitement was kept at a high pitch by the determination of Gruber to leave eventually, despite his many changes of opinion and the obstacles he had encountered. But when on November 13, 1838, a "Rescript" was issued to the clergy of the land urging them to a greater zeal in promoting true Christianity, a storm broke loose against the aged Superintendent Hesekiel, who was considered responsible for the Rescript. Superintendent Schuderoff wrote a pasquil against his superior and against the duke. The entire liberalistic church element was up in arms. G. F. Löber feared that Hesekiel might be forced to leave the country.[2]

On March 18, 1839, the dispute was submitted to the theological faculties of the universities of Jena, Berlin, Göttingen, and Heidelberg for their opinion. The documents in the case and the answers of these schools were printed in a volume, called *Bedenken der Theologischen Facultäten der Landesuniversität Jena und der Universitäten zu Berlin, Göttingen und Heidelberg über das Rescript des Herzoglichen Consistoriums zu Altenburg vom 13. Nov.*

---

[1] Fischer, *op. cit.*, 71.

[2] G. F. Löber to G. H. Löber and Christiane Löber, May 28, 1839, in Löber-Eichenberg (ed.), "Ein Briefwechsel," *Mitteilungen . . . Kahla,* VII, 148—151.

1838 (den kirchlichen Separatismus in der Ephorie Ronneburg betreffend) und über zwei verwandte Fragen, which has been cited a number of times above. The reply from Jena was made on April 6, that from Göttingen on May 2, that from Berlin on May 16, and that from Heidelberg on May 27, 1839.[3] The volume appeared in the summer of 1839 and was advertised by a Saxon newspaper in the same issues which carried the first accounts of Stephan's dismissal.[4] The dates just given of course remove the possibility that Hesekiel or the consistory took these steps in order to keep G. H. Löber in the country, as has been claimed.[5] Meanwhile, as early as May, 1839, individuals from Saxe-Altenburg began to follow the first detachments of emigrants. The Sachau family of Roda was one of these; another was a convict named Todt, who left for America and the Saxon colony with his daughter, when he was released from prison with the condition that he emigrate.[6]

In Saxony itself the repercussions of the emigration had begun even more promptly — or perhaps it would be more accurate to say that they had never ceased. Pleissner had dated the foreword to his book at the "beginning of October," in 1838,[7] although it was not published until the following year. L. Fischer's *Das falsche Märtyrerthum* was completed on "Wednesday after Palm Sunday" (March 27), 1839,[8] and by that time Pleissner's *Die kirchlichen Fanatiker im Muldenthale* was already in circulation. Both of these men testified that numbers of other people were still planning to follow the emigrants if the first reports from America were even moderately favorable.[9] But, however optimistic these first or later reports may have been, they were overshadowed by the startling news of Stephan's removal, which followed.

The sensation created in St. Louis by the dismissal of Stephan was paralleled in the immigrants' former home when the reports of this event burst into print before the Saxon public, and "in a few

---

[3] *Bedenken der theologischen Facultäten,* 101, 136, 161, 174.

[4] *Dresdener Anzeiger,* July 19, 1839.

[5] Lochner, "Ottomar Fürbringer," *Der Lutheraner,* XLIX, 163.

[6] G. F. Löber to G. H. Löber and Christiane Löber, May 29, 1839, in Löber-Eichenberg (ed.), "Ein Briefwechsel," *Mitteilungen . . . Kahla,* VII, 148—151.

[7] Pleissner, *op. cit.,* p. viii.

[8] Fischer, *op. cit.,* p. vii.

[9] *Ibid.,* 71; Pleissner, *op. cit.,* 51, 93.

months Dresden hummed with the disclosures." [10] Unfortunately it was the presentation of the *Anzeiger des Westens* which gained currency in Dresden. Probably the first article to appear in Saxony on the deposition of Stephan was printed in the *Sächsische Dorfzeitung* of Dresden on July 11, 1839. This paper based its report on a communication from St. Louis of May 28, 1839. The *Leipziger allgemeine Zeitung* reprinted the information from the *Dorfzeitung* on the following day, July 12. In that same issue the controversy began which was certain to be occasioned also in Germany by the latest developments in the Missouri colonies. For "A Friend of the Truth" protested in the *Leipziger allgemeine Zeitung* that the information in the *Dorfzeitung* of the previous day was incorrect and unreliable. The defense of Stephan made by this writer was reprinted in the columns of the *Dresdener Anzeiger* on July 15.[11] Stübel reported that on the next day the declaration made in the *Anzeiger des Westens* of June 1, 1839, also was carried by the *Dresdener Anzeiger*.[12]

On July 17 the *Dresdener Anzeiger* carried two arresting advertisements in bold type, one by the publishers of the *Sammler* and the other by the printing firm of Arnold, which together occupied almost a full page. These advertisements offered for sale reprints of the articles in the *Anzeiger des Westens* of June 1, 1839, at one and two groschen respectively.[13] Similar material on the emigrants was advertised in the *Dresdener Anzeiger* of the next two days by the *Sächsische Dorfzeitung* and by the printing firm of Heinrich in

---

[10] Hansen, *op. cit.*, 138.

[11] *Dresdener Anzeiger*, July 15, 1839. In the article from the Leipzig paper, quoted by the *Dresdener Anzeiger*, the issue of the *Sächsische Dorfzeitung* is identified merely as "No. 19." However, this evidently was the issue of July 11, since it was quoted in the *Leipziger allgemeine Zeitung* on July 12; and further, because the next issue of the weekly, No. 20, came out on July 18, as is evident from the *Dresdener Anzeiger*, July 18, 1839.

[12] Stübel to Vehse *et al.*, Sept. 12, 1839, Bound MSS., VI, C. H. I.

[13] *Dresdener Anzeiger*, July 17, 1839. The significance of these advertisements in portraying the sensation created by the news is best described in the words of Herbert Albrecht, who, as a student in Germany, provided the copies used by the present writer: "The reason why I paid 10 Marks to have photo-copies made of the pages is that a mere copying of the material would have weakened the effect. The large print is very rare in the *Anzeiger* [*Dresdener Anzeiger*] up to this time, and what you see in No. 198, p. 5 & 6, is highly unusual — in fact perhaps the first time in the history of the paper up to that date, that anything was ever printed so boldly." Albrecht to Forster, Dec. 26, 1938.

Dresden.[14] Then, on July 26, the *Sächsische Dorfzeitung* again inserted an advertisement in the *Dresdener Anzeiger,* taking cognizance of the assertions of people like the "Friend of the Truth," that these communications were untrue. Attention was called to the verification which the *Sächsische Dorfzeitung* itself had received in letters from Perry County. These letters, it was announced, were being made the basis of further articles in the *Dorfzeitung's* issue of that week, No. 21 (July 25).[15]

With the matter receiving such publicity, it is easy to believe Stübel, who related that all Dresden knew of it at once, as soon as the fateful copy of the *Anzeiger des Westens* arrived. Stübel also mentioned specifically the wide circulation given the articles in the *Anzeiger des Westens* through reprints such as *Authentische Nachrichten.*[16] The floodgates of speculation and exaggeration were now opened, and Vehse was probably not far from right when he said that it would require a volume to correct all the errors that became current.[17] Stephan agreed that rumor had run wild. Of course, to a man who wrote: "I have done no harm to anyone," whatever was unfavorable to him was false, but the "craziest slander" of all, in his estimation, was the allegation that he had turned Roman Catholic.[18]

The persons involved in Stephan's removal were slow to let themselves be heard from and to give accurate information. The first news which Stübel received directly from any of his former friends was a letter written by Vehse on July 16, 1839, the same day on which the article from the *Anzeiger des Westens* appeared in Dresden. In Germany, as in the *Anzeiger des Westens,* some of the leaders, specifically Marbach and the candidates who had been closest to Stephan, were accused of having known of Stephan's immorality even before the emigration took place.[19]

The former associates of the emigrants, who still bore the name

---

14 *Dresdener Anzeiger,* July 18, 19, 1839. Heinrich offered for sale: *Authentische Nachrichten über die Amtsentsetzung P. Stephans in Amerika.* The articles from the *Anzeiger des Westens* contained in this pamphlet are covered more completely in G. Günther's work, frequently cited above.

15 *Dresdener Anzeiger,* July 26, 1839.

16 Stübel to Vehse *et al.,* Sept. 12, 1839, Bound MSS., VI, C. H. I.

17 Vehse, *op. cit.,* 26.

18 Stephan to Flügel, Oct. 12, 1841, MS., C. H. I.

19 Stübel to Vehse *et al.,* Sept. 12, 1839, Bound MSS., VI, C. H. I.

of Stephanites in Germany, were deeply shocked to hear the news of developments in Perry County. Delitzsch began his first letter to F. W. Barthel, after learning of Stephan's deposition, with the words: "With a bleeding heart I take up my pen to write to you," and spoke of Stephan in very severe terms.[20] The first letters from America were by no means apologetic. On December 8 Delitzsch wanted to know: "Why do all the letters coming from your new home contain, instead of humble confessions of sin according to the divine command (James 5:16) even justifications?"[21] It cut him to the quick, he said, that he found more jesting than serious thought in the letters of the colonists during the first months. These confessions were to follow later — several years later — but at this time the colonists were in no such mood.

Delitzsch found furthermore that the exigencies of frontier life were changing the outlook in the settlements and intruding themselves upon the people's own preoccupation with religious questions and with their supposed martyrdom in Saxony. He lamented the fact that "The letters which I read from our people in America no longer breathe the former spiritual life, not to speak of a new one."[22] Despite his obvious concern about and kindly feeling toward F. W. Barthel and his family, Delitzsch found an absence of the former spiritual attitude even in Barthel's letters. Some of the people in Germany, for instance Delitzsch again, found it strange that, in view of the circumstances, Keyl was still urging people, specifically Delitzsch, to come to America, in spite of what had happened. While some people responded to such urgings, Delitzsch and the Leipzigers did not. Delitzsch reported: "We have abandoned the plan to emigrate since God has spoken so thunderously that the Old and the New World have heard."[23] The effect on non-Stephanites was similar. Hansen generalized: "A great number of Saxons who were wavering between the Old and the New World decided not to go."[24]

---

20 Delitzsch to F. W. Barthel, Dec. 8, 1839, MS., C. H. I.

21 *Ibid.*

22 *Ibid.*

23 *Ibid.* Keyl, of course, was not the only one who displayed this attitude. See also Christiane Löber to G. F. Löber, n. d. [September—December, 1839], Christiane Löber to relatives in Germany, Dec. 4, 1839, in Löber-Eichenberg (ed.), "Ein Briefwechsel," *Mitteilungen . . . Kahla,* VII, 152—156, 163—167; Bekenntniss, MS., C. H. I.

24 Hansen, *op. cit.,* 138.

Nevertheless, Delitzsch and others still regarded emigration to America as a possible last resort; for he spoke of "Perry County . . . whither also we may flee, if we are deprived of the little which still remains for us here." [25] That another emigration seemed to be a possibility, that is, that conditions were growing more hopeless for the conservatives after — and partly as a result of — the removal of a large number of them in the Stephanite emigration, is indicated by the fact that Guericke was expecting to leave Prussia, and Rudelbach was being forced into a more determined and aggressive position than he had heretofore occupied.[26]

The Leipzig group of "Stephanites" was faring well. Without entering any "rapport" with the "Modernists" ("Neugläubigen") the group had within a year grown to its former size, despite the loss of a considerable number of its most active members in the emigration. Only one defection, that of Merchant Schwabe, was reported, while over a dozen names of former acquaintances of the colonists, whom the latter had condemned for their refusal to subject themselves to Stephan and to follow him to America, were mentioned as still being associated with the conservative group which sent greetings to the emigrants. Included were the familiar names of Rudel, Israel, and Wolf. But "among those of the Dresden congregation left behind there is dissension." [27] Of the Dresdeners, only Stübel merited a special word of commendation from Delitzsch.[28]

When reports reached the Saxons in Missouri of the reception their action had received in Germany, of the disruption and dissension among their former friends, of the controversy that had arisen in Saxe-Altenburg, and of the accusations which were being leveled against some of them, it naturally added to their concern, depression, and emotional instability. This effect, of course, was especially pronounced in those who were being criticized most sharply in the homeland.[29] However, since word of the develop-

---

[25] Delitzsch to F. W. Barthel, Dec. 8, 1839, MS., C. H. I.

[26] *Ibid.*

[27] *Ibid.*

[28] *Ibid.*

[29] Stübel to Vehse *et al.*, Sept. 12, 1839, Marbach to — ("Hochgeehrter Herr Geheimrath"), May 8, 1840, Marbach to — ("Geehrte Frau Präsidentin"), n. d. November 1839—1841, Marbach to Stübel, n. d. [November 1839—1841], Bound MSS., VI, C. H. I.

ments in Germany was not received in Perry County until several months later, conditions and attitudes in the settlements were different by the time the letters from Germany arrived than they had been when the people in Germany had written. By the fall of 1839 the holier-than-thou attitude, which accompanied Stephan's removal, had begun to give way in the face of the administrative-theological controversy. The disturbance and confusion created in the minds of all because of the dispute raised by Vehse, and the distress caused by the unfavorable external circumstances of the colonists, dominated their thinking and absorbed their attention. These factors, together with a sense of regret — and, in some cases, of shame — which was beginning to take hold of many people as a result of Vehse's preachments and the critical if kindly letters received from their former associates, prevented many of the colonists from writing. The result was misinterpretation and unhappiness on the other side of the Atlantic, where the anxiety of many people was pitiable. A few phrases from the letter of Delitzsch, previously cited, are significant.

> From Gönner I have received no letter. Cannot Böhlau write to his poor, sorrowing mother? Have Geier, Schieferdecker forgotten me altogether? . . . Zink's mother-in-law wants a *certificate* of the death of her daughter. . . . What is Lawyer Marbach doing? What Klügel? What my Ferdinand Walther, my dear friend, to whom I owe so much? Why do the two Pastors Walther not write to their poor parents? Eva Bischoff will not come since her fiancé is delivered from the bonds of this body.[30]

Stübel also complained. He had not heard from Marbach and received many requests for information, most of which he could not answer. He requested specifically that the people write and satisfy their relatives.[31]

Until the end of 1839 the scruples as to the justifiability of the emigration, which later beset those who participated in it, do not seem to have seriously troubled anyone but Vehse, H. F. Fischer, and Jäckel. Accordingly, in spite of their adversities, at least some of the immigrants, as has just been noted, found it possible to urge their relatives and friends to follow them. Isolated individuals or

---

[30] Delitzsch to F. W. Barthel, Dec. 8, 1839, MS., C. H. I.

[31] Stübel to Vehse *et al.*, Sept. 12, 1839, Bound MSS., VI, C. H. I.

families followed the Saxons to Missouri from time to time during the year after the emigration, but they did not constitute a noteworthy addition to the colonies. However, one large and important group came late in 1839. Pastor Gruber was not to be deterred by the fact that Duke Joseph continued to be personally opposed to emigration from Saxe-Altenburg, nor by the reports of Stephan's dismissal, nor by the warnings of some of his more realistic friends in America that the *Gesellschaft* was still unprepared to take care of any considerable number of people and that he should postpone his departure.[32]

Perhaps the deciding factor in making the vacillating Gruber drive ahead with such unaccustomed resolution was that retreat was difficult for him. Not only had he taken steps to leave already in the previous year, but he had also tendered his resignation. This resignation was accepted as early as May, 1839, and Gruber's release was granted, effective August 1.[33] Therefore, by the time the startling developments in Perry County became known in Altenburg, the bridges were burned behind Gruber. That the same is true of the people who went with him is less clear, although it is likely in many cases. In any event, by September, 1839, Gruber was in Bremen arranging for the transportation of his group, and by December 12, 1839, he and his people arrived in Perry County, traveling, like those who had preceded them, via Bremen and New Orleans.[34]

The actual number of the people constituting this group is not definitely known. Vehse set the figure as high as 150, but unfortunately he is not reliable in particulars of this kind, and the number given by him is nowhere substantiated.[35] At the time Gruber arrived, Pastor Löber made this entry into his diary: *"Gruberus meus* cum suis et 129 Lutheranis (Summa 140) ad novam nostram

---

[32] G. H. Löber to relatives in Germany, Sept. 10—30, 1839, in Löber-Eichenberg (ed.), "Ein Briefwechsel," *Mitteilungen . . . Kahla,* VII, 156—162; Bekenntniss, MS., C. H. I.; Vehse, *op. cit.,* 26.

[33] G. F. Löber to G. H. Löber and Christiane Löber, May 29, 1839, in Löber-Eichenberg (ed.), "Ein Briefwechsel," *Mitteilungen . . . Kahla,* VII, 151.

[34] Stübel to Vehse *et al.,* Sept. 12, 1839, Bound MSS., VI, C. H. I.; Excerpts from G. H. Löber's Diary, Dec. 12, 1839, MS., C. H. I. Vehse gave December 13, 1839, as the date of arrival, and has been followed in this error even by present-day writers. Vehse, *op. cit.,* 26; Burgdorf, "Corrections of, and Additions to, Saxon Centennial Calendar, 1839," *Concordia Historical Institute Quarterly,* XII, 14.

[35] Vehse, *op. cit.,* 26.

patriam Deo adjutore feliciter advenit." [36] These figures cannot be correct either, since Gruber, his wife, and eight children made a total of ten persons, who, when added to 129, did not yield the "Summa 140" of Löber. If this were the only discrepancy, it could be dismissed as minor. But several years later, in 1844, when Löber made the only list known to exist of Gruber and his followers, 125 persons appear, as given in the list of Gruber's group used in this study. Löber made the puzzle even more involved when he stated in another document, drawn up at the same time as this list, that the total numer in Gruber's group was 141.[37] Thus the composite of Löber's computations is an alleged total of 139 at a time when he claimed 140, and an actual total of 125 at another time when he claimed 141. The last-named figure is the one which has been used most consistently by writers since the day of the Saxons.[38] The list of 125 is in all probability the most reliable, although the bare possibility must be conceded that there were fourteen to sixteen persons more in the group.

Gruber was not alone in his tenacious resolve to leave Germany. Vehse on returning still found the idea of emigration strongly entrenched in Altenburg, which Gruber had forsaken only a few months before. Plans were also being entertained in Württemberg, Baden, and Prussia, from the last of which Grabau had emigrated less than a year prior to this time. The Saxon archivist, of course, had a ready answer to such plans, in the form of a resounding "No." [39] At least equally as eloquent as Vehse's anti-American propaganda, however, was the practical lesson conveyed to potential emigrants by the return to the homeland of a number of the Stephanites who had left so hopefully a few months before. Some of these people were so impoverished that it became necessary to take a public collection for their relief.[40] Within a year or two even the Missouri colonists were advising against their own urgings to come to America. At the same time a more objective portrayal of con-

---

[36] Excerpts from G. H. Löber's Diary, Dec. 12, 1839, MS., C. H. I. The figure 140 is found also in one other place, Bekenntniss, MS., C. H. I.

[37] Nachrichten an unsere Nachkommen, MS., C. H. I.

[38] Schieferdecker, *op. cit.*, 16; Köstering, *Auswanderung,* 35; L. Fürbringer, "Vor hundert Jahren, 7, Die Anfänge des Kirchenwesens in Perry County," *Der Lutheraner*, XCIV, 215.

[39] Vehse, *op. cit.*, 25, 29.

[40] G. F. Löber to G. H. Löber, April 1, 1840, in Löber-Eichenberg (ed.), "Ein Briefwechsel," *Mitteilungen . . . Kahla*, VII, 167—168.

ditions by some emigrants gave a more accurate picture of life in the New World and curbed the zeal of the overenthusiastic.[41]

Nevertheless, interest in the Stephanite movement did not wane appreciably for a few years, albeit such interest found largely literary expression. Von Polenz completed *Die Öffentliche Meinung und der Pastor Stephan* on November 13, 1839, and published it anonymously early in 1840 (not later than March), approximately at the time when Vehse was returning.[42] In that same year Hengstenberg wrote a series of articles, based largely on the books by Fischer and von Polenz, under the title of "Der Pastor Stephan," which ran through eight issues of the *Evangelische Kirchen-Zeitung,* beginning on April 1.[43] Meanwhile the "war of pamphlets," as Hennig called it, which was referred to above, was raging unabated.[44] The return of Vehse and the appearance of his work have already been related. It is worth adding, however, that *Die Stephan'sche Auswanderung nach Amerika* was promptly subjected to an enthusiastically critical review by Rudelbach in the third *Quartalheft* of the first volume of his and Guericke's *Zeitschrift für die gesammte lutherische Theologie und Kirche.*[45] Thereby Rudelbach probably earned the distinction of being the first writer among many who would demonstrate the rather obvious fact that Vehse's position was not impregnable, without, however, giving Vehse due credit for recognizing, and having the courage openly to defend, certain principles which it took his fellow immigrants much longer to discover. By 1841 at least two other small works by Lommer and by Niedner had appeared.[46]

---

[41] J. K. A. Höhne and J. G. Höhne to their brother, Sept. 26, 1841, quoted in *Die Ameise,* Jan. 10, 1842.

[42] Von Polenz, *op. cit.,* iv; Hengstenberg, "Der Pastor Stephan," *Evangelische Kirchen-Zeitung,* XXVI, 209.

[43] Hengstenberg, "Der Pastor Stephan," *Evangelische Kirchen-Zeitung,* XXVI, 209—213, 217—220, 228—231, 233—235, 241—245, 249—254, 257—267.

[44] Hennig, "Die Auswanderung Martin Stephans," *Zeitschrift für Kirchengeschichte,* LVIII, 158—159.

[45] Rudelbach, "Die Stephan'sche Auswanderung nach America," *Zeitschrift für die gesammte lutherische Theologie und Kirche,* I, No. 3, pp. 133—134.

[46] G. H. Löber to G. F. Löber, Aug. 26, 1841, in Löber-Eichenberg (ed.), "Ein Briefwechsel," *Mitteilungen . . . Kahla,* VII, 184—190. Schneider also cites articles in the *Berliner Allgemeine Kirchenzeitung,* III (1841), in the *Allgemeine Kirchenzeitung,* XIX (1840), XX (1841), and in the *Bremer Kirchenbote* (1841), which dealt with the Stephanite emigration. Schneider, *op. cit.,* 104. Some of the many "confessions" later written by the emigrants were also printed in German periodicals and papers, giving further publicity to the movement.

In later years the accessions by immigration to the Saxons and to the church which they helped found were many. But Gruber's was the last organized movement which joined the settlements in Missouri. After a year or several years had passed and it was noted in Saxony that two of the most important lay leaders, Vehse and Marbach, had returned, other prospective emigrants became reluctant to undertake the venture.[47] Also in Saxe-Altenburg interest gradually waned. By August, 1841, General Superintendent Hesekiel had died, a new man was occupying his place, and the ruffled spirits in the duchy were again becoming more quiet.[48]

By the time the Grubers reached Perry County in December, 1839, the situation in the colonies again had changed somewhat. Of course the hardships of the early months were by no means entirely overcome. As remarked when the difficulties in the settlements were discussed above, the circumstances there described generally applied for a period of several years. However, beginning with the end of August, 1839, some progress was noticeable. It is necessary to understand the extent and the limitations of this progress from 1839 to 1841 in order to appraise the development both of the movement itself and of the ideas nurtured within it.

In the fall of 1839 the people of southeastern Missouri, and with them the colonists, so wrote Christiane Löber, enjoyed, "as the Americans themselves had to admit in astonishment, a more productive year than they had seen for a long time." [49] She continued the account in her letter to Germany:

> This disposes these people, who are mostly very good people anyway, so kindly toward us that they aid us in many ways with victuals and other assistance. They give our people large wagonfuls of apples and sacks of flour, and one may stay with them as long as one likes to gather supplies for the winter; as I have already done on two occasions; when, it is true, I reciprocated by doing some knitting and sewing for them, by which one does them a great favor, but for which one is nevertheless amply rewarded. Yes, dear sister, you would earn much with your skill. Besides they readily take into their employ the old as well as the young, because they are German. They would even like to marry them. But there

---

47 G. F. Löber to G. H. Löber, April 1, 1840, in *ibid.*, 167—168.

48 G. F. Löber to G. H. Löber, Aug. 13, 1841, in *ibid.*, 180—184.

49 Christiane Löber to G. F. Löber, n. d. [September—December, 1839], in Löber-Eichenberg (ed.), "Ein Briefwechsel," *Mitteilungen . . . Kahla,* VII, 152—156.

> are so many of our own unmarried men that there would not be nearly enough girls in the congregation . . . Oh, it is not at all difficult to make a living here, if only we were better established.[50]

Even though the facts related were no doubt strictly true, this was, by and large, much too sanguine a picture of the conditions in which the average Saxon immigrant found himself. The impression created was much more favorable than other facts, equally true, justified. In her last words, Christiane Löber had hit upon the fundamental difficulty in the settlements during the first winter — lack of proper preparation, resulting from disorganization. The example of the Löber family, on whom more information is available than on any other, will serve to illustrate these observations.

Earlier in the same letter just quoted, this obviously cheerful woman had voiced one of her rare complaints when she had showed some concern that the house was not yet finished, although winter was at their door. Plainly even she and her relatives, who were among the most fortunately situated immigrants, were not as well established as they should have been. Yet the Löbers did not have to experience the abject poverty of some of their fellow immigrants, for they had received money from Germany. They were thus enabled to have a two-story home constructed for them on the Altenburg land, where the family was to live and where Pastor Löber was to serve as minister. The cost of erecting the log-cabin structure, whose cracks were stopped up with clay, was about $10.00. Since a hundred feet of poplar or oak board cost only $1.50, even a board house could be put up for no more than twice what the Löber house cost.

One handicap was that in summer, specifically in August, the American workmen or settlers simply refused to undertake any building for the Saxons because of the heat. The Saxons found by experience that the refusal was justified. Thus even the Löbers were unable to move into their home until November 25—27, after the cold weather had set in. On December 4, more than a week later, only one room of the four in the Löber residence was habitable, and consequently it had to serve the family for all purposes.

---

50 *Ibid.* A portion of this letter is also quoted in translation in Dau (ed.), *op. cit.*, 18.

Meanwhile, Christiane, who had an independent income, had bought a little land, also in the Altenburg area, and was having a second house constructed for herself. House and lot together cost $30.00.[51]

Keyl was more fortunate than the Löbers. When the land was divided in Frohna, where he was to serve as pastor, he received a parcel on which there already was a small house, and this, of course, became his home.[52] Other immigrants did not fare as well as these two pastors, however. The Büngers barely succeeded in erecting a log cabin before winter set in. Ernst was supporting the family with his limited medical skill. Johann Friedrich was occupied with his work on the "College" a considerable part of the time. But Theodor and Herman, with some assistance from their candidate brother, had managed to put up a house into which the large family could move before the weather became too cold. Even then, the Büngers had to take in the orphaned Theodor Schubert and care for him.[53] Overcrowded conditions in these humble homes were no exception. By 1841 the two Höhne families, although each had erected a barn, were still living together in a one-room log cabin with dimensions of twelve by eighteen feet.[54]

Yet, as evident from the case of the Büngers, the hospitality of the immigrants was not noticeably abridged by their straitened circumstances. On December 4, when the Löbers were still living in one room, Christiane remarked that when the Grubers arrived, they might have one of the other three rooms for their temporary use until they should become established in their own home.[55] Probably Christiane did not expect that the Grubers would put in their appearance quite so soon — namely, eight days later. Finished or not, the Grubers did move into the Löber home at once and remained

---

51 Christiane Löber to G. F. Löber, n. d. [September—December, 1839], G. H. Löber to relatives in Germany, Sept. 10—30, 1839, Christiane Löber to relatives in Germany, Dec. 4, 1839, in Löber-Eichenberg (ed.), "Ein Briefwechsel," *Mitteilungen . . . Kahla*, VII, 152—167; Excerpts from G. H. Löber's diary, Nov. 27, 1839, MS., C. H. I. Actually Christiane Löber, in her letter of December 4, wrote that the family had moved into its home on December 25. However, the date of her letter and other evidence prove this to be a mere slip, and that she intended to write November 25.

52 Köstering, *Keyl*, 58.

53 C. F. W. Walther, *Bünger*, 54—55.

54 J. K. A. Höhne and J. G. Höhne to their brother, Sept. 26, 1841, quoted in *Die Ameise*, Jan. 10, 1842.

55 Christiane Löber to relatives in Germany, Dec. 4, 1839, in Löber-Eichenberg (ed.), "Ein Briefwechsel," *Mitteilungen . . . Kahla*, VII, 162—167.

as guests until April 21, 1840, when they moved into a house of their own in the settlement that had meanwhile been founded by the people of Gruber's group.[56] Arriving, as they did, in early winter, in settlements where there was not even adequate shelter for those already living there several months, these newcomers merely added to the privations which had to be endured by all. By February 2, 1840, however, the Gruber group was ready to organize a separate congregation with fifteen (voting) members. This step, of course, meant that another settlement had been founded, which, like the others, took its name from the colonists' former home and was called Paitzdorf. The new hamlet (the present Uniontown) was located about eight or nine miles from Altenburg.[57]

The fact that by the spring of 1840 the colonists had weathered the first year in their new home, unfortunately did not mean that their most serious difficulties were overcome. The threat of sickness, for instance, had by no means diminished. A great many of the settlers were afflicted with boils, and almost every one of them, it seems, contracted fever of some kind — either "cold fever" or "nervous fever," as G. H. Löber described them. Of these fevers the former was not considered serious, while the latter was very painful and only too often fatal. Both types lasted eight to fourteen days and were combated with liberal doses of quinine.[58]

G. H. Löber's assurances to his relatives that these and other prevalent sicknesses were not serious if properly cared for, were premature. Likewise Christiane's optimistic assertion that the deaths in the colony were diminishing, was mournfully recalled a few months later, when Christiane herself succumbed to illness during the night from April 7 to 8, 1840, and was laid to rest two days later. Then her brother sadly admitted that health conditions were still poor and that the death rate continued high in the settlements.[59] Others agreed with Löber's later judgment, rather than

---

56 G. H. Löber to relatives in Germany, April 29, 1840, *ibid.*, 169—173.

57 Nachrichten an unsere Nachkommen, MS., C. H. I.; Vehse, *op. cit.*, 26; *Gedächtniss-Feier . . . 1839—1939*, p. 40.

58 G. H. Löber to relatives in Germany, Sept. 10—30, 1839, Christiane Löber to relatives in Germany, Dec. 4, 1839, in Löber-Eichenberg (ed.), "Ein Briefwechsel," *Mitteilungen . . . Kahla*, VII, 156—167; Keyl to Marbach, Aug. 26, 1841, Bound MSS., VI, C. H. I.

59 G. H. Löber to relatives in Germany, Sept. 10—30, 1839, Christiane Löber to relatives in Germany, Dec. 4, 1839, G. H. Löber to relatives in Germany, April 29, 1840, in Löber-Eichenberg (ed.), "Ein Briefwechsel," *Mitteilungen . . . Kahla*, VII, 156—167, 169—173.

his earlier one. As already remarked, Seelitz was especially hard hit. In this settlement conditions seem to have been appalling. Pastor Bürger, his wife, and their children were all ill with fever at the same time and apparently did not even have an adequate supply of water. As late as October, 1840, Mrs. Bürger gave birth to a child without benefit of physician or midwife. The child died at birth, the mother two weeks later.[60]

The problem of earning a livelihood presented even more serious difficulties. There was real privation, and stark hunger was not unknown. Reverting again to Christiane Löber's letter, quoted above, the trouble was not that a living could not be made in Perry County, but that the immigrants were not properly equipped to do so. There was practically no livestock in the settlements, and the only land which had been fenced in by December, 1839, was the plot of sixteen acres belonging to the church at Altenburg. The Löbers had bought two cows and two calves by the fall of the first year, but less wealthy families, like the Höhnes, had to defer getting even draft oxen until 1841, although it meant that until that year the eight cleared acres of the sixty-four acres which the Höhne brothers held jointly had to be worked with a hoe. The two oxen that the Höhnes finally acquired after several years cost them $40, and the plow in which they then also had to invest, cost $10. Obviously this was a major outlay for the struggling settlers, and, under the circumstances prevailing in the colonies, it is not surprising that it took several years before some of them were able to acquire stock and equipment.

The Höhnes found that the land was good when cleared. The first two years corn was planted, a crop probably dictated by the fact that without draft animals it was virtually impossible to clear the land properly, while hills of corn could even be planted between the trees, if necessary. But the third year, after the yoke of oxen had been acquired, they planted wheat and began a simple rotation of crops. However, in the agricultural field the immigrants were at a considerable disadvantage in competing with their American neighbors, most of whom had fifty to a hundred acres cleared and

---

[60] E. M. Bürger, Selbstbiographie, 132, MS., E. J. Buerger Papers, Ellicottville, N. Y.; E. M. Bürger, *op. cit.*, 16, 46; Nachrichten an unsere Nachkommen, MS., C. H. I.; J. K. A. Höhne and J. G. Höhne to their brother, Sept. 26, 1841, quoted in *Die Ameise*, Jan. 10, 1842.

one or more slaves to help work them. The Saxons were disinclined on principle to become slaveholders, but their poverty was an even more effective barrier, for a slave cost the prohibitive price of $800 to $900. The American farmers were very self-sufficient, produced most things they needed from their own land, and made every effort not to pay out any of their hard-earned cash. The Saxons, perforce, emulated these practices. There was indeed little money circulating in the entire area. Taxes, the Höhnes admitted, were low, but the effects of the panic of 1837 were still noticeable, and the Höhnes hoped for relief under the new President, Tyler.[61]

By the fall of 1841 economic conditions generally were improving somewhat in the settlements, and the hope seemed justified that soon each of the immigrant Saxons could be working his own land. Yet some of them still had only a negligible acreage and sustained themselves and their families by working for the meager hire of farm laborers. Whenever a family was not able to work a piece of land for itself, hunger threatened. The Büngers are supposed to have been saved only by the charity of an American who was a stranger to them. The kindness of American neighbors generally to the Saxons was described in the afore-mentioned letter of Christiane Löber. The Saxons in St. Louis also helped out their country cousins with money, food, and clothing to the best of their ability.[62] All such aid combined, however, was inadequate to take care of the needs of the completely destitute in the poverty-stricken hinterland.

In the face of such severe difficulties and privation, it was not surprising that many people should wish to leave. Desertion from the ranks of the *Gesellschaft* had occurred ever since the *Olbers* had landed in New Orleans, but prior to the dismissal of Stephan there had been only isolated cases. After it became apparent that the Saxons were headed for serious trouble, and when internal dissension arose within the immigrant group, the number of those who severed connections with the *Gesellschaft* rose markedly. No

---

[61] G. H. Löber to relatives in Germany, Sept. 10—30, 1839, in Löber-Eichenberg (ed.), "Ein Briefwechsel," *Mitteilungen . . . Kahla,* VII, 156—162; J. K. A. Höhne and J. G. Höhne to their brother, Sept. 26, 1841, quoted in *Die Ameise*, Jan. 10, 1842.

[62] Bekenntniss, MS., C. H. I.; E. M. Bürger, Selbstbiographie, 128, MS., E. J. Buerger Papers, Ellicottville, N. Y.; Köstering, *Auswanderung,* 32—33.

record indicates when each of these persons left, still less what his motives were. Consequently it is impossible to cite specific figures on any given period. But contemporary accounts indicate the general trend here described.[63] Several specific cases illustrate the tendency to leave after Stephan's fall.

One of the first persons to turn his back upon America was Gotthold Günther, brother of Louise Günther. Being entirely without means, he was forced to appeal to other sources for assistance. Although Günther was certainly prepared to meet the requirements of Wilhelm Weber and his committee-to-break-up-the-Saxon-*Gesellschaft,* it does not appear that Weber's estimable group was of any help to Günther. It is conceivable, of course, that Günther did not appeal to them, although, in view of his favorable comment upon their action, it seems unlikely that he would not avail himself of the offer they had made. As a matter of fact, it was the Roman Catholics who took care of Günther's return. In St. Louis Father Lutz provided the young man with funds to get to New York and with a letter of introduction which assured him of assistance from that point to his native land. Günther probably was one of the first persons to leave the group after the events of May and June, 1839. He took his departure from St. Louis on July 7, 1839.[64] His book was published in Germany later the same year, under the title: *Schicksale und Abenteuer der aus Sachsen ausgewanderten Stephanianer. Ihre Reise nach St. Louis, ihr Aufenthalt daselbst und der Zustand ihrer Colonie in Perry-County.*

Another of the more prominent cases of defection from the *Gesellschaft* — and, strangely, also involving the attentions of the Roman Catholics to the Saxon movement — was that of Pastor Örtel. He took part in the removal of Stephan and stayed long enough after that event to witness the outbreak of quarreling among the leaders of the Saxon settlements. Then, in October, 1839, Örtel left Missouri and returned to New York. There for a time he served a group of Lutheran emigrants from Prussia who had been a part of the Grabau emigration to western New York and Wisconsin. The branch of this movement served by Örtel had remained

---

[63] G. H. Löber to relatives in Germany, Sept. 10—30, 1839, Christiane Löber to relatives in Germany, Dec. 4, 1839, G. F. Löber to G. H. Löber, April 1, 1840, in Löber-Eichenberg (ed.), "Ein Briefwechsel," *Mitteilungen . . . Kahla,* VII, 156—168; Nachrichten an unsere Nachkommen, MS., C. H. I.

[64] G. Günther, *op. cit.,* iv—viii.

in the port of entry. However, as early as March 15, 1840, Örtel embraced Roman Catholicism. Subsequently he became editor of a Catholic periodical. In this capacity he had occasion to clash with the Saxons at times, since they also entered the field of publication within a few years. Eventually Örtel again returned to the Lutheran Church.[65]

Examples of others who left at this time are Karl Bergt, who returned to Germany out of deference to his father's wishes, and Mrs. Nagel, who also returned to Germany and to the husband and family she had deserted.[66] Stephan's son Martin returned to Germany in 1841 to study architecture, but he later returned to the United States. Furthermore, some people, who had sufficient funds left, sought escape by moving away and purchasing land elsewhere. Among these it appears there were several of the Hoffmanns, who, like others of the Saxons, moved to Illinois.[67]

Such losses were partly compensated for by the fact that a few new immigrants joined the movement. The individual families from Saxe-Altenburg and Gruber's group have already been mentioned. In addition, another Harnisch family came over with the Prussian group via Buffalo and joined the Saxons in Perry County, and two families from Bavaria and Württemberg, who had emigrated previously and had first settled elsewhere in the United States, came to Perry County in April, 1840.[68]

However, there was also a brighter side to what was, on the whole, a rather somber picture of the physical condition of the colonies. As just indicated, some of the immigrants had enough money left to establish themselves in more favorable locations. Others, who could not finance a complete change, still managed to acquire additional land of their own in the immediate vicinity.

---

[65] C. F. W. Walther to O. H. Walther, May 4, 1840, MS., C. H. I.; Schieferdecker, *op. cit.*, 16; Rathermann, "Professor Maximilian Oertel," *Der Deutsche Pionier,* XV, 62.

[66] Johanna Christiana Nagel (Karl Gottlob Nagel) to the Saxon congregation in St. Louis, March 12, 1842, MS., C. H. I.; C. F. W. Walther to Emilie Bünger Walther, Oct. 11, 1851, May 26, 1860, in L. Fürbringer (ed.), *op. cit.,* I, 14, 148.

[67] G. H. Löber to relatives in Germany, Sept. 10—30, 1839, in Löber-Eichenberg (ed.), "Ein Briefwechsel," *Mitteilungen . . . Kahla,* VII, 156—162; C. F. W. Walther to F. Lochner, Aug. 20, Sept. 22, Oct. 7, 1846, in L. Fürbringer (ed.), *op. cit.,* I, 30—35.

[68] G. H. Löber to relatives in Germany, April 29, 1840, in Löber-Eichenberg (ed.), "Ein Briefwechsel," *Mitteilungen . . . Kahla,* VII, 169—173.

J. G. Palisch had forty acres of government land entered in his name as early as June 18, 1839. Similarly, Keyl bought seventy-seven acres on July 20 of the same year, Jacob Seibel forty acres on April 11, 1840, Wilhelm Bergt forty acres on April 30, 1840, and Gottfried Nönnig eighty acres on May 22, 1840.[69] Moreover, the inventiveness and adaptability of the people began to assert itself, and many articles which they could not afford to purchase were supplied by their own hands. Thus the immigrants were, for example, within a few months making their own lime, and were manufacturing stoves of tile or of sheet iron at the modest cost of $2.00 and $5.00 respectively.[70] It may also be remarked that the dangers most feared by anxious relatives in Germany — Mexican soldiers, wild animals, and Indians — gave the settlers no trouble.[71]

The condition of the colonies, especially their economic status, was, of course, bound up with the question of the joint land holdings — from which, in turn, the general subject of finances is inextricable. It was remarked above in passing that by 1841 the situation, so far as the land was concerned, was beginning to resolve itself to such an extent that individual holdings for all were, or soon would be, a possibility. This result, of course, had been the aim of the petitioning creditors in 1839, when they took the land question into court. The original intention was to cancel 100 thaler of each creditor's deposit, giving him in return a small piece of land and a very little cash from the Credit Fund.[72] Most likely this plan was never carried out. However, the division for Altenburg and Dresden had been largely agreed upon already by the time the original bill in chancery had been filed, and it will be recalled that the court had directed a similar agreement be reached on Seelitz and Nieder-Frohna.

This division of land had not yet been made in March, 1840, so the plaintiffs had to ask for continuance of their case until the next term, on the grounds that it had not yet been possible to get into

---

69 Abstract of Original Land Entries in Perry County, Missouri, 130, 133—134, MS., Office of the Clerk of the Perry County (Mo.) Court, Perryville, Mo.

70 Christiane Löber to relatives in Germany, Dec. 4, 1839, in Löber-Eichenberg (ed.), "Ein Briefwechsel," *Mitteilungen . . . Kahla*, VII, 162—167.

71 G. F. Löber to G. H. Löber, May 29, 1839, G. H. Löber to relatives in Germany, Sept. 10—30, 1839, in *ibid.*, 148—151, 156—162.

72 J. K. A. Höhne and J. G. Höhne to their brother, Sept. 26, 1841, quoted in *Die Ameise,* Jan. 10, 1842.

touch with all concerned and to secure their approval.[73] The fixing of boundaries and the distribution of land in Seelitz and Nieder-Frohna was no doubt effected at a meeting of creditors held June 25, 1840. On this occasion the creditors also decided that all mineral rights on the land to be disposed of should be retained by them for a period of twenty-five years.[74] Thus the idea, of which notice was taken above, is encountered again that Perry County offered prospects of becoming a profitable mining region. It is not known that any of the creditors ever benefited from this stipulation.

The method by which apportionment to individuals was made is given neither in the court records nor in those of the Saxons. However, a letter from H. F. Fischer written as early as July 16, 1839, indicated that possible landholders had been asked to state their preference. At the same time it was understood that the possibility of eventual division by lot was being considered.[75] In view of the fact that this system was probably used in the case of the Altenburg and Dresden land, it is likely that it was used also with that in Seelitz and Nieder-Frohna. The creditors wisely did not keep all the land for themselves. Besides the entire section at Wittenberg reserved for sale as lots, they also decreased the size of their own potential proportionate holdings by permitting those who did not have a credit balance with the Fund to participate in the distribution. Thus, instead of concentrating all land in the hands of a few creditors in ratio to their investment, a more equitable division was effected. Since such non-creditors had to pay for the land received, the creditors also got some money, and the Credit Fund could show a profit of $3,462.65¾ by 1845.[76] Of course, as the date indicates, not all this money had come to the Fund at the time of assignment of land in 1840. It is doubtful that many non-creditors could pay in cash. Furthermore, some of the $3,462.65¾ probably was realized from sale of lots at Wittenberg over a period of years.

---

73 Petition for continuance, Palisch *et al.* vs. Bimpage, Circuit Court of Perry County, Mo., exercising chancery jurisdiction, March term, 1840, MS., C. H. I. This manuscript is in the original form, as drawn up by the creditors in German. Undoubtedly an English translation was presented to the court, but appears not to have been preserved.

74 F. W. Barthel to Niemann, Nov. 1, 1840, Bound MSS., 19, C. H. I.

75 H. F. Fischer to F. W. Barthel, July 16, 1839, Bound MSS., 13, C. H. I.

76 "Länderey-Conto," List of Saxon Emigrants, 1839, MS., C. H. I.

The aim naturally was to populate Wittenberg as rapidly as possible, so that money would be coming into the Fund, houses would be built, a market be erected, trade be developed, and the dreams of the colonists as founders of a city come true. The development of Wittenberg would also have the welcome effect of reducing the amount of the assessment per person for the landing place, school, church, and roads. Consequently, the Wittenbergers and the creditors made it a rule that anyone buying one of the lots for sale there would have to put a building on it within two years. Some of the St. Louis Saxons were willing to invest the little money they had on hand in these lots, but found the obligation to undertake construction within the time stipulated too burdensome. The St. Louisans asked for exemption from this rule, but the request was granted only in specific cases for a special reason, and to gain exemption it was required that a purchaser state a definite time at which he did expect to build.[77]

The assumption seems justified that the creditors paid rather heavily for the land they received, and Pastor Bürger stated so outright.[78] Nevertheless, this was the only way in which they could realize anything at all on their investment, and so they could be glad to salvage at least that much. Besides, it was difficult to fix the value of the land arbitrarily then and even more precarious to judge the action later. Accordingly, any desired effect could be produced by manipulating the figures. For instance the lower the value placed on the land, the greater the creditors' losses, in the form of unpaid balances, could be made to appear. Thus Köstering claimed that while Keyl paid into the Credit Fund 5,360 thaler, he received land to the value of $600.[79] These figures appear much farther apart than they actually were. The one was stated in thaler, the other in dollars. The facts that all of Keyl's expenses had been defrayed from the amount invested and that in addition a part of his investment had been repaid to him, are ignored. Moreover, Keyl received 320 acres, and to value them at $600 is rather wide of the mark. Government land could be purchased approximately at that figure, but not land with any improvements whatever, and Keyl's had a house on it. At

[77] F. W. Barthel to Döderlein, March 11, 1840, MS., C. H. I.; Erstes Protokollbuch, Feb. 17, March 9, 1840, MS., Trinity Church Records, St. Louis.

[78] E. M. Bürger, Selbstbiographie, 127, MS., E. J. Buerger Papers, Ellicottville, N. Y.

[79] Köstering, *Keyl,* 59.

about the same time that the distribution of land took place, the Löbers sold that which had been bought by Christiane, and it brought $3.00 an acre.[80] The loss of the creditors was considerable, but it has at times been exaggerated.

The ultimate allotment showed Altenburg to be the largest settlement in the original area of 4,475.88 acres. Altenburg comprised 1,559 acres, Dresden 1,158.08, Seelitz 758.80, and Nieder-Frohna 360. Wittenberg, of course, consisted of the 640 acres set aside for development at the landing place.[81] Neither Johannisberg nor Paitzdorf were within the original boundaries of the colony, and their exact size is unknown. It is fairly safe to say, however, that of the two Paitzdorf was the larger, but that even it did not exceed Altenburg in area. Certain land was also set aside in three of the original settlements for specific purposes. Seelitz reserved 7.20 acres as school land. In Dresden 143.52 acres were designated as commons, four acres as school land, twenty acres "for Parochial land," and forty acres "was set apart for a Lutheran church." Of the Altenburg land sixteen acres went for church and school purposes.[82] These were no doubt the sixteen acres referred to above and mentioned by Löber as early as September 30, 1839. This indicates that at least partial division had been made long before the creditors filed the bill in chancery.

After the summer of 1840, when distribution of the remaining land was made, nothing further was done for several months. Then on November 2, 1840, two deeds were executed, one to H. A. Döderlein, another to Sophie Schneider.[83] But not all the land had then been surveyed, nor was this accomplished by the middle of the next month.[84] Most of the land was not deeded to individuals until June 15, 1841, and even Döderlein's and Sophie Schneider's deeds were then entered a second time. It may therefore be said that the actual distribution to all participants in it was effected on that

---

80 G. H. Löber to G. F. Löber, Dec. 16, 1840, in Löber-Eichenberg (ed.), "Ein Briefwechsel," *Mitteilungen . . . Kahla,* VII, 174—179.

81 Report of the Commissioners, May 11, 1847, Palisch *et al.,* vs. Bimpage, Circuit Court of Perry County, Mo., exercising chancery jurisdiction, May term, 1847, MS., Circuit Clerk and Recorder's Vault, Perryville, Mo.

82 *Ibid.*

83 Record of Deeds, III, 413—414, MS., Perry County (Mo.), Circuit Court Records, Perryville, Mo.

84 G. H. Löber to G. F. Löber, Dec. 16, 1840, in Löber-Eichenberg (ed.), "Ein Briefwechsel," *Mitteilungen . . . Kahla,* VII, 174—179.

date. Seventy-two separate deeds (sometimes more than one to the same individual) were executed by Bimpage as administrator of the estate and acting in his capacity as representative of the commissioners.[85] His services did not meet with unqualified appreciation. The Höhnes suspected (but offered no proof of) fraud in these transactions.[86]

Actually the transfer of deeds should have concluded all dealings in regard to the land question. However, a few oversights by the commissioners necessitated further action. On May 13, 1846, the Perry County Circuit Court in chancery sitting was petitioned by the same thirty-nine plaintiffs to the effect that, since Bimpage and Gottfried Schlimpert, two of the commissioners, had died, John Seibel and Diedrich Witler (?) be appointed as new commissioners, to take the place of the deceased.[87] On May 15, 1846, the court, having found the facts as alleged by the plaintiffs, made the appointments requested in the petition. The court, furthermore, instructed the commissioners to report on the work of the previous commission, complete the business of the commission, and report back to the court.[88] Almost exactly a year later the commissioners made the report. Several corrections had become necessary, but by and large the work of the previous commission was allowed to stand. By making the report, the commission provided the only record that can be found of the solution finally reached in one of the colonists' most vexing problems, that of the joint ownership of land.[89]

Resolving the issue of land distribution implied the abolition of the Credit Fund. The communal system embodied in the idea of

---

[85] Record of Deeds, III, 520, IV, 23, MS., Perry County (Mo.), Circuit Court Records, Perryville, Mo.

[86] J. K. A. Höhne and J. G. Höhne to their brother, Sept. 26, 1841, quoted in *Die Ameise,* Jan. 10, 1842.

[87] Petition for appointment of new commissioners, May 13, 1846, Palisch *et al.* vs. Bimpage, Circuit Court of Perry County, Mo., exercising chancery jurisdiction, May term, 1846, MS., Circuit Clerk and Recorder's Vault, Perryville, Mo.

[88] Order of the Circuit Court of Perry County, Mo., May 15, *ibid.* The order of the court, which should undoubtedly be a part of the chancery record, is actually entered upon the petition itself and exists only in that form. However, it is attested to as an accurate copy by John W. Noell, Clerk of the Court, with his signature, August 25, 1846.

[89] Report of the Commissioners, May 11, 1847, Palisch *et al.* vs. Bimpage, Circuit Court of Perry County, Mo., exercising chancery jurisdiction, May term, 1847, MS., Circuit Clerk and Recorder's Vault, Perryville, Mo.

the Fund had been based upon several major objectives: the transportation of individuals and their baggage to the United States; the purchase of common supplies, both in Saxony and the United States; the purchase and sale of land; and the transfer and safekeeping of funds. By the time the land had been distributed in 1841, most of these objectives had either been fulfilled, abandoned, or rendered unnecessary. Cash was lacking, and the Fund was largely a bookkeeping agency. Only a few vestiges of the system remained to be removed.

Approximately at the time the distribution of land took place — the exact date is not known — it was also decided that work was no longer to be done on a communal basis. This decision was a necessary consequence of the assumption of full property rights over the land by the creditors. Landowners now worked their own land. Others either were without work, were hired as laborers, or rented land and worked it themselves. Since considerable work had been done in the past on a communal basis, some adjustment had to be made. The new order was made retroactive, and laborers were paid for work done ever since the colonies had been founded. Something of this kind may have been contemplated from the outset, for throughout 1839 and 1840 numerous bills had been handed in to the Credit Fund by all who had worked for the *Gesellschaft*.[90] These accounts were now to be settled. In reality, of course, an actual transfer of cash was involved in very few cases. The sums to which the workers were entitled were merely credited to their individual accounts. As most such accounts showed a deficit, the transaction was merely a means of reducing the debts of an individual and helped balance the books — at the expense of the creditors. Yet even to the creditors the deductions for work done were not a total loss, for improvements had been made upon the land which eventually fell to their lot.

Another vestige of Stephanite days was the property of the *Gesellschaft* purchased with funds from the common treasury. The quantity of such goods bought because the leaders considered them necessary or desirable was augmented by the addition of the per-

---

[90] Numerous specimens of these bills for services rendered are contained in Bound MSS., 19, C. H. I. The other transactions become apparent from List of Saxon Emigrants 1838, MS., C. H. I.

sonal effects confiscated from Stephan and the effects of some of the passengers on the *Amalia,* whose baggage had gone on another boat and was now declared forfeit to the *Gesellschaft* because its owners were still indebted to the Credit Fund.[91] Other property to be disposed of was that of persons who had died and upon whose estates either the *Gesellschaft* or heirs in Germany or the United States had claims. Finally, some people wished to sell their effects in order to obtain money to return to Germany.[92] Since such matters could not be disposed of by manipulating the bookkeeping of the *Gesellschaft,* as many other financial problems were, outright sales became necessary.

The first auction in the colonies was held as early as July 6, 1839, and netted the *Gesellschaft* $1,488.27¼.[93] The total figure appears sizable, but prices brought by individual items were pitiful at times. Bidding, indeed, was so low that the Credit Fund repurchased some of its property at the auction and subsequently entrusted it for sale to "the Store," which was stocked with these and other items that were currently in greater demand. The store was placed under the management of Böhlau and Nitzschke, the former Leipzig and Dresden merchants.[94] The stock of this store of the *Gesellschaft,* valued at $1,117.76¾, was placed on the shelves for sale on January 21, 1840. The items acquired at the auction apparently moved no more quickly through the store, and enough was still left on August 25, 1840, to warrant a second auction on that date. Again the *Gesellschaft,* through the store, had to bid in on its own goods. When Nitzschke and Böhlau made their accounting to the creditors on December 4, 1840, they succeeded in making their books balance at the original figure of $1,117.76¾, but most of the stock which the *Gesellschaft* was trying to unload was still there. The suggestion of the storekeepers that they be permitted to continue operating was therefore adopted, although by this time the *Gesellschaft* had to meet the competition of a second store, which had been established during 1840.[95]

---

[91] See for instance the account of Karl August Weinhold, List of Saxon Emigrants 1838, MS., C. H. I.

[92] Dathe to Marbach, Jan. 16, 1841, Bound MSS., VI, C. H. I.

[93] List of Saxon Emigrants 1838, MS., C. H. I.

[94] Financial report of the store, Dec. 4, 1840, Böhlau and Nitzschke to the Creditors of the Credit Fund, Dec. 30, 1840, MSS., C. H. I.

[95] *Ibid.*

This difficulty of disposing of the goods which the *Gesellschaft* had purchased not only indicates the impractical nature of the articles acquired, but even led the *Gesellschaft* into some questionable practices. For instance, the books of Candidate Fröhlich, now deceased, which he had offered as security for the money advanced to him, were sold at one of the auctions (probably that in July, 1839); and although there were legitimate claims upon the Fröhlich estate by other individuals, the *Gesellschaft* pocketed the proceeds. Döderlein's strong letter of protest to the executors of the estate did not effect a reversal of policy.[96] Other claims were being made, such as Tirmenstein's upon Stephan, set forth in a letter to the administrators of Stephan's property.[97] But it is doubtful that individual claims against Stephan were allowed. These instances, however, show how confused the financial situation was during the years after Stephan's deposition, even giving occasion for some differences between the Perry County and St. Louis colonies.[98]

Another opportunity for bickering over finances was provided by the loss of the *Amalia*. The vessel had carried 3,000 thaler specie, the baggage of some of the immigrants, who were on other ships, and much of the most valuable material purchased by the *Gesellschaft,* such as the entire musical equipment, which alone was valued at 962 thaler. The insurance was far from adequate to cover the financial loss sustained, and the conflicting claims of the *Gesellschaft,* of individuals whose property had been on the *Amalia,* and of the heirs of those who had perished in its sinking created a serious problem. Once more the St. Louis and Perry County groups clashed. F. W. Barthel, representing the latter colony, felt the claims of the *Gesellschaft* should be satisfied before all others. He found the views of "the gentlemen (3)" in St. Louis (H. F. Fischer, Vehse, and probably Döderlein) "narrow" and "limited," because they held that the claims of the heirs in Germany should be

---

[96] Döderlein to the executors of the Fröhlich estate, Dec. 4, 1839, Bound MSS., 19, C. H. I.

[97] Tirmenstein to the administrators of Stephan's property, Feb. 28, 1840, *ibid.*

[98] Erstes Protokollbuch, Feb. 17, March 9, 1840, MS., Trinity Church Records, St. Louis; Dathe to Marbarch, Jan. 16, 1841, Tschirpe to Marbach, June 27, 1842, Bound MSS., VI, C. H. I.; Döderlein to Barthel, Sept. 9, 1839, Bound MSS., 13, C. H. I. See also the collection of letters in Bound MSS., 19, C. H. I., many of which deal with the financial problems of this period.

satisfied first. Vehse, on the other hand, exclaimed in disgust: "And this calls itself the old-Lutheran evangelical church!" [99]

While this quarrel was going on in Missouri, Gruber was making unsuccessful attempts in Germany to secure the *Amalia* insurance money payable there, in order to finance the transportation of his people to America. However, Stübel, who was acting as agent for the *Gesellschaft* in this matter, prevented the execution of such a plan. Actually the insurance was available in November, 1839, one year after the *Amalia* sailed.[100] But the questions revolving about this money dragged on for over a year beyond that date. The final outcome is not entirely clear, but a compromise between the Perry County and St. Louis viewpoints appears to have been reached. Of the fourteen separate accounts of *Amalia* passengers, only two showed a credit balance, amounting together to \$683.55¼. This amount the *Gesellschaft* paid the respective heirs on or before December 31, 1840. The twelve remaining accounts showed a combined deficit of \$1,198.48. Three of these were made to balance by applying some of the *Amalia* insurance money. The other nine were left in the red, with a total loss to the *Gesellschaft* of \$1,073.56¼.[101]

Few, if any, questions connected with the Credit Fund were ever definitively settled. However, the important development in the field of joint finances is clear enough — the transformation of the system from that of a communal treasury to what was practically no more than a central bookkeeping agency. This change was brought about largely by the events of 1839 to 1841. The question of credits and debits, which of course, persisted, received occasional attention in later years. The last general accounting was made in June, 1845. The record at that time showed that, despite numerous adjustments and transfers of credits, many accounts, both of those who owed the *Gesellschaft* and those whom the *Gesellschaft* owed, did not balance. Although the *Gesellschaft* as such in 1841 assumed the deficit of \$2,505.30¼ in the account of "Church and School," the debit in the *Gesellschaft's* account nevertheless was reduced between 1839 and 1845 from \$7,067.62 to \$1,338.79½. These figures, of course, did not take into account the possible claims of the

---

99 F. W. Barthel to O. H. Walther, Sept. 19, 1839, Döderlein to F. W. Barthel, Sept. 9, 1839, H. F. Fischer to F. W. Barthel, July 16, 1839, Bound MSS., 13, C. H. I.

100 Stübel to Vehse *et al.*, Sept. 12, 1839, Bound MSS., VI, C. H. I.

101 List of Saxon Emigrants 1838, MS., C. H. I.

creditors against the Credit Fund. Thus while the *Gesellschaft* as an organization more than broke even after 1839, it was still far from solvent in 1845, and in fact never recovered its solvency.[102]

Meetings were still held in an attempt to straighten out the group's involved finances even after the last accounting of 1845.[103] Their success is doubtful. The ultimate outcome seems to have been that the matter finally was left in a state of indefinite suspense. The Credit Fund thus came to an inglorious end. The true story of its failure is told even more forcefully in the unrealized dreams of its founders than in the obligations it never succeeded in meeting. Both the Fund and the plans built upon it died a lingering but certain death. And while the unfinished business of the *Credit Casse* could remain forever unfinished, the hardships and bewilderment created by its cruel failure could not soon be forgotten.

Meanwhile, the Perry County colonies gave little indication of material prosperity from 1839 to 1841. By August of the latter year, Wittenberg, which was to have been the trade center of the settlements, could boast of only fifteen houses and the two stores mentioned before.[104] In May, 1840, the members of the New York group who were members of C. F. W. Walther's congregation in the settlement of Dresden, branched off and founded a hamlet in Cape Girardeau County, called Johannisberg. This new settlement did not prosper any more than those previously founded. It was not even an independent parish, although a separate school appears to have been maintained. By the end of 1841, Seelitz, Dresden, and Johannisberg had all been made branches of Altenburg, leaving as independent parishes only Altenburg, Frohna, Paitzdorf, and possibly Wittenberg, although the last named was usually dependent upon Altenburg also.[105]

The social life of the settlements seems to have been distinctly limited. There was a high degree of co-operation and hospitality among the people, as shown by several instances already described. Some effort at holding regular gatherings also appears to have been

---

102 *Ibid.*

103 Erstes Protokollbuch, Jan. 12, 19, 26, 1846, MS., Trinity Church Records, St. Louis, Mo.

104 Bekenntniss, MS., C. H. I.

105 C. F. W. Walther to O. H. Walther, May 4, 1840. The elders of the Johannisberg congregation to the St. Louis congregation, June 17, 1840, Nachrichten an unsere Nachkommen, MSS., C. H. I.; J. K. A. Höhne and J. G. Höhne to their brother, Sept. 26, 1841, quoted in *Die Ameise*, Jan. 10, 1842.

made. But the severe demands of frontier life did not allow much time for contact, and the rigorous routine of work necessary for eking out a living was faintly reflected in the remark of the Höhne brothers that a lazy man had no chance to make his way in this country.[106] Although by the end of September, 1839, each of the settlements had its "judge" and its "sheriff," [107] civil government hardly existed. The real unifying factor in the settlement was the common origin of the people, and the chief form of expression for this unity was in the field of religion and education.

Until the fall of 1839 church was held in the open "camps" of the settlers. When the Löbers moved into their new home, they immediately made the second floor of the residence available for services.[108] In Frohna, Keyl's home performed a similar service for his congregation.[109] The schools fared little better than the churches during the confusion of the first few years. With collapse of the system of joint finances in the summer of 1839, educational obligations fell upon the individual congregations, and all of them responded by founding parish schools. For some time these schools were held in the open, in private homes, or in the "College" which was being founded, as the occasion and circumstances allowed. The first school building at Altenburg was not dedicated until December 12, 1841. The meager equipment in these schools consisted largely of slates and pencils, and the teachers obviously worked under the severest handicaps.[110]

Amid the handicaps and hardships described in the foregoing, the plans for a college nevertheless were being carried out. As early as August, 1839, the four men primarily responsible for the erection of the building drew up the following announcement for insertion into the *Anzeiger des Westens:*

---

106 J. K. A. Höhne and J. G. Höhne to their brother, Sept. 26, 1841, quoted in *Die Ameise*, Jan. 10, 1842.

107 G. H. Löber to relatives in Germany, Sept. 10—30, 1839, in Löber-Eichenberg (ed.), "Ein Briefwechsel," *Mitteilungen . . . Kahla,* VII, 156—162.

108 *Ibid.;* Nachrichten an unsere Nachkommen, Excerpts from G. H. Löber's diary, Nov. 27, 1839, MSS., C. H. I.

109 Document placed into the cornerstone of the Frohna church, April 29, 1855, MS., Kirchen-Buch von Frohna, Concordia Church Records, Frohna, Mo.

110 G. H. Löber to relatives in Germany, Sept. 10—30, 1839, in Löber-Eichenberg (ed.), "Ein Briefwechsel," *Mitteilungen . . . Kahla,* VII, 156—162; J. K. A. Höhne and J. G. Höhne to their brother, Sept. 26, 1841, quoted in *Die Ameise,* Jan. 10, 1842; Statements for Wittenberg, Altenburg, Dresden, and Seelitz schools, n. d., Bound MSS., 19, C. H. I.

We, the undersigned, intend to establish an institution of instruction and education, which distinguishes itself from the ordinary elementary school especially by including, besides the usual elementary studies, all branches of a *Gymnasium,* which are requisite for a genuinely Christian and scientific education, such as: Religion, the Latin, Greek, and Hebrew, German, French, and English languages, History, Geography, Mathematics, Physics, Natural History, fundamentals of Philosophy, Music, Drawing. In the branches named the pupils at our institution will be sufficiently advanced so that after completion of a full course they will be prepared for university studies. The esteemed parents who wish to entrust their children to our institution, are asked to obtain further information from Pastor O. H. Walther in St. Louis, Poplar Street No. 14, between 1st and 2d Streets. — God willing, instruction will begin on October 1 of this year.

In the settlement of the German Lutherans in Perry County, near the Obrazo, August 13, 1839.

C. Ferd. W. Walther,
Ottomar Fürbringer,
Th. Jul. Brohm,
Joh. Fr. Bünger.[111]

The date on which this notice was inserted into the *Anzeiger* is not definitely known, but on September 19, 1839, O. H. Walther wrote to the *Anzeiger des Westens,* requesting that the notice be run for one year, and agreeing to pay $1.00 for the service on the first of each month.[112] Whether this was actually done, it is impossible to say. Approximately at the same time, however, O. Fürbringer was informing Delitzsch in Germany that the plans were for starting a *Gymnasium* at the present time but eventually broadening the scope of the institution to make of it a full university and theological seminary. From Fürbringer's description it is doubtful that the training of ministers was at that time a primary object of the institution's founders. He also urged Delitzsch to accept a professorship in the proposed *Gymnasium,* but unfortunately could offer his friend no salary.[113]

---

111 A photostatic copy of this notice, as it appeared in print in the *Anzeiger,* is contained in *Lutheran Witness,* LVII, 445. The text was quoted in German in M. Günther, *op. cit.,* 35, and was translated into English in Polack, *Walther,* 44—45. This latter work was consulted in making the translation which appears above.

112 O. H. Walther to the *Anzeiger des Westens,* Sept. 19, 1839, MS., C. H. I.

113 O. Fürbringer to Delitzsch, Sept. 7, 1839, quoted in L. Fürbringer, "Aus vergangenen Tagen und vergilbten Blättern," *Der Lutheraner,* LXXXVI, 118.

However, all talk about opening the school was useless until sufficient funds could be acquired to complete the building and procure at least a minimum of equipment. Work had to be held up, therefore, until the Saxons in St. Louis stepped into the breach in November, 1839, with a donation of $35.50, which made possible completion of a structure that apparently had been dedicated already in October. In his letter of thanks for the financial assistance received, J. F. Bünger wrote to St. Louis on November 19 from the "Luther-College near Wittenberg"; he and several others were then living in the building. Bünger assured the donors that the one-and-one-half-story building was "adequate and comfortable" and that classes would begin no later than December 1.[114]

In spite of Bünger's assurances, however, G. H. Löber could not record the opening of the log-cabin school until December 9, 1839. On that date he wrote in his diary: *"Initium Gymnasii nostri, quod Angli vocant College."*[115] The first enrollees were Franz Julius Biltz, J. A. Müller, C. H. Löber, Herman W. Bünger, Theodor Schubert, Theobald von Wurmb, and an American lad named Price. Although the institution was not intended to be co-educational, the limited educational facilities in the colonies necessitated instructing also some of the girls in the "College." During the first few years of its existence the school was attended by four girls: Lydia Bünger, Martha Löber, and Maria and Sarah von Wurmb.[116] For some time the chief difficulty in keeping the institution alive was that of maintaining a teaching staff. At first the founders, C. F. W. Walther, Brohm, Fürbringer, and J. F. Bünger, took over the teaching duties. But by the middle of 1841 all but Brohm had left for other fields of activity, and the latter, with assistance from Pastors Löber and Keyl, had to carry on alone.

The obvious contrasts between the group in Perry County and the one in St. Louis, the one in a virtual wilderness, the other in a commercial and population center, were heightened by the kindness of Christ Church. The use of the Episcopalian congregation's building gave the Saxons in the city the advantage of being able to build

---

114 J. F. Bünger to "friends in St. Louis," Nov. 19, 1839, MS., C. H. I.; "J. S.," "Unsere Synode," *Der Lutheraner*, LXXIV, 161.

115 Excerpts from the diary of G. H. Löber, Dec. 9, 1839, MS., C. H. I. See also L. Fürbringer, "Unser theologisches Concordia-Seminar zu St. Louis und sein gesegnetes Wachstum," *Lehre und Wehre*, LXII, 434.

116 *Ibid.;* C. F. W. Walther, *Bünger*, 57.

their own congregational life at a time which was critical to them. Repeatedly during the first two years it appeared that the St. Louis Saxons would find themselves without a place of worship. Each time that Christ Church indicated its desire to terminate the inconveniences to which its hospitality was putting it, the Saxons appealed to the German Protestant congregation for use of its building. Each time the immigrants met with a rebuff, not always couched in courteous terms. And just as regularly Christ Church relented and permitted the use of its buildings for an additional period of time.[117]

The rather heavy expenses for a group in the situation of the St. Louis Saxons were met largely from the Sunday collections, which were augmented sufficiently by the donations of outsiders to enable the congregation to carry on until it could become self-sustaining.[118] Such assistance was all the more important as the immigrants themselves were experiencing considerable difficulty in obtaining employment. On more than one occasion they issued warnings or complaints to their Perry County associates that living in the city was not altogether as attractive as it appeared. Two years after arriving in St. Louis, Dathe wrote to Marbach: "Many healthy, active, and skillful people are running around without work." [119] During the early period in St. Louis, Gönner at times supported himself as a barber, and Geyer worked part of the time in a pickling plant.[120] However, it probably was not necessary for the congregation to make the general appeal to the public for financial aid that O. H. Walther contemplated on September 19, 1839.[121]

The St. Louis congregation was not highly organized during the years from 1839 to 1841. At first the pastor, O. H. Walther, did not

---

117 Bishop Kemper to O. H. Walther, Feb. 20, 1840, O. H. Walther to the vestry of Christ Church, Feb. 26, 1840, The elders of the Saxon congregation to the elders of the German Protestant congregation, Sept. 1, 1840, The elders of the German Protestant congregation to the elders of the Saxon congregation, Sept. 24, Nov. 3, 1840, The elders of the Saxon congregation to the vestry of Christ Church, Nov. 4, 1840, MSS., C. H. I.; Erstes Protokollbuch, March 9, Sept. 28, Nov. 2, 1840, MS., Trinity Church Records, St. Louis.

118 Document . . . des Grundsteins . . . St. Louis . . . 22. Juny 1842, MS., C. H. I.

119 Dathe to Marbach, Jan. 16, 1841, Bound MSS., VI, C. H. I. See also K. E. Schuricht to F. W. Barthel, May 1, 1840, Bound MSS., 19, C. H. I.

120 "Pastor Carl Ludwig Geyer," *Der Lutheraner*, XLIX, 35.

121 Draft of a petition by O. H. Walther to the public for financial assistance, Sept. 18, 1839, MS., C. H. I.

have a written call, and it was not decided to extend one to him until October 19, 1840.[122] The congregation had no constitution and did not appear to desire one. It is not surprising that O. H. Walther made little progress with his plan of establishing a governing body ("Behörde") fashioned after the Saxon consistory.[123] In regard to polity, the atmosphere which pervaded the religious activities of the St. Louis group was a curious mixture of legalism, inherited from its Stephanite days, and of liberalism, developed as a reaction against the same experience. The first board of elders was not elected until February 10, 1840.[124] Nevertheless, the essentials of congregational life did not suffer. Services were conducted frequently and regularly. It has already been noted that a school was promptly opened, and this project was never allowed to lapse, although Geyer was replaced as teacher by J. F. Bünger during the summer of 1840.[125] The first indication of organizational work within the congregation is noticeable in the field of charities. The founding of a society for the care and support of the sick took place in August, 1839. It would be a mistake to conclude, however, that in this and similar endeavors the Saxons were thinking only of themselves. A special collection for survivors of a steamboat disaster was announced by O. H. Walther on December 29, 1839.[126] All possible assistance was also given to needy fellow immigrants in the Perry County colony.[127]

On January 21, 1841, the pastor of the St. Louis group, O. H. Walther, succumbed to a brief illness. What might have been a serious blow to the congregation became a milestone in its progress when the call was promptly extended to the brother of the deceased, C. F. W. Walther. Although this action was taken on February 8, Walther did not accept until the latter part of April. The controversy among the immigrants was reaching a crisis during these months, and for this reason, as well as because of his personal

---

122 Erstes Protokollbuch, Oct. 19, 1840, MS., Trinity Church Records, St. Louis.

123 *Ibid.*, March 9, 1840.

124 *Ibid.*, Feb. 10, 1840.

125 Geyer to the Saxon congregation in St. Louis, March 9, 1840, The Saxon congregation in St. Louis to J. F. Bünger, May 4, 1840, MSS., C. H. I.

126 O. H. Walther, Zur Agende, Aug. 10, Dec. 29, 1839, L. Fürbringer Papers, St. Louis.

127 The Seelitz and Altenburg congregations and Pastor Gruber to the St. Louis congregation, June 29, 1840, MS., C. H. I.

scruples at the time, C. F. W. Walther did not feel that he could leave for a new charge. But the St. Louisans wisely decided to wait, and the day after successful conclusion of the Altenburg Debate (April 15 and 21), in which Walther played the dominant role, he left for St. Louis, where he formally accepted the call on April 26.[128] The events leading up to the Altenburg Debate, however, were part of the religious controversy described above, and a resumption of the narrative dealing with that controversy from the time of Vehse's departure is necessary.

---

[128] The call of the St. Louis congregation to C. F. W. Walther, Feb. 8, 1841, C. F. W. Walther to the St. Louis congregation, n. d., MSS., C. H. I.; Erstes Protokollbuch, Jan. 25, Feb. 22, March 8, April 26, 1841, MS., Trinity Church Records, St. Louis; M. Günther, *op. cit.*, 48—50; Hanser, *op. cit.*, 18, 20—22.

CHAPTER NINETEEN

ZION RE-DEFINED

THE RELATIVELY COMPLACENT attitude of both clergy and laity toward the religious problems raised by Vehse vanished from the scene with him. The people were first in coming to the realization that much of what Vehse and his two companions had said was true, and in sharing the feeling of these critics that many things still going on were un-Scriptural and wrong. This change in attitude led to the natural conclusion that the Protest of Vehse and his friends merited a treatment quite different from that given it by the clergymen — not an anathema, but careful study, not condemnation, but at least qualified commendation. The St. Louis congregation acted upon this conclusion by writing to Perry County for the text of the Protest, which they apparently had not yet been given an opportunity to study when Vehse left, in December, 1839, although his views in general were known to them. The manuscript was received several months later, in March, 1840, and the congregation had it copied at a cost of $2.00.[1]

Vehse's ideas were important for the eventual reconstruction of the religious life of the Saxons. But both Vehse's actions and his writings had an even more fundamental and far-reaching effect in the stimulus they gave to the critical line of thought in the colony than in the positive statements made and the conclusions drawn from them. For Vehse's written "Protest" and the implied protest of his withdrawal were the spurs which roused the people and the pastors from their lethargy into a less smug and more analytical attitude. Soon everything connected with their religious status was being questioned: not only the position and action of the pastors and the relation of the people to them, but the actions and beliefs of the people themselves as well. In fact, the people spared themselves less than did the pastors; it was not merely the desire to

---

[1] Erstes Protokollbuch, Feb. 17, March 9, 1840, MS., Trinity Church Records, St. Louis.

shift blame upon the clergymen which occasioned all the furore, but an honest search for truth. The problems raised dealt largely with the collective and individual culpability in the immigration, the justifiability of leaving Germany, the correctness or error in Stephanism, the relation of the people to their former leader, the question of the personal faith of individuals, and the nature of the Church and the ministry. The development of an attitude which was both predicated upon and strengthened by examination and criticism of such vital matters, meant that the hierarchical system was doomed, if not already destroyed.

Had the pastors remained as sure of themselves and their position after Vehse's departure as they had been when they opposed him, the phase of the controversy which occupied all of 1840 and 1841 would have had an unpredictable outcome, but certainly a very different one. However, a development parallel to that among the laity was disturbing the placidity of even the clerical temperaments. If the assurance with which the ministers had rejected the Protest and similar representations was ever altogether genuine, they experienced a remarkable change of heart immediately after the conclusion of their tilt with Vehse and the others. A day of penance was observed jointly by the congregations in Perry County on November 29, 1839 — a matter of days after rejecting Vehse's objections and receiving his last communication, and more than two weeks before he left. At these services the pastors made partial confessions of their responsibility for what had occurred, confining their statements largely to the obvious, i. e., admission of a reprehensible subservience to Stephan.[2]

However, this and similar gestures were not sufficient to satisfy either the clergymen themselves or their parishioners. The fact was, the pastors were uncertain individually and in disagreement among themselves and with their people as to just what was wrong, wherein they had erred and still did err, what they ought to admit and what not.[3] This uncertainty and lack of consensus among the pastors reacted unfavorably upon the people, who neither knew nor could explain exactly what they thought about themselves or the pastors, or what they expected of the latter. But while there was no una-

---

2 Excerpts from G. H. Löber's Diary, Nov. 29, 1839, MS., C. H. I.

3 C. F. W. Walther to O. H. Walther, May 4, 1840, MS., C. H. I.

nimity among the people, the scruples, vacillation, and uncertainty of the clergy naturally tended to lower respect for them and to prompt the people to become more extreme in their views and more exacting in their demands. Partial confessions from the pastors fanned the growing flames of resentment at those who had deceived, misled, and — some said — defrauded them.

The danger in the situation was that with neither side certain of its ground, or able itself to attain a clear viewpoint, positive thought and constructive action were difficult. Each party reacted unfavorably upon the other and forced it farther and farther in the direction of extremes to which the originator of the entire tempest, Vehse, would probably not have thought of going. This psychological interaction of the various factions can hardly be measured, but must not be overlooked. Had someone with some self-assurance arisen to call a halt, it is probable that order could have been restored long before the spring of 1841. The absence of such a check meant that the entire group of colonists drifted rapidly into a state of chaos.

Chaos does not lend itself to description except to say that it is characterized by the absence of order. That there was little order in the religious affairs of the colonists, or in the thoughts and feelings of the leaders and people, for almost two years, will be abundantly clear from a recital of some of the principal events — which, in consequence, were none too well ordered either. One thing is clear in these occurrences, however, namely, that the administrative issues were receding into the background. The reasons for this development are threefold: First, despite the fundamentally secular character of the controversy originally, the later pronouncements for public consumption by both sides had emphasized the religious aspects of their quarrel and couched their statements in religious phrases, which at least the majority of the people accepted at face value. Secondly, many of the administrative questions underlying the initial clash between Vehse and the clergymen had been, or were being, removed between 1839 and 1841, for instance, the communal system, the joint ownership of land, and the hierarchical system. These questions were gradually but uniformly being settled, not to the advantage and under the control of the pastors, but along the general lines of arrangements suggested by Vehse. Thirdly, with the recession of these matters from the field of vital issues, the religious aspects of the controversy stood out in correspondingly bolder relief and were proportionately more important not only to the ministers, but to the average man as well.

The vital importance of such questions to the colonists at a time when complete preoccupation with more material matters might be expected, is, by implication, as strong a proof as any ever advanced, of the religious motives of at least a majority of the members of the *Gesellschaft.* Again the importance of Vehse's work must be pointed out. Had the pastors now been willing to give consideration to Vehse's views, at least on the religious affairs of the *Gesellschaft,* they would in all likelihood have arrived at approximately the position he had occupied, and arrived there peacefully. Rejection of even fair objections deprived the ministers of any ground upon which to stand. They did not win the struggle for control, and so the hierarchical system became an impossibility. They had nothing to substitute for it. Nevertheless they felt, at least for a time, that they could not take the same position as Vehse. Even in May, 1840, the pastors were seeking to discredit Vehse's Protest,[4] although later they closely approached the views expressed in it. The intransigence of the ministers in 1839 left anarchy as the alternative.

As early as on December 4, 1839, before Vehse left, even ingenuous Christiane Löber noted widespread dissension.[5] It did not take long before there were further demands upon the pastors for statements from them as to their responsibility in producing the undesirable circumstances in which the colonists found themselves.[6] Such statements were not long in coming, and they continued throughout 1840. When the declarations took the form of admission by individuals of having erred, they were called "confessions." When the object was rather to formulate the writer's opinion of the principles in which the *Gesellschaft* had erred, according to which matters ought to be corrected, or which defined the nature of relations between clergy and laity in the *Gesellschaft* at the present time, the term "thesis" was employed.

---

[4] *Ibid.*

[5] Christiane Löber to relatives in Germany, Dec. 4, 1839, in Löber-Eichenberg (ed.), "Ein Briefwechsel," *Mitteilungen . . . Kahla,* VII, 162—167.

[6] Winter to Guericke *et al.*, April 28, 1841, *Zeitschrift für die gesammte lutherische Theologie und Kirche,* II, No. 3, pp. 116—132.

A flurry of such theses now began to appear.[7] A statement by Brohm followed the appearance of Vehse's Protest, setting forth primarily Brohm's personal scruples. A reply to Brohm was written. Spröde was next, releasing a set of theses that constituted his first, but not his last, blast against the clergy. Wege stated his position in writing. Bürger produced a number of statements on what he considered wrong.[8] The St. Louis congregation in 1839 and 1840 resolved to observe days of humiliation and repentance. O. H. Walther improved upon these opportunities by preaching sermons both years on the subject of the congregation's actions and status. These sermons were regarded as "confessions," and the one of 1839 was sent to Germany and printed in *Der Pilger aus Sachsen.*[9] Marbach came out with a presentation of his views and wrote a number of remorseful letters to Germany.[10] Keyl wrote his oft-quoted *Bekenntnisse,* a confession, although it did not appear until later.[11]

Some of the leaders and candidates either could not reach a clear position, vacillated between various views which were current, or enunciated views slightly different from those of the leading protagonists of the various factions. Fürbringer, however, made a "confession"; and generally, C. F. W. Walther judged, the candidates were ahead of the pastors in recognizing and admitting what was wrong; although some tried to remain in favor with all factions,

---

[7] Keyl, *op. cit.,* 17—18. Numerous statements of views on theological questions, the emigration, Stephanism, and similar matters, many of them undated and unsigned, are among the miscellaneous, unbound manuscripts in the Concordia Historical Institute, and in Bound MSS., VI, of the same collection, which contains ten separate manuscripts of this kind.

[8] Winter to Guericke *et al.,* April 28, 1841, *Zeitschrift für die gesammte lutherische Theologie und Kirche,* II, No. 3, pp. 116—132; Notes on a reply to Brohm's statement on Stephanism, n. d., Bound MSS., VI, C. H. I.; C. F. W. Walther to O. H. Walther, May 4, 1840, MS., C. H. I.; Bürger, *op. cit.,* 14—16, 20—41.

[9] Erstes Protokollbuch, Nov. 16, 1840, Nov. 15, 1841, MS., Trinity Church Records, St. Louis; G. H. Löber to G. F. Löber, Aug. 26, 1841, in Löber-Eichenberg (ed.), "Ein Briefwechsel," *Mitteilungen . . . Kahla,* VII, 184—190; Rudelbach in Keyl, *op. cit.,* 1; O. H. Walther, Zur Agende, Sept. 22, 27, 1839, MS., L. Fürbringer Papers, St. Louis; Predigt bei der . . . Bussfeier . . . d. 22. Nov. 1840. Gehalten von Otto Hermann Walther, MS., C. H. I.

[10] Winter to Guericke *et al.,* April 28, 1841, *Zeitschrift für die gesammte lutherische Theologie und Kirche,* II, No. 3, pp. 116—132; Marbach to — ("Geehrte Frau Präsidentin"), n. d., Marbach to Stübel, n. d. [November, 1839—April, 1841], Marbach to — ("Hochgeehrter Herr Geheimrath"), May 8, 1840, Bound MSS., VI, C. H. I.

[11] Keyl, *op. cit.,* 20.

like Klügel, of whom Bürger said that he "wriggled like an eel." [12] Other men, like Winter and Nitzschke, attempted to minimize their responsibility or the gravity of the situation.[13]

In the early months of 1840 Löber, Keyl, and Bürger drew up a formal withdrawal of their condemnation of Vehse's various writings, and on June 29 they sent the letter to the St. Louis congregation. The three pastors admitted that their unjust insinuations had been aimed at Vehse, and that they themselves had merited the distrust of the people, to whom they herewith apologized. Approximately at the same time both Keyl and Bürger sent separate letters of apology to St. Louis.[14] When Elder Niemann of the St. Louis congregation forwarded this letter to Jäckel (who was then in St. Louis, although he did not join the Saxon congregation until later), the latter replied that, while he had made copies for Vehse and Fischer, now both in Saxony, he would not answer for them, but speak only for himself in saying that he found the statement by the clergymen entirely unsatisfactory and very unlike Herman Walther's, which he considered adequate.[15]

The candidates also made a joint declaration in addition to their separate statements. Early in April of 1840 the candidates then in Perry County formally pledged themselves in writing to refrain from all preaching for the time being. Thereby they made it impossible for the Dresden (Perry County) congregation, which wished to call one of them, to procure a pastor, and threw the whole question of calls into the center of the controversy.[16] Fürbringer adopted a curious course of action in accepting a call to Elkhorn Prairie (Venedy), Illinois, without ordination, although he considered or-

---

[12] E. M. Bürger to the Saxon pastors in Missouri, Nov. 3, 1842, C. F. W. Walther to O. H. Walther, May 4, 1840, O. Fürbringer to C. F. W. Walther, Jan. 9, 1841, MSS., C. H. I.; Winter to Guericke *et al.*, April 28, 1841, *Zeitschrift für die gesammte lutherische Theologie und Kirche*, II, No. 3, pp. 116—132; Minutes on a conference at Dresden, Perry County, Mo., March, 1841, and an "Explanation of the Minutes," probably written by Marbach, Bound MSS., VI, C. H. I.

[13] Winter to Guericke *et al.*, April 28, 1841, *Zeitschrift für die gesammte lutherische Theologie und Kirche*, II, No. 3, pp. 116—132; C. F. W. Walther to O. H. Walther, May 4, 1840, MS., C. H. I.

[14] G. H. Löber, Keyl, and Bürger to the Saxon congregation in St. Louis, June 29, 1840, Bürger to the Saxon immigrants in St. Louis, June 29, 1840, Keyl to the Saxon immigrants in St. Louis, July 1, 1840, MSS., C. H. I. In Bürger, *op. cit.*, 14—16, his letter is quoted.

[15] Jäckel to Niemann, July 9, 1840, MS., C. H. I.

[16] C. F. W. Walther to O. H. Walther, May 4, 1840, MS., C. H. I.

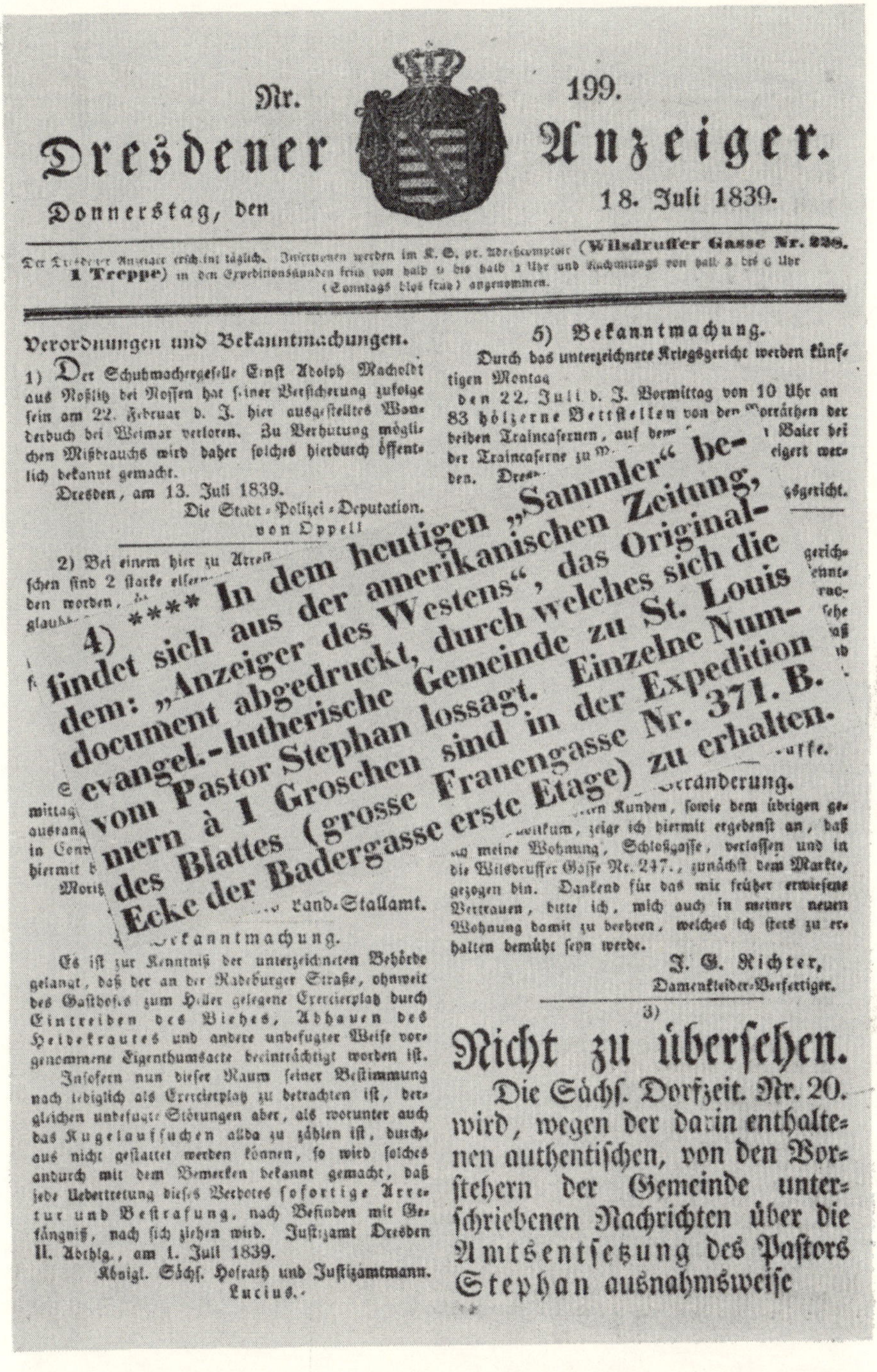

Nr. 199.

Dresdener Anzeiger.

Donnerstag, den 18. Juli 1839.

Der Dresdener Anzeiger erscheint täglich. Insertionen werden im K. S. pt. Adreßcomptoir (Wilsdruffer Gasse Nr. 238. 1 Treppe) in den Expeditionsstunden früh von halb 9 bis halb 1 Uhr und Nachmittags von halb 3 bis 6 Uhr (Sonntags blos früh) angenommen.

Verordnungen und Bekanntmachungen.

1) Der Schuhmachergeselle Ernst Adolph Macholdt aus Noßlitz bei Nossen hat seiner Versicherung zufolge sein am 22. Februar d. J. hier ausgestelltes Wanderbuch bei Weimar verloren. Zu Verhütung möglichen Mißbrauchs wird daher solches hierdurch öffentlich bekannt gemacht.

Dresden, am 13. Juli 1839.

Die Stadt-Polizei-Deputation.
von Oppell

2) Bei einem hier zu Arrest ... schen sind 2 starke eiser... den worden. ... glaub...

... Land-Stallamt.

...ekanntmachung.

Es ist zur Kenntniß der unterzeichneten Behörde gelangt, daß der an der Radeburger Straße, ohnweit des Gasthofes zum Hiller gelegene Exercierplatz durch Eintreiben des Viehes, Abhauen des Heidekrautes und andere unbefugter Weise vorgenommene Eigenthumsacte beeinträchtigt worden ist.

Insofern nun dieser Raum seiner Bestimmung nach lediglich als Exercierplatz zu betrachten ist, dergleichen unbefugte Störungen aber, als worunter auch das Kugelaufsuchen allda zu zählen ist, durchaus nicht gestattet werden können, so wird solches andurch mit dem Bemerken bekannt gemacht, daß jede Uebertretung dieses Verbotes sofortige Arretur und Bestrafung, nach Befinden mit Gefängniß, nach sich ziehen wird. Justizamt Dresden II. Abthlg., am 1. Juli 1839.

Königl. Sächs. Hofrath und Justizamtmann.
Lucius.

5) Bekanntmachung.

Durch das unterzeichnete Kriegsgericht werden künftigen Montag den 22. Juli d. J. Vormittag von 10 Uhr an 83 hölzerne Bettstellen von den Vorräthen der beiden Traincasernen, auf dem ... Baier bei der Traincaserne zu ... eigert werden. ...

...gericht.

...Veränderung.

...ren Kunden, sowie dem übrigen ...publikum, zeige ich hiermit ergebenst an, daß ... meine Wohnung, Schloßgasse, verlassen und in die Wilsdruffer Gasse Nr. 247., zunächst dem Markte, gezogen bin. Dankend für das mir früher erwiesene Vertrauen, bitte ich, mich auch in meiner neuen Wohnung damit zu beehren, welches ich stets zu erhalten bemüht seyn werde.

J. G. Richter,
Damenkleider-Verfertiger.

3)

Nicht zu übersehen.

Die Sächs. Dorfzeit. Nr. 20. wird, wegen der darin enthaltenen authentischen, von den Vorstehern der Gemeinde unterschriebenen Nachrichten über die Amtsentsetzung des Pastors Stephan ausnahmsweise

4) *** In dem heutigen „Sammler" befindet sich aus der amerikanischen Zeitung, dem: „Anzeiger des Westens", das Originaldocument abgedruckt, durch welches sich die evangel.-lutherische Gemeinde zu St. Louis vom Pastor Stephan lossagt. Einzelne Nummern à 1 Groschen sind in der Expedition des Blattes (grosse Frauengasse Nr. 371. B. Ecke der Badergasse erste Etage) zu erhalten.

Early reports in Dresden of the Crisis in the Gesellschaft's *affairs. The superimposed advertisement is from the preceding issue of the same paper, July 17, 1839. Reprints from the* Anzeiger des Westens *being offered in this notice by the* Sächsische Dorfzeitung *contained the statements given on pp. 413f.*

PLATE XXIV

5) Wichtige Nachricht.

In der Arnoldischen Buchhandlung wird so eben ausgegeben:

Authentischer Abdruck der im, zu Saint-Louis (Missouri) erscheinenden Anzeiger des Westens v. 1. Juni 1839 enthaltenen Erklärungen der geistlichen und weltlichen Vorsteher der nach Amerika ausgewanderten sogenannten altlutherischen Gemeinde über die Amtsentsetzung des Pastors Stephan.

Preis: Zwei Groschen.

---

6) In einigen Tagen erscheint und ist beim Herausgeber, sowie in allen Buchhandlungen für Drei Groschen zu haben:

Dresden

im Festgewande des 6. Juli 1839.

Ein Blatt in den Kranz vaterländischer Erinnerungen für Zeitgenossen und Nachkommen.

Von

Friedrich Koitzsch.

Mit zwölf in Kupfer gestochenen Abbildungen herausgegeben von

P. G. Hilscher.

In Partieen für Schulen hat Unterzeichneter den Preis pr. Exempl. ohne Kupfer zu Einem Groschen, und pr. Exempl. mit Kupfern zu Zwei Groschen bestimmt.

Bestellungen nimmt von heute darauf an

P. G. Hilscher,

große Frauengasse, Ecke der Badergasse, Nr. 371. erste Etage.

---

7) So eben ist erschienen und in der Grimmer'schen Buchhandlung, Schloßgasse, Stadt Gotha gegenüber, zu haben, Preis 3 Groschen:

Predigt am 6. Juli 1839,

am Gedächtnißtage der vor 300 Jahren in Dresden eingeführten Reformation in der evangelisch-reformirten Kirche daselbst gehalten und auf ausdrückliches Verlangen dem Druck übergeben von

Ernst Volkmar Kohlschütter,

Prediger der reformirten Gemeinde.

Familien-Nachrichten.

1) Bei ihrem Weggange von Dresden nach Oschatz empfehlen sich Verwandten und Freunden

Benjamin Richter,
Mathilde Richter,
geb. Frauenstein.

Dresden, am 15. Juli 1839.

---

2) Nach Gottes weisem Rathschluß entschlief in eine bessere Wel. unsere innigstgeliebte Tochter Anna in einem Alter von 6 und ½ Jahr. Den innigsten

Daring advertising for Saxon newspapers in 1839. This page reflects the Dresdener Anzeiger's *treatment (on July 17) of the news that Stephan had been deposed*

PLATE XXV

4) Nr. 20. der Sächs. Dorfzeitung enthält die

vollständige

authentische Darstellung der Amtsentsetzung des P. Stephan; sowie auch ein Verzeichniß der am 6ten Juli aufgestellt gewesenen Transparents. Einzelne Nummern sind in allen Buchhandlungen à 1 gl. zu haben.

Heinrich'sche Buchdruckerei,
Neustadt, Markt Nr. 53.

[illegible]

3) Im Verlage der Unterzeichneten ist erschienen und in der Arnoldischen, Wagner'schen und Grimmer'schen Buchhandlung, so wie in der Walther'schen Hofbuchhandlung zu haben:

Die

Schicksale und Abenteuer

der

aus Sachsen nach Amerika ausgewanderten

Stephanianer.

Ihre Reise nach St. Louis, ihr Aufenthalt daselbst und der Zustand ihrer Colonie in Perry-County.

124 Seiten. Preis 8 gl.

Der Leser findet in diesem Schriftchen ein treues Gemälde von den traurigen Schicksalen einer über [illegible] Köpfe zählenden Gemeinde, welche in ihrer beispiellosen Verblendung von ihren Lehrern und Führern zum Gegenstande einer [illegible] Speculation gemacht wurde; er findet ferner einen schaudererregenden Blick, wie weit sich ein Lehrer des göttlichen Wortes verirren konnte, und wie nöthig es ist, sich vor jenen scheinheiligen Heuchlern zu hüten, welche ihre Werke im Finstern treiben.

Heinrich'sche Buchdruckerei,
Neustadt, Markt, Nr. 53.

4) Ueber die Wohlbeleibtheit

10) Stephaniana.

Das mehrfach ausgebreitete Gerücht, als seyen die aus dem „Anzeiger des Westens" mitgetheilten „Erklärungen" in Betreff des Erbischofs Stephan unecht, wird durch mehrere in diesen Tagen eingegangene Briefe von Gemeindegliedern aus St. Louis und Perry County hinlänglich widerlegt. Das Nähere findet man in der heute ausgegebenen Sächs. Dorfzeitung Nr. 21.

Sustained repercussions in the homeland. See pp. 475ff. The Sächsische Dorfzeitung, *one of the first in the field with the piquant news (July 11), is still hawking its wares in the* Dresdener Anzeiger *of July 19, 1839. Within a week letters, which carry more detailed accounts, are offered to corroborate the newspaper stories, to overcome incredulity, and to step up circulation ("10 Stephaniana"). Three months later, G. Günther has returned and is exploiting the excited interest of the city with his sensational "Schicksale und Abenteuer der . . . Stephanianer,"* Dresdener Anzeiger, *October 29, 1839.*

PLATE XXVI

The Altenburg Debate, according to a scene from the centennial film Call of the Cross, *1938. The figure at the right represents Marburg, that at the left Walther.* *(See page 523)*

PLATE XXVII

dination so highly important that he wished to have Rudelbach write to O. H. Walther in St. Louis to authorize the latter to do it. (This because Rudelbach was a "Superintendent" in the Saxon State Church and therefore qualified to perform or authorize such a rite, in the Fürbringer version of the episcopal succession.) Without ordination Fürbringer felt he should not accept. However, the final result was that he went nevertheless, took office August 23, 1840 (after having preached there in May), but was not ordained until 1843. This interesting bit of casuistry apparently can be rationalized only by concluding that Fürbringer considered it bad to serve a congregation without proper ordination, but that if he decided to serve a congregation — for whatever reason — he would rather serve it unordained than ordained by the wrong people. Stephanism was not dead! The inconsistencies of this incident gave Grabau a just cause for complaint.[17] Schieferdecker did not carry his scruples that far. He was ordained in June, 1841, and served a congregation in Monroe (St. Clair County), Illinois, beginning with that year.[18]

In addition to this brief enumeration of statements and positions, three separate cases will be cited as particularly illustrative of various trends: those of Löber, Bürger, and C. F. W. Walther. Löber offers the clearest example of the gradual change in attitude which was taking place. On September 30, 1839, in the midst of the controversy with Vehse, Löber was still certain that the emigration had been right. On April 29, 1840, he stated that he was no longer certain that the departure of the Saxons had divine approval, although he still insisted that his own motives were unselfish. By December 16 the "Lossagung vom Stephanismus," or Renunciation of Stephanism, which was Löber's work, was completed, and its author said he recognized his guilt ever more clearly. He asked forgiveness of his brother, G. F. Löber, and of his former congregation, which he had left. He also sent a letter of apology to Duke Joseph, in which he even expressed his willingness to re-enter the service of the Church in Saxe-Altenburg. The "Lossagung" was originally written by Löber alone for the benefit of the Perry

---

[17] O. Fürbringer to C. F. W. Walther, Jan. 9, 1841, MS., C. H. I.; Erstes Protokollbuch, Nov. 13, 1843, MS., Trinity Church Records, St. Louis; Lochner, "Ottomar Fürbringer," *Der Lutheraner*, XLIX, 179.

[18] Erstes Protokollbuch, June 7, 1841, MS., Trinity Church Records, St. Louis; Schieferdecker, *op. cit.*, 24; Mannhardt, "Gemeinde Chronologie," *Deutsch-Amerikanische Geschichtsblätter*, V, No. 4, p. 18.

County colonies only. A joint statement by all the pastors was to be sent to Germany, and O. H. Walther was commissioned by his colleagues to discharge this distasteful duty. Later, when O. H. Walther died without having produced a satisfactory document and it seemed desirable to make some statement, Löber's Lossagung was circulated and signed by the other pastors and by most members of Löber's congregation.[19]

The second example is that of Bürger, who was in some respects the weakest, most vacillating, and most pitiable figure among the clergy, and perhaps in the entire *Gesellschaft.* On three separate occasions he apologized to his congregation in Perry County. When, in November, 1840, he formally offered to resign from his congregation because he considered himself unworthy to serve it, the latter replied with the request that he stay nevertheless, and he resumed preaching in December. However, by December 5 he again was assailed by doubts, suspended his preaching, withdrew from pastoral activity, and sent his people to other pastors, who were taking some of his dissatisfied parishioners away from him anyway. Some of the people in Seelitz were bitter against Bürger and reviled him in public, he claimed, because they had incurred heavy financial losses. By February 28, 1841, Bürger again assembled his congregation, preached a penitential sermon, and read two documents to them, which denounced Stephan and the emigration, and called on others to admit the correctness of his charges publicly. To this outburst the congregation agreed to reply in a fortnight, but when it failed to do so, Bürger, who was now living with an English family near Dresden, two miles from his former parish (his wife had died), found it difficult to serve the five members who requested him to do so.[20]

The third example, that of C. F. W. Walther, illustrates most

---

[19] Winter to Guericke *et al.*, April 28, 1841, *Zeitschrift für die gesammte lutherische Theologie und Kirche*, II, No. 3, pp. 116—132; O. Fürbringer to C. F. W. Walther, Jan. 9, 1841, G. H. Löber's Introduction to Lossagung vom Stephanismus, MSS., C. H. I.; G. H. Löber to relatives in Germany, Sept. 10—30, 1839, April 29, 1840, G. H. Löber to G. F. Löber, Dec. 16, 1840, Aug. 26, 1841, in Löber-Eichenberg (ed.), "Ein Briefwechsel," *Mitteilungen . . . Kahla,* VII, 156—162, 169—179, 184—190.

[20] E. M. Bürger, Selbstbiographie, 130—140, MS., E. J. Buerger Papers, Ellicottville, N. Y.; Bürger, *op. cit.*, 14, 16—19, 41. The two documents referred to, which Bürger read to the congregation, are given in full in *ibid.*, 20—41. See also Winter to Guericke *et al.*, April 28, 1841, *Zeitschrift für die gesammte lutherische Theologie und Kirche,* II, No. 3, pp. 116—132; C. F. W. Walther to O. H. Walther, May 4, 1840, MS., C. H. I.

clearly the deep personal sense of remorse and inner disturbance gripping some of the men who were responsible for the emigration. "Dr. Walther's" admirers are prone to emphasize his work in 1841 and, in fact, to view that effort in the light of his later achievements and qualities, to describe him as calm and poised, his mind as analytical and logical.[21] However, Ferdinand Walther betrayed his true nature and feelings in a letter to his brother, which is not only a revelation of the writer's character, but also an illustration of the emotional-religious turmoil of the times. No one who wishes to examine more closely either this phase of the Stephanite immigration or the life of Walther, can fully comprehend the abject misery of the people without having read this ten-page letter. Excerpts from it will serve to illustrate many of the generalizations here made regarding the mental depression of the colonists during these years.

After the admission that he did not see the true nature of the emigration at first, that he would not have been able to bear it if he had, and the remark that "a heathen would have been horrified" by the emigration, Walther continued to list the errors of the movement:

> Of primary importance is our unfaithfulness toward the first congregations which we left contrary to God, His will, and His Word, and our oaths to which [the congregations] we broke. Thereupon follow the horrible ruptures of marital relations, the shameful abandonment by children of old, sick, weak parents who required care. Thereupon follow the shameful idolatry with Stephan, the sectarian exclusiveness, the condemnation of other upright people, the departure from many essentials of the Lutheran Church, and who will name it all? Every sad look of a member from our congregations is to me like an accuser before God; my conscience blames *me* for all the broken marriages which occurred among us; it calls me a kidnapper, a robber of the wealthy among us, a murderer of those who lie buried in the sea and the many who were stricken down here, a member of a mob, a mercenary, an idolater, etc. I now no longer dare to say: our emigration was premature; it is a big question whether we pastors should ever have emigrated, whether we should not perhaps have tolerated all restrictions, so long as they did not require something plainly sinful, in order that we might at

[21] Köstering, *Auswanderung*, 38—39; Hochstetter, *op. cit.*, 20—21, 72. These authors have found many imitators.

> least as faithful shepherds have cared for, protected, and watched over the little good which was still present in the German congregation.[22]

The result of attitudes such as this, was that all of the pastors felt their position untenable. Bürger's several resignations have been mentioned above. Löber also tendered his resignation, but the congregation refused to accept it. Keyl had a similar experience, as did C. F. W. Walther.[23]

The ingredients in this witch's cauldron of confusion, uncertainty, remorse, self-recrimination, attack, counterattack, confession, anathema, and all the other component parts of the bitter religio-factional feud which sapped the remaining strength of the colonies, combined to produce a pitiable and morbid situation. Whatever their original opinion may have been, the final result with many people was a deep mental depression, a desperate discouragement, a miserable bewilderment, and a sense of individual guilt that found expression in confessions even among the women.[24] Many felt that they could resolve the conflict within themselves only by returning to Germany. But as their poverty placed this remedy beyond their reach, the resulting psychological impasse left them utterly frustrated and unstrung. It was the last stage in the seemingly inexorable succession of steps toward disintegration of the *Gesellschaft,* which had been in progress ever since the days when Stephan overstepped the bounds of reason in his demands on his followers and thereby provoked revolt.

Everyone had now been so completely unnerved by the tempest that literally no one knew where he stood. Had the pastors the right to serve congregations? Had they been justified in leaving their congregations in Germany? Or ought they return? Had the entire emigration been justifiable? Had their idolization of Stephan

---

[22] C. F. W. Walther to O. H. Walther, May 4, 1840, MS., C.H.I. Several other portions of this letter are quoted in M. Günther, *op. cit.,* 36—40.

[23] C. F. W. Walther to O. H. Walther, May 4, 1840, MS., C.H.I.; Keyl, *op. cit.,* 17—18; C. F. W. Walther to O. Fürbringer, April 14, 1840, in M. Günther, *op. cit.,* 41—42; K. Gruber, "Ehrengedächtniss des . . . Gotthold Heinrich Löber," *Der Lutheraner,* VI, 146.

[24] C. F. W. Walther to O. H. Walther, May 4, 1840, O. Fürbringer to C. F. W. Walther, Jan. 9, 1841, Nachrichten an unsere Nachkommen, MSS., C.H.I.; Dathe to Marbach, Jan. 16, 1841, Marbach to Stübel, n.d. [November, 1839—1841], Marbach to — ("Geehrte Frau Präsidentin"), n.d., Marbach to — ("Hochgeehrter Herr Geheimrath"), May 8, 1840, May 10, 1841, Bound MSS., VI, C.H.I.

deprived them of the claim to being Christians? Were they a church or a mob? Were they the Lutheran Church or a Stephanistic association? Had they the right, if they were congregations, to call pastors and teachers? Had they the right to depose those now in office? If they had this right, were they obliged to do so? What of the tarnished record of these men? More fundamentally: What was a church? What was the office of the ministry? What were the distinguishing characteristics of each? What were the rights and obligations of both clergy and laity? These and a thousand questions agitated the minds of the people, who were beset by economic difficulties, remorse of conscience, and shame before the public.[25]

The extreme views possible on these questions were: First, that all that had been done by the group was justifiable, and that hence all was well, from the moral standpoint, in both the religious and secular life of the colonies; and secondly, that all that had been done in regard to the emigration was wrong, and that the colonies were no longer Christian congregations, but separatistic mobs, and their pastors impostors. The multitude of conclusions, all negative, to be drawn from the second position just stated, are obvious. Actually none of the many opinions was quite as clear as either of these completely positive or negative hypothetical attitudes. The first thesis, in fact, was probably not even represented, and all positions were variants of the second, depending upon the degree of error the individual believed it necessary to admit for himself or attach to others. Thus the polemics were limited to a quarrel about *how bad* matters were, with the implied alternatives, not the *status quo* or reform, but reform or dissolution.

The most extreme critics were two members of C. F. W. Walther's congregation at Dresden, Spröde and Marbach. Spröde had shown some signs of personal animosity toward Walther already at the time both were in Perry County. The New York leader drove matters so far that Walther refused him unqualified absolution, an

[25] Naturally not all the various positions adopted by individuals and the questions that were raised can be described in detail. Practically every reference given in those portions of the study dealing with the religious controversy could be cited here. However, the following are representative: Minutes of a conference at Dresden, Perry County, Mo., March, 1840, Marbach to Stübel, n. d. [November, 1839—1841], Bound MSS., VI, C. H. I.; C. F. W. Walther to O. H. Walther, May 4, 1840, Nachrichten an unsere Nachkommen, MSS., C. H. I.; Schieferdecker, *op. cit.*, 18—19.

action Walther later repudiated. Because of Spröde's violent temper, Walther refused to deal with him except by correspondence. Spröde reacted by nurturing a bitter enmity toward Walther and by forcing him to vacate the house he was occupying on "Johnson's Farm," Spröde's property.[26]

In the case of Marbach, there is no evidence of such personal issues. He was in all probability a conscientious objector to the existing state of affairs. His spirit was crushed by a sense of guilt, doubts as to his spiritual life, and the shattering of his dreams and ambitions. Marbach was deeply disturbed, groping for security and certainty, trying to regain confidence in himself and in some form of religious system. His extremism in some points was mainly a reflection of his own remorse. Meanwhile, he confined his attacks, however sharp, to doctrinal questions and to matters of polity.[27] In such legitimate criticism he enjoyed the substantial agreement of Bürger and the more qualified support of Barthel.[28] These three men finally became the nucleus of that group in the colonies which generally adopted the more extreme views on the evils of the emigration and its consequences, and gradually began to organize and formulate such views into reasonably clear statements.

For a long time the Marbach group and Spröde encountered no effective opposition. Their natural antagonists, the pastors, were themselves too insecure and confused to offer cogent counterstatements. On the practical question of what course to pursue, Löber, Keyl, and Gruber attained a measure of agreement.[29] Generally they adopted as their policy a kind of passive resistance, the underlying strategy of which was to admit only as much as was absolutely necessary (or not even that much) and to ostracize from their circle

---

[26] C. F. W. Walther to O. H. Walther, May 4, 1840, C. F. W. Walther to Spröde, n. d. [May—December, 1841], MSS., C. H. I.; Minutes of a conference at Dresden, Perry County, Mo., March, 1840, and "Explanation of the Minutes," probably written by Marbach, Bound MSS., VI, C. H. I.; C. F. W. Walther to O. Fürbringer, April 14, 1840, in M. Günther, *op. cit.*, 41—42.

[27] C. F. W. Walther to O. H. Walther, May 4, 1840, MS., C. H. I.; Marbach to — ("Hochgeehrter Herr Geheimrath"), May 8, 1840, May 10, 1841, Bound MSS., VI, C. H. I.

[28] C. F. W. Walther to O. H. Walther, May 4, 1840, MS., C. H. I.; E. M. Bürger, Selbstbiographie, 129—134, MS., E. J. Buerger Papers, Ellicottville, N. Y.; Bürger, *op. cit.*, 14—41; Minutes of a conference at Dresden, Perry County, Mo., March, 1840; Bound MSS., VI, C. H. I.

[29] C. F. W. Walther to O. H. Walther, May 4, 1840, MS., C. H. I.

those who failed to support them, e. g., Bürger.[30] In view of his later eminence it is interesting to speculate whether the same fate would not have overtaken C. F. W. Walther, who also had not attained full agreement with the others even while co-operating with them at the level of practical politics, had he not been removed from the scene of active controversy by a serious illness of almost a year, from 1840 to 1841. At times he was forced to suspend his ministerial activities and to seek rest and recuperation in the home of his sister, Amalia Walther Keyl.[31]

By early 1841 matters were approaching a crisis. The colonies were on the verge of dissolution both as religious and civil communities. The Marbach-Spröde faction had refused to take part in the religious life of the Perry County settlement for about a year and had conducted separatist devotional meetings of its own. The pastors were unable to cope with the situation, and the doubts and scruples of their opponents were shared by a majority of the people. In St. Louis, O. H. Walther had died on January 21, and the congregation, still formally unincorporated, was left without a pastor for months when C. F. W. Walther tentatively declined the call. Some of the candidates had left or were leaving, just as Vehse and a few others of the more capable men had done. Almost the sole mitigating circumstance in the rather hopeless outlook of the Saxons was that, under the stimulus of men like Bürger, discussions were still being carried on between the various groups.[32]

In March of 1841 one such conference was held at Dresden, Perry County, with Löber, Keyl, Gruber, Bürger, Marbach, Brohm, and Wege present. A protracted exchange of views ensued during which Marbach gave expression to his now familiar negative outlook, climaxed by the contention that there really "was no church among them." This decisive statement forced certain of the other

---

30 E. M. Bürger, Selbstbiographie, 134—140, MS., E. J. Buerger Papers, Ellicottville, N. Y.; Bürger, *op. cit.*, 42—43.

31 O. Fürbringer to C. F. W. Walther, Jan. 9, 1841, MS., C. H. I.; Erstes Protokollbuch, April 26, 1841, MS., Trinity Church Records, St. Louis.

32 Winter to Guericke *et al.*, April 28, 1841, *Zeitschrift für die gesammte lutherische Theologie und Kirche*, II, No. 3, pp. 116—132; G. H. Löber to G. F. Löber, Aug. 26, 1841, in Löber-Eichenberg (ed.), "Ein Briefwechsel," *Mitteilungen . . . Kahla,* VII, 184—190; C. F. W. Walther to O. H. Walther, May 4, 1840, G. H. Löber to Demme, Aug. 2, 1841, MSS., C. H. I.; Marbach to — ("Geehrte Frau Präsidentin"), n. d., Marbach to Stübel, n. d. [November, 1839—1841], Bound MSS., VI, C. H. I.; Bürger, *op. cit.*, 41.

men to reveal what their position was, even when they could not clarify why they assumed it. Löber, Keyl, and Gruber could not prove Marbach wrong, but refused to agree with him. Brohm agreed with neither side, wanted to share the standpoint of the pastors, but actually shared the doubts of Marbach. Wege adopted Marbach's views unqualifiedly. Bürger went a step farther, not only expressing agreement with Marbach, but carrying this agreement into practical application, with the announcement that he was formally severing all relations with the ecclesiastical life of the community. The seriousness of the dissension disrupting the Saxon group can be gauged from the confused incompatibility evident in this conference.[33] Even then at least two other opinions were not represented, namely Spröde's and C. F. W. Walther's. However, Spröde's extremism could well be dispensed with, and Walther's position was soon to become evident.

It was in these dark days that C. F. W. Walther came forward with a series of propositions which were to prove the fundamental factor in saving the colonies. The idea he advanced was by no means a new one, for it was contained in more than embryonic state in Vehse's writings. Walther was ready to admit his indebtedness to the Dresden archivist. Keyl and Bürger joined in this acknowledgment.[34] Later writers with a less meticulous sense of fairness, however, have given Vehse little credit. It is not difficult, of course, to find "errors" or "un-Lutheran" points in Vehse's statements. That type of criticism was indulged in already by Rudelbach in 1840.[35] But this fact cannot be made the excuse for a presentation which confines itself to pointing out such features of Vehse's work, while slighting or even ignoring Vehse's very real contribution. Such presentations are perhaps motivated by an admiration of Walther, which leads to a deliberate or unconscious unfairness that Walther himself would have repudiated.

The ideas Walther enunciated constituted his first real contribution in the field of religious thought and ecclesiastical polity.

---

[33] Minutes of a conference at Dresden, Perry County, Mo., March, 1840, and "Explanation of the Minutes," probably written by Marbach, Bound MSS., VI, C.H.I.; Winter to Guericke *et al.*, April 28, 1841, *Zeitschrift für die gesammte lutherische Theologie und Kirche,* II, No. 3, pp. 116—132.

[34] Köstering, *Auswanderung,* 43; Keyl, *op. cit.,* 17—18; Bürger, *op. cit.,* 14.

[35] Rudelbach, "Die Stephan'sche Auswanderung nach Amerika," *Zeitschrift für die gesammte lutherische Theologie und Kirche,* I, No. 3, pp. 133—144.

The fact that his views attained lasting importance invites a portrayal which leads to the misconception that C. F. W. Walther attained religious and intellectual maturity with little or no assistance.[36] However, Walther was too big a man to be incapable of further development. The Walther of the emigration years — including 1841 — was definitely not the Walther of succeeding decades, and it is no tribute to the man to picture him so. What Walther actually accomplished in 1841 was, first of all, that he gave a new direction to a line of thought which had already been laid down by Vehse; that he eliminated a few of its extremes and thus developed a position far more acceptable to the reasonable elements in both major factions; and that he defended this theological standpoint, and its practical application to life in the communities, with clarity and ability.

When Walther received the impetus toward his distinctive theories is not entirely clear. Usually it is said that he arrived at his convictions as a result of an intensive study of Luther during the months of his convalescence at Keyl's.[37] This case constitutes the second time in Walther's life that Luther's writings are introduced by his biographers at a crucial moment to help him out of some spiritual dilemma. Marbach, Bürger and others were studying Luther; it is entirely possible that Walther was doing the same.[38] But in Walther's case results were very different. Already before the middle of 1840, during his period of deepest despondency, Walther had displayed a balance not usual among the disputants when he remarked, despite his own views on the emigration, that to *require* people to say now that the emigration was "devilish" was just as wrong as it previously had been to call it divine. Even at this relatively early date he inclined to the theory of the sovereignty of the congregation.[39]

Theologically, Walther's position was based upon an elaboration

---

[36] Köstering, *Auswanderung*, 38—39; Hochstetter, *op. cit.*, 20—21, 29, 72; Schieferdecker, "Synodalrede," *Verhandlungen . . . des westlichen Distrikts der . . . Synode von Missouri . . . 1856*, p. 7; Th. Buenger, "Festival Address . . . Commemorating the Centennial of . . . Concordia Seminary," *Concordia Theological Monthly*, X, 607.

[37] Köstering, *Auswanderung*, 40—41.

[38] C. F. W. Walther to O. H. Walther, May 4, 1840, MS., C. H. I.; E. M. Bürger, Selbstbiographie, 132—134, MS., E. J. Buerger Papers, Ellicottville, N. Y.; Bürger, *op. cit.*, 19.

[39] C. F. W. Walther to O. H. Walther, May 4, 1840, MS., C. H. I.

of Vehse's position that the immigrants were a group of Christians and by that simple fact "a church." Vehse had used his thesis chiefly as an offensive weapon against the pretensions of the episcopacy and its clergy. Walther, while agreeing with Vehse, stressed rather the constructive effect of the conclusions to be drawn. His aim was not annihilation — either of his opponents, as it had been Vehse's, or of the colonies, as it now was Marbach's — but pacification. Vehse's program had failed. Marbach's (and Spröde's), however, was well on the way toward success. It was abundantly clear to the young pastor that by adopting hierarchical ideas of the nature of the Church, insisting upon theories of the episcopal succession, overemphasizing the office of the ministry, or indulging a spiritual hypochondria to the point where it induced a verbal flagellantism in the group, it was possible to produce a spasm of ecclesiastical nihilism during which the Saxon colonies would, in fact, die a convulsive death.

Walther was not interested in helping to produce such an outcome; he sought just the opposite — a set of ideas which would reunite and stabilize the colonies. Therefore he argued that even when all the faults of the emigration were granted, such error did not *per se* demonstrate the absence (although admittedly the adulteration) of Christianity. Indeed, the evidence was all to the contrary; it seemed demonstrable that there were many sincere Christians among the colonists. It was vital to remember, furthermore, that belonging to an organized church body did not constitute one a Christian, but that a body of Christians could organize at any time to constitute a church. "A church," the word which seemed to have become the shibboleth of the controversy — "a church" was still extant among them. If this were so, they must possess all the rights of such a body and could exercise all its functions; specifically, they could call pastors and teachers and provide for the administration of the Sacraments and other rites normally connected with the existence of an organized congregation, or a "church." In practical application it meant the identification of the characteristics and powers of a congregation and "*the* church." [40] This was a modest

---

[40] A number of preliminary drafts of theses by C. F. W. Walther, similar to those presented at the Altenburg Debate, have been preserved. They show how fundamental were the principles stated above in formulating Walther's opinion during this time. MSS., C. H. I. See also Köstering, ***Auswanderung*,** 41—52.

platform when contrasted with the bombastic claims of being "the church" which characterized the period of the emigration. But it was an ambitious platform when contrasted with the claims of those who said the *Gesellschaft* was nothing.

Walther was aided in securing the acceptance of his views by the fact that he had the opportunity of stating them under rather dramatic circumstances. The occasion was a formal discussion arranged between the opposing groups. Walther was chosen to represent the moderates, Marbach the extreme faction. Neither of these two men could reflect all shadings of opinion prevalent among those who regarded them as their spokesmen, but views in the colonies tended more and more to focus upon a moderate and a radical position, with Walther and Marbach carrying the burden of the debate.

The event took place in the log-cabin "College" at Altenburg on April 15 and 21, 1841, in the presence of as large a group as could be crowded into the single room of the building. The sessions at times were stormy, especially when Bürger was accused — unjustly, he claimed — of calling the Eucharist a "comedy." The accusation was sustained by the other pastors on the statement of two laymen; and, in the uproar which followed, Bürger at first could not even succeed in gaining the floor. By the time he did, it no longer was possible for him to efface the impression which had been made.[41]

However, Marbach and Walther were heard. Marbach's line of argument is familiar enough. Walther's has just been described, and a further discussion of it is unnecessary, except to state the separate points upon which Walther based his appeal.

I

> The true Church, in the most real and most perfect sense, is the totality (Gesamtheit) of all true believers, who from the beginning to the end of the world from among all peoples and tongues have been called and sanctified by the Holy Spirit through the Word. And since God alone knows

---

[41] Winter to Guericke *et al.*, April 28, 1841, *Zeitschrift für die gesammte lutherische Theologie und Kirche,* II, No. 3, pp. 116—132; Excerpts from G. H. Löber's diary, April 15, 21, 1841, MS., C. H. I.; E. M. Bürger, Selbstbiographie, 134—140, MS., E. J. Buerger Papers, Ellicottville, N. Y.; Bürger, *op. cit.*, 42—43; Schieferdecker, "Synodalrede," *Verhandlungen . . . des westlichen Distrikts der . . . Synode von Missouri . . . 1856,* pp. 7—8.

these true believers (2 Tim. 2: 19), the Church is also called invisible. No one belongs to this true Church who is not spiritually united with Christ, for it is the spiritual body of Jesus Christ.

II

The name of the true Church belongs also to all those visible companies of men among whom God's Word is purely taught and the holy Sacraments are administered according to the institution of Christ. True, in this Church there are godless men, hypocrites, and heretics, but they are not true members of it, nor do they constitute the Church.

III

The name Church, and, in a certain sense, the name true Church, belongs also to those visible companies of men who have united under the confession of a falsified faith and therefore have incurred the guilt of a partial departure from the truth; provided they possses so much of God's Word and the holy Sacraments in purity that children of God may thereby be born. When such companies are called true churches, it is not the intention to state that they are faithful, but only that they are real churches as opposed to all worldly organizations (Gemeinschaften).

IV

The name Church is not improperly applied to heterodox companies, but according to the manner of speech of the Word of God itself. It is also not immaterial that this high name is allowed to such communions, for out of this follows: —

1. That members also of such companies may be saved; for without the Church there is no salvation.

V

2. The outward separation of a heterodox company from an orthodox Church is not necessarily a separation from the universal Christian Church nor a relapse into heathenism and does not yet deprive that company of the name Church.

VI

3. Even heterodox companies have church power; even among them the goods of the Church may be validly administered, the ministry established, the Sacraments validly administered, and the keys of the kingdom of heaven exercised.

VII

4. Even heterodox companies are not to be dissolved, but reformed.

VIII

> The orthodox Church is chiefly to be judged by the common, orthodox, public confession to which its members acknowledge and confess themselves to be pledged.[42]

Marbach was no mean disputant, but Walther proved to be a match for him. While Marbach was not, properly speaking, convinced by Walther's argumentation, he at least was silenced. However, the great majority of the audience, and the colonists generally, were won over by Walther's presentation of the case, while the pastors, Löber, Gruber, Keyl, and C. F. W. Walther, were now more united than at any time since late 1839.[43] If there was any single factor which saved the colonies from complete dissolution and from the corrosive forces of further internal controversy, it was the Altenburg Debate. The principles laid down by Walther on this occasion were basically those which he later developed in his famous writings: *Die rechte Gestalt einer vom Staate unabhängigen evangelisch-lutherischen Ortsgemeinde,* and *Die Stimme unserer Kirche in der Frage von Kirche und Amt.* Furthermore, these same principles constituted the broad outlines upon which the majority of the colonists now reached agreement and upon which they built their congregations and the larger synodical organization that claims them as their nucleus.

The victory in the Altenburg Debate laid the foundations for the ecclesiastical edifice which Walther was to spend his life in building. And while superlatives must be used with caution in the life of the man who has been called "the outstanding figure in the history of American Lutheranism," this contribution may well be called his greatest, insofar as it was the *sine qua non* of all that was to follow in his eventful life as leader of the Saxons and of the Missouri Synod. For this was what he now became, the leader of the clergy and of the colonists in their subsequent development. Other factors, such as his transfer to St. Louis, were also instrumental in changing his station. But his prestige rested upon the

---

[42] The above translation is from Polack, *Walther,* 49—50. There is another translation in *The Concordia Cyclopedia,* 15. The theses are given in the original German in Köstering, *Auswanderung,* 51—52. See also *ibid.,* 41—50.

[43] Winter to Guericke *et al.,* April 28, 1841, *Zeitschrift für die gesammte lutherische Theologie und Kirche,* II, No. 3, pp. 116—132; Nachrichten an unsere Nachkommen, Excerpts from G. H. Löber's diary, April 15, 21, 1841, MSS., C. H. I.; Keyl, *op. cit.,* 17—18; Schieferdecker, *op. cit.,* 20—21.

fact that he emerged from the chaos of two years of controversy with the most lucid presentation of what the majority of the people felt to be a Scriptural solution for their emotional-doctrinal dilemna and the only plan for a church polity which was workable under the circumstances. These achievements raised him immeasurably in the eyes of all of his associates.

Walther's own character and capabilities, like his theories of church government, at least in their practical application, were still in the formative stage. Both the man and his ideas were to experience numerous modifications and considerable growth before they attained their full stature, but they had produced their first important results. Even Walther realized this, and, feeling that he had now attained clarity within himself, as well as in relation to his colleagues and the people, he accepted the call to St. Louis and became his brother's successor. Walther left for St. Louis the next day after the conclusion of the debate, that is, on April 22, 1841. Before leaving, he saw Marbach and reaffirmed that cordial relations with him had not been destroyed. On that occasion Marbach said he was satisfied that Walther's position on Church and Sacraments was essentially correct.[44] Walther also tried to see Spröde at this time, but was unsuccessful and had to leave for St. Louis without having reached an understanding with him. With this step the activity for which he became known and the rise of the Saxon colonies to national importance begin.[45]

Once Walther had established the fundamental premise: There is a church among us, and secured its acceptance by a majority of the colonists, other problems could be adjusted with comparative ease. It became far less important than formerly to determine the exact degree of complicity in, and responsibility for, the unhappy events of the Stephanite era. Again, whether the pastors *were* pastors was not significant if the congregations in their own right could bestow such office upon them. Other adjustments of attitude and polity resulted. Theories could be changed suddenly, but the resultant modification in policies and methods of procedure — in short, the emergence from years of confusion and chaos — required time. The first reaction was a tremendous relief that warfare was now

---

[44] Winter to Guericke *et al.*, April 28, 1841, *Zeitschrift für die gesammte lutherische Theologie und Kirche*, II, No. 3, pp. 116—132.

[45] C. F. W. Walther to Spröde, n. d. [May—December, 1841], MS., C. H. I.

over. But demobilization was a slow process. A period of transition was necessary before progress could begin. Even Walther had some trying times with himself and his congregation, and felt despondent at times.[46]

There are numerous indications that there was by no means perfect unanimity among, or equanimity in the minds of, the leaders. Confessions were still much in vogue. Keyl finally completed his afore-mentioned "Bekenntnisse," dated "end of August, 1841," and sent them to Rudelbach, who printed them, with a foreword of his own, in the *Zeitschrift*.[47] Even before this Keyl had written letters of apology for his association with Stephan and for all he considered wrong in the immigration. These statements were addressed to his former congregation in Germany (April 27, 1841), to his fellow emigrants, and to all whom he had offended.[48] Pastor Löber's letter to Duke Joseph had been delivered by G. F. Löber, and after the conclusion of the debate the Perry County pastor was finally assured of his former sovereign's good graces and good wishes in his new field of activity.[49] Gruber, who had also written to the duke, had received a similar answer already by the time the debate took place.[50]

Some things, of course, the pastors would never admit. On August 26, 1841, Löber wrote to his brother, and in condemning Vehse's book, which had appeared the previous year, he said: "I must also declare it as downright incorrect and untrue that we pastors were acquainted with Stephan's hierarchical plans already in Germany and afterwards in St. Louis." [51] Such an assertion was particularly ill-advised in view of the actual facts, as described above, both in Germany and in St. Louis, and Löber's own damaging signature, together with that of his colleagues, to the declaration that the establishment of the episcopacy had long been resolved

---

46 Winter to Guericke *et al.*, April 28, 1841, *Zeitschrift für die gesammte lutherische Theologie und Kirche*, II, No. 3, pp. 116—132; Gönner to C. F. W. Walther, May 12, 1841, MS., C. H. I.

47 "Offene Bekenntnisse des vormaligen Pfarrers Keyl," *Zeitschrift für die gesammte lutherische Theologie und Kirche*, III, No. 1, pp. 94—114.

48 *Ibid.*

49 G. F. Löber to G. H. Löber, Aug. 13, 1841, G. H. Löber to G. F. Löber, n. d. [1842?], in Löber-Eichenberg (ed.), "Ein Briefwechsel," *Mitteilungen . . . Kahla*, VII, 180—184, 190; K. Gruber, "Ehrengedächtniss des . . . Gotthold Heinrich Löber," *Der Lutheraner*, VI, 146.

50 G. H. Löber to G. F. Löber, Aug. 26, 1841, in Löber-Eichenberg (ed.), "Ein Briefwechsel," *Mitteilungen . . . Kahla*, VII, 184—190.

51 *Ibid.*

among them. Löber finally sent off his "Lossagung vom Stephanismus," or Renunciation of Stephanism, on April 29, little more than a week after the Altenburg Debate. The explicit instructions which he gave his brother-in-law, to whom the document was entrusted, provided that only a few close friends were to see it, and sought to prevent its circulation or publication. None the less, it became one of the most widely circulated statements regarding the emigration.[52] Winter's letter, frequently quoted in these pages, was written during the last days of April, just after the conclusion of the debate; it also contained qualified confessions.[53] Klügel and a few others carried on the Spröde-Marbach-Bürger tradition, and Wege still wished to return to Germany.[54] The desire to make a further joint declaration in the *Pilger aus Sachsen* could not be realized as late as August, 1841, because there still was not sufficient unanimity to do so.[55] But Brohm did draw up a "confession" for insertion in this same publication.[56]

Meanwhile, however, as an aftermath of the years of bickering, several of the most troublesome characters removed themselves and the disturbing element of their presence from the scene. Notable among those who left were Marbach, Spröde, and Bürger. Spröde merely moved to St. Louis, where he continued to cause trouble; but at least the Perry County settlements were relieved of him. Bürger, whose ideas were still extremely indistinct, who was unable to agree with the new standpoint, and who was still not able to convince anyone else of the contrary, was finally dismissed by three of his remaining five members — in writing on April 23, 1841, and orally in a stormy session some time later. After the conclusion of the debate,

---

[52] *Ibid.;* Excerpts from G. H. Löber's diary, April 29, 1841, G. H. Löber to Demme, Aug. 2, 1841, G. H. Löber's Introduction to "Lossagung vom Stephanismus," MSS., C. H. I.; G. H. Löber to Guericke, April 28, 1841, in *Zeitschrift für die gesammte lutherische Theologie und Kirche,* III, No. 3, pp. 111—115; Keyl, *op. cit.,* 1; K. Gruber, "Ehrengedächtniss des . . . Gotthold Heinrich Löber," *Der Lutheraner,* VI, 146.

[53] Winter to Guericke *et al.,* April 28, 1841, *Zeitschrift für die gesammte lutherische Theologie und Kirche,* II, No. 3, pp. 116—132. See also Winter, "Berichtigung," *ibid.,* III, No. 4, p. 171.

[54] G. H. Löber to G. F. Löber, Aug. 26, 1841, in Löber-Eichenberg (ed.), "Ein Briefwechsel," *Mitteilungen . . . Kahla,* VII, 184—190; Wege to Marbach, Sept. 12, 1841, Bound MSS., VI, C. H. I.

[55] G. H. Löber to G. F. Löber, Aug. 26, 1841, in Löber-Eichenberg (ed.), "Ein Briefwechsel," *Mitteilungen . . . Kahla,* VII, 184—190.

[56] Erstes Protokollbuch, Nov. 15, 1841, MS., Trinity Church Records, St. Louis.

Bürger returned to St. Louis, where he was detained for several months by illness and business affairs. He then left Missouri with Marbach and Stärtzell, intending to return to Germany.[57] In the case of both Marbach and Bürger, it was their lack of equilibrium rather than their maliciousness that made them dangerous to the settlements at a time when these required, above all, stability. Stephan's first lieutenant had become suspicious of everything and everyone that seemed too firmly established or too complacent, and he had come to adopt a purely negative attitude.

For some time before he actually did so in 1841, Marbach had been turning over in his mind the idea of returning to Germany. At first, after the deposition of Stephan and the abysmal failure of the emigration, in which Marbach had placed his highest hopes for a brilliant career, the thought of facing his former associates was unbearable to him. Only in the late months of 1839 and in 1840 was he persuaded by his wife's urgings to write to some of his friends in Germany again. During the next year and a half he gradually resumed his contacts in Saxony and made cautious overtures to government officials to determine what he might expect his political and professional status to be when he returned — a wise precaution in view of the difficulties he later experienced on this score. Finally, Marbach appealed directly to the king and evidently felt sufficiently encouraged to venture back into his former sphere of activity.[58]

Accordingly, after the Altenburg Debate, where his views failed to carry conviction even with himself, Marbach determined to follow both his personal inclinations and his wife's preference by returning to his homeland. Although he liked the United States well enough, the Doctor of Laws had been making a very meager living at farming, and the practice of law in America was too different from practice in Saxony for him to step into it readily. The emigration had by this time cost the lives of two more Marbach chil-

[57] J. K. A. Höhne and J. G. Höhne to their brother, Sept. 26, 1841, quoted in *Die Ameise,* Jan. 10, 1842; Winter to Guericke *et al.,* April 28, 1841, *Zeitschrift für die gesammte lutherische Theologie und Kirche,* II, No. 3, pp. 116 to 132; Bürger, *op. cit.,* 43—46.

[58] Stübel to Vehse *et al.,* Sept. 12, 1839, Marbach to Fredrick Augustus II, May 10, 1841, Marbach to — ("Hochgeehrter Herr Geheimrath"), May 8, 1840, May 10, 1841, Marbach to — ("Geehrte Frau Präsidentin"), n. d., Marbach to Stübel, n. d. [November, 1839—1841], Marbach to Brunner, n. d., Brunner to Marbach, Dec. 23, 1841, Mellwitz to Brunner, Dec. 24, 1841, Bound MSS., VI, C. H. I.; C. F. W. Walther to O. H. Walther, May 4, 1840, Delitzsch to F. W. Barthel, Dec. 8, 1839, MSS., C. H. I.

dren. Thus, within the space of only a few years the unfortunate mother of this family, who was seriously opposed to the adventure from the outset, had to sacrifice five of her children to it. It was no wonder she wished to return; it was a wonder she retained her sanity. The Marbachs had been selling some of their effects ever since January, 1841. Although some things could not be disposed of until they were already back in Germany, they succeeded in winding up most of their business affairs within a few months. By the end of August they were leaving Perry County, and by the middle of September, Marbach, fortified with a letter of introduction from Spröde and in the company of the Bürger and Stärtzell families, began the homeward journey via Buffalo and New York City.[59]

The improvement in the religious atmosphere of the settlements over the former legalistic, schismatic Stephanism, is revealed in the relations between the clergy and candidates, who remained, and Marbach, whom many of them had bitterly opposed. There was no hard feeling, and several of them wrote him very cordial letters just before his departure, or saw him in person. In Germany, Marbach seems to have succeeded even in re-establishing friendly relations with the Stephan family. He again entered the service of the Saxon government. Walther renewed the intimate relationship which had existed between them when he returned on a visit to Germany in 1851—1852. In 1860 Walther was present at the death (June 6) and burial of his "dearest friend in Germany" and "one in his lifetime frequently misunderstood." [60]

With the departure of Marbach the Saxon immigration lost one

---

[59] Dathe to Marbach, Jan. 16, 1841, Marbach to Stübel, n. d. [November 1839—1841], Marbach to — ("Hochgeehrter Herr Geheimrath"), May 8, 1840, Spröde to Evers, Aug. 30, 1841, Receipt for $16.00, J. F. Bünger to Marbach, Sept. 3, 1841, Bound MSS., VI, C. H. I.; G. H. Löber to G. F. Löber, Aug. 26, 1841, in Löber-Eichenberg (ed.), "Ein Briefwechsel," *Mitteilungen . . . Kahla,* VII, 184—190; J. K. A. Höhne and J. G. Höhne to their brother, Sept. 26, 1841, quoted in *Die Ameise,* Jan. 10, 1842; Ahlfeld, "Grabrede . . . dem . . . Franz Adolph Marbach . . . gehalten," *Der Lutheraner,* XVII, 10. See also *ibid.,* XLI, 38; L. Fuerbringer, *Persons and Events,* 93.

[60] C. F. W. Walther, "Editorielle Correspondenz," *Lehre und Wehre,* VI, 194; C. F. W. Walther, "Reisebericht des Redakteurs," *Der Lutheraner,* VIII, 105; Ahlfeld, "Grabrede . . . dem Franz Adolph Marbach . . . gehalten," *ibid.,* XVII, 9—10; Keyl to Marbach, Aug. 26, 1841, Julie Stephan to Marbach, April 14, 1843, Brohm to Marbach, Sept. 2, 1841, Wege to Marbach, Sept. 12, 1841, Bound MSS., VI, C. H. I.,; Winter to Guericke *et al.,* April 28, 1841, *Zeitschrift für die gesammte lutherische Theologie und Kirche,* II, No. 3, pp. 116—132.

of its most colorful and typical figures. He had shared each of the successive phases in the development of the Saxon community: Stephanism and religious zealotry; ambitious planning, unsound finances, and economic failure; and, in the latter years, emotional self-recrimination, and the tension of serious religious controversy. Marbach's elimination of himself as a factor in the future of the settlements is strikingly symbolical and marks the end of a period. The negative phase of the movement was past; the positive was beginning; the way was open for constructive development. While that development has been examined closely in the preparation of the present study, tracing it here would carry the discussion beyond the proper scope of this volume. However, the Saxon immigration does deserve a closing word on its ultimate significance.

Within a relatively short time the Saxons, much the wiser for their harrowing experiences, again constituted a united, compact, energetic group, once more looking forward to rendering spiritual service to their fellow immigrants, rather than looking backward at the tragic interlude of the episcopacy. More than that, they had been purged of their fantastic notions of exclusiveness and semi-autonomy, and while they certainly were not ready to conform to their environment, they were prepared to integrate themselves with it. Stephan and what he had stood for were gone but not forgotten. The Codes and what they had stood for were not gone, but were forgotten. Although sacrificing no element of their Lutheran theology, the Saxons nevertheless began their evolution of a thoroughly democratic form of ecclesiastical organization.[61] This may seem a common idea in American Protestantism today. But to the recent German immigrant of the 1840's, habituated to the episcopal polity or to the paternalism and institutionalism of the state churches in his homeland, this idea was a sharp departure from accustomed habits of thought. It is worth noting that these new, hard-won conclusions of the Saxons established principles well

---

[61] The question of whether the product of this process — that is, polity in the Missouri Synod — ever was completely "democratic," and whether such impulses in this direction as are to be found in the Missouri Synod were entirely, partly, or inconsiderably influenced by the environment of political "democracy" in contemporary America — these questions are taken up in the latter chapters of Mundinger's *Government in the Missouri Synod*. However, the contrast between the autocratic — or, at best, aristocratic — rule of the Stephanite period and the large measure of truly popular control which now developed, is so pronounced as to make all other distinctions of secondary importance for the present study.

suited to the area in which they were to operate. On this basis the Lutheran Church had finally come to Missouri and to the West. And, thanks in part to these principles, it had come to stay.

The achievements of the Saxons during the next few years are a bright closing chapter in their history. In spite of the fact that almost all denominations were already strongly represented in Missouri when they came, the Lutherans experienced a steady growth which soon put them on equal terms with all but the largest church bodies. In the years from 1841 to 1847 four of the original Perry County settlements survived as communities and parishes. They succeeded in maintaining the "College" until 1843. Then the St. Louis group assured the venture of sufficient support to guarantee its continuance not as a *Gymnasium,* but rather as a theological seminary. In this, as well as in other respects, the center of gravity in the Saxon movement shifted to the colony in St. Louis. There, under the leadership of C. F. W. Walther, a strong congregation was built up, which began establishing branch schools and churches even before 1847. In 1844 *Der Lutheraner* was founded by Walther as the organ of the Saxons in defending and publicizing an aggressive, confessional Lutheranism. It is still in publication. Largely through the *Lutheraner* it became possible within less than three years to bring together several elements into a single synodical organization. These elements included not only the original Saxon pastors and candidates, who were by now serving scattered parishes from Missouri to New York City, but also active and capable German missionaries, such as Wyneken, Sihler, and the emissaries of a prominent German clergyman, Wilhelm Löhe. Accordingly the Evangelical Lutheran Synod of Missouri, Ohio, and Other States was founded in Chicago on April 26, 1847.

In 1947, when the representatives of this church body again assembled in Chicago for its centennial convention, it was overwhelmingly the largest Lutheran synod to have developed in the United States. In size the organization was slightly surpassed only by the United Lutheran Church, which was a merger of forty-five synods. The more than one and a half million members of the Missouri Synod constituted between a fourth and a third of the total membership of Lutheran church bodies in the United States. It had 4,215 clergymen actively engaged in its 5,685 congregations, and carried on synodical work calling for an outlay in excess of

$10,000,000. A distinctive feature of the group was its educational system. In this field about 2,800 teachers were serving 1,200 parish schools. Thirteen colleges and seminaries for the training of church workers were maintained in the United States and Canada, six in foreign fields. A large publishing house in St. Louis served as a nerve center for the Church's educational, administrative, and propaganda activities, not the least of which were the fifteen periodicals designed for the needs and interests of the group. The statistics of mere mass may, however, be less important for illustrating the vitality of this church body than the fact that the tenth decade of its history (1937—1947) showed a larger percentage of growth than any other in the preceding fifty years.[62]

But the contributions of the Saxons as a group, and the ultimate importance of the synodical organization which they were instrumental in founding, were not primarily quantitative, but qualitative. This fact was strikingly illuminated already twenty-five years ago by the observations of H. H. Maurer. His words have lost none of their validity as a mature appraisal of the group he was evaluating, although it is necessary to recall that he wrote in the terms of a generation which had been chauvinistically concerned about "hyphenate Americanism" and had put the safety catch of the quota system on the door of American immigration. Despite the physical changes of the intervening years in completing the transformation of this immigrant Church into an indigenous institution, Maurer could say even then:

> It should be appreciated that . . . the group [the Missouri Synod] is a culture-group of no small significance. It is by far the most compact German culture-group in the United States . . . It is perhaps the only separate culture-group which has a perfect organism for self-perpetuation on such a high and well-rationalized plane. It is an exceedingly compact and well-knit body. It is perhaps needless to add that it has little or nothing in common with any other German culture-group, for . . . it was 'made in America.' . . . The [group] mind, then . . . if it is 'from Missouri' [i. e., the Missouri Synod] is not necessarily German. . . .
>
> We are here in the presence of a sectionalism which springs from the subsoil of historical experience. . . . They [the Saxons] were the pioneers of fundamentalism and the founders of a mighty church in America. . . . The conserva-

---

62 *Statistical Yearbook . . . 1947,* pp. 139—141, 147, 179, 193, 195, 200.

> tion of German-language nationalism has never been its aim. . . . A large and fairly compact moral block in the Middle West is being dominated or influenced today by the pattern here discussed, and that block, the German, the Swedish, the Norwegian Protestant farmer element, is pivotal in relation to the Middle West; and so is the Middle West to the nation. Today the gravitation of that block, its leverage, concerns the statesman and the politician.[63]

As a group the Saxons merged their identity with that of the larger organization. But as an influence they remained so distinct that the term "Missourian," which was first used as the designation for a religious group in reference to them, soon came, by transfer, to be applied to the entire synod. At the meeting which marked the centenary of this synod, there was an insistent demand for adopting a name less provincial in its connotations. It was felt that the title "Evangelical Lutheran Synod of Missouri, Ohio, and Other States" was not representative of a Church which now covered not only the forty-eight States, but many foreign fields as well. With an unintentional touch of ironic humor, the members of the body eventually decided upon a new name, "The Lutheran Church — Missouri Synod," which was geographically more limited than the old. But in so doing they had, with a conscious sense of historic values, retained that part of their name which reflects, as no other can, both the origin and the emphasis of their Church. For the fact remains that the Saxons had made Missouri its cradle and its capital.

---

[63] Maurer, "Studies in the Sociology of Religion," and "The Political Attitudes of the Lutheran Parish in America," *American Journal of Sociology,* XXX, 550, 670—671, XXXI, 49—50, 498, XXXIII, 569.

APPENDIX A
LISTS AND TABLES

INTRODUCTION

The data given in the appended lists of colonists and the accompanying tables based upon them have been carefully checked against all sources known to be extant at the present time. No contemporary lists made by the Saxons nor any compiled subsequently have been as accurate or complete as those given here.[1] Actually, a comprehensive list of all the colonists has not previously existed; all such lists have been fragmentary.[2] Individual points of

[1] The information in the Lists and Tables has been obtained from the following sources: The manifests of the vessels which brought the immigrants, i. e., List . . . of . . . passengers . . . *Copernicus* . . . New Orleans, List of Passengers . . . *Olbers* . . . New Orleans, List of Passengers . . . *Republik* . . . New Orleans, Report of . . . Passengers . . . *Johann Georg* . . . New Orleans, MSS., C. H. I.; Passenger lists of the *Olbers, Johann Georg, Amalia, Republik,* and *Copernicus,* Bound MSS., I, C. H. I.; Passenger list of the *Amalia,* Bound MSS., 13, C. H. I.; Passenger list of the *Amalia* in Sauer to Marbach, July 1, 1839, Bound MSS., Invoices, C. H. I.; Passenger list of the *Amalia* in G. Günther, *op. cit.,* 123; A list of emigrants by E. M. Bürger, n. d., A list of emigrants by G. H. Löber, July 8, 1838, Anmerkungen to this list of emigrants by G. H. Löber, July 14, 1838, Passenger list of the *Republik,* List of Saxon Emigrants, List of the New York group I and II (Two partial lists of this group were made after their arrival in Perry County.), Application of Timken, Böschen, Grother, and Holschen for admission to the Association, March 17, 1839, G. H. Löber, Tagebuch and Brohm, Journal, *passim,* C. F. W. Walther, Seelenregister der . . . Gemeinde . . . in St. Louis . . . 1842, MSS., C. H. I.; miscellaneous freight lists and financial accounts in Bound MSS., 5, and Bound MSS., 8, C. H. I.; fourteen lists of passengers on various ships, of emigrants in various locations in Germany, of financial accounts, and of freight, Bound MSS., 10, C. H. I.; Verzeichnis derjenigen Lutherischen Hausväter, welche im Jahre 1838 aus Deutschland nach Missouri ausgewandert sind, Verzeichnis derjenigen lutherischen Hausväter, welche im Jahre 1839 uns nachgekommen und jetzt in derselben County wohnhaft sind. These two lists were probably prepared by G. H. Löber in the year 1844. The first list is one of the few to include the additions in St. Louis and the members of the New York group, and it is the only one which makes a systematic attempt to indicate who left the *Gesellschaft.* The second list is the only one which includes the names of those who came with Gruber. Contained in Bound MSS., I, Trinity Church Records, Altenburg, Mo. There are copies of the last two manuscripts in the Concordia Historical Institute.

[2] In recent years several attempts have been made to compile lists of the five ships which left in 1838, but they have lacked both completeness and accuracy. Stegen, "The Settlement of the Saxon Lutherans in Perry County, Missouri," 55—83, MS., M. A. thesis, Indiana University, 1933; "Members of the Saxon Immigration," *Concordia Historical Institute Quarterly,* XI, 33—47.

difference from previous lists or discrepancies in statements about the immigrants are far too numerous to be indicated each time. Occasionally attention has been called to such matters in the text of the preceding study when this seemed desirable because of the importance of some point or by way of illustration.

The totals given will probably be accepted by all who examine the sources. It would be possible to list for the *Amalia* fifty-eight or even fifty-nine passengers, if three men (Schützler, Ries, and Berje) were included; they were probably on the ship, but they were not members of the *Gesellschaft* and therefore have no significance for the history of the Saxons. The discrepancies in the totals given for the Gruber group have been discussed above.

The list of "Additions in St. Louis" is entirely new and has appeared in part only in Löber's list of 1844. Löber gives no indication that they were added to the roster of members only after the arrival of the Stephanites in America. It may be that this list of later accessions should be larger and that other people also joined during the sojourn in St. Louis. Perhaps the three names (five persons) Thormeier, Theis, and Theis (Nos. 285—287) found in Löber's list of 1844, but not to be found elsewhere, belong into this category. However, only those which can be definitely shown to have joined at the time in question are given here. Naturally, the many "additions" which were made from the St. Louis population in later years are not included; rather, the classification was confined to those people who joined before settlement was effected in April and May, 1839, and who therefore can properly be called colonists.

The arrangement of names is alphabetical according to surnames. Within these groups, however, the alphabetical arrangement was abandoned in favor of grouping by families, which in turn are indicated by the spacing. Single persons of any age not accompanied by their parents, the heads of families, and the parents, brothers, and sisters of the latter are always given full listing, with the exception of women who by marriage entered another family group. The wives and children (unless the latter are heads of families themselves) are always indicated by indentation without the repetition of the family name. Within a family the children are listed according to their ages. Frequently it is easier to suspect a family relationship, especially that of brothers and sisters, because of similarity of names, ages, and places of residence, than it is to prove it. Unless the evidence is clear, the separate listing has been retained.

Specific facts regarding the individual immigrant sometimes defied accurate determination. The spelling of family and Christian names is anything but uniform in the records of the Saxons and is not even consistent in the several signatures of the people concerned. (See the footnote on Stärtzells.) Usually the variation is not important enough to prevent the identification of persons by anyone wishing to consult the list. In those few cases where the difference in spelling affected the position in the list materially, the variant has been inserted at the proper place. Otherwise the principle was followed of accepting and listing only the spelling indicated by the strongest documentary evidence. Strict adherence to this principle at times led to some admittedly strange results, such as the various spellings of Johanne or Johanna; Christiane, Christiana, Christine, or Christina; Marie or Maria; Rosine or Rosina; Karl or Carl; Karoline, Karolina, Caroline, Carolina, or simply Lina; and others. It even happened that such variants occurred within the same family (*e. g.*, Schlagenhaus). However, a reproduction of the contemporary listing seemed preferable to an attempt at standardization a century later, particularly since such standardization would actually constitute greater inaccuracy and violation of source material than would the inconsistency in spelling which actually existed. No difficulty is created in the identification of a single individual as a result of this lack of uniformity. The similarity of Christian names, both in the group at large and within the separate families, is striking, the difficulties this circumstance created, obvious. The Christian names here given are the correct ones; however, their proper order was not always clear because the full name was not always (sometimes never) given in any one source. This fact, combined with the German custom of using a persons's second or third name most frequently in everyday parlance, make certainty of the correct order almost impossible in some cases.

Ages were also dealt with rather carelessly in the lists of the Saxons. All available evidence was carefully balanced in order to achieve the most accurate results possible on the basis of the contradictory figures. The point of time chosen for a computation of ages was January, 1839, the month of arrival in New Orleans.

A half year or more was counted as a full year except in the case of infants under one year. When children were less than one-fourth year old on arrival, their ages are not listed at all, in order not to affect the average of ages.

The listing of occupations is usually clear; there is never any question that the person was by profession what he is listed here as having been. However, some men may have followed another trade or calling also and therefore be described differently in another list. In such cases only one profession, that in the most reliable source, has been accepted and listed. In this connection particular care must be exercised when using the manifests for the ships in New Orleans, some of which give the occupations. At times, when entering the country, a man who had been a craftsman or white-collar worker in Germany gave his occupation as that of farmer because it was his intention to become one in America, an intention that may or may not have been carried out. Similarly, the custom among independent European craftsmen of also engaging in agriculture often leads to variant listings.

Concerning the data given here on the place of residence in Germany, especially the tabulation according to countries, the following facts must be borne in mind: First, in none of the lists is more than the mere name of the community given; the name of the country is almost never listed. Secondly, great liberties were taken with the spelling of place names, and inconsistencies are numerous. Thirdly, some of the localities mentioned, being only small hamlets, do not appear even on detailed maps; some no doubt have disappeared, others have been incorporated in larger communities, or have been renamed. Fourthly, the emigrants were frequently listed not according to their place of residence, but rather by the nearest point of rendezvous, such as Dresden, Magdeburg, Halle, and Leipzig; their real place of origin is discovered only from a variant listing or a personal letter. Consequently in the future some revision may be possible in the listing of locations if further letters or documents are brought to light. Where the name of a point of rendezvous or the name of a larger neighboring city was listed along with that of a smaller place, the latter is always considered to be the emigrant's home, since there could have been little other reason for listing the smaller locality. Any future revisions, it is fairly safe to assume, will not add to the totals of the larger cities, but to those of the smaller communities.

The listing according to ships is accurate as given here, although it disagrees with the manifests of three of the four ships which arrived at New Orleans. Only the *Olbers'* passenger list was really correct, as regards both names and total number of persons. For the sake of brevity, in the list which follows, only the first letters of the ships' names were used, "C" for *Copernicus,* "JG" for *Johann Georg,* "O" for *Olbers,* and "R" for *Republik.* The other letter is for the river boats, "R" for *Rienzi,* "C" for *Clyde,* "S" for *Selma,* "K" for *Knickerbocker.*

The lack of uniformity in the form of these lists is a result of the fact that not all information is given for all immigrants. For instance, Löber's list of 1844 does not give the ages of anyone, nor does it give the names of members of a family, except in the cases where a separate financial accounting was made. Since Löber is the most complete source for both the New York group and Gruber's group, some information is lacking in those lists.

The asterisks in the lists stand for the following:

* Left the colonies by 1844, either by returning to Germany or by severing connections with the *Gesellschaft.* For this information Löber is again largely responsible, although some has been added in the present list. There were probably more defections than these, but unless it can definitely be shown that a person left, he is listed as still with the group. The suspicion that this information is incomplete is strengthened when one notices that not a single person in Gruber's group is supposed to have left in more than four years, according to Löber's information. An asterisk does not appear next to the name of a person who merely moved away from St. Louis or Perry County, but maintained friendly relations with the Saxons (*e. g.,* Ahners). Such a procedure would have eliminated most of the candidates.

** Died en route.

*** Born en route.

The tables are based almost entirely upon the information in the separate lists. In such cases where data were unavailable or obviously impossible to give, the space was left blank. A zero was inserted only when it was clear that there were no persons in that classification, although the possibility existed.

LIST ONE

Passengers on the *Copernicus*, *Johann Georg*, *Republik*, and *Olbers*

Name	Age	Occupation	Former Place of Residence	Ship
Ahner, August Friedrich, Sr.	34	Weaver	Burgstädt	C-R
Johanne Christine	31		"	C-R
Ahner, AugustFriedrich, Jr.	27	Weaver	"	C-R
Friedericke Dorothea	33		"	C-R
Friedrich August	3		"	C-R
Amalia Theresia **	1		"	C
Gotthilf Traugott ***				C-R
Arndt, Carl Friedrich	36	Weaver	Frankenberg	JG-C
Johanne Dorothea Christiane	36		"	JG-C
Carl Friedrich	15		"	JG-C
Wilhelmine	7		"	JG-C
Augustin, Christian Gottlieb	19	Cartwright	Piesern	O-S
Barthel, Christ. Sophie	76		Leipzig	O-S
Barthel, Friedrich Wilhelm	47		"	O-S
Caroline Juliane	34		"	O-S
Richard	11		"	O-S
Mathilde	9		"	O-S
Theodor	7		"	O-S
Marie	5		"	O-S
Martin	½		"	O-S
Barthel, Carl Gottlieb	43	Weaver	Frankenberg	JG-C
Johanna Juliana	35		"	JG-C
Amalie Auguste	13		"	JG-C
Carl August	12		"	JG-C
Friedrich Rudolf	9		"	JG-C
Juliana Friederika Auguste **	½		"	JG
Benedict, Maria Rosine	70		Seelitz	C-R
Bergfeld, Johann Gotthilf *	34	Game Warden	Wildenfels	C-R
Johanne *	29		"	C-R
Marie Sophie *	7		"	C-R
Gotthilf *	5		"	C-R
Bergt, Wilhelm Adolf	27	Weaver	Burgstädt	C-R
Bergt, Christian Adolf	23	Weaver	"	C-R
Bergt, Carl Adolf	21	Weaver	"	C-R
Biehle, Johann Friedrich	35	Mason	Beesen	R-K
Johanne Friederike	36		"	R-K
Friedrich Wilhelm	12		"	R-K
Auguste Caroline	11		"	R-K
Friedrich Christoph	6		"	R-K
Heinrich Ferdinand	2		"	R-K
Johanne Friederike	½		"	R-K
Biltz, Julius	13		Mittel-Frohna	O-S

Block, Rosine	36	Maid	Eichenberg	R-K
Bock, Michael, Sr.	50	Farmer	Jonaswalde	C-R
Bock, Michael, Jr.	21	Farmer	"	C-R
Böhlau, Friedrich Aug. Ferdinand	35	Merchant	Leipzig	JG-C
Böhme, Carl Gottlieb	51	Wagon Master	Dresden	JG-C
Johanna Christina Sophia	42		"	JG-C
Christiana Emilie Carolina	25		"	JG-C
Emma Juliane	19		"	JG-C
Amalia Auguste	18		"	JG-C
Christine Amalia Marie	11		"	JG-C
Carl Martin Johann	9		"	JG-C
Böhme, Wilhelm August	28	Blacksmith	Unter-Neusulza	R-K
Johanna	40		"	R-K
Carl	5		"	R-K
Bertha	4		"	R-K
Maria	2		"	R-K
Ludwig	½		"	R-K
Bolz, Johann Traugott	25	Furrier	Lützen	JG-C
Böttcher, Heinrich Wilhelm	28	Shoemaker	Dresden	O-S
Brohm, Theodor Julius	30	Cand. of Theol.	"	O-S
Bünger, Christine Emilie	26		Etzdorf	C-R
Bünger, Ernst Eduard	21	Medical Student	Dresden	O-S
Bünger, Theodor Ernst	17	Farmer	Seidnitz	O-S
Bünger, Clementine Friederike	15		Nieder-Frohna	O-S
Bünger, Herman Wilhelm	13		Bräunsdorf	O-S
Bünger, Lydia Ottilie	11		Dresden	O-S
Bürger, Ernst Moritz * [3]	33	Clergyman	Lunzenau	C-R
Johanne Christiane Henrietta *	27		"	C-R
Paul Theodor *	3		"	C-R
Martin *	1		"	C-R
Burkhardt, J. Christian Gottlieb	56	Weaver	Nieder-Frohna	JG-C
Maria Rosine	50		"	JG-C
Christian Gottlieb	16		"	JG-C
Johanne Eleonore	9		"	JG-C
Christian Friedrich	5		"	JG-C
Burkhardt, Johann Gottfried	29	Weaver	"	JG-C
Johanne Karoline Concordia	27		"	JG-C
August Herman	1		"	JG-C
Buschner, Johann Frd.	38	Valet	Dresden	O-S
Darnstädt, Johann Georg Gott.	24	Joiner	"	C-R
Dathe, Johann Gotthold *	35	Turner	Pürsten	C-R
Däumer, Johann Christian	25	Shoemaker	Eichenberg	R-K
Dellit, Andreas Franz David	31	Baker	Dresden	O-S

[3] Bürger and his family left in 1841, but later re-established contact with the Saxons; he subsequently became a pastor in the Missouri Synod.

Döderlein, August Heinrich	33	Merchant	Leipzig	O-S
Drenkhahn, Heinrich	23	Joiner	Lübeck	C-R
Eisenschmidt, Friedrich Bernhard	23	Carpenter	Kösen	R-K
Estel, Johann Andreas Gottfried	45	Joiner	Dresden	O-S
Johanne Karoline	43		"	O-S
Martin Andreas, Jr.	23	Joiner	"	O-S
Magdalene Elizabeth	19		"	O-S
Marie Karoline	13		"	O-S
Martin Johann	10		"	O-S
Theodosius Christian	8		"	O-S
Immanuel Friedrich	6		"	O-S
Paul Martin	4		"	O-S
Sophie Johanne	1		"	O-S
Fiehler, Johann Gottlob	30	Blacksmith	Mannsdorf	C-R
Justina	28		"	C-R
Ernestine	3		"	C-R
Fischer, August Adolf	29	Furrier	Halle	R-K
Sophia	29		"	R-K
Fischer, Heinrich Ferdinand *	40	Merchant	Dresden	O-S
Julia *	34		"	O-S
Fischer, Johann Friedrich	38	Weaver	Wansleben	R-K
Maria Dorothea	38		"	R-K
Friedrich Albert	12		"	R-K
Christiane Maria	11		"	R-K
Friedrich Ferdinand	6		"	R-K
Alvina Friederike	½		"	R-K
Fischer, Johanna Sophia	39	Midwife	Lunzenau	JG-C
Johanne Caroline Sophia	8		"	JG-C
Johann Ehregott	½		"	JG-C
Fischer, Julius	16	Turner	Dresden	O-S
Fritzsche, Johann Gottlob *	36	Miner	"	JG-C
Eva Rosine Wilhelmine *	39		"	JG-C
Henriette Rosine *	13		"	JG-C
Karl Wilhelm *	7		"	JG-C
Friedrich August *	5		"	JG-C
Fritzsche, Regine	33	Maid	Dresden	O-S
Fröhlich, Friedrich August Ernst	28	Cand. of Theol.	Ronneburg	O-S
Fuhrmann, Johann Christlieb	33	Laborer (Invalid)	Zetteritz	C-R
Fürbringer, Ottomar	28	Cand. of Theol.	Eichenberg	R-K
Gäbler, Johann Gottlob	40	Locksmith	Wilschdorf	O-S
Geihsler, Carl Gotthilf	35	Carpenter	Dresden	O-S
Juliane	21		"	O-S
Gentzsch, Karoline Hanna	30	Maid	"	O-S
Geyer, Carl Ludwig	26	Cand. of Theol.	Pirna	JG-C
Geyer, Natalie Henriette	23		Nieder-Frohna	JG-C

Gönner, Jakob	31	Cand. of Theol.	Leipzig	O-S
Göring, Rosine	45	Midwife	Jonaswalde	C-R
Gottlieb	18	Shoemaker	"	C-R
Gottfried	12		"	C-R
Justine	11		"	C-R
Gräber, August	46	Shoemaker	Dresden	O-S
Grafe, August Johann Christian	36	Royal Groom	"	JG-C
Juliana Frieder. Wilhelmine	43		"	JG-C
Juliane Friederike	12		"	JG-C
Rosamunde	9		"	JG-C
Anna Therese	7		"	JG-C
Grobe, Maria Rosine	28	Maid	Nieder-Frohna	O-S
Grosse, Christiane Magdalene	53		Leisnig	JG-C
Ferdinand Friedrich	27	Shoemaker	"	JG-C
Moritz Ernst	25	Shoemaker	"	JG-C
Friedrich August	23	Shoemaker	"	JG-C
Gube, Johann Georg	52	Farmer	Seidnitz	O-S
Günther, Johann Samuel	60	Joiner	Dresden	O-S
Friederike (Wife)	35		"	O-S
Louise *	30	Maid	"	O-S
Gotthold *	28	Lithographer	"	O-S
Immanuel	8		"	O-S
Martin	7		"	O-S
Theodor	5		"	O-S
Benjamin	2		"	O-S
Hache, Theodosius Liebgott *	16		"	O-S
Häcker, August Friedrich	56	Merchant	"	O-S
Christiane Sibille	55		"	O-S
Friedrich Wilhelm	24	Joiner	"	O-S
Hahn, Christ. Auguste Wilhelmine	24	Maid	"	O-S
Hänigen, Benjamin Ferdinand	36	Joiner	"	O-S
Hänschen, Johann David	36	Lithographer	Leipzig	JG-C
Friederike Wilhelmine	38		"	JG-C
Johanne Henriette	15		"	JG-C
Juliane Wilhelmine	14		"	JG-C
Sophie Charlotte	6		"	JG-C
Marie Louise	4		"	JG-C
Gustav Traugott	2		"	JG-C
Harnisch, Gottfried Daniel	47	Shoemaker	Dresden	O-S
Johanne Friederike Juliane	46		"	O-S
Johann Adolph	12		"	O-S
Anna Dorothea	6		"	O-S
Harzdorf, Johanne Christine	27		Nieder-Frohna	JG-C
Friedrich Gottlieb	6		"	JG-C
Maria Theresia	4		"	JG-C
Haupt, Christiana Rosine	25	Maid	"	R-K
Heiner, Karl Johann Christian	43	Carpenter	Naumburg	R-K
Johanna Regina	45		"	R-K

Heinig, Johann Gottfried	47	Weaver	Nieder-Frohna	JG-C
Johanne Christiane	37		"	JG-C
Johanne Eleonore	11		"	JG-C
Friedrich Wilhelm	4		"	JG-C
Heinig, Johann Gottfried	37	Weaver	Mittel-Frohna	JG-C
Heinrich, Friedrich Herman *	24	Shoemaker	Lunzenau	C-R
Wilhelmine *	22		"	C-R
Helbig, Johann Gottlieb	40	Weaver	Mittel-Frohna	JG-C
Johanne Christiane	32		"	JG-C
Hellwig, Johann Gottlieb	48	Teacher	Dresden	O-S
Hempel, Johanne **	22	Maid	Mannichswalde	C
Henning, G. Chr. Friedrich	47	Farm Laborer	Eichenberg	R-K
Hermann, Marie Rosine	57		Naumburg	R-K
Rosette	31		"	R-K
Eleonore	30		"	R-K
Adolf	19	Painter	"	R-K
Herman, Rosalie *	21	Maid	Dresden	O
Hinkelmann, Johann Christian	44	Farm Laborer	Zassnitz	C-R
Hoffmann, Carl August	34	Weaver	Frankenberg	JG-C
Hoffmann, Carl Friedrich Gottlieb	33	Weaver	"	JG-C
Hoffmann, Carl Heinrich	25	Weaver	"	JG-C
Hoffmann, Christian Friedrich, Sr.	42	Weaver	"	JG-C
Johanna Eleonore	36		"	JG-C
Henriette Agnes	18		"	JG-C
Friedrich Ernst	17	Weaver	"	JG-C
Friedrich	11		"	JG-C
Juliane	9		"	JG-C
Amalie	7		"	JG-C
Auguste	5		"	JG-C
Emilie	2		"	JG-C
Hoffmann, Gottfried Benjamin	34	Weaver	"	JG-C
Hoffmann, Christiane Rosine	30		"	JG-C
Hoffmann, Johanna Rosina	68		"	JG-C
Hofmann, Christian Gottlob	40	Merchant	"	O-S
Amalia Rosine	31		"	O-S
Hofmann, Johanne Rosine	31		Halle	R-K
Julius Bernhard	13		"	R-K
Hofmann, Juliane Christiane	27		Frankenberg	JG-C
Höhle, Johann Gottlob *	26	Vinedresser	Kleinpestitz	JG-C
Höhne, Johann Gottlieb	39	Merchant	Dresden	O-S
Concordia Wilhelmine	45		"	O-S
Elias Fürchtegott	10		"	O-S
Johanne Constantine	8		"	O-S

Höhne, Johann Karl August	44	Merchant	"	O-S
Christiane Amalia	39		"	O-S
Hölzel, August Friedrich	26	Weaver	Burgstädt	C-R
Christiane Wilhelmine	26		"	C-R
August Wilhelm	3		"	C-R
Friedrich Adolf	1		"	C-R
Höschel, Friederike Sophie	28	Maid	Dresden	O-S
Illgen, Georg	38	Brewer	Reust	C-R
Illgen, Michael	36	Miller	Weida	C-R
Illgen, Friedrich August *	30	Miller	Reust	O-S
Jäckel, Gustav	32	Cashier	Dresden	O-S
Jahn, Gottfried	39	Shoemaker	Reichstädt	C-R
Dorothea	41		"	C-R
Justine	14		"	C-R
Sophie	8		"	C-R
Christina	6		"	C-R
Friedrich	4		"	C-R
Johannsen, Johann Martin	25	Shoemaker	Dresden	C-R
Just, Johann Gottlieb I	33	Shoemaker	"	O-S
Just, Johann Gottlieb II	30	Shoemaker	"	O-S
Kämpfe,				
Johann Samuel Gottfried	28	Farmer	Kleinpestitz	JG-C
J. F. Juliane Christiane	23		"	JG-C
Johann Samuel Gottfried	½		"	JG-C
Keyl, Ernst Gerhard Wilhelm	35	Clergyman	Nieder-Frohna	JG-C
Amalie Ernestine	22		"	JG-C
Stephanus	½		"	JG-C
Klemm, Johann Ferdinand *	39	Court Footman	Dresden	O-S
Klotzsch, Ernst August F.	38	Baker	Leipzig	JG-C
Johanne Friedrike	30		"	JG-C
Klügel, George	66	Farmer	Paitzdorf	C-R
Eva Rosina	60		"	C-R
George	38	Farmer	"	C-R
Wilhelm	37	Farmer	"	C-R
Gottlob	26	Farmer	"	C-R
Justina	22		"	C-R
Klügel, Gottlob	32	Cand. of Theol.	Dresden	O-S
Knoll, Justina G. (Nee Nönnig)	28		Jonaswalde	C-R
Knorr, Christian Friedrich	32	Weaver	Göritzhain	C-R
Johanne Rosina	36		"	C-R
Johanne Sophie	10		"	C-R
Johanne Eleonore	8		"	C-R
Christian Friedrich	3		"	C-R
Koch,				
Johann Friedrich Wilhelm *	25	Teacher	Langenchursdorf	JG-C
Agnes Amalia *	24		"	JG-C

Köppel, Johann Friedrich	47	Shoemaker	Kahla	R-K
Maria Susanna	57		"	R-K
Kramer, Gottfried	62	Cartwright	Paitzdorf	C-R
Johann Gottlob	28	Cartwright	"	C-R
Wilhelm **	24	Cartwright	"	C
Krause, Emil Ernst Lebrecht	17	Joiner	Dresden	O-S
Kretzschmar, Johanna Rosine	52	Midwife	Kolkau	JG-C
Kühling, Johann Gottlieb *	38	Carpenter	Naumburg	R-K
Johanna *	48		"	R-K
Caroline * (Foster Child)	10		"	R-K
Kühn, Gottfried	24	Weaver	Nieder-Frohna	O-S
Kühn, Johann Adam	44	Weaver	Sornzig	C-R
Johanna Elizabeth	44		"	C-R
Amalia Friederika	18		"	C-R
Johanna Christiane	18		"	C-R
Johanna Rosine	14		"	C-R
Johanna Eleonore	10		"	C-R
Karoline	7		"	C-R
Emilie Juliane Wilhelmine	5		"	C-R
Johann Adam	2		"	C-R
Kühnert, Johann Christlieb	43	Mason	Kolkau	C-R
Maria Rosine	41		"	C-R
Johanne Juliane	13		"	C-R
Johann Christian	12		"	C-R
Kunath, Andreas	40	Carpenter	Leuteritz	JG-C
Landgraf, Christian Friedrich	34	Weaver	Mittel-Frohna	JG-C
Johanne Christliebe	24		"	JG-C
Lange, Johann Wilhelm	49	Shoemaker	Dresden	O-S
Leonhardt, Johann Chr. Ehrenfr.	39	Saddler	Wiederau	C-R
Christiane Amalia	39		"	C-R
Wilhelm Bruno	14		"	C-R
Liebernickel, Johann Daniel	37	Farm Laborer	Göritzhain	C-R
Johanna Juliana	35		"	C-R
Johanne Rosine	12		"	C-R
Johanna Christiana	10		"	C-R
Johanna Eleonora	8		"	C-R
Johann Ehregott Lebrecht	2		"	C-R
Lindner, Johann Christ. Gottlob	24	Weaver	Mittel-Frohna	JG-C
Lindner, Johann Samuel	34	Weaver	"	JG-C
Löber, Johanne Christ. Magdalene	43		Eichenberg	R-K
Löber, Gotthold Heinrich	42	Clergyman	"	R-K
Wilhelmine Sophie	40		"	R-K
Christoph Heinrich	10		"	R-K
Martha Marie	8		"	R-K
Gotthilf Simeon	4		"	R-K

Lorenz, Johann Gottfried	28	Shoemaker	Lunzenau	C-R
Lorenz, Johanne Rosine Maria	26		"	C-R
Lorenz, Johanna Christiane	16		"	C-R
Löschner, Friedrich Wilhelm *	40	Painter	Königsbrück	O-S
Marbach, Franz Adolf *	40	Lawyer	Dresden	O-S
Louise *	36		"	O-S
Gustav *	10		"	O-S
Klara *	6		"	O-S
Victor *	5		"	O-S
Martin **	2		"	O
Markwort, Heinrich Gottfr. Chr.	26	Tailor	Hornburg	C-R
Martin, August Wilhelm	21	Weaver	Mittel-Frohna	O-S
Martin, Carl Gottlob	17	Weaver	"	O-S
Martin, Christiane Wilhelmine	20		"	R-K
Meding, Joh. Christ. Magdalena	70		Lunzenau	C-R
Johann Gottfried Leonhard *	40	Shoemaker	"	C-R
Christian Gottlob *	37	Shoemaker	"	C-R
Meinecke, Carl Wilhelm	42	Shoemaker	Dresden	C-R
Mende, Christian Gottlieb *	41	Cooper	Naumburg	C-R
Christiane *	43		"	C-R
Christiane Henriette * [4]	18		"	C-R
Wilhelmine *	13		"	C-R
Johanne *	11		"	C-R
Gottlob *	9		"	C-R
Herman *	7		"	C-R
Friederike *	5		"	C-R
Miehsler, Johanne Christiana	24	Maid	Nieder-Frohna	R-K
[Möding: see Meding.]				
Müller, Christian Gottfried	50	Farmer	Piesern	C-R
Eva Rosina	45		"	C-R
Johann Gottlieb	21		"	C-R
Karl Gottlob	19		"	C-R
Rosina Maria	15		"	C-R
Karl Wilhelm	10		"	C-R
Müller, Johann Christian	58	Tiler	Planena	R-K
Maria Christiana	50		"	R-K
Friederike Rosamund	25		"	R-K
Johann Christian Friedrich	23		"	R-K
Johanna Christiana Amalia	21		"	R-K
Friedrich Gottlieb **	18	Tiler	"	R
Friedrich Wilhelm	13		"	R-K
August Ferdinand	11		"	R-K
Rosine Auguste	7		"	R-K
Müller, Sophia Fr.	22	Maid	Rothenstein	R-K
Mylius, Traugott	47	Lacemaker	Möhrsdorf	R-K

[4] Henriette Mende rejoined the St. Louis congregation by 1842.

Nagel, Johanna Christiana *	40		Bräunsdorf	JG-C
Karl Gottlob	22	Weaver	"	JG-C
Naumann, Johann Christ. Traugott	28	Weaver	Mittel-Frohna	JG-C
Neumüller, Johann Gottlob	27	Shoemaker	Dresden	O-S
Niedner, Caroline Fr. Henriette *	49		Bräunsdorf	JG-C
Carl August *	30	Mason	"	JG-C
Adelheid Bertha Mathilde *	23		"	JG-C
Emma Louise *	17		"	JG-C
Laura *	13		"	JG-C
Niemann, Johann Chr. Friedrich	34	Shoemaker	Dresden	O-S
Christiane Henriette	34		"	O-S
Marie Elizabeth	6		"	O-S
Friedrich Martin	1		"	O-S
Infant **				O
Nitsche, Michael Carl	20	Farmer	Heukewalde	C-R
Nitzschke, Carl Julius Otto	33	Bookkeeper	Dresden	O-S
Nönnig, Gottfried	57	Farmer	Jonaswalde	C-R
Susanna	56		"	C-R
Gottfried	30	Farmer	"	C-R
Rosine	22		"	C-R
Otto, Justina	50		Jena-Löbnitz	R-K
Otto, Johann Gottfried	43	Farmer	"	R-K
Palisch, Johann Gottlieb	33	Farmer	Löbtau	JG-C
Johanna Christiana	32		"	JG-C
Carl Gottlieb	11		"	JG-C
Ernst Adolf	10		"	JG-C
Amalia Wilhelmine	8		"	JG-C
Ernestine Wilhelmine	6		"	JG-C
Emma Maria	5		"	JG-C
Auguste Therese	3		"	JG-C
Palitzsch, Johann Gottlieb	22	Farmer	Kleinpestitz	JG-C
Palitzsch, Johanna Julianne	20		"	JG-C
Paul, Johann Christoph	50	Laborer	"	JG-C
Johanne Rosine Friederike	40		"	JG-C
Pfau, Gustav	30	Engraver	Dresden	O-S
Philipp, Heinrich Robert Jacob	23	Tailor	Lunzenau	C-R
Pietzsch, Johann Gottlieb	54	Miller	Klein-	O-S
Eva Rosine	62		Zschachwitz	O-S
[Piltz: see Biltz]				
[Polz: see Bolz]				
Poppitz, Johann Christian	56	Farmer	Pürsten	C-R
Johanna Sophia	53		"	C-R
Rosina Maria	26		"	C-R
Johann Christlieb	25	Farmer	"	C-R
Johanna Rosine Maria	21		"	C-R
August Wilhelm	17		"	C-R

Poppitz, Johann Gottlob	32	Shoemaker	Lunzenau	C-R
Pötzsch, Auguste	31	Maid	Dresden	O-S
Pötzsch, Emilie Ernestine	21	Maid	"	O-S
Pröhl, Christian Heinrich *	22	Shoemaker	Mittel-Frohna	O-S
Pürfurst, Friedrich	29	Shoemaker	Dresden	O-S
Putzer, Friedrich Traugott	46	Sieve Maker	Naumburg	R-K
Johanne Dorothea	39		"	R-K
Eleonore Auguste	14		"	R-K
Friedrich Traugott	11		"	R-K
Pauline	6		"	R-K
Maria Amalie	2		"	R-K
Quast, Johann Martin	27	Shoemaker	Baruth	JG-C
Quellmalz, Christian Gottfried *	50	Shoemaker	Dresden	O-S
Amalia Wilhelmine *	40		"	O-S
Carl Friedrich *	15		"	O-S
Wilhelm Cornelius *	13		"	O-S
Ernst Wilhelm *	10		"	O-S
Anna Amalia *	5		"	O-S
Reihsner, J. Karoline	36		"	O-S
Richter, Christiane Dorothea	33		Nieder-Frohna	O-S
Richter, Amalie Henriette	22		"	O-S
Richter, Carl Friedrich, Sr.	63	Weaver	Frankenberg	JG-C
Rahel Rosine	63		"	JG-C
Rahel Elizabeth	34		"	JG-C
Friedrich Wilhelm	29	Weaver	"	JG-C
Richter, Johann Christian	53	Farmer	Striessen	O-S
Johanne Sophie	54		"	O-S
Richter, Karl Gottlieb	32	Shoemaker	Kolkau	C-R
Richter, Johann Christlieb	25	Shoemaker	"	C-R
Römer, Ernst August Ferdinand	31	Merchant	Dresden	O-S
Johanne Henriette	27		"	O-S
Johanne	4		"	O-S
Amalie	2		"	O-S
Martin Stephan ***				O-S
Römer, Johann Karl David	23	Saddler	"	O-S
Roschke, Carl Eduard	23	Tailor	Ronneburg	JG-C
Saalfeld, Charlotte Sophie	59		Kahla	R-K
Johann Christian Friedrich	19	Locksmith	"	R-K
Saupe, Johanne Rosine	35	Seamstress	Kolkau	C-R
Scheel, Johann Friedrich	37	Shoemaker	Lützen	JG-C
Joh. Friederike Elizabeth	9		"	JG-C
Scheffler, Johanne Karoline	46	Maid	Dresden	O-S
Schieferdecker, Georg Albert	23	Cand. of Theol.	Falken	C-R
Schlegel, Herman Victor von *	31	Lieutenant (Prussian Army)	Magdeburg	O-S

Schlimpert, Christian Gottfried	36	Farmer	Bräunsdorf	C-R
Johanne Christiane	34		"	C-R
Johanna Karoline	12		"	C-R
Amalia Therese	8		"	C-R
Ernestine	3		"	C-R
Ernst **	1		"	C
Schlimpert, Johann Gottlob	46	Farmer	Zassnitz	C-R
Johanne Sophie	46		"	C-R
Johann Traugott	22	Smith	"	C-R
Carl Gottlob	20	Farmer	"	C-R
Johann Wilhelm	17	Farmer	"	C-R
Johanna Rosine	15		"	C-R
August Julius	12		"	C-R
Ernst Ferdinand	11		"	C-R
Karoline Wilhelmine	7		"	C-R
Gottfried Heinrich	6		"	C-R
Theresia Amalia	3		"	C-R
Schmeiszer,				
Johann Carl Gottlieb	34	Painter	Dresden	O-S
Christiane Caroline Sophie	37		"	O-S
Maria Emilie Magdalene	7		"	O-S
Marie Elizabeth	6		"	O-S
Johanne	4		"	O-S
Christiane Constanze	½		"	O-S
Schmidt, Bernhard	54	Butcher	Kahla	R-K
Schmidt, Eva G.	61		Nöbdenitz	C-R
Johann	31	Blacksmith	"	C-R
Justine	17		"	C-R
Schmidt, Georg Joachim	42	Locksmith	Kahla	R-K
Maria	33		"	R-K
Gottwerth	4		"	R-K
Eva Magdalena	1		"	R-K
Schmidt, Johann Gottfried	29	Shoemaker	Altenhain	JG-C
Schmidt, Maria	63		Paitzdorf	C-R
Gottfried	36	Blacksmith	"	C-R
Johann	34	Glazier	"	C-R
Gottlob	30	Blacksmith	"	C-R
Justina	26		"	C-R
Michael	22	Joiner	"	C-R
Schnabel, Carl August *	40	Physician	Breitenbrunn	O
Eleonore *	42		"	O
Ottomar *	15		"	O
Amandus *	14		"	O
Carl August Albrecht *	10		"	O
Clemens *	6		"	O
Cölestine *	2		"	O
Schneider, Friedrich Ehregott *	60	Physician	Wiederau	C-R
Friederike Amalia *	38		"	C-R
Emma Christine *	21		"	C-R
Ida Rosalia *	12		"	C-R
Bertha Amalia *	11		"	C-R
Minna Pauline *	6		"	C-R

Schneider, Johanne Sophie	45		Dresden	O-S
Schönborn, Friedrich August	28	Weaver	Burgstädt	O-S
Schröter, Johann Karl Eduard	21	Shoemaker	Grünberg	C-R
Schubarth, Linna Wilhelmine	23		Nieder-Frohna	JG-C
Schubert, Georg Philipp	29	Joiner	Dresden	O-S
Schubert, Johann Gottlieb	35	Weaver	Stein	C-R
Christiane Rahel	39		"	C-R
Wilhelmine (Rath)[5]	17		"	C-R
Johann Julius	12		"	C-R
Schubert, Maria	15		Waldenburg	O-S
Schubert, Theodor	10		"	O-S
Schuberth, Ferdinand Wilhelm	24	Weaver	Nieder-Frohna	JG-C
Schulze, Juliane Henriette	27	Maid	Dresden	O-S
Schumann, Elias	36	Farm Laborer	Hohenkirchen	C-R
Johanna Christiane	37		"	C-R
Johanne Rosine	8		"	C-R
David	6		"	C-R
Johann Gottfried	4		"	C-R
Schuricht, Johann Gottlob	50	Weaver	Wallbach	O-S
Anna Rosine	57		"	O-S
Johann Gottlob **	28	Miller	"	C-R
Johann Gottlieb	26	Laborer	"	C-R
Friedrich Wilhelm	23	Weaver	"	C-R
Karl Ehregott	20	Clerk	"	O-S
Johann Traugott	17	Clerk	"	O-S
Johann Fürchtegott	15	Clerk	"	O-S
Johanne Rosine	13		"	O-S
Schütz, Julius	36	Cand. of Theol.	Leipzig	O-S
Schütz, Mathilde	33		"	O-S
Seidel, Franz *	28	Town Councilor	Wildenfels	C-R
Minna *	26		"	C-R
Arthur *	3		"	C-R
Seifert, Johanne Christliebe	22	Maid	Nieder-Frohna	R-K
Sittner, Christina Rosine	23	Maid	Bräunsdorf	JG-C
Stärtzell, Johann August, Sr.* [6]	57	Blacksmith	Bautzen	O-S
Johann August, Jr.*	25	Veterinarian	Dresden	O-S
Johanne Christiane *	21		Bautzen	O-S

---

[5] Wilhelmine Rath was evidently not a daughter of the Schuberts, but traveled with them and used their name. Whether she was an adopted child or one of several girls who made their way out of the country without the consent of their parents is not clear.

[6] This name offers the outstanding example of variant spellings in the lists of the Saxons. At least seven forms are found: Sörtzel, Stärtzel, Stärtzell, Stärzel, Sterzel, Störtzell, and Störzel. Since not even the members of the family were consistent in the spelling of their own name, there can be no objection to any of these forms.

Stengel, Johann Adam	30	Shoemaker	Thierstein, Bav.	O-S
Stephan, Martin *	61	Clergyman	Dresden	O-S
Martin	16		"	O-S
Stiegler, Johann George	50	Cooper	Langenchursdorf	JG-C
Johanna Sophia	37		"	JG-C
Johann Traugott	12		"	JG-C
Johann Gottlieb	4		"	JG-C
Storll, Johanne Sophie	45	Maid	Lunzenau	C-R
Johann Gottfried	22		"	C-R
Stumpf, Fr. Traugott Carl *	23	Mason	Dresden	O-S
Swart, Doro	9		Leipzig	O-S
Teichmann, J. Ch. Gottfried	36	Tailor	Bräunsdorf	R-K
Tennstädt, Fr. Albert W.	62	Farmer	Planena	R-K
Dorothea Elizabeth	64		"	R-K
Tenz, Ernst Moritz	31	Joiner	Dresden	O-S
Tirmenstein, Samuel	44	Coppersmith	"	O-S
Therese Christine	30		"	O-S
Maria Anna	13		"	O-S
Elizabeth Juliana	11		"	O-S
Concordie Christine	9		"	O-S
Samuel Martin	8		"	O-S
Esther Therese	7		"	O-S
Gustav Adolf	4		"	O-S
Anna Susanna	2		"	O-S
Martin Paulus	½		"	O-S
Ulich, Christian Friedrich	33	Millwright	Kolkau	C-R
Ulich, Friedrich August	26	Weaver	Nieder-Frohna	O-S
Vehse, Carl Eduard *	36	Curator of the Saxon State Archives	Dresden	O-S
Mathilda Charlotte *	9		"	O-S
Völker, Karoline Louise	21		Nieder-Frohna	O-S
Walther, Johanne Chris. Karoline	26	Seamstress	Mittel-Frohna	JG-C
Walther, Otto Herman	29	Clergyman	Langenchursdorf	O-S
Walther, Carl Ferdinand Wilhelm	27	Clergyman	Bräunsdorf	JG-C
Weber, Ernst Moritz Johann	15	Joiner	Dresden	O-S
Weber, Johann Christoph	46	Farmer	Planena	R-K
Dorothea	51		"	R-K
Friedrich Wilhelm	22	Farmer	"	R-K
Sophia	20		"	R-K
Christiane	18		"	R-K
Ludwig	16	Farmer	"	R-K
Amalia	12		"	R-K
Christian Adolf C.	6		"	R-K

Wege, Emil Julius Moritz	38	Cand. of Theol.	Dresden	O-S
Weidlich, Friederike Pauline	30	Maid	"	O-S
Weinhold, Johann Heinrich	21	Miller	Nieder-Frohna	JG-C
Weise, Johann Christian *	34	Butcher	Langenchursdorf	R-K
Auguste *	34		"	R-K
Hermann *	5		"	R-K
Oscar *	4		"	R-K
Adelheid *	3		"	R-K
Moritz *	½		"	R-K
Weise, Carl Gottlob	24	Weaver	Bräunsdorf	R-K
Caroline	26		"	R-K
Christiane	2		"	R-K
Friedrich	½		"	R-K
Wesser, Johann Gottlieb	24	Weaver	Ronneburg	C-R
Winter, Johann Friedrich Ferd.	30	Teacher	Planena	R-K
Winter, Rosine	27		Leipzig	O-S
Wirth, Caroline Sophie	61		Kahla	R-K
Wilhelm	24	Watchmaker	"	R-K
Auguste	22		"	R-K
Wunderlich, Johann Carl	35	Farmer	Eichenberg	R-K
Maria Elizabeth	32		"	R-K
Christian	9		"	R-K
Heinrich	8		"	R-K
Dorothea	5		"	R-K
Henriette	3		"	R-K
Wunderlich, Johann Nicolaus	75	Farmer	"	R-K
Wurmb, Johanna von	35		Meura	R-K
Maria	8		"	R-K
Theobald	6		"	R-K
Sara	4		"	R-K
Zeibig, Carl Gottlieb	28	Miller	Eschdorf	O-S
Henriette Wilhelmine	25		"	O-S
Karl August	2		"	O-S
Ernst Wilhelm **	1		"	O
Zeising, Christian Albert * [7]	9		Leipzig	JG-C
Zeising, Emilie Juliane *	3		"	JG-C
Zink, J. Carl Gottlieb Traugott *	37	Tailor	"	JG-C
Dorothea *	37		"	JG-C
Anna *	5		"	JG-C
Zschörner, Fr. August	38	Miller	Klein-Zschachwitz	O-S

[7] In several lists the two Zeisings are listed with the Zink family. However, they were not children of the Zinks.

LIST TWO

Passengers on the *Amalia*

Name	Age	Occupation	Former Place of Residence
Domschke, Johann		Joiner	Lauske
Wife			"
Andreas		Joiner	"
Child			"
Maria			"
Her Child			"
Ehrenhaus, Juliane	44		Dresden
Emilie Florentine	25		"
Klara Maria	18		"
Maria Juliane	9		"
Christine Emilie	8		"
Eichler,		Tailor	Grumbach
Heil, Johanne Christiana			Mittel-Frohna
Heine, Johann Samuel	39	Mason	Beesen
Friederika	41		"
Hinkelmann, Karl Wilhelm [8]		Shoemaker	Rochlitz
Hofmann, Johann Fried. Jakob	45	Shoemaker	Dresden
Johanna Christine Dorothea	43		"
Johann Carl Friedrich	14		"
Christine Juliane	9		"
Hubert, Heinrich Wilhelm		Joiner	Halle
Wife			"
Child			"
Child			"
Child			"
Josing, Johann Julius	39	Shoemaker	Dresden
Christiane Louise	36		"
Johann Jonathan	9		"
Maria Magdalena	5		"
Kobrasch, Karl Gottfried	48	Miller	"
Johanne Sophie (Daughter)	20		"
Karl Friedrich	13		"
Kokuschke, Johann		Farmer	Welttheuer
Wife			"
Child			"
Child			"
Lindner, Ther. (Stepchild of J. C. Heil)			Mittel-Frohna

[8] Apparently this man's name was Wilhelm Augustin, but he consistently used the name Hinkelmann. List of Saxon Emigrants, MS., C. H. I.

Meister, Johann Georg		Weaver	Lunzenau
Wife			“
Fr. Erdm.		Stud. of Theol.	Dresden
Nöbel, Johanna Sophie			Göppersdorf
Christian Gottlieb		Bookbinder	“
Johanne Christiane			“
Karl August			“
Weinhold, Karl August	51	Carpenter	Dresden
Rahel Dorothea	49		“
Christiane Dorothea	24		“
Johann Traugott	18		“
Karoline Sophie	17		“
Karl Heinrich	11		“
Rahel Maria Magdalene	4		“
Welzel, Mathilde Fried. Aug.[9]	32		“
Marie	2		“
Welzel, Karl Wilhelm	31	Cand. of Theol.	“
Welzel, Bernhard Oswald	17	Stud. of Theol.	“
Zöge, Johann Gottfr. Andr. Karl	25	Teacher	“

LIST THREE

Additions in St. Louis

Name	Age	Occupation	Former Place of Residence
Böschen, Klaus *	50	Farmer	Morbedorf, Hannover
Metta Margaretha *	46		“ “
Metta Adelheid *	18		“ “
Metta *	15		“ “
Klaus *	12		“ “
Anna *	10		“ “
Conrad *	7		“ “
Grother, Lütje	50	Farmer	Moringen, Hannover
Anna	53		“ “
Heinrich	20		“ “
Anna	17		“ “
Grünhagen, Johann Friedrich			“From Pommerania”
Höhne			“ “
Holschen, Johann	36	Farmer	Grasdorf, Hannover
Margaretha	23		“ “
Timken, Jacob	58	Farmer	Darmstadt, Hannover
Adelheid	14		“ “
Jacob	12		“ “
Heinrich	8		“ “
Hanna	4		“ “

[9] Not “Wetzel” as in Dau (ed.), *op. cit.*, 7; P. E. Kretzmann, “The Saxon Immigration to Missouri, 1838—1839,” *Missouri Historical Review*, XXXIII, 159.

LIST FOUR

The New York Group

Name	Age	Occupation	Married or Unmarried	Children	Former Place of Residence
Axt, Heinrich Georg	28	Lacemaker			
Becker, Christoph		Tanner			
Becker, Johann		Shoemaker	Wife	2	
Bertram, Eduard		Merchant			
Bischoff, Georg		Shoemaker			
Bünger, Christiane	50		Widow	2	Etzdorf
Johann Friedrich	28	Cand. of Theol.			Dresden
Agnes Ernestine	19				"
Bürger, Georg		Tailor	Wife		
Elgen, Andreas	58	Weaver			
Elgen, Christian			Widower		
Fischer, Jacob		Blacksmith	Wife		
Geisel, Conrad		Weaver	Wife	3	
Grahs, Chr.		Blacksmith	Wife	1	
Grebing, Hartmann		Shoemaker			
Happel, Wilhelm	24	Shoemaker			
Heid, Gottl.	23	Tailor			
Hoffmann, William		Hatter	Wife	1	
Kalbfleisch, Christine	22				
Kalbfleisch, Conrad		Tailor	Wife	1	
Kampmeier, Rudolph		Tinsmith	Wife	5	
Kaufmann, Anton		Laborer	Wife	5	
Kluge		Saddler	Wife	3	
Koch, Rudolph		Weaver			
Kohtz, Louis Fd.* [10]		Papermaker			
Körner, Christ.*		Butcher			
Meng, Jacob *		Shoemaker			
Motz, Heinrich		Cartwright	Wife		
Müller *		Teacher			

[10] *Ibid.*

Neidenberger, Matthias		Tailor			
Örtel, M. Jacob Maximilian *		Clergyman			
Paar, Andreas		Shoemaker	Wife	1	
Reng, Mar.		Maid			
Roth, Georg		Laborer	Wife	4	
Rudloff, Christian Ferdinand *		Butcher			
Rudloff, Franz *		Baker			
Rühle, Maria Josephine	22	Maid			
Schirmer, Christoph		Tailor	Wife	1	
Schlagenhaus, Johann Georg	27	Shoemaker	Wife	2	Leidringen
Katherine	30				"
Catherine Margarethe	6				"
Christiane Friederike	3				"
Schmidt (Female)			?	1	
Seibel, Jacob		Tailor			
Seibel, Johann		Cooper	Wife	1	
Spröde, Fr.*		Baker	Wife		
Stephan, Michael	28	Brazier	Wife	1	Kleeberg
Eva Margarethe	28				"
Jakob	6				"
Tüffel			Widow	2	
Walther, Georg Jacob		Hatter			
Weiler, Georg		Tinsmith	Wife	2	
Wichmann, Hermann Wilhelm		Hatter			

LIST FIVE

Gruber's Group

Name	Occupation	Married or Unmarried	Children	Former Place of Residence
Bracher, J. Peter	Weaver	Wife	2	Gera
Bräunlich, D. Fr.	Weaver	Wife	2	Ronneburg
Burkhardt, J. Gottl.	Mason	Wife	4	Zwötzen
Engert, August Fr.	Shoemaker	Wife	4	Lunzenau
Flamme, Wilhelm	Blacksmith			Merseburg
Frenzel, J. Gottl. I	Weaver	Wife	2	Bernsdorf
Frenzel, J. Gottl. II	Weaver	Wife	3	Stein

Gerhard, Fr.	Blacksmith			Utschen
Gerhard, Justine	Seamstress			Heukewalde
Gerhard, Marie	Seamstress			"
Göthe, Johann Gottl.	Cartwright	Wife	3	Heiersdorf
Grosse, Gottl. Fr.	Tailor	Wife	4	Ronneburg
Gruber, Karl Fr.	Clergyman	Wife	8	Reust
Hartenbach, Sophie				Bräunsdorf
Hecht, Fr.	Weaver	Wife	4	Mittel-Frohna
Hemmann, Gottfried	Farmer	Wife	5	Paitzdorf
Hesse, Georg	Farmer			Hafelbach
Hopfer, Michael	Cooper	Wife	2	"
Jacob, Michael	Farmer			Reust
Jäger, Gottfried	Farmer	Wife	2	Paitzdorf
Kramer, Ros.			1	"
Lindner, Eleonore				Bräunsdorf
Lorenz, Gottfried	Tailor	Wife	4	Stein
Matthes, L. Gottl.	Shoemaker			Lunzenau
Müller, Gottfried	Cartwright			Mittweida
Müller, Gottfried	Farmer			Paitzdorf
Müller, Johann Gottl.	Mason	Wife	2	Langenchursdorf
Niedner, Moritz	Typesetter			Bräunsdorf
Nitsche, Eva				Heukewalde
Nitsche, Georg	Farmer			"
Piehler, Georg	Tailor			"
Rechnitz, Joh. Ros.				Piesern
Richter, J. Gottl.	Gardner	Wife		Barthelsdorf
Schiehsler, Mich.	Farmer	Wife	8	Langenchursdorf
Schneider, Ad. Gott.	Teacher			Lunzenau
Schumann, Georg				Ronneburg
Sittner, Johann Gotth.	Mason	Wife	4	Göritzhain
Theilig, Gottfr.	Tiler			Rüchersdorf
Wagner, Theodor	Student of Chemistry			Dresden
Weber, August	Laborer (Blind)			Zwötzen
Wunderlich, Gottl.	Farmer	Wife	4	Waldsachsen

TABLE ONE

Statistics on Colonists Who Left Bremen in 1838

	Copernicus	*Johann Georg*	*Republik*	*Olbers*	*Total for C., J. G., R., and O.*	*Amalia*	Total
Embarked at Bremen	177	140	111	181	609	56	665
Born en route	1	0	0	2	3	0	3
Died en route	4	1	1	4	10	56	66
Arrived in New Orleans	174	139	110	179	602	0	602
Maximum total	178	140	111	183	612	56	668

TABLE TWO

Sex, Age, Marital Status, Size of Families, Etc., of the Various Groups of Colonists

	Total for *C., J. G., R.,* and *O.*	*Amalia*	Additions in St. Louis	New York Group	Gruber's Group	Total
Total persons	612	56	20	103	125	916
Male	338	23	11	42	34	448
Female	274	26	9	29	26	364
Sex not stated	0	7	0	32	65	104
Age: 1—12	179	8	6	3		196
Age: 13—24	128	8	6	5		147
Age: 25—40	209	7	1	6		223
Age: over 40	96	7	5	2		110
Age: unknown	0	26	2	87	125	240
Average of known ages	25.05	24.87	25.17	25.13		25.05
Married couples:						
without children	17	1	1	4	1	24
with children	65	7	2	15	18	107
Aver. no. of children	3.72	2.59	3.5	2.2	3.56	3.11
Widows and widowers	13	2	0	2	0	17
Divorced	4	1	0	0	2	7
Unmarried mothers	0	2	0	0	0	2
Marital status not clear	15	2	3	17	16	53
Children of the three preceding classes	44	11	4	5	1	65
Children, age 1—18 unaccompanied	11					11
Unmarried persons,						
age: 1—24	302	17	11	4		334
age: 25 and over	114	3	0	1		118
age: unknown	0	13	0	41	69	123
Total	416	33	11	46	69	575
Severed relations with the group by 1844	94		7	9	0	110

TABLE THREE

The Colonists' Former Place of Residence

	Total for *C.*, *J. G.*, *R.*, and *O.*	*Amalia*	Additions in St. Louis	New York Group	Gruber's Group	Total
Bavaria						
Thierstein	1					1
France						
Kleeberg				3		3
Hannover						
Darmstadt			5			5
Grasdorf			2			2
Morbedorf			7			7
Moringen			4			4
Total			18			18
Kingdom of Saxony						
Altenhain	1					1
Baruth	1					1
Bautzen	2					2
Bernsdorf					4	4
Bräunsdorf	21				3	24
Breitenbrunn	7					7
Burgstädt	14					14
Dresden	136	29		2	1	168
Eschdorf	4					4
Etzdorf	1			1		2
Frankenberg	32					32
Göppersdorf		4				4
Göritzhain	11				6	17
Grumbach		1				1
Grünberg	1					1
Heiersdorf					5	5
Hohenkirchen	5					5
Kleinpestitz	8					8
Klein-Zschachwitz	3					3
Kolkau	10					10
Königsbrück	1					1
Langenchursdorf	13				11	24
Lauske		6				6
Leipzig	29					29
Leisnig	4					4
Leuteritz	1					1
Löbtau	8					8
Lunzenau	18	2			8	28
Mittel-Frohna	14	2			6	22
Mittweida					1	1
Möhrsdorf	1					1
Nieder-Frohna	32					32
Piesern	7				1	8
Pirna	1					1
Pürsten	7					7

Reichstädt[11]	6					6
Rochlitz		1				1
Rückersdorf					1	1
Seelitz	1					1
Seidnitz	2					2
Sornzig	9					9
Stein	4				11	15
Striessen	2					2
Waldenburg	2					2
Waldsachsen					6	6
Wallbach	9					9
Weida	1					1
Welttheuer		4				4
Wiederau	9					9
Wildenfels	7					7
Wilschdorf	1					1
Zassnitz	12					12
Zetteritz	1					1
Total	460	49		3	64	576
Württemberg						
Leidringen				4		4
Lübeck	1					1
Pomerania			2			2
Prussia (and the Saxon Province)						
Beesen	7	2				9
Halle	4	5				9
Hornburg	1					1
Kösen	1					1
Lützen	3					3
Magdeburg	1					1
Mannsdorf	3					3
Merseburg					1	1
Naumburg	23					23
Planena	20					20
Wansleben	6					6
Total	69	7			1	77
Saxon Duchies						
Barthelsdorf					2	2
Eichenberg	17					17
Gera					4	4
Hafelbach					5	5
Heukewalde	1				5	6
Jena-Löbnitz	2					2
Jonaswalde	11					11
Kahla	12					12
Mannichswalde	1					1
Meura	4					4
Nöbdenitz	3					3
Paitzdorf	15				14	29
Reust	2				11	13
Ronneburg	3				11	14
Rothenstein	1					1

11 There was a Reichstädt also in Saxe-Altenburg.

Unter-Neusulza	6					6
Untschen					1	1
Zwötzen					7	7
Total	78				60	138
Born en route	3					3
Original place of residence not known				93		93
GRAND TOTAL	612	56	20	103	125	916

TABLE FOUR

Occupations of the Colonists

	Total for *C., J. G., R.*, and *O.*	*Amalia*	Additions in St. Louis	New York Group	Gruber's Group	Total
Agriculture						
Farmers	29	1	4		8	42
Farm Laborers	4					4
Gardeners					1	1
Vinedressers	1					1
Total	34	1	4		9	48
Crafts and Trades						
Bakers	2			2		4
Blacksmiths	7			2	2	11
Bookbinders		1				1
Braziers				1		1
Brewers	1					1
Butchers	2			2		4
Carpenters	5	1				6
Cartwrights	4			1	2	7
Coopers	2			1	1	4
Coppersmiths	1					1
Engravers	1					1
Furriers	2					2
Glaziers	1					1
Hatters				3		3
Joiners	12	3				15
Lacemakers	1			1		2
Lithographers	2					2
Locksmiths	3					3
Masons	5	1			3	9
Millers	7	1				8
Millwrights	1					1
Miners	1					1
Painters	3					3
Papermakers				1		1
Saddlers	2			1		3
Shoemaker	32	3		7	2	44
Sieve makers	1					1
Tailors	5	1		6	3	15
Tanners				1		1
Tilers	4				1	5

Tinsmiths				2		2
Turners	2					2
Typesetters					1	1
Wagon masters	1					1
Watchmakers	1					1
Weavers	40	1		3	5	49
Total	151	12		34	20	217
Laborers and Personal Servants						
Laborers	3			2	1	6
Valets	1					1
Royal Grooms	1					1
Court Footmen	1					1
Total	6			2	1	9
Merchants	8			1		9
Professions and Government Employees						
Bookkeepers	1					1
Cand. of Theology	9	1		1		11
Cashiers	1					1
Clergymen	6			1	1	8
Clerks	3					3
Curator of Saxon State Archives	1					1
Game Wardens	1					1
Lawyers	1					1
Officers, Prussian Army	1					1
Physicians	2					2
Precentors					1	1
Tax Officials	1					1
Teachers	3	1		1		5
Town Councilors	1					1
Veterinarians	1					1
Total	32	2		3	2	39
Students						
Students of Chemistry					1	1
Students of Medicine	1					1
Students of Theology		2				2
Total	1	2			1	4
Women						
Maids	20			2		22
Midwives	3					3
Seamstresses	2				2	4
Total	25			2	2	29
GRAND TOTAL	257	17	4	42	35	355

APPENDIX B
THE CODES

INTRODUCTION

This set of Codes is an unusual group of documents in the history of American immigration. Dreams of a German-controlled community or even a state were not infrequent among the immigrants of the nineteenth century. But seldom, if ever, were plans as complete and far-reaching as those of the Saxons actually formulated. The Codes are a detailed statement of the plans of the committee for the people under its leadership, beginning with the time of embarkation in Germany and extending indefinitely into the future as a compact, autonomous colony in the United States. A rather accurate estimate of the viewpoints, the character, and the tendencies of the *Gesellschaft* could be gleaned from these sources alone. When the Codes are combined with a narrative of the actual events, they place beyond question the nature of several phases of the emigration, primarily its theocratic organization. The hierarchical cast of the movement throws its shadow not only upon Stephan, its chief author and beneficiary, but also upon the other leaders, pastors, laymen, and candidates, all of whom shared the advantages from, and the responsibility for, the arrangement. This subject and other important features of the Codes have been discussed at greater length in the preceding study.

All these Codes are contained in Bound MSS., IV, C. H. I. For several of them there are additional drafts, unbound. When it is clear which of them was the revised form, the later version has been used, as a more accurate statement of the development of the plans of the *Gesellschaft*. In the cases where such a selection was impossible, the text fortunately agreed verbatim except for two unimportant details. Partial translations have been made before,[1] but

[1] The first such translation was probably that of the Code for the Credit Fund, referred to above. The text of the Brief Outline of the Emigration Code was printed in Vehse, *op. cit.*, 159—163; it has been translated in C. W. Eifrig, "A Valuable Historical Find" [?], *Lutheran School Journal*, LXX, 454—457. See also Th. Buenger in Dau (ed.), *op. cit.*, 8—9; Polack, *Walther*, 29—30; P. Kretzmann, "The Saxon Immigration to Missouri, 1838—1839," *Missouri Historical Review*, XXXIII, 160.

they were not used, because the purpose and method of the translations here are somewhat different.

English documents of a similar nature can be printed without losing their character, simply by copying exactly the text, spelling, punctuation, and form of the original; style, quality, and flavor then take care of themselves. Translation, however, automatically eliminates such a procedure. In fact, a free translation — especially if it had made all the corrections in the original German, and standardized spelling, punctuation, and form — would have amounted to a paraphrase in some instances and transformed the Codes from German documents by the Saxons in 1838 into English documents by Americans a hundred years later. Instead, the effort was made to retain as much as possible of the tone and individuality of the original manuscripts.

In every sentence and paragraph of a Code, the reproduction here has striven to convey both the form and the meaning as accurately as that is possible in another language. This task was rendered exceptionally difficult by the illegibility (handwriting and condition) of portions of the manuscripts, and by the indistinctness of some of the phraseology. At times this indistinctness resulted from a ponderous style. Sometimes the difficulty was caused by the attempt of those who drafted the Codes to use a quasi-legal phrasing, or by their confusion of political and ecclesiastical terms. In still other cases the conclusion is inescapable that the leaders of the emigration themselves had only a very hazy idea of what they were trying to express. To give only one example: The word *Gemeinde* still has, and at that time had even more generally, at least the two meanings of "congregation" and "civil community." A choice is not difficult in itself, since the distinction between the two concepts is clear. But the use of the term in these Codes, which were designed for a form of theocratic organization in which the civil and the ecclesiastical were inextricably intertwined, is indistinct, to say the least. A considerable carelessness on the part of the Saxon leaders in the use of the term makes some confusion inevitable. Thus *Gemeinde* might mean: the entire body of people under Stephan's leadership, as a religious group; the same people as a secular society, or the *Gesellschaft;* a ship's company; a ship's company as a religious unit under the leadership of a pastor; the entire group of emigrants envisioned as a political unit after settlement had been effected; the same group as a religious organization; the individual congregational groups within the settlements; or, conceivably, designations for still other possible groups which did not occur to the translator. Similar words are *Kirche* and *Ordnung*. The Stephanite conception of these terms has been discussed above. Occasionally the construction was unclear or unmistakably incorrect. Usually the cardinal principle of the translator to reproduce what the text wishes to say provided the solution. But German case endings may change the meaning of an entire sentence, and the language of the Codes is something less than flawless. When the nebulous hopes of dreamers about communal society are conveyed in the cant of the religious zealot, the result is not likely to be distinguished for its precision.

Considering the quality of the original, adherence to it could not always be carried out within the English sentence, which had to conform to the rules of English sufficiently to be intelligible. But the original could be followed absolutely in all Code, chapter, and paragraph headings. All numbers are given as in the original, either in numerals or as words. Sentences were broken up very rarely, though at times this device was unavoidable. If duplicating the length of the German sentence did not clearly detract from the clarity of the original text, then the translation retained the Saxon expansiveness of style. The result is admittedly not always succinct, modern English, but it was felt that the purpose was to present an accurate reproduction of what the Codes were and said as the Saxons drew them up, and not to improve upon them or revise them. The translated Codes as they stand here have striven to reproduce, at the same time with the meaning, the character, style, and form of the original Codes as nearly as possible — an accuracy that is their due as historically significant documents.

Brief Outline of the Emigration Code

Par. 1. *Confession of faith*

All the undersigned accept with upright hearts the tenets of the Lutheran faith, as contained in God's Word of the Old and New Testaments, and set forth and confessed in the Symbolical Writings of the Lutheran Church. They therefore accept these writings in their entirety and without any addition. They accept these writings according to the simple sense of their wording, as they have, since their origin, been unanimously and uniformly understood and applied — during the 16th, 17th, and the first part of the 18th century by the entire Lutheran Church, and from that time on by all who have not departed from the old, pure, Lutheran faith.

Par. 2. *Emigration — its cause, purpose, and goal*

After the calmest and most mature reflection they find themselves confronted with the impossibility, humanly speaking, of retaining this faith pure and unadulterated in their present homeland, of confessing it, and of transmitting it to their descendants. They are, therefore, constrained by their conscience to emigrate and to seek a land where this faith is not endangered, and where they consequently can serve God undisturbed, in the manner which He has graciously revealed and established, and enjoy undisturbed the unabridged and pure means of grace (which God has instituted for the salvation of all men), and preserve them thus unabridged and pure for themselves and their descendants.

To these means of grace belong primarily:

the office of reconciliation in its entire scope and with unrestricted freedom, pure and free *divine worship*, unabridged and pure *preaching* of God's Word, unabridged and pure *Sacraments, pastoral ministration* and the *care of souls* without let or hindrance.

A land such as they seek is the United States of North America, where complete religious and civil liberty prevails and energetic and effective protection is given against foreign countries as nowhere else in the world. These States they therefore have chosen as the goal, and, indeed, the only goal, of their emigration, and consequently as their new home.

Par. 3. *Ecclesiastical and Civil Code*

On the basis of the confession of faith made in Par. 1, and of the purpose of the emigration stated in Par. 2, the undersigned solemnly promise to subject themselves with Christian sincerity and willingness to the ecclesiastical and civil codes which are to be established, as well as to the school code and especially to the system of church discipline to be introduced.

Par. 4. *Place of settlement*

The place of settlement in the United States of America shall be chosen in one of the Western States: in Missouri or Illinois, or perhaps in Indiana.

Par. 5. *Itinerary*

The city of St. Louis in the State of Missouri, centrally located in all these States and also their commercial center, shall be the immediate goal of the journey. From this city a survey can be made for the site to be selected for the settlement in the afore-mentioned states.

The port of embarkation in Europe shall be Hamburg [sic], the port of debarkation in the United States of North America, New Orleans, and from there the journey shall continue by river steamer on the Mississippi to the afore-mentioned immediate goal of the journey, St. Louis.

Par. 6. *Purchase of land*

With St. Louis as headquarters, a tract of contiguous land shall be purchased by a committee of the entire body of emigrants, and, after deduction of what must be reserved for church, school, and community, separate plots of this land shall be sold to each individual according to his needs. These lands collectively shall form the township, or area of the city.

Each one is at liberty to purchase as much land as he pleases outside the township.

Par. 7. *Assumption of all church and community expenditures for 5 years*

The undersigned bind themselves for five years jointly to raise all church and community expenditures, as these will be fixed from year to year by a committee to be established by church and community. Each one shall contribute in proportion to his means. These contributions shall be apportioned with Christian fairness and care, partly according to the value of the real estate (tax on immovable property), partly according to the amount of the other property and income (tax on movable property). Land which members of the community own outside of the township shall likewise be liable for these expenditures according to a fair proportion.

Par. 8. *Mutual support*

The undersigned, who solemnly promise to conduct themselves in a Christian manner toward each other at all times, do indeed obligate themselves to mutual assistance and support by word and deed, as is proper among Christians. But in order to avoid misunderstandings, let it be noted that no kind of joint ownership of property shall ever take place or be permitted; rather, each one is and shall remain empowered to make disposition of his private property as he sees fit.

Par. 9. *The Credit Fund*

For temporarily defraying the expenditures necessary for the needs of church, school, and community, to support indigent emigrants through cash advances, and to purchase the afore-mentioned contiguous tract of land, a Fund for Cash Advances, or a Credit Fund, shall be established. Accordingly, the expenses noted will be met with cash advances from this Fund, and for each disbursement which this Fund makes, especially also for loans to indigent emigrants, the whole community, as well as the land to be purchased, is surety, however, with the exception of that portion of land which is to be transferred to church and school.

Whatever is left over, after the deduction of all expenses and losses and of that portion of the land to be bought which is to be transferred to the church and school (cf. Par. 6), will in due time be distributed among those who deposit money in this Fund, in proportion to the amount of the deposit.

The amount of these deposits, of which the capital of the Fund consists, depends upon the free will of each individual.

Par. 10. *Christian simplicity in all transactions*

In all dealings, in all promises and assurances, Christian simplicity, integrity, and truthfulness must obtain, and therefore all formalities and red tape which are not indispensable shall be avoided.

Par. 11. *Freedom of participation*

The undersigned herewith declare, affirm, and testify before everyone that complete freedom of choice was allowed each one of them either to go along or to stay at home; that no one urged another to haste, but that they rather made it the duty of one another, frequently and thoroughly to consider the matter, and by all means most carefully to weigh all difficulties which might arise; and that, accordingly, each one made his decision with complete freedom and calm consideration, without haste and deliberately.

Code for the Credit Fund of the Lutheran "Gesellschaft" Emigrating with Herr Pastor Stephan to the United States of North America

Par. 1. *Capital of the Credit Fund*

The capital of the Credit Fund shall be raised by voluntary contributions of the members of the *Gesellschaft,* which contributions are to be administered, bear interest, and be repaid according to the stipulations of this Code.

Par. 2. *Purposes of the Credit Fund*

The Credit Fund is intended

1. to make cash advances on collateral for the following purposes:
   a. for the needs of church and school.
   b. for the needs of the civil community.
   c. for indigent emigrants belonging to the *Gesellschaft,* [i. e.] for transferring them from their present place of residence to St. Louis and vicinity, for their own person, and for the possessions requisite for their needs.
   d. for whatever is required to tide these people over from the time of debarkation in St. Louis to the time that settlement has been effected.
   e. for construction of the requisite dwellings and acquisition of cattle and implements for the initial settlement.

2. to buy a tract of contiguous land, if possible a whole township, in its entirety and at one time, in order that the members of the *Gesellschaft* may live together in one place, separate from strangers. Separate plots from this entire tract are then to be sold to individual members. This land shall become the property of the Credit Fund, except for those parts of it which are transferred to church, school, and community for their needs, or sold to individual members of the community for their private use.

3. to keep and administer, for the time being, possible donations for benevolent purposes.

4. to keep in trust and transport to America money or valuables, in return for an adequate remuneration for such service.

How much shall be used from the Credit Fund for the purposes mentioned above under 1. and 2., depends in each case upon the appropriation of the participants in the Credit Fund, who shall decide on the matter by absolute majority. Absolute majority consists in this, that more than half are agreed. In order to have a vote, a clear credit of at least 100 thaler is required.

Par. 3. *Security for the capital of the Credit Fund*

The whole community, as well as the land to be purchased, shall be security for all cash advances made by the Credit Fund.

When making sales to individual members of the community, the Credit Fund, according to American law, for its own protection, shall retain ownership of the plot of land that has been sold until the buyer has paid the purchase price; meanwhile the buyer shall pay as rent the sum which the interest on the entire purchase price (or as much as is still outstanding) amounts to, and the plot of land may be purchased by no one else, nor may the purchase price be raised. The detailed conditions are to be arranged at the time of each individual purchase and specified in the deed to be drawn up.

Par. 4. *Losses and profits of the Credit Fund — Division of the profit*

The Credit Fund shall carry the following obligations:

1. Loss of interest

a. on those sums of money which must lie idle in the fund from time to time.

b. on that portion of the capital which is used for the purchase of land, insofar as that land is not in turn sold or rented.

c. since compound interest may never be charged, the Credit Fund shall cancel the interest on interest where interest payments are overdue or have been deferred.

d. as long as the borrower is unable to earn anything, computation and collection of interest shall be made according to Christian equity with all possible considerateness; this applies especially to the transportation costs to be advanced. Interest charges on this money shall not begin until one month after arrival in St. Louis.

2. The expenses arising from the administration of the Credit Fund shall be shared equally by the Credit Fund and by the *Gesellschaft*.

3. The Credit Fund shall deed to the church, school, and community, free of charge, as much of the land to be purchased as is necessary for the erection of all necessary buildings and the construction of squares and streets.

All losses, expenses, and cessions which the Credit Fund must bear shall be covered by the proceeds of the sale of land. In selling this land the value [desirableness] of the respective plot to be sold shall be the criterion, and on this basis the price of the sale is to be determined in Christian fairness.

If the Credit Fund through the sale of the land makes enough profit that not only all the losses, expenses, and cessions to be borne by it are covered, but that a clear surplus remains, half of this surplus shall be given to the church for the creation of a church fund, a fourth shall be given to the community for the creation of a community fund, and the remaining fourth shall be divided in proportion to the size of the contributions among those who have made such contributions to the Credit Fund.

Par. 5. *Interest payment on contributions*

Contributions, that is, money which is paid into the Credit Fund for the duration of its existence, shall draw interest according to the custom of the country, *i. e.*, according to the rate of interest prevailing in the State in which settlement takes place. Interest shall begin a month after arrival in St. Louis and be paid by the Credit Fund semiannually.

Until this time no interest shall be paid, because while en route no interest can be earned.

On money which is lent the Credit Fund for a limited time only, interest shall be paid according to a rate to be agreed upon.

On money which is entrusted to the Credit Fund for safekeeping or for transfer only, interest shall not be paid at all; rather, as has already been mentioned, a suitable remuneration is to be made for the service in such cases.

Par. 6. *Administrative Board*

The Credit Fund shall be administered by a board of its contributors. This board shall consist of nine persons, who are to be chosen by absolute majority of the contributors from their own midst. These nine persons shall elect one of their number as chairman. The chairman shall appoint another member of the board as his substitute for occasions when he is unable to attend.

All business matters shall be discussed by the board, and business shall be conducted in accordance with resolutions adopted as a result of the discussions of the board.

Par. 7. *Supervision of the administration*

A committee chosen by the church and the community shall supervise the administration. This committee and the board shall jointly establish a set of regulations, the purpose of which shall be, that the administration always be conducted in a Christian and God-pleasing manner, and that the necessary consideration for the welfare of the church and the community be shown. This set of regulations shall serve the board as a guide in the administration and consequently is to be observed by it at all times. Self-evidently it [the set of regulations] may not conflict with any of the stipulations of this present Code. All cases not covered by this set of regulations, as well as all contested cases, are to be submitted to the committee for clarification and, depending upon the circumstances, for decision.

Par. 8. *Administrative officials*

For conducting the financial affairs and keeping the accounts, one person shall be engaged provisionally, as salaried cashier and bookkeeper, to whom paid assistants may be given as the circumstances require. But as soon as the community government has been established, the community treasurer shall receive this office. However, he will self-evidently keep the bookkeeping, financial, and accounting affairs of the Credit Fund separate from those of the community treasury. The treasurer will receive from the board a set of instructions which he is to observe in carrying on his business. In all cases not covered by the set of instructions, he is to obtain a brief written resolution from the board and observe it as well as all other written resolutions of the board.

The resolutions along with the instructions serve him as vouchers in rendering his accounts, and consequently as justification.

Par. 9. *Special functions of the chairman of the board and his substitute*

The chairman of the board, or his substitute, shall direct the entire administration. He shall exercise supervision over the fund and the bookkeeping, and shall revise it from time to time according to his discretion. Furthermore, he is to sign all resolutions and other declarations of the board, as well as the instructions for the treasurer and bookkeeper, and all documents to be drawn up by the Credit Fund, the latter jointly with the treasurer. He is also to sign all receipts and vouchers for expenditures together with the treasurer. Meetings of the board are called by him, and he shall discuss with it all business matters the performance of which the board does not, in accordance with a business code which is to be drawn up, assign to him without further discussion. Finally, he shall have the deciding vote in case a tie occurs in the voting of the board. For their services he and his substitute are to receive an adequate compensation.

Par. 10. *Financial statements and repayment*

During the course of the first month in St. Louis the first financial statement shall be made, a year later the second, and so on, until the Credit Fund has been liquidated.

Every financial statement is to be made before the assembled board in the presence of the committee of the church and the community.

As soon as it becomes evident from one of these financial statements that the Credit Fund is no longer in need of capital, this capital will be divided according to the contributions made and paid back. This procedure shall be continued until the contributions have been repaid in full. At the wish of the contributors to the Credit Fund [the order of] repayment of the contributions can also be decided by lot.

Whatever remains after repayment of the contributions, is to be considered as profit; on the other hand, if the Credit Fund should not be able to repay the contributions in full, the debit is to be regarded as a loss.

Par. 11

This present code shall be submitted for approval to both the church and the community.

Traveling Regulations for the Lutheran "Gesellschaft" Emigrating with Herr Pastor Stephan to the United States of North America

Par. 1. *Beginning and duration of these regulations*

These present Traveling Regulations become operative as soon as the *Gesellschaft* is completely assembled, which will take place either at Magdeburg, or Hamburg, or Bremen — at the latest beginning with the time of embarkation.

They become inoperative as soon as settlement has been effected and the Community Code is introduced. Until that time they take the place of the Community Code.

Par. 2. *Duties of the "Gesellschaft" in general*

The *Gesellschaft* will everywhere (on the journey and in those localities where it will remain only temporarily until settling permanently) strive for a quiet, peaceable, and honorable behavior, as befits Christians (especially such as the gracious God is delivering after such long spiritual and physical distress), and as wisdom demands especially urgently, in view of the unfavorable sentiments prevailing now and then against emigrants to America.

Par. 3. *Government of the "Gesellschaft"*

The chief management of all affairs of the entire *Gesellschaft* shall be exercised by its primate, who accordingly will combine in his person the supreme authority in spiritual and civil matters.

All arrangements for worship will emanate exclusively from him until the Ecclesiastical Code comes into existence after permanent settlement has been effected.

For his assistance in conducting the civil affairs of the *Gesellschaft* he shall, however, nominate an administrative board of eight persons (clergymen and laymen) to the *Gesellschaft*, and when it has approved the persons nominated, induct them into office before the assembled *Gesellschaft*.

This board, in turn, shall with the approval of the primate, appoint subsupervisors, who are to exercise immediate supervision over the members of the *Gesellschaft* as to morals, order, safety, sanitation, and health.

Should a second, third, and fourth ship be chartered for the migration, then, after election of the primate, a clergyman shall also be appointed to the supreme leadership in spiritual and civil matters of the persons on these ships. This clergyman will likewise have a board of eight persons at his side, which board shall also again choose subsupervisors for the immediate supervision of the members of the *Gesellschaft*.

Par. 4. *Office of the subsupervisors or inspectors*

Subsupervisors shall be appointed, so that there will be one for every fifteen to twenty persons. Obedience is due in the first instance to them in all disciplinary matters. The subsupervisors shall receive definite instructions on the scope of their functions from the board, are to seek the help of a member of the board in all disputes arising which they cannot settle, and if the matter cannot even thereby be settled, bring it before a meeting of the board and await its further instructions in the case. Complaints against these inspectors shall be lodged with a member of the board, who shall at once attempt mediation and, if this should fail, likewise bring the matter before a session of the board for decision.

Par. 5. *Office of the members of the board — Meetings of the board*

The board, consisting of eight persons, is to be appointed by the primate with the approval of the *Gesellschaft,* as mentioned before (Par. 3.), and it will depend solely upon him whether, in view of the available persons, he considers it advisable that it be composed of an equal or an unequal number of clergymen and laymen. This board, under the chairmanship of the primate, shall conduct the chief management of the civil affairs of the *Gesellschaft,* provide instructions for the inspectors subordinate to it, support them in the administration of their office (Par. 4.), and remedy the complaints lodged against them; its decision is final in all cases.

Sessions of the board depend upon the volume and urgency of business and are to be held, as a rule, at least twice a week.

The primate may appoint a substitute for these sessions, who will preside in his place. However, the substitute shall not make any decisions in important matters without the primate. If two members of the board vote for it, his decision must be sought.

Par. 6. *The person of the primate and access to him*

The primate shall at all times be treated by members of the *Gesellschaft* with the reverence due his high office and great wisdom; he shall receive the title "Very Reverend Sir"; offenses against his person and disobedience against his orders shall be punished with severe civil and ecclesiastical penalties.

Only his *Herr* colleagues in office and the members of the board will be granted immediate and free access to the primate — on ship also the cabin passengers, and otherwise those to whom he expressly grants it. All other members of the *Gesellschaft* shall appear before him only after previous announcement.

Par. 7. *Business of the clerk*

The minutes of the sessions of the board and all secretarial work necessary for the board shall be attended to by a clerk to be appointed by the board.

Par. 8. *Procedure in disputes among the members of the "Gesellschaft"*

All misunderstandings occurring between members of the *Gesellschaft,* if they cannot be settled by the individual subsupervisors and board members, shall be brought before the meeting of the board, which may, as it sees fit, summon the parties before it and have them deal with each other.

The parties are to be satisfied with the decision of the board, which shall be rendered according to God's Word and Christian fairness.

Par. 9. *Assessment of penalties*

Transgressions of God's Commandments and of these Traveling Regulations, recalcitrance against the order of the primate, the board members, and the subsupervisors shall be punished the first time with a reprimand, in recurring cases with a sharper reprimand before the assembled board, and, if even this does no good, with confinement or with separation from the *Gesellschaft* for a certain period of time.

A sentence of complete expulsion of a person from the *Gesellschaft* can be imposed only by the primate.

Par. 10. *Special arrangements for the voyage*

On the ship (where there are three places to accommodate the *Gesellschaft,* cabin, steerage, and deck) the following arrangements will be made. In the cabin the primate shall exercise the highest supervision directly. In steerage, where the other members of the *Gesellschaft* are accommodated, at least one member of the board must remain at all times to exercise supervision. Likewise on the deck, to which all ship passengers have access at their pleasure, a member of the board is always to be present. The members of the board are to exercise this office of high supervision in steerage and on the deck in rotation.

Par. 11. *Supervision of the women*

Since the women in steerage sleep together, separate from the men, supervision is necessary here for the duration of the night, especially in emergencies. The board shall therefore, with the approval of the primate, select several older, experienced women, who will exercise supervision at nighttime and assist in emergencies.

Par. 12. *Supervision of the children*

Children as well as parents are under the supervision of the inspectors and members of the board, and the parents are responsible for their children [and they are responsible to the parents for their children]. This, however, does not exclude the parents from immediate supervision, so long as the children are in their company. During the voyage the children shall receive necessary instruction. During such instruction, and when they are playing together in the absence of their parents, they are under the sole supervision of the *Herrn* candidates, and the latter are responsible for them.

Par. 13. *Care of the sick*

Immediately when someone is taken ill, the subsupervisors shall notify the board, which will endeavor to provide the necessary medical attention. Separate nurses shall be appointed for men and women, and will receive adequate compensation for their services. However, if the patient has relatives and friends, he may have himself attended by these.

Care is to be taken that as far as possible the sick enjoy the requisite rest.

Par. 14. *Conduct toward the captain and crew*

The captain shall be treated with Christian modesty and deference. Since he has free and unlimited power in whatever pertains to the piloting of the ship, willing obedience shall be rendered to all his orders pertaining to such piloting of the ship.

In order to avoid quarrels, and also because it is disagreeable to every captain if passengers converse with the sailors, absolutely no one is to associate with the crew.

Par. 15. *Conduct in a storm*

Should a storm strike the *Gesellschaft* on its crossing to America (which God forbid!), its most active and fit men, especially the young people, who are to be selected for this purpose in advance, shall place themselves at the disposal of the captain in order to assist him according to his direction, which is to be followed implicitly. The remaining, weaker members of the company, the women and the children, are to be kept separate. They are to call upon God for gracious deliverance, as befits Christians, and avoid as much as possible that disturbance and confusion should result from their outcries and running about.

Par. 16. *Care of baggage*

For his immediate use every passenger has permission to have the necessary things (small trunks, carpetbags, and traveling bags) with him; but in order not to further diminish the narrow space in the ship's quarters, [he is] to keep them together and in order as much as possible. The bulk of the baggage (trunks and chests) will be stored in the hold. A special overseer, with several assistants to aid him, shall be placed in charge of this baggage. He is to exercise the necessary supervision especially in loading and unloading.

Par. 17. *Journal of the voyage*

A journal of the entire voyage, beginning with the time when the *Gesellschaft* has gathered, is to be kept on each ship by two persons to be appointed by the primate.

Par. 18. *Arrival in New Orleans*

In New Orleans, where with God's help the *Gesellschaft* will land, a few days will be spent in order to rent the steamboats necessary for the journey on the Mississippi and in order to make the necessary purchases. According to the contract made with the captain, living on the ship and meals on it will still be free for three days; the latter, meals, will also be available for a brief additional time at a low cost. Whoever wishes to live in the city and take his meals there, must do this at his own expense. At a specified time all shall put in their appearance promptly for the journey on the Mississippi.

Par. 19. *Journey on the Mississippi*

The same arrangements as for the ocean voyage apply to the trip on the Mississippi.

Par. 20. *Arrival and sojourn in St. Louis*

In order to enjoy the necessary rest from the hardships of the voyage, the *Gesellschaft* will remain in St. Louis for a time, living in houses, some of which will be rented and some of which will be selected by the friends from Berlin, who have gone ahead.

Par. 21. *Excursions into the vicinity*

After the maps of government land in the land office have been examined, excursions into the surrounding territory shall be made as soon as possible by groups of three, five, or ten men, as may be expedient, in order to purchase the land necessary for a settlement. In this matter the preliminary surveys of the Berlin friends will serve as a guide. Those sent out for the purchase of land will be provided by the board with special instructions and full power to act.

Par. 22. *Division of the "Gesellschaft"*

The other members of the *Gesellschaft*, who do not participate in these excursions, will partly (insofar as the craftsmen are concerned) try to support themselves by the practice of their trade in St. Louis; partly (insofar as those skilled in agriculture are concerned) try to rent land in the neighborhood or find employment with the farmers in the immediate vicinity; partly (so far as the more well-to-do are concerned) live in St. Louis at their own expense.

Par. 23. *Support of those incapable of working and the unemployed*

Those indigent members of the *Gesellschaft* who are incapable of working, as well as those who are unable to find employment, will receive the necessary support advanced from the Credit Fund and will be quartered in St. Louis or the vicinity.

Par. 24. *Counsel for the people living outside of St. Louis*

In order that the people who leave St. Louis will not be left entirely without association and counsel, the greatest possible care is to be taken that the members of the *Gesellschaft* shall not take up their residence in complete isolation, too far either from one another or from the city of St. Louis. The individual groups of people leaving St. Louis to seek work will be conducted by leaders, to be appointed by the board. After those whom they are conducting are provided for, these leaders shall rent land, or hire themselves out, or return to St. Louis, if their presence is required there.

Par. 25. *First arrangements on the site of the settlement after purchase of the land is completed*

As soon as the contiguous tract of land to be purchased by the *Gesellschaft* has been bought, all able-bodied men housed in St. Louis up to that time, as well as all those who have been scattered in the country, shall go at once to the site of the settlement under the leadership of one or more members of the board, in order to put up the necessary buildings and prepare for the cultivation of the land.

Par. 26. *Departure of the entire "Gesellschaft" for the site of the settlement and the expiration of these regulations*

When the most necessary dwellings and all preliminary work necessary for receiving the entire *Gesellschaft* have been completed, the departure of all members of the *Gesellschaft* for the site of the settlement will take place. As soon as they have moved in, the Community Code goes into effect, and these present Regulations cease to be operative.

Regulations for Settlement of the Lutheran "Gesellschaft" Emigrating with Herr Pastor Stephan to the United States of North America

CHAPTER I. *Regulations for the purchase and division of land*

Par. 1. Maximum land holdings

In order to leave room for those who will follow later, and also to prevent any inordinately great and oppressive ownership of land from developing in the Christian-civil community to be established, a maximum will be set for the amount of real estate which an independent member of the *Gessellschaft*, who has attained his majority (twenty-five years), may acquire in the contiguous tract of land to be purchased. This amount shall be [the area seeded by] 120 to 160 Dresden *Scheffel* [82.3 to 109.73 acres].

Par. 2 a. Minimum land holdings

On the other hand, to prevent the danger of impoverishment, a minimum amount of real estate will be fixed, which every adult and independent member of the *Gesellschaft*, especially every craftsman, must own in order to keep a few cows and pigs and a garden, so that in an emergency he can earn his bread even if he is entirely alone — also to have a meager subsistence in case of feebleness and in old age. This amount shall be 10 to 20 Dresden *Scheffel* [6.84 to 13.68 acres].

Par. 2 b. Besides this maximum and minimum, two classes of fields of medium size at 70 to 80 and 20 to 30 *Scheffel* [47.86 to 54.7 and 13.68 to 20.51 acres] shall be laid out and distributed.

Par. 3. Distribution of the land

The distribution of the land shall be made by lot under the guidance of a board of eight persons, half of whom shall be elected from well-to-do members of the *Gesellschaft* (the contributors to the Credit Fund), and half from those without means. The election is to be conducted by the primate, who is also to exercise general supervision. In the case of a tie he shall cast the deciding vote.

Par. 4. Choice of land in the distribution

In order to permit everyone to get equally good land, care shall be taken that no one receives all good or all poor ground, but that the proper proportion be observed. Therefore plots which are separated, not immediately adjacent, must be accepted.

Par. 5. Claim to the maximum

The amount of the real estate which may be acquired in [that part of?] the contiguous tract of land purchased which will constitute the area of the city, is conditioned by the size of the contribution to the Credit Fund. Only those can receive the maximum who pay at least (?) 1,000 thaler into this fund, and pay it, furthermore, under the condition that this money remain at the full and free disposal of the fund for the purpose of transporting those without means, because Christian fairness and justice demand that he who sows shall reap, and that he who bears the greatest burdens shall also enjoy the greatest fair advantages.

Par. 6. Claim to land near by

Those who are received into full citizenship in the community (see Par. 2 of the Code for the Civil Community) acquire the right to have the greater portion of their land assigned to them in the immediate vicinity of the projected city, whereas the associates and those who are subsequently received into the community must be satisfied with the more distant land.

Par. 7. Portions to be reserved

a. Main church in the area of the community

Before proceeding with the distribution of the land among the individual members of the *Gesellschaft*, those portions are to be set aside which will become the property of the main church, as well as those which will be owned jointly by the entire community.

Par. 8. Continuation

b. Four branch churches

To provide for the event that it should please God to let his people increase, additional portions of land will be reserved for four other churches, which shall be located at a suitable distance from the main church.

Par. 9. Continuation

c. Public buildings, streets, canals, mills, etc.

Furthermore, the space necessary for the common purposes of the community, public buildings, streets, canals, etc., shall be determined as accurately as possible in advance. Likewise on the river where the settlement is to take place, the necessary space for building mills at regular intervals shall be reserved.

Par. 10. Communal woodlands

The communal woodlands for the lumber and fuel necessary for the community shall be bought outside the limits of the city, in order that the space within the city limits for those who will follow will not be lost.

CHAPTER II. *Plan of the city*

Par. 1. Nature of this plan

On the site of the settlement a city will be laid out, but not with immediately adjacent houses, rather with gardens between them, so that there shall be a garden for each home.

Par. 2. Public buildings

A church shall be the first of the public buildings constructed, thereafter a town hall and the seminary together with the school. The other buildings of the church, the various educational institutions, a combined poorhouse, hospital, and orphanage, and a retreat for widows without relatives, the aged, etc., will be built in the course of time, and as conditions and means permit.

Par. 3. Lecture hall and recreational center

As soon as practicable a public lecture hall and recreational center with many rooms and extensive gardens shall be established, for recreation, whenever desired, and for maintaining community spirit.

Par. 4. Playgrounds

For the children, especially for those of parents from the working classes, public playgrounds shall be constructed, where old and otherwise incapacitated men and women will exercise supervision in the absence of the parents. These grounds shall be laid out in such a manner that they provide shelter from the heat of the sun, can be heated in winter, and in moderate temperature provide open rooms. The arrangement shall be such that the children who cannot yet walk, those attending school, and the adults can stay in separate rooms.

Par. 5. Cemeteries

The cemeteries shall be laid out next to the churches.

Par. 6. Height and specifications of the houses

The houses may not be built over two stories high and must be as spacious, dry, and light as possible. The windows may not be too low nor the roofs of straw. All refuse will be removed at the rear.

Par. 7. Streets

The streets will be laid out twenty to one hundred paces broad, provided with parkways, and interrupted by squares.

CHAPTER III. *Means of sustenance and occupation*

Par. 1. Agriculture and stock raising

The colony to be founded shall be based chiefly upon agriculture and stock raising, but in addition to these, truck gardening and arboriculture, flax raising, silk culture, the production of oil, and vine culture shall also be carried on. Attention shall also be given to the cultivation of medicinal herbs (rhubarb, opium, castor-oil plants, etc.), and botanical gardens shall be laid out for that purpose.

Par. 2. The arts and crafts

The arts and crafts shall be pursued as comprehensively as possible, however, without reintroducing the European excess, and with consideration chiefly for necessity and utility.

Par. 3. Inadmissibility of factories

Factories may absolutely not be established. On the other hand, large-scale production in the crafts is permitted within certain limits, which are to be fixed by regulation.

Par. 4. Trade

Next to agriculture and the various crafts, trade shall be one of the chief sources of sustenance. However, care shall be taken that it does not pass through too many hands in order to avoid the raising of prices and the adulteration of wares. Too extensive and too hazardous commercial speculations are urgently to be warned against.

Par. 5. Monopolies

Brewing on a large scale, manufacture of spirits, milling, the manufacture of bricks, and tanning on a large scale remain communal matters provisionally and for the first years. These five crafts shall be carried on by persons responsible to the community, and the products they put out shall be sold for the benefit of the community in order to cover a part of the common expenses with the resulting profit.

Par. 6. Hired help

As soon as possible a fair scale of wages for hired help shall be fixed in accordance with conditions in the country. This hired work may not last more than eight hours a day. The community council shall exercise supervision so that unhealthful or excessive work is not demanded.

Par. 7. The poor and beggars

The poor who are no longer able to work will be taken under the protection of the church, and through its mediation they will receive the necessary care from the community. As soon as possible, a poorhouse shall be erected. Beggars who are capable of working are absolutely not to be tolerated.

CHAPTER IV. *Police ordinances*

Par. 1. Prohibition of theaters and dance halls.

Theaters and dance halls may never be constructed.

Par. 2. Forbidden games

Lotteries, all games of chance, and cardplaying are summarily forbidden. On the other hand, the following are permitted: Billiards, bowling, draughts, pigeon shooting, and shooting sports.

Par. 3. Prevention of excesses

All cursing, the use of shameful words, as well as uncharitable taunting and ridicule, are emphatically forbidden in order to prevent, as far as possible, angry disputes and excesses.

Par. 4. Regulations for clothing

Regulations shall be established for clothing. In order to prevent extravagance, a maximum shall be set for prices on clothing, which may not be exceeded. All clothing which is injurious to health and is against Christian decency is forbidden. Corsets and their equivalents, such as dresses stiffened in the upper part with whalebone, are entirely forbidden to the women, as especially harmful to their health.

Par. 5. Penalties

Definite penalties for transgressions of the regulations in the preceding Pars. 1 to 4 are to be made public. They are to consist in admonition, in fines, and if deemed advisable, expulsion from the community.

Code for the Civil Community

(Community Code? Municipal Code?? Outline of the Local Statutes for the Community at N. N.??)

Par. 1. *Citizens and associates*

The members of the community fall into two classes, citizens and associates.

A citizen is he who has been accepted as a permanent member of the community and is in full possession of the rights of the community, particularly the right of acquiring permanent possession of land and property within the limits of the city. The extent to which the exercise of these rights is conditional is stated in this code.

An associate is he who is accepted as a member of the community for only a stipulated length of time, or upon recall, under conditions stated in the letters patent to be issued to him. An associate shall be excluded from all participation in the administration of the community but shall contribute toward the public obligations and expenditures as well as the citizens, since he also enjoys the advantages of association with the community.

Par. 2. *Admission of citizens and associates*

Whether a person is to be admitted as a citizen or as an associate depends upon the free judgment of the community.

For admission as a citizen, however, it is requisite by all means that the prospective member present a recommendation from the primate or his representative (or the entire ministerium?) in which his [the applicant's] orthodoxy and Christian integrity is attested. As a testimony of his admission he receives a certificate of citizenship.

For admission as an associate, a simple permit issued by the primate or his representative (or the entire ministerium?) is sufficient. Upon admission he [the associate] shall receive letters patent.

Par. 3. *Community administration — Community council — Electoral franchise*

The citizens shall elect from their midst a community council, which is to attend to all public affairs of the community. In this the council is to be guided:

1. By God's Word;

2. by the laws of the United States and in particular of that State in which the *Gesellschaft* will settle;

3. by this code and the amendments to be made to it from time to time;

4. by the council's code, which is to be drawn up by the council and approved by the community.

In order to take part in the election of a council, as well as to be eligible for election to the council himself, it shall be required in this as in all other elections that a citizen have reached the age of twenty-five years and have not been excluded from participation in the Lord's Supper by the church.

Par. 4. *Council Code*

The community council shall consist, for the first, of nine persons, inclusive of its first member, the mayor. Immediately after their election and induction into office they shall draw up the afore-mentioned council code and submit it to the voting citizens for examination and ratification.

Par. 5. *Election procedure — Inauguration of the council*

The first election of the council by the community shall take place under the direction of the primate [(] or his representative, or a deputy of the ministerium?). All future elections shall be under the direction of a committee of the council. On the occasion of each election everyone entitled to the vote shall present his certificate of citizenship to the election committee, for without it he will not be permitted to vote. In the first election, however, by way of exception, this will not be necessary, for at that time the division of the community into citizens and associates cannot yet have been completed.

The council should always be inducted, *i. e.*, installed, in its office and calling by a deputy of the clergy in the presence of the assembly of voting citizens.

Par. 6. *Length of the term for which the council is elected*

A new council shall be elected every three years. All members of the retiring council may be re-elected. A member of the council who is, during his term of office, formally excluded by the church from partaking of the Lord's Supper, must forthwith resign his position, and a new member shall be elected to the council for the balance of the term.

Par. 7. *Participation of the voting citizens in the administration of the community*

The voting citizens shall represent the community in all respects. Concerning all taxes (and in fact concerning all receipts and expenditures of the community which become necessary from year to year) the council shall draw up an estimate annually and submit it to the citizens' assembly — that is, the assembly of enfranchised citizens — for examination and approval. In this as well as in all citizens' assemblies the mayor shall preside, but have no right to vote, except in the case of a tie, when it is his prerogative to cast the deciding vote. The calling of this assembly is likewise a function of the mayor.

The council is furthermore required to render account of its administration annually before the citizens' assembly and to receive from it the sanction of its [the council's] administration for its justification. Also, at these assemblies all such matters shall be brought up for discussion in which the council considers it desirable to obtain the opinion of the citizenry. Citizens and associates shall be admitted by the council subject to approval by the citizens' assembly.

Finally, amendments to this code can be made only by common consent of the council and the citizens' assembly.

Par. 8. *Chamber of guardianship (Guardianship office?)*

The education of fatherless orphans shall be supervised by the church. The clergyman who has been commissioned for this shall, however, have a member of the council assigned to him for keeping records and accounts. This clergyman and the council member together shall constitute the guardianship office, which shall procure the guardians and exercise supervision over them. Also the guardians for other persons requiring guardianship, such as the absent, the feeble-minded, the infirm, shall be procured and supervised by the guardianship office.

The guardianship office shall draw up guardianship regulations, get the opinion of the council and of the citizens' assembly, but thereafter shall present them to the church for its sanction. After this sanction on the part of the church has been given, these guardianship regulations have the force of law.

Par. 9. *Chamber of justice — Court of appeal*

A committee of the council shall pass judgment as a chamber of justice or a municipal court in all legal disputes and crimes that may occur, which God forbid. From decisions of the municipal court appeal may be taken to the council, and likewise complaint may be made to the council concerning the chamber of justice. The decision of the council is final. All verdicts are to be executed by the chamber of justice. The court of appeal as well as the chamber of justice shall make public from year to year the rules of procedure and judgment, the judicial code. This judicial code must be drawn up by the court of appeal and the chamber of justice according to the Word of God, also taking into consideration the laws of the land, and must then be discussed, approved, and confirmed by the council in its official capacity and by the citizens' assembly. To this discussion, approval, and confirmation the court of appeal and the chamber of justice are to refer for justification in their publication [of the judicial code].

In cases in which the judicial code or other existing laws are not adequate, the Word of God shall be applied, taking into account also the laws of the land, instead of applying the laws directly as a basis of judgment.

In order that God's Word may in no case be interpreted or applied falsely, the opinion of the ministerium shall be sought for instruction, both in the drafting of the judicial code and in those cases in which the Word of God is applied directly in rendering a decision.

In any event, it must be stipulated in the judicial code that, before the beginning of actual judicial procedure, an attempt shall have been made at reconciliation, notice of which shall have been given to the ministerium, in order that it may, if it sees fit, deputize a clergyman to guide the attempted mediation.

The stipulations regarding the relationship between the community courts and the courts of the State, which will be necessary in criminal cases and in litigation between members of the community and non-members, will temporarily have to be held in abeyance.

Par. 10. *Scope of the council's jurisdiction*

The jurisdiction of the council, *i. e.*, its right to govern, and the judicial competence of the council, as well as of the community courts (guardianship office, the chamber of justice, the court of appeal, etc.), extend over the entire territory of the city and all inhabitants thereof. Excepted, however, are the plots of ground which have been ceded to the church and school, and likewise, as far as persons are concerned, the servants of God's Word, candidates of the ministry, seminary students, and teachers and pupils at higher and elementary schools. Over these persons and areas the church has exclusive jurisdiction.

Par. 11. *Books of trade and account*

As long as the Credit Fund exists, books of trade and account are to be kept by the Credit Fund. After the latter is liquidated, they are to be transferred to the council.

Par. 12. *Secretary of the council (City Clerk) Chamberlain (City Treasurer)*

The council shall appoint a secretary for keeping legal records and minutes, and a chamberlain for keeping the accounts and conducting the financial affairs. Both shall be paid from the community treasury, and shall hold office subject to a one-year notice of dismissal. Depending upon circumstances, both may be given salaried assistants.

Par. 13. *Literary board*

The right of freedom of the press may not be restricted in any way. However, the printing offices which will be founded shall be required to submit a copy of every item of printed matter to the literary board before circulation. This board shall consist of a committee from the ministerium and a committee from the council. Each of these two committees shall have the right to confiscate printed matter as soon as it is directed against the existing constitutions of the church and the community, against the old Lutheran confession of faith, and against genuinely Christian morals. One who has in mind doing something of that kind can, of course, not be prevented from having it printed outside of the city limits, but the community cannot become partner to such action by consenting.

As soon as a printed item has been confiscated, it may not be circulated, but is rather to be placed under the seal of the literary board.

The persons involved are not prohibited from bringing suit in the court having jurisdiction (against the ecclesiastical committee before the ecclesiastical court, against the members of the council's committee before the secular courts), and these courts are to assess damages against the defendants if they do not adequately justify their action, to the extent of the damages from such action incurred by the persons involved.

The literary board is to draft a set of regulations which shall have the force of law, if accepted on the one hand by the church and on the other by the council and the assembly of citizens.

Par. 14. *Regulations*

The relationship of the entire community, and especially of the council (as well as that of corporations within the community, *e.g.*, the Credit Fund), to the church shall be determined by regulations that will be established in the nature of a contract.

Par. 15. *Withdrawal and expulsion from the community*

During the first five years after that day on which settlement has been effected, no one may sever his connections with the community *Gesellschaft* by withdrawal. If he does so, all his property is impounded as collateral for all community expenses which are to be met until the expiration of the five years.

In the same manner, the property of the person who is expelled against his own will remains impounded.

After the expiration of the five years the [period of] impounding is restricted to the duration of the current fiscal year, unless there are special obligations for a further impounding.

Whoever has been excluded by the church from all means of grace and all Christian association ceases to be a member of the community, whether he be citizen or associate, and must leave the city limits.

Par. 16. *Revision*

This present code shall be revised by the council and the assembly of the citizens triennially. However, in exceptional cases an extraordinary revision may take place sooner, upon proposal by two thirds of the council and of the assembly of citizens.

BIBLIOGRAPHY

Primary Sources

MANUSCRIPTS

Concordia Historical Institute

Bound MSS., No. 9, Fasc. I, Verhandlg. u. Correspondenz d. Auswanderung betr.

Bound MSS., No. 17, Fasc. II, Applicationen, an der sächsischen Auswanderung teilzunehmenden.

Bound MSS., No. 12, Fasc. III, Protokolle über die Vorberatungen zur sächs. Auswanderung.

Bound MSS., No. 4, Fasc. IV, Gemeinde Verfassungs Sachen.

Bound MSS., No. 11, Fasc. V, Untersuchung P. St. betr.

Bound MSS., Fasc. VI [Correspondence and Documents on the Saxon Immigration, 1838—1841].

Bound MSS., No. 3, Verzeichniss von Stephan's, Meisters und Kokuschke's Effecten.

Bound MSS., No. 5, Acta, Berechnungen über Reise- Fracht- Elb- Weser- und Seeschiff-fahrts- Proviant- Zehrungs- und dergleichen Kosten während und nach der Auswanderung enthaltend.

Bound MSS., No. 6, Belege zur Cassenführung des Herrn Fischer in Dresden.

Bound MSS., No. 8, Miscellanea enthaltend Abschriften von Subrepartitions-Tabellen sub A—D, G—I.

Bound MSS., No. 10, Passagier-Listen und Passagier-Güter von den Seeschiffen.

Bound MSS., No. 13, Acta, die Assecuranz der Effecten und Contracten des Schiffs "Amalia" s. w. d. a. betr.

Bound MSS., Auszug der Acta Ephoralia den des Mysticismus und Separatismus öffentlich beschuldigten Herrn Pfarrer Keyl betreffend, No. 18, Niederfrohna.

Bound MSS., No. 19, Belege zu Verträgen in Credit-Cassen-Angelegenheiten.

Bound MSS., Auszug aus den Acten der evangel. Superintendur Chemnitz betreffend Wahl, Ordination und Amts-Einführung des sel. Professor Dr. C. F. W. Walther ins Pfarramt zu Bräunsdorf in Sachsen sowie den Zwist zwischen den Nagel'schen Eheleuten 1836 bis 1838.

Bound MSS., Abschrift der Acten betrffd. die Beschwerde des Gärtners J. Gottlieb Pester in Bräunsdorf gegen den Herrn P. Walther, daselbst.

Bound MSS., Acta, die anderweite Besetzung der Stelle eines Pastor vicarius zu Langenchursdorf mit dem Candid. Theol. Heinrich Theodor Füllkrus aus Waldheim betr.

Bound MSS., Invoices.

The title is misleading. This volume contains a variety of letters and documents relating to the emigration before 1838 and the contacts after 1841 leading to the organization of the Missouri Synod.

Bound MSS., Vehse, Carl E., Fischer, Heinrich F., und Jäckel, Gustav, Fasciculus, die von Herrn Dr. Vehse und 2. Genossen eingegebene Protestation gegen das Stephansche System des Kirchen-Regiments betr.

Unclassified Manuscripts

Most of the material in Concordia Historical Institute relating to the Saxon immigration belongs into this category. Several thousand such items — varying in size from a fragment of paper to a large volume — were examined; several hundred were cited. As there is no more specific identification, they were designated merely as "MSS., C. H. I."

Among these manuscripts were some of those most important for the history of the Saxon movement, including Brohm's journal of the voyage, all or part of Löber's diaries for the years 1831, 1834—1836, and 1838—1841, all the documents relative to Stephan's elevation to the episcopacy, excerpts of court records in Germany, most of Stephan's accounts, most of the financial records of the *Gesellschaft,* ships' manifests and other lists of emigrants, partial minutes of the committee, contracts for the ships, and most of the extended accounts of the emigration by the emigrants themselves, such as Lossagung vom Stephanismus, Bekenntniss, Nachrichten an unsere Nachkommen, and Marbach's An meine . . . Landsleute.

The Hanewinckel Notes, consisting largely of excerpts from court records in Saxony, deserve special mention here. Formerly in the possession of L. Fürbringer, this 201-page booklet has, since his death, been deposited with the Concordia Historical Institute. The contents of the Notes largely, though not wholly, parallels material contained in Bound MSS., V, C. H. I., and in copies of court records secured by the present writer through other channels. As the manuscript became available for use in this study only after all other research had been completed and did not materially change any of the conclusions, it is cited only infrequently. Its importance, however, should not be overlooked.

Saxon State Archives

Hauptstaatsarchiv, Hausarchiv Friedrich August II, No. 151.

Landeskirchenamt, Stephanakten, vol. I.

Perry County (Missouri) Court Records

County Court Records, Office of the Clerk, Abstract of Original Land Entries in Perry County, Missouri.

Circuit Court Records, Circuit Clerk and Recorder's Vault:

Chancery Record, Johann Gottlieb Palisch *et al.* vs. Henry C. Bimpage (with exhibits and supplementary documents).

Johann Gottlieb Palisch *et al.* vs. Henry C. Bimpage, Bill in Chancery, No. 28 (with exhibits and supplementary documents).

Martin Stephan vs. Fredrick William Barthel, *et al.* (File No. 600).

Martin Stephan vs. Gotthold Henry Loeber, *et al.* (File No. 601).

Church Archives

Trinity Church Records, Altenburg, Missouri.

Concordia Church Records, Frohna, Missouri.

Trinity Church Records, St. Louis.

Private Collections

Edgar J. Buerger Papers, Ellicottville, N. Y.: Bürger, Ernst Moritz, Selbstbiographie von Ernst Moritz Bürger Luther. Pastor emer.

Louis Fürbringer Papers, St. Louis:

Bünger, Johann F., Diarium per iter Dresd. in Americam 1838 et 1839. Reise-Tagebuch.

Walther, Otto H., Zur Agende Dom. II. p. Trinitatis 1839. ad Dom. I, p. Epiph. 1841.

UNITED STATES GOVERNMENT DOCUMENTS

House Docs., 25 Cong., 3 Sess., No. 210; *ibid.,* 42 Cong., 1 Sess., No. 1.

Senate Docs., 26 Cong., 1 Sess., No. 594.

Department of State, Census Office, *Census of 1840,* Washington, D. C., 1841; *ibid., Census of 1850,* Washington, D. C., 1853.

NEWSPAPERS

Anzeiger des Westens (St. Louis), 1838—1846; *Täglicher Anzeiger des Westens,* 1846—1847.

Chemnitzer Anzeiger (Chemnitz, Saxony), 1838.

Daily Commercial Bulletin (St. Louis), 1840.

Daily Missourian (St. Louis), 1844; *Daily Morning Missourian,* 1845—1846.

Daily Missouri Republican (St. Louis), 1839—1847.

Daily Pennant (St. Louis), 1840.

Die Ameise (Saxony), 1842.

Die Deutsche Tribüne (St. Louis), 1844—1847.

Dresdener Anzeiger, 1839.

Evening Gazette (St. Louis), 1838; *Daily Gazette,* 1838; *Daily Evening Gazette,* 1838—1844.

Leipziger allgemeine Zeitung, 1837.

Mill Boy (St. Louis), 1844—1845.

Missouri Argus (St. Louis), 1838—1841.

Missouri Reporter (St. Louis), 1843—1846.

Native American Bulletin (St. Louis), 1842.

New York Observer, 1839.

Old School Democrat And St. Louis Herald, 1843; *St. Louis Democrat,* 1844.

Penig-Bornaisches Volksblatt (Saxony), 1836.

People's Organ (St. Louis), 1842, 1844—1846; *Daily People's Organ,* 1842—1844; *People's Daily Organ,* 1846.

Politische Weltschau (Saxony), 1839.

St. Louis American, 1845—1846; *St. Louis Daily American*, 1846—1847.

St. Louis Daily Union, 1846—1847.

St. Louis New Era, 1840—1845; *St. Louis Daily New Era*, 1846—1847.

Slasher (St. Louis), 1844.

Vereinigtes Wochenblatt Rochlitz, Geithain, Geringswalde, Hortha und Waldheim (Saxony), 1838.

Weekly Reveille (St. Louis), 1844—1847.

CONTEMPORARY BOOKS AND PAMPHLETS

Allen, Thomas, *The Commerce and Navigation of the Valley of the Mississippi; and also that Appertaining to the City of St. Louis*, St. Louis, 1847.

Arends, Friederich, *Schilderung des Mississippithales, oder des Westens der Vereinigten Staaten von Nordamerika*, Emden, 1838.

Authentische Nachrichten über die Amtsentsetzung P. Stephans in Amerika. Auszug aus dem in St. Louis erscheinenden "Anzeiger des Westens", Neustadt-Dresden [1839].

Bedenken der theologischen Facultäten der Landesuniversität Jena und der Universitäten zu Berlin, Göttingen und Heidelberg über das Rescript des Herzoglichen Consistoriums zu Altenburg vom 13. Nov. 1838 (den Kirchlichen Separatismus in der Ephorie Ronneburg betreffend) und über zwei verwandte Fragen, Altenburg, 1839.

Bedingungen der Ueberfahrt von Bremen nach den Vereinigten Staaten von Nord-Amerika, Bremen [n. d.].

Bromme, Traugott, *Missouri und Illinois. Taschenbuch für Einwanderer*, Baltimore, 1835.

Bürger, Ernst M., *Sendschreiben an die evangelisch-lutherische Kirche zunächst in Wisconsin, Missouri, Preussen und Sachsen*, Leipzig, 1846.

Catalogue of the Officers and Students of the St. Louis University, St. Louis, 1840, 1842.

Delitzsch, Franz, *Lutherthum und Lügenthum*, Grimma, 1839.

———, ——, *Wer sind die Mystiker?*, Leipzig, 1842.

———, ——, *Wissenschaft, Kunst, Judenthum. Schilderungen und Kritiken*, Grimma, 1838.

Duden, Gottfried, *Bericht über eine Reise nach den westlichen Staaten Nordamerika's und einen mehrjährigen Aufenthalt am Missouri (in den Jahren 1824, 1825, 1826 und 1827) in Bezug auf Auswanderung und Uebervölkerung*, Elberfeld, 1829.

Eliot, William G., *A manual of prayer for public and private worship; with a collection of hymns*, St. Louis, 1842.

Fischer, Ludwig, *Das falsche Märtyrerthum oder die Wahrheit in der Sache der Stephanianer. Nebst etlichen authentischen Beilagen*, Leipzig, 1839.

[Flagg, Edmund,] *The Far West*, 2 vols., New York, 1838.

Fürbringer, Louis, ed., *Briefe von C. F. W. Walther*, 2 vols., St. Louis, 1915, 1916.

Green, James, *Green's St. Louis Directory (No. I.) for 1845*, St. Louis, 1844.

Green, James, *Green's St. Louis Directory, for 1847,* St. Louis, 1847.

[Günther, Gotthold,] *Schicksale und Abenteuer der aus Sachsen ausgewanderten Stephanianer. Ihre Reise nach St. Louis, ihr Aufenthalt daselbst und der Zustand ihrer Colonie in Perry County,* Dresden, 1839.

Haan, Wilhelm, and Ramming, Carl, *Kirchlich-statistisches Handbuch für das Königreich Sachsen,* Dresden, 1838.

Hall, James, *Notes on the Western States,* Philadelphia, 1838.

Hasse, H. G., *Abriss der meissnischen-albertinisch-sächsischen Kirchengeschichte,* Leipzig, 1846.

Keemle, Charles, *The St. Louis Directory, for the Years 1838-9,* St. Louis, 1838.

———, ——, *The St. Louis Directory, for the Year 1840-1,* St. Louis, 1840.

Keyl, Ernst G. W., *Offene Bekenntnisse des vormaligen Pfarrers Keyl in Niederfrohna über seine Gemeinschaft mit Stephan und die darin begangenen Versündigungen,* Zwickau, 1894.

Kirchenbuch für den evangelischen Gottesdienst der Königlich Sächsischen Lande auf allerhöchsten Befehl herausgegeben, 2 vols., Dresden, 1812.

Königl.-Sächs: Allergn: concessionirter Dresdner Historischer Stadt und Land Kalender 1839 [n. d.].

Lenz, T. W., *Reise nach Saint Louis am Mississippi,* Weimar, 1838.

Lütkemüller, Ludwig P. W., *Die Lehren und Umtriebe der Stephanisten,* Altenburg, 1838.

Lyford, William G., *The Western Address Directory,* Baltimore, 1837.

Peck, John M., *A new Guide for Emigrants to the West,* Boston, 1836.

Pleissner, Georg, *Die kirchlichen Fanatiker im Muldenthale,* Altenburg, 1839.

[Pöschel, Friedrich,] *Glaubensbekenntniss der Gemeinde zu St. Johannis in Dresden zugleich als Widerlegung der ihr und ihrem Seelsorger, dem Herrn Pastor Martin Stephan in einigen öffentlichen Blättern gemachten Beschuldigungen,* Dresden, 1838. [Usually Pöschel is regarded as the author of this volume. However, according to K. W. Welzel's testimony before a Dresden court, March 14, 1836, three other candidates for the ministry belonging to Stephan's circle at this time were also active in the preparation of this publication, namely, Brohm, Wege, and Welzel himself. The nature and extent of their contribution was not specified. See Hanewinckel Notes, p. 121, MS., C. H. I.]

Proceedings of the St. Louis Chamber of Commerce, in Relation to the Improvement of the Navigation of the Mississippi River, and its Principal Tributaries and the St. Louis Harbor, St. Louis, 1842.

Rudelbach, Andreas G., *Die Sacrament-Worte oder die wesentlichen Stücke der Taufe und des Abendmahls, historisch-kritisch dargestellt,* Leipzig, 1837.

St. Louis Business Directory for 1847, St. Louis, 1847.

St. Louis Directory for the year 1842, St. Louis, 1842.

Scheibel, Johann G., *Archiv für historische Entwickelung und neueste Geschichte der Lutherischen Kirche*, Nürnberg, 1841.

Schilling, Ernst M., *Handbuch des geistlichen Geschaeftstyls und der geistlichen Geschaeftsverwaltung*, Leipzig, 1830.

Skillman, W. D., *The Western Metropolis; or St. Louis in 1846*, St. Louis, 1846.

Stephan, Martin, *Der christliche Glaube in einem vollständigen Jahrgange Predigten des Kirchenjahres 1824 über die gewöhnlichen Sonn- und Festtags-Evangelien*, 2 vols., Dresden, 1825, 1826.

———, ——, *Herzlicher Zuruf an alle evangelischen Christen*, Dresden [n. d.].

———, ——, *Wir sind Pilgrime in dieser Welt, eine Predigt*, Dresden [n. d.].

Vehse, Carl E., *Die Stephan'sche Auswanderung nach Amerika. Mit Actenstücken*, Dresden, 1840.

[Von Polenz,] *Die öffentliche Meinung und der Pastor Stephan*, Dresden, 1840.

Walther, Otto H., *Exulanten-Lieder auf dem Meere. Eine kleine Beisteuer zum geistlichen Schiffsvorrath der um ihres allerheiligsten Glaubens willen mit dem treuen Knecht Gottes und Zeugen der Wahrheit, Martin Stephan, aus Sachsen nach Nordamerika fliehenden apostolisch-lutherischen Gemeinde, den 31. October 1838*, Bremen, 1838.

Wetmore, Alphonzo, comp., *Gazetteer of the State of Missouri*, St. Louis, 1837.

Ziehnert, Johann G., *Praktisches Evangelisches Kirchenrecht*, 2 vols., Meissen, 1826, 1827.

Secondary Works

PERIODICALS

American Historical Review, vol. LIII, New York, 1948.

American Journal of Sociology, vols. XXII, XXX, XXXI, XXXIII, Chicago, 1918—1929.

Biblical Repertory and Princeton Review for the Year 1853, vol. XXV, Philadelphia, 1853.

Catholic Cabinet and Chronicle of Religious Intelligence, vol. I, St. Louis, 1843.

Concordia Historical Institute Quarterly, vols. III, VII, XI, XII, XIII, St. Louis, 1930—1940.

Concordia Theological Monthly, vols. I, III, IX, X, St. Louis, 1930—1939.

Das Westland. Nordamerikanische Zeitschrift für Deutschland, vol. I, Heidelberg, 1837.

Der Deutsche Pionier. Eine Monatsschrift für Erinnerungen aus dem Deutschen Pionier-Leben in den Vereinigten Staaten, vols. III, VI, XV, Cincinnati, 1872—1884.

Deutsch-Amerikanische Geschichtsblätter, vols. V, XX—XXI, Chicago, 1905, 1922.

Evangelische Kirchen-Zeitung, vols. XXIII, XXVI, Berlin, 1838—1840.

Lehre und Wehre. Theologisches und kirchlich zeitgeschichtliches Monatsblatt, vols. VI, VII, XVI, XXXIII, XXXVI, XLVII, LXII, St. Louis, 1861—1917.

Der Lutheraner, vols. I—XCIV, St. Louis, 1844—1938.

Lutheran School Journal, vol. LXXIV, St. Louis, 1939.

Lutheran Witness, vols. XXX, LVII, St. Louis, 1912—1939.

Mississippi Valley Historical Review, vol. XXXVI, Cedar Rapids, Iowa, 1949.

Missouri Historical Review, vols. IX, XII, XIV, XV, XVI, XVIII, XIX, XXIV, XXXIII, Columbia, Missouri, 1914—1938.

Missouri Historical Society Collections, vol. III, St. Louis, 1908—1911.

Missouri Medical and Surgical Journal, vol. I, St. Louis, 1847.

Mitteilungen des Vereins für Geschichts- und Altertumskunde zu Kahla und Roda, vol. VII, Kahla, Germany, 1912.

Public School Messenger, vol. XXXV, St. Louis, 1938.

St. Louis Catholic Historical Review, vols. I, V, St. Louis, 1918—1923.

St. Louis Magnet, Designed to Illustrate the Philosophy of Human Nature, vols. I, II, St. Louis, 1845—1846.

Sechzehnter Synodal-Bericht des Iowa-Districts der deutschen evang.-lutherischen Synode von Missouri, Ohio und anderen Staaten, versammelt zu Lowden, Cedar Co., Iowa, vom 21. bis 27. August 1901, St. Louis, 1901.

Theological Monthly, vol. II, St. Louis, 1922.

Theological Quarterly, vol. III, St. Louis, 1900.

Verhandlungen der Zweiten Sitzung des westlichen Distrikts der Deutschen Evang.-Luth. Synode von Missouri, Ohio und andern Staaten, im Jahre 1856, St. Louis, 1856.

Zeitschrift für die gesammte lutherische Theologie und Kirche, vols. I, II, III, Leipzig, 1840—1843.

Zeitschrift für die historische Theologie, vol. XII, Leipzig, 1842.

Zeitschrift für Kirchengeschichte, vol. LVIII, 1939.

BOOKS

Amrhein, Hans, *Die deutsche Schule im Auslande,* Leipzig, 1905.

Andrees Allgemeiner Handatlas in 139 Haupt- und 161 Nebenkarten, Leipzig, 1906.

Annual Review, History of St. Louis, Commercial Statistics . . . From the Missouri Republican, January 10, 1854, St. Louis, 1854.

Bek, William G., *The German Settlement Society of Philadelphia and its Colony, Hermann, Missouri,* Philadelphia, 1907.

Bente, C. F., *American Lutheranism,* 2 vols., St. Louis, 1919.

Breckenridge, James M., *William Clark Breckenridge,* St. Louis, 1932.

Campbell, Robert A., ed., *Campbell's Gazetteer of Missouri,* St. Louis, 1875.

Celebrating the 100th Anniversary of the Saxon Immigration 1839—1939, Cape Girardeau, Missouri, 1939.

Clapham, J. H., *The Economic Development of France and Germany 1815—1914,* Cambridge, 1921.

Crawford, Ruth, *The Immigrant in St. Louis,* St. Louis, 1916.

Culmer, Frederic A., *A New History of Missouri,* Mexico, Missouri, 1938.

Dallmann, William, Dau, William H., and Engelder, Theodore, eds., *Walther and the Church,* St. Louis, 1938.

Dana, Charles A., ed., *The West; or, the States of the Mississippi Valley, and the Pacific,* New York [1853].

Das Ortsbuch fuer das deutsche Reich, Berlin, 1938.

Dau, William H., ed., *Ebenezer: Reviews of the Work of the Missouri Synod during Three Quarters of a Century,* St. Louis, 1922.

Denslow, Ray Vaughn, *A History of Royal Arch Masonry in the State of Missouri,* 2 vols., 1932.

Douglass, Paul F., *The Story of German Methodism,* New York, 1939.

Douglass, Robert S., *History of Missouri Baptists,* Kansas City, Missouri, 1934.

———, ——., *History of Southeast Missouri,* 2 vols., Chicago, 1912.

Edwards, Richard, and Hopewell, Menra, *Edwards's Great West,* St. Louis, 1860.

Erhorn, Irmgard, *Die deutsche Einwanderung der Dreissiger und Achtundvierziger in die Vereinigten Staaten und ihre Stellung zur nordamerikanischen Politik,* Hamburg, 1937.

Fairchild, Henry P., *Immigration,* New York, 1913.

Faust, Albert B., *The German Element in the United States,* 2 vols., Boston, 1909.

Ferenczi, Imre, and Willcox, Walter F., *International Migrations,* vol. I, New York, 1929.

Fritschel, Georg J., *Geschichte der Lutherischen Kirche in Amerika,* Gütersloh, 1896.

Fuerbringer, Louis, Engelder, Theodore, and Kretzmann, Paul E., eds., *The Concordia Cyclopedia,* St. Louis, 1927.

Fuerbringer, Louis, *80 Eventful Years,* St. Louis, 1944.

———, ——, *Persons and Events,* St. Louis, 1947.

Gebauer, Heinrich, *Die Volkswirtschaft im Königreiche Sachsen,* 3 vols., Dresden, 1893.

German Engineers of Early St. Louis and Their Works, St. Louis, 1915.

Grabau, Johannes A., *Lebenslauf des Ehrwürdigen J. An. A. Grabau,* Buffalo, 1879.

Gräbner, August L., *"Bis hieher." Kurzgefasste Geschichte der Missouri-Synode,* St. Louis, 1897.

———, ——., *Half a Century of Sound Lutheranism in America. A brief Sketch of the History of the Missouri Synod,* St. Louis, 1893.

Gräbner, Theodor, *Lutherische Pioniere. I. Unsere Pilgerväter,* St. Louis, 1919.

Gruber, J. L., *Erinnerungen an Professor C. F. W. Walther und seine Zeit,* Burlington, Iowa, 1930.

Guericke, Heinrich E. F., *Handbuch der Kirchengeschichte,* 3 vols., Leipzig, 1867.

Günther, Martin, *Dr. C. F. W. Walther,* St. Louis, 1890.

Hagenbach, Karl R., *History of the Church in the Eighteenth and Nineteenth Centuries,* 2 vols., New York, 1869.

Hall, Prescott F., *Immigration and its Effects upon the United States,* New York, 1907.

Hansen, Marcus L., *The Atlantic Migration 1607—1860,* Cambridge, 1940.

Hanser, C. J. Otto, *Geschichte der Ersten ev.-lutherischen Dreieinigkeits-Gemeinde in St. Louis, Mo.,* St. Louis, 1889.

Hawgood, John A., *The Tragedy of German-America,* New York, 1940.

Hennig, Karl, *Die sächsische Erweckungsbewegung im Anfange des 19. Jahrhunderts,* Leipzig, 1929.

Henderson, W. O., *The Zollverein,* Cambridge, 1939.

Herford, C. H., ed., *Germany in the Nineteenth Century,* London, 1915.

Herzog, J. J., and Plitt, G. L., *Real-Encyclopädie für protestantische Theologie und Kirche,* vol. XIV, Leipzig, 1884.

Hiersemann, P., *Chronik der Kirchengemeinden Niederfrohna und Mittelfrohna mit Fichtigsthal,* Limbach, 1899.

Hill, Walter H., *Historical Sketch of the St. Louis University; the Celebration of its Fiftieth Anniversary or Golden Jubilee, on June 24, 1879,* St. Louis, 1879.

History of Southeast Missouri, Chicago, 1888.

Hochstetter, C., *Die Geschichte der Evangelisch-lutherischen Missouri-Synode in Nord-Amerika,* Dresden, 1885.

Hogan, John, *Thoughts about the City of St. Louis,* St. Louis, 1854.

Hundertjährige Gedächtniss-Feier der Sächsischen Einwanderung 1839—1939, Cape Girardeau, Missouri, 1939.

Hyde, William, and Conard, Howard L., *Encyclopedia of the History of St. Louis,* New York, 1899.

Janzow, C. L., *Life of Rev. Prof. C. F. W. Walther, D. D.,* Pittsburgh, 1899.

Kargau, Ernst D., *St. Louis in früheren Jahren, Ein Gedenkbuch für das Deutschtum,* St. Louis, 1893.

Kluge, K. A., *Geschichte der christlichen Kirche von der Reformation bis auf unsre Tage,* Leipzig, 1856.

Körner, Gustav P., *Das deutsche Element in den Vereinigten Staaten von Nordamerika,* 1818—1848, Cincinnati, 1880.

Köstering, J. F., *Auswanderung der sächsischen Lutheraner im Jahre 1838, ihre Niederlassung in Perry-Co., Mo., und damit zusammenhängende interessante Nachrichten,* St. Louis, 1867.

———, ——. ——., *Leben und Wirken des Ehrw. Ernst Gerhard Wilh. Keyl,* St. Louis, 1882.

Krauss, E. A., *Lebensbilder aus der Geschichte der christlichen Kirche,* St. Louis, 1913.

Kuhn, William F., *Centennial History of The Grand Lodge, Free and Accepted Ancient Masons of Missouri 1821—1921,* St. Louis, 1921.

Lamprecht, Karl, *Deutsche Geschichte,* 12 vols., Berlin, 1907.

Mauelshagen, Carl, *American Lutheranism Surrenders to Forces of Conservatism,* Athens, Georgia, 1936.

Mayer, Otto, *Das Staatsrecht des Königreichs Sachsen,* vol. IX, Tübingen, 1909.

Mayo-Smith, Richmond, *Emigration and Immigration,* New York, 1907.

M'Clintock, John, and Strong, James, *Cyclopaedia of Biblical, Theological, and Ecclesiastical Literature,* vol. IX, New York, 1894.

Memorial Volume of the Diamond Jubilee of St. Louis University, St. Louis, 1904.

Mezger, G., ed., *Denkstein zum fünfundsiebzigjährigen Jubiläum der Missourisynode,* St. Louis, 1922.

Monroe, Paul, *Founding of the American Public School System,* New York, 1940.

Moore, Robert, *Vital Statistics of St. Louis since 1840* [n. d. — Reprinted from the *Journal of the Association of Engineering Societies,* XXXIII, 1904].

Münch, Friederich, *Der Staat Missouri; ein Handbuch für deutsche Auswanderer,* Bremen, 1866.

———, ——, *Der Staat Missouri, geschildert mit besonderer Rücksicht auf teutsche Einwanderung,* St. Louis, 1859.

Mundinger, Carl S., *Government in the Missouri Synod,* Concordia Historical Series, vol. IV, St. Louis, 1947.

Neve, J. L., and Allbeck, W. D., *History of the Lutheran Church in America,* Burlington, Iowa, 1934.

Parrington, Vernon L., Jr., *American Dreams,* Providence, Rhode Island, 1947.

Polack, W. G., *The Building of a Great Church,* St. Louis, 1926.

———, ——. ——., *The Story of C. F. W. Walther,* St. Louis, 1935.

Ritters Geographisches-Statistisches Lexicon, 9th edition by Johannes Penzler, 2 vols., Leipzig, 1910.

Rösener, Paul, *Unser erster Emigrantenmissionar, Pastor Stephanus Keyl,* St. Louis, 1908.

Rosenthal, Hildegard, *Die Auswanderung aus Sachsen im 19. Jahrhundert (1815—1871),* Stuttgart, 1931.

Schaff, Philipp, *Germany; its Universities, Theology, and Religion,* Philadelphia, 1857.

Scharf, John T., *History of Saint Louis City and County,* 2 vols., Philadelphia, 1883.

Schieferdecker, G. A., *Geschichte der ersten deutschen lutherischen Ansiedelung in Altenburg, Perry Co., Mo.,* Clayton County, Iowa, 1865.

Schnabel, Franz, *Deutsche Geschichte im neunzehnten Jahrhundert,* 4 vols., Freiburg, 1937.

Schneider, Carl E., *The German Church on the American Frontier,* St. Louis, 1939.

Schuyler, Montgomery, *Historical Discourses Delivered at the Semi-Centennial Celebration of Christ Church, St. Louis,* St. Louis, 1870.

Seeberg, Reinhold, *Die Kirche Deutschlands im neunzehnten Jahrhundert,* Leipzig, 1903.

Sihler, William, *Lebenslauf von W. Sihler,* vol. I., St. Louis, 1879.

Statistical Yearbook of The Lutheran Church — Missouri Synod for the Year 1947, St. Louis, 1948.

Steffens, D. H., *Doctor Carl Ferdinand Wilhelm Walther,* Philadelphia, 1917.

Stephenson, George M., *A History of American Immigration 1820—1924,* New York, 1926.

Stevens, Walter B., *Centennial History of Missouri,* 5 vols., St. Louis, 1921.

———, —— ——., *St. Louis The Fourth City, 1764—1909,* 5 vols., St. Louis, 1909.

———, ——, ——., *The Building of St. Louis,* St. Louis, 1908.

Stielers Hand-Atlas, 100 Karten in Kupferstich mit 162 Nebenkarten, Gotha, 1914.

Stöckhardt, Georg, *Die kirchlichen Zustände Deutschlands,* Zwickau, 1892.

Taylor, J. N., and Crooks, M. O., *Sketch Book of St. Louis,* St. Louis, 1858.

Treitschke, Heinrich von, *Deutsche Geschichte im Neunzehnten Jahrhundert,* vols. IV, V, Leipzig, 1907—1908.

Uhlhorn, Friedrich, *Geschichte der deutsch-lutherischen Kirche,* vol. II, Leipzig, 1911.

Verfassungsurkunde des Königreichs Sachsen vom 4. September 1831, Dresden, 1875.

Walther, Carl F., *Kurzer Lebenslauf des weiland ehrwürdigen Pastor Joh. Friedr. Bünger,* St. Louis, 1882.

———, —— ——., *The Proper Distinction Between Law and Gospel,* St. Louis, 1929.

Ward, Adolphus W., *Germany. 1815—1890,* vol. I, Cambridge, 1916.

Wegener, W., *Memorial Sketch of Dr. C. F. W. Walther,* St. Louis, 1911.

Williams, Walter, and Shoemaker, Floyd, *Missouri, Mother of the West,* 5 vols., New York, 1930.

Wittke, Carl, *We Who Built America,* New York, 1939.

Wolf, Edmund J., *Die Lutheraner in Amerika,* New York, 1891.

Yeaman, W. Pope, *A History of the Missouri Baptist General Association,* Columbia, Missouri, 1899.

MANUSCRIPT

Stegen, E. F., The Settlement of the Saxon Lutherans in Perry County, Missouri, M. A. thesis, Indiana University, 1933.

TOPICAL INDEX

Not all names of emigrants appear in the Index. But they can almost always be found in the Lists of Appendix A, which see.

Similarly, the Codes are not broken down into the individual subjects with which they may deal, but are listed rather as units, reflecting their incorporation in full, in Appendix B.

Statistical information is compiled in the Tables of Appendix A.

Administration Board 440 f.

Agenda, revision of, 1812 26, 78, 81

Altenburg (Mo.), largest settlement 444, 494; boundaries and "special partition" fixed and agreed upon after a survey by Bimpage 456; Dresden, Seelitz, Johannisberg, become branches of 500

Altenburg Debate 523 ff.

Altenburg (Germany). See Saxe-Altenburg

Amalia (ship) 149, 168; sum spent for use of 169; date of departure 193, 201; passengers 200; vainly waited for 209; immigrants on the *Olbers* left word for the *A.* before leaving New Orleans 217, 218, 220; sinking of the ship and the impression on the immigrants 362; unnecessary supplies bought in Germany went down with the *A.* 368; bickering over financial losses in the sinking 498; insurance money 499; list of passengers 554

Americanization 213

Ammon, C. F. von, prominent rationalist 25, 30, 57

Angelrodt, E., Prussian consul in St. Louis 260, 458

Antipfaff, Der 263 ff., 317

Anton, King of Saxony 7, 85

Anzeiger des Westens 229; disapprobation of the Stephanites 240 ff.; the first German-language newspaper west of the Mississippi 250; Heinrich Bimpage its founder 259; its first successful rival 261; brings the *Explanation* of the pastors 413; new attacks on Saxons by the *A.* 434, 458 ff.

Arndt, Joh. 38

Aufklärung, the Age of "Enlightenment" 10, 13; reflected in the theology of the University of Leipzig 25

Barthel, Friedrich Wilhelm, tax official at Leipzig, a lay member of the *Erweckung* movement 57; treasurer of the emigrants 58, 126, 163; Marbach's assistant at New Orleans 216; in trouble, as the treasurer, on account of Stephan's expenditures 224, 292, 361; accounts showing decrease of the Credit Fund 371; against Stephan 390; receives letter from Delitzsch 477

Basel Mission Society 307

Bavaria, family from, came to Perry Co. 490

Bay of Biscay storms 214

Beichtgeld 33

Bergt, Wilhelm, of the better situated economically 491

"Berliner," see the New York group

Bibliography 584

Biltz, Franz Julius 153 (note), 503

Bimpage, Heinrich, publisher of the *Anzeiger* 259; connected with the land purchase committee 378, 387; read the Sentence of Deposition 413, 455 f.; deceased 495

Böhlau, F. A., member of the Leipzig group 58, 192; operating store 497

Bohemia, Lutheran refugees to Saxony from 28 f.

Breslau 27

Brief Outline of the Emigration Code 133 ff., text 566 ff.

British Empire, attitude of emigrants toward 137f.
Brohm, Theodore Julius, becomes Stephan's secretary 42, 71, 117, librarian 118; ecclesiastical affairs his department 125, 215, 280; misgivings 285; offered his services to a missionary named Wyneken, in Indiana 457; joins efforts with O. Fürbringer and J. F. Bünger to provide a *Gymnasium* course 457; a statement following Vehse's Protest 511, 528
Bromme, Friedreich, author, his sympathies for the "persecution" suffered by the Stephanites 150
Bünger, Agnes 151, note 77, 197
Bünger, Ernst 409f.; practicing medicine 450f.
Bünger, Johann Friedrich, becomes closely associated with C. F. W. Walther 44, 125; reached Missouri with the Spröde group 196, 197, 404—407; participates in starting the *Gymnasium* 457; teacher after Geyer 505
Bürger, Ernst Moritz 41, 75, 80, 156, 176, 178, 179; Bürger and his contingent passengers of *Copernicus* 193; on January 19, 1839, the first Stephanites, led by Bürger, reached St. Louis on the river steamer *Rienzi* 203, 279, 293, 358; disagrees with Stephan 390; not mincing words about the nature of Walther's assignment 403; subscribed the Sentence of Deposition 418; the first of the clergymen to abandon the approved clerical position 470; produced a number of statements on what he considered wrong 511; penitential sermon 514; leaves Missouri with Marbach 529; later re-established contact and subsequently became pastor in the Missouri Synod 541
Burschenschaftler, German immigrants 254f.

Canary Islands 208
Christ Church. See Episcopalians.
Church of the Holy Ghost, German Protestant, in St. Louis 308, 343
Cincinnati 127
Code for the Civil Community, text 579ff.
Codes 133ff.; text 564ff.
College. See *Gymnasium*
"Concordia-hours" 66.
Confirmation of Stephan's Investiture 299ff.
Clyde, steamboat 206.
Copernicus (ship) 148; cost of voyage 169; date of departure 192; number of passengers 199; made the voyage in the shortest time 202; list of passengers 540ff.
Council, the 416ff.
Credit Fund 123f., 162; maximum actually attained 164; funds designated for the "church" 168, 169; contributions 361; shrinkage 362; exposed to the caprice of Stephan 363; expenditures 363ff.; confused statements about the Fund 369; contributions to augment it 372; no help promised the New York group from the Credit Fund 406; after the removal of Stephan the matter of most pressing importance was that of finances 432; cash still remaining in the C. F. 440, 451, 453; profit shown by 1845 492; abolition of 495f., 497; transformation from a communal treasury to what was practically no more than a central bookkeeping agency 499, 500; Code for the Credit Fund, text 568ff.
Cuba, the voyagers on the *Republik* are enchanted by the view of 208

Daily Missouri Republican 236f., 268f.
Delitzsch, Franz, a scholar and a Stephanite 20; eminent philologian and Old Testament exegete 51; did not join the emigrants 176; letter to F. W. Barthel after learning of Stephan's deposition 477, 478, 479
Dittrich, Caroline, applies for admission to *Gesellschaft* but accuses Stephan 72, 394
Döderlein, A. H., merchant at Leipzig 58, 165; deed executed to 494
Dreissiger, the revolutionary forebears of the Forty-Eighters 247, 255
Dresden (Saxony). See separate topical headings
Dresden Mission Society 30
Dresden (Mo.), settlement 445; survey by Bimpage 456; comprised 1,158.08 acres 494; members of New York group branch off to found the hamlet Johannisberg, Dresden becomes a branch of Altenburg 500; conference at D. 519
Dresdeners and Leipzigers 40

Duden, Gottfried 4; *Bericht über eine Reise nach den westlichen Staaten Nordamerikas,* the work Kurtz advised Stephan to read 88 f.; reaction to Duden's account 98

Ecclesiastical Code 135
Economic conditions confronting the immigrants 325 ff.
Economic motives in the emigration 154 ff.
Eichler, passenger on the *Amalia* 200, note 141
Einsiedel, Count Detlev von, the highest-ranking layman among Stephan's followers 7, 56; brought Pastor Benjamin Kurtz of the General Synod together with Stephan 57; his resignation from the Royal Saxon cabinet was a real blow to the Stephanite movement 85; 127
Emigration of Stephanites, European background 1 ff.; development of the emigration idea 83; the idea not made widely known before 1836 96; Missouri unanimously regarded as the most suitable destination 97; a "Constitution for the Lutheran Church after It has Safely Landed" 98; a "sign" indicating the date for actual departure was to be awaited 99, 104; as to religious motives leading to emigration 105 ff.; planned with complete detail yet completed within a short period 113 ff.; money placed in the "bank" 115; meeting of first leaders 117; no one was to be solicited to join the "Auswanderungs-Gesellschaft" 119 (but compare 152 f.); basis on which to negotiate with the officials for permission to emigrate 122; the "bank" or "Credit Fund" 123 f., 162; personnel of the reorganization 124; Emigration Code 125, 133, 160; settlement in Missouri 127; contact with Americans, Messrs. Kimm and Rivinus 128; fare from a German port to New Orleans 131; policy of purchasing an entire township 132; intention to found a semiautonomous theocratic community 135; organization of the "Auswanderungs-Gesellschaft" 137 ff.; meeting about ships and route to be taken 140; the Bremen route chosen 143; number of emigrants 143, 148, 149; cabin and steerage passengers 144; public opinion, favorable and contrary 146 ff.; additional ships chartered 148 f.; families disrupted 151; the great bulk of the Stephanites not wealthy 154 f.; economic motives played a part 156; finances 161; sums spent for each of the five ships' companies 169; parting and departing 171 ff.; conservatives who did not join the emigration 177; difficulties of getting permission to emigrate 178 ff.; the first ships left the third of November, 1838 188; the general plan for moving the emigrants 188 ff.; the order in which the ships left 192 f.; number of emigrants 198, 200; localities from which the emigrants came 200; Table III, Appendix A, 560; *Lebewohl der aus Sachsen nach Nord-Amerika ziehenden altlutherischen Gemeinde* 201; the voyage from Bremerhaven to St. Louis 202; arrival in St. Louis of the group led by Bürger 203; first Stephanites reach St. Louis under Bürger 203; St. Louisans dispense advice 204; further arrivals 206 ff.; the *Selma* reaches St. Louis; the passengers reunited with their fellow immigrants of the three preceding detachments 225; interest in the Stephanite emigration did not wane in Germany for a few years after the Bishop's deposition 482; former place of emigrants' residence 560; Emigration Code 566
Engel, guardian of Schubert children 194
Engelmann, Georg 4, 251, note 19, 260, 267
Episcopal polity, introduction of planned 173; Stephan's Investiture 288 ff.
Episcopalians, Christ Church, hospitality shown the Saxons 321, 435; further extension of the privilege 460; the kindness of 504
Erie Canal, in the journey of the Spröde group 407
Ernst, shipbroker 210
Erweckung, the strongest force opposing Rationalism 14, 15, 19, 31
Exter, H. W., captain of the *Olbers* 216

Financial situation confused during the years after Stephan's deposition 498
Fischer, Heinrich Ferdinand, a Dres-

den merchant 58; with Marbach and Jäckel worked out a tentative plan for the emigration in accord with Stephan's wishes 113, 116, 124, 125, 131, 139, 215; his duty on the *Olbers'* landing at New Orleans 216, 220; refused submission to Stephan 292, 304; disagreement with Stephan 390, 402; resigns from the newly created Administrative Board 440, 441 f.; participates in Protest with Vehse and Jäckel 464 ff.; about land apportionment 492
Fischer, L., an opponent of Stephanism 19, 22, 64, 109, 182; *Das falsche Märtyrerthum* 474
Forty-Eighters 245, 247
Fourth of July 275
Francke, A. H., 36, 38
Fredrick Augustus I adopts Catholicism to qualify for the Polish crown (1697) 20
Fredrick Augustus I (III), his long reign 1763—1827 6
Fredrick Augustus II 7, 126
Fresenius, Joh. Phil. 38
Frey & Company, New Orleans 128, 131
Fröhlich, Friedrich A. 49
Frohna 500
Frontier neighborliness of the English, Scotch, Irish, and French in Southeastern Missouri 449
Fürbringer, Ottomar, brought into touch with Stephan through Welzel 43, 126, 175; report to Stephan 210, 213; helps in founding the *Gymnasium* 457, 502; a "confession" 511; to Venedy 512 f.

Garlichs, Hermann, Evangelical pastor 317 ff.
Gempp, Dr., in close relation with the Stephanites as physician of the *Gesellschaft* 347; inclined to join the *Gesellschaft* 360; agreed to serve the immigrants in their financial difficulties 372, 375; chose to remain in St. Louis 450
German press in the West 237 ff.; in St. Louis 250 ff.; anti-clerical and anti-religious 261 ff.; in politics 268 ff.
German Immigration Society of St. Louis 211
German immigrants, and political parties 267 f.; education among 341 ff.; religious conditions among 307 ff., 315 ff.
German immigration to U. S. 3 f., 246 ff.
Germans in Missouri before 1839 245 ff., 249 ff.; in St. Louis 250 ff.; *Vereinsmeierei* 258; prominent individuals 259.
Germany, economic conditions 7; religious conditions 9 ff.
Geyer, Carl Ludwig, cousin of the Walthers 50; in the early period, worked part of the time in a pickling plant 504
Giessen Gesellschaft 250, 253
Gönner, Johann Jakob, first rector of the college in Perry County 50, 71; in the early period, at times supported himself as barber 504
Grabau, J. A., Prussian emigrant pastor 17, 481, 489, 513
Gräber, assigned to Stephan's personal service 216
Gratiot estate 375 f.
Gruber, J. L. 71, 180
Gruber, Theodor Carl Friedrich, emigrated 1839 53; slow to accept Stephan's leadership 55 f., 198, 473, 480; list of his group 557
Gube, J. G., a wealthy farmer 59; member of the larger group of leaders 117, 124, 125, 215; leads the committee who was to seek suitable land 375; the land in Perry County was all in Gube's name, and he bought much of it himself 378; signed the Sentence of Deposition 418; died 453
Guericke, H. E. F., 16, 18; relation to Stephan 65
Günther, Gotthold, and his book *Schicksale und Abenteuer* etc. 489
Günther, Louise 72, 101, 216, 355, 426 ff.
Gymnasium, constructed and opened by candidates, 1839 457, 502 f., 532

Hagemann, Otto, ship agent in Bremen 142, 143
Hahn, Wilhelmine 392, note 6, 427
Harless, G. C. Adolph von, *Zeitschrift für Protestantismus und Kirche* brought Muldenthal Statement 177
Harms, Klaus, his new set of ninety-five theses 17
Hattstädt, O., "Vor hundert Jahren" 303
Health conditions, in St. Louis 331 ff.; in Perry County 450, 486
Hellwig, Johann G. 97, 100
Hengstenberg 18, 163
Hermann, Mo., German settlement 250, 262, 315

Hermann, Rosalie 220
Hesekiel, Superintendent 79; "Rescript" urging the clergy of Saxe-Altenburg to a greater zeal in promoting true Christianity 473; his decease 483
Heyer, Evangelical pastor 318, 320
Hoffmann, J. G. 188, note 93
Hofmann, C. G. 215
Höhne brothers 485, 487
Höschel, Sophie 101, 103, 354, 392, note 6, 427

Illinois, considered as a site for settlement 128, 130, 377; Germans in 255
Indiana, considered as a site for settlement 128, 130
Indians, fear of discourages emigration 127, 129; moving through St. Louis 229; fears of unfounded 491
Insurance on the cash the *Gesellschaft* carried to the United States 169, 221
"Investiture," Stephan's, text of 288ff.; "Confirmation" of 299ff.
Irish immigration to St. Louis 245

Jäckel, Gustav 59; from December, 1837, on the secretary for all official meetings and transactions 113, 116, 120, 124; signed proceedings on *Olbers* 215, 220; confronted Stephan, together with Vehse, with a statement of the financial status of the *Gesellschaft* 371; resigns from the newly created Administrative Board 440, 441; participates in Protest with Vehse and H. F. Fischer 464ff.
Johann Georg (ship) 148; amount paid for voyage 169; date of departure 192; C. F. W. Walther, passenger 195, 196, 199; sixty-four days crossing 202; reached New Orleans January 5, 1839 206; list of passengers 540ff.
Johannisberg in Cape Girardeau County 500
Joseph, Duke of Saxe-Altenburg 175, 179, 193, 480, 513

Karlowitz, von 101, 184f.
Kayser brothers, Alexander and Heinrich 260, 267, 273
Keyl, E. G. W. 39; first contact with Stephan 40; a clash followed by a return to friendship 40, 65, 72; his parish 73, his sermons attract widespread attention 74; the Muldenthal Pastoral Conference 75, 76; mission and Bible societies 78; official acts for people across the border from Prussia 79; the right to supervise the school in his parish is taken from him, later partially restored 80, 175; his sermons in St. Louis censored by Stephan 357; disagreement with Stephan 390; signed the Sentence of Deposition 418; commissioner with Bimpage and Schlimpert to lay out land and to give deeds 457; bought seventy-seven acres 491; sum paid into the Credit Fund 493; his *Bekenntnisse* 511, 527
Kimm & Tewes, Saxons' contact with St. Louis 128, 129, 131; Kimm reports the *Olbers* could be contracted for 142; help the Stephanites at their arrival in St. Louis 206, 221; Kimm approached for advice in the purchase of land 374; his sensible advice was disregarded 378, 405, 460
Kirchenverein des Westens 308, 318ff.
Klemm, assigned to Stephan's personal service 216
Klügel, Gottlieb 50; substitutes for Stephan 102; carried on the Spröde-Marbach-Bürger tradition 528
Knickerbocker, river boat 212f.
Koch, Heinrich, the prolific and poisonous pen of 241, 243, 263f., 308, 346, 348, 349, 350; why he was given free rein by the *Anzeiger* 351; at meeting of German citizens 458
Körner, Gustav 255, 426
Köstering, *Auswanderung* 25, 303, 393
Krafft 18
Krause, W. E., lawyer for Stephan 168, 176
Krause, E. L., the pastor of a group of "Old-Lutherans," who wished to be incorporated into the Stephanite *Gesellschaft* 191
Kretzschmar, Friedrich 259
Kribben, Christian 260, 264
Kühn, a candidate of theology 36ff.; 52, 53, 75
Kurtz, Pastor Benjamin, of Hagerstown, Md., meets Stephan 57; gives an account of the interview 84; Stephan reopens to him the question of emigration to the United States 86ff.

Land, purchase of 373ff.; amount of 378ff.; cost of 379ff.; apportionments, method of 492; land set aside for specific purposes 494
Lane, D., ranking magistrate of St. Louis 400, 401
Leipzig, fair 1; University of 7, 25; group of Stephanites at 36ff.
Leonhardt 128, 130, 205f.
Lindenau, von, progressive Saxon statesman 7, 93f.
Liturgy, revision of, in Saxony 1812 26
Löber, Christiane, informative portrayal of life in the colonies 483ff.; one of her rare complaints 484; notes widespread dissension 510; her death 486
Löber, G. H., in touch with Klaus Harms 18; biographical sketch 53f.; doubted whether Stephan could be trusted 55, 65; deception "incomprehensible" 71; conducted devotional meetings 76; his diary 96, 175, 179, 180; late in arriving at Bremen 193; arrives on the *Republik* with Candidate Fürbringer and Teacher Winter 206; his searching sermon leads to confessions of women 392f.; subscribed the Sentence of Deposition 418; Löber visits Stephan 424; "Lossagung vom Stephanismus" 513, 528; letter to Duke Joseph effects assurance of his former sovereign's good graces 527
Lodges 310
Löhe, Wilhelm 532
Lüdering, J. D., and Co., ship brokers 142, 145
Lütkemüller, Ludwig P. 49, 146f.
Lutheraner, Der 238, 532
Luther's Catechism, printing bill of the *Gesellschaft* 168
Lyceum 340f.

Managing Committee (Administrative Board) 434
Marbach, Franz Adolph 58, warns von Uckermann not to doubt Stephan 64, 72; comes to Stephan's defense 92, 93; from December, 1837, until December, 1838, Stephan's right-hand man 113, 116, 119, 120, 121f., 123, 125, 127, 128, 132, 134, 138; instructed with Fischer to leave for Bremen to close the deal for at least the *Olbers* 144f.; clergymen instructed to ask their respective governments for releases from office 145; where M. seriously differed from Stephan before the embarkation at Bremen 157; his unique position betwixt clergy and laity 174; when the *Olbers* docked at New Orleans, M. was to attend to paying the duty on the baggage 215; opposition to Stephan 283, 285f.; petitions the Episcopal congregation for the use of its new church 320; second phase of the contest with Stephan 359, 390; asks Mr. Sullivan of St. Louis for advice on the proper method of dealing with Stephan 400, 416; his relation to the Credit Fund 471; remorseful letters 511; conscientious objector to the existing state of affairs 518; was silenced in Altenburg Debate 525; cordial relations with Walther not destroyed 526, 530; notable among those who left the *Gesellschaft* 528; returns to his homeland, re-entering the service of the Saxon government 530
Marbach, Martin 214
Maurer, H. H., his appraisal of the Saxons 14, 533
Michigan, as an area for immigration 128
Mississippi River, traffic on 222f., 227f.
Missouri, considered as a site for settlement 97, 127ff.; plan for a German state in 253; temperance movement 310; education in 336ff. See also separate topical headings, such as Germans in Missouri.
Missouri Synod 532ff.
Muldenthal, Pastoral Conference 75, 100; difficulty in persuading Muldenthalers of the necessity of emigrating 107; denounced the extremism of Stephanites 177
Müller, Heinrich 38
Müller, teacher with New York Group 205, 422
Münch, Friedrich 246, 254, 277, 314, 316

Nagel, Johanna C. 490
Native Americanism 249, 271ff.
New Orleans, interesting impressions it made upon the immigrants 209f., 217; prices for some commodities 218

New York group of immigrants 397; arrival of over one hundred, with them the three Büngers 404 ff., 407 f.; called the "Berliner" 445, 446; list of the N. Y. group 556
Nieder-Frohna (Mo.), "special partition not yet agreed upon" 456, 492
Niemann, Christiane H. 218
Nitzschke, Julius Otto, a factor at the royal china warehouse in Dresden 59, 90, 96, 100, 101, 103, 125; assistant of Marbach at New Orleans 216; questions the propriety of Stephan's conduct 391; operating store 497
Nollau, Rev. E. L. 309, 318
Nönnig, Gottfried, able to buy eighty acres 491

Occupations of the colonists 154 f., 232 ff., 562
Olbers (ship) 142, 143; the contract drawn up and signed 145, 162; cost of voyage 169; date of departure 193; Stephan, O. H. Walther, Marbach, and other important personages were assigned to this ship 193, 199; date of sailing 201; sixty-four days in crossing 202, 209; all authority and initiative was vested in the group on this ship 214; severe sea storms 214; letter of thanks to Captain H. W. Exter, containing indication that Stephan considered the possibility of bringing to the U. S. other members of his family 216; passengers 540 ff.
Olshausen, Theodor 259
Örtel, Maximilian, emissary of the *Barmer Missionsgesellschaft,* with Spröde in New York 205; with Rudloff to St. Louis 206, 406; signed the Sentence of Deposition 418; returned to New York, embraced Roman Catholicism and returned to the Lutheran Church 490

Paitzdorf 500
Palisch, Johann Gottlieb 375, 418; given the power of attorney 453; had forty acres of government land entered in his name 491
Palm, Wilhelm, citizen at St. Louis 259, 270, 458
Panic of 1837 325
Passenger lists, List I, Appendix A 540 ff.
Perry County, Mo. 378 ff., 382 ff.; condition of the soil, grassland, game supply 443; settlements 445 f.; housing for settlers 449; lots laid out 456
Pfau, Gustav, a painter at the Royal Art Gallery in Dresden 59, 125, 354
Picker, Rev. F. 309
Pietism 10, 31; of the old school 38
Pietsch, J. G. 162, 362
"Pledge of Subjection to Stephan" 224; text of 293 ff.
Pleissner, warned against the hierarchy 442; *Die kirchlichen Fanatiker im Muldenthale* 474
Polenz, von, *Die Öffentliche Meinung und der Pastor Stephan* 482
Pöschel, Candidate F. W., made possible the publication of Stephan's sermons by his stenographic notes 49; probably it was he who wrote the *Glaubensbekenntnis der Gemeinde zu St. Johannis* 90
Pötzsch, Auguste 392, note 6, 427
Press, The, in St. Louis 236 ff.; reactions in the German press 474 ff.
Prices of commodities, in New Orleans 218; in St. Louis 326 ff.
Protest by Vehse against arrogation of power by clergy 399 ff., 402, 411, 416 ff., 431, 436 ff., 461 ff., 507 ff.
Prussian emigrants 191, 481; at Buffalo 490
Prussion Union 16, 17

Rambach, J. J. 38
Rationalism 10 ff.; found wanting 14, 15; continues strong in Saxony 19, 20, 22, 23, 25; Rationalistic textbooks introduced in schools 79
"Regulations for Settlement," text 576 ff.
Religious Conditions in the West 305; churches in St. Louis before 1847 306; Synod of the West 307; German Protestant congregation, unionistic 307 f.; *Kirchenverein des Westens* 308, 318; no lack of religious activity 320
"Renunciation of Claims" on the *Gesellschaft* by Stephan 421
Republik (ship) 149; sum spent for voyage 169; date of departure 192, 199; crossed in sixty-two days 202; arrival 207; accounts of Löber, Fürbringer, and Winter 208 ff.; Appendix 535; List of passengers 540 ff.
Rienzi, steamboat 203
Ries, G. 200

Roman Catholics, their attentions to the Saxon movement 489
Rudelbach 18, 19, 34; the Muldenthal Pastoral Conference 75, 177; objects to the *Agenda* of 1812 81; quoted by Scheibel 388; his critical review of *Die Stephan'sche Auswanderung* 482
Rudloff, Ferdinand, baker, with Spröde 205; with Örtel to St. Louis 206; his letter to the leaders of the emigration 221

Sagner, Ben. 360, 459
St. John's Church, Dresden, 28f., 32f.
"Salaries" paid the Stephanite clergy et al. 362ff.
St. Louis 127; first direct contact with 128f.; the river front 227; the beginning of mail service on river boats 228; extent of the city (1839) 229; steady stream of immigrants pouring in 231, 327; the St. Louis area well suited to the Saxons 232; Irish immigrants 245; increase in population 230, 251; the Nativists 273f.; churches in St. Louis 306; housing in St. Louis 328ff.; educational policies 335ff.; libraries 341; "German School Association" 342; parish school 343; one of the first concerns of the Saxons to establish a school 344; labor conditions, strikes 349; between one hundred and two hundred of the Saxons chose to stay in the city 404, 412; newspapers 236ff.; it becomes clear that the best thing would be to let the St. Louis membership remain there 436; citizens of German extraction hold meeting for the purpose of "helping" the Saxons 458; other St. Louisans who materially helped 460; Saxon congregation in 504ff.; list of additions in St. L. 555
Saxe-Altenburg, religious conditions in 20, 54, 78f.; reaction to emigration in 473f., 483. See also Joseph, Duke of Saxe-Altenburg
Saxon Bible Society 30
Saxons, The, and their new home 226ff.; the St. Louis area well suited to them 232; craftsmen the largest single group 232f.; an occupational group well suited to the needs of the community 233; the ratio of females to males was forty-five to fifty-five 234; "a host of children" 235; public opinion, list of newspapers in St. Louis 236ff.; have made permanent contributions to the religious life of America 248; enjoyed, in St. Louis, complete freedom from criticism on the part of the English-language press or the English-speaking populace 252, 277; establishing the episcopacy 278ff.; first service at (Episcopalian) Christ Church 321f.; problems of communal living in St. Louis 325ff.; hard beginnings 325; a time of business depression following the Panic of 1837 326; high rents 327; housing problem 329; scarcity of fuel 331; high death rate 332, 334; rumblings of discontent 334; educational policies 335ff.; one of their first concerns was to establish a school 344; public interest centered in them at the time of their arrival 345; Dr. Gempp defends them against Koch 347; their own defense in the *Anzeiger* 348, 388; revolt brewing in consequence of the bishop's bearing, some people leave 356; additions of members in St. Louis 360; losses 361; purchase of land 372; committee whose duty it was to seek suitable land 374f.; the favorable offer of the Gratiot estate, but purchase not made 376; the new settlement finally located in Perry County, Missouri 378ff.; public statement in the *Anzeiger* 401; Stephan's expulsion 411ff.; the explanation of pastors and laymen in the St. Louis *Anzeiger* 413; lay leaders' conception of their position 414; transfer by two boats of members from St. Louis to Perry Co. 415; the Sentence of Deposition 418; the difficult times after the fall of Stephan 428ff.; the matter of most pressing importance was that of finances 432; the folly of concentrating the people in Perry County is officially recognized 436; clerical authority continues 436, 438; laymen attempt to abrogate the hierarchical system 439; "calls" issued to the pastors 444; Perry Co. settlements 447ff.; experience with the frontier problems 448; diverse misfortunes 449; division of the land 452; abandonment of the formal plans for establishing a school on

the model of the German *Gymnasium* 457; Vehse's six "theses," a new phase of the controversy between laymen and pastors 461 f., 464, 465 f., 467, 469; disorganization and reorganization 473; German newspapers after Stephan's removal 475; humble homes of the pastors in Perry County 485; sicknesses 486; problems of earning a livelihood 487; economic conditions improving 488; desertion from the ranks of the *Gesellschaft* 489; some left, others joined the movement 490; there were those who had enough money left to establish themselves in more favorable locations 491; first auction held 497; social life 500; church in open "camps" till 1839, then in parsonages; schools little better, first building at Altenburg, December, 1841 501; announcement in the *Anzeiger des Westens* for the erection of the "College" 500 f.; O. Fürbringer urges Delitzsch to accept a professorship in the proposed *Gymnasium* 502; Saxons in St. Louis donate $35.50, which made a completion of the College structure possible 503; the first enrollees and teachers 503; Vehse's Protest 507; problems dealing with the collective and individual culpability in the immigration, the nature of the Church and the ministry, etc. 508; a day of penance is observed 508; the entire group of colonists drifts into chaos 509; letters of apology sent to the St. Louis congregation by Löber, Keyl, Bürger 512; resignations of the pastors 516; the Altenburg Debate 523 ff.; again constituted a united, compact, energetic group 531; began their evolution of a thoroughly democratic form of ecclesiastical organization 531; bright closing chapter in their history 532; continuance of their college as a theological seminary 532; Appendix: Traveling Regulations for the *Gesellschaft* 572; Regulations for Settlement 576; Local Statutes 579

Saxony, political conditions 6 f.; economic conditions 8 f., 154; religious conditions 19 ff.

Scheibel, J. E. 27

Scheibel, J. G., leader of the anti-Rationalists 16, 18; breaks with Stephan 65, 99, 177, 178; an article of his reprinted in the *Anzeiger* 388

Schieferdecker, Georg Albert 50; 513

Schlegel, von 361

Schlimpert, Christian Gottlieb, signed the Sentence of Deposition 418; given the power of attorney 453; commissioner with Keyl and Bimpage for laying out land into parcels and to give deeds 457; deceased 495

Schnabel, Dr. C. A. 220, 222

Schneider, Dr. Friedrich E. 361 f.

Schneider, Sophie, 362, 427, 494

Schubert, Mr. and Mrs. 45, 194

Schubert children, Marie and Theodor 194 ff., 355, 485, 503

Schurz, Karl 246

School, a source of controversy in Saxony 79 f.; one of the first concerns of the Saxon immigrants 345; in Missouri and St. Louis 337 ff.; among Germans 341

"School and church code" 118

Schützler, C. A. 200

Seelitz (Mo.), settlement 445; low-lying, unhealthful 450; "special partition not yet agreed upon" 456; system of apportionment of land by lot 492; becomes a branch of Altenburg 500

Seibel, Jacob, owned forty acres 491; appointed commissioner 495

Seidel, Franz 147

Selma, the steamboat that took *Olbers* passengers up the Mississippi 219 ff.; "one of the larger of those mighty American water palaces" 222; serious difficulties impeded progress up the river 223; arrival at St. Louis 278

"Sentence of Deposition," pronounced upon Stephan 418

Siebenhaar, Superintendent 49, 73 f.

Sihler, W. 69, 532

Slavery, slave market in New Orleans 217; as an issue in the churches 313; in the newspapers 313 ff.; Saxons against slavery on principle 488

Spener, Philipp Jakob 38

Spröde, F., under his leadership a small group of people emigrated in 1836 to the United States 99; a letter from 129, 130; his trip to Germany to confer personally with Stephan 131; connection with Rudloff and Örtel in New York 205 f.;

return to Germany 221, 302 f.; 405; signs the Sentence of Deposition 418; his first blast against the clergy 511; personal animosity toward Walther 517; left Perry Co. for St. Louis, where he continued to cause trouble 528
Stärtzell 101, 125, 190, 529, 551
Statistical information on colonists, Tables in Appendix A 559 ff.
Steamboat races 211
Stephan, Martin, his youth 27, call to St. John's, Dresden 28; constructive, peaceful years 29; work in the Dresden Mission Society 30; religious gatherings in addition to the regular church services 32, 66 ff.; St. as preacher 33; charges against him 34; his reply 35; his followers 36; impressed most noticeably the young and unstable 52; achieved his greatest success with professional men, students, merchants, and officials in the government service 59; even less consistent than the average person 60, an "ordained spellbinder" 61; the members of his own congregation often could not get into the pews of their own church 62; at first allowed undue veneration, later accepted it as his due 65; after about 1832 resistance to him was almost negligible 65; walks at night 68; family life 69; in 1830 first mentioned his plan of emigration to Keyl 85; advised by Benjamin Kurtz that such a colony should be established on the banks of the Missouri River 88; the martyr complex developing 89, 121; arrested by the civil authorities for the first time 90; his defense 91; before emigration St. was never convicted of a single criminal charge, however small 94 f.; placed under a virtual house-arrest 103; his final decision in calling for a general emigration 104; "care of the person of the Herr Pastor" fell to Dr. Stübel 118; instructions to Spröde in New York 130; his wishes followed in determining the itinerary of the emigration 141; disbursements from the Credit Fund 167; direct references to St. as the "bishop'" 172; permission for his leave in doubt 182 ff.; finally, after a plea to his sovereign it is given 186; stormy sea passage 214; made bishop, just after the *Olbers* had entered the Gulf of Mexico 215; his expenses 224; the first few weeks in St. Louis 278; determines to establish himself as the sole authority 286; Stephan's Investiture 288 ff.; Pledge of Subjection 293; Confirmation of Stephan's investiture 299; problems of his administration as Bishop 352 ff.; the "protocol" 353; a bishop's vestments and accompanying paraphernalia 353; an episcopal residence in the prospective colony 354; "soirees" given by the Bishop 354; began to re-establish the way of life to which he had become accustomed in Germany; nocturnal strolls, etc. 355; interference and domination in private and family affairs 358; he became *the* hierarchy 359; leaves St. Louis for Perry County 385 ff.; his residence near the landing place 387; immorality comes to light 392 f.; disciplinary action against him 397 ff.; his expulsion 411 ff.; the Sentence of Deposition 418; his Renunciation of Claims on the *Gesellschaft* 421; taken across the Mississippi to the Illinois shore 423; attempts of resuming relationship with the *Gesellschaft* 423 f.; his declining years 427
Stephan, Martin, Jr. 216 f., 355, 490
Stephanism, rise of, in Saxony 1810 27; transformation into separatism 60; far-reaching plans 276; establishing the episcopacy 278 ff. See also *Stephan, M.,* and the *Saxons*
Stöckhardt, G., *Die Kirchlichen Zustände Deutschlands* 11
Storekeepers 497, 500
Stübel, Dr. 58, 117; eventually remained in Germany 118, 121 f., 124, 125; finally withdrew 176
Sullivan, involved in the purchase of land 379; adviser to Saxons 400 f.
Supernaturalism 11
Symbols, pledge to them 23
Synod of the West 307

Tennstädt, Mr., received repayment in full of his investment in the Credit Fund 414 f.
Tholuck 18
Tribüne, Die Deutsche 236, 261, 264, 268

Uckermann, Baron von, product of the Saxon *Erweckung* 57, 64, 126; did not emigrate 176, 177

Umlaut ä, ö, ü, type used in this study 11

Union of the Protestant churches in Prussia 16, 110

Vehse, Dr. Carl Eduard, curator of the Saxon State Archives 58; with Marbach defends Stephan 93, 118, 120, 122, 123, 124, 125, 127; apprehensions concerning Spröde's trustworthiness 129; signed the proceedings that declared Stephan bishop 215, 224, 285 f., 292 f., 353, 363; statements concerning the Credit Fund 269 f.; disagrees with Stephan 390; his book 396; theological controversy between him and the clergy 399, 401 f., 415; the Sentence of Deposition 418; a central figure in the movement as long as he was with the immigrants 436, 440, 441; move to change the structure of the *Gesellschaft* 452; his set of six "theses" 461 f.; "Protestationsschrift" 462; assertion of the doctrine of the universal priesthood of all believers 463, 464; flat assertion that the emigration was wrong 469; returns to Germany 470; his book *Die Stephan'sche Auswanderung* 471 f.; his Protest takes effect after his departure 507 ff.; Walther draws the constructive conclusions 522

Vles, John J., Saxon consul in New Orleans 210, 217, 219, 362, 372

Völker, Louise 354 f., 392, note 6, 427

Wall, Rev. G. W. 307 ff.; his "German Protestant church" strongly opposed to the Stephanites 345

Walther, Amalia 45

Walther, Carl Ferdinand Wilhelm 2, 25, 39, 46; why he felt himself indebted to Stephan 47, 63; tutor in the home of Friedemann Löber 48; pastor at Bräunsdorf 49, 71, 74, 75; Muldenthal Conference 75, 76; refused to permit the use of Rationalistic textbooks 80; his farewell sermon 178; was granted a formal release by the consistory 179; the Schubert children 194; on the *Johann Georg* 195; the Pledge of Subjection 303 f.; hears from Löber what charges the women made against the leader 393; representative of the pastors to deal with Stephan 397, 399, 403; letter to the New Yorkers 406; informs Bünger 409; the Sentence of Deposition 418; pastor in Dresden, Perry Co. 457; succeeds O. H. Walther at St. Louis 505; judges the candidates were ahead of the pastors in admitting what was wrong 511; letter of deep feeling of regret 515; call to St. Louis 519; his study of Luther; rise to eminence 521 ff.; the Altenburg Debate 523 ff.; doctrine of the Church 523 ff.; his famous books *Die rechte Gestalt* and *Kirche und Amt* 525; the fundamental premise "There's a church among us" 526; under his leadership a strong congregation in St. Louis was built up 532; the Evangelical Lutheran Synod of Missouri, Ohio, and Other States founded (1847) 532

Walther, G. H. W. 46, 179

Walther, Konstantine 194

Walther, Otto Hermann 45, 75; poems by him, printing paid by the *Gesellschaft* 168, 175, 179; was to look after the interests of the emigrants 191; his *Exulanten-Lieder* 192; the Schubert children 194; Stephan seldom preached while at sea, leaving the pastoral duties largely to O. H. Walther 215; on committee with H. F. Fischer contracting for the *Selma* 219; attends Stephan 278; Stephan's investiture 288, 292; subscribed the Sentence of Deposition 418; call issued to O. H. Walther, who was now to serve St. Louis 458; Vehse's six "theses" 461, 463 f.; officially reproved by the St. Louis congregation for his Stephanism 469 status of the St. Louis congregation 505; Pastor O. Walther succumbs to a brief illness 505; preaches sermons regarded as "confession" 511

Weber, Wilhelm, publisher and editor of the *Anzeiger* 259; at the meeting of German citizens aiming to "help" the Saxons 458

Wege, Moritz 40, 50, 97, 215, 354; states his position in the controversy 511

Weidlich, Pauline 354, 427

Welzel, Karl Wilhelm 40; lost his life on the *Amalia* 50; member of the larger group of leaders 117, 118,

125; instructions to him 218; the sinking of the *Amalia* 363
Welzel, Mathilde 183
Winter, J. F., a teacher at Plenena, induced a considerable number of Prussians to join the Stephanite venture 56, 65, 71, 149; arrives with Pastor Löber and Candidate Fürbringer 207; correct description of Stephan's treatment of the pastors and candidates 359; on sending C. F. W. Walther to Perry Co. for an interview with Stephan 403; most observant chronicler 443; his remarks concerning the laymen's Protest 471, 512, 528
Wisconsin, as an area for immigration 129, 253
Wittenberg, the landing place 445 f., 447; unhealthful, low-lying hamlet 450; 640 acres to be set aside for 456; sale of lots at 492; town remained small 500
Württemberg, 481; family, having originally settled elsewhere in the U. S., came to Perry Co. 490 f.
Wyneken 457, 532

Zeibig, E. W. 214
Zöge, Johann G. 97
Zollverein 8

PGIL2024USA